Best wishes to all stud
at Woodbrooke College.

Serge Bowsby

D1645187

BIRMINGHAM WORKING PEOPLE

A History of the
LABOUR MOVEMENT IN BIRMINGHAM 1650 – 1914
by
GEORGE J. BARNSBY

INTEGRATED PUBLISHING SERVICES
141 HENWOOD ROAD
WOLVERHAMPTON
W. MIDLANDS WV6 8PJ

ACKNOWLEDGEMENTS

I wish to gratefully acknowledge assistance in publishing this book from the following organisations: Twenty-Seven Foundation, Transport & General Workers' Union (Midland Region), TUC (West Midlands Regional Council), NALGO (Wolverhampton Branch), and NUPE (Birmingham).

I also wish to thank Dorothy Thompson, who was always at the end of a telephone to answer numerous queries, and also three people who believed in this project from the beginning and whose support has helped me: Tony McNally, Nick Matthews and Chris Roseblade.

Lastly, my heartfelt thanks to all those Sponsors, who responded to the call for assistance in publishing this book; their names appear individually at the back of the first impression of the book.

942.4.

To the working people of Birmingham. This book is produced by a Birmingham printing Co-Partnership and set in the Baskerville type of the Birmingham master printer and Secularist.

© 1989 George J. Barnsby.

ISBN 0 905679 06 7

BIRMINGHAM WORKING PEOPLE
A History of the
LABOUR MOVEMENT IN BIRMINGHAM
1650 – 1914

CONTENTS

ILLUSTRATIONS

Sources of Illustrations. The map is taken from Arthur H. Driver's *Carrs Lane 1748–1948*. Pictures 1 to 4 from R.K. Dent's *Old and New Birmingham*. Picture 7 from *Bisset's Magnificent Directory 1808*. Pictures 8 to 10 are from the Birmingham Reference Library collection and 14 from the Birmingham Museum and Art Gallery collection. Picture 11 is taken from a TUC collection and 12 and 14 from John Corbett's *Birmingham Trades Council*. The cover picture of the *Gathering of the Unions,* again from the Birmingham Reference Library collection, is engraved: "Drawn from four sketches taken during the three successive meetings in May 1832 by Henry Harris, Birmingham. Printed by Hullmandel. Published August 20 1832 by the artist 20, Hagley Row, Birmingham."

INTRODUCTION

This book began life almost ten years ago with a study of secularism as being the bridge between Chartism in the 1840s and the re-emergence of Socialism in the 1880s.

It then went on to describe the deepening and broadening of the socialist and labour movement up to 1914. At this point it became clear that any idea of taking the narrative beyond 1914 would have to be abandoned both because this would take several more years to complete and also it would make a book too long to be read and too costly to produce.

But when the limits forwards had been established other problems still nagged. The most serious was the misleading character of existing narratives of Chartism. These not only distorted the history of the movement in the town but also adversely affected national analysis of the movement. So an initial decision was taken to summarise briefly the well known events of 1837 – 39 and research more extensively the period 1840 – 1860. However, the events of 1837 – 39 proved so important from the point of view of working class influence and hegemony that this period also had to be re-written. Misrepresentation of the events of 1848 has been so blatant that received opinions regarding the national movement have here been challenged; and the continuity of Chartism in Birmingham up to 1860 was so extensive that this has become the longest chapter in the book.

Another problem was Owenite Socialism in Birmingham. In this case it has been conceded that Birmingham made notable contributions to the national movement through the development of Labour Exchanges operated on the principles of the exchange of labour equivalents through labour notes, but the later period of militant atheism and its links with subsequent Secularism had never been explored. The basic reason for this was the same as that of the distortion of Chartism, namely, that despite the valuable sources of working class history in the Birmingham Reference Library, the principal sources lie in the working class newspapers in the British Newspaper Library at Colindale in London. These had been neglected in the years before extensive microfilming and cheaper photo-copying have made these sources more easily available.

The last problem that nagged was the so-called 'mob politics' of the eighteenth century and its almost complete cessation after 1815 with the pioneer development of 'modern' working class organisations and practice. This produced the first two chapters of the book. Chapter one involved an appraisal of the highly significant work of R. B. Rose and John Money on eighteenth century Birmingham political organisation. But the first few pages of J.T. Bunce's *History of The Corporation of Birmingham* pointed to an even earlier development of the radical tradition in Birmingham during the middle ages through the work of Toulmin Smith on Gilds and Thorold Rogers on medieval prices, wages, standards of living and democratic movements. These were part of a now almost forgotten traditional radical historiography which investigated the origins of village communities in communally owned tribal lands and administration through folk moots etc. by such historians as Seebohm and Gomme and the 'old-fashioned' constitutional histories of Sir Henry Maitland and William Stubbs. The works of all these authors would be found on the bookshelves of the well read worker-artisan from the 1880s to the outbreak of World War II.

A second set of questions regarding this book relates to Ideology, defined here as the particular framework of ideas through which objective reality is perceived. The author comes from the general working class secular tradition of atheism. Specifically he subscribes to the Marxist materialist view that in order to survive humankind must work and co-operate with other people. For this reason this book is structured around the development of the productive forces. In the period of industrial capitalism, for instance, political developments are set against three Long Depressions in the period 1812 – 1845 then the Great Expansion of 1845 – 1875 and then the Great Depression of 1875 – 1885.

This is quite enough (some will say too much) ideological baggage to carry around, so the facts as they emerge have been allowed to speak for themselves, in the belief that this is indeed possible. The result is a 'narrative' style of history. This approach has been reinforced by a desire to present the actions of the participants from the viewpoint and aspirations of the time, and not as later generations would perceive them.

One point, however, must be clearly understood. It is no part of my intention to present 'both' sides of the question. Middle class Whig and Tory ideas permeate and distort virtually all we read of national and local history. Capitalist wealth controlled livelihoods, the national and local states, education and information media. These shaped, and still shape, working class lives and opinions.

The facts and opinions presented here have had to be dug out from a buried past, much like an archaeological excavation. They are here presented for public viewing many for the first time since they occurred. I have neither the time nor the inclination to double the size of the book by presenting an equivalent amount of anti-Labour history. Those who want such a point of view can find it in the standard texts, most of which are cited in the bibliographical notes attached to each chapter.

From the foregoing it will be seen that this book can be 'read at a number of different levels'. The most important intention, however, is that it be used as a gazeteer or reference book to which the reader can turn for basic information on what was happening in the labour movement in Birmingham at any particular period, year, month or even week, between 1650 and 1914.

John Wilkes.

Richard Webster. Jeremiah Vaux.

James Bisset.

James Sketchley.

James Murray.

John Freeth.

John Collard.

John Miles.

John Toy.

Joseph Fearon.

Joseph Blunt.

THE FREETH CIRCLE: FROM THE TONTINE PICTURE BY ECKSTEIN.

PART 1
INDUSTRY AND POLITICS
1650 – 1850

Chapter One
EARLY RADICALISM
1650 – 1800

Radical Origins

Birmingham Radicalism was shaped by three revolutions — the English Revolution of the seventeenth century and the American and French Revolutions of the eighteenth century. The English Revolution, sweeping away the feudal debris of centuries and opening up the way to the development of Britain as the first developed industrial nation of the world, was the last great 'western' revolution fought out under a religious ideology. The American and French revolutions were the first that were secular both in form and content. Birmingham radicalism therefore combines, perhaps more than any other area of Britain, progressive religion (mainly Old Dissent) together with increasingly important forms of Secularism. The latter were adopted by working people first to assist the growth of capitalism, and later to develop the fully secular principles of Socialism to protect themselves from the dire consequences of capitalism and then to struggle for complete mastery of their conditions of life through a new, more humane, classless system of society. It is the interplay of these forces and not the misleading myth of 'class harmony' (which still dominates the writing of Birmingham history), that this book sets out to describe and analyse.

Birmingham developed as one (and not at first the most important) of a cluster of industrial villages. When it was visited by Leland in the sixteenth century he gave the following description:

> There be many smiths in the town that use to make knives and all manner of cutting tools and many lorimers that make bits, and a great many naylers; so that a great part of the town is maintained by smiths, who have their iron and sea-coal out of Staffordshire.

An artisan population owning the tools of their trade, was already supplemented by a propertyless proletariat of journeymen, apprentices and labourers.

Birmingham also developed as a 'free' town without the restrictions of merchant and craft gilds. The only gild that did thrive was the Gild of the Holy Cross, described by Bunce as 'an endeavour to develop by the union of all classes a kind of local government'. This gild was peculiar to Birmingham. Although without religious or trade regulating functions, it had powers of local government and could undertake trading enterprises in the interest of the community. The earliest record of this gild, 1392, had another democratic feature distinguishing it from the normal merchant and craft gilds with their insistence on protections from 'foreigners' (i.e. strangers from outside the town):

> The bailiffs and commonalty of Bermyngeham found a Gild of lasting brotherhood of bretheren and sisteren among themselves in the said town

to which shall belong as well . . . men and women of other towns of the
neighbourhood who are well desposed towards them.

Bunce goes on to say that Toulin Smith conjectured 'not without reason'
that:

> . . . the Birmingham people had been influenced by the teachings of
> Wicliff, who from his Lutterworth vicarage, would be known to the
> midland district and that works such as the Vision of Piers Ploughman,
> and other attacks on the superstition, ignorance and corruption of the
> priesthood, had operated in the same direction and that, as a
> consequence, the merely religious foundation offered no attractions to
> the townsfolk.

The government of Birmingham devolved largely on this Gild through a
Master and Wardens, but important decisions required the consent of the
'bretheren and sisteren'. The Gild built a hall known as the Gild Hall or
Town Hall. It maintained two priests at St Martin's, not to pray for the
souls of the dead, but to act as part of the town government. The Gild
maintained a bellman, a midwife and an organist. The remaining funds
of the Gild were laid out in alms houses, gifts to the poor and the repair
of roads and bridges.

These latter details are known from the 1536 Report of Henry VIII's
Commissioners who misrepresented the Gild as a religious one, and its
possessions were therefore seized as part of the Reformation.

The next year under Edward VI the Gild lands were restored to
maintain the Free Grammar School and this remains to the present the
constitutional position. In addition, the democratic tradition persisted
with Lenches Trust which had been set up in 1525 to supplement the
work of the Gild of the Holy Cross in repairing roads and bridges. This
was outside the remit of Henry VIII's Commissioners and thus escaped
their attentions, to survive into modern times.

It is highly unlikely that medieval Birmingham was actually ruled by
such democratic principles; much more likely that Master and Wardens
from the richer merchants and craftsmen dominated the scene. Yet such
a democratic local 'constitution' would set barriers to arbitrary action and
also create traditions which could be appealed to and broadened.

What is certain is that this radical-democratic tradition continued into
the next vital stage of development, that of the English Revolution of
1640 to 1688. Birmingham was a bulwark of support for Parliament
against the king and arbitrary Stuart rule. This was in accord with the
general national position of trading and manufacturing communities
being the firmest support of Parliament against the king.

Clarendon, the royalist historian, writes of 1642, just before the first
main battle of the civil war at Edgehill, that Birmingham was 'a town so
generally wicked that it had risen upon small parties of the King's and
killed or taken them prisoners and *sent them to Coventry* declaring a more
peremptory malice to his majesty than any other place'. The other
industrialised townships of the west midlands were equally in support of
Parliament and while the battle of Edgehill was inconclusive from a
national point of view, it determined that Royalist influence in the west
midlands would remain in isolated strongholds such as Dudley Castle and
Aston Hall.

In April 1643 Royalist forces commanded by Prince Rupert attacked the town giving rise to such Parliamentary accounts as:

> Prince Rupert's burning love to England discovered in Birmingham's flames; or a more exact and true narration of Birmingham's Calamities under the barbarous and inhumane Cruelties of Prince Rupert's forces. Wherein is related how that famous and well affected town of Birmingham was unworthily opposed, insolently invaded, notoriously robbed and plundered and most cruelly fired in cold blood the next day by Rupert's forces.

This has the flavour of war-time propaganda but another contemporary account states that about one hundred dwellings were burned in the Dale End, Welsh End and Moor Street districts. Prince Rupert also attacked the town on two other occasions. But Aston Hall, defended by the royalist Holte family, was reduced in 1643 and Edgbaston Hall was taken about the same time by Parliamentary troops under the well-known Tinker Fox of Walsall. It would seem therefore, that military operations in the Birmingham area were largely determined from Coventry (also giving rise to the well-known expression of 'being sent to Coventry') and from the military committee at Stafford. Insufficient has been researched on Parliamentary rule in Warwickshire, but mention of Tinker Fox suggests that it is likely to have paralleled that of Staffordshire where the military and political conditions for defeating the Royalists demanded a considerable extension of democracy. This caused grave disquiet among the traditional aristocratic, landlord and merchant ruling classes. Indeed an accusation of misappropriation of funds by Fox when in occupation of Edgbaston Hall made by the Warwickshire County Committee is much more likely to reflect political intrigues which eventually gave rise to the compromises of 1660 and 1688 than any dishonesty on the part of Fox. Fox, although not an itinerant tinker in the modern sense, was representative of the 'lower orders' whose military efficiency and energy were necessary to win the military campaigns against the king and who consequently staked claims to a substantial share of local government both during and after the civil wars.

The changes that occurred in England in the 16th and first half of the 17th centuries were so fundamental that they need to be briefly summarised before attempting to relate them to a Birmingham radical tradition.

Henry VIII's Reformation settlement led to democratic developments in religion which spilled over to politics and science. It also created a land settlement giving those who had purchased church lands a vested interest in its continuance. The brief counter-Reformation under Mary (1553 – 58) emphasised an increasing economic differentiation between a more feudal, backward north and the rapid development of industry and trade in London and the south of England. Under Elizabeth (1558 – 1603) the main threat to the Reformation came from Catholic powers abroad and merged into a patriotic struggle for national independence. Its symbol was the defeat of the Spanish Armada and it saw the early development of an overseas empire.

The first Stuart kings (James I & Charles I) came from backward Scotland with feudal ideas of the divine right of kingship and a

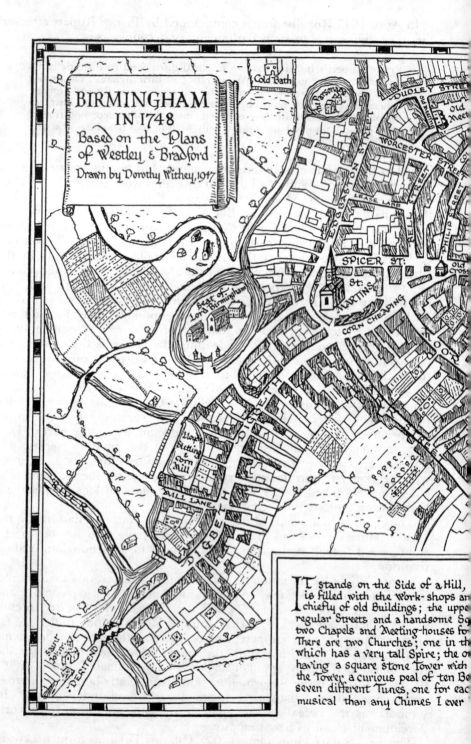

BIRMINGHAM
IN 1748

Based on the Plans
of Westley & Bradford

Drawn by Dorothy Withey, 1947

Cold Bath

The Parsonage

Seat of
Lord Birmingham

DUDLEY STREET

Old
Meet

WORCESTER STREET

EDGBASTON STREET

LEASE LANE

BELL STREET

PHILIP STREET

SPICER ST.

St.

St. MARTINS

Old
Cross

CORN CHEAPING

MOOR

DIGBETH

Floot
Slitting
& Corn
Mill

MILL LANE

DIGBETH

RIVER

Saint
Johns

DERITEND

IT stands on the Side of a Hill,
is filled with the work-shops an
chiefly of old Buildings; the uppe
regular Streets and a handsome Sq
two Chapels and Meeting-houses fo
There are two Churches; one in th
which has a very tall Spire; the o
having a square stone Tower with
the Tower a curious peal of ten Be
seven different Tunes, one for eac
musical than any Chimes I ever

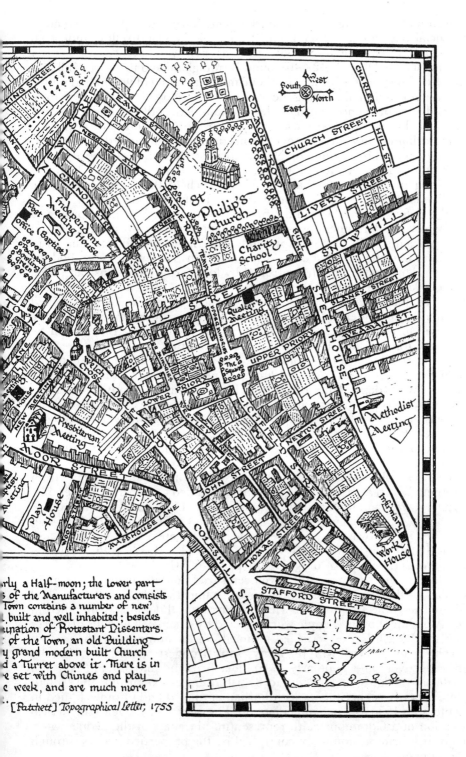

...rly a Half-moon; the lower part
...s of the Manufacturers and consists
...Town contains a number of new
...built and well inhabited; besides
...nation of Protestant Dissenters.
...of the Town, an old Building
...y grand modern built Church
...d a Turret above it. There is in
...e set with Chimes and play
...e week, and are much more

[Patchett] Topographical Letter, 1755

determination to rule without Parliament. They attempted to create a financial base for arbitrary power by illegal taxes and selling industrial monopolies. The inevitable outcome was civil war.

The first civil war (1642 – 46) found Birmingham and the west Midlands divided. There was a Roman Catholic minority many of whom had shown great heroism in maintaining the old faith, but many of them were in exile abroad and could only return on the coat-tails of the other Catholic powers, of which France was the most powerful in the 17th and 18th centuries. The Parliamentary forces ranged from the Anglican landed aristocracy, through the whole gamut of Nonconformist Puritan sects representing merchants, farmers, manufacturers, artisans and labourers. Roughly speaking it can be said that the zeal of each of these elements in the Parliamentary cause was in inverse proportions to their wealth.

The defeat of Charles I in the first civil war created as many problems as it solved. Parliament was then divided between Presbyterians and Independents. The former represented the richer London merchants in England and the established reform church in Scotland. They stood for a more democratic church controlled by local presbyteries instead of the bishops and king who controlled the Anglican church. But they also required that everyone should be compelled to belong to this unified church. The Independents favoured freedom of religion and were opposed to any state church. Victory in the civil war had been won by Oliver Cromwell and his New Model Army. But this had required the active participation of the 'lower orders' of society and had led to the democratisation of the army to a degree never achieved either before or since. The Independents of Cromwell representing largely the gentry, more prosperous farmers and provincial merchants were faced with an increasingly powerful left-wing of Levellers, Diggers etc, who introduced Agitators (virtual political commissars) into the army and demanded such advanced radical civil measures as annual parliaments and universal suffrage.

Charles I played each party off against the other, after his escape from captivity began a second civil war, this time aided by Scots Presbyterians. Charles was again defeated and the logic of events demanded his execution. This occurred in January 1649 and a Commonwealth was set up. But this, however, alienated moderate Independents and had also necessitated the removal of Presbyterian MPs. Pride's Purge left a Parliamentary rump of only 60 Independent MPs.

The Revolution might still have been saved, and the whole subsequent history of the working class movement changed, if Cromwell had allied himself with the Leveller left-wing. But its radical demands embodied in the Agreement of the People were rejected by Cromwell and his grandees and the Levellers were crushed militarily in the summer of 1649.

This left Cromwell with the army as his strongest power base. He used this effectively and popularly to conquer Scotland and Ireland and also to defeat the latest challengers to British overseas expansion, the Dutch. But successive experiments with Parliament failed and Cromwell died in September 1658 as a personal dictator. The only alternative to the radical solution of a Commonwealth representing the mass of the people was a modified form of monarchy controlled by the propertied classes through Parliament.

The restoration Parliament of 1661, however, was a vengeful Cavalier one. It passed legislation aimed at destroying Nonconformity by insisting on the use of the book of Common Prayer within the Anglican church and excluding from national and local government all those who refused or remained outside the established church. These acts powerfully influenced the future development of Birmingham, specifically the Five Mile Act which forbad all ministers refusing to sign the Act of Uniformity to reside within five miles of any corporate borough, which Birmingham of course was not.

Charles II's long reign (1660 – 85) saw a series of intrigues with France to make himself independent of Parliament and restore the Roman Catholic faith, but he pursued them with sufficient caution to die (of apoplexy) in his own bed. It took his stiff-necked brother James II, just three years of the same policy to unite the divided ranks of Protestantism to the point of inviting Mary (a daughter of James I) and her Dutch husband William to become joint sovereigns, and James fled.

The correlation of these national events with the search to find a continuing (or changing) radical tradition in Birmingham constitutes an immense agenda of historical research much of which remains to be done. However, enough has already been stated to indicate that such a correlation exists. What can be added here is that from the time and as a consequence of the failure of the English Revolution to provide democratic Parliamentary solutions representing the whole nation until the time when the working class would create its own institutions of trade unions, co-operatives and political parties, it was inevitable that the influence of the 'lower orders' should be asserted as 'mob politics'. It is that phenomenon which dominates the politics of eighteenth century Birmingham.

Central to all questions, is the growth of Birmingham. The best guesstimates show:

1640	1000	houses :	5300	inhabitants.
1720	1900	houses :	11400	inhabitants.
1750	4058	houses :	23688	inhabitants.
1785	9500	houses :	52250	inhabitants.

Thus in the 80 years between which Prince Rupert burned a tenth of the town, and 1720 the population doubled. It only took thirty years to double it again and in the next thirty years it more than doubled again. This should be compared with national population growth in England and Wales. In 1660 the population was about 5 millions, by 1700 about 5½ millions, by 1750 6½ millions and by 1800 9 millions. Thus between the English Revolution and the French Revolution national population had doubled, but Birmingham's population had increased tenfold. The significance of this, both in terms of the influence of Birmingham on national development and also the qualitative change that it represents in the structure of the labouring population is immense.

Radical Institutions

In searching for the institutions through which radicals worked it is natural, at this stage, to turn first to religion. Our guide here is William

Hutton, first historian of the town and himself part of the radical tradition. Hutton, born in Derby served two terms of seven year apprenticeships — in the silk mills and as a stockinger. He first visited Birmingham in 1741 and came to live here in 1750. He prospered as a stationer and bookseller, became a landowner, entered public life and died in 1815 celebrated as an author and literary figure. His *History of Birmingham* written in the early 1780s is discursive, opinionated, a joy to read, and the bedrock still of eighteenth century Birmingham history.

His section on Places of Worship opens:

> In a town like Birmingham, unfettered with charteral laws, which gives access to the stranger of every denomination for here he finds a freedom by birthright; and where the principles of toleration are well understood, it is no wonder we find various modes of worship. The wonder consists in finding such agreement in such variety.

The development of the Anglican church demonstrated its ability to resist the encroachment of nonconformism. In addition to the parish church in the Bull Ring and St. Philip's, there was St. John's chapel Deritend (technically in Aston) an ancient foundation of 1382, but rebuilt in 1735, St. Bartholowmew's was a new foundation built in 1749 serving the east of the growing town. The rapid population growth of the 1770s led to two new foundations in that decade — St. Mary's and St. Paul's.

The first Nonconformist chapels were Presbyterian. Hutton writes:

> After the extinction of the Stuart race, who bore an invincible hatred of presbyterianism, the dissenters from the establishment procured a licence for a meeting at the bottom of Digbeth, which yet bears the name of Meeting-house yard. Here the rigid sons of worship paid a weekly attendance. The place is now a workshop . . . Instead of an impression on the heart it is now stamped upon the button . . . Another was erected in the reign of King William, now denominated the old meeting . . . This is large and much attended.

This was followed by New Meeting erected in 1730. Presbyterianism in Birmingham developed towards Unitarianism and, as an offshot of Old Meeting, Carrs Lane meeting was erected in 1748. Of this Hutton reports:

> This residence of divine light is totally eclipsed by being surrounded with about forty families of paupers, crowded almost within the compass of a giant's span, which amply supply the congregation with noise, smoke, dirt and dispute.

The first Baptist meeting was founded in Cannon Street in 1738. Hutton again, this time displaying his prejudices:

> Some trifling differences arising in the congregation to which the human mind is everlastingly prone, caused discontent; Individuals began to sting each other, which in 1745, produced a swarm.
>   The destitute wanderers therefore, erected for themselves a small cell in Freeman Street, where they hived in expectation of harmony. Over this little society of separatists presided a journeyman woolcomber. What elevation he bore in the comb-shop during six days of the week, history is silent; but having the good fortune to procure a black coat and a white

wig, he figured on the seventh with parsonic elegance ...
Although the teacher might possess some shining qualities at the comb-pot, he did not possess that of protecting his flock, who in 1752, silently retreated to their original fold in Cannon Street ...
The growing numbers of this prosperous society induced them, in 1780, to enlarge the place of worship ... in which is observable some beauty, but more convenience.

The Quakers built their meeting in Bull Street, as early as the 1650s and Hutton tells us that in the 1780s it was, 'A large, convenient place, and notwithstanding the plainness of the profession, rather elegant. The congregation is very flourishing, rich and peaceable ... they are the only christian sect who have never exercised the cruel weapon of persecution.'
Methodism was a much later schism from the Anglican church, originating in the eighteenth century. Its first public meeting house was in Steelhouse Lane which it occupied for many years, the wags of the day observing, Hutton tells us, 'they were eat out by the bugs.' He continues. 'They therefore procured a cast-off theatre in Moor Street, where they continued to exhibit till 1782; when, quitting the stage, they erected a superb meeting house in Cherry Street.' Hutton at this point, before briefly mentioning the Roman Catholics and Jews, sums up his view of the development of religion in Birmingham as follows:

Thus our composite order of religion, an assemblage of the Episcopalian, the Presbyterian, the Independent and the Baptist, fled from the buffeting of the vulgar, and now take peaceable shelter from the dews of heaven.

This suggests a lessening of religious intolerance, but also the development of all these denominations, as middle class institutions, none of them serving the needs of most working people. The completion of Hutton's survey does not alter this picture. Of the Roman Catholics he says they formerly occupied a religious place of worship in Masshouse Lane, 'but the rude hand of irreligion destroyed it. There is now none nearer than Edgbaston.' He goes on to philosophise on the change of fortune of the Roman Catholics. 'Three hundred years ago Birmingham did not produce one person of a different persuasion; but now, out of 50,000 people, we have not 300 of this.'
Of the Jewish Synagogue Hutton writes with the deplorable anti-semitism of the age:

We have also among us a remnant of Israel. A people who, when masters of their country were scarcely ever known to travel, and who are now seldom employed in anything else. But though, they are ever moving, they are ever at home; who once lived the favourites of heaven, and fed upon the cream of the earth; but now are little regarded by either; whose society is entirely confined to themselves, except in the commerical line.
In the Synagogue, situated in the Froggery they still preserve the faint resemblance of the ancient worship. Their whole apparatus being no more than the drooping ensigns of poverty ... The proverbial expression 'as rich as a jew' is not altogether verified in Birmingham, but perhaps time is transferring it to the Quakers ...
It is rather singular that the honesty of a jew, is seldom pleaded but by the jew himself.

This failure of religion to satisfy either the spiritual or material needs of increasing numbers of working people marks a turning point in the secularisation of society and led to a search for more satisfactory institutions.

The natural alternative to the church as the fount of local authority was the much more democratic tavern, and Birmingham radical politics in the eighteenth century were largely organised through public houses and Coffee Houses, the first of the latter appearing in Birmingham, according to Hutton, in 1777. The organ of political influence was the Club.

The longest lived Club in Birmingham was the Bean Club. This began soon after 1660 as a loyalist club and was the focus of Tory politics for nearly two centuries. Because of the limited appeal of Toryism within Birmingham it perforce spread its influence into the west midlands to try to counteract Birmingham radicalism.

The most remarkable of the radical Clubs was the one associated with John Freeth's Leicester Arms tavern on the corner of Lease Lane and Bell Street. This tavern had been in the hands of the family in the first half of the eighteenth century and John Freeth took it over from his mother in 1768. By this time Freeth had already established himself as the most famous of Birmingham's poets and much of the contemporary radical history of Birmingham is encapsulated in the ballads set to music and sung by the Birmingham rhyming songster.

At Freeth's tavern the London and provincial newspaper were kept, and later, reports of the debates in Parliament, which at the time was itself a contentious, democratic issue. From the 1770s Freeth's Tavern (or Coffee House as it was often called) was the centre of the Birmingham Book Club, from which the Birmingham Library originated in 1779, whose most famous director was Joseph Priestley.

Freeth's was only one of many taverns where radical politics were organised. Formal debating societies emerged. One of these was the Robin Hood Free Debating Society originating in 1774 and meeting at the Red Lion. It modelled itself on similar Robin Hood Societies in other parts of the country. Its debates gave support to John Wilkes and expressed sympathy for the American colonists. It disappeared in 1775, but a Society for Free Debate persisted until 1789 linked with those who frequented Freeth's Coffee House.

The Robin Hood Society charged an admission fee of 6d. (which could be offset by 'the customary allowances'), but women were admitted free and allowed to speak. Despite this high admission charge the debates were widely attended by 'poor apprentices and mean mechanics'. This disturbed the more middle class elements who complained of 'tumultuous proceedings', bad language (a swear box with a fine of 1/- was instituted to overcome this), and a 'lack of cleanliness where ladies are present.' These complaints of unruly behaviour, lack of oratorical and debating skills etc. are interesting. They are difficulties well-known to modern teachers of working-class children (particularly in the 'lower' streams) attempting to develop discussion and debating techniques. But they almost never apply to adult trade union and political discussion, where high standards are the rule and not the exception.

These problems were more closely addressed by the Amicable Debating Society which was also started in 1774. It met at Mr Aston's

Coffee Room in the Cherry Orchard. The Amicable attempted to keep better order by publishing the rules and electing members of the Society. It tried to avoid the charge that it was thereby suppressing free speech by admitting non-members, but making an admission charge to them of 1/-.

From 1790 – 91 the Debating Societies met with the same problems as all other radical institutions — reactionary political interference and heckling and the threat of legal suppression.

Discussion required to be supplemented by the printed word. In the second half of the seventeenth century there were two printers in Birmingham. By the 1730s there were seven booksellers in the town. In 1743 Thomas Aris, a Londoner, took over an existing newspaper to provide the town with its permanent, weekly paper, *Aris's Birmingham Gazette*. Thomas Warren, one of the town's booksellers, had been hiring out books from 1729 and other circulating libraries appeared at that time.

By far the most important printer and publisher in Birmingham was John Baskerville. He was born in nearby Wolverley in 1706. In 1726 he became a writing master in Birmingham and then, as an artist of talent, he became a japanner. In 1775 he leased land which he gave the name of Easy Hill, built a house and continued as a japanner for the rest of his life. Hutton says of Baskerville's resplendently japanned coach:

> . . . his carriage, each panel of which was a distinct picture might be considered the pattern-card of his trade, and was drawn by a beautiful pair of cream coloured horses.

From 1750 his artistic skills turned his thoughts to printing. Several years of experiment followed during which £600 was sunk 'before he produced a single letter to please his fastidious taste,' and some thousands of pounds before 'a shallow stream of profit began to flow', Hutton informs us. His printed works began to appear in 1757 with a magnificent edition of Vergil. In 1763 he issued his immense folio the Cambridge edition of the Bible. He died in 1775, the most celebrated name in English printing after Caxton. His masterpieces can be viewed today in the Heslop Room of Birmingham University Library.

Baskerville was a Deist and disciple of the third Earl of Shaftsbury. He was a friend of radicals and freethinkers throughout the world (including Voltaire, and Benjamin Franklin) as well as those of Birmingham. The terms of his will were made subject to the 'express condition'.

> That my wife in concert with my executors do cause my body to be buried in a conical building on my own premises heretofore used as a mill, which I have lately raised higher and painted, and in a vault which I have prepared for it. This doubtless to many may appear a whim, perhaps it is so but it is a whim for many years resolved upon, as I have a hearty contempt for all superstition, the farce of a consecrated ground, the Irish barbarism of sure and certain hopes etc. I also consider revelation as it is called, exclusive of the scraps of morality casually intermixt with it, to be the most impudent abuse of common sense, which ever was invented to befool mankind.

The carrying out of these instructions, like those of the great ironmaster, John Wilkinson with his iron coffin and burial in his garden, led to later complications. Baskerville's body was eventually moved from Easy Hill and, according to the account in *The Great Silver Manufactory*, the churchmen, reluctant to place him in consecrated ground, buried him in a plot of land under which ran one of Birmingham's canals. The land was purchased some twenty years after by a business man who exposed the embalmed body of Baskerville to the public for a fee. The religios eventually claimed him, as they did Wilkinson, when a gentleman obtained permission from the rector of St. Philip's to have his body placed in a vault, the property of the church warden, George Baker.

Baskerville's influence continued after his death through other printers that he had attracted to the town, and those who, like Robert Martin, learned their trade at Easy Hill and acted as Baskerville's general manager from 1758; or Christopher Earl who also kept the Engine Tavern at Dale End, another noted centre of a radical club.

Newspapers and printing led to magazines; a shortlived fortnightly in 1764 called the *Birmingham Register* reprinted the celebrated No 177 of the *North Briton*, which was the centre of the Wilkes agitation. At the end of the 1760s a number of magazines developed including the *Repository*, descended in part from the *Birmingham Register*, which supported the American rebels. Also circulating in Birmingham was *The British Museum*, a publication of the Robin Hood Society of London, reporting and sharply commenting on, Parliamentary proceedings. The *Birmingham and Stafford Chronicle* from 1773 continued this tradition.

Reading was supplemented by borrowing. Libraries can be traced back to at least 1658 when the Rev. Thomas Hall, a leading Presbyterian during the Civil War and Commonwealth, gave the best of his books to 'the library at Birmingham'. Further libraries based on churches and churchmen developed. The most significant, however, was the Birmingham Library, founded in 1779 by nineteen subscribers, eighteen of whom were Dissenters. Entrance fee was 1 guinea and subscription 6/- a year. In 1780 Joseph Priestley undertook direction of the library and it grew steadily. The library came under the influence of the Church towards the end of the decade and played a part in the Priestley Riots of 1791. After 1795 most of the Dissenters withdrew to form their own Birmingham New Library. By 1800 eight or nine commercial libraries supplemented the older ones, catering largely for lighter tastes in reading especially fiction. But James Belcher, operating one of these commercial libraries, developed as the most radical printer and bookseller in Birmingham. Political literature was available from Belcher's from 1775. He was concerned with mechanic's education long before the days of Mechanic's Institutes and in 1816 he and his sons published a catalogue of their Artisans' Library.

Another important literary development was the Book Club. These probably originated in the 1740s to enable people to buy the serialised novels of the day and the Birmingham Book Club was at the centre of reform politics in the town from the 1760s.

Visiting lecturers and showmen also played a part in general enlightenment and entertainment. At first these visited taverns and coffee houses and from these developed specialised institutes such as 'academies' and theatres.

The role of the inn and tavern in the development of radical politics is impossible to assess, but it was clearly crucial. John Freeth celebrates the enormous number of these establishments and the delights of the only town official with a pleasurable function — the ale taster:

> Of all civil officers annually chose,
> There's none in the kingdom equal to those,
> Whose duty requires little more than to rove,
> And taste at their pleasure what Englishmen love.
>
> From Bord'sley to Hockley our province extends,
> I wish we had time to address all our friends;
> Of houses all freecost, to visit, 'tis clear,
> The number is more than the days of the year.

Hutton enumerates some of the Clubs operating from inns and says 'perhaps there are hundreds of these societies in Birmingham . . . some of them boast the antiquity of a century.' The largest number were the friendly societies or sick clubs. How many of these were trade unions and how far back trade union origins in Birmingham can be traced are matters of dispute. Most of our evidence, both direct and indirect, tends to come from the early nineteenth century. For instance, the Carpenters and Joiners Sick Society meeting at the Turks Head, York Street in 1809 and the Friendly Society of Cabinet Makers at the Lamp Inn, Bull Street in 1810 could hardly have been anything else, especially as the dates given occur during the period when trade unions were illegal. The best evidence, however, is the indirect evidence of societies registering to protect their funds. This shows the number of clubs registering was 22 in 1795; this fell to an average of three in the years 1799 – 1824 when trade unions were illegal; It rose to the phenomenal figure of 102 in 1824 when the Combinations Acts were repealed. As well as friendly societies and trade unions, Hutton also mentions the following: book clubs, breeches clubs, 'cloathes' clubs, watch clubs, clock clubs, and even rent clubs. For the more affluent there were building clubs whose members balloted for houses as they were completed and even capital clubs with a similar ballot when the subscribed capital reached £50.

The plethora of radical institutions outlined above, developing between the period of the English Revolution and the French Revolution, makes nonsense of any notion that radical politics in Birmingham could not be efficiently organised. 'Mob politics' there were but the apparatus for direction was at hand. This will become even clearer as we move from the organisation to the stuff of eighteenth century politics and attempt to differentiate more clearly between radical and working class politics.

The Standard of Living 1700 – 1800

Eighteenth century politics in Birmingham can, with considerable justification, be treated in its two separate halves. One reason is that of working class welfare. National indices of prosperity suggest that the first half of the century saw rising living standards, while the second half, despite the enormous aggregates of wealth accruing from the Industrial Revolution, was a period of declining living standards. Using such local indices as there are available, the same will be found true of Birmingham. Other reasons for treating the two halves of the century separately are the increasing tempo of change in the second half of the century and with

this, the increasing importance of Birmingham in the national economy
and its influence on national policies.

1700 – 1750

While it is true that throughout the eighteenth century the Birmingham
economy was one of small workshops rather than large factories, it is a
mistake to imagine the typical Birmingham worker as a skilled artisan.
Elrington and Tillot suggest that 60% of the working population were
labourers, journeymen and apprentices, and only 25% small craftsmen.
Within that 60% were many desperately poor people living on the verge
of subsistence at the best of times, and liable to starve in bad times. The
control of the growing population posed problems of social control which
were the constant preoccupation of the 5% or so of the population who
were men of real substance controlling the town administration. Glimpses
of the problem can be seen from the description previously given, of the
colony of paupers surrounding Carrs Lane. The exercise of control is
clear from the following extracts from the preface of a contemporary
account of the 1791 Priestley Riots:

> It may not be improper to inform strangers that manufacturers and
> labouring class people in this town are brought up in earliest habits of
> industry; that at 5 or 6 years they become useful in the manufactories
> in which children of both sexes are usually placed; and that the attention
> their employment requires together with necessary relaxations from
> business leave little or no time for improvement of the mind:- they are
> taught to act, not to think.

Data to assess the living standards of Birmingham working people are
almost completely absent. Full employment in Birmingham depended
crucially on both home and foreign markets. Wars could open new
markets formerly held by trade rivals, or close existing ones by action of
enemy fleets. Wars caused a boom in war supplies, particularly guns, but
they could also cut off the lucrative peacetime market for sporting guns.
It is impossible to draw conclusions from national trends in trade and
exports for Birmingham as information regarding the relative importance
of, for instance, the American market compared with the East Indian
market is not known. Domestic markets were crucially dependent on
harvests; so much of working class income went on food that rises in the
cost of grain lowered demand for other consumer goods. The price of
grain on the Birmingham market is available for each week of each year.
But to date, these prices have not been collated and averaged over periods
long enough for them to be used to estimate local living standards, and
national figures or those from nearby areas, which may be very
misleading, have to be used. The same is true of the prices of other goods
and it is also true of wages. Only one local index of well-being has been
found. This is expenditure on the Poor Law. William Hutton gave the
amount spent on the Poor Law for most years from 1676 to 1780. If we
assume that our figures of population for the same period are fairly
accurate, we can calculate Poor Law Expenditure per Head of the
Population. Hutton also remarks on 'times of exceptional scarcity'. With
these, and such other local information as comes our way, we can look

at each decade of the first half of the eighteenth century and make some estimate of general well-being.

Both 1699 and 1700 were years of exceptional Poor Law expenditure at 6d and 7d per head respectively. Expenditure moved back to a 'normal' level of 5d per head in the middle years of the first decade. It rose to 6d and 7d again for 1707 – 1709. The latter were years of bad harvests nationally when the national cost of living rose by 25%.

In the second decade, poor law expenditure in Birmingham rocketed to 9d in 1710 and 10d in 1711. The average for the years 1712 – 1718 was 7d. This rose again to 10d in 1719.

For the years 1720 – 1722 poor law expenditure was 8d and 9d. But Hutton's poor law figures fail us for the years 1723 to 1738. Nationally, there were bad harvests in 1727 – 1728, and 1728 was one of Hutton's years of 'great scarcity'.

The 1730s seems to have been a tranquil decade. The national cost of living fell and foreign trade increased. Birmingham seems to have shared the general prosperity, for when poor law expenditure appears again in 1739 it is down to 4d per head.

The beginning of the next decade was more difficult. 1739 and 1740 were both years of bad harvests. 1740 saw hunger riots on a national scale that E.P. Thompson has described as Risings of the People. But there were no riots in Birmingham, although 1741 was one of Hutton's 'times of remarkable scarcity.' The rest of the decade gave poor law expenditure in Birmingham at the remarkably low level of 4d and 5d per head.

In summary it can be concluded that the economic situation was difficult from 1700 to 1730, particularly the crisis years of 1718 – 1722, but, the 1730s and 1740s were decades of 'full employment'. Using the Gilboy national cost of living index (really a London index) and assuming the stationary wage rates over long periods which were normal for the eighteenth century, it can be shown that the national standard of living was virtually unchanged between 1700 and 1730 but then rose by about 8% for labourers and perhaps 10% for craftsmen. If we try to compare this national result with the Birmingham position we find we are not only handicapped by having neither local price nor wage material, but also our only Index — poor law expenditure — disappears for the years 1723 to 1738. However, if we make the reasonable assumption from the figures we do have that poor law expenditure fell from 8d per head to 6d in the 1720s and from 6d to 4d in the 1730s we get a sharper rise in the standard of living in Birmingham of 20% in 1750 over either 1700 or 1730.

For confirmation of such conjectures one would look to the political activity of the period. Such activity as is recorded tends to be in the first decades when living standards were stationary. The focus still tended to be religious. The Jacobite rebellion of 1715 caused some stir in Birmingham, but by then support for Church and King meant, to most people, Anglican church and Hanoverian king, not Catholic church and Stuart king, and 'the mob's' dissatisfactions were being vented on the Dissenters rather than the Catholics.

Trouble began with the coronation of George I in November 1714. Some hundreds of people attacked the houses of noted Dissenters, William Guest and Thomas Gisburne, and also John Murdock. They defended themselves vigorously with shot guns and swords. The Jacobite invasion of 1715 brought riots to Birmingham in July, when the Presbyterian Old Meeting House was destroyed. The riots were not brought under control for ten days.

In 1745 it was alleged that there was some support for the Young Pretender, and supplies of arms were seized. But Birmingham contributed supplies to the Protestant forces of the Duke of Cumberland which spent several days in Birmingham during December. This time there was no outburst against Dissenters.

This seems to be about the sum total of significant, recorded political activity in Birmingham in the first half of the eighteenth century.

The Standard of Living 1750–1800

The second half of the eighteenth century is probably the most important period in the history of Birmingham. The most remarkable change was the effect of the technical innovations and the scale and scope of trade brought about by the Industrial Revolution. But these changes, enormously increasing the wealth of the town were accompanied by a succession of bad harvests, and a series of wars which seriously disrupted trade. But above all, the developed capitalist system brought to fruition by the Industrial Revolution, brought with it the cyclical movement of boom and slump which has been, and continues to be, its curse for those who possess nothing but their labour power and must sell this as a commodity to an employer.

We will again review the period decade by decade. The first half of the 1750s seems to have been tranquil with a stable national cost of living similar to that of the seventeen thirties and forties. But 1756 and 1757 saw hunger riots, and were years of Thompson's Risings of the People and Hutton's 'times of remarkable scarcity'. Poor Law expenditure per head of the population doubled from about 5d to 10d and this proved to be a point of no return.

In the 1760s there were local hunger riots in 1762. In 1766 hunger riots in Birmingham, the midlands, and other parts of the country brought disturbances greater than any known in England since the Civil Wars. Bad harvests continued in 1767 and 1768. In these years the poor law expenditure in Birmingham climbed to 13d per head.

The 1770s brought another series of bad harvests from 1772 to 1775 with 'times of remarkable scarcity' in Birmingham in 1774. More ominously, in 1772 Matthew Boulton was reporting to the Earl of Dartmouth that 'trade was dead' in Birmingham; the industrial cycle had begun. This is the last decade for which there are local poor law figures; expenditure per head rose to 17d in 1779, with an average for the decade of 14d.

In the 1780s there were hunger riots in Birmingham in 1782 and a bad harvest the next year also.

The 1790s have been described by Langford as 'the dreadful decade'. He referred not only to the economic situation, but also the political situation which began with almost universal rejoicings at the outbreak of the French Revolution in 1789, brought the infamous Priestley Riots of 1791, the war with France from 1793 with its consequent nationalism and jingoism and with it, national efforts to destroy radicalism root and branch from 1795. The latter part of the decade also brought bad harvests in 1795 and 1796 with hunger riots in the former year. The next two years saw some improvement, but had harvests in 1799 and 1800 brought hunger riots again in the latter year.

With the disappearance of poor law expenditure figures, we are obliged to look for other indices to roughly measure the standard of living in Birmingham. The sources we have is the Gilboy 'national' cost of living index used for the first half of the century. This, as already stated, is mainly a London cost of living. But we now have some wage figures, not for Birmingham, but for areas near to Birmingham. The only wage figures which give a long run of years are contract building labour employed by corporations such as colleges or churches, also general labour on agricultural estates. Bernard Eccleston has collected such wage figures from 1750 for five midland counties. None of these figures is for Birmingham, but I have selected his figures for locations nearest to Birmingham. For building labour the nearest area is Stratford-on-Avon. From these average wages and from the Gilboy cost of living we can construct the following index of real wages:

Real Wages for Building Craftsmen and Labourers by decades 1750 – 1800

	Craftmen	Labourers
1750s	100	100
1760s	107	94
1770s	106	99
1780s	110	94
1790s	101	92

The above figures suggest that craftsmen increased their standard of living by a maximum of 10% from the 1750s to the 1780s but were falling back to the 1750s standard as prices rose steeply in the 1790s. Labourers, on the other hand, failed to maintain their 1750s standard of living and by the 1790s were 8% worse off. The frailties of such an index are obvious. The figures apply only to building labour, the cost of living index is a mainly London one. But it is from such frailties that the most positive statements regarding the general standard of living in England have been proclaimed. This first attempt to measure the standard of living in Birmingham will be refined as we proceed. It should be noted that such standards applied only to those who were in work. Also that charting improvements and deteriorations in real wages says nothing about the actual standard of life at which people lived. Both of these problems will also be addressed as we proceed; the latter when we examine more closely the Hunger Riots.

Political consciousness developed sharply in the 1760s. The domestic issue that stirred artisan and middle class radicals alike was the Wilkes and Liberty agitation which began in 1762 as a campaign for press freedom. It developed into a question of the right of electors to choose their MP and then merged with the democratic cause of the American colonists for freedom. It was perhaps the latter aspect that moved the Birmingham middle class most deeply, involving as it did the economic issues of expanding markets for its exports and the necessity to import American bar iron in the decades before the Watt/Wilkinson improvements to the steam engine and Cort's puddling process eventually brought vast streams of British iron on tap.

The other issue raising political consciousness in the 1760s was the high cost of living and the Hunger Riots in the town. We know that there were Hunger Riots in Birmingham in 1756, 1757, 1762 and 1763, but no detailed records of these riots survive. The riots of 1766, however, have been fully explored because they were so widespread and disturbed the social order so deeply. The first question to be asked is whether what are normally called 'food riots' were in fact Hunger Riots, as I prefer to describe them. This involves an examination of the extent to which food prices rose in times of scarcity and also the percentage of workers' incomes spent on food.

Material for answering the first question comes from John Money and others. Money carefully charted the changes in wheat prices on the Birmingham corn exchange for the period 1763 to 1769. He showed wheat at a 'normal' average price of 32/-d per quarter in 1763/4; it rose steadily thereafter to a peak of 60/-d in December 1766; it then fell back to 56/-d early in 1767 and peaked again in March at 76/-d. It was down again to 48/-d at the end of the year. The price eventually stabilised in 1769, when it was much above the 1763/4 level at between 40/-d and 48/-d per quarter. These prices for wheat must be married to prices of bread, and there is not always a direct correlation. Our only guide here is John Freeth the Birmingham poet who, in his annual rhyming invitations to the annual Birmingham Book Club dinners, sometimes referred to bread prices. In Birmingham, the standard was the 6d loaf and it was the weight of this loaf that was altered as the authorities set the price. Freeth tells us that the 'normal' price for bread was 12 ounces for 1d. This gives a 6d loaf of 4 ½lbs; but in 1792 the 6d loaf weighed 3lbs and by 1799 it weighed only 2lbs. How much bread did a family consume? Eden tells us that it was between 1lb and 1 ½lb per person per day. This is confirmed for Birmingham where at one time there was a 'self-denying ordinance' to try to limit individual consumption to 10 ounces per day. If we take a family of five and assume that their individual bread consumption is 1lb of bread per day, this means a family consumption of 35lbs of bread per week.

To find the percentage of their wages that working people spent on bread we will take a Birmingham building craftsman and a labourer and assume that they earned the same amount as building workers at Stratford-on-Avon. In the 'normal' year of 1764 with wheat at 32/-d a quarter and the 6d loaf at 4½lbs it would mean that the labourer would spend 3/10d or more than 63% of his 6/-d weekly wage on bread. However, in 1766, the year of the Hunger Riots, his bread would cost him 7/-d which is more than his total income. The building craftsman would spend 43% of his wages on bread in 1764 but 78% in 1766. These amounts spent on bread are so enormous and the conclusion that rises in the price of bread would lead to hunger is so inescapable that the assumption made must be questioned. Did Birmingham building workers earn more than those at Stratford-on-Avon? Figures from the late nineteenth century suggests that they did and that there was a 2d differential per day in favour of Birmingham; but when the first figure for a wage of Birmingham bricklayers and carpenters surfaces in 1770 from Arthur Young, these workers actually earned less than those in Stratford.

However, Arthur Young also tells us that Birmingham manufacturers paid wages between 7/-d and £3 per week. If we take a more optimistic view and assume that 7/-d was the wage of a Birmingham building labourer and that there was a 2 to 3 differential between labourers and craftsmen it could then be estimated that the labourer spent 55% of his income on bread in 1764 and 100% in 1766, the craftsman would have spent 31% and 61% of his wage on bread in the same years.

But it was not only bread; a very large percentage of income was spent on other foods. As a reminder of this it is instructive to look at the amount spent on food at a well-endowed but quite spartan trade school for working class children near to Birmingham.

Cost of keeping five Scholars at the Oldswinford Hospital School 1760.

Amount spent on Grain	Total Amount spent on Food.
3/6d per week	12/6 per week

The amount spent on grain (the school baked its own bread) was 50% of a labourers wage and the total amount spent on food was 5/6d more than the wage of a labourer and 2/-d more than the wage of a craftsman; and 1760 was a fairly 'normal' year for grain prices.

Working Class Politics 1750 – 1800 — The Hunger Struggles

Such figures provide overwhelming evidence that rising food prices meant for many people actual starvation and food riots were in fact Hunger Riots. It is this latter title given to the article by Dale Edward Williams analysing the events of 1766 and we turn now to the mechanics of the Hunger Riots.

Williams reported public disorder in 1766 on a scale not seen since the Civil Wars; widespread disturbances, not only throughout the midlands, but simultaneously in the south west, along the Thames valley and in East Anglia. The background was not only one of bad harvests and soaring food prices, but also economic depression at the end of the 7-Years War (during which Wolfe and Clive had laid the basis for a vast expansion of the British empire). Midland disturbances began in Birmingham on the 28th of August and at first concerned the price of butter and cheese. Crowds in the market took butter from vendors attempting to sell it at 10d per lb. and sold it at 7d. The proceeds they returned to the original vendors. The leaders of the protest said that they would attend at the market each day to see that the lower price was maintained. On 1 September 'Regulators' attended the market and ensured that bread was sold for 1d per lb. They also lowered the price of cheese and spirits. It is then alleged that some of the crowd became unruly and were taken to jail. Soon after this, one of the 'Confederates' mounted the wall on a ladder and made 'such dreadful threats' to the prison keepers' wife that she released the prisoners. The authorities then took action. 'Local inhabitants were summoned to give assistance in case of further incident'; bakers were made to agree to provide good household bread to the poor at 1d per lb and local farmers were assured that their persons and property would be protected in the market place. John Wyrley, the sole JP in Birmingham, speaking for the 'principal inhabitants' promised constant attendance at the market and prompt action against future offenders in breach of the peace.

This seems to have satisfied the Birmingham people and action moved on to the neighbouring areas. We follow some of this to show both the variety of actions available to the protestors and also the varying customs of each market. At Stourbridge on 15 September a dispute arose at noon over the high price of butter which, at that hour, was purchased by poorer people. Before this was settled a dealer outbid two poor women for a bag of wheat. At this, the poor immediately became riotous and obliged the farmers to sell wheat at 5/-d per bushel.' (45/-d per quarter). On 19 September three hundred Kidderminster rioters were joined by many others at Stourbridge where they persuaded country people to bring their butter to the market and sell it for 6d per lb. Wheat was sold at 5/-d per bushel. The next day similar events occured at Bewdley and the following week spread to Tamworth and Worcester. At the latter place, the local newspaper reported that 'it does not seem to be the intent of the poor to plunder the property of others, they only desire . . . to be provided with the necessaries of Life at a reasonable price.' That Saturday the mayor and justices of Worcester went round the several markets of the town and 'caused the king's proclamation regarding forestalling to be read.' Action continued in Coventry and Bedworth; engrossers were informed against and the magistrates made to order that no wheat should be lodged in inns or private houses, but brought direct to the market. On 26 September 150 Bedworth colliers came to Coventry market demanding that the mayor issue warrants to search several houses where they suspected cheese was stored. At one of the houses they found about 7cwt of cheese which they took to the market and sold for 2½d per lb. returning the money to the vendor. But at another house, where a much larger amount was found, the cheese was sold and the money not returned. The following day the Assize of Bread was fixed.

In the last days of September actions became widespread and Birmingham was again involved. On Monday 26 September 'a great number of the poor' assembled at the Birmingham cheese market and forced sales at 2 ½d per lb and then went to the hucksters' shops to enforce a price of 6d per lb for bacon. In this instance the crowd was 'overpowered by the civil magistrates authority' and the ring-leaders (two chimney sweeps and two labourers) were committed to jail. Troops were moved into the town from Shrewsbury. A subscription was then opened 'to supply the poor with inexpensive bread'.

The next market day in Birmingham a common labourer, 'said to be a Dudley man,' raised his standard, an inverted mop, and called out 'Redress of Grievances', after which 'parties went round to stallholders and grocers forcing them to sell bread, cheese, bacon and other provisions at fixed prices.'

At Hanbury, a meeting of farmers on 29 September met in the vestry of the church and agreed to bring their corn to Bromsgrove market on all market days to Christmas and sell it at 5/-d per bushel.

Despite the continued rise of prices, disturbances ceased in the west Midlands and in October 'more serious riots' moved to the east Midlands.

These events of 1766 in the west Midlands establish a number of points. They establish the range of food prices which were considered normal. They also show that in neighbouring incorporated towns such as

Coventry and Worcester much of the ancient legislation against forestalling, regrating and the establishment of the 'just price' could still be enforced in times of crisis, and apparently be made to operate successfully, provided sufficient force was brought to bear by working people. In Birmingham which, of course, was not an incorporated town, the administration wriggled and twisted to try to avoid regulating trade even when the necessary force was being exerted, but it is clear that there was both a tradition demanding controls, and also town officials whose duties included, or could be stretched to include, such popular controls. The main official was the High Bailiff, whose job was, according to Hutton, 'to inspect the markets, to see that justice took place between buyer and seller and to rectify the weights and measures used in the manor.' There were also the High Taster, who we have already met, who 'examined the goodness of beer and its measure', and the Low Taster who inspected the meat on sale and destroyed that which was unfit.' It is interesting to note that although there was no Assize of Bread, that a 'just' rate of 1d per lb should be established.

The 'Food Riots' of 1766 in Birmingham are also interesting because in examining these events it is difficult to find a 'riot'; there is plenty for the bourgeois local paper, Aris' Gazette, to describe as a 'riot'; much that was disturbing to the town administration and presumptuous on the part of 'the lower orders'; much to make officials nervous, call in and use the military and thus create the conditions for a 'riot'; but the main impression of the events of 1766 is of the orderly and disciplined action of working people taking action to invoke both their rights not to starve and also assert their ancient liberties. Finally, the events of 1766 in Birmingham represent a water-shed. The cost of food was never to return to the 'normal' level, and consequently the custom of unchanging wage rates over many decades had to be challenged and the unceasing fight of workers to keep their wages abreast of the cost of living was inaugurated.

The next decade, the 1770s however, provides little political activity of note. There was a series of bad harvests from 1772 to 1775 and 1774 was one of Hutton's 'times of remarkable scarcity', but riots did not recur. The two main democratic issues of the decade — Wilkes, and the revolt of the American colonies — tended to unite the different sections of Birmingham radicals who can roughly be separated out into the middle class political radicals of Dissent, the middle class economic radicals of entrepreneurs developing the Industrial Revolution (including Boulton, Watt and those in the Lunar Society), and the artisan and worker radicals. But this was also the decade which fashioned the banners under which the two main classes would fight their future ideological battles, the doctrines of Adam Smith and Tom Paine.

In the 1780s Hunger Struggles occurred in Birmingham in October 1782 when bread was 2d per lb. These struggles seem to have been initiated from the Black Country. A party of colliers marched into Wednesbury, 'waited upon the principal Maltsters and Gentlemen of the town', and persuaded them to reduce the prices of malt and flour. The miners then marched to Birmingham and were met in the Bull Ring by an officer of the town who demanded what they meant coming to the town in that hostile manner. The Leader replied that they did not come with the intention of committing depradations, but to regulate the price of malt, flour, butter, cheese, etc. The officer stated that he would do everything in his power to lower the prices of the articles complained of, 'as much as the times would admit of.' He then signed a paper to that effect and the miners were conducted a little way out of town. In the meantime, the Gentlemen of the Association and the military were drawn up in the Square and sent a message to the town officers stating that they were ready to march to their assistance. To convince the 'daring invaders' that they had sufficient force to disperse them if necessary, they 'paraded through the streets with drums beating etc.' Two days later, 'a very numerous and respectable meeting of the Officers and other Inhabitants of the town which included many of the principal retailers,' unanimously resolved to recommend that bread be sold at 8½ lbs for 1/-d, malt at 5/6d per bushel, and cheese at 3½d her lb. Also at this meeting 140 of the 'principal inhabitants' of the town were sworn in by the magistrates to act upon all emergencies when called upon.

These proceedings also initiated, as usual, an unbuttoning of pockets and 18 November the public were informed that 'several humane and public spirited Gentlemen had set on foot a Subscription for raising a sum of money to purchase flour, malt, etc. and dispose of it at a reduced price to the industrious poor inhabitants'. A meeting took place in December to discuss the subscription and the relief of distress during the winter, but 'the meeting was not so numerous as might reasonably be expected in so considerable and opulent a Town'. However, over £1,300 was subscribed in three weeks to sell 6lb 9d loaves to the poor for 6d. Distress was so bad in the winter that in January a meeting was held to discuss a new Workhouse.

Radicals and the Anti-Slavery Agitation.
In the 1780s the campaign began for the abolition of the slave trade. This issue tended not only to unite all the radicals but also the evangelical Tories. It was the high point of class collaboration in the town. Birmingham's participation and economic interest in the slave trade, ranging from the baubles and 'toys' for which slaves were bought, through to the provisions of guns and manufacture of the chains, handcuffs, and iron collars with which the slaves were shackled is well documented. Less well-known is the degree of support to abolish the trade.

Thomas Clarkson, the national leader (with William Wilberforce), came to Birmingham in 1787, the year of the foundation of the Society for the Abolition of the Slave Trade. Here he seems to have contacted the Quaker community, mentioning particularly the Lloyd family of John, Sampson and Charles. The next move came in January 1788 and was initiated by the Rectors of St Martin's and St Philip's. A public announcement by them noted that the slave trade was liable to be the subject of a parliamentary enquiry in the near future; it stated that they believed that the slave trade had long been a disgrace to Europe as well as violating Christian law, and informed that a meeting had been held in Birmingham in November which had sent 100gns to the National Society and had appointed the two signatories to remain in consultation with London and take any further steps they might think proper. On 23 January Dr Priestley delivered a sermon to the text 'And have made of one blood all nations of men to dwell upon the face of the earth,' which he subsequently published. At the end of January a meeting was held which passed the following resolution:

> First, That the practice of going to Africa to purchase Men to sell as Slaves should be publicly execrated.
> Second, That as Englishmen and Christians it behoves us to exert our best Endeavours to Abolish Slavery.
> Third, That it is the Duty of this Meeting to petition Parliament to take into consideration the inhuman practice of purchasing harmless Men, Women and Children, to sell in British Dominions for Slaves, and to restrain the Cruelties that are inflicted upon them . . .

A very vocal opposition to Abolition developed in the town, their views expressed (unusually anonymously) through the local press. Their two main arguments were that Abolition was not practicable and also that it would damage the trade of Birmingham. This anonymous opposition eventually prevailed on the Constables to convene a town meeting in May at the Public Office in Dale End:

> . . . to take into consideration a Petition to Parliament that the African Slave Trade (which is so greatly and extensively beneficial to this Town and Neighbourhood), may not be abolished, but undergo such Regulations only as are conducive to Humanity.

This meeting was packed by the supporters of Abolition and so many people attended that it was necessary to adjourn the meeting to the Hotel, Temple Row. Samuel Garbett was then elected to the chair and the first request was to the Constables to reveal the names of those who had called the meeting. A list of eight names was then read out, most of them manufacturers involved in the slave trade. Then the original resolution in favour of Abolition was passed, and finally the following resolution passed 'by a very great Majority':

> That no opposition having been made to this Petition (favouring Abolition'— GB) either at the time or since . . . and the House having now discovered a disposition to comply with the very numerous Petitions in favour of the oppressed Africans, it would be highly improper for the town of Birmingham to present a Petition directly contrary to the former . . .

After this, an African, Gustavus Vasa, came to Birmingham and strengthened the campaign for Abolition with the 'circulation of a narrative'. When he left, he thanked all those who had helped him, noting, in addition to the activists already mentioned, Matthew Boulton, Rev. J. Riland, William Russell, John Taylor, Samuel Galton and others. Vasa was apparently an African of substance for he went on:

> . . . these acts of Kindness and Hospitality have filled me with a longing desire to see these worthy friends on my own Estate in Africa, when the richest Produce of it should be devoted to their entertainment; they should there partake of the luxuriant Pineapples and the well-flavoured virgin Palm Wine, and to heighten the Bliss, I would burn a certain kind of Tree, that would afford a Light as clear and brilliant as the Virtues of my Guests.

The Parliamentary campaign for Abolition involved great expense in procuring witnesses and paying their expenses etc. and Birmingham assisted with public subscriptions. In April 1791, Wilberforce introduced his Bill for the Abolition of the Slave Trade, but it was defeated in the House of Commons by 163 votes to 88. The Abolitionists retorted with a national campaign to boycott West Indies rum and sugar. Two more years of agitation followed before Wilberforce could introduce another Bill. This one passed in the Commons, but was rejected in the Lords. By this time larger events were overshadowing Abolition. It was to be another thirteen years before success was achieved, the final Bill enacting that no vessel with slaves should be cleared from any port within the British dominions after May 1807, and no slave should be landed in British colonies after 1 March 1808.

First Reactions to the French Revolution
Returning to the 1780s, it is clear from the early stages of the campaign for Abolition that politics continued to be organised mainly from the Clubs, and it is still difficult to find recorded activities of artisans and other working class radicals. The advent of the French Revolution was to change all that. A year before this, however, came the centenary of the revolution of 1688.

The centenary celebrated was not the real revolution of 1642 – 46. The real revolution had economically undermined the relics of feudalism and cleared the way for the development of capitalism. Politically, it had exploded for all time the pretensions of kings to rule by divine right and established the principle of rule by parliament. But in making the revolution, the 'lower orders' who did the fighting and dying had asserted their claims to a share in the government. After the wars Levellers, Diggers, Ranters etc. had reasserted Socialist principles which could be traced back through More's Utopia, the Lollards, early Christianity and even primitive Communism before class societies emerged. Such democratic pretensions were crushed, but the price paid was compromise with the aristocratic landed interests, first in 1660 and then in the definitive bourgeois 'Glorious Revolution' of 1688.

One hundred years of development in Britain since then had almost totally obscured the socialist tradition. It had also obliterated the Jacobite tradition, and with it, the original differences between Whigs and Tories. For both parties in 1788 King and Church meant Hanoverian king, the constitutional settlement of 1688 and Anglican church. Dissenters also supported the Constitution and monarchy, so the celebrations of 1788 included all Birmingham opinion apart from a handful of die-hard Jacobites on the one hand and the advanced democrats in the Clubs and taverns whose voices we do not hear, on the other.

The main celebration in the town was a centenary Dinner organised by the town authorities at the Hotel, Temple Row. A slight snag (or was it advantage?) was that the actual days of the celebration, 4 and 5 November, included Guy Fawkes night and the authorities issued the following notice:

REVOLUTION JUBILEE AND GUNPOWDER PLOT. The Officers of the town respectfully inform the Public that no Illuminations, Bonfires or Fireworks, will take place on the celebrations of the above days on Tuesday and Wednesday next, and hereby give Notice that proper

People will be stationed in different parts of the town to apprehend all
Persons letting off Serpents, Rockets etc. and such as are found
offending will be prosecuted to the utmost rigour of the Law.

These dampeners on the exuberance of the population could not be
maintained and in fact the Hotel, the Clubs and the main streets of the
town were illuminated. The following is how the official celebrations were
reported:

On Tuesday and Wednesday last that happy era of civil liberty, the
Revolution of 1688, was celebrated with great concord and festivity. The
morning of Tuesday was ushered in by the ringing of bells and other
demonstrations of joy; and at three o'clock the assembly of Gentlemen,
who had met together to commemorate the day by dining at the Hotel,
was more numerous and respectable than any ever known in the Town.
It consisted of the High Sheriff and Members for the County, of the
Magistrates and principal persons of the Town and neighbourhood, and
of persons of every persuasion. The majority of the company was dressed
in blue coats, with orange capes, having on beautiful emblematical
buttons, manufactured by ingenious gentlemen of the town. They
likewise wore, pendant on an orange ribbon elegant silver medals, which
were struck upon the occasion . . .
   Our High Bailiff, Henry Clay Esq., presided at the dinner, which did
credit to the Master of the Hotel; and after the cloth was drawn the
following toasts were given:-
   The King and a speedy restoration of his health — The Glorious
Revolution and the immortal memory of the Great King William the
Third — Old England and its Constitution — Queen and Royal Family
— The Prince of Wales and perpetuity to the Brunswick line — May the
unanimity of this commemoration seal the extinction of parties —
   . . . The town and trade of Birmingham and may commerce ever
support and be supported by freedom . . . etc. etc.

We are also told that 'At the Free-masons and other taverns different
companies likewise met to commemorate the day'.

   The celebrations were the high point of unity in the town. The very
next year class harmony was cracked by the French Revolution, and in
1791 it was shattered by the Priestley Riots, the worst the town has ever
known.

The Priestley Riots 1791

   The Priestley Riots occurred over the position of the Dissenters, which
was particularly strong in Birmingham. The Presbyterians had evolved
into the Unitarians who dominated much of the political life of the town.
Quakers, such as the banking family of the Lloyds dominated much of
the economic life, although the greatest economic influence, Matthew
Boulton, was an Anglican. However, despite their influence, the
Dissenters were numerically a small minority in the town.

   The greatest of the Dissenters, Dr Joseph Priestley the Unitarian,
straddled three worlds. The first was that of world-famous chemist and
scientific participator in the developing Industrial Revolution, an influence
partly expressed by his membership of the Lunar Society in Birmingham.
Secondly, Priestley was a controversial and trenchant theologian with a
large published output of sermons and pamphlets. Thirdly, Priestley was
a radical democrat and a consummate political organiser.

The increasing convergence of Whig and Tory politics, led Dissenters to believe that the time was ripe for them to develop a campaign against the remaining restrictions on them. Their immediate target became the Test and Corporation Acts which reserved all state and municipal offices to Anglicans. In 1789 a vote to repeal the acts had been lost in the House of Commons by only twenty votes and it was felt that a national campaign would bring success. Birmingham Dissenters, led by Priestley and William Russell emerged as leaders of the campaign.

Beginning with a Birmingham Committee of the Seven Congregations of the Three Denominations (Presbyterian, Baptist and Independent) they spread such committees through the midlands and then nationally. But by 1790 reaction to the French Revolution was dividing opinion into traditional radicals who welcomed the equality and freedom brought by the Revolution, and reactionaries who saw the spectre of the democracy of the real English Revolution being revived. In January 1790 the Rev. George Croft, rector of St. Martin's, was accusing the Dissenters of weakening the fabric of Christianity, and the next month Spencer Madan, the rector of St. Philip's, was warning that 'Presbyterian principles are undoubtedly Republican'. The year also brought the first of a stream of publications from the fictional Nott family, pseudo-artisans and populist Tory reactionaries, which played a significant role in mobilising working class Toryism in the town.

In order to analyse the forces at work on Birmingham public opinion at the time of the Priestley Riots, it is necessary to follow the course of the French revolution to its second anniversary in July 1791. Pre-revolutionary France was ruled by an absolutist king, supported by the superior Roman Catholic clergy (the First Estate) and a swollen class of nobles with unchecked authority and exemption from taxation (The Second Estate). The smaller landlords, free tenants and free citizens constituted the Third Estate. The vast mass of the population — serfs and labourers — were unclassified, totally without rights but payers of the taxes which supported the feudal state. The revolution followed almost exactly the course the English revolution had taken one hundred and fifty years earlier. It was a revolution of the middle class (Third Estate) to abolish feudalism and establish the 'freedoms' necessary to develop capitalism. In doing so it faced the same problem as the English revolution — the need to mobilise support of the 'lower orders' who then made democratic demands the middle class were not prepared to concede.

The revolution began in May 1789 when, as a last resort to rescue the country from dissolution and bankruptcy, it became necessary for the king to convene the States-General (Parliament) for the first time since 1614. The Third Estate immediately took control and constituted itself the National Assembly of France. The king then attempted to close it down and the Third Estate then took the celebrated Tennis Court Oath at Versailles pledging itself not to separate until it had given France a constitution. Continued intrigues of the king led to an uprising in Paris and on 14 July the Bastille, the royalist prison and symbol of reaction, was stormed. In August came the main measures of the revolution, the abolition of serfdom, the Declaration of the Rights of man Liberty, Equality, Fraternity (taken from the American revolution) and in December the church lands were expropriated to the state.

JOSEPH PRIESTLEY, LL.D.

From an engraved portrait after Fuseli, in the possession of W. Bates, Esq., B.A

Richard Brinsley Sheridan.   Dr. Priestley.   Sir Cecil Wray.   Charles James Fox.   J. Horne Tooke.   Dr. Theophilus Lindsey.

"A BIRMINGHAM TOAST, JULY 14, 1791."

From the original etching by JAMES GILLRAY: Drawn on wood by G. H. Bernasconi.

1790 was a year largely of peaceful development in preparing a Constitution and it also saw a hothouse development of democratic public opinion directed largely through the Clubs that sprang up, notably the federation of Jacobin clubs across France, representing the views of the Third Estate. The first anniversary of the revolution saw a vast demonstration at the Champ de Mars where Louis XVI swore to uphold the constitution decreed by the Assembly.

But the king continued to plot against the revolution, the main difference between him and Charles I earlier being that Louis had somewhere to go, namely the border where foreign governments and French emigrees were gathered to overthrow the revolution. In June 1791 the king fled from Paris, where he had previously been brought from Versailles by the women of Paris to prevent such an action. He was discovered and brought back. This raised the question of what was to be done with the royal family and, as in England earlier, led to the emergence of parties advocating the deposition of the king and establishment of a Republic on the American model. Such was the state of affairs in France when Birmingham democrats proposed in July 1791 to celebrate the second anniversary of the revolution.

To complete the picture, two momentous events in England must be mentioned. Initially the French revolution had been supported by almost all sections of public opinion, but in November 1790, Edmund Burke, previously a democrat who had supported the American revolution, published his *Reflections on the French Revolution* which attacked the revolution and became immediately the bible of all reactionaries. Within three months, Thomas Paine had replied with his *Rights of Man*. This electrified democratic opinion and by 1791 was said to be flooding Birmingham from the publishers and booksellers of the town. The influence of Paine on the democratic movement can hardly be exaggerated. Some people influence one revolution and achieve immortality; this artisan and gentle revolutionary who never advocated anything more violent than universal peace, civilisation and the ending of poverty, decisively influenced three revolutions. Paine became first the ideologue of the American revolution and a prime mover of the American constitution with his *Common Sense,* then the spokesman for liberty throughout the world and member of the French Assembly with his *Rights of Man* and finally, in 1794 with his *Age of Reason* showed that the bible was not the word of God and thus became a founding father of British and world Secularism.

It was under these circumstances that the 'friends of freedom' announced their personal proposal to hold a public dinner at the Hotel, Temple Row on 14 July 1791 to celebrate the second anniversary of the fall of the Bastille.

This event was immediately associated with Priestley who had himself produced an 'able reply' to Burke's *Reflections* and as a result had been nominated a citizen of France. The attack on Priestley had been building up throughout the year. In one of his pamphlets the doctor had rather rashly compared the progress of free enquiry with the action of gunpowder:

> The present silent propagation of truth may even be compared to those
> causes in nature which lie dormant for a time, but which in proper

circumstances act with the greatest violence. We are, as it were, laying gunpowder, grain by grain under the old building of superstition and error, which a single spark may hereafter inflame, so as to produce an instantaneous explosion; in consequence of which, that edifice, the erection of which has been the work of ages, may be overturned in a moment, and so effectually, as that the same foundation can never be built on again.

Churchmen and others immediately misrepresented this as 'A New Gunpowder Plot for blowing up all the churches in the Establishment'. Another critic added a rhyme:

> E'en now is your church undermined,
> With Priestley's Polemical Nitre,
> Which exploded you'll presently find
> The red night-cap take place of the Mitre.

Controversy with the learned doctor was even being seen as an avenue of preferment within the church and, as Hutton remarked, Priestley had 'already made two bishops and there were still other heads which wanted mitres and others who cast more humble eyes upon tithes and glebe lands.'

The dinner became an event of national importance. A bitter cartoon by Gilray was circulated widely in the country and in Birmingham representing the national 'Jacobins' at a similar dinner drinking 'A Birmingham Toast' by Priestley with a silver salver in his hand proposing The Head Here, (implying the King's Head Here) and such national figures as Fox saying 'My Soul and Body on the Toast' and Sheridan (the playwright) saying 'I'll pledge you that Toast', etc. Finally, a forged handbill brought from London, was circulated and became the main weapon of those opposing the celebration. It extolled the revolution and went on:

> But it is impossible to forget that our own Parliament is venal? Your Minister hypocritical? your clergy legal oppressors? the reigning family extravagant? the crown of a certain great personage becoming every day too weighty for the head that wears it? . . .
> But on the 14th of this month, prove to the political sycophants that you reverence the Olive Branch; that you *will* sacrifice to public tranquility, till the majority *shall* exclaim *The Peace of Slavery is worse than the War of Freedom* Of that moment let tyrants beware.

On the morning of the 14th July the Dissenters published a notice in the *Birmingham Chronicle*:

> The friends of the intended festivity finding that their views and intentions, in consequence of being misconceived by some and misrepresented by others, have created an alarm in the minds of a majority in the town and, it is thought, endangered its tranquility, inform their neighbours that they value the peace of the town far beyond the gratification of a festival, and have therefore determined to give up their intentions of dining at the hotel upon this occasion; and they very gladly improve this renewed opportunity of declaring that they are to this hour ignorant of the author, printer or publisher of the inflammatory hand-bill circulated on Monday.

But Mr Dadley, the proprietor of the Hotel, argued that there was no danger of serious disturbances and that the dinner should go on but break up early. This advice was taken and at 3 pm 'about eighty gentlemen sat down to dinner'. Ordinarily, Joseph Priestley might have been present, (although 'public assemblages of a political or convivial nature were not the chosen recreation of the philosopher and theologian'), but he stayed at home on this occasion.

The dinner was chaired by Capt. James Keir, the noted chemist, glass manufacturer at Stourbridge, chemical manufacturer at Tipton, member of the Lunar Society and an Anglican. Among the eighteen toasts drunk at the dinner were the following:

1. The King and Constitution
2. The National Assembly and Patriots of France, whose virtue and wisdom have raised twenty six millions from the mean condition of subjects of despotism, to the dignity and happiness of free men.
7. The true Friends of the Constitution of this Country,who wish to preserve its spirit, by correcting its abuses.
8. May the people of England never cease to remonstrate, till their Parliament becomes a true National Representation.
9. The Prince of Wales.
10. The United States of America. May they forever enjoy the liberty which they have so honourably acquired.
16. Peace and Good-will to all mankind.
17. Prosperity to the town of Birmingham.
18. A happy meeting to all the Friends of Liberty on the 14th July 1792.

A crowd had hissed and hustled the diners as they went into the Hotel, but when the dinner broke up at 5 pm they found much greater difficulty getting to their homes. The mob seemed intent on finding Priestley and watched the Hotel until 8 pm. When they did not find him they attacked the place where the dinner had been held despite pleas of 'Don't break Dadley's windows, He's a Churchman'. Foiled in their attempts to find Priestley, they next attacked the building in which he ministered, the New Meeting in Moor Street, and burned it to the ground. Meanwhile another crowd attacked the Old Meeting and razed that to the ground.

The two mobs then merged to attack Priestley's house at Fair Hill and set it alight, burning or destroying priceless manuscripts and scientific equipment. Priestley and his family had left about an hour before the attack and were at James Russell's house at Showell Green.

The next morning the Church and King mob reassembled despite feeble attempts of the town and church authorities to control the monster they had created. The first target was Baskerville House, formerly the residence of the great printer but then much enlarged and occupied by J. Ryland. It was estimated that about one thousand rioters were at this house, many of them drunk by looting the wine and that seven persons were burned to death in the cellars. Special constables were sworn in, but they could not save Baskerville House. The next target was John Taylor's house at Bordesley Hall and the final attack of the day was on William Hutton's premises in the High Street. Hutton had not believed that his property was in danger since he was not a Unitarian but an Independent worshipping at Carrs Lane. But Hutton's offence was that he was the originator of and propagator for the Court of Requests, known as the

Conscience Court where suits for non-payment of debt could be brought cheaply, and the large number of cases brought there against the poor had undermined his popularity.

The third day of the riots was the worst. Hutton's private house on Bennett's Hill suffered first, followed by James Humphrey's at Sparkbrook. William Russell's (necessitating further flight of Joseph Priestley, his wife and their daughter), James Russell's, Mr Hawke's, John Taylor's and the houses of various dissenting ministers.

The fourth day was the Sabbath and began with an 'Important Notice to the Friends of Church and King', signed by the magistrates and main clergy of the town. It requested that the burning stop, not because it was illegal, but because the expense of it all would fall not on the victims but upon the body of local rate payers! This appeal fell on deaf ears and further houses and meeting places were destroyed. It was only when the mob was preparing to set the torch to Edgbaston Hall, the residence of Dr William Withering, that the announcement of the approach of a body of soldiers led the rioters to finally disperse.

The victims of the riots had scattered, some, such as the Priestleys and Russells to London. But within a few days, most returned to Birmingham to seek legal redress and to begin a political counter-offensive.

Priestley wrote a long Address to the Inhabitants of Birmingham published in the *Birmingham Gazette* on 25 July attacking those who had misrepresented the Dissenters as enemies of the Constitution, especially the Rector of St. Martin's and again denied any knowledge of the forged handbill which had played such a fatal part in the tragedies. He stated that the books, manuscripts and scientific equipment destroyed was probably the most priceless collection ever brought together by a private individual. He also maintained that the rioters had hindered their cause more than that of the Dissenters since, 'nothing but reason and argument can support any system of religion.'

Only twelve of the rioters were arraigned at the Warwick Assizes of August 1791 and only four were found guilty and sentenced to death, two actually being hanged. The leniency of the Court passed into national hunting parlance when it was said of foxes in a hopeless position that 'only a Birmingham jury can save him now.'

The claims of the victims for compensation were heard at the Warwick Assizes of 1792. Total claims were made of £35,000 of which £27,000 was allowed. The largest claim was John Taylor's for £13,000 of which £10,000 was allowed. Hutton's was the next highest claim at £6,700 of which £5,400 was granted. Priestley claimed £3,600 and was granted £2,500. The main costs of the trial, borne by the Dissenters, were £13,000.

Controversy raged as to who was responsible for the riots. Suspicion falls upon the government. They had a vested interest in crushing both dissent and sympathy with the French Revolution; the tardiness with which troops reached Birmingham only on the fourth day gives weight to this. But with recent experience of the Gordon Riots in 1780, the government in London understood better than the local Church and King zealots that mobs might be mobilised and incited, but controlling them was a very different matter. Most culpable were the local civic authorities who took no effective steps to prevent the riots occuring, and the local

church authorities who recklessly fanned animosity towards the
Dissenters. With hindsight it might also be said that Priestley misjudged
the general political situation and some of his utterances could have been
framed more diplomatically. On the other hand, Priestley was a very big
fish, a national leader, even though he operated in the small pond of
provincial society, and national resources were brought to bear to
discredit him.

Working Class Politics during Birmingham's 'Reign of Terror' 1792 – 1800

The 1791 Riots mark a turning point in the democratic history of
Birmingham. For almost a generation a 'reign of terror' as Langford
called it, descended. Control of the town passed to Tory reactionaries,
democratic activity was stamped out by the Combination Acts at the end
of the decade and the suppression of all progressive political activity. In
addition, the development of the French Revolution and the looming
spectre of the Good Old Cause of the English Revolution led the high
bourgeoisie of Birmingham away from the radicalism which had to a
considerable extent united them with their artisans, to an unerring aware-
ness of their class position, in this period during which the working class
was emerging. This was to change the direction of the radical tradition
in the town.

Democracy did not die in the town without a struggle, however. The
details of radical activity after 1791 have been unravelled by John Money
and there are further Hunger Struggles to consider.

Whether Priestley's proposed Warwickshire Constitutional Society
ever got off the ground is unclear, but democratic activity was carried out
with the Society for Constitutional Action of which William Russell had
been a leading member since 1783. In June 1792 600 copies of a letter
from Tom Paine to the government defending his cheap edition of *The
Rights of Man* circulated in Birmingham through such channels. The two
Meetings of Unitarians met together in a temporary building in Livery
Street until rebuilding was complete, and the minister who took
Priestley's place after he had emigrated first to France and finally to
America, continued his work. William Belcher was arrested for selling
The Rights of Man in December 1792 and defended himself by stating that
the book was on sale in every bookshop in Birmingham. The key event
was the formation in November 1792 of the Birmingham Society for
Constitutional Information led by John Harrison and Thomas Prosser.
This linked with the London Corresponding Society and is therefore the
first clearly working class political society of which we have notice.

This activity was buoyed up by the continuing development of the
French Revolution. In July 1792 the coalition powers led by Austria and
Prussia declared that they had taken up arms to end anarchy in France.
They threatened the destruction of all towns that resisted and prepared
to march on Paris from Moselle, the Rhine and the Netherlands. As these
armies advanced on Paris, the city rose in arms to resist, the first Paris
Commune was formed and in August Louis XVI was arrested. In early
September the first 'massacres' of the fifth column of aristocrats and their
supporters occurred. On 2 September the French levies won the
resounding victory of Valmy and put the invading armies to flight. On 21

September the Convention, elected by universal suffrage, proclaimed the Republic. In January (the same month that had seen the execution of Charles I) 1793 Louis was executed. In June 1793 the Jacobins, representing the French middle class supported by the sans-culottes came to power and the revolution reached its highest point.

These events alarmed the British authorities. Home Office spies locally controlled by John Brooke, infiltrated the Birmingham Clubs, notably the Society for Free Debate.

Reactionary Clubs were formed; the Church and King Club was formed by Edward Carver and John Brookes at Hobson's Tavern, Worcester Street, and the loyal True Blues at the Union Tavern in Cherry Street. By December 1792 the Birmingham Association for the Protection of Liberty and Property had been formed. Such organisations, more closely controlled than the Mob of 1791, tended to take to the streets and act as stormtroopers, hence Langford's 'reign of terror', and retaliation by Jacobins brought a state of gang warfare to Birmingham. It was claimed that there were about 400 True Blues mobilised in groups of 20 who operated in collaboration with the local authorities.

Attempts were made to make peace between Church and Dissent, but the position of the Dissenters, made clear by William Russell, was that although they were loyal to the Hanoverian succession and to the constitution, certain 'abuses' had crept in since 1688 which called for Parliamentary reform as the only remedy for the country's discontents; they were 'enemies of sedition', but opposed to the government's present prosecution of printers and booksellers and they supported the freedom of the press.

In March 1793 pressure was put on the Clubs and 120 innkeepers agreed not to offer their facilities to constitutional societies. Later the same month Harrison and Kilminster, the leaders of the democrats, were ambushed after a meeting at the Hare and Hounds, Hill Street, and a gang led by Woolridge, the town gaoler, and Barr, the Constable, beat them up and robbed them. They were then arrested, kept in solitary confinement and interrogated by Joseph Carles for four hours the next day.

The democrats then took their campaign into the workshops and manufactories. They distributed to every workman a broadsheet demanding annual parliaments and the vote.

The next complication was that the financial and moral support of the reactionary British government for the enemies of the revolution led the French government to declare war on Britain. This brought jingoism into play, but also resulted in mass unemployment in Birmingham. In March 1793 the factory campaign in Birmingham continued with a Letter to the English Nation. This pointed out that the war had already put 10,000 out of work in Birmingham and warned that if the French were unable to defeat the coalition of powers waging war against the revolution, then they would call upon the Americans to return the support they had been given for their revolution and Britain would again be defeated and disgraced as she had been in the American War of Independence.

Regular contact between the Birmingham Society for Constitutional Information and the London Corresponding Society was commenced. Similar societies throughout the country poured petitions to Parliament demanding annual parliaments and universal suffrage. Birmingham's petition was said to contain 2,720 names. John Kilminster was convinced that the Church and King mob was being overcome. But in August an allied victory at Valenciennes brought jingo celebrations, and the mob was out in the streets again in October resisting the collection of the special rate to compensate the victims of the Priestley Riot. In the autumn a Convention in Edinburgh was convened. This represented a possible alternative Parliament if reform was refused, and opened out revolutionary possibilities to which the government was always sensitive. But Birmingham did not send a representative to this Convention, pleading expense as an excuse.

Mass unemployment, large increases in taxes, further attacks on the freedom of the press and the continuing high cost of bread strengthened support for the 'Jacobins', and the ideological struggle for the control of the 'Mob' became crucial. The actions of the mob can best be regarded as the direct, organised exercise of power by the mass of the population excluded from political power. Spies and informers began to report such 'mixed' slogans as 'God save the King and Tom Paine for Ever', or 'No Presbyterians and Tom Paine for Ever'. The revolution in France also continued to exercise contradictory influences on people's minds. On the one hand, 1794 was the year of the Terror with the mass guillotining of the internal enemies of the revolution; on the other hand it was also the year of the Law of the Maximum which fixed the price of bread and other necessities of life and unemployment melted away with the fixing of a minimum wage and the decreeing of an 8-hour day.

In 1795 a particularly bad harvest brought matters to a head and Hunger Struggles returned to Birmingham. At the bottom of Snow Hill there was a corn mill and bakehouse owned by Packard which supplied a considerable number of people with flour and bread. On 29 June 'a mob (principally composed of women) assembled . . . round the mill and began to break the window of it.' Two magistrates went to the mill and began to remonstrate with the women, but 'a rabble, urged on by furious women, made their way into a part of the premises and the persons of the magistrates were endangered by the stones and brick ends which were thrown in every direction.' The military and Yeomanry were sent for 'and the mill saved from destruction', although the crowd broke into the counting house to find the account books. The riot act was then read and the military cleared the premises. Later in the day another attack was made on the mill and 'some of the leading rioters', were arrested. To take them to the lock-up, the constables ordered the soldiers to load their weapons. Despite this, a rescue attempt was made, and the soldiers, again on the orders of the constables it was alleged, fired on the crowd, killing two men. This ended the violence, but led to 'written papers' protesting at this outrage. Brooke, the reactionary coroner, returned a verdict of justifiable homicide on the deaths of the men. Two women and a man, said to be the ringleaders were committed to Warwick gaol to face charges which carried the death penalty. The democrats response to this was given by Kilmister the following month:

> In the late disturbances in Birmingham, the chief arguement of the rioters to the magistrates was, 'You did not shoot us when we were

rioting for Church and King and pulling down the presbyterian meetings and dwelling houses, but gave us plenty of good ale and spirits to urge us on. Now we are rioting for a big loaf we must be shot at and cut up like Bacon Pigs'.

As the decade ground on repression multiplied. From 1793 habeas corpus had been suspended, prosecutions for 'sedition' multiplied and the rights of free speech and public meetings restricted. The continuing influence of the English Revolution, working through the French one, was attested to by the formation of a Birmingham Association for the Protection of Liberty and Property against Republicans and Levellers. This federated with other associations of the same name in other parts of the country. All the leading Birmingham reactionaries joined the committee, notably Brookes the coroner, Carles, and Spencer and the principal Anglican clergy of the town — Madan, Croft, Curtis and Burn.

The democrats replied after the 1796 riots by forming the Birmingham United Corresponding Society. Two London delegates, John Binns and John Gale Jones attended meetings which were held in parts in order to try to comply with the new sedition and treason laws limiting meetings to fifty persons. Both were arrested and committed for trial. Binns was brought to trial at Warwick in August 1797, but the jury refused to convict — an important victory for the democracy at that time. The Society played its part in a national campaign for the dismissal of the Pitt ministry and helped to collect about 4,500 signatures to a Birmingham petition in August. The Society met at Parr's Cottage of Content, and the last notice of it, in September 1797, stated that it was 'daily increasing in numbers.'

1797 was the year of the financial panic in England and the suspension of cash payments by the Bank of England. It was also the year of the Nore and Spithead naval mutinies. In Birmingham mass unemployment and misery was bringing about the conjunction the authorites always dreaded — that between the political movement and the industrial. In 1798 there was legislation to suppress 'seditious and treasonable' societies, with new laws to muzzle the press. The following year every printer had to be registered and licenced. In 1799 Corresponding and similar societies were totally banned and the final attempt made to extinguish radical activity completely with the Combination Acts of 1799 and 1800 which banned trade unions.

Despite this almost total repression radical sentiment and activity continued. Slogans scratched on walls through the town changed significantly from the early 1790s when they had been 'Church and King' and 'Damn the Jacobins'. By 1800 it was such 'seditious utterances' as 'No War', 'Damn Pitt', and 'No K.. g, Lords or Commons'. The Hunger Protests of 1795 and 1800 brought wall slogans such as 'No damned rogues in Grain', and 'No Badgers'. The two agitations came together with such slogans as 'Large Loaves, Peace, No Taxes, No Tithes, Free Constitution'. Finally, despite the Combination Acts, trade union activity continued, as will be shown.

Chapter Two
WORKING CLASS CONSCIOUSNESS
1800 – 1830

The War Years 1800 – 1815

The last chapter has indicated how the radical-democratic tradition in Birmingham developed and then was challenged from the 1790s — ideologically by the theories of Burke and Adam Smith, and politically by nationalism, pro-war jingoism and religious conservatism. When this failed to defeat the countervailing ideology of Thomas Paine, revolutionary tradition and hunger protest, the direct force of the state was used to forcibly stamp out all democratic organisations of protest. This too failed. The present section traces how, in the complex conditions of war and repression, continuity of the radical tradition was maintained.

The raw material of the narrative of this struggle has been set out in considerable detail by Rose, Langford and Dent, so that only the main outlines and inter-connections need be made here.

The development of Corresponding Societies in Birmingham from 1794 and their link-up with the London Corresponding Society and those of other towns marks the emergence of Birmingham artisan and worker influence from the local Clubs of Birmingham on to the wider national stage. Bad harvests and distress in the first years of the nineteenth century brought further trade union and political pressure in Birmingham. The two years of peace from March 1802 to May 1804 brought some relief as trade expanded. When war was resumed it soon brought the Berlin Decrees from Napoleon in 1806 banning all trade with Britain and its colonies. These were followed by the retaliatory Orders-in-Council the next year which devastated Birmingham trade and industry. There was perhaps a brief respite in 1809 and 1810, but in 1812 the USA entered the war against Britain and all was economic gloom until the end of the war. In these circumstances workers and artisans continued the Corresponding Society tradition from 1811 by forming the Artisan Committee. This marked the emergence of George Edmonds, a Birmingham Baptist minister's son, into political activity. The Committee was hounded by the magistrates and their informers, but survived to pass the torch on to the Hampden Club which in 1815 was responsible for the petition against the Corn Laws (forbidding the importation of corn into Britain until it reached the famine price of 80/-d (£4) a quarter). This was said to have been signed by 48,600 persons, almost the entire adult population of Birmingham.

Trade union activity also continued during the war, despite its illegality and the fearsome penalties which were liable to follow prosecution. Much of this activity was probably under the cover of Friendly Societies some of which continued to be set up and register their rules during the years of trade union illegality from 1799 to 1824. By combing *Aris's Birmingham Gazette,* Rose has identified the following trades which combined and struck work between 1800 and 1810 — shoemakers, tailors, brushmakers, journeymen cabinet makers, journeymen tailors and candlestick makers.

Others combined to petition their masters for wage increases, and the trickle became a flood in 1810, one of the few years of prosperity. At this time brass founders claimed that they had not had an advance of wages for more than 50 years, steelyard makers for 40 years and brushmakers for 30 years. Among the trades combining were metal platers, scalebeam and steelyard makers, iron spoon makers, journeymen bone and ivory brushmakers, turners and toymakers, cast-iron hinge makers, mathematical instrument makers, brassfounders, spurmakers, bayonet filers, gilt and plated buttonmakers, journeymen of the horn, button and hard white metal spoon trade, bellows pipe makers and steel grinders. In addition, at least thirteen other groups of workers obtained increases of wages, although less certainly as a result of combination.

Besides these increasingly 'modern' methods of improving economic conditions, traditional methods continued and there were hunger protests in 1800, 1810 and 1812.

Reform and New Traditions — the first Long Depression 1815 – 22

After the Napoleonic Wars, instead of the expected boom in trade, depression and mass unemployment continued. This was the first of three Long Depressions, as I have called them, in the first half of the nineteenth century. They may be considered to be 'classic' examples of the trade cycle in the second wave of capitalist expansion after the distorting effects of war have been removed. The case of Birmingham demonstrates most clearly the basic causes of capitalist crises. These are the imperative of ever expanded reproduction of capital resulting in the grossest inequalities of income. This is combined with blind production for markets, domestic and foreign. Together, these result in disproportionalities in production which prevent the surplus value in goods produced being realised. Unsold goods accumulate and mass unemployment is the inevitable result.

Each of these Long Depressions brought an upsurge of working class activity which drew on the radical democratic traditions of the town; but the half century 1800 – 1850 is particularly notable for adding to those traditions and producing organisations and forms that were unique. And because the Industrial Revolution came first to Britain and the British were therefore the first working class in the world, these innovations were later taken over and adapted by working class movements throughout the world.

The most striking characteristic of the period after the Napoleonic Wars is the changed form of politics. Out went 'mob politics' and riots. In came new, modern institutions — working class newspapers, trade unions, co-operative organisations, Socialist policies and working class political parties.

Conditions of mass unemployment and hunger were exacerbated by the insistence of the reactionary government of Lord Liverpool that all protest was evidence of insurrectional intent to be met, not with reform, but with repression. The Hampden Club remained the main artisan/working class political organisation and its hounding by the local authorities continued. In January 1817 came the first of the famous series of mass meetings on Newhall Hill with Birmingham acting as the focus of the protest movement of the whole of the west Midlands from Coventry to the Black Country. Twenty thousand people are said to have attended this meeting which demanded universal suffrage and annual parliaments and protested against distress.

1819 brought another surge of radical activity. In July, at another mass meeting on Newhall Hill, Sir Charles Wolesley was elected Legislatorial Attorney and directed to attempt to take his seat in Parliament as MP for Birmingham. This was the second of two alternative radical strategies for reform to which the government was acutely sensitive and always acted fiercely. The first strategy was the setting up of an alternative assembly to Parliament, such as a Convention; the second was the election of alternative representatives as MPs. The above meeting was notable for the presence of Major Cartwright, radical MP and father of the Six Demands which were to become the basis for Chartism. Also present was T.J. Wooler, editor of *Black Dwarf,* the most important 'seditious' working class newspaper of the time.

By this time the working class press was widely distributed in Birmingham. The other influential, national 'seditious' newspaper was that of the Tory Radical, William Cobbet whose *Political Register* circulated in circles wider than working class ones. But Birmingham also had a radical press of its own. From 1811 to 1814 there had been the *Midland Chronicle,* controlled by the Birmingham radical W. Hawkes Smith, who also printed and published the *Birmingham Inspector,* in 1817. In 1818 – 19 the *Birmingham Argus* appeared, whose printer George Ragg, was prosecuted and sentenced to twelve months imprisonment. This was followed by newspapers, variously titled, controlled by George Edmonds in 1819 – 20.

1819 was also the year of Peterloo, the outrage at St Peter's Fields, Manchester, in which eleven demonstrators were killed and something like 400 wounded by Yeomanry sabre charging a peaceful crowd. This led to a vast protest and solidarity movement throughout the country, including Birmingham. But the government followed it up with the most repressive legislation of the period, the notorious Six Acts, which made legal protest all but impossible and included a new tax of 4d per copy on all newspapers.

The *Birmingham Argus* was the paper of a new, radical political organisation, the Union Society. This replaced the Hampden Club and was the forerunner of the Policital Union, destined to play so important a part in Birmingham politics. The Union Society claimed 2800 members and acquired its own premises with proposals for a library and reading room and a Sunday school.

Such activities alarmed the authorities and repression was immediate. A Birmingham Association for the Refutation and Suppression of Blasphemy and Sedition was started and Anglican reactionaries such as Edward Burn, perpetual curate at St Mary's and J.H. Spry of Christ Church thundered from their pulpits on the duty of obedience to established governments.

Prosecutions began from the middle of 1819. Joseph Russell was prosecuted for selling the celebrated lampoon of Liverpool, Castlereagh and Eldon (the government ministers) in Hone's *Political Litany,* even though Hone had been acquitted by a London jury of seditious or blasphemous intent. Russell, who had two motherless children, was sentenced to eight months imprisonment. Other local prosecutions at the time were those of George Edmonds the bookseller, Osborne, Joseph Brandis, R. Mansfield and George Ragg who was sentenced to 12 months imprisonment. The chairman of the Union Society, Charles Whitworth, was also arrested.

The organisers of the meeting that elected Sir Charles Wolseley Legislatorial Attorney felt the full force of government fury. Major Cartwright, Wooler and the Birmingham radicals Edmonds and Maddocks were indicted before a grand jury at Warwick Assize in 1820. It resulted in a fine for Major Cartwright and imprisonment for the other defendants.

Radical activity was not stamped out, however. At the end of 1822 the Birmingham Union and Patriots' Friends' Society gave a public dinner to welcome Wooler on his release from Warwick goal. In July 1823 the Birmingham Union Society of Radical Reformers gave a dinner for Henry 'Orator' Hunt, the hero of Peterloo, at which George Edmonds took the chair and Ragg, Russell, and Brandis were present. Earlier in the year there had been an enthusiastic crowd in the Bull ring to welcome back George Edmonds from Warwick gaol.

By 1822, however, the slump was over, a short period of expansion followed and the progressive movement became bogged down in the unedifying contest between the dissolute Prince Regent and his equally reprehensible wife, Caroline. This came to a head with the campaign in 1820 to deprive her of the privilege of queen, and closed with her death the next year.

So ended another phase of the struggle for Parliamentary reform. Again it had been unsuccessful. But any 'equipoise' in Birmingham reflected not the balance of class forces in the town, but the direct intervention of the coercive power of the state.

The Reform Bill of 1832 and the second Long Depression 1829 – 33.

An important reason for the failure of the reform movement up to this time was the absence of a viable alternative system to capitalism. The following period was to see the inexorable development of the productive forces of capitalism reach such a stage that both the first possibilities of replacing the system began to emerge, together with the strengthening of the propertyless factory proletariat forces towards the point where they would be the leading force in change. Birmingham played an important national part in these developments within the co-operative and Owenite Socialist movements. But while this was occurring, Birmingham was also to play a leading role in the 'Jacobin'/working class alliance which produced its greatest triumph in the passing of the Great Reform Bill of 1832.

The background to the Bill is a series of working class struggles which originated in the period of expansion in the 1820s between the two Long Depressions. The first was the ending of the Combination Acts and the extraordinary development of trade unionism facing a lengthy period when they were no longer illegal, but not yet legal. Another was the battle for press freedom against the 'taxes on knowledge'. A third was the further development of Union Societies under working class and radical control which finally culminated in the middle-class led Birmingham Political Union.

Enough has already been said to establish the continuity of trade unionism during the period of illegality from 1799 to 1824. The antiquity and ubiquity of such trades and crafts as brush makers, carpenters and many others suggests that organisation in some of these pre-date the Industrial Revolution even in Birmingham. The development of trade clubs and societies between 1790 and 1826 was comprehensively examined in a Birmingham University BA thesis by J.W. Nicholas in 1949 and the latest historian of this early period is Clive Behagg. Nicholas used the statistics of societies registering their rules with the Registrar of Friendly Societies to indicate trends in trade unions development. These figures are not conclusive, since not all societies registering were trade unions, and not all trade unions registered, but the correlations are so striking as to give the figures a high significance. Societies registered in 1795 totalled 22. In 1799 when trade unions were made illegal the total was down to two. During the years of illegality registrations range between none and five. But in 1824, the year of the repeal of the Combination Acts, no less than 102 societies registered. The next year that total was 22 and in 1826 it was eight. This emergence of 'friendly societies' registering their rules was accompanied by an unparalleled spate of trade societies negotiating wage increases by a variety of methods ranging from orthodox demands for increased pay, through to the normal channel for artisans of demanding an increase in the price paid to them for their product by merchants or manufacturers, on to one society which announced that if the masters lowered the price paid to them, they would lower the quality of the product they made by an equivalent amount. Some further detailing of this trade union activity gives only a glimpse of the total amount of activity, but a vivid picture of the hundreds of crafts in Birmingham which were capable of organising themselves. In July the Hammer, Compass Pincer, Saddlers Tools and Heavy Steel Toymakers secured a pay rise. In August platers were negotiating with masters to raise prices. In September Button Stampers and Tool Makers' Journeymen called a meeting at the Swan Tavern, Church Street. The Union Society of Jewellers were meeting at the Roebuck, Cock Street. More significantly, there was clear evidence of crafts combining into trades, at least for purposes of wage negotiations. In Novemeber 1824 there is the first mention of Engineers as meeting at the King's Head, Alison Street. In April 1824 Sadlers and Harness Makers and Whipthong workers were demanding increases. In May the building tradesmen of Operative Carpenters Plumbers, Painters and Glaziers and Bricklayers were all demanding increases. This activity laid the basis of the famous Builders Union of 1833 – 4 in Birmingham which led on to the vast Grand National Consolidated Trade Union of the same year.

Such trade union activity continued until the end of 1825 when the economic boom broke in December.

The 1820s and 1830s were also important decades in the struggle for a free press and against the newspaper stamp duty. The problem for the government was that the readership of the 'seditious and blasphemous' press was as high or higher, than readership of the capitalist press, and this was probably as true of Birmingham as it was of the Black Country. Cobbett's *Political Register* evolved from a Tory radical background and circulated from 1802 to 1835, except for a short period from 1817 when repression led Cobbett to flee to America. After the Napoleonic Wars, from exposing government corruption and rural starvation; the *Register* espoused Parliamentary reform and became a leading radical journal of the working class. This background of Cobbett's gave him influence in 'respectable' as well as radical circles. Even before the demise of Wooler's *Black Dwarf* in 1824, Richard Carlile's *Republican* (1819 – 26) and later Henry Hetherington's *Poor Man's Guardian* (1831 – 35) became the main working class newspapers.

Carlile initiated from London 'the battle of the unstamped', by selling his paper unstamped, going to prison, and then relying first on his family and then a seeming never-ending stream of volunteers to continue the paper and maintain his business, until they, too, went to prison. This battle was also sustained outside London. In Birmingham, Guest claimed to be the first person locally to have distributed the unstamped press. He was among the 500 or so who went to prison for selling the *Poor Man's Guardian*. The expansion of Guest's business led other publishers, printers and booksellers to follow his example. The importance of the *Guardian* was that it was the organ of the National Union of the Working Classes, branches of which were set up in Birmingham and the midlands. Trade unionists were catered for by the successive papers of John Doherty such as the *Voice of the People* published from Manchester. Doherty pioneered some of the earliest attempts to form general unions, notably the National Association for the Protection of Labour, of which a midland association existed at the end of the 1820s.

These and other working class newspapers are our main source of knowledge of the labour movement and it must be stressed that it is the neglect of these sources (which, until the micro-filming of these papers in recent years, were available only at the British Newspaper Library in London) and reliance on the press sources in Birmingham Reference library alone, which account for the incomplete and sometimes widely misleading versions of Birmingham labour history in the past, notably of Owenite Socialism and Chartism. This stricture applies particularly to the use of the *Birmingham Journal* (1825 – 59). This began life as a high Tory paper, became the mouthpiece of the Birmingham Political Union between 1829 and 1842 and ended its life in 1859 by becoming the *Birmingham Post*. More genuinely reflecting working class opinion were the local Owenite papers, the *Birmingham Co-operative Herald* (1829 – 30) and the *Birmingham Labour Exchange Gazette* (1833). In 1831 there was also the *Midland Representative & Birmingham Herald*, edited by Bronterre O'Brien, who was later to be known as the Schoolmaster of Chartism.

All the above developments of press, trade unions and political organisation demonstrate a confident development from innovation to consolidation. It indicates a considerabled growth of class consciousness during the short period of economic expansion and comparative prosperity of the mid 1820s.

During the same period a reactionary Tory banker was metamorphosising into the most important middle class radical that Birmingham was to produce after Joseph Priestley and before Joseph Chamberlain. This was Thomas Attwood. He had been a leader of commercial opinion from at least 1812 when he had led a public campaign against the government's Orders-in-Council and its renewal of the East India

Company's monopoly. With the growing importance of Birmingham, the informal eighteenth century arrangement whereby one of the two Warwickshire MPs was deemed to represent the interests of Birmingham and other industrialised parts of the country, no longer sufficed and Attwood was slowly won to the cause of parliamentary reform and direct representation of Birmingham. A second, and perhaps even more impelling motive with Attwood, was his unorthodox monetary views, for which he unsuccessfully struggled to gain support, and he was eventually outraged when Wellington treated them with contempt. Attwood gathered round him a core of Birmingham supporters for his currency scheme — Joshua Scholefield, Charles Jones, Benjamin Hadley and Thomas Clutton Salt — who came mainly from the ultra-Tory camp and so it might well be said that the leaders of the Birmingham Political Union were firmer for currency reform than they were for Parliamentary reform. This is one of the reasons for the apostasy of these middle class leaders in 1839 when they deserted Chartism.

Attwood advocated a paper currency. The immense economic upheavals after the Napoleonic Wars had led to the restoration of the gold standard in 1819 and thus the liability of debtors who had contracted debts at very high prices in a period of paper money to repay in 'prices' (ie of the goods they sold or the wages they received) which had fallen steeply. This, Attwood held, was not only a gross injustice which bound together both manufacturers and workers, but meant that there was insufficient purchasing power to buy goods produced and mass unemployment resulted. Attwood's solution was to issue sufficient paper currency to enable the goods to be bought.

The theory is plausible, but false. In the first place it assumed that the fall in prices was the result of the return to gold, and that control of the money supply could have prevented this. It is a mono-theory of the causes of crisis which has surfaced in modern times under the guise of Monetarism. In the second place, it is a variant of all trade cycle theories which seek to find a cause extraneous to the actual mechanism of capitalism itself, such as defects in the monetary or banking systems, or the fault of greedy trade unionists, or harvests and sunspots etc. Although any one or a combination of such reasons might spark off depression, the basic cause, Marx held, lay within the operation and turnover of capital itself; value and surplus value had been created in the manufacture of goods, and neither could be realised because inequalities of income, falling rates of profit and disproportions in production require that vast masses of capital and goods must be destroyed before profitable investment is again possible. The search for a cure to the capitalist trade cycle is as vain as the medieval alchemists' quest to turn base metal into gold. Only the abolition of capitalism itself will abolish the trade cycle.

In December 1829, Attwood and his middle class supporters met to plan 'a general political union between the lower and middle classes of the people . . . for an effective reform in Parliament and the redress of public wrongs and grievances'. The 'lower class' parent of the body was, however, the earlier political unions and when the Birmingham Political Union (BPU) was launched at Beardsworth's Repository the next month, George Edmonds and William Pare were elected to its 36 member political council.

The 1832 Reform Act was a key event in the struggle for Parliamentary reform forcing the landlord dominated British parliament to partially yield its monopoly and share it with the rising capitalist class. The background was the prolonged slump of the second Long Depression which began at the end of 1826, but whose trough in the years 1830 to 1832 created unbearable conditions of mass unemployment and starvation. There was also the rick-burning and arson from the desperate rural areas and the French Revolution of 1830 to remind most reasonable people of the possible consequences of delayed reform.

During 1830 large numbers of Political Unions were formed throughout the country, and those in the west Midlands, at least, modelled themselves on the Birmingham one. So the objects and rules of the BPU were of particular importance. Among the objects were the following:

1st To obtain by every legal and just means, such a REFORM in the COMMONS' HOUSE OF PARLIAMENT as may ensure a REAL and EFFECTUAL REPRESENTATION of the LOWER and MIDDLE CLASSES of the people in that House.

2nd To inquire, consult, consider and determine, respecting the rights and liberties of the industrious classes, and respecting the legal means of securing those that remain, and recovering those which are lost.

3rd To prepare Petitions, Addresses, and Remonstrances to the Crown and the Legislative Bodies respecting the preservation and restoration of PUBLIC RIGHTS and respecting the repeal of bad laws, and the enactment of good laws.

4th To prevent and redress as far as practicable all LEGAL PUBLIC WRONGS AND OPPRESSIONS, and all LOCAL EN-CROACHMENTS upon the rights, interests and privileges of the community.

5th To obtain the repeal of the MALT and BEER TAXES; and in general to obtain an alteration in the system of taxation, so as to cause it to press less severely upon the industrious classes of the community, and more equally upon the wealthy classes.

Attwood's currency plan was the sixth objective and was formulated as follows:

To obtain the reduction of each separate Tax and Expense of the Government in the same degree as the legislative increase in the value of money has increased their respective values, and has reduced and is reducing the general prices of labour throughout the country.

The seventh objective was to promote peace, union and concord 'among all Classes of his Majesties subjects'. The eighth was to collect and organise the peaceful expression of public opinion. The ninth to promote the return of upright and capable members of Parliament. The tenth and last was to obtain an effectual Parliamentary investigation into the situation of the country with a view to relieving the national distress, of rendering justice to the injured and bringing to trial any individuals, of whatever station, found to have acted from criminal or corrupt motives.

This was an admirable programme of reform in the old radical democratic tradition: but the emerging working class would not want all their eggs in that particular basket. Nor would it attract the high bourgeoisie, who in most towns held aloof from the Political Unions at this stage.

The Constitution of the BPU was 'essentially popular'. Membership was open to all who agreed to abide by its rules and pay a minimum quarterly subscription of 1/-d although more was expected where this could be afforded. Government was by a Political Council of not less than 36 individuals chosen at a general annual meeting occurring in July. Rule 16 clarified the attitude of the Union to all other classes of society:

> The subscriptions of noblemen and gentlemen are invited in support of the Political Union, the objects of which being strictly conservatory are calculated, in restoring the just rights and interests of the Industrial classes to confirm the Constitutional Privileges of the Aristocracy, and to preserve every class of the community from the common anarchy which threatens all.

The duties of the members of the BPU were to be good, faithful, and loyal subjects of the king, to obey the laws of the land, and where these ceased to protect the rights, liberties and interests of the community to endeavour to get them changed by peaceful and legal means only.

The duties of the members of the Political Council were to endeavour 'to the utmost of their powers' to promote the objects of the Union by peaceful means only; not to promote private objects of their own; to watch the proceedings of the legislature and present Petitions etc. whenever the rights of the lower or middle classes were invaded and to endeavour to preserve the peace in Birmingham during any political convulsion brought about by distress occasioned by the mismanagement of public affairs.

The final document, signed by Attwood as chairman, and Benjamin Hadley as secretary, ended with an additional regulation giving details of a medal to be struck for every member of the Union. It showed the Union Jack, 'a standard which has nobly supported the national honour in foreign climes and which will, we hope, be equally efficacious in the great moral contest for recovering the national liberty at home'. The obverse of the medal showed the British Lion arousing himself from slumber with the legends above, 'The Safety of the King and People', and below 'The Constitution, nothing less and nothing more.' The reverse of the medal showed the royal crown and the words, 'Unity', 'Liberty', 'Prosperity'. 'God Save the King', and 'Birmingham Political Union 25th January 1830'.

The 12,000 people who crowded Beardsworth's Repository to accept this Constitution listened for seven hours and finally adopted a petition praying that the House of Commons take into consideration 'the distresses of the kingdom and the grievances of the people'. These were stated to be:

> Overwhelming taxation, an enormous and unconstitutional standing army, bands of useless and unmerited placemen and pensioners, profligate expenditure of the public money, an ill-regulated Establishment Church, and an arbitrary change in the value of money.

This meeting had a wide effect on the rest of the country. It was fully reported by the national press and many Political Unions on the Birmingham model were formed. The first great demonstration of the BPU was on Monday May 17th 1830. The following paraphrases Dent's account.

Early in the morning the busiest streets of the town were thronged with the members of the Union from outlying districts and hundreds pressed into the rooms to enlist under the banner of political freedom among whom was the member-elect of 1819, Sir Charles Wolesley. The day was regarded as a public holiday, shops were closed, the town was in general commotion, not a few of the more timorous respectabilities professing to entertain fears of disturbance. But that was a thing of bygone days; the people under their new leader had learned the value of peaceable demeanour and the power of moral force.

A monster procession was organised, headed by a band playing God Save the King and marched to Beardsworth's Repository where not less than 18,000 people were present. Attwood said that the formation of the BPU had resounded not only throughout England but into Europe. We have given the enemy a tremendous blow. This must be repeated again and again until success is achieved, by strictly legal methods. But for our prudence and caution respecting those inexplicable laws which like 'devil-traps' hedged about the reformers on every hand we should have been destroyed like the Reformers of old 'and I picked out from among you and in all probability lodged in a dungeon'.

Dent ended his account:

> The Reformers little thought ... that before another public gathering should be held, the King whose powerful influence had ever been on the side of repression and political injustice, would have passed out of the world; yet such was the case. On the wild and stormy night of 26th June, George IV died ... and the Liberals looked forward to the dawn of a more hopeful state of things.

Constitutionally, at that time, the accession of William IV necessitated a general election. Its result was a House of Commons in favour of Reform. This encouraged the BPU to make the first annual general meeting another great demonstration. Sir Francis Burdett, the noted Parliamentary radical, was invited to be the guest of honour. Again the town was given over to political display and demonstration. Again, 20,000 people crowded in to the Repository. Sir Francis was 'called to the chair and made a vigorous and telling speech concerning the corrupt practices that prevailed at elections; pocket boroughs, the Corn Laws and kindred topics'. Edmonds, Attwod and others also addressed the meeting which was rounded off by the presentation to Mr Beardsworth, 'the proprietor of the large and most suitable building in which all their public meetings had been held', of 'a handsome silver service.'

In the evening there was a dinner which 'passed off in an admirable manner.'

> It was not judged advisable to invite the neutral milk-and-water like friends of Reform, or probably a much larger number of Respectables, as they are called, might have been brought together. The band of the

Union (which had just been provided with a splendid uniform) played a selection of patriotic airs; the speeches were of the usual after-dinner type and included many loyal toasts ... and the members of the organisation were by this pleasant reunion bound more closely together.

That same evening 'while English liberals were dining together in peace and amity, their brethren in France were striking a glorious blow for freedom, hurling the last of the Bourbons from the throne, and declaring once more the liberty of the people.'

In the following months the agitation of the BPU was stepped up. In October the French Revolution was celebrated by a dinner at Beardsworth's. The same month they petitioned the king to dismiss the ministers and a few weeks later the Peel-Wellington administration resigned and the fires of reform were truly lit when the Grey reform government was formed. In December 1830 another large gathering at Beardsworth's adopted the famous Petition of Right which was entrusted to the Earl of Radnor to present in the Lords and the Marquis of Blandford to present in the Commons. It claimed as the birthright of every Englishman:

1st   The right of having all PLACEMEN dismissed from the House of Commons agreeably to the Great Constitutional Act of Settlement which places the present illustrious family on the Throne.

2nd   The right of having TRIENNIAL or more frequent Parliaments ... as secured by 6th of William and Mary cap 2.

3rd   The right of sitting and voting in the Commons, when lawfully chosen without the QUALIFICATION OF PROPERTY, which was fixed unconstitutionally by the Act of 9th of Queen Anne.

4th   The right of having all the Knights, Citizens and Burgesses of the House of Commons paid the REASONABLE WAGE OF ATTENDANCE ...

5th   The right of having the large towns and populous districts of the country represented in the House of Commons in place of those decayed boroughs which return members to Parliament, although now containing but few inhabitants.

6th   The right of every man to have a vote in the election of members of the House of Commons, who is in any way called upon to contribute to national or local taxation, direct or indirect; by which your petitioners understand that either all taxes ought to be taken off from those articles necessary for the subsistence and comfort of working men, or that all working men who are compelled to pay such taxes should have a vote ...

7th   The right to have elections free and unbiassed, and ... to have arrangements ... as may effectually prevent all force, fear or intimidation, and all bribery or undue influence from acting upon the minds of electors.

Here was indeed a radical programme with practically all the points which were soon to become the People's Charter. The treatment of the suffrage is interesting; not necessarily manhood suffrage, but the ancient (and American Revolution) principle of no taxation without representation.

The first Reform Bill was presented to Parliament by Lord John Russell on 1 March 1831. The second reading was carried by a majority of one in the fullest House of Commons ever known of 603 MPs. This brought national celebrations, including Birmingham, with a general illumination of the town. The ministers were later defeated, however, on business relating to the Bill and they resigned. The king refused to accept this and ordered a new election to test public opinion on the matter. This brought new rejoicing in Birmingham and 'the belfries were broken into and the bells set ringing merrily, to the horror and disgust of their clerical custodians'. The BPU issued an Address to the Electors of the Kingdom urging them to vote only for candidates pledged to 'the whole Bill and nothing but the Bill.'

The result was an even larger number of MPs returned pledged to Reform, and a second Bill was introduced in June 1831. This Bill was successfully carried until it reached the Committee stage where it met with every kind of objection. The political council of the BPU addressed a Petition to the House of Commons contrasting the tardiness of the reform proceedings with the 'rapidity with which measures of penalty and spoilation have been enacted in the past'. Eventually, in September 1831, the Bill was passed by 345 votes to 236. Again there were great rejoicings in the town. But there then arose the certainty that the Bill would be rejected in the House of Lords.

Immediately the first of what was to become a series of great meetings was called on Newhall Hill for 3 October 1831. Although hastily summoned, estimates of attendance varied between 50,000 and 150,000 people. Shops and factories were closed, church bells were rung and slogans displayed. This Birmingham demonstration was only one of many, but it was reputed to be the largest, and certainly the best organised political gathering ever held in England up to that time and had enormous national influence. A Petition to the Lords approved by the meeting urging them to pass the Bill was referred to in the debates in that House by Lord Eldon and others as illegal and treasonable. On 7 October the Lords rejected the Bill.

Political anger erupted and the national standing of the BPU was probably enhanced by its insistence on supporting the government and also its insistence on 'law and order' when Political Unions elsewhere were demanding direct action. These included the more radical elements within the BPU. Russell was already printing notices, 'No Taxes paid Here' and George Edmonds was urging people to withdraw their money from the banks. An Address by the BPU to The People urged the formation of Political Unions in every town and village. It ended:

> Friends, Countrymen and Brothers! Listen to us. The SWORD must not be drawn in England. The terrible KNELL of the TOCSIN must not sound. The tears of the Widow and Orphan must not mark our course. These are the last dread alternatives of an oppressed nation. The influence of the Oligarchy, aided by a corrupt and degenerate bench of BISHOPS, has obtained a momentary triumph in the House of Lords. By the power of the King and of the Law we will humble the Oligarchy in the dust. Our gallant neighbours the French effected a glorious revolution by lifting the Barricades, cemented by the best blood of the nation. We will have no BARRICADES. Without blood — without

anarchy — without violation of the law, we will accomplish the most GLORIOUS REFORMATION in the History of the World. GOD BLESS THE KING.

By order of the Council
Thomas Attwood, Chairman.
Benjamin Hadley, Secretary.

The third Reform Bill was introduced by the government in December 1831. It passed its third reading on 19 March 1832. In the House of Lords the 2nd Reading was carried by a minority of nine on 14 April. But the Bill then had to go to the Committee stage. To convince the Lords of the strength of support for Reform in the country, the BPU called the second, and most famous, of the Newhall Hill meetings for 7 May 1832. It was probably the most decisive event in the Reform agitation with attendance variously estimated up to 200,000. The meeting was held, as usual, on a Monday. Crowds began to arrive on the Saturday. On Monday the marching contingents poured into Birmingham. The Eastern Division, including the Political Unions from Coventry, Warwick, Bedworth, Kenilworth, Leamington and Stratford-upon-Avon, numbered 5,000. The Southern Division representing Bromsgrove, Redditch, Studley, Worcester, Droitwich and Alcester, numbered 10,000. The Grand Western Division including Stourbridge, Dudley, Harborne, Cradley, Lye Waste, Oldbury, Rowley Regis, Halesowen etc. was two miles long, exhibited 70 banners and numbered about 25,000 people. Overshadowing all, however, was the great mass migration representing the rest of the Black Country. The Great Northern Division including Wolverhampton, Bilston, Sedgley Willenhall, Wednesbury, Walsall, Darlaston and West Bromwich numbered no less than 100,000 people. It exhibited 150 banners and 11 bands of music. The procession was four miles long and the whole of the road for that distance was virtually jammed. This vast column had set out from Wolverhampton at between 6 and 7 am. These details are given for the benefit of those who lightly claim that attendance figures for these meetings are exaggerated. The commitment of working people to assemble in Wolverhampton or Coventry at about 5 am, march to Birmingham, listen to speakers and then walk back home, suggests dedication to a cause, (or economic desperation) and capacity for organisation which it ill becomes chair-borne modern historians to belittle or deride.

The actual proceedings at this historic May 7 demonstration also deserve to be recalled. They began 'from the whole concourse, like the surging of the sea' with the singing of the Hymn of the Union. This had six verses of a Call, the first of which was:

> Over mountain, over plain
> Echoing wide from sea to sea,
> Peals, and shall not peal in vain,
> The trumpet call of liberty!
> Britain's guardian spirit cries —
> Briton's awake! awake! arise!

This was responded to by three verses of the Answer:

> Lo! we answer; see! we come
> Quick at freedom's holy call.

> We come, we come! we come, we come!
>   To do the glorious work of all.
> And hark! we raise from sea to sea
>   Our sacred watchword, Liberty!

The main speech by Attwood reiterated his constitutional stance:

> . . . the people of England stand at this very moment like greyhounds on
> the slip; and that if our beloved King should give the word, or if the
> Council should give the word in his name and under his authority, the
> grandest scene would be instantly enacted that was ever witnessed on this
> earth before.

Other speeches were more militant. Richard Fryer, the Wolverhampton
banker, who was the second speaker, suggested that in the case of reform
being refused a Grand National Council of Political Unions be
immediately assembled. Even Joseph Parkes spoke of a 'violent
revolution which may at once destroy public credit, depose the borough
mongers and utterly destroy their wicked domination'. The
demonstration ended with the Vow 'the vast sea of faces, upturned to
heaven, with heads reverently uncovered uttering with one voice':

> In unbroken faith, through every peril and trial and privation we devote
> ourselves and our children to our country's cause.

News of this great event, described this time by the Tory *Wolverhampton
Chronicle* as 'the greatest political meeting ever held in this or any other
country', was reported not only throughout Britain, but also in Europe,
thus influencing Reform movements abroad.

But the Lords were not converted, and on the very evening of the
Birmingham demonstration, the government was defeated on the Bill. The
next day Lord Grey went to Windsor with the Cabinet's ultimatum on
the creation of peers. The King asked for a night to consider this, but then
declined and on May 9th, he accepted the resignation of the ministry.

These events produced a genuinely revolutionary situation. In the
more proletarianised parts of the country there were reports of drilling,
arming and marches on London. In Birmingham, the movement was still
controlled by the constitutionalist middle-class, but their leadership rested
on the mass base of working people.

On 10 May Birmingham was given over to politics. Most factories and
workshops were closed. The muffled bells of St. Philip's tolled through
the town and a black flag floated from its tower. The BPU called the third
of their great demonstrations, officially reported as follows:

BIRMINGHAM POLITICAL UNION

> At a meeting of the Town and Neighbourhood of Birmingham held
> suddenly and spontaneously, to the number of 200,000 people at
> Newhall Hill this 10th day of May 1832. Thomas Attwood in the chair,
> it was resolved unanimously that the following Address and Petition be
> presented to the House of Commons.

The Petition stated that they were struck with alarm at the 'awful
intelligence' of the resignation of the Ministry as a result of persevering

with a Bill of Reform already twice passed by the House. That under these circumstances the life and property of no man in England was safe. The House was looked upon 'as the last remaining stay of Constitution' and urged not to shrink from the great duties imposed on them, to support the Rights of the People. The Petition then went on to discuss necessary measures. First the House was urged to take whatever measures might be necessary for the Safety and Liberty of the country. Next that the Bill of Rights declared that the people of England 'may have arms for their defence, suitable to their condition and as allowed by law', and apprehended that 'this great right will be put in force generally'. Finally, the Petition urged the Honourable House to beseech his majesty not to allow the resignation of his ministers, to create sufficient Peers to allow the Bill to be passed and that the House 'will instantly withhold all supplies and adopt any other measures which may be necessary to carry the Bill and to ensure the safety and liberty of the country'.

It was at this point of the crisis that the high bourgeoisie of Birmingham decided to join the BPU, and from a Council meeting later the same day it was announced that, 'A body of gentlemen, to the number of 500 and upwards . . . comprising the professions and mercantile interests of the town', had enrolled and made the following declaration.

> We, the undersigned . . . who have hitherto refrained from joining the Birmingham Political Union, deem it our duty to our country at this awful crisis to come forward and join that body for the purpose of promoting the further union, order and determination of all classes in support of the common cause of Parliamentary Reform.

Not the least of their reasons for joining was that the leadership of the Birmingham movement was passing into more radical, working class, hands. Shops and houses were displaying posters printed by Russell stating 'No Taxes paid here until the Reform Bill is passed.' All through the night of 10/11 May the death bells tolled from Birmingham churches.

On 11 May there was better news. The House of Commons had passed a vote of confidence in the Grey government. The town responded by unmuffling the bells and celebrating.

Meanwhile, the deputation from the BPU was in London. The request that the House support the Grey administration had already been carried out. The deputation had been welcomed by Lord Grey and they had also met representatives of the City of London and also the London friends of reform. It was later stated by Francis Place that at this meeting, on May 11th, Joseph Parkes had pledged that in the event of Wellington taking office, any 'general rising of the people' would be led by Birmingham. Rumours circulated both in Birmingham and throughout the country that a great march of the BPU, two hundred thousand strong would set off for London and camp at Hampstead Heath until the Bill became law. In response to this, warrants were actually made out for the arrest of the Birmingham leaders, but remained unsigned in the Home Office papers.

The official response of the BPU was to draw up their famous Solemn Declaration against the Duke of Wellington, to be adopted by all Political Unions, throughout the country. This first set out the grounds for the 'alarm and horror' against the Duke. These included his avowal of arbitrary principles; his activities against Reform; his being a pensioner of foreign despots, exposed to their influence and thus unfit to govern a free people; his 'expressions amounting to those of regret' that the Irish people would not break the law; his general support for arbitrary despots in Europe; and his incompetency to govern England by any other means than those of the sword'. The Declaration went on:

> For these and various reasons, we hereby solemnly declare our fixed determination to use all the means that the Constitution and Law have placed at our disposal, to induce His Majesty to reject from his councils that faction, at the head of which is the Duke of Wellington ... and we declare ... that public excitement and agitation can never be allayed until the great Bill of Reform be carried into law by that Administration by whose wisdom and virtue it was first introduced.

The Declaration ended by 'confidently calling on our fellow-countrymen throughout England, Scotland and Ireland' to sign it. Thus invoking memories of the Old Scottish Covenanters, other reformers in Birmingham led by W. Redfern prepared a Solemn League and Covenant '... to Stand, Abide and Hold-fast, the one by the other, in using all feasible and lawful ways and means with which God or Nature, Chance, or Circumstances, may furnish us, for the assertion and vindication of all such our just rights and liberties'.

In London Wellington was having difficulty forming a government and not the least of his fears was for the reliability of the army. In Birmingham the Scots Greys were stationed, among them private Alexander Somerville. He told how, on Sunday 13 May the barracks was closed and orders given to sharpen their swords. Not only was this the first time since the Battle of Waterloo that such an order had been given, but the swords were to be sharpened in such a way that jagged wounds would be inflicted by any thrust. Some of the soliders, Somerville says, wrote to the King, Wellington and the War Office, stating that so long as the people marched peaceably to London, the Scots Greys would not interfere with them. Similar letters were written and dropped in the streets of Birmingham. Many of the soldiers became members of the Political Unions and wrote letters to the newspapers in favour of Reform. Alexander Somerville wrote one such letter which concluded. 'The Duke of Wellington, if he sees or hears of this, may assure himself that military government shall never again be set up in this country'. This letter appeared in an anti-Reform newspaper on 27 May. His commanding officer took immediate action. Somerville was courtmartialled the next day at an hour and a half's notice and received one hundred lashes. He was then sent to hospital. George Griffith reporting this writes:

> The illegal and inhuman conduct of the commanding officer being made known to the public through the newspapers, a ferment took place among the people, quite unparalleled ... great fears were entertained for the safety of the officers in the barracks. The fuel thus added to the fire of the Reform movement was terrific, and had it not been for Somerville's urgent requests to the people to keep the peace, the barracks no doubt would have been turned into a heap of ruins.

Returning to events earlier in May. Work and government in Birmingham was now at a standstill. Nearly everyone in the streets wore

BPU medals or Union Jack ribbons. Moods swung between deep despair and ecstatic hope. Monday 15th was a day of gloom. Attwood's house was guarded and the family was expecting his arrest for high treason and sedition. But the next day news was received of a Commons motion that it would never accept a Reform Bill from Wellington, thus making it highly unlikely that a Wellington government could be formed. This news was brought to Birmingham by Parkes at 6 am on 16 May and touched off demonstrations of joy and relief. The church bells were unmuffled and rung. Crowds collected outside Attwood's house at Harborne and a procession with banners and bands, gathering strength as it went, proceeded to the old meeting place of Newhall Hill. Here it was joined by large numbers from the surrounding areas, and when proceedings began there were about 60,000 people present. Attwood spoke and claimed that Birmingham had been responsible for this great national victory of peaceful and constitutional struggle. A memorial to Lord Grey was then determined on and Attwood, Scholefield and Parkes named as the deputation to present it. They left for London at 6.30 the same evening on what was to become a triumphal procession.

Others, however, were less convinced that victory had been won. George Edmonds and other radicals were backing national calls for a run on the banks and this action was already beginning to bite. In fact, when the Birmingham delegation reached London, Wellington had still not admitted defeat and it was not until the night of 17 May that he went to the King and told him that he could not form an administration and the return of Lord Grey became inevitable. Even then, Wellington was not finished. The recall of Grey was made conditional on a compromise whereby the King made an unconditional pledge to create the new peers necessary to pass the Bill, but this would be withheld if Wellington and the House of Lords agreed to cease to oppose the Bill. Wellington reneged on this promise by marching his followers out of the House of Lords. This new crisis led Attwood, now in the heady atmosphere of London, to talk in terms of a gigantic meeting of one million people joining him at Hampstead Heath 'in a grand exhibition of Reform feeling.'

On 18 May William gave Grey the necessary unconditional pledge to create the peers necessary and resistance from the House of Lords collapsed. Grey immediately re-introduced the Bill and it proceeded on its way through the Parliamentary procedure.

Attwood was now fully convinced that it was the efforts of the BPU that had been mainly responsible for this victory for Reform, and much of the country agreed with him. Attwood and his delegation were feted wherever they went. Lords Grey and Holland received them 'with every mark of respect.' Enthusiastic welcomes came from both Houses of Parliament and even royalty itself. There were dinners and receptions from the London radical leaders. The 'highlight' of the visit however was on 23 May when the Corporation of London presented Attwood with the freedom of the City and gave a banquet at the Mansion House for the visitors.

The journey back to Birmingham was equally triumphal. Whole villages turned out to greet them, others presented addresses, or raised arches of evergreens. Dent reports the reception in Birmingham:

But when they reached home the joy of the inhabitants knews no bounds.
The whole population turned out to meet them as they entered the town
on May 28th; banners hung from almost every window; every peal of
bells in the town clanged out a joyous reception to the deputation and
the thunder of artillery echoed the same greeting; but these were both
drowned in the deafening cheers of the populace, as from two hundred
thousand throats the victors' return was hailed and the final vanquishing
of their opponents was celebrated. Such a scene was never before
witnessed in Birmingham; and at length, when from the pressure of the
multitude the pole of Mr Attwood's carriage was broken, the people
joyfully harnessed themselves thereto and wheeled, or rather carried the
conveyance up the Bull Ring into New Street.

A week later the Reform Bill passed the third reading in the House of
Lords and on 7th June received the royal assent.

To what extent this victory was due to the peaceful and constitutional
pressures exerted by the political unions throughout the country and to
what extent by the more radical pressures of the spectre of financial ruin,
the threat of the defection of the army and the fear of revolution, remain
moot points. The extent to which the victory was due to the leadership
and nationwide influence of the Birmingham Political Union is even more
problematic, but there can be no doubt that the radical tradition in the
town had once again triumphed and that the BPU exercised a very
considerable national influence on the passage of this historic Bill.

The result of the Act was that Birmingham for the first time in its
history was represented in Parliament, by two MPs. In addition, the
vote was granted to all £10 householders within the Parliamentary
borough. Attwood and Scholefield were nominated by the BPU as the two
Liberal candidates and they were returned unopposed at the general
election which did not take place until the following winter.

The parliamentary position following the passing of the Act proved
satisfactory neither to the middle class nor the working class. For the
former, the redistribution of seats nationally did not go far enough to
ensure domination of capitalist interests over landlords and aristocracy;
nor did the extension of the franchise go deep enough into the
'respectable' working class to produce Liberal rather than Tory
governments. To the working class it became immediately obvious that
they had once again been the troops doing the fighting only to gain
victory for their Liberal capitalist employers, who in important respects
were even worse than the Tory landlords. Employers opposed factory
reform and were immediately responsible for the infamous Poor Law Act
of 1834.

In Birmingham the radicals had expected that the second Parliamentary candidate with Attwood would have been a representative of the
working class, George Edmonds. Even this was not to be, however, as it
would have led to the complication of a Tory candidate putting up and
a contested election running the risk of not returning the two Liberals.
Because of the uncontested election we shall never know what meagre
number of working class voters were enfranchised as £10 householders.

But one of the decisive victories of the century had been won. Equally
decisive elements of independent working class organisation and ideology
had been developed. The second Long Depression was ending and the
middle years of the 1830s, like those of the 1820s were years of capitalist

expansion during which other key working class innovations gestated to reinforce the radical tradition, notably Owenism and the first Socialists in Britain. When the third Long Depression occurred at the end of the 1830s independent working class activity had fully evolved. The result was Chartism.

Chapter Three

CO-OPERATION & OWENITE SOCIALISM IN BIRMINGHAM

1828 – 1842

Co-operation is the essence of Socialism. Trade unionism is the first 'primitive' response of workers engaged in commodity production (and who therefore have themselves become commodities) to protect the value of their labour and the conditions under which it is sold. Political activity is the search for organisational forms to affect the existing machinery of control. Radical and working class politics in England at least from 1600 to the present time have been almost entirely dominated by a single aim — the Reform of Parliament. This is not necessarily 'reformism' — in the 1640s reform of Parliament was fought out in revolutionary civil wars — but it does largely account for the peculiar shaping of the English political mind, its general indifference to politics except in terms of Parliament. Co-operation however is the *practical* art working out different forms of *social* organisation to the existing one. In all three spheres — politics, trade unionism and co-operation — the British working class as the first developed working class in the world pioneered organisations which subsequently became common to working people in other countries. The 1830s and 1840s were quite astonishingly innovative decades as far as the development of forms of working class struggle were concerned. The developments in co-operation at this time were probably the most daring of all drawing to it the trade union movement and first defining the political system which would replace capitalism — socialism. These developments are indissolubly connected with the ideas of Robert Owen and give him his abiding and towering importance in the movement. Nor is the fact that Owen's socialism, (along with that of Fourier and St. Simon) is scientifically defined by Marx as Utopian to be taken as a term of abuse; it reflects the period at which these ideas were developed.

The first recorded co-operative in Birmingham is probably the striking journeymen tailors of 1777 who appealed publicly, over the heads of the master tailors, for the public to deal with them directly.

More clearly co-operative was the Birmingham Flour and Bread Company established in the year of scarcity, 1795. This was aimed at defeating the corn badgers and millers in the town who refused to grind additional flour and thus bring down the price. It's aim was to raise £6,000 or £7,000 in £1 shares limited to £20 per person and the low denomination of the share indicates that artisan and working class participation was possible. It became the Union Mills and in 1779 paid a dividend of 10%.

The first co-operative clearly identified with the ideas of Robert Owen was the Birmingham Co-operative Society and Trading Fund Association established in 1828. The rules, drafted by John Rabone, defined a co-operative society as being 'for the purpose of avoiding some of the evils which men are exposed to when acting singly and to obtain some of the advantages which otherwise they must be deprived of.' The objects of the society were: 1. a mutual protection of the members against poverty, 2. the attainment of a greater share of the comforts of life and 3. the attainment of independence by means of common capital. This common capital was to be obtained by weekly subscriptions. It was to be utilised first for extending trade, then in manufacturing for the society and finally in the purchase of land and living on it in community of property. Thus the ultimate aim of the co-operators was socialism and it was the Owenites who were first called and accepted the name Socialists. The president of the Birmingham society was William Pare, a young man who was to become one of the closest of Owen's advisors and the vice-president was James Guest the celebrated radical bookseller of the town.

In October 1831 the second Co-operative Congress was held in Birmingham convened by William Pare who was made secretary. By this time the Birmingham society had embarked on a farming project stated to have been in the nature of an experiment for the guide of other societies; this at a time when the society's capital was not much more than £100. At the Congress it was reported that there were four societies in Birmingham. These were not all Owenite societies. The Handsworth Economic Union had been started in 1830 by work people at the Boulton and Watt engineering works. It seems to have been a purely trading co-operative with the business like rule that no dividend was payable until the capital of the society had reached £3 per member.

The only information concerning the Owenite society at the Birmingham Congress was that it had thirty members and possessed a library of 170 volumes. Before the Birmingham Congress a proposal had been put in *Carpenter's Political Letter* that 200 societies be approached to supply £30 each and to start a Community with this £6000. Owen, in his grand way, ridiculed the smallness of the scheme. Nevertheless at the Congress a committee was appointed to prosecute it and three local men were appointed to the Committee.

Owen's ideas, as usual, were moving beyond the reality of the situation and the question being asked was, 'Have you discussed Exchange?' This referred to the Labour Exchanges using Labour Notes which were established in various parts of England, the most successful being the one in Birmingham. The Labour Note was to be the quick route to Socialism, money being superseded by the direct exchange of labour and capitalist enterprises being replaced with Socialist communities. The proposed direct exchange of labour was, as the perceptive author of the *History of the Birmingham Co-operative Society* saw, probably the most original and far reaching of all the working class innovations of this period. It failed at this time and, as Marx was later to show, the direct exchange of labour is not possible. But to have acted upon the theoretical premise that the exchange of goods through money is in fact the exchange of human labour was, and remains the fundamental reality of any society that produces commodities for exchange and the only basis on which an objective analysis of capitalism can be made.

The Birmingham Labour Exchange was mooted when the London Labour Exchange was already in operation. Robert Owen came to Birmingham in November 1832 and spoke at a mass meeting of 8,000 people at Beardsworth's Repository, Moseley Street. Owen was supported not only by the Birmingham leaders of Owenite Socialism — Pare, George Edmonds, Rabone, Hawkes-Smith etc. — but also by the powerful bourgeois Reformers of the town. Attwood who linked the Owenite reforms with his own currency views, was at the meeting and the chairman was G.F. Muntz. The appeal for £2,000 in £20 shares shows that the scheme was not only supported by the trade unions who could buy quarter shares, but its success depended on merchants being willing to effect wholesale exchanges and manufacturers and others in the town being willing to accept Labour Notes.

The Labour Exchange was formally opened on 12th August 1833 at the Old Coach Yard, Bull Street. On the opening day deposits totalled 18,000 hours and exchanges 9,000 hours. This continued to be the pattern, exchanges never exceeding half the deposits. The Exchange remained open, however, until the middle of 1834 and it closed voluntarily with all debts discharged, its share capital repaid and a balance of £8 donated to the Birmingham General Hospital. This episode of Exchange ranks as one of the most important contributions of Birmingham to the development of the working class movement.

There was little sense of failure or disappointment among Socialists at this time for by then further immense schemes were in operation. The years of slump 1829–33 fueled not only the politics of Reform and the social organisation of Co-operation, but also an upsurge of militant and innovative trade unionism in which Birmingham played an outstanding part.

In 1831 a Great Operative Builders' Union was created. In 1833 it published a manifesto in which it announced that it had formed itself into a National Building Guild of Brothers to erect buildings throughout the country (a) cheaper than any master builder (b) to keep builders and their families in infancy, illness and old age (c) to eliminate unemployment in the trade (d) to pay fair wages (e) to determine speed of work (f) to educate both builders and their children (g) to unite with other producers of real wealth (h) to replace the present artificial, inaccurate and injurious circulating medium (i) to remove the causes of individual and national competition which results in war (j) to give to present masters who understand their business a more secure position than they have now under the system of competition between master and master (k) to exhibit by our new organisation and practical operations, the means by which the interests of the classes may be united and all become useful members of the great Association for the Emancipation of the Productive Classes. Another vast scheme of Owenite reform was under way.

The propagation of this Owenite gospel in Birmingham was in the hands of the partnership of architects and master builders Hansom and Welsh. Joseph Hansom in particular had a large national influence on the Builders' Union.

In September 1833 Edward Welsh wrote:

> My partner and myself with his (Owen's) assistance are endeavouring so to organise the great working masses of Builders in the Kingdom as to place them in a permanent position of comfort and happiness — and to destroy that ruinous system of competition amongst their guides which

has reduced them to misery and involved us in almost incessant anxiety and care.

The previous month Hansom had written to Owen:

> We have been reading your Manifesto this morning together and were particularly struck with the force of its truth. There does seem to be a *new life* producing to us, and a *new light* wherewith to see things. That which under the old system had the operation of evil, impels us to the good and correct course . . . . The Builders are a beautiful class of men to operate with their minds less sophisticated than others, and yet tutored to a great extent in practical knowledge . . .

In June 1833 the masters nationally had combined to present the Document to all its workers. It read:

> We, the undersigned do declare that we are not in any way connected with the General Union of the Building Trades and that we do not and will not contribute to the support of such members of the said union as are or may be out of work in consequence of belonging to such union.

This was replied to with a savage strike which lasted sixteen weeks, the union calling out the trades separately so that the other trades continued in employment although work at the sites ceased. In August, when signs of peace were appearing Messrs. Walthen, one of the largest contractors in Birmingham and successful rival of Hansom and Welsh for the grammar school contract had discharged all their workers belonging to the union. The trade in Birmingham was instantly in uproar and Owenite influence became paramount. A deputation of building workers went to see Hansom and Welsh. Welsh then drafted a document, which, as was intended, made peace with Walthen impossible:

> Sir,
> We the delegates of the several Lodges of the Building Trades elected for the purpose of correcting the abuses which have crept into the modes of undertaking and transacting business, do hereby give you notice that you will receive no assistance from the working men in any of our bodies to enable you to fulfil an engagement which we understand you have entered into with the Governors of the Free Grammar School to erect a New School in New Street, unless you comply with the following conditions.
> Aware that it is our labour alone that can carry into effect what you have undertaken, we cannot but view ourselves as parties to your engagement, if that engagement is ever fulfilled; and as you had no authority from us to undertake such an engagement, nor had you any legitimate right to barter our labour at prices fixed by yourself, we call upon you to exhibit to our several Lodges your detailed estimates of quantities and prices at which you have taken the work, and we call upon you to arrange with us a fixed percentage of profit for your own services in conducting the building and in finding the material on which our labour is to be applied.
> Should we find upon examination that you have fixed equitable prices which will not only remunerate you for your superintendence but us for our toil, we have no objection upon a clear understanding to become parties to the contract and will see you through it, after your having entered yourself a member of our body and after your having been duly *elected* to occupy that office you have *assumed.*

Owen was immediately brought to Birmingham by Hansom and shown that the town was won for Owenism and at the same time a special delegate meeting of the Manchester and Birmingham Lodges showed that the two largest provincial centres were with him. Owen left Birmingham with a recommendation to the London operatives and meetings there convinced him that he could take his final step and take control of the Grand Lodge or Builders' Parliament scheduled to meet in Manchester in September. Here the Grand National Guild of Builders was set up.

With this, and even more grandiose schemes, in view, Owen was prepared to sacrifice the Labour Exchanges, these being '. . . but a bagatelle — a mere pawnbroker's shop in comparison with the superior establishments which we shall speedily have it in our power to institute.'

Owen, Hansom and Welsh had dominated the Builders' Parliament and it was fitting that notwithstanding the existing problems in Birmingham, the Guild there should start the most ambitious of the organisation's projects — the building of a Guildhall at the cost of £2000. Work began on the 28th November 1833 when a large procession marched to Broad Street, headed by a local band. The carpenters, bricklayers, painters, masons, slaters, plumbers and glaziers attended in aprons and with their banners; the labourers had provided themselves with a strange banner representing O'Connell and Polish officers, with suitable mottoes. Other trades, unconnected with building, attended and heard a speech, in pouring rain, by Joseph Hansom, who laid the foundation stone. Beneath it he placed a box containing a parchment, recounting the occasion of the building and concluding: 'In a confident hope, therefore, of success, this work is commenced, being, as it is believed, the beginning of a new era in the condition of the whole of the working classes of the world.'

Difficulties arose however. Serious attempts to hamper work at the grammar school were abandoned as work was concentrated on the Guildhall. In February 1834 even this work was at a standstill and Hansom wrote to Owen:

> With you I wish to commune, not so much relative to my own condition as on the topic of the Trades Union and most of all with regard to the Birmingham Operative Builders' Guildhall. It stands, it progresses not. To please my partner, and his friends, and the Commissioners of this Town, I have for the last 6 to 8 weeks been at Anglesey forwarding the Mason's work at the Quarries, and it is likely that unless I take some proper step now, that I shall be punished and justly for my subservience — unwilling tho' it be — to a party I can never respect but always despise, and for my apparent abandonment of the Trades when my presence was almost as necessary to them as the keystone to the Arch . . .
>
> It is of vital importance to the question, the grand question of the *Independence of Labour* and to the Regeneration of the Country, that this project of building the Guildhall should not be defeated. The Men have already spent a considerable sum in labour and I have invested also a large sum in material — more I cannot do — but the men can and will complete it, if a few hundred pounds could be procured for the remaining materials — at the utmost £500.

A contributory cause of the problems was the defection of Welsh. He had married on the day the foundation stone of the Guildhall had been laid, and his enthusiasm for the cause declined from that day, according to

Hansom. He took advantage of Hansom's absence to seize the title deeds to the Guildhall as security for materials advanced by the firm. Work was eventually restarted on the Guildhall, but it was never completed. This was done by a new landlord and the building stood as a warehouse in Shadwell Street until the clearances of recent years.

In April 1834 the Second Builders' Parliament met in Birmingham, but the only record of its proceedings is a document stating that the Builders' Union at Birmingham was determined to found schools for their members' children and also to establish science lectures for their members.

Owen, in February 1834, unruffled by the problems of the builders, passed to an even larger project — the uniting of all the unions which had sprung up into one big union, the Grand National Consolidated Trades Union. To Owen's disgust, the Builder's Guild did not join the GNCTU and no record of activities of this most celebrated of trades unions in Birmingham has been found.

The vast scale of the GNCTU presented problems from the start. Apart from the strikes and lock-outs with which it had to contend, employers reverted to prosecutions for illegal oaths. Here the most notorious case was that of the Tolpuddle Martyrs. Owen's demands for allegiance to his theories (notably the acknowledgement that labour was the source of all wealth, and that man's character was formed for and not by him) and also his intrigues, completed the havoc. The GNCTU was wound up in August 1834. The Builder's Guild proved only slightly more resilient; it survived until January 1835.

Even then, Robert Owen was not deterred. From 1832 to 1834 the paper of Owen was *The Crisis*. In the middle of 1834 Owen announced that the *Crisis* was over and the *New Moral World* was about to be ushered in, and from 1834 to 1845 this newspaper was the vehicle of Owen's ideas to the world. On May Day 1835 Owen founded the truly apocalyptic Association of All Classes of All Nations with himself as the Rational Social Father. The objects of this Association were:

> . . . to effect peaceably and by reason alone an entire change in the character and conditions of mankind by establishing over the world the religion of charity, combined with a well-devised, equitable and natural system of united property without infringing on the rights of any private property now in existence. These objects to be obtained by a 'central Association with branches in all parts of the world creating new public opinions in favour of an entire change in the character and conditions of man by meetings, discussions etc. and by founding Communities of United interest.

Birmingham retained the important position it had gained in the earlier Co-operative period. The Second Co-operative Conference had been held in Birmingham in October 1831 vying with Reform as the focus of working class attention. William Pare was now one of the most intimate of Owen's advisers. Co-operation in Birmingham continued to flourish both at the more mundane level of consumer societies and in its advocacy of Community. After 1835 Congresses continued to be held annually, but after that date were known as Socialist congresses instead of Co-operative ones and it is from this time the term Socialist enters widely into political thought and language.

Birmingham was registered as No. 4 branch of the Association of all Classes of All Nations. It began with its own Social Institute in Well Lane with meetings held three times a week, twice on Sundays and once on Wednesday evenings. In 1837 the secretary was Richard Bewlay, there were 95 paying members and 30 subscribed to the National Community Friendly Society, their total subscriptions amounting to £1-13-0d. This Friendly Society had been set up at the Third Socialist Congress in 1837 to purchase land to set up Communities.

Birmingham's importance was such that the Manchester Congress in 1838 decided to transfer the headquarters of AACAN to Birmingham. With this went also the printing and publication of the *New Moral World*. The Central Boards of both the Association and the paper were set up at 30 Bennetts Hill. On a motion by Pare, the Manchester Congress also set up two other organisations to promote the work of AACAN. These were the Socialist Missionary Society and a Tract Society; socialist Bishops were also to be created. In fact, the full-time workers of the organisation were always subsequently referred to as Socialist Missionaries and nothing further is heard of the Tract Society.

The 1839 Socialist Congress met in Birmingham. The High Bailiff refused the use of the Town Hall for the Congress and subsequent public meeting, on the grounds that the purpose of Owen was to subvert the foundations of religion and attack a most vital part of our social relations. The use of the Royal Society of Arts and the Museum in Temple Row were also refused and the Congress was eventually held at rooms in Great Charles Street, it lasted for sixteen days! At this Congress AACAN and the National Community Friendly Society were amalgamated to form the Universal Community Society of Rational Religionists. Another item on the agenda was a report by the estates committee on its extensive enquiries for suitable land to establish Communities. As a result of that report, an estate of 500 acres was purchased at Tytherley in Hampshire and the celebrated Queenwood Estate came into existence. The first batch of members of the National Community Friendly Society took possession in October 1839. Harmony Hall, the palatial building for the colony was designed by Joseph Hansom. The Birmingham Society of Rational Religionists sent £80 to the Community as well as a large number of presents including mathematical instruments, rat traps and a patent cork screw.

The New Moral World was published from June 1838 by Guest, the radical Birmingham publisher and printed by Frances Basset Shentone Flindell at 38 New Street, but a month later the printing was transferred to Joshua Hobson of Leeds until it was brought back to London in October 1841. In April 1839 the Birmingham Socialists bought for £800 Lawrence Street Chapel, which had originally been built by the Southcottians, and converted it. The building was enlarged to hold 1,000 in 1840.

Some efforts were apparently made in Birmingham to realise the Community ideal, one being the purchase of Union Cottage in Vauxhall Road where ten or twelve young men furnished the cottage, appointed a housekeeper and pooled their resources to live the common life.

But the main activity of the Birmingham branch of Rational Religionists, as for most others, was not to support Queenwood or promote Community and communal living, but to educate the public through meetings, classes and social activity on their own premises; and when the general public were less receptive, to educate themselves (self-improvement). The main emphasis was on rational, secular thought and radical social reform which, inevitably, brought them into conflict with organised Christianity, belief in God, the scriptures and revealed religion. These conflicts they entered into with great gusto. This gives substance to Chartist, and later, charges of sectarianism; on the other hand, they were both advocating and practising on a small scale, the alternative society of Socialism. This early flowering of Socialism was brief, its peak being 1839 to 1840. The strength of Socialism in Birmingham, unlike that of the Black Country, was that it was firmly rooted in the co-operation of the earlier period and a uniquely bourgeois-radical support or semi-support system.

Information regarding Birmingham from the *New Moral World* is more plentiful for 1842 than for the previous years. This is strange, because the movement elsewhere at this time was in rapid decline.

In January 1842 we learn that attendance at lectures is very full, the audiences are the most respectable part of the working class and some middle class. Later the same month we are told 'Mr Hulse is now secretary of the branch. We are now entering new candidates and some old members who left are coming back.' At this time George Alexander Fleming was the Social Missionary and he reported lecturing in Derby, Coventry and Birmingham, but declared that the position in Coventry was 'not satisfactory'. Later in the year night classes and Sunday schools were operating in Birmingham, helped by Frederick Hollick. But the students were giving some trouble and 'we found it necessary to stop the tickets of some and to remonstrate with others to preserve order in the Society.' Hollick was a young man, much the same age as Holyoake and both were self-educated working men who had come up the same way via the Birmingham Mechanics Institute.

In September 1842 there was a long report from the latest Social Missionary, Thomas Simmons Mackintosh, stating that Sunday, evening and day schools were all operating in Birmingham and that a social and party had attracted upwards of 800 people. There had been dancing on the green, cricket playing, football, archery etc. 'A beautiful balloon 36ft in circumference ascended with a rabbit in a little car. At a considerable altitude the balloon disengaged from the car and the rabbit descended by parachute.' The party had lasted from 11 a.m. until dusk.

As not infrequently occurs, indications of widening support and promising developments are not fulfilled and the above proved to be the last report of Socialism in Birmingham. It raises a number of questions regarding the differences of development with other parts of the country and particularly the adjacent Black Country. Birmingham Co-operative Socialism (to coin a phrase) was extremely important for the whole period 1824–1842. This begins with the 'Brighton period' (Co-operation modelled on the pre-Owenite principles of Dr King), on through the Owenite Socialist days of 1831–34 of Labour Exchange – Labour Notes/Builders Guild/GNCTU, re-emerging again in a strong, leading position in 1839 to 1840. All of this was basically working class activity and organisation which could only be matched nationally by, perhaps,

Manchester, and with only pale reflections of these activities in the Black Country. From 1839 to 1842 however, Birmingham reverts to the radical middle class/working class alliance of 1832 and it is the early stages of Chartism in which Birmingham takes a leading national role. This contrasts strongly with the Black Country where Chartism is embryonic in the early years up to 1839, but emerges as a leading centre in the period of the 2nd Petition and General Strike of 1841 – 42, continuing important thereafter until the total demise of Chartist organisation in 1860. The middle class alliance in Birmingham, however, collapsed in 1839 (as it did after 1832) with the defection of the middle class leaders led by Attwood. On the other hand, Black Country Owenite Socialism flourished in 1839 – 40 compared with Birmingham and declined with the rise of Chartism. What remains after these differences are noted is a correlation between the decline of Socialism and the rise of Chartism (and vice versa) for each area. But one is not the cause of the other, for both the aims and the personnel of the two movements remained stubbornly separate. Owenite Socialists did not become Chartists, nor did Chartists become Owenite Socialists. The only other comment that might be made is that whenever the Birmingham working class united with the middle class it was building on sand. In the Black Country there were no such snares and temptations; the working class either organised itself or there was no organisation at all.

What is clear is that Birmingham, in this period, produced a considerable number of leaders of working class origin for the Socialist cause. These included George Edmonds, probably John Rabone (the first man to popularise the term 'Christian Socialist'), William Pare, Joseph Hansom, the Holyoake brothers and Frederick Hollick.

Another intriguing difference between Owenite Socialism in Birmingham and the Black Country is that the ferocious, unremitting opposition that Black Country Socialism faced does not appear to have been repeated in Birmingham. The most virulent and unprincipled opponent of Socialism was John Brindley, who was for a time a teacher, at the Oldswinford Hospital School in the Black Country. Brindley both led and encouraged opposition in that area. William Pare, in Birmingham suffered from that other national opponent of Socialism, the Bishop of Exeter, and was forced to resign his Registrarship of Birmingham after 1840, but Brindley met with less success in Birmingham than elsewhere.

Brindley's forte was the marathon debate lasting over several nights with Socialist leaders at which violence usually erupted and at one meeting in Bristol Robert Owen nearly lost his life. Lloyd Jones undertook one of these marathons with John Brindley in Birmingham in May 1841. At least 3,000 people were present each evening at the three night debate of Jones and Brindley and there was some violence. There had also been a debate two years previously in January 1839 between Brindley and Robert Owen himself at Birmingham Town Hall, but violence there also seems to have been contained. The reasons for the differing degrees of violence reflect the differences of social structure and response. Birmingham leaders such as Pare and Hawkes-Smith were 'moderates' in the matter of engaging religionists in controversy and thus avoided provoking extremists such as Brindley. There was also less organised hostility to Socialism from the clergy of the Church of England in Birmingham where they were both less influential and effective; in the Black Country the ministers of the Church of England were the 'black slugs' teaching obedience to church and state on Sundays and savagely sentencing working people for the rest of the week in their role of justice of the peace. Reactionary Methodist influence was also less in Birmingham than in the Black Country. Also despite the church and king mob tradition of the Priestley Riots, the Unitarian, Quaker, Birmingham Political Union radical influence in the town provided a radical and religious spectrum which ranged all the way from progressive Anglicans to an actual merging with the Radical Religionists. This made it difficult for the Bishop of Exeter to find support in the town for the suppression of Socialism. Finally there was the character of Brindley himself; no one could be sure to what extent his opposition to Socialism was from pure religious conviction and to what extent he was an adventurer making a good living (like many a later one) out of his anti-Socialism.

Robert Owen

Chapter Four

CHARTISM

The Chartists created the first national working class political party in Britain and because the Industrial Revolution occurred first in Britain creating the first industrial proletariat in the world, Chartism was the first working class political party in the world. Given this national and international significance of Chartism it is not surprising that its aims and achievements have been distorted as well as celebrated.

The two most important distortions are firstly that the movement was a failure, and secondly that Chartism ended in 1848 with a fiasco of a meeting on Kennington Common when the Petition was bundled into a cab examined and found to have a large number of fictitious signatures, and was contemptuously rejected by Parliament. On the first distortion, it is difficult to see how a movement which had Six Points, five of which have long since become the law of the land, can be considered a failure. On the second, the tenacity of the myth is mainly due to a failure to produce local narratives of the movement to dispel the distortion; for Chartism continued to exist as the main working class political party until 1860, albeit at a lower level of activity after 1848, which itself was lower than in 1842. During the period 1848–1860, however, Chartism survived in most industrial areas, and in periods of crisis, such as during the Crimean War, was capable of mobilising working class support on a scale almost as significant as in 1842.

The distortions arising from the lack of such a local narrative for Birmingham have been particularly serious; not only have they reinforced the national misrepresentation of the movement, but also added two further myths. One, that because of its class structure, Birmingham was unable to sustain a working class leadership. Two, that Birmingham Chartism developed under middle class leadership and when that leadership reneged in 1839 the movement came to an end. The modern villain of the piece in Birmingham was Trygve R. Tholfsen who in 1958 wrote:

> On the spectrum of Victorian politics Birmingham stands at one extreme
> — the exemplar of class harmony and co-operation. Where other towns
> were torn by strife and discord, here the forces of cohesion and stability
> were triumphant. An alliance between the middle and working classes
> remained the cardinal fact of political life from Thomas Attwood's
> Political Union to Joseph Chamberlain's caucus.

Such gross distortions of the class realities of Birmingham are no longer acceptable, but modifications of the myth still dominate the perceptions of Birmingham history. The following does not claim to be a complete narrative of Chartism in Birmingham, but it does cover the whole period 1837 to 1860.

National and Municipal Politics 1832–1839.

To explain how Attwood and the middle class leaders of the Birmingham Political Union came to embrace Chartism, it is necessary to understand their preoccupations between 1832 and 1837. Once the worst of the 'rotten boroughs' in a Parliamentary sense had been removed by the 1832 Reform Act, the government determined to end the 'rottenness' in the municipal sense. This included both boroughs with ancient charters and the newly enfranchised towns such as Manchester and Birmingham whose local government was controlled by self-perpetuating oligarchies. Legislation would therefore have to embrace both the replacement of old charters and the granting of new charters, and it was on these twin objectives that the 1835 Municipal Corporations Act was to founder. Birmingham was at the heart of the Royal Commission whose enquiry and report preceded the Act, in the person of Joseph Parkes, who was both secretary to the Commission and who played a large part in drawing up the subsequent Birmingham Charter.

Although the Municipal Corporations Act as passed in 1835 detailed the powers of new corporations, an unsatisfactory feature was that instead of automatically granting such Charters, these had to be applied for. Herein lay vast regions for small minorities to object, opportunities which the Tory minority in Birmingham were not slow to seize.

It was not until March 1837 that the first moves were made in Birmingham to obtain a Charter from the Crown. The strongest argument for the Charter was the existing government of Birmingham:

> We have our Court Leets and our bailiffs, chosen by themselves; our Street Commissioners, chosen by themselves; our Town Hall Commissioners, chosen by themselves; working in the dark, unseen by the public eye, irresponsible to the public voice, appointing their own officers, levying taxes at their pleasure, and distributing them, without check or control, as their inclination shall determine.

The main arguments of the Tory opposition to the Charter were to be that the town was well-enough governed by the existing structure, that the proposed corporation would have few powers, that it would be expensive and create yet another tier of taxation, and perhaps the most telling of all, that the whole history of the development of the town had been its openness without the shackles of charters or corporations.

Incorporation went ahead, however. Despite determined opposition both locally and in Parliament, a Charter was granted in October 1838. Its main feature was to incorporate all the inhabitants into a corporate body entitled the Mayor, Aldermen and Burgesses of Birmingham. The town was divided into thirteen wards, ten of which were within the parish of Birmingham and in addition, Edgbaston, Deritend and Bordesley, and Duddeston and Nechells, the two latter electing six councillors thus giving a Council of Mayor, 48 councillors and 16 aldermen. The first elections, instead of being held under household suffrage were confined to the £10 householder, as for Parliamentary elections, which excluded all but a tiny minority of working people. The elections were held in December 1838. All seats in all wards were contested by Tories and all seats in all wards were won by Liberals. This completely Liberal council met the following week and proceeded to transact its business. The first matter was to swear in its members as required by the 1835 Municipal Corporations Act. This included the following statement concerning the Church of England:

I, AB, do solemnly and seriously, in the presence of God profess, testify
and declare, upon the true faith of a Christian, that I will never exercise
any power, authority or influence, which I may possess by virtue of (my)
office to injure or weaken the Protestant Church, as it is by law
established in England; or to disturb the said Church, or the bishops, or
the clergy of the said Church, in the possession of any rights or privileges
to which such Church or the said bishops and clergy are, or may be, by
law entitled.

W. Harrold immediately said that he could not make the declaration.
Joseph Sturge, the Quaker, also refused, saying that he had such strong
feelings against establishment and felt so strongly that there would be no
peace in the country while the present system existed that he was
determined to do all he could, in a lawful manner, to make a change. He
could not make the declaration in the morning and vote against Church
rates in the evening. William Pare, the Deist, saw the matter differently,
however. They only declared that they would not injure the church in
their corporate capacity; they did not surrender their private judgement
or individual rights as citizens. Harrold then declared his scruples
removed and all councillors, with the exception of Joseph Sturge and his
brother Charles, took the oath.

The next business was the election of aldermen. Joseph Sturge and
others argued that only councillors should be eligible to maintain the
principle of popular election. Philip Muntz, whilst agreeing that rejected
Tory candidates should not be elected, thought it unwise to reject good
men who had not offered themselves as candidates. Eventually sixteen
aldermen were elected including two non-councillors. The five with the
highest votes were Philip Muntz, Thomas Bolton, William Scholefield,
Benjamin Hadley and Joseph Sturge.

Scholefield, who up to this point had been acting as Returning Officer,
was then unanimously elected Mayor. The Council then proceeded to
elect its officers. For Town Clerk, William Redfern was nominated by
Bolton and Muntz, and Solomon Bray was nominated by Hadley and
Salt. In support of Redfern, his eminent services in promoting the
Charter were urged, and after Bray's nomination had been put and
negatived, Redfern was elected unanimously. R.K. Douglas was elected
Registrar of the Mayor's Court and George Edmonds was nominated as
Clerk of the Peace. Edmond's election was urged on the grounds that he
was the oldest man in Birmingham who had stood on the platform of
religious liberty and had suffered imprisonment for it. Hadley added that
not only in Birmingham, but friends of freedom throughout England
would rejoice at the result of the labours of Edmonds. He had been one
of the great pioneers in the battle for freedom. His election was not
proceeded with, however, it being pointed out by the Town Clerk that the
appointment could not be made until a request for Quarter Sessions had
been made and granted. The meeting then adjourned. Elections to fill the
vacancies left by aldermen took place within a few days. Again all seats
were contested and again, all Liberals were returned.

When the new councillors came to take the oath more objections arose.
David Burnett, who was a Jew, objected to the phrase 'on the true faith
of a Christian'. He, like the Sturge brothers was allowed to declare in his
own way 'at the risk of incurring any personal penalty to which he might

be exposed by so doing.' Another new councillor, Captain Moorsom, was an anti-Establishment Churchman, who objected to the Oath, and he also was allowed to take his place.

Moorsom raised the next question of principle when he asked the Town Clerk:

> Do you consider it the undoubted and inalienable right of the Council to discuss and pronounce an opinion upon all questions of general policy, foreign or domestic, of municipal and fiscal regulations, of religious and civil liberty; on every question, in short, which affects the welfare of society?

The Town Clerk hedged in his reply giving it as his opinion as a lawyer that the only duties the town council were competent to perform were strictly of a local nature, but adding:

> ... when he considered what had been the almost uniform practice of municipal corporations for ages past, and how important a part they had played on some of the most momentous occasions of our history ... he felt warranted in saying that they were not bound to confine themselves within the strict limits prescribed by the Municipal Corporations Act, but that it was competent for them to deal with matters of a general and national nature.

This matter was immediately put to the test by an application from the Anti-Corn Law Association for an interview with the Council with a view to inducing them to use 'all means in their power for the total repeal of corn and provision laws'. After discussion on the principle of dealing with such matters, a deputation consisting of Joshua Scholefield, the MP, and several others including Councillor George Edmonds was received, and at the next meeting a motion by Joseph Sturge was accepted that the Mayor be requested to convene a town meeting to discuss petitioning Parliament for the Repeal of the Corn Laws. This establishment of the principle that the Council was competent to discuss any question of political or public importance led to the first major disagreement on the Council, for at a meeting of the Duddeston and Nechells Radical Reform Association a resolution was passed in January:

> This meeting utterly deprecates the attempts now being made by short-sighted men to distract, by the agitation of party and class questions, the attention of the people from the momentous constitutional struggle in which they are engaged ... That it would ill become the municipal representatives of this great and enlightened borough to sanction the interested movements of the Whig Corn Law intriguers; and that the high reputation of our important town demands that the first political act of its corporate body should be in aid of the legal and peaceful movement which is now being made by suffering millions to acquire their indefeasible right of suffrage.

In other words, at this stage the working class was demanding that the Council reinforce the leading role of the Birmingham Political Union in developing the local and national Chartist movement and not allow itself to be diverted by the Anti-Corn Law Leaguers.

At this point we can leave this apparent democrat's paradise created by

Birmingham radicalism. It seemed that all the worst fears and nightmares of the Whigs and Tories had been realised.

No one could have foreseen that this whole democratic structure was to collapse like a house of cards; that the town council was to be rendered powerless and penniless by a challenge to its powers of levying rates; that for several years it would face the ignominy and ridicule of challenges to the principles and details of the town Charter; that this would generate a powerful Tory opposition in the town and that the corporation that would eventually emerge would be one shorn of most of its democratic features. At this point we can turn to Chartism.

The First Stage of Chartism to 1839.

We have seen how, when economic expansion was resumed in 1833 and in the wake of the disillusionment with the 1832 Reform Act, the working class broke off its alliance with the middle class to develop its own organisations. These included the further development of trade unions, and Owenite Labour Exchanges culminating in the 'syndicalism' of the Grand National Consolidated Trade Union. In addition, it was the working class in Birmingham who bore the brunt of the struggle for a free press against the 'taxes on knowledge'.

For overall leadership, the working class organisations in Birmingham after 1832 turned to the National Union of the Working Classes and Others. The title suggests the new relation of class forces — unity with the middle class if they wanted it, but under the leadership of the working class. This also represented the situation in Birmingham. The difference between middle class leadership of the Birmingham Political Union in 1832 and BPU 'leadership' of Chartism in 1839 was that in 1832 the middle class were the decisive force in the alliance of classes, but in 1839 working class influence was paramount. The National Union of the Working Classes subscribed to a labour theory of value with its slogan — Labour is the Source of Wealth. Its programme was Universal Male Suffrage at age 21 with one year Parliaments, Vote by Ballot and No Property Qualifications; in other words four points of what was to become the six points of the People's Charter. The organ of the NUWC was the *Poor Man's Guardian*.

The whole of the issue of the *Guardian* of 3 November 1832 was taken up with a report of the formation of the Midland Union of the Working Classes, a branch of which was set up in Birmingham. It was specifically stated that the new organisation implied no hostility to the Birmingham Political Union, but that organisation it claimed was now inactive and working people had been much deceived by the Reform Act. The statement endorsing these views was signed by J. Larkin as chairman of the Non-Electors, H. Watson, chairman of the United Trades, T. Baker, chairman of the Unemployed Artisans and R.J. Edwards, secretary of the United Committees. Edwards was elso elected, at this meeting, secretary of a strong midland committee consisting of Massey (treasurer), Morrison, Watson, Whitworth, Bewley, Skillicorn, Larkin, May, King, Rose, Orford, Baker, Haden, Adams, Bridges, Cleaver, Chilton and Pessineur. The *Poor Man's Guardian* besides being the organ of the Union of Working Classes also served those Political Unions which had survived under working class control (for instance, in the Black

Country, Wednesbury and Dudley). It also supported the Secularism of Owenism exemplified by such reports as one in September 1833 'The March of Methodism. It seems that this new description of locusts is spreading with fearful rapidity', or a verse a year later:

> Robert Owen wise and good
> Better known than understood
> Too often putting wisdom's tools
> Into the hands of fools.

In March 1833 the Birmingham Political Union demonstrated that it was not dead by organising another monster rally on Newhall Hill attended by 200,000 primarily on the internationalist issue of protest against the Irish Coercion Bill. This was an issue which united both classes. Present at the meeting were ·members of the Political Council of the BPU including Attwood and Muntz and also, as the main attraction, the Great Liberator himself, Daniel O'Connell, with Dr Wade and other 'friends of Ireland'. The meeting decided to petition the king asking him to 'dismiss his ministers' — the very same ministers who only a year before had been the heroes of the Reform Act. This Petition had still not been presented in June, Earl Fitzwilliam declining to do so and sending a twelve page letter of his reasons for not doing so, but Attwood had presented a Petition to Parliament by then 'against all restrictions on importation of animal and vegetable food' (a euphemism for Repeal of the Corn Laws). The Political Council of the BPU had also protested against the conduct of the police at the late Coldbath Fields. This last was a sweetener to the working class. Coldbath Fields had been a miniature Peterloo at which the police had violently broken up a peaceful public meeting; more significantly, however, it had been called by the National Union of the Working Classes to discuss preparations for the calling of a National Convention, an issue on which both Whig and Tory governments were excessively sensitive, but one to which the leaders of the BPU were beginning to return.

The disillusion with the government encouraged the Birmingham Tories to raise their heads and resuscitate the old Loyal and Constitutional Society. In December 1835 they celebrated their first anniversary with a dinner at the Town Hall with 850 guests. The Liberals replied with a dinner at the same venue with 900 guests among whom were Daniel O'Connell and Sir Charles Wolseley. But the working class topped this with a Town Hall dinner in February 1836 organised by the town's Committee of Non-Electors with 1000 guests.

At the end of 1836 a decisive new factor appeared. The short-lived expansion from the end of 1833 to the end of 1836 came to an end and the third Long Depression began which was to last into 1843. The return of starvation and mass unemployment to the town hastened the transition of the working class to the politics of Chartism. It also gave a renewed credibility to Attwood's currency theories. These can be simplified into the two propositions that the slump was one of poverty in the midst of plenty i.e. of Underconsumption. Secondly that it could have been prevented, and could be cured, by adapting the money supply to the requirements of consumers to buy, which would then allow investors to profitably invest.

In May 1837 the Liberals created a new society, the Reform Society, and inaugurated it in June with a 50,000 meeting on Newhall Hill. The meeting adopted the policy of Household Suffrage, Secret Ballot, Triennial Parliaments, Payment of Members and the Abolition of Property Qualifications i.e. almost five of the Six Points. At the same meeting a Women's Political Union was established. This meeting was dominated by the leaders of the BPU and the constitutional character of the new association was emphasised when the proceedings commenced with 'a solemn prayer from the whole of the vast assembly, heads bared, for the recovery of the King, who lay dying'. This did not prevent 'drastic preparations by the military authorities with the dragoons kept in readiness to mount, booted and saddled and provided with ball and cartridges.' Happily, Dent concludes his report, 'as on all previous occasions, military intervention was wholly unneeded.'

The election of July 1837, necessitated by the death of William IV, first brought violence back to the town. Dent's biased and myth creating report says that crowds of 'noisy and turbulent people' gathered at the Royal Hotel, the defeated Tories' central committee rooms, ridiculing the defeated party. About 7.30pm it seems the Tories sallied forth from the Hotel and set about the opposition. 'The crowd becoming angry at this rather rough usage . . . immediately hurled a shower of brickbats at the Hotel windows thereby doing considerable damage'. The dragoons were called for from West Bromwich where they had been kept in readiness and their commanders went to see Attwood at the Clarendon Hotel requesting him to use his influence to disperse the crowd. This Attwood did and only a few stragglers remained, to whom the Riot Act was read. The next morning crowds again gathered at the Royal Hotel to view and add to the damage. The Riot Act was again read and the crowd was dispersing when 'at an inopportune moment', a troop of the Worcestershire Yeomanry rode through the streets 'attracting still larger crowds hooting and pelting them with small pebbles until they were forced to take refuge in the Hen and Chicken's yard'. Attwood was brought to attract the attention of the crowd in New Street while the frightened Yeomanry escaped.

Dent goes on to say 'it was stated' that the Yeomanry had been ordered to load with ball and on the throwing of the first stone to fire upon the crowd. To which a Liberal newspaper replied:

> Yes, the crowd would have scampered . . . pistols to pebbles are mighty odds. But the crowd would have re-assembled; and they would have assembled in arms. There are at least 100,000 muskets in Birmingham and 40,000 men who known how to use them.

From this sort of reporting the myth of working class Chartism representing 'physical force' and Attwood and company 'moral force' was passed on to another generation by Dent. The reality was more complex and it is necessary to consider the evolution of Attwood's thinking under the impact of his disillusionment with Parliament, the question of the municipal charter, and the renewed significance of his currency theories under the impact of the third Long Depression. These, together with a more realistic understanding of working class politics and power will allow us to see how the first stage of Chartism was created.

The basic purpose of the Reform Association formed in May 1837 had been to consider the declining state of trade. It had gone on to define its Reform programme and went on to agree that, if 4,000 people enrolled, it would reconstitute the Birmingham Political Union. Six weeks later there were 5,000 members and the BPU was formally revived. This was not universally welcomed by the Birmingham working class since this also revived the 'dictatorship of the Political Council'. (Shades of Joseph Chamberlain's future Junta). The Political Council at that time consisted of 35 middle class members and no working men. Attwood later stated that 'the very essence of the Birmingham Union, under the law, was unlimited obedience to their leaders who formed the Political Council'.

Independent working class activity at this time included a petition with 13,000 signatures, organised by the Working Men's Memorial Committee requesting a joint meeting of masters and men to discuss distress. This took place on the 30th May. In October the Working Men's Memorial Committee called a town's meeting to petition parliament over distress. At this meeting, very blunt class positions were put by such speakers as John Collins and Thomas Baker regarding employers' policies of low wages and hostility to trade unions. The BPU supported this petition whose presenters had a very unsatisfactory meeting with Lord Melbourne. This further emphasised the necessity for the vote for working men and raised the vexed question of what could be done if Parliament failed to enact measures to relieve poverty and expand trade. On both these issues the Birmingham Political Union was changing its attitude. Salt in April had declared that physical resistance was a duty where the government violated the law; the BPU was also moving towards the acceptance of manhood suffrage which it had previously resisted. This was endorsed in January 1838 together with the idea of lobbying other towns for a projected National Petition for political reform. On this basis, the Working Men's Memorial Committee committed itself to association with the BPU.

Meanwhile, the reformed parliament had produced but a puny number of radical MPs with any working class sympathies whatever. By the middle of 1837 these included J.A. Roebuck, J.T. Leader, Sir William Molesworth, Colonel Thompson, Thomas Wakley, Sharman Crawford, Joseph Hume and Daniel O'Connell. This number was reduced by the election of July 1837, so that when a mildest possible motion for 'the better representation of the people' was moved in the new Parliament, only 22 members voted for it. Discussion between the London Working Men's Association and this most unsatisfactory band of Parliamentary radicals had, however, resulted in agreement on a programme of Reform of the Six Points of what was to become known as the People's Charter. These six Points were: Universal Manhood Suffrage, Annual Parliaments, Vote by Ballot, No Property Qualifications for MPs, Payment for Members and Equal Voting Districts. The last point was not universally agreed since, before the Famine decimated the population of Ireland, one third of members of Parliament would have been Irish. This People's Charter was published in May 1838.

In the same month, the National Petition was launched in Birmingham by the BPU. There was no necessary connection between the Charter and the Petition. Attwood's mind was on a repeat performance of 1832. A massive Petition with millions of signatures, backed by a Convention elected by millions of citizens would, Attwood argued, exert such mass, peaceful pressure that the government would not be able to resist their demands. Working people and their leaders, however, were sceptical; the 1832 Reform Act had simply installed their employers in Parliament and the result had been such measures as the hated Poor Law. Collaboration with the middle class was difficult enough in Birmingham; in the factory districts it was all but impossible. The BPU therefore had to re-establish its credibility with the working class, and where it did, it was often only on the basis that Petitioning parliament would be tried 'just once more'.

The National Petition was a sonorous, eloquent document, written presumably by R.K. Douglas, the editor of the *Birmingham Journal*. It described Britain as a land with enterprising merchants, skilful manufacturers and workmen proverbial for their industry, dwelling in a land abundantly furnished with materials of commerce, enjoying for twenty years a profound peace, but now overwhelmed with public and private suffering. They were bowed down under a load of taxes, traders trembled on the brink of bankruptcy, workmen were starving and capital brought no profit. They had searched long for the causes of such distress and could observe none in nature or in Providence. It could only be, therefore, that the energies of a mighty kingdom had been wasted in building up the power of selfish and ignorant men. The good of the nation had been sacrificed to the interests of the few. It had been the fond hope of the people that a remedy would have been found in the Reform Act of 1832. The people had been utterly and basely deceived. The Reform Act had transferred power from one domineering faction to another and left the people helpless as before. 'We tell your Honourable House that the capital of the master must no longer be deprived of its due reward; that the laws which make food dear, and those which by making money scarce make labour cheap, must be abolished; that taxation must be made to fall on property, not on industry; that the good of the many . . . must be the sole study of the government.'

This Petition, smuggling in as it did, both Corn Law repeal and Attwood's currency theories, ended with the demands, of which there were only three of the Six Points — Universal Suffrage, the Ballot and Annual Parliaments.

The People's Charter was widely disseminated throughout the country by the London Working Men's Association; the BPU widely circulated the Petition and Chartism was launched with the collection of signatures to the Petition, elections to the National Convention and the raising of the National Rent which was to sustain those elected to the Convention.

The first great meeting of Chartism is reckoned to be the mass demonstration organised by the working class of Glasgow attended by 200,000 people on 28 May 1838. The main guests were the leaders of the BPU; Attwood, Douglas, Edmonds, Muntz and Collins were all present.

Attwood was rapturously received. He outlined his plans. The Petition was to be signed throughout the country and he calculated that there would be two to three million signatures. This petitioning process was to be continued again and again, and should parliament still not concede the popular demands, the working men, with such of the middle class as might favour their views, should proclaim a solemn and sacred strike from every kind of labour. Gammage's account goes on to say that Edmonds, Muntz and Douglas all followed in the same strain to the great delight of the meeting and none of these gentlemen seem disposed to pass over the obstacles. Attwood said they would have all the aristocracy, nine tenths of the gentry, the great body of the clergy and all the pensioners, sinecurists and bloodsuckers that feed on the vitals of the people, against them. But, Gammage shrewdly concludes, 'he never seemed to contemplate the greatest obstacle of all, the newly enfranchised middle class'.

All through the summer and autumn vast rallies were held throughout the country, organisations formed, signatures collected and delegates to the Convention elected. In August it was Birmingham's turn. There was another huge turn-out, this time at Holloway Head. Attwood again outlined his plan, stressing the need for peaceful agitation, but again advocating a general strike if such pressure failed. This time Gammage commented, however, that such a strike was bound to lead to the very violence that Attwood was condemning if he were not to act like the good old Duke of York, marching his men to the top of the hill and then marching them back again. But this Birmingham rally was basically different from the others which Attwood had dominated since the early days of the BPU. At this rally there were elected Convention delegates from all parts of the country and national decisions were to be taken on this day. Among those delegates, and making the first of his many decisive interventions in Birmingham Chartist politics was Feargus O'Conner. O'Conner distrusted the middle class, was at odds with Attwood's friend, Daniel O'Connell, and bitterly opposed to the Anti-Corn Law agitators, one of whose key figures was Joseph Sturge. In his speech O'Conner took on where Attwood had left off. When Attwood presented the Petition, 500,000 men should accompany him to Parliament and declare that they were waiting for an answer in Palace Yard, O'Conner suggested. Such a speech was more to the liking of the Birmingham working class. All ended in harmony, however, at this meeting. The Muntz brothers, Douglas, Clutton Salt, Edmonds, Hadley, Pearce and one working man — John Collins were elected as Birmingham delegates to the Convention. The national delegates at this Birmingham rally then endorsed the National Rent to come into operation in October 1838. This was fixed at £2-10-0d. for every one thousand of population. When amounts reached £5 they were to be paid into a London bank and entered into an account in the name of the Muntz brothers and R.K. Doulgas of Birmingham. From this August meeting, however, tension gradually built up between the leadership of the BPU and the working class whose undisputed leader by now was Feargus O'Conner. This should not be interpreted as a simple split between moral and physical force factions. It was a difference between responsible working class leaders building a movement which took as its watchword 'Peaceably if we may, Forcibly if we must' and those who by ruling out from the beginning any possibility of having a resort to force condemned the movement to impotence.

Nor was it O'Conner who imported into Birmingham concepts of physical force. He was frequently in Birmingham at this time, had good

relations with Attwood and on occasions attended the fortnightly meeting
of the BPU Political Council. At one stage O'Conner referred to himself
as a 'follower of Messrs Attwood and Fielden'. But working class activity
and leadership dominated Birmingham politics at this time. The BPU
Political Council met on Tuesdays, and the Working Men's Committee
and also its sections throughout the town met every Thursday. Harmony
was maintained, however, even after September 1838 when the
Manchester Anti-Corn Law Association was founded and Sturge and
others unsuccessfully tried to get repeal of the Corn Laws accepted in both
the BPU and the town council.

Open conflict first appeared over the question of the National Rent. As
middle class influence waned, so did middle class attendance at the BPU
Political Council meetings. In November, Henry Watson and Thomas
Baker, two working men on the BPU Council, proposed a system of
district meetings to raise the Rent more efficiently. This was rejected and
Watson complained that if the proposal had been made by a wealthy
middle class member, it would have been passed. As a result of this, the
Working Men's Committee took the matter over and made themselves
responsible for collecting the Rent. This was by now pouring in from
Birmingham's trade union branches, teachers, factories, friendly societies,
money clubs and, not least, from the Women's Political Union, which by
March 1839 had collected £32 through Mrs Oxford.

In February 1839 the Chartist General Convention of the Industrious
Classes, at last opened in London. It was a staid gathering of 53 delegates
29 of whom were middle class and only 24 working men. It was constantly
under threat of being declared illegal. At its opening, the Petition
contained just over half a million signatures. Of these, the largest number
were from Birmingham and district — 94,643, of which 24,000 were
women. Birmingham and district also contributed £167 of a National
Rent total of £967. Because many districts were still unorganised, one of
the first decisions of the Convention was that the presentation of the
Petition be delayed and some of the delegates sent as missionaries into
their areas to develop this work. Of the Birmingham delegates elected in
August 1838 only Douglas, Hadley, Salt and Collins attended. They were
all given Birmingham and district to develop and in addition, Hadley was
also made responsible for Reading and Collins for Cheltenham and
Coventry.

The remaining delegates at the Convention continued their deliberations. William Lovett was elected secretary. The delay in presenting the
Petition was not to the liking of the more militant members as it extended
the life of the Convention beyond that intended with a drain on the
National Rent, and a depleted membership made for indecisive
discussion. The main question before the Convention was the vexed one
of what to do if Parliament rejected the Petition. The various proposals
eventually appeared as the celebrated Manifesto of Ulterior Measures,
but before this could be discussed, more urgent matters arose. As the
missionaries went about their work of developing new areas and
collecting more signatures, numbers of Chartists were being arrested.
Towards the end of April O'Connor brought to the attention of the
Convention the fact that a jury at King's Bench, in the case of the arrest
of one of the more prominent northern leaders J.R. Stephens, had

declared the Convention illegal. O'Connor therefore proposed that the Convention move to Birmingham, where it would be better protected by the militant workers of that town. As a result of objections by Lovett and others the motion was postponed.

On May 1 the Petition, which now had 1,283,000 signatures and was nearly three miles long, was taken to Attwood's London address to be presented to Parliament by him and Fielden the following Monday. Attwood raised objections, however. Lord John Russell's resignation was expected on that day and presentation would have to be postponed. Attwood also objected to introducing a Bill entitled the People's Charter in the House on the grounds that he did not agree with all the Six Points, especially the one calling for Equal Electoral Districts, which would have given the Irish 200 MPs. Lovett, who was present at these discussions, concluded that Attwood was more interested in his currency schemes than in the Charter.

On May 10, Henry Vincent, the most personable and eloquent of the Convention delegates, was arrested. O'Connor again brought before the Convention his proposal to move to Birmingham and this time he was successful. The outcome was the importation of a force of London police which resulted in the so-called Bull Ring Riots. To explain this event adequately it is necessary to return to the question of Birmingham's municipal Charter, and also the complete loss of control of Birmingham Chartism by the middle class which led to the resignation of their delegates in March 1839.

We left the town charter at the point where there seemed to be almost unlimited scope for the development of local democracy and therefore the continuance of the middle class/working class alliance. The Charter had granted a democratic council elected on a franchise of household suffrage i.e. a vote for all householders paying rates. Although in most cases the 'head' of the household with the vote would be a man, some 'heads' would be women and this would raise the case for universal suffrage. Additionally, there was no property qualification for Councillors; the Council was to be competent to determine its own composition through declaration if oath were objected to and making no claims for the established church, so that the Council was open to Nonconformists, Catholics, Jews and Secularists; and the Council was to be competent to act upon matters both local and national if these bore upon the welfare of the burgesses. But, equally important, one of the crucial intentions of the Municipal Corporations Act of 1835 was that the new Corporations should at once create their own police forces and these should, as was traditionally the case, *be completely under the control of the local authority through a local Watch Committee.* There was even to be the possibility of direct election of magistrates.

The first challenge to the Charter came on the question of police powers. In January 1839, the borough council had nominated 21 borough magistrates, all of who were middle class Liberals. In applying to the Home Secretary for the grant of Quarters Sessions to the town, the Home Secretary had altered the list and approved it only with six Liberals removed and three Tories and three Whigs in their place. In July 1839 the London police were brought into Birmingham not by the town council, who were not consulted on the matter, and soon regretted it, but by direct application of the Mayor and borough magistrates to the Home Secretary. To add insult to injury, the magistrates then urged the moneyless borough council to immediately raise a police force 'to preserve the peace and to protect the property of the borough'. The council agreed that this was 'highly expedient', but added that this should be delayed until their power to levy rates had been granted. Matters were then complicated by the so-called Bull Ring Riots of 8 to 15 July and rejection of the Chartist Petition in the same period. After the Birmingham 'riots' there were strong debates in Parliament. In the Lords, the Duke of Wellington was particularly vitriolic claiming that 'he had seen many towns taken by storm, but never had such outrages occurred in them as . . . in Birmingham'. The government offered a way out of the town's difficulties in raising a police force. This was to grant the council a loan of £10,000. This was acceptable to the town council and the Home Secretary, Lord John Russell, who then moved a Bill to this effect. During the proceedings Sir Robert Peel asked whether the force was to be under the control of a Stipendiary Magistrate or the Corporation and local magistracy. The Home Secretary confirmed that it would be under the control of the Corporation. Peel then rejoined that he thought it would be better to have the police under the control of a paid magistrate, as in London.

This point was taken up by the Tory opposition in Birmingham who then drew up a Petition to the Queen that the whole Birmingham charter be annulled on grounds that it had not promoted good order, offices of honour and emolument had been monopolised and the town threatened with heavy rates. No such direct challenge to the charter was likely to succeed however, and hopes would be even slimmer if the powers of the town council were legitimised by the granting of a loan for the police. A more direct attack on the police bill was therefore necessary. Birmingham Tory discussions with Peel then produced a radical new amendment to the Bill. Peel proposed that control of the Birmingham police be vested not in the town council, but in a Government Commissioner. His grounds were a precedent in the case of Dublin, a 'doubtful validity' of the Birmingham charter, and the partisan character of the Birmingham magistrates with their connections with 'the party of violence', the Chartists. Such grounds were vigorously contested in Parliament by both the town's MPs and other radicals. But the Home Secretary was now colluding with Peel and a new Bill was brought in embodying these changes. A Chief Commissioner of Police with a salary of £800 a year was to act as a JP for the county town of Warwick under the direction of the Home Secretary, with sole and full authority over the Birmingham borough police.

These proposals not only struck at the roots of democratic local control, but also brought credibility to the notion that the town charter itself was 'of doubtful validity'.

A nation-wide protest then followed, because the Police Act applied not only to Birmingham, but to other towns, notably Manchester. Birmingham town council pointed out that not only was it to be deprived of the ancient right of controlling its local community, but made the instrument of its own degradation by having to raise local rates for this purpose. Powerful support came from the City of London, (which to this day controls its own police), by a Petition to Parliament presented by its Sheriffs demanding that the House of Commons 'sanction no invasion of the ancient and salutary rights of local government inherited by the people of this country from the earliest times as an essential principle of our free Constitution'.

The bill was contested bitterly through every stage of both Houses. In August, the MP for Coventry was taunting Russell with following Peel 'who was known to desire a government police', and thanking the Corporation of London 'who had preserved their own liberties intact for seven hundred years', for their support. In the Lords, Wellington, venting his spleen on Attwood and the Birmingham radicals, was the main supporter of the Bill. Lord Brougham proposed compromises — that the town council appoint the Police Commissioner with the approval of the Home Secretary and that the proposed salary of £800 be reduced to the £400 paid in Liverpool, which was a larger town than Birmingham at that time. All to no avail. The police force imposed on the town by the end of 1839 was not only an authoritarian, centrally controlled force, but was clearly seen as an instrument set up primarily to control working class activity.

At this point we return to Chartism and the loss of control by the Birmingham middle class leaders of the BPU. Working class leadership had been decisively demonstrated at the August 1838 Holloway Head rally. Under the impact of the slump and recurring visits of Feargus O'Connor it developed with astonishing rapidity in the following months. We have already noted the early breaches in November 1838 over the National Rent and the increasing tendency for the middle class leaders to absent themselves from the proceedings of the Political Council of the BPU. In January 1839, when Attwood put in a rare appearance at the Council, he feared that 'dangerous and imprudent men' would gain control of the Convention. However, when the Chartist Convention opened in London in February 1839, the *Birmingham Journal* reported its early proceedings favourably, if not enthusiastically. But under the blows of early discussion of 'ulterior measures' at the Convention, criticism of delegates such as Salt for not being energetic enough in developing the movement in the surrounding area and increasing domination of the BPU by the working class, the middle class delegates Douglas, Hadley and Salt resigned from the Convention on 28 March 1839.

These resignations caused scarcely a ripple. John Donaldson, one of the working class leaders, wrote to the Convention asking it to send a deputation of enquiry to Birmingham. This was granted and a Birmingham Observational Committee was set up to oversee Birmingham interests in the meantime. Among the new leaders, besides Donaldson, were John Fussell, Edward Brown, John Powell and Henry Wilkes. A preliminary meeting was held at Holloway Head at which the middle class leaders were castigated as betrayers of the movement and using the people as tools for their own purpose. The arrival of the deputation of enquiry was the occasion of another Holloway Head rally with Feargus O'Connor as the main speaker. Here a motion of censure against the resigned delegates was passed and at another Holloway Head meeting on April 22, Brown, Powell and Donaldson were elected to join John Collins as the four Birmingham Chartist Convention delegates.

This transition to a completely working class leadership was celebrated by a ceremonial burning of the *Birmingham Journal,* and those who wish from April 1839 to trace the actions and aspirations of working people in Birmingham must symbolically follow that example and turn to the Chartist papers, above all Feargus O'Connor's *Northern Star* for enlightenment.

By May 1839 the situation in Birmingham was indeed much more militant than in London. From January the Birmingham working class had taken to meeting in the Bull Ring to discuss politics and to have read aloud — for the benefit of both those who could not and those who could read — the working class newspapers of the week. These meetings began at 8pm and were at first attended only by 200 to 300 people. But during the sessions of the Convention the meetings had become nightly and vast crowds of several thousands assembled. In early May the Bull Ring meetings began to be held twice a day — from 1 to 2 pm as well as 8pm. At this point the magistrates, egged on, they claimed by complaints from shop-keepers in the vicinity, decided to put an end to such meetings. On 8 May a Caution was posted in the Bull Ring stating that it had been represented to the magistrates that meetings were being held at which not only were so many people assembled that the public thoroughfare was impeded, language highly inflammatory and seditious was used, and residents in the vicinity put in fear that their businesses would be injured, but that peace and order in the town were endangered. It was therefore desirable that such meetings in the Bull Ring and elsewhere be discontinued. The JPs therefore 'earnestly cautioned' all persons attending that they bore a heavy responsibility. This order was signed by the Mayor and JPs Gem, Barlow and Ryland.

Arrangements for these meetings were, at this time, largely in the hands of John Fussell, who at once began to negotiate with the magistrates. The Mayor said that it was not their intention to ban meetings everywhere and Fussell apparently undertook to find a more suitable site than the Bull Ring. But twice daily meetings continued in the Bull Ring and on Saturday 11th another notice was posted stating that those attending meetings in the Bull Ring were liable to be prosecuted. This fresh warning was again signed by the Mayor, William Scholefield, but also by a larger number of magistrates including Philip Muntz who had been one of the original delegates elected to the Convention.

The Chartists then resolved to put this matter to the Convention due to arrive in Birmingham on Monday 13th. When the Convention did arrive it received a great reception. The crowd originally waiting in the Bull Ring, moved to Freeman Street, and then to Duddeston Row railway station where the delegates were met. A procession was then formed which marched through the town to Holloway Head. It was estimated that there were 30,000 people in New Street and between 100,000 and 150,000 at Holloway Head. The Convention renewed its deliberations in Lawrence Street Chapel on 13th May and this further increased excitement in the town.

The town authorities had also made arrangements to receive the Convention. These included strengthening the military force in the town by two or three companies of riflemen from Weedon barracks, the sending of cavalry to Weedon and the swearing in of 2,300 special constables, including 1,000 Chelsea pensioners. The town was therefore an armed camp. Fussell was unable to address the Convention on the question of Bull Ring meetings, but privately met with some delegates who advised transferring meetings to Holloway Head. Meetings were held there on the Tuesday and Wednesday, but while Holloway Head was suitable for large rallies, being outside the town centre it drew smaller crowds for routine meetings and a resolution was passed to meet at the Horse Market.

The Mayor and JPs had made one other arrangement undisclosed at the time. They had brought back from London two police officers who advised the arrest of Fussell and Edward Brown which was carried out in the early hours of Thursday 16th May. Fussell was charged with 'incitement to resist the authorities by force' on the grounds that he had been the main speaker at the Holloway Head welcome to the Convention and had allegedly said that he would speak at the Bull Ring, if this were sanctioned by the Convention. When Fussell appeared before a full bench of magistrates the same day, the principal witnesses were the two London police officers, who were immediately recognised by Convention delegates. The case was a complete frame-up, the two main witnesses having taken separate notes, but having then compared them and produced a joint report. This procedure was subsequently characterised by the town council report on the Bull Ring riots as 'unprecedented and highly dangerous kind of evidence' and was deduced to be the reason why the case against Fussell was ultimately dropped. These arrests aroused deep anger and larger crowds gathered on 17th May when Fussell and Brown again appeared before the local magistrates, this time defended by Feargus O'Conner. Both were remanded on bail, Fussell's fixed at £400, but Brown's at £800, both reduced by half on appeal. Fussell's bail was found at once, but Brown went to gaol until his could be raised.

The main business of the Convention in Birmingham was to discuss the Manifesto of Ulterior Measures. This took the form of a rousing statement urging the justice and necessity of the Six Points being accepted by Parliament. It was followed by a list of possible actions which could be taken in the event of the Petition being rejected. These were to be discussed at Simultaneous Meetings throughout the country over Whitsun at which the measures would be put and the degree of support for each gauged.

The measures listed were:

1. Withdraw all savings from banks etc.
2. Convert all paper money into gold or silver.
3. Abstain from labour for a Sacred Month, at the same time abstaining from all intoxicating drink.
4. Provide themselves with arms to defend the laws and constitutional privileges bequeathed them by their ancestors.
5. Support Chartist candidates at the next General Election, who, if elected by the show of hands, would meet together in London as the true representatives of the people.
6. To deal exclusively with Chartists (i.e. to boycott all anti-Chartist trades people).
7. Support by all and every means the great objects of the People's Charter and accept no measures offering less.
8. Obey all just and constitutional requests of the majority of the Convention.

The whole tenor of the Manifesto makes nonsense of the supposed division of Chartists, made at the time and ever since, between Physical and Moral Force men. The Manifesto was drawn up by William Lovett, the 'moderate' and contained the slogan of all responsible working class leaders, 'Peaceably if we may; Forcibly if we must'. To further emphasise this responsible character of the agitation resolutions were passed proposed by Bronterre O'Brien as follows:

1. That peace, law and order continue to be the motto of this Convention so long as our oppressors act in the same spirit, but should our enemies suppress our lawful agitation by lawless violence we shall deem it the sacred duty of the people to meet force with force.
2. That in accordance with the above, the Convention employ only legal and peaceful means; that people proceed to meetings soberly, orderly and unarmed; to treat as enemies of the cause any who provoke a breach of the peace by exhibiting staves, pikes, pistols or any other offensive weapon.
3. That marshals and others in charge of meetings give effect to the foregoing and consult with local authorities before the meetings take place.

The Convention then adjourned until 1 July.

The Simultaneous Meetings produced such vast crowds in some towns and were held in so many places down to tiny villages that this must be regarded as the most wide-spread mobilisation of working class support ever achieved up to that time. At Kersal Moor 500,000 were said to have gathered, and on Peep Green, West Riding 200,000. O'Connor later reported that together with the Birmingham meeting, he had addressed nearly one million people at those three meetings alone. These meetings were invariably peaceful, but nevertheless there were arrests of Chartists across the country.

The Convention re-convened in Birmingham on 1 July. By then Attwood had presented the Petition in Parliament, but the debate on it was still to come. The question of the Convention returning to London to be at the centre of these proceedings was raised, but O'Connor and others maintained that it was even more necessary to remain in Birmingham in view of the arrests and the evident intent of the government to put down Chartism by force. So the Convention remained in Birmingham and turned its attention to the results of the Simultaneous Meetings (which had not been simultaneous). Most of the reports gave general support to the many measures suggested by the Manifesto, but were vague on such crucial specific actions as the Sacred Month.

A specific motion was put by Dr. Taylor and seconded by O'Connor that an address be issued to the country calling for people to withdraw their money from the banks, to run for gold, to start exclusive dealing, to give up all excisable luxuries and to use their constitutional privilege of arming themselves as speedily as possible, if the Petition were rejected. Collins and Lovett supported Taylor's motion, but Lovett thought only the Sacred Month would be effective. This should be approached by bringing some trades out at first, requesting all others to support them and from this, to gauge the strength for a general strike. This proposal was accepted by Taylor. With regard to when these measures should begin, Lovett said that the Petition was due to be discussed in Parliament on 12 July and the debate should be fixed in the light of the result on August 1st. Taylor accepted this if the date were put forward to 13 July. This was agreed and Dr Taylor's resolution was then agreed unanimously.

The Convention also discussed their legal position in Birmingham and the continuing meetings in the Bull Ring where militancy was rising even higher with the return of the Convention. The eventual, unanimous decision was that to deprive the magistrates of all excuse for interfering with their proceedings, they would organise processions through the streets and hold their meetings outside the town.

But the magistrates were not to be appeased. On July 4 the mayor and two JPs met the Home Secretary and requested a force of London police. They returned the same day with 60 men. The next day the mayor gave written instructions to the two Inspectors in charge, Martin and Partridge. They were to proceed to the Bull Ring and if there were no speakers they were 'to do all you can, quietly and temperately, but firmly and decisively to disperse the crowd.' If meetings were being addressed the speakers or leaders were to be arrested. Should any extraordinary features arise, they were to adopt such a course as necessity and the law would justify, and use as little violence as was consistent with the attainment of the desired end.

When the London police reached the Bull Ring on the night of the 5th July they found a peaceful meeting in progress being addressed by Fussell. In flagrant disregard of their instructions, they immediately set about the stunned people with their truncheons, who fled in all directions. The police might have been expected to content themselves with such a 'victory', but in their ardour they pursued the crowd out of the Bull Ring and thereby dispersed themselves. The crowd then fought back, the police were defeated and fled to the Public Office. The police obviously vowed vengeance and in the language of the report commissioned later by the town council they subsequently acted as though martial law were in force in the town and that all civil rights were utterly at an end. Working men going about their ordinary duties were ordered about, pushed and struck. It was a police reign of terror lasting until 15 July when matters came to a climax.

But meetings in the Bull Ring continued. On July 8th while a meeting was in progress, another attempt to clear the crowd was made. This time a Convention delegate Dr Taylor was arrested, together with a number of local Chartists. The next day the Convention passed three resolutions drafted by Lovett:

1. That this Convention is of opinion that a wanton, flagrant and unjust outrage has been made upon the people of Birmingham by a bloodthirsty and unconstitutional force from London, acting under the authority of men who, when out of office, sanctioned and took part in the meetings of the people; and now, when they share in the public plunder, seek to keep the people in social slavery and political degradation.

2. That the people of Birmingham are the best judges of their own right to meeting in the Bull Ring or elsewhere ...

3. That the summary and despotic arrest of Dr Taylor, our respected colleague, affords another convincing proof of the absence of all justice in England, and clearly shows that there is no security for life liberty or property till the people have some control over the laws they are expected to obey.

These resolutions, signed by Lovett, were taken to James Guest, the printer, by John Collins. The printer was then arrested and released only when he had been obliged to name the messenger who had brought the manuscript. The authorities then sent for Salt, one of the erstwhile Convention delegates, to identify the signature of Lovett, and both Lovett and Collins were then arrested. They appeared before magistrates, including Philip Muntz, another resigned Birmingham Chartist delegate, committed for trial and granted bail at £1,000.

Three days later the Petition was introduced into Parliament by Attwood. He said that the nearly 1,300,000 signatures on the Petition were the elite of the working class who could read and write; that the Reform Act of 1832 had failed to produce a legislature which understood the wants and conditions of working people; that four fifths of manufacturers and merchants at that time faced ruin. Twenty million working people were convinced that only the vote for all working men could achieve the necessary changes in the conditions of the people, that no force could cow them, and if it were not granted peaceably, it would be taken forcibly.

A few MPs showed sympathy. Disraeli traced the origins of the Charter to the invasion of the people's rights, notably the Poor Law; C.P. Villiers, the Wolverhampton MP did not see how the House could oppose consideration of such a gigantic Petition; but when the second Birmingham MP, Josiah Scholefied, rose to speak members were baying for a division and the Petition was rejected by 235 votes to 46.

The Convention moved back to London on 10th July, but the police and military terror in Birmingham continued. Events came to a head on the evening of 15 July. By that date, the bail of Lovett and Collins had been raised and the news went round that they were entering the town. A large crowd gathered in the Bull Ring. Versions of what happened then vary. Lovett says that the police attacked crowds in the Bull Ring and if John Collins' brother had not hurried to meet them and divert them, they would have run into the trouble and no doubt have been blamed. Gammage says that police attacked the crowds in the Bull Ring and that pent-up feelings of rage burst out; that there were cries of 'put out the gas' and the police were powerless. Houses of anti-Chartists were fired and their contents brought into the Bull Ring and set alight. Meetings continued to be held in the days that followed and a large number of the gentry fled the town including the mayor. The town council report unearthed only one person who claimed to be an eye witness. His testimony was that crowds had gathered in the Bull Ring to welcome back Lovett and Collins from Warwick gaol and had moved in procession into Digbeth when a statement was made that police were attacking in the Bull Ring. They then turned back, shops were broken into and set alight. The Riot Act was read, police and military called, the crowd were soon dispersed and there was no violence thereafter.

The so-called Bull Ring Riots, more properly called the Bull Ring Police Assaults, have a significance as great as that of the equally misnamed Priestley Riots of 1791. Locally they demonstrate the hegemony of working class influence in Birmingham at that time which could only be broken by armed force. This state of military and police occupation continued for many months. Nationally the effect of the Bull

Ring Police Assaults was to set in motion a movement of protest comparable to those generated by the Peterloo Massacre of 1819. The effects of such protests can be seen directly in the stimulation of a previously non-existent movement in Bilston and some other Black Country towns which were to take over the leadership of Chartism in the west Midlands in the subsequent phase.

The Second Stage of Chartism 1840 – 1842.
The first stage of Chartism is conventionally considered to have ended in 1839 with the rejection of the first Petition and the arrest of the main Chartist leaders after which the movement is said to have 'collapsed' until a new upsurge began with their return from gaol. This is a half truth, and there is plenty of evidence of the continuation of the movement in Birmingham.

Among the most impressive is the reports of police spies at Chartist meetings, some of which were published by Dorothy Thompson in her *Early Chartism*. These convey the atmosphere in which Chartist activity was carried out when meetings were known to be infiltrated by spies and provocateurs in a town occupied by police and military. They also demonstrate the impressive scale of working class activity in the face of that terror. For instance, Tongue, the spy, reports meetings at Allison Street on Saturday 2nd November 1839, and a committee meeting the next day with a meeting in the evening attended by about one hundred people. On Monday 4th was another meeting, Tuesday a members' meeting, Wednesday another members' meeting, Thursday 7th a meeting with 120 to 130 people present, and so on.

1840 was a year of sustaining the families of gaoled Chartist victims and discussion on the future of the movement. In January at one of the weekly meetings at Lawrence Street chapel support for the family of John Collins was discussed together with similar support for Thompson who was a Birmingham gunmaker (always an occupational group vulnerable to police frame-ups) who had been sentenced to eighteen months imprisonment at Chester Assizes. With indecent haste, the Bull Ring 'rioters' had been tried at Warwick Assizes in September 1839. Howell, Roberts, Jones and a boy named Aston were sentenced to death, but later reprieved and transported for life. The families of Thompson and Roberts were both said to have been in great distress. On the trial of Roberts the *Northern Star* reported that he was 'condemned to death on the evidence of a once noted prize-fighter, but now of the Bludgeon Corps, although twelve witnesses swore that he (Roberts) never left his home at the time of the disturbances'. Also in January 1840 Frost, Williams and Jones were sentenced to death for leading the Newport Uprising. They also were later reprieved and transported for life. Their conviction gave rise to the greatest national solidarity and protest movement since the case of the Tolpuddle Martyrs and committees met weekly throughout the country for many years to agitate for their return.

In March 1840 George Julian Harney addressed the Lawrence Street Chartists before going for his trial. Harney had been indicted in Birmingham when he had been a delegate to the Convention and he was defended by George Edmonds. Also in March, Birmingham Chartists were experimenting with new forms of organisation. A new Charter

Association had been set up at Mr Groves' meeting room in Ladywell Walk. Its members were to pledge themselves to peaceable methods only and were to purchase a 1d ticket stating, 'I voluntarily give up all intoxicating drink, tobacco, snuff, tea, coffee and all excisable articles until the five points of the People's Charter becomes the law of the land.' Members were to meet weekly in private houses and anyone bringing arms or arranging secret meetings was to be prosecuted.

In April 1840 Harney and the two local men Edward Brown and Henry Wilkes were tried. Harney and Wilkes were both acquitted on the grounds that after their arrests they had abstained from Chartist activity. But Edward Brown, arrested it will be recalled with John Fussell in welcoming the Chartist Convention to Birmingham, had a very rough deal. Firstly he was accused by fellow Chartists of using for his own purpose funds collected by him at a dinner. This had first been raised by the police spy, Tongue. Brown denied the allegation in a letter to the *Northern Star*. Then, at his trial Brown paid the penalty for defending himself vigorously. He was charged with sedition which the prosecution, unsuccessfully, tried to get raised to treason. Brown stated that he had said and done nothing that Attwood and the Recorder at that particular Assizes (Davenport Hill) had not said and done in 1832. In spite of this it took the jury only five minutes to find him guilty; hardly surprising since at least two jurymen had been heard to say that all Chartists should be hanged. Brown, who had a family of seven children, went to Warwick gaol for eighteen months.

From August 1840, some Chartist leaders were being released. First to emerge from incarceration were Lovett and Collins. Their reception in Birmingham was tumultuous and probably marks the high point of working class hegemony in Birmingham. Gammage has described in detail the procession two miles long into Birmingham, with its marshalls on horseback at the front and rear, its bands and banners, its marchers of Chartists and trades from Birmingham and the surrounding areas, its carriages, drawn by four greys, of victims and their families, delegates from England and Scotland etc; and its crowds 'exceeding by one half' that which welcomed Attwood to Birmingham after his Reform Act triumphs of 1832.

By the end of 1840 there were signs that the Birmingham Co-operative and Owenite Socialist movement was joining forces with Chartism. In November, a Birmingham Co-operative Society for the Better Distribution of the Necessities of Life among the Working Classes was set up, and in the same month John Pare was associated with a meeting at Bill's Coffee house, Moor Street, which voted to turn itself into a Birmingham branch of the National Charter Association with Pare as treasurer. By December, the Frost, Williams and Jones Restoration Committee was finally established at the Jerusalem Chapel School Room in Newhall Street, soon to become the Birmingham Christian Chartist Church.

1841 was the year when the main Chartist leaders were released from gaol, bringing with them differing thoughts regarding the organisation of Chartism. Some of those were sharply reflected in Birmingham.

One centre of these differences was the Birmingham Christian Chartist Church. This was formed by Arthur O'Neil in December 1840. O'Neil was a theology student turned Chartist active in the organisation of

Christian Chartism in Scotland, where it was most influential. O'Neil came to Birmingham as a delegate to the Lovett-Collins release celebrations and stayed in the town to become a leading local and national figure. Birmingham Chartists had reorganised themselves in accordance with the Manchester Conference plan of August 1840. This had decided to set up one single National Charter Association of Great Britain, thus attempting to overcome the problems of a national political party with local branches which would certainly have been declared illegal at that time. It was formed to achieve the People's Charter and only peaceful and constitutional means were sanctioned. The governing body was to be a national Executive elected annually by all members. The Executive would appoint Councils with a sub-secretary and sub-treasurer for each locality. This fiction of one centralised body was not only a highly original solution to the problems of illegality, but had the happy additional result that every locality had to submit its list of local Council nominees to the Executive and these lists were published in the *Northern Star*. We therefore have the names, and usually the occupations, of all leading Chartists throughout the country. The undisputed leader of the NCA was Feargus O'Connor who retained the unswerving devotion of majority Chartists in Birmingham, as in most of the rest of the country, almost to the unfortunate end of his political life. Councillors in Birmingham at first tended to use that title to further the belief that the Chartist councillor was more representative of the people than the town councillors elected by the £12 householders. The Manchester plan also envisaged standing Chartist candidates in all parliamentary constituencies who would go to the public show of hands and if so elected consider themselves the duly elected legitimate MP for the constituency. But these ambitious plans to create shadow national and local administrations never came to full fruition.

1841 began with a great national demonstration at Holloway Head. This had originally been mooted by Mansfield chartists who recalled the key role played by the Birmingham working class in both 1832 and the Chartist petitioning of 1839. Unfortunately, it was hardly the time of year to organise a national demonstration. The weather on New Year's Day was particularly bad; the *Birmingham Journal* tried to discredit it by calling it a 'gathering of physical force Chartists', and in view of the fact that even the *Northern Star* made no estimate of attendance, it must be assumed that it was not one of the largest Holloway Head gatherings. The chairman of the meeting was John Collins, and Arthur O'Neil attended as a delegate from the Peace Society.

Another complication arose in January with the setting up of a Birmingham Total Abstinence Chartist Association. Teetotal Chartism was the brain child of Henry Vincent, the most silver-tongued of all Chartist orators, who had been converted while in prison. The secretary of the Birmingham association was John Pare and they met at the Association rooms 17 Little Charles Street.

Yet another complication was that Lovett and Collins in Warwick gaol had worked out a totally different plan of Chartist organisation which centred entirely around education and propaganda. This envisaged a one penny per week subscription from every Chartist to finance missionaries, to print tracts, to establish libraries and erect public halls and schools for the mental, moral and political education of the people on an ever-increasing scale as enlightenment spread. Such worthy objects were defended by Lovett and Collins with the less worthy argument that the Manchester scheme had not been declared legal and a blank refusal to join the NCA.

Feargus O'Connor and NCA Chartists were vehemently opposed to any dilution or compromising of working class Chartism by Christian, Teetotal, Educational or any other middle class brands. Their view was that such varieties were useful adjuncts as long as their advocates adhered to the main NCA body. But this the minorities refused to do. The first attempt to reconcile the differing views was made in March 1841 by George White. White was another experienced and powerful Chartist import into the area. In January 1841 O'Connor appointed White *Northern Star* correspondent for the Birmingham area. After five weeks with the main Chartist body in Birmingham, White felt strong enough to call a rally at Holloway Head to try to resolve differences, offering a dissolution of the local NCA council to facilitate unity. The first resolution agreeing 'never to cease peaceful, legal and constitutional exertions until the Charter, the whole Charter, and nothing but the Charter' was the law of the land, passed unanimously. But a second motion, moved by White, proposed the adoption of the Manchester plan for the Birmingham Association. To this John Collins proposed the setting up of a Committee to examine the legality of the NCA and this was supported by O'Neil. The original motion was passed with about 75% of the crowd agreeing with it. White then urged that all present should join the NCA.

The same week, another aspect of unity arose. A Chartist soiree was held at the Lawrence Street chapel where 360 people including 'upwards of 100 well-looking and well-dressed females' gathered. The chairman was William Mogg of Wolverhampton, reflecting the growing importance of Black Country chartism, and Charles Southwell responded to the various toasts. Southwell was the Owenite Socialist missionary in the town and his presence reflected the rapprochement of Socialism with Chartism which might have changed the history of both movements. This time it was George White who refused unity using the standard Chartist argument that while they met at Lawrence Street Chapel they were held up to be Socialists and infidels. Chartists were therefore resolved to have their own rooms in Freeman Street.

Disagreements continued over a proposed Restoration Demonstration for the return of Frost, Williams and Jones. Collins and O'Neil said they would attend, although they condemned the violence of the Newport Uprising.

The growth of Chartism from the beginning of 1841 was rapid. The movement was stirred by the death in prison of John Clayton, a Sheffield Chartist. John Barrett, the secretary of the Birmingham NCA, painted a portrait of Clayton, and at the Christian Chartist Church, O'Neil conducted a funeral service so crowded that several females fainted. In January, Dean Taylor had been appointed missionary in Birmingham and he was joined in March by William Martin. District organisation was established in these months covering the major towns from Coventry to the Potteries. One of its most important functions was to work out quotas and collect the finances to support these missionaries.

The NCA continued to seek unity and criticise the separatists. In April an NCA deputation 'waited on Collins' to try to persuade him to join them. His negative reply and response that he was seeking the opinion of the parliamentary radical J.A. Roebuck regarding the legality of the NCA 'provoked disgust among members of the deputation'. O'Connor attacked the lack of logic of the Christian Chartist Church not joining the main body of Chartists. 'Were the rest of us infidel Chartists, then?' O'Connor asked in one of his weekly *Northern Star* letters read and applauded at a weekly NCA meeting. George White took a more direct and blunt line. He stood up at a Birmingham Chartist Church meeting and asked whether it was true that O'Neil had called him a spy? O'Neil replied that he had not done this in public, but said so privately. Martin subsequently defended George White's conduct and added, if Christian Chartists why not Jewish, Catholic etc. Chartists? Martin later elaborated this criticism in a large Freeman Street meeting with about one hundred female Chartists when he said that Birmingham had been selected as the headquarters for Rational, Teetotal, Educational, Household etc. Chartism but this was slipping through their fingers'.

In May 1841 another NCA branch was started meeting at Dartmouth Street. In June George White and Dean Taylor began open-air meetings at Gosta Green. The same month an enquiry came to Freeman Street from the Chartist church regarding their plans for standing a Chartist candidate at the forthcoming general election. This letter was rejected, White saying that the NCA was going to set up a Committee of Non-Electors to consider this matter and they would have nothing to do with a 'hole-in-the-corner self appointed Committee'. This meeting was duly held in a large field at the rear of Duddeston Row railway station called by a placard of the NCA signed by George White. A Non-electors Committee of 40 people, all NCA members previously chosen, was set up! The next week George White agreed to stand as the Chartist candidate and it was further agreed to vote only for those who supported the Six Points. At the election, George White addressed a large crowd, but he did not go on to the show of hands at the poll. This was presumably because Muntz and Scholefield supported all or most of the Charter.

Meetings continued during the summer at Duddeston Row, White stating that since they were prevented from using the town hall and every other public building, they would meet there every Monday evening.

In July Edward Brown, who had reason to consider himself one of the worst treated of Chartist prisoners, was released from his eighteen months in gaol. For him there was no such great reception as Lovett and Collins had received. But when Feargus O'Connor was released from York prison after serving his twelve months, vast demonstrations were held throughout the country. These included 'a triumphal entry into Birmingham' at a Holloway Head rally. Women and children were brought in from all over the district on the Sunday, but the men marched in from Coventry, Wolverhampton and other towns the next day. The arrangements for this demonstration had been in the hands of a Committee headed by John Mason, a new district lecturer from Newcastle-on-Tyne who stayed in the town and played a distinguished role in west Midlands Chartism over the coming period. Mason's committee later gave special thanks to the Birmingham trades for their banners etc. at the O'Connor demonstration. A balance sheet was also issued showing receipts at £18 and expenditure £22.

John Fussell, who had been arrested with Edward Brown but escaped imprisonment, had moved to London and become a leading Chartist there. He returned to Birmingham to speak at a meeting and was delighted with his reception saying that he thought he would have had to defend himself against attacks. This was a reference to accusations, made originally by the police spy Tongue, that both he and Brown were involved with the police. However, the difference between Fussell's reception and Brown's may be accounted for by the fact that at a Duddeston Row meeting addressed by Henry Vincent and only luke-warmly reported in the *Northern Star* ('most people had left because of the rain'), Edward Brown had said that although he supported the NCA he preferred the Lovett-Collins plan.

Chartist growth continued through the autumn of 1841. Freeman Street seems to have been the main NCA headquarters with meetings on Mondays, Wednesdays and Sundays, but there were other sections at the Brittania Inn Peck Street, Parkes Coffee House Upper Windsor Street, the Fox Inn· Swallow Street and 'others were about to be opened'. Freeman Street meetings were said to be crowded, but most important of all, a section had been opened at the Ship Inn, Steelhouse Lane, that was to have an unbroken existence into the middle 1850s. In addition, the Frost, Williams and Jones committee, of which James Guest the Birmingham printer and bookseller was national treasurer, met either at Lawrence Street chapel or at the Chartist Church, thus keeping the channels of communications open between the NCA, Christian Chartism and Owenite Socialists as the movement entered the decisive year of 1842.

Events in Birmingham, as elsewhere, continued to be dominated by the third Long Depression. This had begun at the end of 1836 and continued into 1843. It has not so far been possible to find indices to measure the depth of the Depression in Birmingham as has been done for the Black Country, but 1842 was perhaps the worst year of the whole century, and coming after so many cumulative years of mass unemployment gives reality to the expression the Hungry Forties. Those who measure the deprivation from wage indices alone might convince themselves that a fall in wages from 5/-d. per day to 2/6d. or even 2/-d. might involve hardship but not starvation. However a fall in wages from 5/-d. a day to nothing for the vast numbers unemployed does mean starvation, whilst a drop from 5/-d a day for a six day week to 2/-d. for a two day week means only slightly longer starvation for those on short time working, which has always been a scourge of Birmingham. But whatever the levels of destitution, neither poverty nor ideology could lift Birmingham Chartism to the national levels of significance that the movement reached in 1839.

However, as has been stated, the legacy of 1839 and the Bull Ring Police Assaults was to spread Chartism in the Black Country and the leading national role of Birmingham was taken over by that adjacent area. The new generation of Chartist leaders in Birmingham, particularly George White, John Mason and Arthur O'Neil not only sustained Chartism in Birmingham, but also played an important supporting role in the Black Country.

We can supplement the names of the above three who were already national Chartist figures when they came to Birmingham with the names of other Chartist militants taken from the Birmingham nomination lists to the NCA General Council published in the *Northern Star*. These were Charles Thorp, Fred Corbett, Walter Thorn, Smith Lyndon (formerly a Dudley stalwart), Thomas Rouse, Thomas Welsford, Charles Stewart, Charles Ashton and E. Spink. A Fussell also remained active in Birmingham. This was James Alfred Fussell; whether he was a relation of the John Fussell who went to London is not known.

Turning to organised Chartist activity in Birmingham in 1842, the year began with skirmishes with the middle class. As the Depression deepened Attwood's currency views were once again pressed and the *Northern Star* reported scathingly that at a Public Office meeting Thomas Salt had informed the public that the distress was due to lack of money! The Anti-Corn Law lobby was also active under these circumstances and the same paper reported that the 'Black Bread and cheap Labour employers were forcing employees to join their organisation.'

The most important middle class initiative in the spring of 1842, however, came from Joseph Sturge. Sturge broke with the Anti-Corn Law movement, became an advocate of household suffrage and started what became known as the Complete Suffrage Movement, promptly dubbed by Feargus O'Connor as the Complete Humbug Movement. Because Sturge lived in Birmingham, because the two main conferences were held in the town and because of the earlier middle class association with Chartism, Sturge and Complete Suffrage are important to Birmingham Chartism. Sturge's movement was attractive to Vincent's Teetotal Chartists and also to O'Neil and the Christian Chartists. O'Connor campaigned vigorously against the first Conference, held in April, urging Chartists to elect delegates to oppose the Sturgeites and even offering himself as a delegate for Bilston to act with others from 'that Prince of Chartist towns.' A committee was set up to organise the conference on which Alfred Fussell managed to get himself elected. When the Conference met it was an all-ticket affair at the town hall to which the public (i.e. the Chartists) were to be admitted only at the end. Sturge spoke, urging working class and middle class collaboration in attaining the main points of the Charter, but no resolutions were put, and so no direct challenge to working class leadership of the movement emerged.

Signature collection to the new Petition was being systematically organised in the district and when a new Chartist National Convention met in mid-April there were about 30,000 signatures from Birmingham. This stimulated recruitment to the movement. It was resolved to call a delegate meeting of trades; each manufactory was contacted following a town hall meeting at which it was stated that 10,000 workers had declared themselves to be Chartists. A new NCA locality at Aston Street became prominent with its meetings said to be 'crowded'. By May, Aston Street was recommending the formation of a Women's NCA branch and another section meeting at the Brittania Inn, Peck Street, became active. At the same place the only regularly reporting and long-lived trades branch of the NCA was set up; this was the Shoemakers' NCA. Dorothy Thompson, however, has identified a Tailors' NCA branch in 1842. Open air meetings were started in May at Duddeston Row and were soon extended to Summer Lane. A large rally at Duddeston Row was called to hear the Birmingham delegate to the Convention, George White, report. Bronterre O'Brien was the other main speaker. The same week there was a 'splendid public dinner' for O'Connor.

In June 1842 the question of the premises at Lawrence Street was being discussed by the movement. It had ceased to be the Socialist chapel, renamed the Hall of Science, and a crowded meeting at the Public Office had met to raise funds to complete and renovate it.

The second Chartist petition was presented to and rejected by the House of Commons in May, but the prolonged and agonising discussions on what to do next which had plagued the 1839 rejection were cut short by the development of the huge strike movement of August and September 1842 which climaxed the second phase of Chartism.

At this time the main locus of events had shifted to the Black Country and it was here that Birmingham leaders became involved. John Mason had become the Black Country paid organiser and the Staffs and Herefordshire delegate to the Chartist Convention. Distress and unemployment was calamitous in the Black Country. In May began the series of strikes which culminated in August with the great Miners' Strike. This merged with the general strike stretching from south Staffs, into the Potteries and joining with the main movement covering the Yorkshire and Lancashire coal and textile areas for jobs, wages and the Charter. This was to be the pinnacle of Chartist achievement and the greatest revolutionary threat to the government.

The strikes in the Black Country began in May with the nailers and chain makers. In Sedgley, 'a little Tory ridden village, the petty authorities had insolently and illegally threatened to arrest the first Chartist who entered the place.' The Chartists held a meeting there and the parish constable intervened to stop it. Onlookers protested and seven people were taken into custody. The speaker, John Mason, was not one of them, but when he attended the hearing he was arrested, charged, committed to the next quarter sessions and bailed. Mason was eventually sentenced to six months imprisonment for 'the new fangled invention of holding an unlawful meeting', as the *Northern Star* put it. The Mason case immediately became a national scandal raised throughout the movement as well as in Parliament.

George White also moved into the Black Country addressing large meetings and co-ordinating this with protest action in Birmingham. A warrant was issued for White's arrest at the height of the miners' strike in August when a large joint Birmingham-Black Country demonstration was organised in Birmingham probably by the Chartist church. The mayor banned the meeting. It took place nevertheless and was addressed by O'Neil and Joseph Sturge who advised the crowd to disperse. When it was learned that large numbers of Black Country miners were marching in O'Neil and Sturge also urged them to disperse. George White denounced this and called a meeting the next night at Duddeston Row. All that day White's house was surrounded by police, but White was not there. Eventually the meeting took place at Lozells where there were 12,000 people present and a procession of miners, led by the Bilston Chartist, Joseph Linney, was met by George White. White evaded arrest until September when he was taken into custody on charges of conspiracy. White was given eight months in prison, which he served in 1843.

Despite the differences between the NCA and the Christian Chartists, Arthur O'Neil played a full part in the agitation for the Charter in the summer of 1842 and in support of the great Black Country strike movement of the time. He was arrested on 26th August after addressing huge meetings in Oldbury and Dudley, despite the fact that they were banned. In evidence, one witness said that he had heard O'Neil at a Cradley meeting say that the situation of the people was like being in a room with an air pump. When the air was removed it was not at first generally felt. Then some one went to the window to open it and found the Duke of Wellington with his sword preventing anyone from opening it. They went to another window and found the Archbishop of Canterbury stopping the air with his surplice. At the last window they found a lawyer stopping it with his wig. In September the Birmingham Christian Chartist Church issued a placard declaring the government unchristian and stating their determination to pay no more taxes. This was signed by O'Neil and had been 'much taken up by the London papers'. O'Neil was sentenced to twelve months imprisonment in Stafford gaol.

As the great national strike movement of August-September ebbed, the government felt itself strong enough to arrest the other national leaders and with this, and the rejection of the Petition, the second phase of Chartism came to an end.

Chartist activity in Birmingham was low key in the autumn and winter of 1842 despite George White still being at large. Again, defence committees raising monies for the families of Chartist prisoners occupied much time including a committee for George White's defence meeting three times a week at one stage. John Mason's family was the one requiring immediate local support and problems arose here over whether monies raised should be used for this purpose or sent to national funds.

National financial problems also arose which embroiled Birmingham. James Leach attacked George White and the Birmingham chartists who had passed a resolution regarding money said to have been wasted by the National Executive. George White, in reply to a letter from John West, stated that he had complained about NCA finances as often as anyone, but he had never included charges of dishonesty. White's letter was unanimously approved by the Steelhouse Lane chartists and at the same time the account of money spent by the NCA executive when it stayed in Birmingham refuted charges of extravagence. This was signed by all those associated with the accounts — Charles Aston, William Hopkins, Henry Creswell, Charles Thorp and the two sub-secretaries of the Birmingham NCA branches, William Talbert and David Potts. How easy it was to run foul of accusations of improper uses of money arose at the same time when George White authorised the payment of £10 to Mrs. Ellis, one of the wives of a victim sentenced to transportation. This payment was approved by the committee, however.

We may close the account of the second stage of Chartism in Birmingham with a report of the second, decisive conference at the end of December with the Complete Suffrage Union. The ostensible point at issue was whether the Six Points of the charter should continue to be presented as Chartism, or under a less 'discredited' name. The real point was whether agitation for the Charter should continue to be working class

led and controlled or merged with middle class support. Delegates were
to be elected in each town of both Electors and Non-electors except where
agreement on joint delegates could be negotiated. O'Connor again made
huge endeavours to see that the 'Complete Humbugs' were defeated.
Eventually 374 delegates assembled 'in a spacious building, formerly
used as a Mechanics' Institute in Newhall Street'. O'Connorites were
there in large numbers, but there was some anxiety as to whether other
brands of Chartists held the balance of power. The main resolution was
moved by the Complete Suffragists proposing a Bill of Rights containing
the Six Points but omitting all reference to Chartism. When William
Lovett rose to speak he was expected to support the Sturgeites as he was
in favour of co-operation with the middle class and had also been a
member of the Complete Suffrage committee which arranged the
conference. He had, however, been offended by the typically high-
handed way his suggestions for the conference had been treated, as well
as understanding that so much working class effort and sacrifice had gone
into promoting Chartism that working people would not give up the
name. So Lovett's support went with O'Connor's, the resolution was lost
and the Sturgeites retired from the Conference to pursue their Bill of
Rights. The Chartists remained to discuss the reorganisation of the
movement. The six Birmingham delegates to the Conference included
Feargus O'Connor, the others being George White, Arthur O'Neil,
Thomas Parkes, John Follows and John Horsley.

The Third Stage of Chartism 1843 – 48.

Reorganisation of Chartism took place in Birmingham in the winter of
1843 after approval of the changes made at the December conference.
These had been concerned with the election and functioning of the
national executive and annual convention and had made no changes in
local organisation. It was agreed that Chartism in the district had been
disorganised ever since the miners' strike of August 1842. A
reorganisation meeting was therefore called in the name of George
Richardson, William Talbot, James Reece, George White, Bates,
Cowen, Murless, Parkes and Saunders at the Royal Oak Inn, Little
Charles Street. At the meeting, John Mason took the chair and Saunders
moved a motion that all localities merge. This was opposed by Joseph
Washbourne of the Shoemakers' and a resolution setting up localities was
passed. A large Birmingham committee was then elected. The complete
list, again giving an excellent indication of Chartist activists at the time
was: William Smith Lyndon, John Williamson, J. Magee, William Chilton,
David Potts, John Follows, Alfred Fussell, John Mason, William Hopkins,
James Reece, Murless, John Newhouse, Thomas Welsford, James Mavitty,
Cowen, William Knight, Thomas Blake, George Richardson, George
White, Richard Thompson, Walter Thorne, Watson, Edward Jones,
Thomas Laughton, Joseph Washbourne, William Bradley, Gibbons, Peter
Higgins, Charles Stewart, Barry, Edward Taylor and Wright.

In February, the municipal ward system of the town was adopted for
the Chartist localities, but it never became possible to carry out such an
ambitious organisation. The important localities at that time were those
meeting at Aston Street, the Ship Inn society in Steelhouse Lane, and the
Shoemakers' society.

An important degree of district organisation was achieved by the setting up of a Birmingham and Midland Counties Charter Association with west midland branches in Birmingham, Dudley, Wednesbury, Walsall, Worcester, Lye Waste and Stourbridge, Coventry, Great Bridge, Oldbury, Smethwick, Bilston, Wolverhampton, Darlaston, West Bromwich, Kidderminster, Bromsgrove, Redditch, Stafford, and Warwick and Leamington. At the first monthly district meeting in April John Mason reported on the state of the movement in Birmingham. They had laid out the town and collectors had been appointed. There was also a monthly conference of all members and the plan was succeeding admirably. At the June district meeting, however, Mason reported that little progress was being made, although open-air meetings had been started. John Chance of Stourbridge, who was in the chair on that occasion, commented on the small attendance and said that it was poverty preventing delegates from attending. The continuance of the Long Depression was also commented on at the July meeting which took place in Wednesbury. Here it was said distress was as great as ever and the mine owners had taken advantage of the late strike to reduce wages even further.

By this time George White was in gaol and fund raising for his defence had included a Grand Ball in April. Chartist public meetings at the time were held in the Mechanics' Institute as the restoration of the Hall of Science went ahead. Early in April it was announced that the Hall would soon be opened for Chartists and others and by the end of the month E.P. Mead, the district lecturer opened his summer campaign 'within the walls of the new Chartist Hall' to numerous audiences. In August there was a great public meeting in the Hall of Science on Thomas Attwood's return to public life. Attwood had taken the Chiltern Hundreds at the end of 1839 after the rejection of the first Petition and on his short-lived return to public life he told a crowded audience that he was not sure of his plans, 'but if people think it excludes the Charter and the working class, their expectations will fail.'

In the summer and autumn regular open-air meetings were held at Duddeston Row with public meetings at the Hall of Science and local meetings during the week, particularly at the Ship Inn and Aston Street. 1843 ended with the announcement of a tea party to welcome George White's release from prison which Feargus O'Connor would attend.

1844 was the first full year of economic expansion in Birmingham. White received a warm welcome on his release from gaol in January. He was met at the station by large crowds and he spoke at the Mechanics' Institute. At the subsequent tea party at the same place the large saloon was 'full to overflowing'. The tea party was a democratic development of mass politics involving both women and children of which George White approved. It took the place of the dinner attended mainly by men which formerly would have been the main function on such occasions.

White quickly returned to activity. Before the end of January he had agreed to speak at the public Chartist lecture every Sunday at the Chartist Room, Peck Lane where he started by stating that real Chartism was the struggle of Labour against Capital. He would also hold open-air meetings (weather permitting) at Duddeston Row. In March a district meeting at Bromsgrove elected George White and John Beale to be delegates to the national Chartist Convention held the next month at Manchester. This was the first of short annual conventions held to help solve the difficult problems of the election and control of the national Chartist executive.

In July, Joseph Sturge wrote to the *Northern Star* stating that he had been selected by a Committee of Electors and Non-Electors to stand as a Birmingham candidate in the next general election. He was of no party; he was opposed to the Poor Law and the ban on public meetings in Birmingham and he endorsed the Six Points of the Charter. Again, this was seen as another middle class attempt to take over the leadership of working class matters. But it again emphasises the problems of establishing a Chartist tradition of fighting general elections in Birmingham where both sitting members and other possible candidates paid at least lip service to the Six Points.

Also in July a tea party for Duncombe was announced which O'Connor was also expected to attend. This matter was not entirely uncontroversial. Thomas Duncombe, the radical MP, had presented the Petition to parliament in May 1842, but was not himself a Chartist. In the autumn of 1843 O'Connor and Duncombe had commenced a tour of agitation throughout Britain but chiefly in the north and it was in Aberdeen that Duncombe took out a Chartist card. Before this, Sharman Crawford, the radical MP for Rochdale had proposed a radical party in Parliament that would disrupt business until the Six Points of the Charter were enacted. O'Connor seems to have favoured Duncombe rather than Crawford as the leader of such a party. Hence the importance of making Duncombe a Chartist. The position was further complicated by a plan for a substantial testimonial to Duncombe for his services to Chartism. Neither the project for the party nor the testimonial was accepted by all Chartists and differences existed in Birmingham.

At this time George White was taking up paid lecturing for the movement and spent less time in Birmingham. Thomas Clark became the paid organiser for Birmingham. In October a 'numerous meeting' held at the Public Office forwarded the proceeds of the Duncombe Testimonial. The notice of the Testimonial had been posted in the London *Times* as well as the *Northern Star* and this had raised the ire of some Birmingham Chartists. But it was defended by William Maurice Langston, a Birmingham cordwainer, who went further to the heart of the matter by saying that he welcomed the support not only of Disraeli and Young England but any other Tory as well. Langston was playing a role of some significance at this time. He seems to have believed that any attempt to develop a radical alliance inside Parliament necessarily involved co-operation with the middle class and this would also affect local strategy. Langston was also a trade unionist and in the period of expanding trade after 1843 the Chartists were paying increasing attention to 'the trades'. Langston also had wider interests. In the summer and autumn of 1844 it was from a Steelhouse Lane locality meeting at Clark's Reading Room that most Chartist activity was reported. Here they were developing a debating society and in September there was a debate Monarchy v Republicanism. John Beale had supported Republicanism, but Langston together with Kettle, both Chartists, spoke up for Monarchy. The previous month at the same venue Langston had lectured, on Democritus who, a modern authority, Bertrand Russell, defines as being of a Greek philosophical school of Atomists akin to modern science, believing that everything is composed of indestructible atoms which are and always have been in motion.

Also in the autumn of 1844 the whole Chartist movement made a great national effort to raise the question of Frost, Williams and Jones to a higher level. Birmingham's contribution was a town's meeting called to memorialise the queen on the release of the victims. This was unanimously accepted in a crowded hall where W. Thomas, Chartist, was called to the chair and the motion put by Langston and seconded by Wilkins, supported by John Mason and McGrath, the new paid organiser for the district.

As a footnote to the changing emphasis of Chartism in these years, it should be noted that O'Connor moved his newspaper from Leeds to London in November 1844 and changed its full title from *Northern Star & Leeds Advertiser* to *Northern Star and National Trades Journal*.

1845 brought further changes in Birmingham chartist activity and localities. A Democratic Chapel emerged in Thorp Street where McGrath lectured in January and T. Clark also spoke on Trade Unions. A Shakesperean locality was opened in Pike Street in January with another national figure, Jonathon Bairstow, speaking on the lofty theme (a certain indicator of lack of militancy in the general movement) of the Incompatibility of Class Legislation with National Morality and Prosperity. The Ship Tavern in Steelhouse Lane locality began reporting and Clark's Reading room in the same street disappears. In March, Thomas Sherwood Kettle lectured at the Democratic Chapel on the Present Position of Chartism. In April, the question of the Charter was again raised publicly at the Public Office on the Registration of the Democratic Vote. Walter Thorne, described not as a Chartist but as a 'highly respected working man', was called to the chair and John Mason was a main speaker. In April 1845 the Chartist annual convention was held, but there was no delegate from Birmingham. Birmingham speakers were faring better in the Black Country than in their own town. In May, John Mason spoke in a Tuesday evening lecture in Bilston to a crowded room on the Benefits of a General Union of Trades, the lecture giving 'the greatest satisfaction'. This meeting was also addressed by Joseph Linney, the Bilston Chartist released from gaol the previous July. The expectation in the Black Country was that 'there will be a powerful movement in the neighbourhood in a short time'. In the Potteries too Chartist activity was reviving with a newly formed Council for the Potteries meeting in May.

This very real trade union based revival of Chartism in the surrounding areas was not reflected in reporting of Chartist activity in Birmingham in the second half of 1845. But in June the Ship Inn had raised the question, 'What should be done about the Co-operative Land Plan?' and from that time there was an added dimension, as well as added problems for Chartist to cope with.

The Chartist Land Plan

This was Feargus O'Connor's last, long-lived, legacy to the British labour movement. The Chartist Land Co-operative was formed in April 1845. It spread with astonishing rapidity. By May 1847 the first Chartist

Land Colony near Watford was built, opened and inevitably called O'Connorville. In January 1848 Birmingham's local estate at Great Dodford, near Bromsgrove was bought and by July 1849 was operating. If one considers the difficulties of establishing a scheme to settle working people on the land and eventually making them freeholders with a vote, by the purchase of shares in weekly instalments of 3d. or more until one complete share was bought upon which one's name went into a ballot for the next allocation of colonists to the land; if one considers the problems of purchasing estates with weekly contributions and rents, contracting for and overseeing the building of substantial cottages and public buildings for six estates and supporting urban settlers through difficult early years of farming, it is clear that no such legal scheme sponsored by Chartists would ever have been allowed to develop. Feargus O'Connor therefore took upon himself the gargantuan labours of originating and bringing to fruition such a scheme whether legal or no. It probably cost him his sanity, but he was rewarded with the loyalty and devotion of the main body of Chartists throughout Britain to the very end. This contrasts starkly with the critics, both outside the labour movement and within it who hounded O'Connor at every step and still manage to misunderstand and misrepresent his achievement.

Chartist localities combined Land Plan support with normal activities. The first matter dealt with in 1846 was a report of the Manchester Convention of which a general meeting at the Ship Inn 'highly approved', and arranged a further meeting to see how its conclusions could be applied to Birmingham. International affairs also preoccupied Chartists at this time. In March it was Polish independence. The Ship Inn were considering holding a public meeting, but this was abandoned in favour of sending to O'Connor a £1 donation to the Polish Regeneration Fund. In April it was the Irish question. A meeting discussed 'the damnable coercion Bill' and Fussell and Potts were deputed to 'wait upon' the committee of the Repeal Association to ascertain whether steps were being taken to hold a public meeting in Birmingham.

In the meantime Land Plan organisation had been set up and Birmingham workers were buying shares. Walter Thorn was the treasurer who was forwarding sums to London. It is noteworthy that Birmingham subscriptions were invariably sent to O'Connor himself and not through other established channels. The first ballot for land at O'Connorville took place in June 1846. No one from Birmingham received land, but there were allottees from Pershore, Worcester and Bilston.

In June, Ship Inn was involved in one of the most serious internal Chartist arguments between O'Connor and Thomas Cooper. Cooper was a bitter critic of the Land Plan who threatened at the forthcoming Leeds Convention to move motions of no-confidence in the Plan and in O'Connor as well as attempting to separate out Land Plan organisation from general Chartist activity. Birmingham expressed complete confidence in O'Connor and declared that Cooper was trying to destroy the character of O'Connor.

By July 1846 further details of the Land Plan were emerging. The Chartist Co-operative Land Society met at 111 Rea Road, which remained the main venue for several years. The sub-secretary was Walter

Thorn. Another ballot took place to allocate Land in August. Again there was no allottee from Birmingham but a Dudley family received a two acre estate and one from Bilston three acres. The annual Chartist convention was brought forward to August 1846 and much of its business was with the Land Company. Joseph Linney attended as delegate from Birmingham and South Staffs. Ship Inn met to consider its proceedings and found that they gave 'general satisfaction', and the treatment of Cooper, who was expelled, was 'highly approved'. The meeting made no mention of Linney's efforts at the Convention on their behalf. Besides supporting the general resolutions, he opposed a proposed change of the method of electing the Executive from a vote of the whole membership to election by the Convention. He also spoke in favour of a new national petition, which was approved at the Convention.

Whether Linney reported personally to the Ship comrades on the Convention we don't know, but he was at the Ship the following week bringing with him 11/-s. for the Mrs. Roberts' fund. This was a project to raise £50 to send Mrs Roberts and her children to join her husband in Australia where he had been transported as a result of the Bull Ring Police Assaults.

The next week Fussell gave an account to the Ship chartists of a demonstration to O'Connorville, the People's First Estate, after which it was resolved that the locality itself should take shares in the Land Company. This was in complete opposition to Cooper's plan that the activities of the Land Company and those of the Chartist localities should be strictly separated.

In October 1846 a letter appeared in the *Northern Star:*

> Fellow Workers,
>   Are you politically dead? Do you not know that there is such a place as the People's Hall, Loveday Street, St. Marys Square intended for moral and intellectual improvement?

The letter went on to say that there were 400 paid up shareholders instead of the 3000 required. That a valuable piece of building was about to be taken out of their hands which was worth £2500 but was mortgaged for £800. If the mortgagee did not received the interest due he was going to sell the mortgage to pay himself. A committee had been set up which would meet every Tuesday and Thursday at the Hall to register shares. No account of the outcome of this appeal has been found, but the building was saved and made more use of by the movement. In December, for instance, a tea party and ball at the People's Hall was part of the arrangements made by a special Chartist Land Society at Rea Street for the forthcoming Land Society conference which was to be held in Birmingham. Also meetings addressed by Philip M'Grath and Thomas Clark were held at the People's Hall.

The situation in the autumn of 1846 was complex. In October a delegate meeting in Birmingham set about carrying out two of the key decisions of the August Convention. These concerned the forthcoming elections and the crisis state of central Chartist finances. A special Birmingham and S. Staffs. committee was set up to 'assist the central committee to send as many members as possible to the House of

Commons and pledge ourselves to do all in our power to collect funds'.
Each location was urged to set up its own election committee. Each
chartist body was to raise 1/-d. (per member?) to be divided among the
Chartist exiles while an additional 1d. per month was to be paid into the
Veterans, Widows and Orphans Fund. But the same resolution insisted
that the secretary accompany the report to the *Northern Star* with some
remarks on the 'apparent apathy in the Districts'. These remarks duly
appeared as follows:

> To the Chartists of Birmingham and South Staffs.
> Brother Chartists,
>   The delegates assembled here feel real regret that so few are
> represented and they sincerely hope that you will shake off your lethargy
> and put your shoulders to the wheel. Will you do your duty or will you
> allow a few men to struggle ardently while you sleep in apathy? Let every
> place in this district be represented at the next delegate meeting in
> Dudley.

Despite the alleged apathy arrangements went ahead in Birmingham both
to collect signatures to the new Petition and also to play host to the Land
Conference. A deputation went to wait on David Malins, the High
Bailiff, to obtain the use of the town hall on Tuesday 8th December for
a public meeting to adopt the Petition. This, as usual, was refused. The
delegate for Birmingham and district to the Land Conference was elected
at a November district meeting; it was George Holloway of
Kidderminster. The Conference opened on the 7th December and the
occasion was taken to hold a 'great meeting' to adopt the Charter. At this
meeting a letter of apology was read from Joseph Sturge. The motion to
adopt the Six Points was moved and seconded by the local Chartists
Thorn and Fussell, but T. Clark raised squarely the issue of the middle
class and the election by stating that the working class had been used by
the middle class to raise them to power and the working class had been
betrayed. There was no sense, he went on, in which the town's two MPs,
Muntz and Scholefield, represented the working people of Birmingham.
Two more local men, Smith Lyndon and Goodwin proposed the adoption
of the National Charter and they were supported by the main speaker,
Feargus O'Connor. O'Connor used the occasion both to stress his
connections with Birmingham and also to answer current criticism of him
regarding Land Company finances. He appealed to the men of
Birmingham who, by the threat of marching to London, had been
instrumental in the passing of the Reform Bill. He went on to say that
he had been a member of the Birmingham Political Union and he had
never been able to get a balance sheet out of them. But he presented his
today. Aristocracy had declared that they held the land on Royal Patent
from the king. But the king of kings had declared land the property of all.
    1847 opened with unfinished business from the Land Conference. At
the usual weekly Ship meeting, Potts was nominated as a scrutineer, and
Fussell and Cartland as auditors for the Land Company. A vote of thanks
was also passed to M'Grath and Clark for their work on behalf of the
Birmingham district NCA while they were in the town for the Land
Conference.
    In February Dr M'Douall was appointed lecturer for Birmingham and

district for a month. In March the first Birmingham man was successful in the ballot for land on the Mathon Estate, near Malvern. This was J. Baker who received a four acre plot. This month also saw the first signs of the impending economic slump. Money continued to be sent to O'Connor regularly from the Land Society subscriptions. In addition, from the Ship, went 10/-d. for 'Daddy' Richards, the old Potteries chartist who was always a cause of special concern to local Chartists and 10/-d. to the victims of the Liverpool trials.

In January 1847 O'Connor had set up a special Land & Labour Bank and a special meeting of Land Society shareholders met in April to determine how they could use the bank. In May a Ship meeting 'crowded to excess', met to hear a report of the settlement of the first batch of pioneers on the First People's Estate at O'Connorville. A motion on the Land and Labour Bank at the same meeting proposed 1. A Money Club be set up for NCA members only. 2. An unlimited number of shares paid for at 3d. a week could be subscribed for. 3. When 20/-d. was in hand members' names would be entered in the ballot. The Rea Street section was urged to follow suit. In May it was announced that No.3 branch of the Land Company located at 98 Hill Street had opened a Co-operative Store. Its secretary was the Owenite Socialist pioneer John Pare. Pare was also enrolling in a National Land Company Operative Benefit Society. Once again, it seems, Chartists and Owenite Socialists were working together in Birmingham. In June a meeting had been held at the house of S. Brindley the Cross Keys, Springhill to set up yet another branch of the National Land Company. The Land Plan was clearly asserting a wide influence in Birmingham, but this held the danger that Chartist activity would be submerged, a danger constantly stressed by George White and one of the few things likely to break the bond between O'Connor and the majority of Chartists as O'Connor placed increasing emphasis on the Land Plan. This was underlined the same month when a letter from the Birmingham Co-operative League stated that at its weekly meeting the fourth number of the *Labourer* had been read after which a motion was passed cordially thanking O'Connor for his exertions on behalf of the people but respectfully suggesting that he carry out more fully the principles of Co-operation. This letter was signed by John Alfred Langford, the secretary who was a middle class co-operator, and who we have met in these pages as an early historian of Birmingham.

The next matter engaging Chartist attention was the growing slump. A public meeting was held at the town hall in June to discuss the best means of relieving distress. The chairman was John Mason. The Chartists moved an amendment to the motion calling for an 'altering currency'. This was no doubt, ironically enough, a version of Attwood's currency scheme. Mason ruled that the amendment was out of order and the mayor was not justified in putting it. This enraged the Chartists who passed a motion at the next Ship meeting that Mason had 'basely deserted the principles he had long advocated and had therefore forfeited the respect of the working classes.' Mason wrote a letter of reply to the *Northern Star* claiming that he had been quoted out of context, but the secretary of the Ship Chartists, John Newhouse, denied this and reinforced the condemnation of Mason.

The general election of 1847 occupied a great deal of Chartist time and

brought a revival of interest in the movement. The outstanding result was
the election of Feargus O'Connor at Nottingham. A Midland Counties
Agitation and Electioneering Committee was set up in June. Birmingham
was not represented at this meeting and its main decision was to plan a
campaign for Joseph Linney to stand in Dudley culminating in a Monster
Camp Meeting involving O'Connor and other national leaders. At a
subsequent meeting in June it was decided to increase the number of
Camp Meetings to three, one of which was to be in Birmingham; both
Ship Inn and Hill Street localities were represented at this meeting.
Despite the brave words of Clark earlier in the year, the Birmingham
sitting members were marked down in the *Northern Star* list as 'Chartist
candidates' since they endorsed all, or most, of the Six Points. Joseph
Sturge, who was standing at Leeds, was similarly treated. Election fever
was therefore confined to the Black Country, where Chartist support was
greater. The O'Connor rally at Dudley was a great success and Joseph
Linney was overwhelmingly elected at the show of hands. This led to a
late fielding of Samuel Cook in Wolverhampton against the Anti-Corn
Law Leaguer and luke-warm supporter of the Charter, C.P. Villiers.
Birmingham was therefore confined to a supporting role which took on
a greater significance after the election when crowded meetings at the
Ship sent congratulations to Feargus O'Connor and pledged themselves
to raise part of the £600 necessary to support him in Parliament.

After the election interest returned to the Land Plan and the more
efficient organising of NCA activity. The annual conference of the Land
Company was held at the Low Bands estate, Worcestershire. It opened
with 46 delegates, none of whom was from Birmingham or the west
Midlands, but on the second day Fussell from Birmingham and John
Chance from Stourbridge attended. At a ballot held during the
Conference John Smith of Birmingham was allocated a two acre plot. The
Conference was reported back to a general meeting of shareholders at the
People's Hall on 7 September and a week later, again at the People's
Hall, there was a public meeting to 're-activate' general Chartist activity.
Later in the month, a dinner was held at the Ship Inn to celebrate the first
anniversary of the Land Company branch at the Ship which had grown
to 300 members.

The autumn and early winter of 1847 brought new evidence of growth
both in Land Plan and general Chartist activity. A public meeting at the
People's Hall in late September resulted in 'considerable numbers
enrolling in the NCA'. The following week another public meeting was
held in the same Hall when the main attraction was the reading of a letter
of the Roberts family, the Australian deportees. 'Considerable numbers'
joining the NCA continued to be reported in October, and it was
cautiously stated that there was 'every probability of cementing a good
union of the working classes in Birmingham'. On 11 October there was
a supper at the People's Hall to commemorate the Land Society and also
O'Connor's election at Nottingham; the Rea Street Land Company
branch cancelled their weekly meeting to attend the celebrations and the
same evening a No.3 Money Club began operation.

1847 was the most successful year nationally for the Land Plan with 600
branches, many thousands of members and two estates, O'Connorville
and Lowbands, operative. Mass unemployment and bitter privation fed

both the Land Plan and general Chartist support. Ahead lay the familiar struggle for economic survival and the collection of signatures to the third Petition. What was not known was that 1848 was to be the year of Revolution.

1848

The year opened with the Chartists, at last, able to use the town hall. At a large and enthusiastic meeting in January chaired by Councillor Baldwin, Feargus O'Connor spoke on both the Land Plan and the new Chartist Petition.

At the end of February the growing ferment in Europe and Ireland which was already stimulating Chartist activity in Britain greatly increased with the news that a republic, based on universal suffrage, had been declared in France. Very large meetings and demonstrations took place all over the country in support of the Charter, to organise the collection of signatures and to plan the Chartist Convention which was to organise the presentation of the Petition to parliament. In Birmingham, another large town hall meeting took place in support of the Charter, again chaired by Baldwin, at which Sturge, Collins and Mason were among the speakers as well as NCA Chartists. O'Connor and Ernest Jones were addressing vast rallies throughout the country, including one attended by 20000 people on Kennington Common in London.

It is against this background that the so-called 'fiasco' of 10 April and the myth of yet another 'end of Chartism' must be considered. On April 4 the national Chartist Convention met to consider the presentation of the Petition and subsequent action to be taken. As always, a basic concern was to keep the number of delegates below 50 at which figure such an assembly was deemed legal. Birmingham and district were represented by James Alfred Fussell and Joseph Linney. During the early sessions, devoted to testing the mood of the country, Linney said that Black Country people were ready to obey the Convention and he felt determined to have the Charter before he left London. Fussell thought that Birmingham people were better off than in former years, that the middle class had declared for the Charter, that Chartists now had the use of the town hall, and he hoped the questions of physical and moral force would not be introduced to destroy the unanimity of the Convention.

The eventual programme decided on by the Convention was:

1. That if the National Petition was rejected by the House of Commons, a National Memorial should be presented to the Queen calling on her to dissolve Parliament and 'call to her counsel such ministers only as will make the People's Charter a Cabinet measure'.
2. That the Convention convene a National Assembly to act permanently until the Charter is the law of the land.
3. That simultaneous meetings be held throughout the country on Good Friday April 21st to elect delegates to the National Assembly.
4. That the National Assembly meet in London on April 24th.
5. That the present Convention continue until the meeting of the National Assembly.

On the presentation of the Petition, it was decided that there would be a meeting on Kennington Common and a procession from there would accompany the Petition to parliament.

The government replied with the vast military preparations that led up to the April 10th meeting. First, by proclamation, they declared the proposed procession from Kennington Common to parliament illegal. Secondly, they passed a Crown and Government Security Bill, opposed by Muntz among others, making 'seditious language' a felony in all parts of the UK punishable by transportation. Police and military were mobilised on an unprecedented scale throughout the country, and in London on the 10th April police armed with cutlasses surrounded Kennington Common, thousands of special constables were sworn in and the army, with artillery, was mobilised. Faced with such preparations only fools would have advocated mass law breaking on the 10th. and the Chartist leaders were no fools.

The procession set out from the Convention rooms at 10a.m. on the 10th. In front was a car drawn by four horses carrying the Petition. Another car, drawn by six horses, followed carrying the Convention delegates with O'Connor and other leaders on the front seat. Then followed the procession which marched through the City and on to Kennington Common where the final assembly was between 150,000 and 200,000. On arrival, O'Connor was informed by the police that the meeting would be allowed, but the subsequent procession to Parliament would not. O'Connor, and most other leaders, accepted this and urged the vast crowd to respect this decision. This they did and the enormous Petition was taken to the House of Commons. The same week it was reported that thirteen clerks had examined the Petition and found that it contained not 5 million signatures as claimed by O'Connor but 1,975,496. Of these signatures some were of such unlikely notables as Victoria Rex and the Duke of Wellington or fictitious names such as Pugnose, Longnose and others more obscene. The folk lore of the third Chartist petition is, therefore, that after the 'fiasco' of the Kennington Common meeting the Petition was subsequently rejected by Parliament amid laughter and derision.

Both of these conclusions deserve re-examination. With regard to the signatures. Given the bitter hostility to Chartism and the Petition there is no reason at all to accept that there were only about 2 million signatures. O'Connor claimed at the time that there had been insufficient time for the clerks to count the signatures and given the known practice of all authorities of deliberately under-estimating attendances at meetings etc. by at least one half, it is likely that there were at least 3 million signatures on the Petition. Even if the figure of 2 million is accepted, the immense achievement of such a total must be recognised. Some of these difficulties will be recognised by anyone who tries to collect signatures today. There are those who agree, but ask what good would their signature do; those who agree with some points of the petition, but not all; those who agree but who prefer to be anonymous or ribald (should Pugnose be rejected in these circumstances?). But the additional problems of signature collection in the 1840s must be considered. In the first place, large numbers of people could not write a signature, or wrote so badly that they would not reveal this deficiency in public. There was also the real fear that a public signature would lead to future victimisation. In addition there was a widespread prejudice against women signing the Petition. The strength of this feeling can be indicated by the fact that one MP calculated that there were scarcely 5 million male adults in the whole United Kingdom; under these circumstances it was difficult to collect signatures from any but the 'advanced' women of the time. Finally the circumstances under which signatures to the three Chartist petitions were collected should be considered. I quote the experience of Birmingham and the Black Country. Signatures to the first Petition of 1839 were widely collected in Birmingham but on a limited scale only in the Black Country. Only for the second Petition of 1842 was signature collection done in a highly organised way with district organisation setting targets and interim reports on the progress of collection throughout the west Midlands. The third Petition was adopted at the Chartist Conference of 1846 on a developing Chartist movement but whose base was weaker than in 1842. There was some district organisation, but the *Northern Star* made little mention of progress in signature collection either locally or nationally. After the Petition had been presented there were statements that in some areas considerable numbers of signatures were still lying in local offices e.g. at Halifax, according to Ernest Jones, and in other areas there is evidence that the feeling prevailed that however many signatures were collected the Petition would be rejected so potential support was regarded as more important than numbers on the Petition. When all these circumstances are considered, two million signatures was a staggering achievement and certainly no 'fiasco'.

Similar considerations apply to the so-called collapse of Chartism after April 10th. The Chartist press gives no support to such a notion. Vast mass meetings were held over Easter to elect delegates to the forthcoming Chartist National Assembly. These highlight yet another problem for the movement when it came to designing measures to be taken if the Petition were rejected. We, with hindsight, know that there was never sufficient total strength within the country to support coercive measures against the government, but the Chartists did not know this and in addition, support ebbed and flowed throughout the country. So in 1839, Birmingham was a great Chartist centre, by 1842 this had moved to the Black Country, but by 1848 neither area played a decisive role. In 1848 London Chartism was much stronger than in 1839 or 1842, reflecting both the European revolutions and events in Ireland, always greater in the most cosmopolitan capital. Locally, the Easter meetings took place in Birmingham, but finds no record in the *Northern Star,* whereas Bilston reported a 'large and enthusiastic meeting'. When the Chartist National Assembly met O'Connor was still insisting on strict legality and limiting the number of delegates to under 50, but on this he was over-ruled and it was at that point that Birmingham and other local delegates were admitted. These included William Insull for Dudley, H. Roden for Birmingham and Carver for the Birmingham district. The business of the Assembly it will be recalled, was to prepare the Memorial to the Queen to dismiss her ministers and to propose other measures. The right to Memorialise the Queen, which was an ancient one, had however, been outlawed by the government's hasty pre-10th April legislation and this created divisions within the Assembly.

Assembly proceedings began on May 1st and the first days were taken up with reports from the delegates. At this time, Scotland was playing a

more advanced and militant role and some localities were reported as
being willing to accept whatever measures the Assembly proposed, but
from other areas it was clear that the majority were opposed to direct
action. The Assembly then adopted a diffuse programme of 1.
Arrangements for the presentation of the Memorial to the Queen, 2.
Practical measures to make the Charter law and 3. Organisation and
policy of the Chartist body. From all this there emerged a resolution to
elect an executive of the Assembly and for the Assembly itself to dissolve,
which it did in the middle of May.

Chartist activity was once again dispersed to the localities where it
continued at various levels from militant and menacing in parts of
Yorkshire, Lancashire, Scotland, east Midlands and London to non-
existent in some other previously flourishing areas. In between was the
low level organised activity in Birmingham and declining activity in the
Black Country.

The government was determined to destroy the movement, but it was
not until after the June days when counter-revolution succeeded in
France and other European countries that it felt strong enough to launch
its main offensive. The Chartist leaders in the militant areas were
rounded up and imprisoned. This, again traditionally, is regarded either
as the end of another phase of Chartism, or, more usually, as the end of
Chartism itself. In fact, Chartism lived for another ten years, and the
down-turn in its activity, like that in 1842, was due more to an up-turn
in economic activity than any other factor.

Before dealing with this last phase of Chartism, we can briefly review
the activities of those Chartists who chose to remain outside the NCA,
notably Arthur O'Neil, John Mason and John Collins.

Arthur O'Neil established the most famous Christian Chartist Church
in December 1840. It was more recognisedly Christian than either the
Owenite Rational Religionists of the 1830s or the later Labour Churches
of the 1890s. O'Neil attracted unmeasured abuse from all Christian
denominations, which must forever stand to the discredit of Christians.
O'Neil was also roundly condemned by O'Connor and all NCA
members. This was because instead of recognising themselves as a
'branch' of Chartists attracting Christians but affiliated to the main body
of the movement, in which role they would have been welcomed, they
prevaricated regarding the 'illegality' of the NCA and were regarded as
those most likely to sell out to middle class influence. In fact, when it
came to the crunch in 1842, O'Neil and the Christian Chartists played
an honourable role in the economic and political struggles of the time and
shared the same fate as Feargus O'Connor, and local NCA leaders such
as Linney. In its early days the Chartist Church operated with working
men pastors, including John Collins, and presumably were attracted to
the Educational Chartism of Lovett and Collins. The Church proselyted
the surrounding areas and at one time had hopes of establishing Chartist
churches in Banbury and Warwick. From 1843 to August 1844 O'Neil
was in prison and the Church seems to have continued, but even when
O'Neil was released, details of the activities of the Church are hard to
come by. In April 1846, O'Neil seems to have had a complete change of
heart when he announced that he no longer believed that the heavenly
word 'Christian' should be an appendage of the word 'Chartist', and

announced that he was dissolving the Chartist church. The next month O'Neil joined the Baptist church and when George Dawson relinquished charge of the Mount Zion chapel in Newhall Street, O'Neil became minister there. For the remainder of his life O'Neil continued an important national figure within the international peace movement, together with Joseph Sturge.

The question arises as to why Christian Chartism established itself so firmly in Birmingham. The best answer that can be given is that the leadership of both O'Neil and Collins established it in the town, the influence and money of Joseph Sturge kept it there, and that it fitted more easily into the radical Christian tradition inherited from Joseph Priestley and the Unitarians than most other towns.

With regard to John Collins, he, together with William Lovett, established 'education Chartism', Lovett returning to London and Collins remaining in Birmingham. Unfortunately, soon after the closure of the Chartist church, Collins was certified insane, and his political influence thus came to an end.

John Mason moved steadily towards co-operation with the middle class governing circles in Birmingham, although, as we have seen, he denied that this meant he had deserted the working class. Whatever his dilemmas, Mason sought a solution in emigrating to America. Before he left he was entertained at a tea-party where the guests included Muntz, Douglas, George Dawson 'and other gentlemen'. He was also presented with a purse containing £40.

The Last Stage of Chartism 1849 – 1860.

The last decade of Chartism spanned the first decade of the Great Economic Expansion which was to last until 1874. Expansion had in fact begun from 1845, but was broken by the short slump of 1847 – 48. The difference between this short slump and the Long Depressions of the earlier part of the century was that living standards did not plummet down to starvation levels in 1847/48 and the overall period 1845 – 55 was probably one of the two key periods of advancing living standards for most workers in the Victorian era of British industrial supremacy. The other period was 1870 – 74, for during the Crimean War there was another slump in 1855 – 56 and the 1860s was a decade of surprisingly high unemployment. So during the last decade of Chartism it was not, for most of the time, the 'knife-and-fork' question which had previously given it its cutting edge, but an abstract political issue attracting a lower level of support. Nevertheless, as will be seen, Chartism remained the dominant working class ideology capable of regenerating mass support on crucial issues.

Chartist activity in 1849 was still dominated by the Land Plan. One of the criticisms Feargus O'Connor faced was that contractors could build on the estates more cheaply than he did. In January a letter in the *Northern Star* from GP of Birmingham enquired why, if contractors could build cottages at half the price, he did not use them. O'Connor's reply was trenchant. He never let contractors build. None of them admitted to being liars and rogues, but all of them were. From October 1847 to June 1848 he had built 165 cottages and two schools at a cost for overseers of £84. He had used the best timber and other materials; contractors would have used the worst materials and made the highest profits. The difference of £62 was the difference between a home and a hovel, O'Connor concluded. Considering the way these cottages have survived to the present day, it is difficult to think that O'Connor was wrong. The matter obviously worried the Birmingham members however, for in February the Rea Street branch was 'Respectfully requesting Feargus O'Connor to reconsider the expense of buildings'. They were 'not activated by factious motives, but by the best interests of the Company'.

The mid-way position of middle class acceptance of the Six Points of the Charter without accepting the name of 'Chartist' continued to dominate Birmingham chartism. In May a meeting was held at the Public Office to petition the legislature for 'full representation of the people as embodied in the People's Charter', with Goodwin in the chair and spoken to by Messrs Dalziell, Ward, Connor, Blaxland, Higgins, Brewster, Rev. O'Neil and Councillor Baldwin. From this list it is difficult to identify the middle class element willing to associate themselves with the Charter, but the town councillor Baldwin is certainly one. The Petition was accepted and forwarded to the MP, Muntz. This initiative was continued with a Chartist public meeting at the People's Hall, when Goodwin read letters from two local councillors pledging themselves to accept the Charter. Another aspect of relations with the middle class arose in July when there was a letter in the *Northern Star* from G.F. Muntz, the Birmingham MP, complaining that he had been cited as a delegate to the 1839 Chartist Convention. O'Connor graciously acknowledged that it was his brother Philip Muntz who had been the 1839 delegate and he added 'As far as I know you have never advocated the Six Points, but I am aware that there is not a more independently minded member in the House.'

In July, at the usual weekly meeting at the Ship it was proposed that every member of the Land Company be levied 3d. for a delegate to the Land Conference. This met the next month at Snig's End and Lowbands, the two adjoining estates between Tewkesbury and Gloucester. The Birmingham delegate J. Smith appeared on the second day of the Conference.

In October the Chartist EC levied Birmingham £4 for Convention expenses. As a comment on the relative strengths of Chartist localities at this time it should be noted that only Manchester and Aberdeen were levied as much.

Also in October 1849 there was a letter from James Taylor of the Birmingham Freehold Land Society which indicated the powerful indirect influence the Chartist Land Plan had in stimulating Land and Building Societies throughout the country. Taylor complained of O'Conner's bias against his Company and stated that in two years they had expended £19,000 in freehold land and granted 426 freeholds to members. This had placed nearly 200 people on the county voting list and the next year there would be 300 more. 'In the name of 1,729 working men of Birmingham who are now candidates for freeholds we ask you to cease opposing us'. O'Connor replied that he had 'neither exulted, crowed, nor clapped my hands at the unjust decision of the barrister', and wished them 'success and ultimate triumph over barristerdom'. This referred to a decision not to legalise the Birmingham society.

The legal position of the Chartist scheme at the time was as follows.

The House of Commons had appointed a Select Committee in May 1848 to enquire into the affairs of the Land Company. This in itself had an adverse affect on recruitment to the scheme. The first part of the enquiry suggested that although decidedly unorthodox, nothing illegal could be connected with either the Company or the Land Bank, and the dominant question became whether the allottees could both pay rent and avoid becoming a charge on the Poor Law by acquiring a settlement in the parishes of the estates. At the time allottees had neither titles to the land nor were they paying rent. The second part of the enquiry concentrated on the legality of the lottery principle and whether 70,000 members, half of whom already had a paid-up share, could be settled on estates (which depended on rents to be raised and the mortgaging of existing estates to buy further estates) within a reasonable number of years. The final decision, in July 1849, was to declare the Company illegal on a negative answer to the last question, but gave 'the parties concerned the option of winding up the Company and thus relieving themselves of the penalties to which they had exposed themselves as a result of their illegalities'. The main parties concerned were the allottees on the land anxious to get a title to their land, the subscribers concerned to get back their share money of £1-6-0d (if fully paid up) or less, and O'Connor and W.P. Roberts, the famous Chartist attorney, in whose names the land was registered.

In December 1849 at the usual weekly meeting of the Ship Inn Chartists and Land Company members, O'Connor's letter in the *Northern Star* was read and approved. This requested allottees to pay six months rent that was owing, or lose a leasehold on their plots. Later in the month, on a sharper note, Ship Inn supported O'Connor's measures to wind up the Land Company, but proposed that he 'get rid of dishonest and ungrateful members located on the estates'.

Also in December there were signs of a Chartist revival in Birmingham. Arthur O'Neil at the Public Office had delivered a 'lengthy and instructive lecture on the People's Charter which gave great satisfaction'.

In January 1850 it was announced that a branch of the Chartist Association under the new organisation had been commenced at The Swan, Warwick Street, for Deritend and Bordesley. Several supporters from the Ship attended and the branch met every Monday evening under the chairmanship of Henry Roden. At the Ship in February the secretary was instructed to write for 30 membership cards for new recruits. Also in February 'the usual weekly meeting' reported yet another Chartist locality at New Summer Street. A resolution from there had condemned Thomas Clark who in resigning from the NCA executive and starting his own National Chartist League was 'likely to lead the movement into disrepute'. This report was signed by G. Sharp (chairman), William Jackson and James Dumain.

In March 1850 Ship Inn reported a collection of 13/-d for 'O'Connor's Libel Case' — actions that O'Connor was increasingly finding it necessary to take against the most scurrilous critics of the Land Company. Ship also proposed a public soiree to commemorate 10 April 1848 — so much for the 'fiasco of Kennington Common'. They also proposed to call a district delegate meeting at an early date.

The national revival of Chartism paradoxically revealed the weakness

of the one issue, one organisation National Charter Organisation. Everyone, including O'Connor, was finding it necessary to co-operate to some
degree with the middle-class elements in support of the Six Points;
Harney, who was now the editor of the *Northern Star* was concentrating to
a greater extent than before on international affairs in the paper; trade
unionism was growing in the wake of economic expansion; and
Republicanism led by Bronterre O'Brien was growing out of what had
been educational Chartism. But Feargus O'Connor was opposed to
Socialism; land nationalisation cut across his Land Company plans to
settle workers on the land and Republicanism was anathema to one who
claimed descent from the ancient kings of Ireland. In addition, O'Connor
was increasingly showing signs of the mental disorder that was to end his
political career. Birmingham chartists were caught up in all these cross
currents.

In March 1850 the Deritend Bordesley district supported recent
changes in the Provisional Chartist executive and also announced a
lecture on the Rights of Labour by Mr. Thompson with Renshaw in the
chair.

Revival went even further in Coventry where a Reading Room and
Library was established in June at the Temperance Hotel, Bishop Street.
But Birmingham reports for the summer and autumn of 1850 are rare
and we are again left to ponder whether this meant that activity collapsed
or whether it was neglect of duty by the corresponding secretary. When
reports resume at the end of the year expansion is still being reported. In
November 'a numerous meeting' at the Ship Inn collected money for
Hungarian and Polish refugees. Nine new members were enrolled. In
December a Ship meeting suggested that given the differences which had
arisen regarding the calling of a national Chartist conference it would be
best for the localities to elect a Provisional Committee of five who would
then determine when and where a Conference should meet. They also
made another collection for O'Connor's libel actions but suggested that
he 'refrain from entering English law courts with his political opponents,
seeing that they are predetermined to carry out their old motto — ruin
him with expenses'.

The Land Plan shared one general characteristic with the Chartist
movement — reports of their demise were greatly exaggerated. After the
declaration of the illegality of the Plan in 1848, attention shifts to the
estates, and for Birmingham this meant Great Dodford. This estate was
· located more closely to an industrial area than any other — 12 miles from
Birmingham. It could therefore supply the nearby urban food market and
also be sustained by local Chartist groups. The estate was bought in
January 1848 and location began in February 1849. By this time
allocation by ballot had been declared illegal and Great Dodford was
therefore settled by 'bonus', plots being granted to the highest bidders,
although one quarter of the estate was assigned to winners in the previous
ballot. Thus the main attraction of the scheme for working men was lost
and most of the estate went to better off workers. In 1850 O'Connor
attempted to sell the estate, but much of the land was withdrawn when
plots sold for less than O'Connor had paid for them. In 1852 the Land
Company was wound up, ground rents being fixed at 4% of capital
values averaging £275.

Chartists reacted vigorously to these problems. The winter of 1849 was particularly severe and Chartists from Birmingham and the Black Country visited the estates and also gave practical help such as the donation of tools etc. In 1850, Dudley chartists led the way by winding up their branch of the Land Company and forming a Redemption League to buy up the shares of all local dissatisfied shareholders and 'present them to O'Connor to be used by him for the furtherance of the glorious Land Plan'. In 1850 at least two organised trips were made to Great Dodford. The first was on the anniversary of its settlement in February and the second in June when 'large numbers of friends from Birmingham and Dudley were delighted by the improved appearance of the estate since our visit last year.'

In January 1851 a Thomas Bardel Brindley of Birmingham was given almost a whole column in the *Northern Star* to state how he had been converted to the virtues of Feargus O'Connor and his Land Plan.

Apart from Land Company activity 1851 yields less evidence of Chartist activity in Birmingham than any other year. In the summer Ernest Jones, the new leader of the movement, was in the west Midlands. He asked the Ship locality to arrange a meeting for him. Jones reported first from Walsall where he had spoken to a crowded meeting where at least 100 had stepped forward to join when some Chartists had refused to enrol them saying that they were in touch with middle class leaders and hoped to win them over 'with a good deal of talk about Unitarians and Baptists etc. which was perfectly unintelligible to me. This miserable, pusillanimous spirit must be put an end to ... By truckling to the middle class no movement yet ever made headway. Jones ended by saying that he had 'never seen a better spirit than in Walsall'.

Of Birmingham, Jones was even more scathing. The previous day he had spoken at the Corn Exchange and reported that 'nothing can exceed the apathy and inertia of this large town'. He had been told that this was the best political meeting for some time. 'If so, all I can say is best is bad. Trade is too brisk'. Jones ended by saying that the temper of the meeting was excellent and eighteen people joined, which was a fair proportion of the audience. In September more ambitious plans were laid for autumn activity. At the usual weekly Ship meeting the secretary was instructed to write to the Executive for 100 monthly circulars and from October a course of public lectures was to be arranged given by all the national Chartist leaders including Reynolds, Harney, Jones, Cooper, Thornton Hunt, Kydd and Feargus O'Connor, if he were in the country.

Mention of the latter brings us to the *Northern Star*. From 1850 O'Connor was less able to direct the paper and it passed to G.W.M. Fleming and Dougal M'Gowan. In January 1852 they bought the paper from O'Connor for £100. From March the name was changed to *The Star & National Trades Journal*. In April 1852 it was sold to Julian Harney who re-named it the *Star of Freedom*. The paper expired in November. But from May 1852 the main Chartist journal was Ernest Jones' *People's Paper*.

The above catalogue suggests that 1851 was a dismal year for local Chartists. It was in November of that year, however, that Kossuth, the Hungarian revolutionary leader, came to Birmingham and the town laid on one of its great traditional demonstrations, mobilising as in the past, its tens of thousands from the surrounding areas.

The early months of 1852 record no Birmingham NCA activity in what was to be the last year of the *Northern Star*. The first number of Jones' *People's Paper* appeared on 8 May. Its first editorial stated that the NCA held the field as the only People's Party; that it had survived all dangers and witnessed the fall of all competitors because it was true to itself in advocating Chartism as the Charter alone. In July it reported that friends favourable to the Charter in Birmingham had met at Mr Wild's Temperance Hotel, 89 Hill Street when a branch of the NCA had been formed. This had been proposed by James Dumayne and seconded by Thomas Scrimshire. The secretary pro. tem. was William Jackson and the branch was to meet every Tuesday evening. From that time on reports of 'the usual weekly meeting at Wild's' appeared in the paper. In August the branch had voted for the new Chartist executive, giving 7 votes to Gammage, 7 to Finlen, 4 to Jones and 3 to Bligh. The next week it was reported that the *People's Paper* had been read and the article on the reign of the Tories much applauded. The following week Ernest Jones' Address to the Readers of the *People's Paper* had been read and 'excited the sympathy of all present'. 4/10d had been collected and it was resolved to take the paper for Mr Wild's Temperance House. The loyalty of Chartists to Feargus O'Connor, who by now had been taken to Dr. Tuke's Asylum was expressed at this meeting:

> . . . knowing the great sacrifices made by that great man Feargus O'Connor and the persecution he has undergone holds it to be ingratitude of the basest kind to allow him to remain as at present almost unobserved and uncared for. It is therefore resolved to form a committee to collect subscriptions on behalf of Mr O'Connor at a special meeting next week when it is earnestly requested that all who have observed that gentleman's honest and straight forward conduct during a laborious life spent in the people's cause will attend.

The committee appointed was: J. Dumayne, W. Jackson, J. Scrimshire, J. Piers, T. Wild, J.N. Ridgway, J. Smith, Mr Woodward (secretary) and J. Brown (treasurer). This committee was to meet every Monday evening from 8 to 10 to receive donations to the Fund.

At this time nation wide controversy was being aroused by a bill to reintroduce a home defence militia in view of the coup-d'etat in France and another Napoleon as ruler. On the 22nd September a 'respectable and enthusiastic meeting' heard Finlen speak on the Militia Bill. The next week the 'largest meeting since 1848' heard Finlen link this matter with the Charter when Finlen spoke for two hours to No Vote, No Musket, after which the following resolution was passed:

> All governments of whatever form attempting to coerce people to obey laws which they have had no part in making are not Governments but Usurpations and have no just claim on the obedience of the people. Any such government calling on the people to arm for purposes of offence or defence ought to be resisted by all constitutional means.

To underline the point it was announced that the next meeting was to be a discussion on Monarchy v Republicanism. In fact this topic was postponed to discuss a letter by Gammage in the *People's Paper* which criticised Ernest Jones.

The year ended with a special committee consisting of Dumain, Jackson, Grimshaw, Wild, Piers, Brown and Barnes elected in Birmingham to extend the circulation of the *People's Paper*.

The continued existence of the *People's Paper* required considerable exertions to extend the circulation and cover the weekly financial deficit. At the beginning of 1853 there were three public agents for the paper — Butterwick of 75 Stafford Street, A. Wilcox of Balsall Street, and W. Jackson at 112 Hill Street. In January 1853, however, in response to further requests from Jones, Birmingham chartists, having again discussed the paper, reported that they considered they had done their share and hoped others would do theirs.

In the spring of 1853, the Chartists moved their usual weekly meeting from Tuesday to Sunday evenings. During March they expressed their continued sympathy with Feargus O'Connor tendering their 'thanks to Dr. Tuke for his kindness to Mr O'Connor in that gentleman's unfortunate affliction' and suggesting that his removal would be unjust and cruel.

In May 1853, Gammage lectured at the Temperance Hall, Ann Street, with Alderman Baldwin, 'whose sympathies have ever been on the side of the people', in the chair. Gammage spoke on 'the people's wrongs and remedies and contended for the People's Charter'. A resolution was passed at the end of the meeting stating that 'the social rights of the people will never be secured until the House of Commons is representative of the national will and the best means of ensuring this is the adoption of the People's Charter'.

By the middle of 1853 there was another national surge of Chartist support. This did not reach Birmingham until the autumn, when Scrimshire, the secretary, announced that at the usual weekly meeting at Wild's on October 4 'business of great importance' would be transacted. By the end of the month William Jackson had been elected secretary and J. Scrimshire treasurer supported by a committee of Brown, Gork, Abjer, Howl, Oxford and Child. This reactivation had been made possible by an influx of members, particularly two from Coventry (which had been for some time the most powerful Chartist location in the west Midlands) — John Oxford and Howl.

The Chartist revival centred around the strikes and lock-outs of 1853 – 54, notably the Preston lock-out, and the powerful solidarity campaigns these events evoked throughout the country. Ernest Jones and the Chartists were able to promote a Labour Parliament around these events aiming to unite the trade union and political wings of the labour movement and again raising the spectre at Whitehall of a ruling class Parliament of the rich at Westminster and an alternative Labour parliament representing working people.

Early in January 1854 the *People's Paper* reported that Johnson and Gork had been active in canvassing and had left 80 – 90 collecting books at various Birmingham workshops and factories and had inundated them with bills. The town was now 'tolerably well organised', it was reported and a public meeting with Ernest Jones and Clark Cropper, a Manchester leader, was to be arranged. Funds were pouring into the *People's Paper* via the Amalgamated Committe of Birmingham. At first each of these contributions were listed in the paper. For instance, one showed donations from Mr Brigg's workmen, Harley's joiners, 5 brushmakers, Pearl Button Makers, Globe Foundry, Turley's factory, but the paper warned they could not continue to give detailed lists since the 'largest newspaper in the world would not allow us to do this'.

Later in January the *People's Paper* headlined 'An Important meeting in Aid of the Labour Parliament and Lock-outs'. It reported a Tuesday evening meeting at the Oddfellows Hall where there was a large attendance despite the fact that Sir Robert Peel had a meeting at the Town Hall the same evening. John Oxford was in the chair and opened the meeting by saying that 'The children in our factories are yearning for education, but this is denied them by the grasping hand of capital which locks the door of knowledge. The child is made the machine. Society is hindered with a fearsome amount of juvenile crime, intemperance, theft and prostitution and the unfailing footprints left on society by the god, capital. The time has come when capital, the offspring of labour, must succumb to labour, the legitimate parent'. Edward Clark Cropper the representative of the Mass Movement Committee of the Strikes and Lock-outs in Lancashire was the next speaker. Hargreaves then stated that he was opposed to the Labour Parliament being brought into the matter and he was opposed to strikes. He was answered by the main speaker, Ernest Jones. Gork seconded the main motion in a 'humorous and effective speech'. The resolution in favour of the Labour Parliament was passed unanimously and three names put forward as possible delegates — John Oxford, Allen and Dalziel.

The Labour Parliament met in March 1854 with John Oxford as the Birmingham delegate. It approved an ambitious paper programme giving itself powers similar to those eventually assumed by the Trades Union Congress. In addition it set up five boards — Agriculture, Manufacture, Distribution, Regulation of the Price of Labour, and Assistance in Strikes and Lock-outs and Labour Legislation. Supreme authority was to be vested in the Labour Parliament which was to meet at least once a year.

Such a grandiose scheme could not be sustained by the movement at that time and instead of it strengthening the local movement, Birmingham was immediately involved in a national quarrel. A letter in the *People's Paper* from Oxford and Scrimshire reported that the previous Christmas a request had been made to them to nominate Bronterre O'Brien as co-editor of the paper. This they had refused because O'Brien had previously stated that he would only contribute to the paper if he were paid. Following this it was alleged that Ernest Jones had duped Oxford into asking for assistance for the *People's Paper* and monies contributed by a Mr. Howell never reached the paper. Oxford and Scrimshire then went on to say that in fact Jones had refused to take the money himself and instead asked for it to be sent direct to the printer, which they did. 'Further, O'Brien spoke in such an insulting manner of Ernest Jones that we are surprised he should want to join that gentleman on the paper'. This letter was followed by comments from the editor:

Consider the villainy. An O'Brien conspiracy requests friends at Birmingham to nominate its chief. Next they launch a falsehood on Jones and accompany it with money to Oxford under the pretence of believing him duped. Mr Oxford is too upright and manly to be duped by O'Brien and his friends.

The national revival of the movement led to a discussion on the high price of the *People's Paper* and proposals were made at a great demonstration at Blackstone Edge to reduce it from 5d. to 3½d. with a £200 fund to support the reduction. The proposal was not considered realistic by Jones, who demanded that the £200 be raised before the price reduction, and £20 be produced immediately. Circulation figures derived from the official stamp returns showed for the second quarter of 1854 the *People's Paper* at 43,000 which was much greater than many other weeklies, and even the renowned Manchester school *Economist* was only 56,000. Divided by thirteen this would give weekly circulation figures of 3,300 and 4,300. Birmingham chartists resolved to turn themselves into a Committee to co-operate with London in raising the fund and Jones promised to reduce the price of the paper on 9 December, if the money had been collected. At the end of November less than £72 of the £200 had been collected, but Jones reduced the price to 3½d on 16 December. The next week he reported a circulation rise of 1,000, but stated that 3,000 more was required. At the end of December John Oxford reported that Birmingham sales had nearly trebled and exhorted, 'Working men, tell us in the columns what you are doing'.

1854 had seen other events which were to sustain the last great surge of Chartism. The Crimean War had started with jingoistic expressions of nationalism even in the *People's Paper,* although these had perhaps more justification than usual, since it promised new revolutionary liberation movements as the 'gendarme of Europe' came under attack. But the euphoria of early victories collapsed under the idiocy of the Charge of the Light Brigade and the great sufferings of the British troops in the winter. These brought great movements of protest which Chartists were to lead. Birmingham was particularly affected by the development of middle class demands for army and civil service reforms under the name of Administrative Reform. Such reforms inevitably raised the question of the franchise and this helped the resurgence of Chartism, but raised again in a sharp way the question of co-operation with the middle class. A second effect of the war was a considerable rise in the cost of food, particularly bread and meat. Food protests were headed by Chartists, notably George White, who returned to Birmingham at this time and briefly published the only local working class newspaper the Chartist movement ever produced — *The Democrat and Labour Advocate.* The paper ended with fierce quarrels between local Chartists.

But a main concern in 1855 continued to be the fate of the *People's Paper.* Strenuous efforts were still being made to raise the £200 fund. In February, Birmingham chartists announced that they proposed a ballot 'for some magnificient framed pictures of democrats' in aid of the fund organised by a committee consisting of Joseph Aston, Thomas Noble, Thomas Scrimshire, John Oxford and Edward Alger. The ballot circulated throughout the country and was drawn in June when it was announced that 800 tickets had been sold of which Bilston with 100 had sold the most. £33 had been raised for the Fund and first prize had been won by Mr. Patterson of Ripponden whose locality had sold the second highest number of tickets.

Circulation of the paper rose, although never sufficiently to cover all its costs. Evidence from the sale of stamps is ambiguous however, as the April returns still showed 43,000. The stamp evidence is best used to show comparative sales and these give the *Nonconformist* 38,000, the *Spectator* 36,000, the *Patriot* 32,000, *United Services Gazette* 28,000, and the *Lancet* 23,000. Such figures always prompted the question among Chartists of why these journals appeared prosperous while the *People's Paper* was always demanding more money. The difference was, of course, that most other journals had large advertising revenues or wealthy patrons.

Expansion in Birmingham continued from the beginning of 1855. In January there was 'a long and able discussion' participated in by Alger, Wild, Perkins, Aston, Noble, Dumain, Oxford, Scrimshire and others as to the most effective way of 'gathering up the scattered elements of Democracy'. They resolved that the Chartist national executive be urged to set up a Democratic Convention to which all societies whether Chartist, Republican or trade unionist etc. be invited. Birmingham expansion coincided with developments in Bilston where new blood in the person of HVM (H.V. Meara) was writing a series of letters in the *People's Paper* on democratic development. The result was local discussion on Meara's ideas, and the establishment of district organisation by June. By this time Birmingham chartists were involved with the Birmingham Administrative Reform Association. A meeting of 4,000 to 5,000 at Bingley Hall was called by 'Muntz, Dawson and the whole commercial class of the town'. The working class was represented by Dalziel, Bower, Hawkins, Rafferty and Oxford. Oxford tried to put an amendment to the main motion in favour of accepting all the Six Points of the People's Charter. This the chairman refused to accept. Dalziel then managed to put an amendment which stated 'while deeply deploring the awful condition to which the nation has been reduced through the imbecilities of the government, we believe that no reform in the administration can be accomplished without a thorough reform of the House of Commons by Manhood Suffrage and the ballot'. The report went on to say that the whole platform was determined to speak against the Dalziel amendment and 'Oxford got hold of the chair . . . but such was the tumult that it became impossible to hear or know what was being voted for. The amendment was lost by 3 to 2, the middle class declaring that the Chartists had been crushed, but it appears the reverse'.

The following week at their usual meeting the Chartists discussed a proposal by one of the committee members of the Administrative Reform Association to call a town's meeting to reorganise the Suffrage Movement. They 'thanked that gentleman' and proposed a preliminary meeting to discuss the matter. On the following Sunday there was a district Chartist meeting in Walsall which Oxford and Alger attended as Birmingham delegates. This meeting passed a resolution damning the Administrative Reform Association, stating that they had no confidence in it, it was not sincere, they repudiated them in toto and advised all localities to bring the People's Charter before any meeting convened by that body. The result in Birmingham was the setting up of a Committee of Observation to monitor the activities of the Birmingham Administrative Reform Association.

By the end of June 1855 Birmingham chartists were reporting growing numbers and the necessity for a larger room. Early in July it was reported that the Chartists were meeting every Monday at the Glassmaker's Hall, Midland Passage.

In July the Birmingham chartists were drawn into a sideshow. John Oxford lectured on David Urquhart, who was gaining considerable national support for his unlikely assertions that Palmerston was an agent of the Tsar.

Chartist growth in Birmingham was again accompanied by arguments, this time Oxford falling out with Ernest Jones. It began with abusive comments by Jones in the *People's Paper* concerning Oxford and the non-arrival of money for the £200 fund. Oxford hit back with a scorching diatribe in the paper concerning Jones. Such personal abuse was both sad and surprising in view of the previous relationship of Oxford and Jones concerning money for the paper. Reaction in Birmingham to the Oxford letter was prompt. A meeting was announced the next week to 'consider the letter of the late secretary' at which 'Mr. Dalziel and his twenty staunch Chartists' were requested to attend. This was signed by J.H. Ridgway as secretary pro tem. In August the *People's Paper* Committee was requested to meet at the house of T. Scrimshire, their secretary, at 22 Nova Scotia Street.

The result was yet another reorganisation of Chartism in November around an almost completely changed slate of members. Ridgway continued as secretary, Alger was treasurer and the committee consisted of T. Taylor, F. Skinner, H. Wolley, M. Divine and A. McCarthy. Meetings were held at the Bird in Hand, Holloway Head every Sunday at 7pm.

This did not solve Birmingham's problems. On 22 December it was announced that a meeting of friends of the People's Charter had met at the Ship Inn and passed the following resolutions. 1. Absolving Mr. Newhouse and the Chartist council from all blame in the matter of the *Democrat and Labour Advocate*. 2. Arrangements for a meeting at the Ship Inn on 23 December to re-establish an organisation of Chartists in Birmingham. Lyndon and Alger also moved that Newhouse act as secretary pro tem. and reports of their meeting be sent to *Reynolds Newspaper,* the *People's Paper,* the *Democrat and Labour Advocate* and the Black Country chartist localities. Jones printed the above details in the *People's Paper* with a note that he had declined to publish the first part of the report because it consisted of an attack on George White to which he would have to be given a right of reply and he (Jones) had no desire to open the columns to such quarrels.

This brings us to the matter of White and his paper. George White had reappeared in Birmingham after an absence of some years during which he had been an active Chartist in other parts of the country. He started a weekly paper, probably in November 1855, called the *Democrat and Labour Advocate*. At least ten issues were printed, but only five survive in the British Newspaper Library. It was a four small page paper priced at 1d. White was the editor and the paper was at first published by John Newhouse the Birmingham chartist and printed by Edward Taylor at 100 Steelhouse Lane. White was, at this time, organising mass meetings in the Black Country on the issue of Dear Bread, addressed by himself and

James Finlen. The 8 December number of the paper announced that 'by
the authority of the democrats at Moxley, Lye Waste, Bilston and
Wednesbury the printing of the paper has been transferred to another
printer. There was no alternative'. The imprint at the end of the paper
showed that it was printed by Samuel Russell 24 Old Meeting Street,
Birmingham, for the proprietor Francis Hazeldine, Cock Inn, Lichfield
Street, Bilston. The same issue carried a letter from White which he said
the *Birmingham Journal* had refused to print except as an advertisement for
12/-d replying to 'an impudent advertisement' in the *Journal* from Edward
Taylor stating that he had only received part of his expenses for printing
the *Democrat*. White went on:

> I employed this man (Taylor) on behalf of the Chartists of this district.
> He made out his account which was paid and for which I hold his receipt.
> It appears strange that I should be publicly defamed for disposing of my
> own property.

White ended by stating that his actions had been endorsed by the Bilston
chartists. This was the last number of the *Democrat* to appear as Russell
then refused to print any more. The controversy rumbled on in the
columns of the *People's Paper*. In January 1856 Dudley chartists heard a
report from George White who advised Hazeldine to sue Russell for losses
incurred in his refusal to continue to print the paper. In April 1856 the
Shelton chartist locality made charges of 'infamous behaviour' against
White stating that they had loaned him the use of types, press and a
house, made him an elector and subscribed more than £20 to his paper.
'His drunken and scandalous behaviour and base ingratitude exceeded
belief. A secret correspondence is being carried on between the little
clique at Soho, Mr Aulton of Walsall and George White'. This brought
a sharp rebuttal from Aulton stating that, far from supporting White, he
had been the first to suffer at White's hands, and if this had been listened
to, Birmingham and Black Country chartists 'would not have suffered so
deeply in pecuniary matters which threw the defrauds on the Shelton
brethren in the shade'. No further details have been found to pronounce
on the charges against George White whose record as a Chartist both in
Birmingham and nationally is outstanding and who is said to have been
imprisoned ten times for his political activities. The language used against
White is typical of the ferocity of debate at the time and it is certain that
at least part of the criticism can be correlated with the differing political
stances of the participants at the time.

   With regard to general Chartist activity, 1856 opened with the Ship
locality in command. A long letter appeared in the *People's Paper* in
January signed by the leading Birmingham personnel — John
Newhouse, William Rudhall, Henry Roden, William Jackson and
William Smith-Lyndon giving an analysis of the Crimean War in its last
months:

> . . . the cause of the people in the last few years has remained dormant
> though not dead through the excitements of war carried on by the
> irresponsible governments of England and France against the despotic
> power of Russia which, even if it resulted in the crippling of the power
> of that autocrat, would still leave the masses of the people in political

bondage as before. We therefore call at the commencement of the new year for renewed determination to persevere in endeavours to obtain our inalienable rights, for now is the time for everyone to give reason for the faith he holds and if he sees no reason to object to Chartism, let him subscribe to the Charter ...

Also in January, James Dumaine died and we catch a rare glimpse of the life of a leading local figure. Dumaine died at the age of 35 leaving a crippled wife and two children. He was a native of Wales and a bootmaker by trade. He took part in the Welsh movement in 1839 with John Frost and others. He had to leave Wales and live in exclusion to prevent being imprisoned. He returned to Wales, but the spirit of persecution was still as great. He was nearly apprehended by government spies but he escaped and later came to Birmingham where he remained an active Chartist, an ardent supporter of Feargus O'Connor and member of the National Land Scheme. 'To elevate suffering humanity was the end and aim of his life. Peace be to his bones'.

In March 1856 a new Chartist locality was formed operating from 5 Summer Street with Thomas Noble as secretary. They reported new members enrolling and a good spirit prevailing. At the end of March they announced a meeting being held at the Ship Inn 'by the enemies of the Chartist movement' with John Oxford in the chair and they invited to attend 'all friends of the democratic movement (to) ... teach these knaves a political lesson'. According to the Summer Street chartists, D.A. Aulton, who was co-operating with John Oxford had written that 'Chartism has long since been at a discount and its name synonymous with blackguardism'. A week later it was triumphantly reported that the Ship meeting had been a miserable failure and 'George Dawson has taken this abortion under his patronage'. This dispute can be dimly followed through Black Country and midland district Chartist politics. Aulton, of Walsall, sent a report of a delegate meeting held in Bilston in March (to which Ridgway and Binney were the elected Birmingham delegates) at which the main proposal had been to form a new midland organisation to be called the Central League of National Chartist Brotherhood. Ernest Jones was upset by the report to the *People's Paper* and refused to print most of it on the grounds of lack of space, but made his own views plain by stating:

> I feel convinced from bitter experience that all such sectional and isolated movements are fatal to Chartism. I do not feel justified in excluding bona fide Chartist matters to make room for programmes in direct contravention with the united movement. I trust that the friends for whose kind sentiments expressed in the resolution I feel thankful will see the justice of this course and abandon isolated action.

Aulton was repudiated by Walsall, but Birmingham chartists remained divided.

In August 1856 there was another fillip to activity with the return of John Frost from transportation. This was an emotional moment after so many years of continuous campaigning. One million people were said to have greeted Frost in London and midland Chartists endeavoured to arrange a similar reception. But Frost was not the militant that he had been and the campaign came to nothing.

1857 – 58 saw the last of the Chartist revivals. Jones stood for Feargus O'Connor's old seat at Nottingham in the general election of 1857. Despite wide popular support he failed at the poll. From that time Jones seems to have accepted the inevitability of co-operation with the middle class, but continued to insist that Chartist organisation be kept intact. In April Jones called for a Chartist conference to decide attitudes to the middle class. This coincided with further problems with the finances of the *People's Paper*. Birmingham Chartists contributed to both Jones' election fund and also to the finances of the paper, but a call in March for democrats to meet at the house of Mr. T. Noble 5, Summer Street 'when business of great importance will be put to them' appears to have failed to produce regular meetings. The revival in Birmingham began in October when a meeting was called in the large room of Mr Groves' Temperance Hotel at 55 Hill Street and where 'a goodly number were present and officials were elected for one month'. These were T. Noble (secretary), J.H. Ridgway (treasurer) and J. Tipping, J. Home and D. Bayley (committee). By the middle of December the first open air meeting had been held at the Old Cemetery to a 'very good muster considering the weather'. Dalziel spoke on the State of the Country, Alger showed the weaknesses of the soup kitchens 'now being established', and Trueman spoke on the Charter.

This revival was based on both the enthusiasm for the Chartist Conference and also the slump of 1857 which had started in 1855. The idea of the Chartist Conference was being widened to that of a Reformers' Conference of Chartists with the middle class. The leading spirits locally were the Dudley chartists who proposed inviting to the Conference the Rev. A. O'Neil, George Edmonds and Clutton Salt. The Birmingham chartists attended district delegate meetings in the Black Country and, as activity increased, the original proposal for one district delegate to the Reformers' Conference broadened to the concept of two Black Country delegates and one from Birmingham.

1857 ended with a notice signed by W. Carroll as secretary pro. tem urging Chartists to meet at Eagger's 27 Duddeston Row. This meeting took place on 16 January 1858. The main item of discussion was the Conference, which was now once again being called a Chartist Conference. This also involved discussing Jones' proposal for a one man Chartist executive. On the latter question Richard Edwards moved that a one man executive was undemocratic, but an amendment by Daniel Bailey and John Hayward that there should be an executive of one and that one should be Ernest Jones was carried with only two against. The delegate meeting, which took place in Bilston at the end of January resolved that local delegates at the Conference should vote for nothing less than Manhood Suffrage and No Property Qualification. Also that local delegates be allowed £3-5-0d each for personal expenses. On the matter of the proposed one man executive they left the question open.

The Conference opened at last on 8 February 1858 and the two local delegates were John Chance the long serving Stourbridge chartist and Daniel Wallwork the leading Dudley chartist at the time. Some middle class radicals attended the Conference, but not the Birmingham ones. The Conference in fact determined what concessions were to be made in return for collaboration with the middle class. The main resolution agreed that Manhood Suffrage and No Property Qualification should be the main demands as the middle class were already in favour of the Ballot, Equal Electoral Districts and Shorter Parliaments, but that agitation for the whole Charter should not be abandoned. The Conference also agreed the one man executive and elected Ernest Jones to the post. Finally, it was agreed to raise a £100 fund to carry out these decisions.

After the Conference, a district meeting took place which approved the conduct of the delegates (Wallwork had spoken in favour of the one man executive) and pledged itself to raise £1 of the £100 fund.

But when the Birmingham report back meeting took place (after three weeks of advertising it in the *People's Paper* under the signature of J. Howe, secretary), the main business was not the Conference but Ernest Jones' financial problems with the paper. By 1857 the price of the paper was up again from 3½d to 5d. stamped and 4d unstamped. Jones' solution to falling sales was not to reduce the price, but to publish also a 1d. paper which would be profitable and enable the *People's Paper* to be subsidised. At the Birmingham meeting, which took place at Alger's, it was moved by Ridgway and Edwards that 'this locality declines to take any steps to support the *People's Paper* at its present price'. This resolution was passed against an amendment of Hayward and Bailey that 'this locality will do its utmost to relieve both the *People's Paper* and its editor from their present difficulties'. An invitation to Jones to speak to the locality was deferred. The meeting also elected a committee of Alger, Edwards and Ridgway to 'draw up a set of rules and get out a membership card' for Birmingham chartists who were now split on the newspaper question. The next week a resolution stating that the locality would do its utmost to assist the bringing out of a 1d. paper was printed under the signature of T. Noble (secretary). Two letters in the *People's Paper* also supported the 1d. paper. One, unsigned, stated that he had persuaded nine of his Birmingham friends to take a copy of the paper for six months. The other, signed C. Wheeler stated that 'if every Chartist will work as hard as I have done, I believe the 1d. paper could become the best circulated in the kingdom'.

On 8 May 1858 the first issue of Jones' 1d. paper, the *London News* appeared and quickly reached a circulation of 16,000. But this failed to solve Jones' financial problems and he sold both papers to Baxter Langley, the owner of the radical *Morning Star,* on the understanding that two columns of the *People's Paper* would be reserved for Jones' to report Chartist activity. This arrangement worked briefly, but by August Jones was quarrelling with Langley who announced that the *London News* would be expanded to eight large pages (the same size as the *People's Paper)* and sold for 2d. in which Chartists would have more space to report. He (Langley) would support the Political Reform League and invited Jones to contribute on Chartism. He also offered to sell the *People's Paper* back to Jones for £100. The Political Reform League was formed in London and the name suggested by Jones himself at a committee of Chartists and reformers set up to carry out the decisions of the Chartist Conference. Joseph Sturge was elected president.

Ernest Jones' reaction to Langley was to start a new small eight page weekly paper published at 2d. called the *Cabinet Newspaper* dedicated to the Union of Classes and the Liberty of Man. The first number appeared on

27th. November 1858 and contained a Birmingham notice urging all Chartists to attend at the house of Thomas Noble at 5 Summer Street, on 'business of great importance'.

From January 1859, however, Chartist activity in the *Cabinet Newspaper* was being reported under the name of the Camden and Midland Reform Union. In April the Union reorganised itself as the Camden Club and Manhood Suffrage Association. Regular reports of its activities appeared until June in the *Cabinet Newspaper* still under a column 'Chartist Activity', but by September the name of the column had been changed to 'People's Movement'.

In January 1860 Jones announced that he was starting a *Penny Times* and from 18th February the *Cabinet Newspaper* disappeared to be replaced by a *Weekly Telegraph*. This can be seen as the final departure of the National Charter Association from history as the new papers lasted only until April. This left remaining local Chartists groups without a national leadership.

That Birmingham chartism survived until the very end is testified to by the last notice of February 1860 which requested 'members of the Chartist locality as established in 1858' to attend at the house of Mr. Alger, 19 Duddeston Row, the notice was signed by J.H. Gunner.

Feargus O'Connor

PART 2
COPING WITH MATURING CAPITALISM 1850 – 75

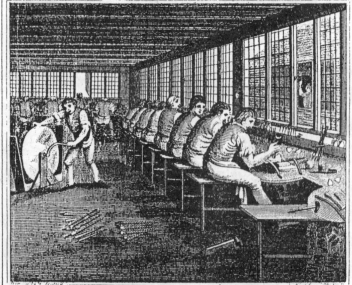

MILL for Grinding FILES.

Birm. Pub. May 1 1800 for J. Bisset's grand National Directory.

Chapter Five

SECULARISM — THE BRIDGE FROM CHARTISM TO SOCIALISM

From 1850 to 1860 Chartism and Secularism co-existed, although the main ideology of working class politics remained Chartist until its disappearance in 1860 when it was replaced by Secularism. This continued until the early 1870s when a powerful Republican movement initiated by Secularists threatened to become a new radical, working class party. This possibility was blown away in 1874 with the onset of the Great Depression. From 1874 to 1884 Secularism resumed its former role as the search for an alternative system of economic and political ideas to' challenge the dominant laissez-faire ideology continued. The search was successful in 1884 with the re-emergence of Socialism. There was a mass defection of working class Radicals from Secularism to the more satisfactory ideology of Marxism with the sudden appearance of the Social-Democratic Federation. Those Secularists who accepted Socialism but rejected Marxism became Fabians. The dominant trend within the rump of Secularism accepted Bradlaugh's anti-socialism, and Secularism thereby relegated itself to the fringe movement where it has remained to the present day.

Before relating these events in detail, Secularism must be more closely defined and the question raised of why the working class crossed from Chartism to Socialism via Secularism.

We have seen how the Catholic-feudal state hegemony was broken from the Reformation and resulted in the development of the radical tradition, particularly in Birmingham. Christianity has always contained the dialectic contradiction of the Communist teachings of its founder and its need to legitimise itself by association with the existing state. The unique advantage of Christianity to all ruling classes was its system of moral blackmail offering everlasting bliss to the faithful and eternal damnation to the infidel. The political and social struggles of the seventeenth century did not break out of the religious framework; but when the rigours of Puritanism were replaced by the cynicism and dissoluteness of much of society after the Restoration and the attacks on religion of the French Enlightenment prepared the ground for the secular revolutions in America and France, widespread religious indifference spread. While these religious backslidings were confined to ruling class statesmen such as Shaftesbury, Bolingbrooke, the elder Pitt etc. the damage could be contained, but when it spread to the 'lower orders' it was a more serious matter.

Secularism displaced religious ideology through the period of three, overlapping, working class agitations. Its prophet was Thomas Paine who was to haunt the ruling classes through the first half of the nineteenth century, as Marx was to haunt them in the second half. The first period was that of the Corresponding Societies in the 1790s. Paine's ideological influence on the American and French revolutions had been expressed through his 'Common Sense' and 'Rights of Man'. It influenced the

Birmingham radical tradition of the middle class through the Lunar Society members, the Joseph Priestley connection etc. This came to an abrupt end with the Priestley Riots of 1791 which closed the era of middle class support for the French Revolution. But working class support, as we have seen, continued, despite mass repression and illegality. During the 1790s Paine published his 'Age of Reason' and this at once became the bible and indeed replaced the bible for the majority of working class activists.

The open Painite tradition was revived after 1815 with the development of the working class press by such papers as *Black Dwarf, Republican* and *Poor Man's Guardian*. These newspapers were invariably labelled by the establishment as 'seditious and blasphemous'. It was while Carlile was in jail for circulating unstamped newspapers that he first read Paine and subsequently published his works. This led on to the epic struggles in London with Carlile's family and then volunteers keeping his shop open as each was prosecuted and sent to prison. In Birmingham, as we have seen, the brunt of these struggles was carried by Guest, Russell and the printers and publishers of the town.

This working class agitation eventually overlapped with the third Infidel movement of Robert Owen. Owen the self-made philanthropic factory reformer created the enormously successful and profitable factory community at New Lanark conducted on humanitarian principles informed by Owen's belief that character was formed by circumstances and not at birth. When it became clear to Owen that other industrialists would admire him, but would not follow his principles, and when his plan to overcome the post-1815 capitalist slump by creating industrial communities was rejected by the powerful of the land, Owen left for America to pursue his principles there.

On his return, in 1829, he found himself the leader of the British trade union, socialist and co-operative movements. Owen was not discouraged by the failure of the Grand National Consolidated Trade Union and the experiment with Labour Exchanges and labour notes, but went on to found in 1835 the even grander Association of all Classes of all Nations which, by establishing the initial colony at Queenwood, was meant to demonstrate the superiority of socialism and peacefully replace capitalism by the development of further colonies. If this were not enough, Owen's views on the formation of character and his 'religion of charity' set the alarm bells ringing; Owen was dubbed an atheist, although he was in fact, like Paine himself, a Deist. The fatal conjuncture of religious and political radicalism, however, aroused the fear bordering on hysteria which led to the victimisation, vituperation and violence on an unprecedented scale experienced by these earliest Socialists. This was not lessened by the enthusiasm which Socialists showed for entering into anti-religious controversy and their palpable neglect of what should have been their first duty — to create further Socialist colonies. One reason for this was the dual role of the Priesthood of spiritual terrorists in the pulpit on Sundays and temporal terrorists for the rest of the week in their role of justices of the peace. In addition, the unremitting hostility of Evangelicals and Methodists alike to all working class aspirations for reform determined that political radicalism and hostility to organised religion should go together.

With the failure of these early attempts at Utopian Socialism, and the expansion of capitalism after 1850, Secularism arose. The name itself is the creation of George Jacob Holyoake who was its first leader. The early leaders of Secularism came mainly from the Owenite tradition and not the Chartist, since the latter movement (although not necessarily its adherents) had nothing to say about religion.

Finally, in this introduction to Secularism in Birmingham, the economic background must be sketched. In view of the fact that G.J. Holyoake was both the national leader of Secularism and also a native of Birmingham who witnessed or participated in all radical movements in the town from 1832, his account of working class conditions is probably the most important that we have.

Holyoake was born in 1817 at No.1 Inge Street, in the centre of Birmingham. His father worked at the Eagle Foundry, Broad Street for more than forty years. Of his father's religious opinions, Holyoake says that in his youth he never remembered his father uttering any expression which implied that he had ever heard of religion. He never said anything for it, nor anything against it. He left all that to his wife. He had a pagan mind and his thoughts dwelt on the human side of life. Holyoake's mother was a horn button maker and a workshop was attached to their house. The horn button trade died out in Holyoake's youth, but as a child he learned the trade at home. As a child, he also began to work at the Eagle Foundry. 'I must have been very young then, as I remember asking my father to let me hold his hand as I went along by his side.' Here he learned the trade of whitesmith.

Eagle Foundry was owned by two men. One was Samuel Smith, a Unitarian, who was 'a placid gentleman'. Of the other, Holyoake wrote:

> Mr Hawkes was the other partner, to whom no workman ever made a request . . . he was an unpleasant person. He was exacting and always spoke with harshness. I saw old men who were in such terror at his approach that they would strike their hands instead of the chisel they were using, and were afraid of dismissal or reduction of wages in consequence of the incapacity he had witnessed, and which his presence caused. Piece-workers and day-workers were so continually subjected to reduced prices and wages that they never felt certain on Monday morning what they would receive on Saturday evening. There were no trade intimations where other employment might be obtained — no energy in seeking it — there was continual resentment, sullenness, and disgust, but no independence or self-dependence. If a man saved a little money, he carefully concealed that he had done so; if he could afford to dress cleanly and moderately well, he was afraid to do so, as his wages were sure to be reduced. I remember a fine, well-built young man coming to the foundry from Sheffield, where there was always independence among the workmen. He undertook the deadliest work in the mill, the grinding. There was great astonishment when he entered the foundry gates wearing a well-fitting, handsome suit of black clothes. The master was as much astonished at his audacity as the men were. He changed his clothes in the mill and put on a rough grinder's dress, mounted before the deadly stones and working like a splashed, mud-covered Hercules — but he would wash, dress and leave the foundry like a gentleman. His employer at once concluded that he had given him too much wages; but the moment a reduction was proposed he resented it, drew the money due to him, and went away entirely. It was almost the only example of independence I remember to have seen.
> One incident occurred which filled me with a lasting indignation. The

younger brother of a man called Barton who had been employed for
years at the mill was found by William Hawkes one meal time, removing
a file from one of the shops. He was an industrious, well-conducted
young fellow — he had not taken the file away, which was worth about
7d. though he probably intended taking it. He was apprehended, and
transported for ten years, on the evidence of the master. A week's
imprisonment would have been sufficient penalty for a first offence in a
mill where theft was unknown. The arbitrary and continual reduction of
prices by the master was a far more serious theft of the earnings of all
the men. That was the way in which employers behaved generally, so far
as I knew them . . .

Holyoake had attended a dame school for a short time before he began
full-time work which was probably when he was eight years old. When
he was ten he began to attend the Carrs Lane (Wesleyan) Sunday school,
of which he has given a chilling report. He later became a child teacher
at a Congregational Sunday School at Harborne, to which he went with
John Collins, the future Chartist leader. When he was sixteen he found
his way to the Birmingham Mechanic's Institute which held nightly
classes in mathematics, science, drawing, Latin, French etc. Here he
came under the influence of Birmingham's two leading Owenite Socialists
— William Pare and William Hawkes-Smith. The religion which
Holyoake had imbibed at the various chapels he had attended for his
elementary education passed into a Unitarian phase as he studied logic
and mathematics at their Sunday school before becoming an Owenite.
With such teaching and the Penny Magazine of the Society for Promoting
the Diffusion of Useful Knowledge, Holyoake gained a thorough
grounding in grammar, logic, mathematics, astronomy and mechanics.

By his twentieth year, in 1837, Holyoake was a Birmingham public
figure. He was on the Committee of the Mechanics' Institute and beside
his full-time work at Eagle Foundry he gave lessons in logic and grammar
at the Unitarian Sunday School. All his study had been, and continued
to be done between 7pm. when he left work and midnight or beyond. His
health broke down and a doctor recommended a walking cure. He left
Birmingham with five pounds in his pocket and went to Manchester (the
Mecca of Owenite Socialism), Liverpool, the Isle of Man, Wales etc. and
returned five weeks later with five shillings. He returned to the foundry
for the winter, but his health was not completely restored and he thought
of emigrating either to India or Australia. In 1839 however, he married
in the Birmingham Registry Office presided over by William Pare and
about the same time, left the foundry. For some time the couple led a
precarious existence as Holyoake applied for and failed to get such jobs
as lodge-keeper at Birmingham Botanical Gardens. For some months in
1840 he taught at a private school, and then became a book-keeper.
About this time Holyoake resigned from the committee of the Mechanics'
Institute as a party in the controversy which was to wreck the movement,
namely its middle class control and failure to provide advanced social
studies. In October 1840 Holyoake became a Social Missionary of the
Owenite Socialists. From this point Holyoake became a national political
figure and his direct connection with Birmingham ceased.

The Owenite Socialists split in 1841 over the issue of whether to declare
their premises as places of religious worship. The atheists opposed this,
and Charles Southwell began a new paper called the Oracle of Reason.

Southwell was prosecuted and sentenced to one year in jail. Holyoake associated himself with Southwell and took over the editorship of the paper. Six months later Holyoake was arrested on a charge of blasphemy and served six months in Gloucester jail.

These prosecutions led to the setting up in the middle of 1842 of the first purely free-thought organisation, The Anti-Persecution Union whose aims were to assert and maintain the right of free discussion, and to protect and defend the victims of intolerance and bigotry. With the decline of the Owenite movement Holyoake emerged as the leading Secularist. He replaced the *Oracle of Reason* with a more moderate paper, *The Movement*, and in June 1846 he began *The Reasoner* with which was merged the remaining newspaper of the pro-Owen faction of the Movement.

Through the pages of the *Reasoner*, the vague outlines of the development of secularism in Birmingham can be traced.

In concluding this introduction, an acknowledgement is necessary. A prior study of Birmingham secularism is an undergraduate thesis by Christine Stephens — *The Secularist Movement in Birmingham and District 1850 – 1885.* This highly competent study researched not only local sources, but also the Holyoake collection at Manchester and some of the main secular newspapers at the British Newspaper Library, particularly the *Reasoner, National Reformer* and *Secular Review.* The author (now Mrs. Turner) has generously allowed me access to her research material, and all my references to the Birmingham paper *Secular Chronicle* 1872 – 1878 are taken from her sources.

I am conscious, however, that some other material which we have both independently researched may appear here due to the fact that Mrs. Turner did not use all the material she collected for her thesis. If this be the case I apologise to her and acknowledge that she was the prior researcher.

Chapter Six

BIRMINGHAM SECULARISM
1850 – 1866

The leading figure in Birmingham Secularism and Republicanism over nearly thirty years was Christopher Charles Cattell. An early peak of Secularist activity came in 1855 – 56 and Cattell was then editing an *Eclectic Journal* produced in Birmingham. Eclectic Societies had existed in various parts of the country from the earliest days of Holyoake's *Reasoner* and annual reports of the Birmingham Eclectic Society for 1846 – 48 have survived. However, it is from 1855 that continual activity can be traced.

In December of that year there was a Birmingham Eclectic Institute in Union Passage, New Street. Holyoake lectured there and at the Oddfellows Hall and at the Public Office on successive Sundays in that month. In January 1856 Cattell was attempting to form a Birmingham and Midland Eclectic Society from friends in the surrounding Black Country areas. This was the first of a number of attempts by Cattell to form, consolidate and extend midland organisation. It is noteworthy that both the Wolverhampton and Dudley representatives who responded to this appeal were Chartists. These were the years of the Crimean War when, after an initial period of jingoism, there was a nation-wide resurgence of Chartism due to high prices and unemployment.

The last three months of 1856 seem to have seen the firm establishment of a Birmingham Secular Society in premises at 15 Hill Street. Every Sunday there was a Grammar and Elocution Class at 10.30 a.m. and at 6.30 p.m. there was a Conversation Class followed by the main meeting of the week. On Wednesdays at 7.30 p.m. there were also lectures and discussions. The joint secretaries of the organisation were Charles Smith and James Brookes. In November a Secularist Day School was opened under the direction of a competetent teacher of twenty years experience who, 'deeming it requisite that Secular education should occupy the place of superstition has discarded every sentiment calculated to injure the minds of the rising generation.' An evening school for adults was opened at the same time and also a Young Men's Class for instruction in reading, grammar, elocution and logic.

These successes appear to have been short-lived. In December the society moved to new premises at 124 Brearley Street. Further moves followed and two years were spent at rooms in Church Street belonging to Mr. Field.

Progress was resumed in 1860 with the acquisition of premises at 91 Suffolk Street. Cattell sent a long report to the *Reasoner* outlining the general difficulties facing all Secularists and describing the facilities at Suffolk Street. The first problem, he said, was to find suitable premises in the centre of the town owned by a landlord who was willing to let them to an infidel society. Then a tenant had to be found to occupy the premises. Finally the finance both to acquire and sustain the premises had to be found. These problems had been satisfactorily solved, Cattell continued. Mr. Ranford had become their tenant in premises which comprised a double-fronted shop with a room above capable of seating thirty or forty people. The premises had been named 'Reading and Discussion Rooms, Suffolk Street' so that no one would be compromised by using the premises as it was hoped to let them to outside bodies when not required by the Secular Society. The shop had been turned into a bookshop selling freethought and progressive literature. This was necessary because no shop-keeper in a central thoroughfare would 'make a show' of such works. The fragility of the experiment was revealed in Cattell's final paragraph which appealed for immediate financial and other support since 'delay may not only defeat our present purpose, but may prevent any similar experiment being made in the same direction for many years to come.' The move was indeed a bold one as the columns of the *Reasoner* at that time advertised only eight Secular Societies in London and twelve in the rest of Britain.

From the early 1860s Holyoake's national influence diminished as a new, more virile champion of Secularism arose. This was Charles Bradlaugh and his newspaper the *National Reformer*. Birmingham secularists were immediately plunged into clerical controversy by a series of lectures in July and August 1860 by the co-editors of the *National Reformer*, Joseph Barker and Iconoclast (Charles Bradlaugh). As a result of these lectures, 'the parsons' scavenger, now proclaiming himself the Rev. Dr. Brindley, had proclaimed an Infidel Revival, which he (Brindley) would fight.' As a result of this the Birmingham Daily Post had shut out all mention of Iconoclast's lectures and all friends of Secularism were asked to rally round the Society and its bookshop which had been expressly established to supply the town and district with secular literature. The Reading Room was also open every day and evening for a subscription of 1d. a week. This report was signed 'Christopher Charles', which was a pseudonym much used by C.C. Cattell to avoid problems at work. In November 1860 advertisements for Birmingham secularism first began to appear in the *National Reformer* and from these we learn that freethought literature was not only available at Suffolk Street, but also at 19 Hospital Street and 13 Key Hill. These were newsagents shops of John Morris, who was also the secretary of the Secular Society.

1861 was a year of great economic distress in Birmingham, but there were few reports of secular activity. From 1862, however, a fuller picture of the Society and its activities emerge.

In January 1862 at the annual general meeting officers and a Committee of eight were elected. Thomas Evans became secretary and Daniel Baker president. Cattell was elected an auditor. The Committee was to meet every Wednesday at 7.30 p.m. At this meeting it was also reported that a long-awaited debate between Holyoake and the Rev. Thomas Ragg had taken place at the Temperance Hall which had 'been filled to overflowing each evening by very respectable and attentive audiences.' Christians of Birmingham were awake and anxious for discussion, Thomas Evans thought. In March, Iconoclast did three lectures at the Oddfellows Hall, Upper Temple Street. These were reported to the *National Reformer* by Thomas Evans and it is worth reproducing some of his remarks, as indicating the flavour of Secularist discourse:

Three lectures were delivered in the Oddfellows Hall on Sunday March 9th by Iconoclast, when, not withstanding the severe wet weather of the morning and afternoon, the Hall was completely full, and in the evening the place was so crowded that many people were unable to obtain admittance.

The subject of the morning lecture was '*Thomas Paine and Martin Luther*' in which the teachings of these great reformers (as they are both considered to be by different classes of people) were contrasted. Paine was shown to be the friend of the people, of humanity, ever working in the great cause of human progress, while Luther, the friend of princes, the reformer who would claim reforms for himself that he would not grant to mankind, was a reformer selfish, pandering to courts and princes, teaching the people rather to kneel and pray, than to rise in noble effort for their own redemption.

Paine the maligned, scorned, calumniated and misrepresented — Luther the lauded, the never-enough-to-be-exalted, the glory of this protestant country and pillar of its church — Luther, who would connive at polygamy or concubinage in a prince, so long as the common people did not know it; who taught one thing to the peer and another to the peasant, and this was their great reformer. The picture of Luther, his doings and his teachings, seemed to be altogether new and startling to the audience, if one can judge from the intentness with which they listened to the recital.

The afternoon lecture on '*Italy; Religion its Curse, Freethought its Salvation*', was the most masterly oration we have ever heard. The graphic description of Italy as it was, with its advanced civilisation, as evidenced by the excavations made in the lava-buried cities of Pompeii and Herculaneum, contrasted with the enslaved and degraded condition of its people after eighteen conturies of Christianity, tended to show that religion had indeed been the curse of that glorious country and its once progressive people. The touching picture drawn by the lecturer of the awful poverty, the inconceivable depths of degradation, and the almost complete loss of power to help themselves, to which religion and its foster-child, priestcraft, had crushed the Italians, was sufficient to move the heart of the most stoical listener to deplore their wretchedness. We have heard a great many lectures and orations, from Mursell, Gough the Temperance orator and John Bright — men renowned for their power to move their hearers; but we think we have never heard one before that commanded such breathlessly intense silence, followed by such hearty, soul stirring applause as the present one . . . .

The evening lecture was an answer to the question '*What did Jesus teach?*' in which the lecturer gave a rapid resume of the alleged teachings of Christ as contained in the New Testament — his treatment of the Syro-Phoenician woman, the Lord's Prayer, the parable of the Talents and the Marriage Supper coming in for special comment. This lecture was delivered with the same earnestness, and listened to with the same marked attention as the preceding ones, with this difference, however, that the first two passed off without hisses or interruptions of any kind, and the opposition (perhaps owing to the sacredness of the day which kept the reverends away) was as weak and feeble as can well be conceived. We have had Iconoclast in Birmingham many times, his audiences being ever on the increase, but he never appeared to greater advantage, or had such crowded assemblies, as on Sunday last. A considerable number of friends attended the lectures from the villages and towns around Birmingham . . . Altogether this was one of the most glorious days for Freethought that has been witnessed here for a long time and will long live in the memories of those who participated in the intellectual feast which our modern Demosthenes provided for them.

In April and May 1862 J. Starling lectured over three Sundays on *Positive Philosophy and Auguste Comte* which were also reported at length by Evans. Also in these months Cattell spoke on *Secularism and Civilisation* and Evans recited Selections from the Poets, a popular speciality of his.

By the summer there was again premises trouble in Birmingham. The Oddfellows Hall was being used for the society's lectures and a grammar class there was being sponsored by the Society. In August it was announced that the monthly members' meetings were being held at the Oddfellows Hall, but the Committee was meeting each Wednesday at Clarke's Hotel, Edmund Street. The society held a discussion, led by Charles, on the best means of raising money for a Secular Hall and a committee of Hackwood, Charles and Hogetts was set up to collect the names of persons willing to subscribe £1 shares to rent or build a suitable hall. If there was a sufficient response the money was to be put into a Building Society. By November the Society was meeting at the Guildhall Assembly Rooms, Constitution Hill.

At this same meeting in August 1862, a crisis in the circulation and finances of the *National Reformer* was also discussed. A further Committee of Morris, Evans, Charles and Hackwood was elected to collect money from all those prepared to buy shares in the National Reformer Company. The Society was already doing all it could to increase circulation, it was asserted, but further suggestions were made. One speaker, a newsagent, offered to deliver the paper at cost price to anyone living within one mile of his house. Another was willing to pay double for the paper. Others suggested that all members take two copies each week and yet another knew that 'many of our Birmingham friends' would take six copies a week 'rather than permit the paper to succumb.'

The autumn of 1862 saw a full programme of meetings of local speakers at the Guildhall Assembly Rooms. Charles gave lectures on *The Living God* and *The Religion of a Secularist*. J. Bolland spoke on *Objections to the Bible* and Smith on *Paine's Works*. There was also some social activity. After one of Charles' lectures 'two of his lady friends enlivened the proceedings by singing some pretty glees.' Thomas Evans gave one of his *Evenings with the Poets*. He commenced with a rhymed address of his own and followed with selections from Shelley (the 6th and 7th cantos from Queen Mab), Hood and Mackay and the comic Ingoldsby Legends of Barham. It was 'a very pleasant evening' Thomas Fayes reported.

1863 was not only a full year, but a controversial one. Much of the controversy revolved around John Bolland, who became secretary of the society in that year. Bolland's weekly reports of meetings to the *National Reformer* tended to contain an unwonted critical note, which led to Bolland being similarly critically reported on by Thomas Evans. The Society was further upset in February by yet another move; this time to the Balmoral Rooms, Great Hampton Row. Bolland was a young, new broom. He was an enthusiastic advocate of open-air propaganda which 'respectable' Secularists decidedly eschewed, contending that it was unproductive and led to rioting and clashes with authority that did more harm than good to the Cause.

Bolland had a good literary style, well displayed in the report below, which nicely points the contrast between Holyoake's more gentle advocacy of secularism and Bradlaugh's abrasive, militant approach:

On Sunday the 15th (of March) Mr. G.J. Holyoake delivered three exceedingly good lectures to very respectable audiences and was listened to with that earnest and marked respect which this gentleman everywhere wins, and so well deserves. Mr. Baker presided, to the great satisfaction of the members, whose esteem he has won as a gentleman and a true Secularist.

Mr. Holyoake wins a hearing by his gentlemanly manner, exactness of speech, facility of expression; and though lacking force, his discourses lack not lucidity of thought, nor solidity of argument. He is not strong, but clear in language; he is not powerful, but polished in eloquence; not bold, but pure in style. Though he could not steer the barque of Unfavourable Views through the troubled waters of popular opinion proudly, majestically, defiantly and rapidly; yet, he could guide it smoothly, gracefully, pleasantly, softly — but slowly. He reasons not to crush, but pierce; not to dispel, but penetrate; not to banish, but expose; not to cast aside, but to examine; not to destroy, but to analyse the wrong, the darkness, the corruption, forms of systems that surround us . . . .

There were many strange faces present, and many grown strange from long absence . . . .

A Christian gentleman at the evening lecture declared that if that was Secularism he was a Secularist, every inch of him. He believed in the equal enjoyment of this world's good things, more action and less prayer, and if the devil brought him a good coat, he would certainly wear it.

Mr. Holyoake replied, and the meeting dispersed, after a pleasant and instructive day. Tea was provided for friends from a distance, and the social chat over the social cup, was not the least agreeable part of this day well spent.

In May, Bolland reported that an advertised speaker, Mr. Hiron, had failed to appear on the grounds that he was not prepared. This reminded Bolland of the story of the man who would not enter the water until he could swim! In June it was the turn of Joseph Barker to be on the wrong end of one of Bolland's blasts; here, however, his criticism was in line with Bradlaugh's opinion of his erstwhile co-editor.

Mr. Barker, that man of many coats and colours delivered two lectures at the Balmoral Rooms. Many came out of curiosity to see this character and were thoroughly disgusted at the amount of cant and humbug more fitting to Spurgeon or Weaver instead of the wise reformer and intelligent leader that Barker aspires (vainly) to be.

The previous month Bolland had been critically reported on by Thomas Evans. Bolland had lectured the Society on *'Man's Ills and Comforts'*. Evans complained that the subject required definitions which had not been forthcoming and instead they were given a rather rambling speech on Christianity. The speaker appeared to be in a blissful state of uncertainty as to what the ills and uncertainties were. Evans concluded that in one so young, Bolland had some merits as a speaker, but he dealt so much in generalisations that it was difficult to follow his reasoning.

In June 1863 Bolland put his case for open-air activity. Birmingham, he said, was advantageously placed for a vigorous Freethought propaganda. There was no lack of men or talent, only of will. They paid heavy rents for halls and enclosed themselves within brick walls during the summer months. He heard people say that outdoor propaganda was not respectable, would lead to popular violence, or that members' personal interests precluded it. 'But you who plead you have families dependent upon you, must consider that your inactivity, cowardice and false decency will afflict your families with evils you now shrink from facing.' It was a source of regret to see the beauty of the weather and the general indifference to any kind of outside gathering. Bolland concluded that it should be left to the Committee to decide, '. . . but if we had the ability and experience of some of our fellow members we would resign our official positions and do our utmost individually.'

Whatever the decision of the Committee was, Bolland himself began open-air activity in June and in this was strongly supported by Thomas Evans. At his first meeting at Gosta Green, Bolland was stated to have been surrounded by a dense mass of persons for two hours. The police, 'who discovered what sort of rubbish he was spouting' wished to drive him away, 'but their stupidity in these matter is proverbial.' Bolland was asked to go to the police station, but he refused 'offering his card instead'.· He was not arrested. Evans ended his report with a rebuke to members:

> If our friend continues to hold Gosta Green pitch next week we hope he will not have to say, as he did last week, that he went alone and unaided.

Opposition appears to have made the Gosta Green pitch impossible to maintain. The next week the Secularists found their platform occupied by Mr.W. Osborne, (a Christian who sometimes attended the secularists' indoor meetings):

> Osborne is the renowned Hebraist of the Brindley, Grant and Cumming school. By his eccentricities and offensive conduct he won the admiration and support of the more ignorant and fanatical Christians. We treated his challenges with contempt. Christians now greatly outnumber us, although we inaugurated these meetings.

A further report stated, 'We were not at our post last Sunday because we were not prepared to meet the *forcible* arguments of Irish popery. We might take up a fresh position in the town or accompany a few friends to nearby towns for a week.'

The Secularists moved to Smithfield Market where Bolland was arrested and fined 5/-d. with 7/6d. costs for speaking to an excited crowd of 500 people. The arrest had been initiated by a weighing machine proprietor who had requested the police to move Bolland on and he had refused to go. By the end of July the Secularists were at the back of the town hall, where Chamberlain Square now is. This was another traditional meeting place of radical and Christian speakers. They found Mr. Flint, a Deist, with a few people round him. The Secularists opened up and when people learned they were atheists, the crowd grew. 'We made many friends and many enemies. We intend next week to speak at the rear of the Town Hall and at Calthorpe Park in the afternoon.'

The outdoor meetings continued in August. Bolland reported:

> Our Sunday meetings are more encouraging. We were first looked on with suspicion, but now the greater part of the crowds show interest. We occasionally meet with zealous Christians unconscious of their opponents' strengths who rush to combat but retire precipitously, although we like some opposition as truth never shows to better advantage than when placed side by side with error. Active friends distribute handbills, tracts and past numbers of the *National Reformer*.

With the autumn programme of lectures, outdoor activity tailed off. Flint lectured to the society on *Moral Evils* in October. Evans reported, 'He is somewhat excitable in his gestures and too emphatic in his declarations, but the lecture was interesting.' In November Holyoake was at the Balmoral Rooms. 'There was a small meeting on account of the wet weather.' In December an additional newsagent handling the *National Reformer* was announced and also the commencement of a singing class on Wednesdays at a charge of 3d. a month.

1864 was a year of quiet activity. The annual general meeting in January elected a committee of twelve with T. Davies as president, and Thomas Evans as secretary. In his inaugural address, Davies objected to Holyoake's views that Christianity was becoming more tolerant and that Freethought propaganda should therefore be less offensive. Evans gave a poetical and historical account of *Witches and Witchcraft*.

Flint, the Deist, seems to have been welcomed as a critical contributor to the Society's proceedings. He had originally been described as 'a vegetarian and teetotaller who objected to the bible because it did not advocate these principles.' In January he reviewed R.T. Loveridge's *Christian Power and Sceptic Weakness* and in May 'We were entertained by our amiable friend, Mr. Flint, on *Dietics*.'

In May a 'more than average attended' general meeting discussed a financial problem in the affairs of the society, but was told that it now had a fair prospect of being solved. Also at this meeting, Evans tendered his resignation as secretary. 'But this was met with such unfeigned regret that Mr. Evans was induced to reconsider the whole position.' For the rest of the year reports in the *National Reformer* however, tended to be signed by the Burns brothers Ernest and Henry and a member using the pseudonym Julian. Also in May the 'renowned Whitsun Fair lecture' was given by John Bolland who spoke on *Catholicism So-called*.

Summer outdoor activity was not on the same scale as the previous year. In June a meeting at Calthorpe Park was advertised, but there was no subsequent report of it.

In August the Society devoted two meetings to the U.S. Civil War. Also in August there was an excursion to Knowle costing 2/-d. including tea.

> We mustered stronger than we had expected. There were many fair faces
> and joyous little ones. We have hitherto neglected such events. We are
> punished by our lack of sociability, friendliness and cheerfulness whenev-
> er these are absent.

The lack of activity in the summer was acknowledged by a report in October, 'After a long interval of relaxation, we recommenced our secular life with a visit from Iconoclast', but reports of autumn activity were sparse. In December Holyoake visited the society with a judicious mixture of biblical criticism and current affairs. In the morning he spoke on *The Effect of Reading the Bible a Second Time*. His afternoon lecture was on *Those who had Abandoned their Principles or whose Principles had Abandoned Them*. This dealt with Thomas Cooper, Joseph Barker, J.B. Bebbington and John Gordon, all of whom had been leading Secularists but had recently returned to or been newly converted to religion. In the evening there was a 'full and warm house' for the *Conversion of Murderers: People who had attended the Execution of Muller.*

1865 was another quiet year. The Society continued to meet at the Balmoral Rooms. Thomas Evans continued as secretary with Ernest Burns as assistant secretary, although Cattell stood in during the summer. Activity was regularly reported, but there was nothing of note. Nationally it was memorable for the demise of *The Reasoner* after twenty years editorship by G.J. Holyoake. By then the paper was reduced to a four page monthly. It was briefly revived in the early 1870s.

The following year was also one of low key activity dominated by the problem of premises. In February 1866, it was announced that the Society had become tenants of rooms in New Meeting Street, Dale End, 'in the very midst of Orthodoxy.'

> It adjourns (sic) St. Michael's Roman Catholic church (formerly Dr. Priestley's chapel). It is by the side of St. Peter's, Church of England and opposite the Sunday schools and back entrance of Carrs Lane chapel (the late John Angel James' Gospel shop). It will be familiar to many friends as having been used for many years by the Unitarians as their school room and they having been scholars. It is nicely fitted up and is altogether the best room that we have had for ordinary meetings. Some friends have incurred liability for the next twelve months, and the rent is twice as much as at Great Hampton Row. Those willing to pay the usual monthly subscription will be entitled to free admission at all meetings, the use of books and every other privilege as hitherto . . .

This report was signed, J. Morris, secretary pro tem. Within a couple of months, however, the Society had moved again to rooms at St. George's Hall, Upper Dean Street. The reasons for this new move do not appear from the reports,, and Cattell's report only tells us that the Hall held five to six hundred people and there that 'friends from a distance need not fear that they would not get a seat.'

In May, a new list of Birmingham outlets for the *National Reformer* showed that it was available from Mr. Small at 310 New John St. West, Ealger of 30 Duddeston Row and W. Jackson, 11 Hill Street. At this time, the weekly Birmingham listing in the Guide to the Lecture Rooms in the paper disappeared. When it reappeared in July it showed that premises had changed yet again and the Society met each Sunday at 6.30 p.m. at the Atheneum Rooms, Temple Row. After the summer recess John Morris (still secretary pro tem) was announcing in some desperation that the Society was meeting at the Great Western Hotel, Livery Street, to make final arrangements for the session's lectures and 'everyone who takes the slightest interest in the movement is specially invited to attend.' Meetings continued every Sunday, but a report in November, plaintive but prophetic stated that:

> Our only work at present is to report what is going on in our locality. Many of our members are involved in local affairs. This is how it should be.

For the mid-1860s lull was coming to an end. The future was to bring the 1867 Reform Act (in which Birmingham played an important part); the fight for the legalisation of trade unions; the Education Act of 1870 and the campaign for secular education in Birmingham (which was central to the activities of the Society); the Franco-Prussian war and the Paris Commune (which sparked the powerful Republican movement); and the years of Joseph Chamberlain's mayorality and civic reforms on the basis of the Great Boom of 1870 – 74. All of these increased the authority of the Secular Society and its members, now nationally organised and centralised under Bradlaugh's leadership.

Chapter Seven

BIRMINGHAM SECULARISM
1867 – 1874

The momentous issues of this period led to a much greater involvement of the Secular Society in political matters. This is clearly seen in the lecture programmes of the Society which, while never deserting the stimulating intellectual combat with the church, became both more directly political and more practical in their polemics against Christianity.

The first of the great national issues to be raised in the Society was the trade union question. The Sheffield Outrages and the Hornby v Close legal decision endangering trade union funds had led to the setting up of the Royal Commission on Trade Unions in February 1867. Concern with these issues, but more immediately, the Master & Servants Acts had led to the setting up of the Birmingham Trades Council in July 1866. This trade union question revealed rifts in the Secularist ranks. Mr. Collins, a trade unionist of many years standing, lectured on the development of his own society. It admitted none but competent and sober workmen, he said, and as a consequence many respectable employers applied to the union when they required labour. In the ensuing discussing, Cattell said that he argued nothing against Mr.Collins' society, but he was opposed to trade unions on principle; they brought about strife; they acted on the principle that there was a natural antagonism between capital and labour; · they sought to raise wages by artificial means. John Morris (now the permanent secretary) reported that Bolland had replied to Cattell 'with a very argumentative speech.'

The early weeks of February 1867 were taken up with attempts to form a Birmingham and District Secular Union. Also in February a public meeting was announced to discuss *Why Should Working Men attend Churches and Chapels?* to which representative Christians had been asked to speak and the Christian public invited to attend. This was a follow-up to a church conference on the same subject in the same hall which Thomas Evans had fully reported in the *National Reformer* of 3 March 1867.

Evans said that he had attended the Conference expecting to see 'a fine array of parsons all brimful of reasons why people should go to places of worship.' Instead he found 'An incommodious building said to be capable of holding one thousand persons crammed with undoubted working men, all apparently anxious to state their reasons (why they didn't go) and the parson-power almost nowhere.' The rector of St. George's, who presided, stated that in preparation for the Conference he had visited 118 houses in his district and had found that 37% of their inhabitants never went to a place of worship, 32% went occasionally and 49% professed to go regularly. Apart from the matter of arithmetic, the rector had serious doubts about the alleged regularity of the 49%. Working men were then asked to give their reasons for non-attendance at worship and Evans reported them as follows:

> The contrast between the wealth of the church and its representatives and the poverty of the people.
> The opposition of ministers and clergy to the political interests of the people.

Philosophical freethinking objections to Christianity.

'These speakers were objected to by many present, but were heard to the end.'

Temperance speakers who wanted total abolition of drink shops and who complained that the middle class gave them too little support.

Those who thought that people were more profitably engaged teaching their own children than sitting in churches listening to uninteresting sermons.

Experiences of vile conduct of clergyman.

Workers from rural areas who claimed that in the countryside the clergy were the greatest oppressors of the poor.

The class system prevailing within churches. Workers were put in the hardest coldest seats where they could hear little. Wealthier neighbours were put in nicely cushioned seats and when the collection was taken 'a gentleman in kid gloves with a plate covered with baize waited upon the best pews, but a fellow in a fustian jacket thrust a long stick with a square box at the end for the coppers of the poor.

Sale of church livings.

The only day of leisure should not be wasted by going to church.

The hypocrisy of the middle class attending church only as a matter of form.

The Conference had been adjourned to the next week, against the wishes of the chairman. The Secularist meeting took place in the middle of March at the Great Western Hotel and seems to have been a much more sedate affair.

John Bolland opened on the Secular side and a gentleman gave his reasons for attending 'God's house'. Evans, Robbins and Shotten spoke on the Secular side against three other Christian speakers. They were all listened to with the greatest interest.

Dialogue between Secularists and Christians was always a tricky matter. T.H. Ashton, the well-known leader of the Birmingham Protestant Union, complained to the *National Reformer* in March that he had received an invitation to speak worded as follows:

Dear Sir,

You are respectfully invited to attend and defend your faith and principles (you can have equal time with the lecturer) if you think they are worth defending; if not stay away.

Under these circumstances, Ashton had refused to debate with Charles Watts the topic *The Character of Christ as Evidence for the Truth of Christianity*. But Ashton invited Secularists to a meeting without charge at which he would reply to Watts.

1867 was the year of the Reform Act which gave the vote to working class male householders in towns. For the Secularists the issue raised the same dilemma that it had presented to the Chartists — whether their principle of Manhood Suffrage was realisable or whether a compromise was a better way forward. The issue had first been raised the previous September, when a motion *Ought Manhood Suffrage become the Law of the Land* was opened in the negative by Cattell. In February the matter was reopened when a Mr. Thomas argued that while the present aristocracy possessed such power in the state, the conditions for the success of the fight for Manhood Suffrage were not favourable and he therefore considered it a waste of time to agitate the question. This appears to have been supported by Cattell, but it is emphasised that Evans, Wilde, Cope, Morris and Hewins all spoke for Manhood Suffrage and this represented the majority view.

The tangled web of the agitation in Birmingham for the Reform Act of 1867 belongs to the history of the Birmingham branch of the National Reform League; but the Secular Society played its part. A key event (as in 1832) was a monster Birmingham demonstration said to have been attended by 200,000 to 250,000 people. At this demonstration there were eight platforms. The Birmingham Secular Society marched with the 1st Division from Vauxhall to Brookfields, where John Bolland was one of the speakers. This was followed by a monster London demonstration supported by London Secularists. But at this time Charles Bradlaugh resigned as a vice-president of the Reform League, to deprive the opponents of reform of the pretext of attacking the Reform League as an irreligious body. This may also have been a reason for a low profile of Birmingham Secularists in the Reform struggle.

In April 1867 at the Society's A.G.M. Thomas Evans was elected secretary and George Brookes treasurer with an enlarged committee of fifteen. The next month the Society was stressing its non-sectarian nature:

> Our members may be Christians, Secularists or Nothingarians. Our mixed Committee represents every creed.

Before Disraeli's Reform Bill became law in August 1867 Birmingham was rocked by another matter. This was the Murphy Riots of June and the political repercussions the riots were to have.

Murphy had been brought to Birmingham by the Birmingham Protestant Association to preach anti-popery. George Dixon, the mayor, had refused to allow Murphy the town hall to lecture in. The Secularists discussed this at their Birmingham Sunday Lecture and Debating Society (inaugurated at the annual general meeting) in mid-May and were thoroughly divided on the issue. John Bolland supported free speech. Cattell said that Murphy's intention was to inflame public minds and he supported the ban. Hewins said that it was not a question of free speech, but a matter of prudence. Thomas Evans thought that Murphy should have been heard and protected. The Birmingham secularists were at this time indulging in some anti-Catholic discussion themselves on the question of *Should the Confessional be Unmasked or Prohibited ?* This proved so popular that the discussion was carried over to the next week.

After Murphy had been refused the town hall he had built a large wooden building in Carrs Lane which he called a Tabernacle, and on Sunday June 16th delivered his first anti-Catholic lecture. A large number of Irish gathered around the place hissing and throwing stones and in the evening smashed the windows of the house of John Ashton at Dale End, who was the father of T.H. Ashton. They also smashed windows elsewhere. The next day vengeance was wreaked by a rival mob taking possession of Park Street and gutting the houses of the Irish living there. In the afternoon the military were called in, the Riot Act read, and the streets cleared. These matters were reported to the Secular Society by Cattell. Birmingham had been disgraced by the worst Christian riots since the Priestley Riots. Murphy was only making converts from the errors of Catholicism to the errors of Protestantism, he contended. Irishmen were making their sermons in stones and bricks and as long as Christianity was an affair of the heart and not of the head, he, Cattell, would oppose it.

After this the society's Sunday lectures moved to less dangerous ground. For two weeks in June they debated *Has Machinery benefitted the Working Classes?* The motion was negatived by one vote. The next debate was *Should Sunday be Protected?* and was opened by Cattell.

The political consequences of the Murphy riots followed adventitiously from the death of William Scholefield, the senior of the town's two members of parliament, who died at the early age of fifty eight. Cattell reported this matter to the *National Reformer*. The Liberal candidate to replace Scholefield was George Dixon, the mayor. As a direct result of the Murphy Riots this had led to an opposition candidate being put up after many years of unchallenged Liberal ascendency. This was Sampson Lloyd, the Tory banker. The Tories were lambasting Dixon as an enemy of free speech because he had refused the town hall to Murphy, but in fact, Cattell reminded his readers, Dixon was a supporter of John Bright and Reform. Ironically, since Murphy had moved to London, the Liberals had taken over his Tabernacle and meetings were held every night in praise of Dixon. Even more ironically, Murphy himself had turned up at a town hall meeting of Sampson Lloyd, but had only sat in the gallery and had not participated in the meeting. Cattell ended by saying that he would report more fully when the poll closed. 'So far only one window has been smashed and nobody killed.'

Cattell's further report did not appear, as by this time it was the close season for the Secularists. But we know from Langford that Dixon polled 5819 to Sampson's 4214 and that the joint election expenses 'reached the enormous sum' of nearly £9,000 of which Dixon spent £3,700. The next month, the Reform Bill becoming law, Birmingham became entitled to a third member of parliament and 1868 saw further election excitement.

In the autumn of 1867 Birmingham secularists returned to activity with growing support. An unfailing indicator of this was the political nature of the discussions. 'One of the best discussions since the Society commenced' was the verdict on a lecture *Ought the Government to Provide a National System of Secular Education?* This was followed the next week by 'an excellent address by John Bolland on *Should Working Men be sent to Parliament?* A rare comment on the working class character of the Society should be recorded:

> This was a most amusing and interesting debate and not nearly as one-sided as one would expect from an audience of working men.

After Charles Watts had spent another Sunday lecturing in Birmingham, Thomas Evans was reporting ecstatically:

> Better lectures better attended by audiences better pleased we have never had.

In December at a meeting to hear a report back from Cattell of the first conference of the National Secular Society, the branch took a decision to formally constitute itself a branch of the National Secular Society. A committee of fourteen was then elected with Daniel Baker as chairman and John Morris as secretary. It was agreed to continue to support the Sunday Lecture and Debating Society as a separate venture.

1868 was a year of consolidation rather than advance. John Morris, the secretary, became a member of the national council of the N.S.S. The first quarter of the year saw visits from the national speakers Charles Watts and Charles Bradlaugh and Cattell gave a series of readings from Herbert Spencer. The Birmingham Society was also active in promoting the development of Secularism which was taking place in the Black Country.

In April, new steps were taken to acquire premises owned by the Society. A resolution was unanimously carried that a Secular Hall Company should be formed under the limited companies act with shares of £1 denomination. Daniel Baker immediately subscribed £50 and David Kirkwood £20. Some eight or ten other members present also agreed to take shares which meant that nearly 100 shares were applied for. 'The meeting was not large, but if the other 60 or 70 members respond, we will soon have a hall of our own.' A flurry of activity followed; a prospectus was issued, an offer by Iconoclast to come and help the company was gratefully received, directors were appointed with David Kirkwood as company secretary and Daniel Baker as chairman and it was announced that the share subscription could be paid in instalments.

This renewed impetus to acquire their own hall was not unconnected with the fact that the Society was again moving its meeting place. The new venue was the Dining Hall, Slaney Street, Snow Hill. A highlight of the use of these premises was a complimentary dinner given to Charles Bradlaugh in July. At this time Bradlaugh was being prosecuted by the government for failing to comply with a law requiring every newspaper to give sureties of £800 against blasphemous or seditious libel. Bradlaugh had always refused to give such sureties on the grounds that they would probably have been liable to forfeiture about once a month; it was only under Disraeli that the matter was pressed to a prosecution which the government was ultimately to lose.

In July 1868 more mundane matters were also dealt with. A balance sheet for the half year showed a deficit of 8/6d. on an expenditure of £30.4.7d. It was also announced that the Sunday Lecture would be suspended until further notice and the committee would continue to meet every other Tuesday in the Dining Hall.

August brought a sobering report from the Birmingham Secular Hall Co. There was the possibility of the present meeting place being lost by conditions being put on the lessee and this made the project of their own hall more urgent. But 1000 shares were necessary to the success of the venture and only 200 had been subscribed to at that time. David Kirkwood's report ended with the never-failing optimism of the committed, 'In such a town as Birmingham we feel sure that the determination to have such a hall needs only to be widely enough known to ensure its perfect success.'

The general election in November 1868 posed questions to the

Birmingham Secular Society which were only partially revealed in the
National Reformer reports. The Birmingham Trades Council had raised the
question of the working man candidate for the third member granted by
the 1867 Reform Act and the most important issue to the Trades Council
was the protection of trade union funds threatened by the Hornby v Close
decision. The expense of £500 for a working class candidate (£300 a year
salary and £200 election expenses) effectively made this impossible. The
Trades Council therefore eventually supported the Liberal trio of Dixon,
Bright and P.H. Muntz despite the fact that none of these would support
the protection of trade union funds, whereas the Tory duo (Sampson
Lloyd and Sebastian Evans) both promised the legal recognition of trade
unions. In fact, an ex-working man candidate did put in an appearance.
This was none other than George Jacob Holyoake, national Secular
leader and Birmingham born working man. Holyoake lectured at the
Town Hall in late October with Councillor Baldwin (himself a Liberal
nominee for the third seat) and president of Birmingham National
Reform League in the chair. This meeting was reported in the *National
Reformer* under the name of the Birmingham Secular Society without
revealing whether the local Society supported Holyoake. Holyoake gave
an address of two hours which, it was announced, would be published.
Holyoake prints this address in his *Sixty Years of an Agitator's Life* (vol II
p.129); it is much abridged, and it makes no mention of the trade union
question. Holyoake goes on to say that the object of his putting up was
to test and advocate the question of working class representation in
Parliament, but finding that there was no strong feeling on the subject,
he withdrew. The nominations were made on the 16th November with
20,000 people present. Voting took place on the 17th and 18th and the
results announced on the hustings were:

Dixon 15098: Muntz 14614: Bright 14601: Lloyd 8700: Evans 7061

The year 1869 began with the Society in confident mood. The A.G.M.
in January accepted the half-yearly accounts showing expenditure £38
and income £37 and noted that 'members participating in local elections
and other business meant that the affairs of the Society had been
somewhat neglected.'

A special vote of thanks was given to George Brookes, (the lessee of the
Dining Hall) for his generous support in allowing the premises to be used
free of cost on many occasions. Officers elected were David Kirkwood
president, Cattell vice-president, Thomas Evans member of the national
council, George Brookes treasurer, and Joseph Morris secretary.
Lectures had been arranged for every Sunday up to the summer 'and
there was a unanimous feeling for an energetic propaganda in this town.'

In February Cattell was advocating a Midland District Secular
organisation based on Oldbury which had a Temperance Hall of its own.
In March the Society reported that 'our present plan is to vary the
subjects for discussion with scientific lectures and political and social
questions rather than allowing theology a monopoly.' This is the sure sign
that the Society was flourishing and during the winter Morris had spoken
on the *French Revolution*; there had been a discussion on *Politics*; Reddalls
had lectured on *Political Economy* ('but had confined himself to the

Malthusian doctrine') and George Brookes had lectured on *Education*. But trouble was again brewing regarding premises. In the spring of 1869 notices of Birmingham meetings disappeared from the *National Reformer*. When they reappeared in May the Society was meeting at the Coach and Horses, Snow Hill. In June the Society had moved again to the offices of *The Radical* newspaper at 50b, New Street. This notice went on to say that unless all members paid their subscriptions it would be impossible for the committee to take a permanent meeting place. Friends were also requested to look out for suitable premises for the Secular Club and Institute. A summer outing was tentatively under consideration and all those in favour of a Sunday out at Dudley Castle were asked to communicate with the secretary, J. Morris. At the end of June it was announced that 'a suitable place had been offered for 500 people and smaller rooms. All it needs is for members to attend.' In July at the half-yearly meeting (Income £27-10-3d., Expenditure £27-18-4d.) a long discussion on the meeting room took place and it was unanimously decided to return to St. George's Hall, but the room would have to be fitted out and furnished. In August a committee was set up to visit all members to raise the £40 necessary for this purpose. Meanwhile the Society continued to meet at the premises of the *Radical*. At the end of August Morris reported that the premises in Upper Dean Street accommodated 600 people and workmen were then preparing the Hall for a September opening at which Bradlaugh would be present. There was a long list of subscribers. There had also been gifts such as draughts boards and pictures, and George Brookes had contributed a quantity of books. Twelve months rent had also been guaranteed. By early September the £40 target had almost been achieved 'but a further £10 could be advantageously expended.' The Hall would be opened on Wednesday 19th. September with Bradlaugh lecturing not on a theological theme, but the highly topical and radical subject of *The Land, The People and the Coming Struggle*. Admission would be 3d. with reserved seats 6d. The premises had unanimously been given the title of the Birmingham Secular Club and Institute as 'better conveying the image of large operations.' From October the Reading Room would be open every day of the week and all day Sundays for reading, chess, draughts etc. A debating or elocution class would be established. Membership fees would be 2d. a week or 1d. for each visit.

The actual opening of the Hall merited a front page *National Reformer* article by Cattell in his best literary style:

> St. George's Hall was opened to the accompaniment of tremendous thunder and a rain storm. Up to the present the Secular party has been at the mercy of landlords and have been liable to eviction at almost any moment. Its position for thirteen years when a few of us met at a barber's shop has been that of a wanderer. Our home now is Upper Dean Street by Smithfield Market, two minutes away from St. Martin's church.
>
> Anyone coming to the town has only to think of the Bull Ring Riots, look at the old church and enquire for Dean St. when he will see a horse on the top of a building and St. George on top of the horse. Beneath this gigantic figure he will find the Secular Society.
>
> A goodly number of people braved the fury of the elements to greet Mr. Bradlaugh who arrived with his habitual punctuality. For the first time we had reporters from the *Daily Post* and the *Daily Gazette* to take down

words with a view to publication instead of for the guidance of local magistrates. This was followed by a supper party. The latter part of the programme was inaugurated by Kirkwood playing Bradlaugh at draughts,
which Kirkwood won.

Whatever the reasons that took the Society from George Brooke's Dining
Hall back to St. George's Hall, the move was a fortunate one and this
remained the Society's meeting place for several years to come.

Activity flourished in the new premises with classes and social activity,
although the early lectures tended to be theological or historical indicating
that political issues were less pressing. For instance, two early lectures
were on *Radical Characteristics* and the more topical question *Vaccination —
A Folly and a Crime*. The first debate at the hall was *The Execution of Charles
I — Was it Justified?* The motion was opposed by the assistant secretary
A.D. Earles, but affirmed by Joseph Morris, supported by Kirkwood and
Reddalls and carried by a large majority. M.V. Mayer, the old Dudley
Chartist spoke on *The People's Charter — Retrospect and Forecast*, concluding
that all the points of the Charter were in a fair way to becoming the law
of the land. Mayer also spoke on Chartism later in the year 'Censuring
the blunders of the physical force leaders and the hollowness of their
utterances.' Such views would have disturbed the shades of Samuel Cook
and Mayer did not go unopposed, 'Mr. Alger at the close speaking a few
words in favour of the physical force policy.' Yet another historical topic
was a lecture by Kirkwood on *The Antiquities of Egypt*.

The premises crisis earlier in the year does not seem to have affected
the Society's summer activity. The proposed summer visit to Dudley did
take place, and the *National Reformer* published a very long article on the
geology of the area, which was of course, highly relevant to the nineteenth
century controversies on evolution. In addition, the Birmingham society
was the mainstay of district Secular activity in the Black Country centred
on the Oldbury Temperance Hall.

The early 1870s brought national political developments in which
Birmingham was deeply involved. 1870 was the year of the Education Act,
1871 was the year of the Franco-Prussian War and the Paris Commune.
This connected with the organisation of the agricultural workers by Joseph
Arch, the attack on landed property and the aristocracy leading to the
demand for land nationalisation. All of this led to the emergence of the
most powerful Republican movement the country had seen since the days
of George IV. This coincided with the period of Joseph Chamberlain's
greatest radicalism and the Birmingham municipal reforms of the years
of Chamberlain's mayorality (1873 – 76).

It was also the years of the legalisation of the trade unions. All this was
played out on the background of the hectic capitalist boom of 1870 – 74
before the crash of the Great Depression.

In all these events, Secularists played an important, but not the leading
role, and some of these developments are best dealt with separately. One
result of this was that it is difficult to find references to purely Secularist
activity until the appearance of the Birmingham secular monthly
newspaper the *Secular Chronicle* which commenced publication in August
1872.

We do know that Secular classes and discussions were maintained at
St. George's Hall and it was not until July 1871 that it was necessary to

make a special appeal for funds. Then G.H. Reddalls, the secretary, explained that the Hall had been opened for almost two years at an annual cost of about £100. Success had been greater than expected, but heavy expenditure in the previous quarter had made it necessary to appeal to all friends. Lists of donations followed. The previous January about sixty people had attended the annual Thomas Paine tea party. In the first six months of 1871 lectures had included Reddalls on *Jesus and his Teaching*, Kirkwood on *The Advance of Organic Life*, Rugg on *Why I became a Freethinker*, Cattell on *Republicanism*, Ernest Burns on *Female Education* and J. Robson on *John Cade*. Activity continued throughout the summer of 1871 with the monthly tea party and entertainment and a visit from Charles Watts.

In September 1871 the Birmingham society hosted the annual conference of the National Secular Society. The considerations behind the decision to hold the conference in Birmingham were, no doubt, the availability of St. George's Hall in Birmingham and also one of the recurrent booms of Secular activity in the Black Country which made the west midlands probably the most important area of Secular activity at that time. There were delegates from Coventry, Dudley, Oldbury, Tipton and Wolverhampton, while Birmingham provided four delegates — Kirkwood, Morris, Cattell and Reddalls.

The Conference ended with a public meeting at which the Hall 'was filled to overflowing.' But the Conference was not a success. It came at a time of national crisis for the N.S.S. Bradlaugh's finances were depleted and he wanted time to restore them. So neither he, nor Charles Watts stood for the new executive. Under the new executive national membership fell and it was not until 1874 when Bradlaugh first contested Nottingham and resumed leadership of the N.S.S. that the organisation began to grow again.

This national trend does not seem to have affected Birmingham and the Black Country. During 1871 St. Georges Hall housed not only the Secular Society but also the Republican Club and the Land and Labour League. Specifically secular activity continued into the later months of 1871 with a lively social life and lectures such as *Science and the Bible* by Kirkwood, Reddalls on *Population* and Evans on the temperance topic of *The U.K. Alliance Programme*.

Secularist progress continued into 1872 and in June a Birmingham Secular Sunday School was set up run by a committee consisting of Kirkwood, Evans, Sedgwick, Cope and Reddalls 'to further this project'.

In August 1872 the cherished project of a Birmingham secular newspaper materialised. This was the *Secular Chronicle* sub-titled *A Monthly Journal Established to Promote Free Enquiry into Social, Political and Theological Questions and as a Record of Freethought Progress*. It cost one halfpenny and was edited by G.M. Reddalls at 135 Digbeth. It ran until 1879.

The first issue of the *Secular Chronicle* contained an article by Thomas Evans explaining his conversion to Secularism. It followed a fairly familiar pattern. Evans had been brought up as a Methodist. Although he tried for many years he 'never received the glorious conviction that my sins were forgiven.' He sought God 'with all the powers of my nature', but did not find him. He thus saw the Christian religion deserting him rather than the other way round. He then became critical of Christians and Christianity. He progressed to scepticism and then to positive unbelief. Paine's Age of Reason and the *National Reformer* landed him in Secularism.

Francis Neale also had an article in this first issue of the *Secular Chronicle*. Like Mayer, Neale had graduated from Dudley Chartism and had become a national secularist figure resident in Birmingham. Neale claimed that not only were the lower classes deeply imbued with the spirit of religious scepticism, but that the upper classes had also succumbed to its all-pervading influence. There was still much to be done however, particularly as Christianity was taught in grand cathedrals and churches whereas Freethought was propagated in ill-ventilated and badly situated halls and many towns had no place of meeting at all. 'Some of our lecturers, though honest and earnest enough, lack that culture, the presence of which is so greatly attractive in Christian teaching' he concluded.

Thomas Evans also had an article on the Birmingham Club and Institute which adds something to what we already know. The Hall seated 400 to 500 persons and the Club accommodated about forty. The Hall was used on Sundays for lectures and discussions and during the week for penny readings, dancing and dramatic entertainment. There was a good stage with proscenium and scenery fitted up at considerable expense. An excellent Dramatic Club of local members produced entertainment every few weeks. A pianoforte was kept in the Hall which was played at the beginning and end of lectures. The club room was used for the usual purposes of reading, chess, draughts, dominoes etc. There was a good little library to which John Stuart Mill had recently presented copies of the whole of his works. It was therefore a properly constituted Working Men's Club offering all forms of refreshment. On the controversial topic of alcoholic drink, Evans goes on to say that no case of excess had ever been known in the three years the club had been opened and they were quite satisfied it was best to keep ale and the like for those members who used it, because when the public-house incentive to drink was taken away alcohol was used as moderately and harmlessly as tea or coffee. Terms of membership were 8/- a year or 2/- a quarter or 8d. a month or 2d. a week.

In the September issue of the *Chronicle* there was an article by Christopher Charles (Cattell) on the famed Birmingham radical preacher of the Church of the Saviour, George Dawson. 'The aspect of the place and the words of the preacher cheer the hearts of the free enquirer.' In the early days Dawson had indeed been the saviour of the church, Cattell went on, when his congregation had met to sing and dance. It was the only body of churchmen and women who dared to be 'jolly' in the sight of God. Sometimes the allusions and illustrations of Dawson were so droll that the congregation laughed. 'Why not? They don't 'fear God' and have no dread of the "other one".' Dawson was also the 'only preacher who speaks uniformly with respect and honesty of the Atheist and Secularist.'

In the Notes of the Month for September 1872 it was reported that the Birmingham Free Library had refused to accept a gratis copy of the Secular Chronicle on the grounds that its policy was not to accept religious papers. This was considered to be an excuse as there were some religious papers there.

The paper printed poetry and an occasional anti-religious joke such as the following. At a revivalist meeting an old lady prayed fervently 'for the young lambs of the flock'. Whereupon another old lady rose and demanded 'who is to pray for the old ewes?'

The autumn programme of the Society was a full one. In September, two important outside speakers lectured — J. de Morgan and Charles Watts — and as a bonus G.J. Holyoake put in an unexpected appearance at de Morgan's lecture on the *Rights of Man*.

In October the members' general meeting reported an expenditure of nearly £300 with a favourable balance of £16. A committee of thirteen was elected, including two ladies, and the officers were J. Morris president, W. Rudhall treasurer, E. Burns secretary, and E. Sedgwick librarian. The local paper gave the full programme of lectures for each month. From these it can be seen that local lecturers from the autumn to the end of 1872 were Mayer, Reddalls, Kirkwood, E. Burns, Morris and A. Mahony fairly evenly balanced between freethought and political subjects such as Mayer's *Politics — Why the People should Study them.*

In 1873 Birmingham Secularism continued its modest flourishing with the strength to nurture the movement in the Black Country and to provide cadres for the Republican movement.

During the winter the dramatic society was put on a firmer basis. 'Knowing Mr. Burns' predilection for the histrionic art, he was prevailed upon to accept its management.' This necessitated his resignation as secretary of the Society and T.E. Green was elected in his stead with J.F. Hipwood as assistant secretary pro-tem. The librarian reported that he was making a new catalogue of books and gifts of scientific, theological, philosophical and historical works would be thankfully accepted. Noting the influx of young people into the Institute he also suggested that literature of a lighter character would also be acceptable.

It was usual for the president to give a formal presidential address each year. For 1873 Thomas Evans chose the topic of *The Progress of Freethought.* He noted that the Sunday opening of the town's Reference Library and Art Gallery was a step in the right direction as was allowing Mr. Bradlaugh the use of the Town Hall. David Kirkwood's debate with Mr Whitmore in the Temperance Hall had been a triumph. But it was in the press that progress was most manifold. They still had to contend with the *British Workman* dealing out old recantation nonsense and the Religious Tracts Society circulating death bed conversion scenes,but truthful pictures of life by Dickens etc. had more meaning for the working man. The publication of *Essays and Reviews* had caused theological discussion and was evidence of growing scepticism. There had also been an article in the *Birmingham Weekly Post* stating that religious liberty was at the root of all freedom. Another important article had been one in the *Daily Mail* on Dull Sermons. The clergy worried about growing scepticism, but was it not possible that the failure of the church to counteract freethought was due in some measure to their inability to make their own great teachings worth listening to? Avowed scepticism was better than pious lethargy. 'If religion is to be vital it must kindle a living fire in the hearts of the people and that it will never do so long as Sunday after Sunday incompetent clergy drone out pious twaddle to sleepy listeners.' Evans also pointed out that Birmingham now had its own freethought journal in the *Secular*

Chronicle which had been praised by both Bradlaugh and Holyoake.

Winter lectures pressed forward this freethought offensive, and put it in its local context. For instance, Cattell lectured on *The Bible, Unfit to be Used in Schools*. He said that a similar notion of the laws of nature as taught by the bible could be gained by a visit to a modern pantomime. In the bible, people could travel through the air, jump out of their graves, live on nothing, walk on the sea, blow down buildings with trumpets and see all the kingdoms of the world without a telescope from the top of a high hill. 'Is this the kind of stuff to put in the little heads of children who will have to earn their bread and cheese by manual labour and mechanical skill?' Cattell ended by urging direct secular representation on the local School Board around the existing programme of the Education League.

There were also lectures attacking pseudo-sciences which some free-thinkers had previously supported. Kirkwood, for instance, lectured against Phrenology which had been much admired by the earlier Owenite socialists and was said to be favoured by women because it disproved any alleged mental inferiority of women. G.H. Reddalls also gave two lectures on *Spiritualism*, 'giving an able exposé of modern spiritualism.' Reddalls also lectured on *The Soul*, Kirkwood on *The Religion of Science* and Reddalls followed up with *Secularism the True Religion*.

Activity continued into the summer. Among the more widely reported meetings was one in June when Evans reviewed T. Brassey's book *Work and Wages*. He said that while not necessarily endorsing all the views of the author, the book was worthy of the attention of working men and contained very valuable information. It was essentially a middle class production advocating fair remuneration of labour from a purely commercial viewpoint, concluding that dear labour was the cheapest labour. E. Burns reported that 'a very animated discussion followed in which Brassey was rather sharply criticised!' This is not to be wondered at as Brassey remains a very potent source for Optimists in the perennial debate on the standard of living in the nineteenth century. Brassey's thesis was that well paid English/Irish railway building navvies were more productive than lower paid railway labour in Europe, S. America and elsewhere.

The summer outing, in August, was to Sutton. The weather was good for the picnic after a rainy week. The party 'strolled through the pleasure gardens of Mr. Cole and then took tea. Afterwards we proceeded through woods and the wild, open common. At 9 p.m. we returned, well pleased with the excursion.' In September another catalogue of books was prepared and gifts again solicited for 'the very respectable library'.

Attendance at the 4th Annual General Meeting in November was 'very good'. The balance sheet showed revenue £329 and expenditure £322 and a committee of the enormous number of 30 was said to have been elected. The officers were Thomas Evans president, W. Rudhall treasurer, Ernest Burns reverted to secretary, George Gosling became assistant secretary and G. Sedgwick remained the librarian.

The triennial School Board elections occupied society members during the autumn and in November Cattell reported a victory for the freethinkers on the Birmingham School Board. This overturned the church and Tory victory in the original elections when Liberal attempts to grab all the seats had resulted in their failure to gain overall control.

Other events during the years had been the loss of David Kirkwood, who emigrated to American in April and gave a farewell address to the Society. In June a national Freethinkers' Benevolent Society had been set up 'to make provision for the sick and poor of the Freethinkers' party'; a local lecture was held in aid of the Fund when Mayer lectured on *Heaven*. Monthly tea parties continued and in December the party was regaled by readings by Mr. Holland of Bilston. This was followed by 'two or three selections by the Secular Glee Club which elicited much approbation'.

The last year of the great Victorian capitalist expansion was 1874. The beginning of the year brought reports of flourishing activity in both Birmingham and the Black Country, but by the autumn activities were much curtailed. Reports for the year are scarce in both the *National Reformer* and the *Secular Chronicle*, and by the end of the year only the Birmingham Secular Club was being advertised in the Guide to Lecture Rooms column in the former journal. From the sparse reports we can cull the following.

In January J. Russell opened a discussion on *Food*. This was topical in view of a recent outcry on the dearness of meat. The lecturer suggested that the best way of bringing down the price was not to buy it. Here was yet another strand of some Secularists' thinking — vegetarianism. In March there was 'an absorbing lecture' on *Shylock*. Shakespeare was a very popular topic among Secularists and they made a considerable contribution to the strong Birmingham tradition of Shakesperean studies. In September George Bill spoke on *Macbeth*.

In June G. Starling lectured on *The Positive Religion of August Comte*. Gosling reported 'a considerable amount of criticism at the end'. Positivist influence, particularly their assistance to the trade unions, was around its peak at the time and its weaknesses as an alternative to revealed religion would be in the minds of Secularists. In July Foote was in the west midlands for a lecture tour, but his Birmingham meetings presumably created little stir as there are no reports of them in the *National Reformer*.

At the end of August the lecture programme for the autumn session was announced, but a notice the following month of a Mutual Improvement class was an unfailing indicator of falling public support.

Chapter Eight
BIRMINGHAM REPUBLICANISM
1870 – 1874

Republicanism revived as a significant political trend in Britain from 1870 with the outbreak of the Franco-Prussian War, the proclamation of the second French Republic and the setting up of the Paris Commune in the autumn. The abiding strength of Republicanism was hostility to the monarchy and the aristocracy as totally incompatible with democratic forms of government. The practical examples of Republics were of the English Revolution of the seventeenth century and the French and American Revolutions of the eighteenth century. The immediate impetus to the growth of Republican sentiment was the overthrow of Louis Napoleon abroad and the unpopularity of the prolonged withdrawal of Queen Victoria from public life after the death of Prince Albert together with persistent rumours of her relations with John Brown. In addition there was a strong land movement attacking landed property and the aristocracy. This demanded land nationalisation both to acquire for the nation the increment of increased land values and also the provision of small land holdings; the latter demand was triggered by appalling rural poverty and the rise of Joseph Arch's Agricultural Union.

In the autumn of 1870 a national monthly journal entitled *The Republican* appeared and adopted the democratic programme of The Land and Labour League formed the previous autumn. The nine point programme of the Land and Labour League included: Land Nationalisation and Home Colonisation; National Secular, Gratuitous and Compulsory Education; A Single Property Tax; Reduction of hours of Labour; Equal Electoral Rights with Payments of Members.

By February 1871 Cattell formed a Birmingham Republican Club which met on the premises of the Secular Society. He became president and G.H. Reddalls secretary. There was a very elaborate constitution and three categories of members — Active, Passive and Honorary — elected by ballots of members. In April the *Republican* was commenting that the Republican Club movement had taken root all over the country with greater speed than the Working Men's Club Union a few years previously. The *Republican*, however, is a disappointing source of information with regard to Republicanism in Birmingham and the Black Country and it is to the *National Reformer* that we continue to turn for information of the local movement. From July 1871 there was a regular weekly Republican Club column in the *National Reformer* and regular reports from Birmingham were printed.

Republicans and Secularists continued to thrive together at St. George's Hall. In October the Town Hall was refused for a Republican meeting and it was reported that they were awaiting the outcome of the election of a new Council and mayor and would then renew their application. Republican subjects became more frequent at Secularist meetings, as for instance in January 1872 when Cattell spoke on the *House of Lords* and in November when E. Burns lectured on *Napoleon*.

The Republicans also took their agitation outside. In August 1872 at the Birmingham Eclectic Club Charles Higgs gave an address on *The American Declaration of Independence*. 'Everything Republican was lustily cheered' it was reported. Birmingham Republicans were also active in promoting Clubs in the Black Country. By December 1872 five local Clubs were reporting in the *National Reformer* — Birmingham, Oldbury, Walsall, West Bromwich and Wednesbury.

Republicanism continued to prosper in 1873. By March the Birmingham Republican Club had moved to its own premises at 42 Newhall Street. In March Cattell lectured at the Secular Club on the Land Question — *Should the Government be the sole Land-owner and Private Property in Land Cease?* Cattell was also at the Birmingham Debating Society the same month speaking on *Is a Republic the best form of Government and is England fit for it?* Cattell was supported by George Bill, J. Lampard, M. Dalzell, E.M. Adams and David Kirkwood. The report stated that this series of meetings began on January 12th and was the most interesting ever held by the Society. The room on each occasion was crowded to its utmost capacity. Also in March an All Saints Ward branch of the Republican Club was formed.

In June, the Birmingham Republican Club was honoured with a message of greetings from Garibaldi to Cattell. By October the Republican Club had moved a little further down the road to 30, Newhall Street. At this time the Club had invited John Bright to put his views on the following questions:

1. Representation of labour in the House of Commons.
2. Payment of candidates' expenses out of rates or taxes.
3. Reduction of our military expenses.
4. The abolition of grants, payments or allowances except to persons who have earned them by adequate and valuable public service.
5. Disestablishment and disendowment of the Church of England.
6. Shorter Parliaments.
7. Extension of the suffrage in the Counties and redistribution of seats according to population.
8. Equitable legislation for both employers and employed.
9. National compulsory, free Education.
10. Absolute and unconditional repeal of the Game Laws.
11. The Land Laws: abolition of primogeniture and entail; a reform that will make the transfer of land cheap, secure and easy so as to allow the acquisition of small-holdings as well as large ones.
12. Mr. Chamberlain's platform, free Church, free land, free labour and free schools.

Cattell reported the remarks of the London *Daily Mail* on this:

> The Birmingham Republicans are not overburdened with modesty. They have actually put a string of twelve political topics to Mr. Bright, upon which they coolly request him to 'state his present views'. Now, as each of these twelve subjects is good for at least an hour's speech, the Birmingham Republicans have imposed upon Mr. Bright, rather a heavy task. However there is nothing like pluck.

Birmingham Republicanism reached its apogee in 1873 and the highlight of that year was the hosting of the first National Republican Conference at St. George's Hall in May. by this time the *Republican* newspaper had disappeared and the Conference was most fully reported in the *National Reformer* where it occupied most of the sixteen pages of that paper despite its black bordered front page being entirely devoted to the announcement of the death of John Stuart Mill.

The location of the Conference in Birmingham reflected the importance of the movement in Birmingham and the Black Country and also the personal influence of Christopher Charles Cattell. According to Bradlaugh, Cattell had inaugurated the first Republican Club in Birmingham and all the others had followed. The number of delegates at the Conference, although larger than the number at the National Secular Society at the same Hall eighteen months earlier, was not great. Eight London bodies were represented, but Mr Le Lubez represented both Deptford and Greenwich's Secular Society and its Radical Association as well as the central council of the Land & Labour League. Also represented were the Universal Republican League German Section, the London Patriotic Society, Mile End Land & Labour League and the Eleusis Club Chelsea. Charles Bradlaugh and G.W. Foote were there not as the two leading Secularists but as delegates from the London Republican Club. Provincial delegates came from thirty-nine localities representing forty organisations. One quarter of these were from the west Midlands. The central Birmingham Republican Club was represented by Cattell, Reddalls and Ubersax. The Birmingham All Saints Republican Club delegates were N. Harrison, Mahony and Potter. Other west Midlands representatives came from Bilston, Kidderminster, the Potteries, Stafford, S. Staffs & E. Worcs Secular Union, Walsall, West Bromwich and Wolverhampton. John Bright, the Birmingham M.P., had been sent an invitation by Cattell, but had sent a very sharp letter of refusal asserting that our forefathers had suffered nearly a century of unsettled government consequent on the overthrow of the monarchy brought on by the folly and the crimes of the monarch of the time and that forty years of improvement gave him the hope of establishing a government good enough to avoid the troubles which he believed inseparable from the uprooting of an ancient monarchy.

The Conference went to great pains to dissociate itself from any image of violence or force. Bradlaugh opened the Conference by expressing his satisfaction at the wide representation from Glasgow to Dover, although they were only there as private individuals. He reminded them that they met in the town so important to the passing of the 1832 Reform Act. Bradlaugh then warned against physical force or illegal methods. He made the interesting distinction that while not absolutely against violence, force was justified only to protect the rights they had, not to try to win those they had not; the place to win new rights was the polling booth.

The main speaker, however, was C.C. Cattell, obviously the driving force behind the Conference. Cattell explained that when he established the Birmingham Republican Club he clearly set out the objectives, and many of the Clubs subsequently established had adopted the same objectives. The purpose of the Conference was now to seek agreement on these objectives and to see what delegates might want to alter or add. These objectives were: to unite all Republicans within a given area; to correspond with Republicans at home and abroad; to collect books, papers etc. on Republican doings and institutions in all countries and all ages; to promote all efforts in Parliament, platform and press tending to Republicanism. The object of actions taken by the Clubs was to teach the best principles of civil government. That the word Republic should be used to signify a Commonwealth in which public affairs shall be managed by persons appointed by the people. That the objects of the Clubs be promoted by intellectual, legal and moral means alone. Cattell continued that his hope was that Clubs should take up questions concerning the industrial class, asserting priority of life and manhood over class and property. He expected such Clubs eventually to supersede Whig, Liberal and Radical Associations, forming one party, that of the People. Cattell suggested that until the movement could afford a daily newspaper, a supplement to be called Republican Reporter might be issued from such a paper as the *National Reformer*. The Republican Clubs should also take up every new issue that arose to avoid the waste and over-lapping of the proliferation of new organisations for every fresh demand.

The Conference then unanimously passed a resolution to set up a national Republican organisation for the carrying out of a political programme upon which all Republican or Democratic Clubs and organisations could agree. The Conference then ran into trouble concerning the name of such an organisation. Charles Watts representing the Republican Clubs of Aberdeen and Plymouth said that by a Republic he understood government by and for the people apart from all class distinction. The members he represented wished him to make clear that they favoured moral and legal means only and did not aim at revolution. It was then proposed that the organisation be called the Universal Federal Republican League. To this Foote and Watts promptly proposed that the name be the National Republican League. Supporters of the former then asked why it could not be called the Federal Republican League and this led on to a lively discussion on what was meant by Federal and whether Scotland, Ireland and Wales should be united in one Republic as in the U.S.A. or whether they should be separate. 'Universal' also came in for criticism. Did it mean that they should always aid Republicans in Poland, Spain, France etc; did universal include Fiji and what did Republicanism mean there? Eventually on the further recommendation of Cattell, the Foote-Watts amendment of National Republican League was carried by forty to one.

A dampener was then put on proceedings by a long, powerful and extremely well constructed speech by H.V. Mayer, the ex-Chartist from Dudley, who pointed out that while he personally was a Republican and wished the Cause well, it must be recognised that those who set out to subvert the institutions of a country required a considerable amount of confidence, audacity or rashness. It must commend itself to the nation at large:

> The cautious will enquire as to its legality, the prudent as to its feasibil-
> ity, the philosophic as to its value and the statesman as to its
> expedience. . .

And then there would be hosts of others who from prejudice, interest or fear would oppose it, apart from the six tenths of the population who had no political opinions or interests at all. Much harm had been done by those Chartists who had demanded 'the whole Charter and nothing but the Charter' and had obstructed or opposed those other movements which between them had well-nigh won the Charter in the intervening years. Mayer ended, a trifle inconsistently, it would seem, by saying that having committed themselves to the Cause there should be no feebleness or half-heartedness and although the task was arduous and great, with courage and perseverance most things were possible.

Cattell then proposed that the movement be divided into districts with radii of about 50 miles and a central executive be elected to meet in London. The former was a favourite organisational device of Cattell's and he spent much of his time promoting Birmingham district or midland district organisation. But an amendment approved a central Executive Council only. Bradlaugh then proposed, rather surprisingly, that until the next Conference, the delegates present constitute the Central Executive with power to add four to their number. This proposal met with opposition, but after an amendment proposing a seventeen strong elected executive had been defeated, the original motion was carried. Bradlaugh then proposed that any Republican Club not represented at the Conference should also have power to add a delegate to the Executive until the next Conference, which he thought should be in a few months' time.

Cattell then pursued his proposal of a Republican supplement to the *National Reformer*. This Bradlaugh strongly deprecated, stating that he had no means of starting a new journal and that the only other possibility of a Republican publication was from capital provided by a foreigner. He, Bradlaugh, would report as much Republican activity as possible, but what he was already doing in the *National Reformer* was as much as could be done. Potential Republican support was wider than that for the *National Reformer*.

> If he could find others to do the work he would hold his tongue about Republicanism because of the stigma that attached to it through his opinions on other subjects...

Cattell then withdrew his resolution.

Mr. Hill (presumably Joseph Hill the Leicester delegate) then complained that the Conference had been convened for Sunday. Some Republicans were sincere Christians and would not attend on that account. Bradlaugh replied that if the objection had been foreseen the Conference could quite as easily have been convened for a Monday. The Conference then adjourned.

The next day the Conference re-convened in the Town Hall Committee Room. Attendance was smaller, those present being exclusively delegates. It first passed a vote of thanks to the *Morning News* and *Daily Post* for their impartial reporting of the previous day's proceedings and a vote of thanks to the *Daily Gazette* for *not* attending 'previous experience having shown that their reports were unreliable.'

The Conference then turned to a series of resolutions prepared by the London Club whose delegates were Bradlaugh and Foote. The first was:

> That this Conference declares the Republican form of government to be the only form worthy of the support of a civilised people; meaning by a Republic or Commonwealth a state or a unity of states which guarantees the fullest individual liberty compatible with general security and in which the sovereign power resides in deputies elected by the people according to equitable principles of representation to the complete exclusion of all

hereditary or class privileges, which are absolutely contradictory to every principle of justice and of reason.

G.W. Foote, moving the resolution said that there might be differences of opinion among Republicans as to the proper sphere of government action, but he thought there was very little doubt in the minds of all present that the chief end of government was to secure the fullest exercise of the faculties of every individual, so long as this did not interfere with its due exercise in other persons. It was absolutely necessary that there should be some distinction between the sphere of individual action and State action. It was always possible to oppose the tyranny of one man who might have usurped power, but this could not be done when the majority of the people constituted the tyrant. The only way to protect the people was to narrow the limit of state action. There were at present many 'shams' but the greatest was that while nominally Parliament had all the power, actually it was vested elsewhere. Mr. Drake, the delegate from the Mile End Land & Labour League, seconded. Walter Rhodes from Leeds supporting the motion read an extract from an old speech of John Bright's showing how much his views had changed. He had done great good in the past and had done indirectly more to create the present movement than any other living statesman (applause.) So they could now afford to let him sit by and rest on the laurels he had gained — (laughter) — while they, who had not gone through so much Court influence as he, would try to perfect another form of government. This resolution was then carried unanimously. Foote then also moved a successful resolution on Universal Suffrage:

> That every human being should have the legal right to vote for the election of all public representatives unless incapacitated by non-age or privation of reason.

Charles Bradlaugh then moved:

> That the special affairs of England, Scotland and Ireland should, if the people of those countries so desire, be managed by local, separate Parliaments, and all Imperial questions be decided by the federal government.

He said that although the resolution was limited to Britain his own sentiments would include India in the same fashion, for he thought every state sufficiently marked by geography and habits should legislate on its own local affairs. This debate was used by those who advocated Home Rule for Ireland to stress that their intention was not to separate from England, but to share her future whether that be monarchical or republican.

The next resolution passed unanimously was one proposed by Austin Holyoake that all persons should be equal before the law and justice should be administered to eliminate the invidious distinction between rich and poor through the costliness of its operations.

The Conference then turned to Land Reform and unanimously passed a motion by Bradlaugh that:

> The tenure of land should be subject to considerations of general utility and that no supposed right of private ownership therein should be

allowed to stand against the economical and social requirements of the
nation; and that all legal causes of land monopoly should be at once
removed, and the land tax be equitably apportioned, as a first step in the
direction of land tenure reform.

Next, the House of Lords was considered. Charles Watts moved:

> That the House of Lords, being a mere relic of feudalism and founded
> upon the exploded hereditary principle should as soon as possible be
> abolished. (Applause.)

Watts said that the resolution demanded the abolition of the House of
Lords as at present constituted. It was quite possible that under a
Republic it would be necessary to have a second chamber but it would
be formed very differently from the present one. This was passed
unanimously.

In the next resolution Birmingham delegates clashed with the London
ones. Le Lebus moved:

> That standing armies are inimical to the moral and industrial welfare of
> the State, and a perpetual menace to its safety, and should, therefore,
> give way to a national citizen force.

Mahony moved an amendment that 'our armies be so constituted that the
greatest portion be occupied in times of peace in commercial industries.'
This found no seconder. Reddalls strongly opposed the original resolution and Cattell moved to substitute 'should be abolished' in place of
'should give place to a national citizen force'. Bradlaugh appeared to
support Cattell. He said that if they looked at it that the Republic they
were to form would require any organised force except that necessary for
the prevention of ordinary crime, then they understood Republicanism
differently from him. Foote favoured a citizen army, for if every citizen
were a soldier, the soldiers could not tyrannise over the citizens. The
resolution, with Cattell's amendment, was carried with four dissentients.

The Conference then moved to education where the Secular/Radical,
Secular/Liberal split was clearly revealed. It was moved:

> That this Conference urges the establishment of a national system of
> compulsory, gratuitous, secular, and industrial education.

Foote objected to the resolution almost entirely. He might not object to
the state making education compulsory but he strenuously objected to any
pauperising measure by which the state would provide free education to
all. Free education meant that children were to be educated by taxation
levied from the mass of the people. By what principle could a man with
two or three children be called upon to pay for the education of another
man's five or six children? Ferguson, the Glasgow delegate pointed out
that having passed a resolution on Federalism it was inconsistent to try
to bind such countries as Scotland or Ireland to secular education when
the vast majority supported religious education. Bradlaugh said that he
spoke with considerable diffidence. He wanted every child to be properly
educated, but Foote had put that which was perfectly true. He objected
to the word 'gratuitous', as whether the cost was to be paid to the
schoolmaster or through the rates, it was not free. They proposed

providing precisely the same facilities to the improvident as to the provident. He thought the matter ought to be referred to the next Conference for the best men on either side to put their views, as he could neither vote for the present resolution nor did he wish to vote against it. Foote than wanted to put an amendment that Bradlaugh's suggestion be acted upon. This was objected to on the grounds that Foote had already spoken in the debate. Eventually, the original resolution was carried by twenty-seven votes to two. So there were obviously many abstentions.

The London motions being disposed of, the Conference then elected G.W. Foote secretary and R.A. Cooper president of the new organisation. Bradlaugh then brought the Conference to its logical conclusion by moving that every borough and county in England should be prepared to stand a Republican candidate 'where other candidates did not come up to certain points in reference to legislation', and this should be done even if it resulted in a victory for the Conservatives. This was carried with acclamation.

The Conference closed, as most such conferences did, with a mass meeting at the Town Hall. Such a galaxy of speakers would have brought a large attendance at any time, but on this occasion it was reported that 'the immense building was crowded with an enthusiastic audience'. R.A. Cooper presiding said that a Conference called by the London Republican Club had been convened in Birmingham to set up a national Republican Party. Harrison, from Birmingham, then moved:

> That this meeting heartily approves of the holding of the Republican Conference in Birmingham and hails with delight the establishment of the National Republican League.

Cattell supported this by asking those who approved of the association to join it. Their ideas were not utopian; they were only carrying forward the work of the men of the old Political Union of the days of 1832. As Republicans they were for peace, law and order and also for universal justice. The resolution was carried with only about a dozen dissentients. Charles Watts then moved 'That this meeting is of the opinion that a Republic is the best form of government and pledges itself to endeavour by all legal and moral means to establish Republican government in England.' Foote seconded him and then the great orator himself rose to support the motion. Bradlaugh was received 'with deafening cheers again and again renewed'. A small number of hecklers tried to interrupt his speech and sang 'God save the Queen', but Bradlaugh brushed this aside. He said that Republican feeling was widespread in the country and asked why this was so. It was because for two hundred years we had been ruled by a family which had neither kith nor kin with us, had lived on our earnings, had grown rich at our cost and had never added to the honour or glory of the country. How could there be loyalty to those responsible for such a war as the Crimean and who, with Hanoverian troops, had hewed down Scotch rebels and hunted Irishmen struggling for their freedom. They did not seek violent means and parliament, which had sanctioned the present monarchy, could also dismiss it. There could be no such armed conflict as there had been on the removal of Charles I because parliament was already in control. Monarchy supported the class of great earls and lords who monopolised the land and grew rich on the unearned income of increased values. He agreed with John Bright that it was easier to uproot monarchy than to establish a new form of government, but as it was impossible to get from this system the legislation necessary for the improvement of the condition of the people, he pleaded for a Republic. Mr. Bradlaugh 'resumed his seat amidst tremendous cheering and waving of hats and handkerchiefs' and the resolution was carried 'with about a dozen dissentients among the many thousands present.'

So the conference had set up a National Republican League, discussed the whole democratic programme, had gained the approbation of at least a large number of the people of Birmingham and dispersed with the highest hopes of new and better government and even the development of a third political party. As we have seen, the movement carried on into the early part of 1874, but by the end of the year it was buried, as were all other progressive developments by the end of the great Victorian expansion and the onset of the Great Depression.

Chapter Nine

SECULARISM AND THE MAIN ISSUES FOR THE WORKING CLASS MOVEMENT
1850 – 1874

An assessment of the importance of Secularism may be gained by attempting to trace Secularist influence over national events of the period in which Birmingham played either a crucial or a leading role. In the first category is Birmingham influence on both the Reform Act of 1867 and the Education Act of 1870. In the latter category is Birmingham influence on the struggle to establish and legalise trade unions; internationalism in general and Birmingham participation in the 1st International in particular; also the development of the Co-operative movement.

Education

Education is the obvious issue where Secularists consistently argued for universal education and that such education should be non-sectarian. Some Secularists indeed argued, as we have seen, not merely that religion should not be taught, but that the bible was an immoral book to which children should not be exposed. Birmingham became the leading centre for the advocacy of free schooling — universal, compulsory and non-sectarian. There were also special circumstances which made Birmingham the centre of the free school movement.

The 1851 Religious Census showed that roughly 25% of the Birmingham population went to church or chapel, half of whom were C of E. Despite this numerical preponderance and a vigorous and costly programme of church building from the 1840s, influence in this period lay not with the Church of England, but with those other religious sects of the town who considered it their Christian duty to involve themselves in the political and social affairs of the world. First among these were the Unitarians, the senior dissenting congregations of the town, some of whose members were Rational Religionists rather than Christians. These were the heirs to the Priestley tradition and it was the sect to which Joseph Chamberlain was attached. Next there were the Baptists dominated by the great influence of Charles Vince. The Independents with their famed chapel at Carrs Lane were served first by the eloquence and learning of the Rev. John Angel James, and after 1859 by the Rev. R.W. Dale, one of the great formative influences on the emergence of the Birmingham Civic Gospel. The greatest influence, however, was George Dawson, orator extraordinary, who from an appointment to the Baptist Mount Zion chapel in Graham Street in 1844 set up his own Church of the Saviour completely free from any sectarianism and where the staple diet was sermons on Thomas Paine and Voltaire. George Dawson was the direct link between Secularists and radical religion in Birmingham.

An important presence in the town was the Quakers led by the Sturge

brothers. Joseph was a leading Anti-Corn Law Leaguer who, unsuccessfully, attempted to unite the Chartists and the middle class in his
Complete Suffrage Union and who linked with Elihu Burritt the world
peace movement, internationalism and the abolition of the slave trade.
Finally there was the residual influence of Arthur O'Neil's Birmingham
Chartist church. O'Neil dissolved the Chartist church in 1846 but remained in Birmingham until his death in 1885 as pastor of Mount Zion
Baptist chapel in Newhall Street. He moved steadily to the right from
1842 when as a 'moral force' Chartist he had stood with Joseph Linney
the militant Black Country Chartist and had been arrested in the General
Strike of 1842. O'Neil met with considerable hostility from George White
and other Birmingham Chartists after 1842. By the 1860s O'Neil was still
a champion of working class education but a supporter of sectarian
schools. O'Neil was an important influence in the Peace Movement and
also in temperance work.

Of the other religious sects, Methodism was wracked with schisms and
politically quiescent. Roman Catholicism, despite its importance as a
leading centre from the sixteenth century, its large influx of Irish in the
nineteenth century, the proximity of its famed college at Oscott and the
activities of John Henry Newman, never acquired the decisive influence
in the town enjoyed by Catholics in such towns as Liverpool and
Glasgow.

So the radical religionists of Birmingham called the tune. This was
united around the rock of Gladstonian liberalism, the radicalism of John
Bright and buttressed by the traditions of Attwood and the earlier
Birmingham reformers. To all this was added the new Civic Gospel and
the incomparable organising talents of Joseph Chamberlain. Thus the
cause of free and secular education in Birmingham came, by the mid
1860s, into the hands of the men of wealth and power in the town and
dwarfed the influence of the Secularists.

A key event presaging the Education Act of 1870 was a series of
meetings in 1867 in Birmingham sponsored by the mayor, George Dixon,
which agreed the following:

> Increased powers are necessary for the extension of the means of
> education.
> That an Act of Parliament is desirable enabling municipal corporations
> to levy rates for this purpose.
> That children of tender years should not be employed unless provision
> be made for their instruction at school.
> That where parents are able to pay for their children's education
> penalties should be inflicted on them if they fail to do so.
> No general system of compulsory instruction is recommended but we are
> of the opinion that an extension of the Industrial Schools Act may prove
> a means of securing the instruction of neglected children.

As a result of these meetings the Birmingham Educational Society was
formed. The original aims were subsequently modified and by the end of
the year the town council had passed a motion that in their opinion:

> ... there should be established and maintained in England and Wales
> a national and compulsory system of education.

Within two years the Birmingham Education Society had evolved into the National Education League, partly as a response to the rival National Education Union sponsored by the religionists to advocate an extension of education through existing voluntary means.

The scale of the initial funding of the National Education League compared with the finances of working class organisations is a stark reminder of how the vast wealth created during this phase of Britain's industrial supremacy stuck to the fingers of the capitalist class and adds point to Joseph Chamberlain's constantly reiterated point during his radical days that property must pay the 'ransom' of increased taxation if they expected to be allowed to hold on to their wealth. From Birmingham the mayor, George Dixon, headed the subscription list with £1000; there were nine other donations of £1000; the Kenricks weighed in with £500 each from three members of the family. The money was to be paid in ten instalments. These immense sums should be contrasted with the £80 painfully collected in pennies and shillings for George Reddall's wife, when her husband died.

This system of large public subscription was to form part of Joseph Chamberlain's system of moral blackmail perfected subsequently through the Birmingham School Board and then the Liberal Association (the direct descendent of the Education League) which maintained Chamberlain's iron hold on Birmingham politics even after he defected to the Tories in 1886.

The Birmingham School Board was set up immediately after the passing of the Education Act of 1870. There were fifteen elected places on the Board and the Birmingham radicals of the National Education League were confident of taking all fifteen places. What they had not allowed for was that, in the interests of minority interests, voting was cumulative and one could 'plump' by giving all one's votes to a single candidate, or distribute them in any other desired way. The final result was a great shock. The Roman Catholics plumped all their votes on Father Michael O'Sullivan and he topped the poll with 35,120 votes. The churches, which had put up only 8 candidates had them all elected, leaving a minority of only 6 seats for the League's candidates. Thus the Birmingham radicals, who had led the fight in the country for a national system of education, had lost control in their own town. It was an error they were not to repeat.

This was the only School Board election for which a Secularist stood independently. This was David Kirkwood who received the very respectable vote of 7,095. Kirkwood was also the only working class candidate, his occupation being given as a gun-action filer.

At the elections for the second School Board in 1873 the radicals put up only eight candidates, all of whom were elected, the churches had 6 seats and there was one Roman Catholic. No Secularists stood. David Kirkwood urged that they should, but he was about to emigrate and so did not stand himself.

After this, church and state co-existed, each party nominating only within its strengths up to the required fifteen and so there were no elections to the third and fourth School Boards. Only in 1882 was there an election when Independents stood on the highly popular platform of retrenchment and a reduction in teachers' salaries! By an unholy alliance of the affluent, who always resent paying rates, and the very poor who were opposed to compulsory schooling, Henry Hawkes, the borough coroner, came top of the poll with 54,490 votes.

With regard to working class representation, there had been a bye-election during the second school board which W.J. Davis had contested as a Labour condidate and lost. Davis, however, as a good Lib-Lab was quickly incorporated into the panel for the third Board and entered, together with T. Bestow, a tin-plate worker, as the first working class representatives on Birmingham School Board.

By 1879, radical ardour had considerably cooled and during the tenure of the fourth Board, the bible was restored to Birmingham schools. Five churchmen voted for the restoration together with George Dixon and J.S. Wright, both Liberals. Only W.J. Davis voted against; the others abstained including the Roman Catholic priest, Father O'Hanlon.

Parliamentary Reform

Reform was always at the heart of Birmingham politics from as early as the 1760s. The Secularists were the heirs to the Chartists' Six Points, believing in Manhood Suffrage or even Universal Suffrage, but constrained as the Chartists were not, by the 'practicalities' which divided opinions regarding collaboration with the middle class. Although the early 1830s and the period of greatest Chartist influence (1839–1848) were the most explosive periods of struggle, the period here under review (1848–1874) saw almost continuous agitation for reform and included the Reform Act of 1867.

After the failure of Joseph Sturge's Complete Suffrage Union, which the middle class saw as an attempt to 'divest Chartism of its ugly element' the story can be taken up in 1848. This was the 'year of Revolution'. In January Feargus O'Connor had held a 'glorious meeting' in Birmingham and in April the third Chartist Petition was presented. The impact of the Chartist Petition was sufficient to lead to the first meeting in May of a middle class Reform League in Birmingham to agitate for household suffrage, vote by ballot, equal electoral districts and triennial Parliaments. This was much closer to the Charter than the Birmingham middle class usually went and the leaders of the Reform League were the Chartist defectors of 1839, Muntz, Scholefield and Douglas together with George Dawson, George Edmonds and T. Weston. This had been preceded by the setting up of a Birmingham Political Council on the lines of the old BPU after the February revolution in France and to counteract 'Chartist violence'. When the excitement of 1848 died down, the reform movement in Birmingham and elsewhere was boosted in 1849 by the rejection by the House of Lords of the Jewish Disabilities Bill after it had passed the Commons. A Reform League meeting in May and a Political Council meeting in June, both at the Town Hall, declared in favour of Joseph Hume's motion in the House of Commons for votes for householders, votes by ballot, triennial Parliaments and equal electoral districts. There was also an open-air Chartist demonstration in June. The scale of this meeting is probably best judged by Dent's comment that a large body of police was mobilised and also two companies of infantry from Weedon. Despite such provocation, their services were not required.

The dilemma regarding the amount of Reform to concede surfaced again with regard to Russell's 1852 Bill to extend the franchise to occupiers of houses of rateable value of £5 in towns. At a town's meeting George Edmonds and George Dawson proposed support for the bill on the grounds that it extended the franchise and did away with the property qualifications for M.Ps. Alderman Baldwin, however moved the following resolution which won the day:

> That in the opinion of this meeting any measure of Reform that does not include the shortening of the duration of Parliament, the abolition of the property qualification of Members of Parliament, universal suffrage, and a fair distribution of members corresponding with the population of each district, will not give satisfaction to the people of this country.

In other words, virtually the whole Charter and nothing but the Charter was still winning the day, but without the dreaded label 'Chartism' being used. This particular Bill fell, however, with the resignation of Russell. In July 1853 one of the periodical revivals of Chartism saw a meeting in the Corn Exchange addressed by Ernest Jones and R.G. Gammage to petition Parliament in favour of the People's Charter. In 1854 Russell introduced a more complicated Bill giving the vote to £6 householders in boroughs who had resided two years and ten months in one place. A town's meeting passed a very weak resolution in favour of that part of the bill that extended the franchise. This bill was also withdrawn.

Despite a very real Chartist revival during the Crimean War, reform was not again raised in Parliament until 1859. In the meantime a Reform Union was formed in Birmingham in January 1858 aiming to unite the middle and working classes. It refused to endorse the Charter, opting for 'a much wider extension of the franchise' and 'a shortening of the duration of Parliament'. An amendment in favour of manhood suffrage and payment of M.Ps. was rejected.

The development of Reform agitation throughout the country led to John Bright being deputed to draw up a Bill. This brought further action in Birmingham with the formation of a Birmingham Reform Association which agreed on three points:

1. A large extension of the franchise.
2. Vote by ballot.
3. A more equal apportionment of members to population.

But these three points were accompanied with a long list of Administrative Reforms, raised sharply by the chaos of the Crimean War, which included national education, internal free trade, reform of the law, lower taxes on earned income, investigation into pauperism and much more.

Early in 1859 Bright did introduce a bill based broadly on the Reform Association programme, but it was superseded by a government Reform Bill, the main characteristics of which were immortalised by Bright as 'fancy franchises' giving the vote to such people as those with £10 in the public funds or £60 in a savings bank or those with pensions of more than £20 a year etc. This bill was unanimously condemned by Birmingham reformers.

1860 opened with a great reform meeting at the Town Hall demanding 'a large extension of the franchise'. In response to widespread agitation the government introduced a Bill, but it was not seriously intended and was withdrawn by the middle of the year.

By now it was becoming clear that until the removal or death of Palmerston nothing could be done. The movement continued in Birmingham with the formation of a Radical Reform League, but it was not until 1865 when Palmerston died that reform became a real possibility.

In 1866 Gladstone introduced a vastly complex Reform Bill into Parliament which Bright did his best to defend, and a town's meeting was persuaded to support it backed by a petition signed by 44,236 people. In June Gladstone's bill was defeated in Parliament. This was followed by mass demonstrations throughout the country. The best known is ·the Hyde Park demonstration of July 1866 when the railings were torn down and the forbidden park occupied. But almost equally important was the Birmingham agitation. Open air meetings were organised almost every week with attendances of up to 10,000. These culminated in the great regional demonstration of August at Brookfields, near Icknield Street East where, in the time-honoured way, the factories closed and the working class contingents poured in from all parts from Coventry to the Black Country and almost 200,000 people assembled.

In 1867 Disraeli became prime minister and introduced in February a number of Resolutions on reform. These were promptly rejected by the newly-formed Birmingham Liberal Association the next day as having the intention of delaying Reform and agitation in the town mounted. On the evening of 12th February a mass meeting at the Town Hall called by the Reform League with speakers such as Thorold Rogers and Ernest Jones endorsed this view. The agitation culminated in an even vaster demonstration at Brookfields attended by about 250,000 people. From six starting points this great mass of people marched to Brookfields where there were eight platforms. An important part in organising this meeting was played by Birmingham Trades Council not yet one year old. Local trade union leaders spoke, and also George Howell and George Odger from the London Trades Council Junta. Also their rival, George Potter, editor of the *Beehive* spoke. Benjamin Lucraft representing the International Working Men's Association spoke as did Roger Bateson, secretary of Birmingham Trades Council. Most fitting of all, the old Chartist leaders spoke — Arthur O'Neil, John Oxford the Birmingham Chartist, and Joseph Linney the great Bilston and Black Country Chartist.

All platforms passed resolutions stating that 'the only true and permanent basis for just and true representation of the people is registered, residential manhood suffrage protected by the ballot.' Other resolutions stated that while desiring to maintain law and order, the continual obstructions to reform and the base treachery of the House of Commons in this matter was exasperating a loyal and industrious people and if persevered with might lead ultimately to anarchy and revolution. Nor was this immense working class gathering in any mood to allow the Liberals to continue their old game of enfranchising the rest of the middle class and only the 'respectable' working class. They 'deeply deplored the defection at the last moment of so large a portion of Liberal members' and in a clear warning even to such 'advanced' Liberals as John Bright, demanded assurances of support to Gladstone which would enable him to secure, without protracted agitation, a satisfactory measure of reform.

It was to be, of course, not Gladstone the Liberal, but Disraeli the wily Tory who was to cut the Gordian knot and pass in August 1867 the Reform Act which gave the vote to male householders in the towns.

Thus the Reform Bill again demonstrated that while the middle class in Birmingham with their enormous financial resources and control of industry and local administration dominated the organisation of limited reforms, it was the mobilisation of working people through their own organisations that was necessary for decisive change. The effectiveness of this latter mobilisation was only made possible by the labour of those who through good times and bad kept working class organisation alive. 1867 should be viewed as a latter day triumph of Chartism, nurtured by Chartists themselves up to 1860 and thereafter by Secularism and trade unionists. These are further reasons to reject the contention that Chartism was a failure.

Legalisation of Trade Unions and Labour Representation

The establisment of trade unions and the fight to get employer recognition of them is the first stage of effective trade unionism. This had begun even before the Industrial Revolution and is a continuing struggle, but much had been achieved by 1850. Legalisation of these trade unions and the necessity for working men to be among the legislators were the main and basic issues of the second half of the nineteenth century.

The first U.K. Trades Union Directory published by the London Trades Council in 1861 showed at least 32 trade societies in Birmingham. One section was the old established trades with a long record of organisation some going back to the eighteenth century such as the Bookbinders Consolidated Union, Boot and Shoe Makers (both Ladies' and Reformed branches), Tailors, Compositors and Printers, Gunmakers and Brushmakers. Then there were the building trades, Carpenters Progressive Society and the Carpenters & Joiners (Old Society) but no Masons or Bricklayers. Loosely linked with these might be classified the Brickmakers and Carvers and Guilders. Then there were other old trades destined to migrate to the Black Country — Saddlers, Whip Makers, Curriers, Ropemakers. Then there were the craft societies which would come and go in Birmingham as fashion or changing technology dictated such as Thimble Makers, Teapot Makers, Steel Pen Tool Makers, Bone Button Makers, Fender Makers, Fender Moulders, File Cutters, Cork Cutters etc. Then there were the Coach Builders and Furniture Platers, Coach; these originated in the luxury trade, but were already building railway coaches and would go on to make cars. Finally there was a group of newer trades or skilled trades which tended to be carried on in the larger Birmingham factories or works, such as the Iron Founders, United Order of Smiths, Engineers Amalgamated, Britannia Metal Workers, the Flint Glass Cutters General Union and the Engine Drivers and Firemen.

All trade unionists knew of and many had personal experience of the total illegality of trade unions from 1799 to 1835-24. But the fact that they were no longer illegal did not mean that they were legal, and the disabilities they suffered from were the same that had made the Combination Acts virtually unnecessary, because the more ancient Master & Servant Acts made almost any significant trade union activity illegal. These Acts mainly concerned breach of contract and default of duty. The former required 'customary notice' of termination of employment, usually fourteen days, before a strike was not illegal. The latter concerned damage to the masters' interests while a strike was in progress. For workers these matters came under the criminal law and masters could insist that magistrates prosecute, and in many cases, the aggrieved employer was himself the magistrate. Vast numbers of mass and individual prosecutions leading to prison sentences occurred under these Acts. Where employers were at fault, however, it was a civil matter and workers were obliged to bring private prosecutions against employers with little hope of gaining redress, but large chances of being victimised.

The Master & Servant Acts were a potent factor in the formation of the Birmingham Trades Council in 1866. The trades council was formed by twenty five delegates representing 4,814 members. The thirteen founder societies of the Council were Cordwainers (four branches), the General Union of Carpenters & Joiners (three lodges), the rival Amalgamated Society of Carpenters and Joiners (two branches), Cabinet Makers, Mill Sawyers, Wood Turners, Basket Makers, Painters, Tailors, Lathe Benders, Birmingham and Dudley Societies of Fire Iron Makers and the U.K.Society of Coachmakers. It was thus quite limited in its initial respresentation, but included some of the largest societies in the town.

The Trades Council was immediately faced with the Hornby v Close court ruling that trade union funds could not be protected through the courts. After this came the Sheffield Outrages leading to demands for the outright banning of trade unions. Birmingham Trades Council lobbied all candidates in the 1868 election on their attitudes to the legalising of trade unions and the protection of their funds. Both Tory candidates agreed to support these demands in their election addresses, but the three much vaunted radical Liberal candidates, including the most 'radical' of all M.P.s., John Bright, refused to do so.

Next came the Royal Commission on Trade Unions requiring enormous mobilisation of resources to prevent all trade unions being tarred with the brush of Sheffield violence. The Commission resulted in the 1871 Criminal Law Amendment Act which in typical Liberal fashion (a) made trade unions legal and protected their funds but (b) made picketing illegal, which vitiated the first. Much activity followed including attempting to stand William Gilliver as a working man candidate supported by benefit, friendly, co-operative, political and trade societies in the town. This fell through as there was insufficient time to organise the collection of the election expenses plus the £500 per year necessary to pay a salary of £300 a year and sustain an electoral organisation in the town. The incoming Tory government in 1875 repealed the Criminal Law Amendment Act, made peaceful picketing legal and passed an Employers & Workmen Act which did away with many of the barbarities of the Master & Servant Acts.

Such an enormous programme of activity for the infant Trades Council required the mobilisation of every section of the labour movement, including the Secularists, but it is clear that Secularist support was marginal to these important developments.

Internationalism and Peace

Internationalism is of the essence of the working class movement. Particular recipients of working class sympathy and solidarity in the early part of our period were the defeated revolutionaries of 1848. The greatest hero was Louis Kossuth, the Hungarian, who had been largely responsible for the March Revolution in Vienna that had toppled the seemingly impregnable Metternich and had gone on to declare a virtually independent state of Hungary. When in 1849 Austrian reaction had recovered its position, its army was sent into Hungary to overthrow the new government. At this time at least three meetings were held in Birmingham. On 23rd May a meeting was held at the Oddfellows Hall. It passed a resolution stating that the struggle was one for national liberty which no free man could look upon with indifference. It pledged itself to aid the Hungarians by all means consistent with citizens of a neutral state. Another meeting was held on June 23rd to petition Parliament to the same end. The third, a town's meeting, held at the Corn Exchange on 13th August passed the following resolution:

> That as Englishmen, as lovers of freedom, civil and religious, as true Conservatives and as friends of progress, this meeting feels it a sacred duty to express their earnest, entire and unreserved approbation of the Hungarian struggle for Independence, and their humble and hearty admiration of Hungarian heroism.
> That we look with deep and unmitigated abhorrence upon the savage and horrible manner in which Austria carries on the war; and as friends of the rights of nations and the freedom of the world, emphatically protest against the unrighteous intervention of Russia.
> That a petition be presented to the Queen, praying the Government to give an emphatic expression to these universal feelings of the people, by immediately recognising the de facto Government of Hungary; and that the Mayor be requested to sign the same on behalf of the meeting, and to secure its presentation.

The Hungarian republic was crushed. On 10th November 1851 Kossuth visited Birmingham:

> The whole town kept holiday; nearly all the manufactories were closed, and a procession of from 60,000 to 70,000 men was formed to meet Kossuth at Small Heath and escort him into the town. Since the day that the Political Union met Thomas Attwood at the same place, Birmingham had not witnessed such a magnificent display of generous enthusiasm. Flags, banners and trade symbols were carried in profusion; six bands of music were placed in different parts of the procession, and almost every person wore the Hungarian tri-colour. The streets were lined with people, every window on the line of route were lined with gazers — men, women and children — all displaying the popular colour. Platforms were erected in every convenient place and were crowded with spectators. As the carriage containing Kossuth passed along the streets he was greeted with the loudest demonstrations of welcome and the heartiest enthusiasm — surpassing in this respect any public event witnessed in Birmingham, not excepting those in connection with the Political Union.

In the mid 1850s, the Crimean War divided the working class and radical movement. For working class militants wars to repress liberty and for colonial expansion were seen as arising from the social system and thus to be condemned. On the other hand, Tsarism was seen as the Gendarme of Europe and the lynchpin of the system of repression which, ever since 1815, had opposed national liberation and unification in Europe. Thus the forcible overthrow of Tsarism was seen as the key to democratic advance everywhere. For these reasons the early stages of the Crimean

War saw a most untypical outburst of jingoism from the most militant
working class newspaper, Ernest Jones' *People's Paper*, and there was a
very substantial Chartist revival during the war. This jingoism quickly
disappeared and the Chartist revival continued on the more substantial
grounds of high war-time prices and misconduct of the war. Adding to
general support for the war was the usual unpolitical social patriotism and
the inescapable fact that wars were always good for the Birmingham
armaments' trade.

Nevertheless, there was never universal support for the war even at the
beginning in March 1854. Opposed to the war was the not inconsiderable
Peace Movement led by Joseph Sturge and the Rev. Arthur O'Neil ex-
Christian Chartist turned Baptist. The mainstay of the Peace Movement,
apart from the pacifist Quakers, was the Free Trade Movement led by
Cobden and Bright which maintained that universal free trade led inevitably to universal peace. All this, together with the religious radicalism
of George Dawson, the Unitarians and others meant that Birmingham
was never strong for the war.

The ramifications of the war widened. In May 1854 a meeting at the
Town Hall chaired by George Dawson heard Stanislaus Worcell of the
Polish Central Democratic Committee and passed the following
resolution:

> That this meeting, believing that the present war cannot be brought to
> a satisfactory conclusion, nor a lasting peace secured, without the
> restoration of the nationality of the Polish people, urges on the
> Government a full consideration of the just claims of Poland; that,
> admiring the undying spirit of the Poles, and sympathising with them in
> their renewed efforts to obtain their lost nationality, this meeting
> promises them all just and practicable aid.

In February 1855 another town's meeting passed resolutions on the
independence of Poland, the raising of a Polish legion to serve in the war
and a petition to Parliament. The next day another town's meeting memorialised 'the legislature on the necessity of prosecuting the enquiries into
the causes of the disasters in the Crimea and on the system of
appointments in the Army and Navy.' This was passed with the 'utmost
enthusiasm'. The idiotic Charge of the Light Brigade had occurred in
October 1854 and the ensuing winter brought great suffering to the
British troops as a result of the lack of supplies and the intense cold. In
May another large and enthusiastic meeting at Bingley Hall set up an
Association for Administrative Reform with a Committee of 150 and
passed the following resolution:

> That this meeting entertains a strong and earnest conviction that the
> disastrous and disgraceful condition in which England has been placed
> in the conduct of the War with Russia, is mainly attributable to the
> inefficiency of the Executive, and the defective system of conducting the
> business of the nation; and that this state of things is the natural result
> of the postponement of merit to family and personal influence in the
> selection of ministers and other public servants.
>   That the monopoly of the honourable and lucrative offices of the State
> by one class, discourages men of ability from qualifying themselves for
> entering the service of the nation; and this meeting, while it disclaims
> any desire to exclude the aristocracy from that share in the direction and

conduct of public affairs, to which their ability or their special fitness may entitle them, is of the opinion that the most prompt and effective remedy for the official mismanagement from which this country is now suffering, is the substitution of the test of merit and fitness for that of rank and family connection in all official appointments....

Administrative reform was to be the kernel of the Liberal struggle against Tory aristocratic control which flowered in the next decade and culminated with Chamberlainism and Republicanism, but it had no immediate effect as the first annual meeting of the Association was attended by only six persons.

But such was the strength of feeling at the time against the conduct of the war and the need for reform that there was a brief flowering of Urquhartism in the town. In July 1855 Urquhart commenced a series of meetings for the impeachment of the previous ministry of Lord Aberdeen, and a committee of such radicals as George Dawson and J.A. Langford was set up to 'watch over the interests of the nation', but this soon fizzled out.

A final effect of the Crimean War on Birmingham was that John Bright was rejected by his Manchester constituents for his opposition to the war and became a Birmingham M.P. in 1858. This was an important landmark in the shift of the centre of gravity of national Radicalism from the Cotton-Free Trade-Peace axis of Manchester, to the wider industrial base of Birmingham.

This transition was completed during the U.S. Civil War (1861 – 65). Sympathy for the north was virtually unanimous among working people and radicals, based both on republican sympathies and opposition to slavery. Town and working class meetings were held when Abraham Lincoln was assassinated; a Birmingham and Midland Freemen's Association whose accounts at one time showed £6,700 collected held a Victory Meeting when slavery was abolished in the U.S.A. During 1865 Elihu Burritt was appointed U.S. Consul in Birmingham which strengthened the international peace movement in Birmingham. But the greatest significance of the US Civil War had been the development of new sources of raw cotton in Egypt and India, thus strengthening imperialist tendencies in Britain. The industrialisation of the U.S. which henceforth absorbed most of its own cotton diminished the economic importance of cotton and Manchester, while immensely widening the US market for Birmingham goods.

Sympathy with the Italian revolution and the unity of Italy was another feature of Birmingham internationalism. In August 1861 Garibaldi was taken prisoner and a town's meeting in September expressed sympathy with him and memorialised the Government to use its influence in having French troops leave Rome. This motion was seconded by F. Wotton, one of the few English Garibaldian volunteers. In 1864 Garibaldi made his famous visit to England which was cut abruptly short for reasons never satisfactorily explained. Birmingham town council invited him to visit the town and he accepted. Committees were formed to meet him, one consisting of the usual town radicals such as Dixon, Muntz, Dale, Timmins etc. The other was a Working Men's Committee. Its chairman was Joseph Jones, (probably the Bilston Chartist barber, for Garibaldi's visit was important for Black Country Chartists) and the vice-chairman was John Oxford, the Birmingham Chartist. Unfortunately, Garibaldi's visit, which would undoubtedly have seen another great Birmingham manifestation of international solidarity, never took place, as he had by then returned to Italy.

1864 is particularly important from the point of view of internationalism for it was the year of the setting up of the International Working Men's Association. This had a much greater effect on national and Birmingham working class politics than is generally realised. It marked the continuance of the influence of Marx and Marxism which had begun with the later stages of Chartism. The First International originated in the development of trade unions and working class parties in Europe in the mid-1860s. An important immediate factor in its formation was the suppression of the Polish insurrection against Russia in 1863. The Birmingham reaction to this event was a town's meeting which formed a committee and set up a relief fund. A Petition was also presented to Parliament requesting that in view of the violation of the 1815 Treaty it was the duty of Her Majesty's government 'to take such measures as may lead to the securing and the maintenance of the national existence of Poland.'

Birmingham trade unionists quickly associated themselves with the International. The organisation was set up in September 1864; in March 1865, a Birmingham delegate to the national conference of the Shoemakers Union, which had received a deputation from the International moved;

> That we cordially agree with the principles of the International Association as represented so eloquently by the deputation from that body and pledge ourselves to join them for the furtherance of those principles and endeavour to spread their liberal and glorious ideas among our constituents.

The resolution was carried unanimously. In November 1865 The Council of the Cordwainers Association was requesting that copies of the rules of the Association and its Inaugural Address be forwarded to the four branches of the union in Birmingham. By May 1866 the Birmingham Cordwainers were sending remittances to defray the costs of the forthcoming Congress of the International at Geneva.

Birmingham Trades Council was formed in May 1866. This added another link in the chain of international solidarity and aid for men on strike. William Gilliver, the first president and later secretary of Birmingham Trades Council, was active in the Peace Movement which was associated (not always amicably) with the International. For instance, in 1867 the Rev. Arthur O'Neil wrote to the General Council of the International asking for the addresses of the continental secretaries for him to transmit peace addresses to them; the General Council took no action. This decision was influenced by the Congress of the League of Peace and Freedom in September 1867. This League was sponsored by the Quaker-pacifist Peace Society together with the Free Traders. Marx had derided it as the 'peace at any price party' and the unanimous decision of the general council had been not to be represented at the Congress although individual members of the International attended in their personal capacities.

By March 1868 Birmingham Trades Council was directly involved with the International. A meeting of the Lynn branch of the International had discussed motions for the forthcoming Conference and had circularised these to, among others, Birmingham Trades Council. They were:

1. That the credit system established on the co-operative principle, facilitated by the use of paper money, would be beneficial to the working classes.
2. Under the present system machinery is very detrimental to the working classes.
3. This meeting is of opinion that it is highly expedient to draw up . a programme for the technical and comprehensive secular education of the working classes.
4. This meeting is of the opinion that there could be no such thing as private property in land originally, and that the sooner it would be converted again into public property, the better it would be for the nation at large.
5. This meeting seeing that the intelligent portion of the working classes view strikes as evils, although under certain circumstances necessary, would be most happy to embrace any means which might be introduced to prevent the same.

As a result of this, the General Council in January 1868 sent out a series of questions to their members requesting their opinion on the following with a view to incorporating these topics into the next Brussels Conference of the Association in September.

1. The practicability of organising a system of credit and co-operative exchanges — facilitated by the use of paper money — amongst the various associations of working men.
2. What are the effects of the use of machinery upon the conditions of the labouring poor?
3. The advisability of drawing up a definite programme for the technical, and a comprehensive secular education of the children of the poor.
4. The land, mines, canals, highways, railroads etc.; ought they to be the property of private individuals and worked for their personal profit, or would it be expedient to convert them into public property and work them for the community at large.
5. The policy of strikes, and the advisability of insisting upon the establishment of the courts of arbitration.

In 1869 Birmingham Trades Council had the honour (a not entirely welcome one in view of the pressure of work on it at the time) of hosting the Second Annual Trades Union Congress. They had written to the International in April stating that expenses of delegates would not exceed 6/-d. and they wrote again in June asking whether the General Council proposed sending a delegate to this working men's congress. No reply is recorded and from the list of delegates at the Congress it does not appear that the International was directly represented, although members of the General Council who attended from other organisations included George Odger (secretary of the London Trades Council), and George Howell (Operative Bricklayers). George Potter the editor of the *Beehive*, the weekly paper of the International also attended. In fact, the International was discussed at the Birmingham TUC and John Hales later reported to the General Council that the following resolution had been proposed by

William Cremer (of the London Trades Council and the first general secretary of the International) and passed:

> That as local organisations of labour have almost disappeared before organisations of a national character, so we believe the extension of the prinicple of free trade, which induces between nations such a competition that the interest of the workman is liable to be lost sight of and sacrificed in the fierce international race between capitalists, demands that such organisations should be further extended and made international. And as the International Working Men's Association endeavours to consolidate and extend the interests of the working masses, which are everywhere identical, this Congress heartily recommends that Association to the support of the working men of the United Kingdom, especially of all organised bodies, and strongly urges them to become affiliated to that body.

The influence of the International was at this time approaching its peak and it produced a document (written by Marx) in reply to a sneer about the ineffectiveness of the International in which it was demonstrated that every significant organisation of the British working class movement had, at that time, its representation on the General Council of the International. These organisations included the London Trades Council, the Reform League, the National Reform Association, the Co-operative movement and the Secular movement.

The climacteric of the International was now approaching which was to bring its international influence to a tremendous peak and then to lose the support of some reformist English trade unions and to send the International to exile and final disbandment in the United States. The event was the Paris Commune.

In July 1870 the First Address of the International Working Men's Association on the Franco-Prussian War drafted by Marx and approved by all members of the General Council, including the English trade unionists Applegarth, Hales and Odger, was issued. This condemned the war as one of aggression on the part of France and self-defence for Germany. Very considerable trouble was gone to to get the widest possible circulation for the Address including the Positivists and the Peace Society. In Birmingham, copies of the Address went to the Birmingham Trades Council and the Plasterers.

By September the Germans had defeated the French armies, Napoleon III had gone and the Republic had been proclaimed. This was received with immense enthusiasm everywhere and greatly stimulated the Republican movement in Britain. In October the International received a letter from Arthur O'Neil requesting the view of the General Council on a proposition for arbitration between the belligerent powers. Their reply was to say that arbitration at that time was out of the question and all that could be done was to hold meetings to compel the British government to recognise the Republic. By this time the Second Address of the General Council of the International on the Franco-Prussian War had been issued, again written by Marx and again supported by the English trade unionists stating that the war of defence had ended with the surrender of Louis Napoleon at Sedan and it was now a war of aggression on the part of Germany for Alsace-Lorraine. The Address ended with the words:

> Let the sections of the International Working Men's Association in every country stir the working classes to action. If they forsake their duty, if they remain passive, the present tremendous war will be the harbinger of still deadlier international feuds, and lead in every nation to a renewed triumph over the workman by the lords of the sword, of the soil and of capital. VIVE LA REPUBLIQUE.

In October 1870 Birmingham Trades Council wrote to the International enquiring about what sum would be considered a donation to join. In fact there was no answer to this question as the International had problems throughout its life in fixing its subscriptions. They were told what the Carpenters and Bricklayers paid, leaving the trades council to fix their own amount 'as their joining would be of more importance than the amount of contributions.' They joined in January 1871 and asked whether £1 per annum would be considered a sufficient contribution. Manchester Trades Council also joined the International at this time and the adhesion of the trades councils of the two largest provincial towns in England was an event of the first importance; sufficient to be reported to the Spanish Section of the International by Frederick Engels as the Corresponding Secretary for that country.

At this point it is necessary to consider the effect of events in France on British politics. From September 1870 when the French Republic was proclaimed until March 1871 there was universal sympathy with France fighting what was now a war of self-defence against an aggressive almost united Germany. In January 1871 Paris surrendered and in February France made peace which included ceding Alsace-Lorraine to Germany and the payment of an enormous indemnity. From this point, however, events changed. The French republican government was now intent on controlling Paris and disarming its National Guard; and it was not averse to using the Prussian troops stationed in France to do it; Paris had no intention of being disarmed. In March the attempt was made to seize the guns of the National Guard, the attempt was unsuccessful, the government retreated from Paris to Versailles and the victors set up the Paris Commune. This was the watershed. The first government representing working men had been set up. This was not the work of the First International and its Jacobin, Blanquist, Proudhonist participants were not Marxists, but it did represent the setting up of the new social order the International advocated and it got all the blame for it. The Commune was therefore instantly anathematized by the ruling classes, although radical middle-class opinion in Britain in general and Birmingham in particular could continue to support Republicanism. There is no evidence that the Birmingham working class deserted the International as a result of the 'extremism' of the Commune; and the atrocities of the authorities culminating in the massacre after the Commune had been suppressed in May 1871 when 25,000 were shot and 13,700 convicted and mostly deported strengthened working class sympathies. On the other hand, however, no open support can be traced. The records of the Trades Council make no reference to the Commune and the minutes of the International make no mention of Birmingham.

The main preoccupations of the General Council of the International during the Commune were the exposing of false documents, the unearthing of police spies and coping with the effects of its continental sections being made illegal. After the Commune it seems to have been 'business as usual' with the International for the British trade unions. This meant support for trade union solidarity and the normal lofty disregard for all the political issues agitating everyone else in the organisation. So in August 1871 Robert Applegarth was confirming his support for the International and promising to attend the General Council, more regularly; it was reported that the ASE was considering affiliation; new British branches of the International had been set up, and Harriet Law was having long discussions at the General Council meetings on education. All this while the International was being torn apart over controversies on Marx and Engels great classic *The Civil War in France* issued as an International document in June 1871; Marx' losing battle with the Bakuninists over the control of the organisation; and Engels grumblings that the English working class had done nothing to help the Commune refugees having left it to the middle class.

Finally it should be noted that the great Republican movement in Britain based on Birmingham did not really get off the ground until after the Paris Commune had been crushed, 1872 – 73 being the most important years. Republicanism in Britain was not killed by the Paris Commune, but by the Great Depression.

The Co-operative Movement

After the immensely innovative decades of the 1830s and 1840s Birmingham settled quickly into the Co-operative retail pattern of the Rochdale pioneer society of 1844. The small size of many of these societies made them inherently unstable, apart from the managerial problems, lack of protection of the law etc. which beset all societies.

In 1846 a Birmingham Co-operative Society was established whose secretary was J.A. Langford. Other Co-ops between 1846 and 1850 can be traced at Selly Oak, Digbeth, Smethwick and Hockley and in 1850 a Coal & Coke Society was formed. In 1852 a Co-operative Flour Mill was started and also the Birmingham Co-operative Friendly Society with George Dawson as president and J.A. Langford vice-president. Within three months the latter had a membership of one hundred members paying a membership fee of 1/-d. and buying by instalments shares of 10/-d. Trading was from a small store on Ludgate Hill opened from 10 a.m. to 8 p.m. on Wednesdays and Saturdays, but only from 6 p.m. to 8 p.m. on other weekdays. In 1856 the Hope Iron Boat Club was established.

In the 1860s retail co-operation was consolidated in Birmingham. In 1861 a new Birmingham Co-operative Industrial Society was formed trading from Steelhouse Lane. Officers were obliged to give ample security and at an adjourned half-yearly meeting at the Ship Inn, Steelhouse Lane, the storekeeper, Mr. Houghton, resigned on the grounds that the 4d. in the £1 on purchases which he was granted was insufficient for him to continue. This meeting was very disorderly, serious charges being levelled against various people connected with the Society. At this meeting, the storekeeper refused to give up possession of the premises on the grounds that he had advanced the only capital the Society had ever had — £45 which he claimed to have loaned to the Society at 5%.

Also in 1861 some Midland Railway workers started the Victoria Co-operative Society at Heneage Street. About 140 members subscribed 3d. per week for 700 £1 shares. This store was at first successful but 'an insane love of dividend' and jealousy among its officials were given as reasons for its demise. The Birmingham Heath Industrial Co-operative Society was started towards the latter end of 1861 and a Smethwick Co-operative Society in the same year. There was also, it seems, a society in Newton Street in 1862 and another at Nechells Green in 1866.

The most successful Society seems to have been the Ladywood Society begun in 1865 with initial resources and capital even smaller than most. Within three years apart from the headquarters in Friston Street it had branches at Bishopsgate Street, Wells Street and Sherlock Street. In 1869 its turnover was £6,881 and a dividend of 1/-d., in the £ was paid. The annual meetings were events of importance attracting the mayor and the local MPs and even Conservative M.Ps. from outside Birmingham. In 1869 the chairman, George Dixon, stated that in the preceding ten years eighteen Societies had been formed in Birmingham at least half of which had failed while three others had amalgamated with the Ladywood Society; at that time there were five Societies in the town.

Ladywood Society continued to prosper until at least 1871. Its 1870 annual general meeting and tea was held at the Town Hall, the Mayor presiding. By 1875 however, the Society had ceased to exist.

The Birmingham Perseverance Society, started in 1867, was also successful intitially. It was an educationally orientated trading society emphasising educational lectures, a library of co-operative works, tracts, and a newsroom open one or more nights a week where articles from the *Co-operator* were discussed. In 1869 there were 121 members with a turnover of £360 usually paying a dividend of 1/3d. This Society, like the Ladywood Society, was represented at the 1871 Co-operative Congress held in Birmingham.

In Handsworth the Economical Society had survived from 1830 until 1855. Co-operation was resumed in this area in 1868 with the formation of the Handsworth Industrial Co-operative Society formed by eighteen men, mostly employed at Tangye's who subscribed 1/-d. each to print circulars advertising their intentions. Within a few weeks over £70 was raised. By 1874 membership was 110, capital £316 and sales £534. The next year it amalgamated with the much larger West Smethwick Society which had been established in 1866 and by 1871 had a turnover of £7,000 from groceries and provisions, butchers' meat and shoes. Membership was 874 in 1880, but even this large Society failed in 1887.

Societies in both Bordesley and Sparkhill were formed in 1860, the latter failed in 1866 and the former was defunct by 1869. In this year three more Societies were formed, another Bordesley Society, the Birmingham Anchor Society and the Ten Acres and Stirchley Society; the last named still survived until recent times.

The Co-operative Congress was held in Birmingham in 1871 attended by 50 local delegates and visitors. Of the three chairmen of the Congress, one was C.C. Cattell, who, together with J.A. Langford must be considered the Birmingham leaders of Co-operation in this period; the two Birmingham giants of the movement were still active, but outside the town, both Holyoake and William Pare having national responsibilities in the movement.

This chapter has indicated the extent of Secularist involvement in the main social and political issues of the day in addition to their ideological function of promoting rational, secular modes of reasoning.

Their achievement in the most difficult years of 1850 to 1875 when British capitalism dominated the world was considerable. Within that secular tradition it is clear that Marxist ideas were taking deep root.

The Great Depression from 1875 was to remake the world, and it is to a detailed analysis of that event that we now turn.

PART 3
THE
GREAT DEPRESSION
1875 – 1900

Chapter Ten

WHAT WAS
THE GREAT DEPRESSION?

The Great Depression exploded on Britain in 1874 like a bolt from the blue. Nothing was ever to be the same again. It marked the end of a thirty year expansion of British capitalism which had begun about 1844. This expansion had been punctured by a number of serious economic crises such as 1847 – 48, the Crimean crisis of 1855 – 58, the cotton crisis of the U.S. civil war 1862 – 63, and the depression of 1866 – 68; but none of these was serious enough to set the capitalist system at risk. The Great Depression was a different matter, however. It marked the end of Britain's world industrial monopoly and it was the beginning of the problems of our basic industries which beset us today. The industrial development of rival powers, notably Germany, France, Belgium and the U.S.A. led to cut-throat competition and falling profit margins. This rivalry led to a desperate search for new markets and exclusive sources of raw materials culminating in the second great rape of Africa (the first had been the slave trade) when that continent was divided up among the warring European powers. It was J.A. Hobson, the British liberal observer who first characterised these new developments as Imperialism, but it was Lenin who sharpened and refined the analysis, the main features of which, as they applied to Britain, were (a) that it marked the end of the competitive stage of capitalism and the development of a monopoly stage (b) that the export of goods was increasingly giving way to the export of capital and (c) that the world was being divided up by the great powers as markets for their goods and this would be followed by the forcible re-division of the world by war. The Great Depression saw a total re-alignment of capitalist politics in Britain when the emerging monopoly elements broke with Gladstone over Ireland to destroy for ever any class basis for the Liberals, and the Conservatives became the unchallenged party of big business. Birmingham, of course, was at the very centre of these developments with Joseph Chamberlain the leading figure both nationally and in Birmingham. The Great Depression saw even more important changes in working class politics. After ten years of depression, socialism re-emerged in Britain with the Marxist parties of the Social Democratic Federation and Socialist League, and by the end of the century British working people had given their final verdict on 150 years of economic development by creating The Labour Party dedicated after 1918 to replacing capitalism with socialism.

Among bourgeois scholars it is fashionable to dismiss the Great Depression. The main grounds for this are (a) that production continued to grow over this period, albeit more slowly (b) that the standard of living of the general population improved during these years and (c) that levels of unemployment were comparatively low. It has been shown that for the neighbouring Black Country area each of the above propositions requires very serious re-consideration because of the faulty nature of the statistical evidence used by Saul and others. The present author seems to have won a sort of academic dispensation to write Great Depression for the Black Country without inverted commas. Birmingham, however, with its thousand trades which, it is asserted, made the town immune from general depression, has been the jewel in the crown of those who would relegate the Great Depression to a myth. A closer examination of economic and social conditions in Birmingham, however, reveals very serious weaknesses in the above thesis, and it will be argued here that there was indeed a Great Depression in Birmingham for the following reasons:

1. That capitalist crises are generated not by external factors such as the money supply or the wickedness of trade unionists and agitators, but within the very mechanism of capitalism itself. This requires that capital must be turned over continuously and on an ever expanding scale. Insofar as this is achieved by increasing mechanisation (Marx' increased 'organic composition of capital') and this is not offset by a cheapening of workers' subsistence costs, this will result in a lower general *rate* of profit which at first may be disguised by an increased *mass* of profit, but eventually the *rate* of profit will fall to the point where it is not longer possible for the system as a whole to produce profitably. This creates unemployment and the spiral of falling incomes popularised by Keynes as the gap between Savings and Investment. The crisis will continue until sufficient capital has been destroyed (in the form of unsold stocks, bankrupted firms and the physical destruction of plant and machinery) for some new investment to become profitable. This will activate the reverse spiral of increasing incomes leading to a new peak of expansion followed inevitably by the next slump. This trade cycle is as real in the 1980s as it was in 1880s, as real in the 1930s as it was in the 1830s. It seems reasonable, therefore to assume that this cyclical development is one of the potential fatal flaws of capitalism bringing poverty, misery and mass unemployment to every generation unless it is superseded by a socialist planned economy which, by producing goods for consumption and not for capitalist profit, will remove the causes of economic crises.

2. That the rate of expansion of capitalism from 1750 to 1900 was not high enough, given the vast inequalities of income that capitalism creates, and the high growth rate of the population, to substantially and permanently raise the standard of living of the mass of the population.

3. That the levels of unemployment in Birmingham (as in the rest of Britain) were substantially higher than has been represented. That this unemployment was likely to have been equal to the levels which prevailed both in the later period of the 1930s and also the earlier period of the dreadful three Long Depressions of 1814 – 19, 1829 – 33 and 1839 – 43 (the actual years will vary slightly between different areas of Britain) which brought starvation and near revolution. Consequently, from 1874 to 1939 the issue dominating the labour movement in Birmingham (as elsewhere in Britain) was always mass unemployment.

4. That the problem with the Great Depression is not to decide whether it existed but when it ended. The terminal date is usually given as 1895, and it is true that this decade did see substantial rises in living standards for those in work. But there continued to be mass unemployment, sweated labour, low wages and falling living standards after 1900 which persisted until the first world war when the destruction of capital both human and physical was sufficient to give capitalism a further upward lurch.

The initial reaction to the Great Depression of 1874 was exactly the same as the reaction to the Great Depression of 1974. From 1870 there had been a hectic four year boom and in that period there had been long overdue improvements in working conditions. Full employment had raised incomes and limited wage increases had been won. Hours, in some cases, had been shortened. Trade unions had won a limited legal status. Some social services had begun to develop; rate borne Poor Law expenditure had risen mainly due to improved treatment of pauper children and the sick; both local rates and national taxation had increased as a result of the 1870 Education Act. Such advances were an immediate target with the onset of the Great Depression and, as in 1974, the immediate reaction was an increasingly conservative one as the capitalists and their newspapers identified their culprits. The Depression was caused by high wages, they claimed; these must be brought down to the level of overseas competitors. The trade unions had become too strong; in their early days they had served a useful purpose, but now they were above the law and their powers must be curbed! Public expenditure must be cut to divert expenditure from the molly-coddling of the poor into industrial development; the virtues (in this case pre-Victorian) of the poor standing on their own feet must be restored. Thus the labour movement of the 1870s found itself under the same ferocious attack as the movement in the 1970s, as capitalism attempted to solve its crisis at the expense of working people and by destroying the limited liberties which working class 'agitators' and 'trouble makers' had won despite unremitting Conservative and Liberal hostility.

We shall consider the Great Depression in detail under the following heads:

1. The deployment of the labour force in Birmingham.
2. The reaction to the economic situation by the Birmingham capitalist class.
3. The reaction of the Trade Unions.
4. Chamberlainism and the political reaction.
5. The working class movement and the Great Depression.

Chapter Eleven

THE OCCUPATIONS OF THE WORKING PEOPLE
1850 – 1900

Problems

The most detailed source for an examination of the structure of the working population is the Occupation Tables of the ten-yearly Censuses. There are considerable difficulties, however, in using successive censuses to make comparisons over time. Some of these difficulties are general and others specific to Birmingham. The schedules of occupations into which employment was grouped were constantly being changed in the search for greater accuracy. The 1841 Census is the local historian's delight because it enumerated virtually every occupation that existed. This was however unsatisfactory from the point of view of national analysis and occupations were more systematically grouped in subsequent Censuses. Another problem is the different age groups into which employment was grouped. For instance, the 1841 Census grouped employment into males under 20 and males 20 and upwards with the same age groups for women. The 1871 Census lists occupations for males and females of 20 years and upwards only. The 1881 Census lists occupations for all males and females irrespective of age. Both the 1891 and the 1901 Censuses list occupations of males and females of 10 years and upwards and the latter further sub-divides these into five sub-age groups.

The problems specific to Birmingham are also serious. When Birmingham became a municipal borough in 1838 it comprised the parish of Birmingham, the parish of Edgbaston and the townships of Bordesley, Deritend and Duddeston-cum-Nechells. But for Census purposes Birmingham was in one registration district, Edgbaston was in another and the townships were in the registration district of Aston. Both the 1841 and the 1871 Censuses analyse employment for Birmingham borough; the 1881 and 1891 Censuses analyse employment for the Sanitary Urban Districts of Birmingham and Aston Manor which are virtually coterminous with Birmingham borough; the 1901 Census is for the enlarged Borough of 1891. For the above reasons it has been difficult to disentangle the total population of 'Birmingham' and this applies with greater force to analyses of occupations of the working population. The analysis below follows the Census tables for the years 1841, 1871 and 1901. For the 1881 and 1891 Censuses it takes only the Urban Sanitary District of Birmingham omitting Aston Sanitary District. This gives a better comparison with the other Censuses. However, for any discussion of *total numbers* for the 1881 and 1891 Censuses the Aston numbers would have to be added. The following discussion is in terms of *percentage of employed persons* and for this purpose the figures given are adequate since the *proportion* of people in employment in both Birmingham and Aston in each trade was roughly similar. There are two exceptions, however, which are important. One is Jewellery where about 35% of workers lived in Aston, and Guns with 25% compared with the general proportion of population of 14% in Aston and the remainder in Birmingham. When writing of these trades, this point will be taken into consideration.

Male Employment

Male Occupations in Birmingham

Numbers in Employment at each Census together with % of Employed persons.

I. Professional.	1841	1871	1881	1891	1901
Connected with the Church	87	214	237	309	353
Legal Prof. Barristers and Solic.	131 }	129	138	171	161
Legal Law Clerks & Others	}	139	307	358	408
Medical Prof. Physicians & Surgeons	15	176	176	253	295
Scientists, Engineers, Surveyors & Architects	197	47	194	277	165
Art, Music, Drama, Literary	225	773	937	1042	1440
Teachers (incl Lecturers & Profs.)	152	212	512	587	555
Other Professional people	260	394	288	677	134
Total	1067 2%	2084 2%	2789 2%	3674 2%	3511 2%
State Employment					
National & Local Govt. Union etc.	77	365	343	511	2204
Police and Prison Service	382	479	525	654	-
Armed forces	266	321	307	261	368
II. Domestic					
Private Servants & Institutional Service	1062	804	1620	1740	2362
III. Commercial					
Agents, Brokers, Factors, Merchants and Salesmen	486	648	804	932 }	2596
Accountants	93	124	153	128 }	
Auctioneers & Valuers	49	80	112	116 }	
Banking & Money Employment	27	109	194	229 }	1158
Insurance & Benefit Societies	-	78	226	556 }	
Commercial Clerks	1370	1651	3709	4712	5548
Commercial Travellers	15	507	974	1255	-
Total	2040 3%	3197 4%	6172 4%	7928 4.5%	9302 5%
Conveyance of Persons, Goods & Messages.					
On Railways	77	1337	2442	3576	5418
On Roads	687	1518	2802	5687	8488
On Canals	281	474	471	535	592
Storage	178	932	719	806	-
Messengers	693	1023	2944	4367	4731
Total	1951 3%	5360 6%	9512 7%	15186 9%	19229 10%
V. Agricultural.					
Farmers, Labourers, Dealers etc.	974	616	537	511	372
Gardeners, Nursery, Grooms	598	864	1115	1124	644
Total	1572 2½%	1500 1¾%	1652 1%	1635 1%	1016 ½%

VI. Industrial Workers.

Building & Construction	3623 5%	6865 8%	9846 7%	11589 6¾%	16205 8½%
Fabric & Dress including:	4003 6%	7351 8½%	8123 5¾%	7963 4½%	7256 3¾%
Boot and Shoe makers	1997 3%	2628 3%	2769 2%	2549 1½%	1754 1%
Tailors	1257 2%	1584 1¾%	1700 1¼%	1945 1%	1970 1%
Food, Drink & Lodging including Publicans, Beer-sellers, Tavern, Hotel & Inn keepers, Maltsters,	3042 4½%	6773 7¾%	8126 5¾%	9403 5½%	11672 6%
Brewers	1129	2029	1975	2112	3178
Butchers	579	882	1258	1509	-
Bakers	391	742	1237	1430	-
Grocers	356	872	1271	1655	-
Minerals, Metals & Machines incl:	–	35483 41%	50911 36%	60287 35%	63583 33%
Brassworkers	3295 5%	4462 5%	9235 7%	11829 7%	-
Iron & Steel Working	-	6990 8%	8328 6%	9909 6%	7023 4%
Jewellery	1572 2%	4471 5%	5788 4%	4431 3%	5588 3%
Guns	2039 3%	4374 5%	3461 3%	3789 2%	3413 2%
Glassworkers	890	1168	1369	1295	1197
Buttonmakers	1734	1333	1491	1134	655
Coaches & Carriages	405	1215 1%	1693 1%	3868 2%	7294 4%
Labourers	3532 5%	4773 5.5%	5286 4%	6406 4%	4367 2%
Total Working Population	65724	87165	140994	174334	193633

The first point to note is that the population was overwhelmingly manual. Heavy and sustained labour was the lot of most workers — when work was available. About 2% were professional people and 3% commercial in 1841 and at the end of the century only the latter figure had changed, rising from 3% to 5%. Thus throughout this half century between 95% and 93% of the working population were manual workers. Most of these were also direct producers of material values and thus of surplus value. Of the non-productive occupations in 1841, professional men amounted to 2%, state employment occupied 1.1%, domestic service 1.6%, conveyance 3% and food, drink and lodging 4%. Thus about 12% of the working population did not directly produce values. By 1901 the non-productive sector had risen to 18.5%. But almost the whole of this increase was accounted for by Conveyance which had risen from 3% to 10% of the employed population.

Taking each of these categories of employment in turn, we will start with professional people. Here it is clear that very little change took place through the period 1841 – 1901. There were 0.5 doctors per 1000 of the population in 1841 and only 0.57 in 1901. The number of scientists and engineers was a standing disgrace and was an important factor in the depth and severity of the Great Depression in Birmingham as elsewhere in Britain. This also highlights the extent to which industrial development was dependent on the intuitive and acquired skills of the workforce. This stricture applies almost equally to men teachers whose numbers rose only from 0.8 per 1000 to 1.1 per 1000 from 1841 to 1901 highlighting the limitations of the 1870 Education Act. The arts appear to better advantage in an area not greatly renowned for its culture, increasing from 1.3 per 1000 of population in 1841 to 2.8 per 1000 in 1901. How this compares with other towns cannot be pursued very far here. I would note, however, that in 1871 Bristol with about half the population of Birmingham had roughly the same proportion of cultural workers whereas it had nearly four times the proportion of those 'connected with the Church' that Birmingham had. The latter suggests that Birmingham was a far less 'priest-ridden' town than some. Bristol at this time also had 49 civil engineers to Birmingham's 38, and 212 barristers and solicitors compared with 129 in Birmingham.

Little need be said of male domestic service in Birmingham. It was 2% of male employment in 1841 and this had declined to 1.5% in 1901. Of the 1620 in 1881, 309 were domestic coachmen and grooms, 165 domestic indoor servants and nearly 700 worked in inns, hotels, clubs, colleges etc. A tiny number was engaged in hospitals and laundry service.

An analysis of commercial occupations in Birmingham is particuarly significant in view of the importance that 'optimists', who assert that the standard of living rose consistently throughout the nineteenth century, place on an alleged upward mobility of employment from lower paid to higher paid jobs. We have already seen that there was no such upward mobility into professional employment. In 1841 about 3% of the employed population were in commercial positions. By 1871 it had risen to 4% where it remained during the first decade of the Great Depression. It then rose to 4.5% in 1891 and 5% in 1901. The number of clerks quadrupled from 1841 to 1901, but the increase had only marginal effects on upward mobility because the absolute numbers are small, the percentage of clerks in the employed population rose only from 2.1% to 2.9% and it is by no means certain that salaries of clerks were superior to wages of workmen. The doubling of employment in Insurance and Benefit Societies between 1881 and 1891 is interesting. The commercial figures throw some light on those responsible for the selling of the vast and varied output of Birmingham. The key figure was the merchant variously known as agents, brokers or factors, together with their salesmen and commercial travellers. One might expect these wholesale dealers to increase rapidly during the great expansion; in fact they increased from 0.7% of the employed population in 1841 to 0.74% in 1871. The Great Depression might have had the conflicting effects of bad trade driving out merchants, or difficulties in disposing of output tending to increase the number of merchants; in fact the figures declined to 0.6% in 1881 and further to 0.5% in 1891. Finally one might expect the end of the Great Depression to bring an increase in the number of merchants both as a result of the expansion of trade and also the greater difficulty in selling arising from the increased foreign competition; numbers here do indeed appear to have risen substantially for although the 1901 Census grouped together merchants with accountants and auctioneers, the great majority were merchants and salesmen suggesting a doubling of this category of employment to 1% of the employed population. Commercial travellers also increased rapidly from a virtually non-existent category in 1841 to 0.7% of the employed population in 1891. Unlike merchants, this growth had been considerable from 1841 and virtually doubled between 1871 and 1881.

Conveyance of persons, goods and messages was the fastest growing sector of employment rising from 3% in 1841 to 10% in 1901. This was a railway led growth, but after 1871 the proportion of road transport workers to railway workers increased and between 1881 and 1891 there was a doubling of road transport. There was also a very large increase in Messengers during the whole of the Great Depression. This was a main source of dead-end jobs for young boys (55% of all messengers in 1901 were between 10 and 15 years) as it was also in the slump of the 1930s and differentiates it from our own Great Depression when youth unemployment is such a serious problem.

Agricultural workers were not important in this period falling from 2.5% of the employed population in 1841 to 0.5% in 1901. Until 1891, however, their absolute numbers increased, the majority of these workers were not concerned with growing food, however, but catered for aesthetic or leisure pursuits of the urban population; thus in 1901 264 males worked on farms but 748 were grooms, gardeners, nurserymen, seedsmen and florists.

Finally, we turn to the main source of Birmingham male employment — industrial employment. The figures for building workers are important. Their numbers should indicate periods of maximum building and periods when building is of less importance. It is also sometimes claimed that construction work does not necessarily follow the pattern of the trade cycle. Something can be said on these points with regard to Birmingham. The town had its maximum nineteenth century population increase of 42% between 1821 and 1831. This was followed by three decades during which growth was about 27% in each decade. Growth in the next two decades fell to 16% and 17% and in the last two decades of the century to 9%. It is perhaps surprising therefore to find the construction industry employing only 5% of the employed population in 1841. The proportion increased to about 8% in 1871 and then fell during the Great Depression to 6.75%. During the middle years of the 1870s there was said to have been a building boom in Birmingham due to the great Improvement Scheme and the building of Board Schools, but if this were so the boom does not seem to have been strong enough to maintain the comparative size of the industry. Growth was resumed in the 1890s.

Another 10% of the working population was engaged in the two industries of (a) Fabric & Dress and (b) Food, Drink & Lodging. This seems to have reached a maximum in 1871 when it was over 16%. Thereafter employment within the two industries diverged, fabric and dress falling as both tailoring and bootmaking located themselves geographically outside our area. Food and drink fell less steeply. The growth in the drink trade slowed during the Depression years. From 5.9 publicans per 1000 of total population in 1871, the proportion of publicans fell to 4.4 in 1891; but by 1901 the figure was back at 6 per 1000 population which was almost as high as the 1841 figure of 6.2. The increase in the number of other food shops looks impressive, but when reduced to shops per 1000 population it seems that between 1841, and 1901 butchers' shops remained constant at 3, bakers' rose from 2 to 3 and grocers' rose from 2 to 3.5.

Lastly, we come to the traditional crafts and trades of workshop and factory. In 1871 more than 40% of the Birmingham male workforce were employed in what can be summed as a Minerals, Metals and Machines category. This proportion continued to decline through the remainder of the century and by 1901 was down to 33%. In 1871 the largest proportion of these worked in Iron and Steel. These were clock and instrument makers, machine makers, toolmakers, tinplate workers, iron makers, blacksmiths and whitesmiths, ironmongers etc. and constituted about 8% of the total workforce. Until 1891 their numbers increased but their proportion declined to 5.75%. By 1901 both numbers and proportion declined to 3.75%. The developing trades were those working in brass. The increased use of brass for gas-fittings, furniture such as bedsteads etc. made Birmingham the leading brass town displacing iron working as the leading category of factory and workshop employment.

The traditional jewellery trade — goldsmiths, silversmiths, lapidary etc. between 1841 and 1871 gave 2% to 5% of male employment. The trade suffered severely during the Great Depression falling to 3% of employment in 1891 and 1901.

Another traditional industry was Gunmaking. This industry was subject to the vagaries of both the demands of the war-mongers of all nations and the standardisation of rifles which began in U.S.A. and led to the setting up of a government factory at Enfield followed by the hasty cobbling together of B.S.A. with a large factory at Small Heath. Thus the era of the Crimean War and the wars of Italian and German reunification led to the maximum growth of the industry in the 1860s and 70s when it employed 5% of the workforce. It subsequently fell below 2% with a downswing in the human slaughter industry and strong Belgian and German competition in the alternative outlet of 'sporting' guns. Expansion was resumed with the Boer War.

The glassmaking industry in Birmingham was almost as large as in its traditional Black Country location of Stourbridge, or more correctly, Brierley Hill. It maintained its numbers quite well during our period, but the proportion of employment it offered fell from 1.3% in 1871 to 0.6% in 1901.

Button making employed about 2.5% of the male workforce in 1841 but fell to negligible proportions by 1901.

The other great growth industry, paralleling the development of road transport was Coach and Carriage building. Employing about 0.5% of the workforce in 1841 it grew to 1% by 1871. It stagnated in the next decade, but gave employment to 2% of the workforce in 1891. By 1901 the Census category had been changed to 'Vehicles'. and employment had doubled to 4%. Of these 4735 were engaged in 'Cycle and Motor Manufacture' and 897 were 'Railway — Coach, Waggon Makers'.

A weakness of the Censuses from the point of view of the social historian is their failure to identify grades of skill. Particularly important in this respect is unskilled labour. Much is made of the growth of skilled and thus higher paid employment as the century progressed, but much less is heard of de-skilling processes which also took place with such technical advance as was made in Birmingham. The 1841 Census shows Labourers as 5.25% of the workforce. From this I have excluded the 663 agricultural labourers. But there are obviously large numbers of labourers enumerated elsewhere under their industries. The largest number would probably be building labourers, but there are many others in local government employment, all factories, in brickmaking and many other employments. The 1871 Census shows a rise to 5.5% and would undoubtedly be greater if those of 20 years and under were known. Subsequently the proportion of 'Labourers' appears to decrease and by

1901 is down to the absurd proportion of 2%. At least in this Census, however, 2538 'Others' appear under House Building, most of whom are presumably labourers. A considerable number of the 1492 under 'Other Works of Construction and Roads' will also be labourers. If one includes the 2538 and only one third of the 1492, the percentage of labourers is near to 4%. In addition, a large number of the big increase in transport workers such as porters on the railways and carriers and carters in road transport were also labourers. The inadequacy of the educational system, the failure of the scientific and technological infra-structure to develop suggests that despite the development of large factories connected with vehicles, work skills where they existed, remained largely intuitive, that there was no large increase in the demand for skilled labour, and the economy continued to depend to an enormous extent on unskilled and semi-skilled labour existing within a low wage economy. These factors were both the most important cause of the depth of the Great Depression and, at the same time, the cause of its continuance in the face of developing industry in other countries. It is only in the last decade of the century when the Great Depression officially ends that some change in this situation occurs. Mass unemployment remained, however, and the limitation of the advances made in that decade are testified to by both the continuance of these economic problems to the present day and the subsequent history of the Birmingham working class movement to 1914 with its emphasis on the organisation of the unskilled and semi-skilled.

To complete the picture of male employment in Birmingham I discuss all other occupations which employed 1,000 or more in 1881. Nearly 2,000 men were employed in books and printing including 1280 newsagents. Nearly 3,000 were employed in furniture making and house decoration including 1,205 cabinet makers and unholsterers, 593 gas fitters, and 325 carvers and gilders. Almost 1,000 were employed in the working of cotton, flax, hemp, carpet making and other textiles, but 816 of these were drapers. Nearly 1,500 worked in grease, gut, bone, horn, ivory, skins, hair and feathers including 459 brush and broom makers. Over 2,250 worked in oils, wood and paper including 232 japanners and 496 wood turners and box makers. Over 1,500 worked in leather of whom 1055 made saddles, harness and whips and about 500 were tanners, curriers and makers of leather goods such as bags and straps. Finally, there were 1,122 undefined General Dealers including 178 pawnbrokers and 582 costermongers, hucksters and streetsellers.

This complete breakdown suggests that while Birmingham was indeed the town of a thousand trades the general economic development and well being of the town was heavily dependent upon a more limited range of trades which provided the bulk of employment.

Women at Home and at Work.
Long and exhausting toil was not only the lot of men, but of the vast majority of women as well. With females work began even earlier than with males; almost from the time that she could walk, a girl would be expected to help with the care of successive new arrivals in the family in a round of errands, housework and child care. It was the girls' education which was liable to be non-existent or interrupted in meeting the ordinary needs or crises of family life.

For most of the century large numbers of young girls would be at work contributing to the family income from the age of six. Under more favourable circumstances, such education as a girl might snatch would end at the age of ten and she would either leave the family for domestic service or she would enter industry at a wage finely calculated by the surplus of supply over demand to provide for her bare subsistence. The only escape from this Scylla was the Charybdis of marriage. Then began the real business of life. First there was the care of a male breadwinner who had to be woken, fed and washed for. Then came the endless round of child-birth, child care and housework which sapped the strength and undermined the health of even the hardiest and most efficient of women. Added to these almost impossible burdens was the necessity for the wife, either in an emergency or permanently to supplement the family income by taking in washing, doing part-time work or taking-in work from one of the sweated industries. During this phase of the family life cycle there was a considerable chance of the wife being widowed which would greatly exacerbate the poverty unless she remarried. By the time the family had grown up all but the strongest and most fortunate of women were worn out. Widowhood became an increasing certainty and the majority of women ended their lives in the direst poverty, dependent on such assistance as the children could or would afford or a few shillings from the Guardians each week with the final resort of the Workhouse. Such was the double oppression of women, alleviated in very many cases by caring and thoughtful husbands and children, but a double oppression never eliminated.

The limitations of the following Census data are even more pronounced for women than for men. The main problems are discussed below.

Female Occupations in Birmingham.
Number in Employment at each Census together with % of Employed Females where appropriate.

	1841	1871	1881	1891	1901
I. Professional.					
Connected with the Church	None	46	98	95	105
Law Clerks	None	1	None	2	8
Art, Music & Drama	33	233	419	539	667
Schoolmistresses & Governesses	409 2.3%	817 2.2%	1395 2.3%	1741 2.3%	1870 2.2%
Nurses & Midwives	176 1%	332 1%	490 0.8%	814 1%	963 1.2%
Doctors	1	-	3	2	2
II. Domestic.					
Wives & Others not Occupied	-	55869	116892	111631	127399
Domestic Service	7696 43%	8947	17933 30%	20393 26%	18337 22%
III. Commercial.					
Clerks	5	41	349 0.6%	1208 1.6%	2683 3.2%
Warehousewomen	332 2%	1388	1661 2¾%	1251	438

	1841	1871	1881	1891	1909
V. Industrial.	-	21833	37495 62%	48662 63%	57097 69%
Textiles & Dress	2772 16%	11016	13872 23%	14146 18%	13180 16%
Food, Drink & Lodging	342 2%	1577	1722 3%	3450 4%	5742 7%
Minerals, Metals & Mines	3879 22%	3974	13167 22%	15560 20%	24207 29%
incl Buttons	1160 6½%	1695	3081 5%	3246 4%	1687 2%
Jewellery	72	796	2857 4.7%	1761 2%	4143 5%
Pen Making	229	929	2233 3.7%	2530 3.3%	2887 3.5%
Burnishers	155	531	1585	2214	-
Iron Manufacture	-	1425	852	1549	-
Guns & Ammunition	55	546	343	114	729
Total Women in Employment	17872	37992	60209	77142	83116
Total Females 10 Yrs & Upward	70670	131414	152431	188773	210515

The key question of how many married women worked can only be
answered directly for 1901. According to the Census for that year 21557
married or widowed women were at work or 19% of all women in
Birmingham married or widowed. This figure is swollen by the large
number of widows, the majority of whom would presumably be forced to
seek employment, since very few would be receiving Poor Law allowances. For other Censuses, employment is divided between the two age
groups of those under 20 and those over 20. To estimate how many of
those over 20 at work were likely to have been married it is necessary to
consider marriage patterns in Birmingham. If we take the whole female
age group of 20 and upwards in 1881 we find:

Married 63% Unmarried 22% Widowed 14%

A further breakdown of the age groups shows:

	Ages						
	15-20	20-25	25-35	35-45	45-55	55-65	65 & Upward
Unmarried Women	12405	7674	4354	1467	779	410	257
Married Women	297	4530	14145	11699	7546	3709	1218
Widowed Women	3	55	579	1485	2275	2611	2735

Almost two thirds of women aged 20 to 25 were still unmarried. Most
women were married between the ages of 25 and 35, but nearly 23% of
that age group remained unmarried. The maximum marriage rate was
80% of the age group 35 to 45 after which the percentage of the age group
married declined as women were widowed:

Women widowed in age group 45-55	21%
Women widowed in age group 55-65	39%
Women widowed in age group 65 +	65%

The main conclusion is that many women tended to marry late in life
after the age of 25 and therefore a very large proportion of those females
over 20 enumerated as being in employment were likely to be single
women. For a closer estimate of married women at work we are forced
back to the 1841 Census. Here the number of females at work aged 20
and over was 12,335, but there were nearly 10,000 women aged 15-20
almost none of whom would be married and another 10,000 aged 20-25

almost two thirds of whom were likely to be single women and then large numbers of the 10,000 girls in the age group 10-15 were likely to have been employed. The conclusion can only be that very few married women went to work. This is unlikely to have been because of deep-rooted attitudes that married women should not go out to work — very little evidence of such attitudes in Birmingham have come my way; it is more likely to have been the normal and inevitable division of labour within working class families of men engaged in exhausting physical labour over twelve hours of each day plus a walk to and from work of 1 to 3 miles each way. Such a regime made it essential that the male wage earner should be serviced by a wife who would cook, wash and clean for him as well as bring up the family. The economic superiority of the man in this partnership would inevitably mean that a greater share of the common burdens would be placed on the woman, but this should not hide the necessity for such a division of labour in the period of the development of capitalism when the amount of surplus value to be extracted from a worker was limited. This situation changed slightly as the century progressed with a limited fall in the number of hours worked, and the boon of fairly cheap transport to work with the development of trams.

This inconclusive argument on the numbers of married women at work might be summarised as follows. In 1841 12% of all females 20 and upwards were enumerated as being at work. In 1901 this percentage had more than trebled and 37% of all females 20 and upwards were at work. In the latter case we know that 19% of all married and widowed women were at work. One might assume that the increase of married women at work proceeded *pari passu* with the increase of total women at work, in which case there would be about 6-7% of married women at work in 1841. But if social attitudes or economic conditions had changed during the half century permitting a greater proportion of married women to work, then the 1841 figure of married women at work would be less.

Turning from the question of who went to work to the question of what work they did, as with male occupations, we shall look first at the professional category. In 1841 there was one female doctor in Birmingham, in 1871 there was none, a maximum of three was reached in 1881, but thereafter it went down to two. There was a steady rise of women connected with the arts, the largest category of which appears as 'Musicians, Music Masters'. Teaching and Nursing have been the two professional occupations in which it has been assumed that opportunities greatly improved during the century. The numbers did, indeed, increase, but the proportion of such professional women within the workforce did not. It is sobering to find that the 409 Schoolmistresses and Governesses of 1841 represented 2.3% of the working female population and this remained virtually constant through the rest of the century. Even the 1871 proportion of 2.2% is valid in this case (only employment over 20 years is given in this Census) as few teachers would be under 20 years. These figures again illustrate (a) the backwardness of the educational system in Birmingham (b) that expansion of school facilities up to 1870 failed even to keep pace with the growth of population and (c) that progress after the 1870 Education Act was extremely slow.

With regard to nurses and midwives, it was not until the 1881 Census that they were upgraded from the status of 'Domestic' to 'Professional'.

The same comments apply as for teachers. Nursing provided 1% of female employment throughout the period 1841 – 1901 and was therefore neither a growth sector for female employment nor an avenue of 'upward mobility'.

In general with regard to professional women in Birmingham, one can only echo what is generally known. Nowhere was the domination of men more jealously guarded than in the (sometimes called 'liberal') professions. The situation with regard to women in general has been little changed since and it is the nineteenth century situation exactly that black women face at the present time.

Overwhelmingly the most important category of work for women was domestic labour. Until the introduction of mass Comprehensive Schooling, the key decision with regard to a child's future was taken at the age of ten. In recent years this was the age at which most children sat the mis-named 11 + examination to determine whether they went to elementary schools to join the mass of hewers of wood and drawers of water, or joined the 5% élite at secondary schools. For most of the nineteenth century such education as the average child acquired ended at the age of ten. Most children then left school for paid employment. With regard to girls, there was a particularly cruel dilemma. Girls earned less than boys and thus the wage earned was even nearer to the absolute subsistence level than for boys. The alternative was to shed the member of the family and, with all the heartache that this usually involved both for the family and the member, to send the girl into the virtual slavery of domestic service. In numbers of cases the slavemaster and mistress would be benign and some skills might be learned in private service; no doubt as many of these virtual slaves could be found to deny their slavery or even enjoy it as could be found among the actual slaves in ancient Greece or Rome, but the sixteen-hour day and almost total control over the life of the girl made domestic service the worst element of women's oppression. In 1841 domestic service accounted for 43% of all females employed. Numbers continued to rise reaching their peak in 1891 but the proportion steadily declined until in 1901, only 22% of the female workforce were domestic servants. Other facts confirm received opinion; most domestic servants were young girls. In 1841, 3151 were under 20 as against 4415 over 20, but we cannot identify the actual ages of those under 20. Domestic servants were overwhelmingly single women; in 1901, 11073 were unmarried compared with 1208 who were married. The same Census also tells us that 5% of those in domestic service were between 10 and 15 years. Finally, domestic service was the refuge of the spinster. In 1901 42% of domestic servants were over the age of 25 and most of these would remain voluntary or involuntary spinsters for the rest of their lives.

We next turn to Commercial employment, which was a considerable growth area of female employment. In 1841 there were just five female clerks in Birmingham, compared with 1364 men. By 1881 this figure had increased to 349. This nearly trebled in the next decade and more than doubled again in the next decade so that in 1901 there were 2686 female clerks, just above 3% of the total female employment. In 1901 only one in three clerks was female, but this proportion had been rapidly rising from less than one in ten in 1881. Higher grade commercial occupations however show no such large increase. In 1841 there were 24 female

Merchants, Agents & Accountants; by 1901 this figure had increased to 77 plus 99 women in banking and insurance. This is an increase from 0.13% to 0.21% of the employed female population.

Women played very little role in Transport which, until 1901, was enumerated under Commercial employment. For instance, in 1881 only 16 women worked on the railways, 7 in road transport and only 8 on the canals. The exception to this was Warehousing. For most of the century women predominated in this occupation. For instance, in 1841 there were 332 warehousewomen to 178 warehousemen; in 1881 there were 1661 women to 714 men. At this point it provided nearly 3% of all female employment. Both the numbers of women and their proportion fell thereafter.

As with Transport, women played a very small enumerated role in the tiny Agricultural occupations of the borough. In 1841 there were 786 male farmers and farm labourers compared with 26 women. In 1901 there were 1016 male farmers, labourers, gardeners, florists etc. and 46 women.

This leaves us with the consideration of Industrial Employment in the town which accounted for approximately two thirds of total female employment. In 1881 the largest component of this industrial employment was Dress and Fabric employing 23% of working women, compared with an almost equal percentage in minerals, metals and mines. The largest categories within the 13872 women working in Dress & Fabric were 5150 milliners and dressmakers, 1429 tailoresses and 1273 seamstresses, shirtmakers and stay makers. By 1901 textile and dress had fallen to 16%, and minerals, metals and mines had become the largest category of female employment at 29%. Food drink and lodging employment was a much smaller proportion of the enumerated female workforce than the male, but its proportion rose through the century from 2% in 1841 to 7% in 1901. Despite the fall-off in the important Textiles and Dress occupations, industrial employment continued to rise until in 1901 nearly 7 in 10 working women were employed in industry compared with less than 4 in 10 in domestic service. The Minerals, Metals and Mines category was mainly responsible for this, its share of the working female population rising from about 1 in 5 for most of the period to nearer 1 in 3 in 1901.

Something must be said about the traditional Birmingham industries and their contribution to female employment. In 1841 the button trade was probably the largest factory/workshop employer of female labour with about 6.5% of the workforce. The trade continued to be important, but the proportion employed seems to have halved between 1891 and 1901 from 4% to 2%. Jewellery was a negligible employer of women in 1841. It rose to nearly 5% in 1881, suffered severely in the subsequent decade (as did male employment), reviving strongly at the end of the century. Penmaking employed about 1% of women in 1841, developed rapidly to a peak in 1881 thereafter holding its proportion of about 3.5% of the female workforce. The gun trade provided very little employment for women but the allied and more dangerous occupation of ammunition and explosives became a predominantly female occupation, although maximum employment of 729 in 1901 represented less than 1% of female employment.

Other trades bring surprises. The development of the brass trade brought a large demand for burnishers and this became virtually a female occupation providing 3% of employment in 1891. Paper bag making was also an important provider of female employment. In 1841 it employed only 9 females. By 1881 it had risen to 1078. By 1901 it had increased 50% when it absorbed 2% of the female workforce. The only other trade providing considerable female employment was french polishing. This rose from 16 in 1841 to 665 by 1881. In 1891 french polishers were combined with upholsterers and furniture dealers in the enumeration and totalled 1384.

This section can be concluded by listing the only other five occupations providing more than 1000 female jobs in Birmingham in 1901:

Trade	Numbers Employed
Saddle, harness, whip & leather trades	1720
Cycle & Motor Manufacture	1409
Tinplate goods	1185
White metal & electro-plate wares	1140
Bolt, rivet, nut, screw & staple makers	1096

Hence, perhaps even more so for women than men, although Birmingham was the city of so many trades, occupations providing significant amounts of employment were limited.

Juvenile Employment

It might be thought that the Census would provide hard statistical evidence on the widespread use of child labour that existed in Birmingham throughout the century. It does not. The reasons for this are varied and complex, but two stand out. First, it is clear that parents were reluctant to register their children as being in paid employment, presumably from real or imagined fears of adverse legal or economic repercussions on such employment. Secondly, the age ranges used within which employment was recorded are so consistently unhelpful in quantifying child labour that it leads to the suspicion that official opinion did not want to use the Census to throw light on this problem.

Only two of the Censuses analysed employment by age groups at all. The first was the 1841 Census which divided both male and female employment into the two age groups of Under 20 years and Over 20. If we try to break down the Under 20 figures further we find that there were 9,401 females aged between 15 and 20. Most of these one would expect to find in employment. But the total number of females under 20 recorded as being employed came only to 5,330. The position is almost as bad with males. The total number of males aged 13 to 20, almost all of whom would need to be employed total 12,582. But males Under 20 at work totalled only 8306. The conclusions drawn from these figures might be either that child employment was not widespread, or that vast numbers of people who ought to be at work were not working. The former conclusion is negatived by the findings of the Child Employment Commissions of the 1840s and 1860s and the Sweated Labour enquiries in the last thirty years of the century. We do know that large numbers of children were neither at school nor at work throughout the century and made life difficult for the police. We would also expect considerable numbers of girls to be kept from school to help in the home and for this not to be recorded as employment; but the known fact that for the majority of Birmingham children schooling finished at the age of ten and work began, we must conclude that the Census figures are faulty.

In the 1901 Census employment is given for both males and females within the 10 to 15 age range. This at least acknowledges that there might be children at work at the age of ten. But the same problems arise. If we take two fifths of the total females aged 10 to 15 of 26,294 and assume that they are the 13-15 age group almost all of whom should be at work they total 15,776; but total females at work aged 10 to 15 only number 5,048. A similar analysis for boys shows 10,450 aged 13 and 14, but only 6,834 boys aged 10 to 15 at work.

The same deficiencies preventing a count of children employed, affect the identification of the industries in which child labour was particularly prevalent. Once again we are forced to an indirect approach which identified those industries where an above average number of the Under 20 age group were employed in 1841 and the 10 to 15 age group for 1901. In 1841 the proportion of the workforce under 20 was 30%. Hence:

1841

Occupations in which females under 20 constitute more than the average of 30%

	%	Numbers employed
Domestic Servants	42%	7566
Button Making	40%	1160
Pen Making	45%	229
Hook & Eye Making	45%	56
Chainmaking	47%	74

In 1901 females employed in the 10 to 15 age group amounted to 6% of employment. Only three industries can be identified here employing more than the average percentage in this age group and domestic service is not one of them:

1901

Occupations in which females 10-15 constitute more than the average of 6%

	%	Numbers employed
Jewellery	12%	2794
Saddlery	13%	Not known
Messengers, Porters and Watchmen	70%	311

The 1841 figures perhaps provide the strongest indirect evidence that domestic service absorbed large numbers of young girls; most of the other trades listed were both factory and domestic trades, but the numbers employed are insignificant except for button making. The 1901 figures perhaps indict the jewellery and saddlery trades, but the only certain conclusion is that the largest proportion of young girls employed was as messengers etc. The demand for this type of labour, however, was insignificant compared with the employment of boys as van boys, delivery boys etc.

The same techniques used for analysing male employment shows that in 1841, 16% were under 20 years of age and in 1901, 4% were aged 10 to 15:

1841

Occupations in which males under 20 years constitute more than the average of 16%

	%	Number employed
Brass trades	26%	3295
Button making	25%	1734
Domestic Servants	31%	1057

The above are the only three trades providing considerable employment where the numbers employed under 20 were above the average. Apart from whether these figures can be correlated with child employment, they have an interest of their own and there are some surprises. For instance, Porters, Messengers and Errand Boys where one would expect to find a large proportion of young people shows that only 93 out of 693 were under 20 giving a percentage of just under the average. Again, Warehousemen, an unskilled job where one would expect large numbers of young people shows a percentage at 8% well below the average with only 15 of the 178 under 20. One also finds that in skilled trades where one would expect a low proportion of workers under 20, that many have a much higher percentage of young people, although the total amount of employment they give is small. For instance 34% of the 131 Goldbeaters were under 20 and, just as surprising, 38% of the 260 printers were under 20. 34% of Founders, 26% of Engravers, 29% in the Glass trades, 33% in Nailmaking, 26% in Bellfounding were other examples of smaller trades employing more than the average of young people.

The 1901 Census is even less helpful in identifying industries employing more than the 4% which was the average of the total male workforce employed in the 10 to 15 age range. Messengers and errand boys constitute 55% of the 3794 people employed. Jewellery is the only other considerable employer of labour having 6% of its 8539 workforce under 20. For some strange reason no less than 150 or 13% of the 1168 males employed in National Government were under 20 and 6% of the 408 in law offices were young persons. For the rest, there are vast agglomerations of industries grouped together such as the 58,462 employed in Metals, Machines, Implements & Conveyances which show only 3% of employees under 20 and there is little else of significance to be gleaned from these figures.

Conclusions

Despite the difficulties and deficiencies of the Census date they provide the indispensable statistical base for comparing trends in employment throughout the expansionary phase of capitalism (1844 – 1874) and the changes which occurred thereafter to 1900. Some of these conclusions are:-

1. That superior employments requiring higher levels of skill and commanding higher wages are difficult to identify at any time from 1840 to 1900. Numbers certainly increased, but these just about kept pace with the increase in population. This appears to be true even of occupations where progress has been generally assumed, notably education and nursing.

    Skills continued to be intuitive and acquired at work rather than formally taught.

2. Those occupations that substantially increased tended to be service industries such as transport and catering where both levels of skills and wages tended to be low. This suggests substantial levels of deskilling to offset against such upward mobility and skill acquisitions as did occur.

3. The division of labour between men and women in the home was such that few married women worked unless dire necessity required this. The number of women in domestic service increased up to the 1890s, but as a proportion of employed women, declined from the 1850s. The proportion of women in industry therefore increased. Such work was overwhelmingly in unskilled and semi-skilled trades. This tended to keep wages of both men and women low. In growth occupations requiring skills absolute numbers were low e.g. female clerks, schoolmistresses and nurses. Their upward mobility would have to be offset to some extent by losses of skilled jobs in dressmaking, millinery etc.

4. The extent of child labour is hidden from us by the age groups under which employment was enumerated, and the apparent reluctance of parents to record that their children were employed.

5. Although Birmingham continued to be the city of a thousand trades, the bulk of employment was confined to a restricted range of trades, so that the immunity of Birmingham from mass unemployment and depression was much less than has been claimed.

Chapter Twelve

THE EMPLOYERS' RESPONSE TO THE GREAT DEPRESSION

Employer Summary of the Depression

Employer response to the Great Depression can best be dealt with through the reactions of the Birmingham Chamber of Commerce. This comprises (a) their day to day reaction through the activities of the Chamber and (b) their evidence to the Royal Commission on Trade and Industry in 1885 involving both their reply to questions asked and the oral evidence given. Under 'employer response' we can also use the reports of the Factory Inspectors, who were all. employer orientated, particularly the inspector Bowling.

Regarding the day to day response of the Chamber of Commerce we can begin with the early seventies. The boom is first commented upon in 1871 when the state of trade was given as 'very healthy'. The following year the Chamber was warning:

> The development of the healthy state of trade has been so rapid that the
> usual relations between supply and demand have been disturbed to an
> inordinate degree. It is impossible to say how soon the 'inevitable
> reaction' will take place.

It then went on to counsel 'extreme prudence and caution in granting wage increases and shorter hours.' In 1873 trade remained 'fairly active', but difficulties were reported from 'advanced costs of labour and the exorbitant price of fuel which has diverted a considerable portion of our trade to foreign countries.' The USA was quoted as a vast market 'now supplying its own needs as well as supplying the colonies and even importing into Britain.' 1874 gave the first hint of the coming slump there being 'considerable depression of some trades in the town.' The crisis developed in 1875 and by the next year there was 'no relief from the depression which the important staple trades and general industries of the town and district suffer.' 1877 brought no improvement 'depression was great and almost universal.' In 1878 'the depression had still not reached its depth' but the Chamber was stoutly resisting protection as a solution, 'after 35 years we have undiminished confidence in the advantages of free trade.' Some causes of the depression were mentioned — the Spanish tariff, famines in India and China, default on foreign loans of £300m, bitter and ruinous disputes between capital and labour and foreign competition. All this had brought 'excess production over demand.' Lack of notice of the depression in 1879 might suggest that it was easing. In fact it was perhaps the very worst year and in 1880 there was 'no change in the almost universal depression.' Not until 1881 was a gradual improvement in trade reported. Remedies were discussed in that year. In discussions there had been large majorities for bimetallism and a demand for increased trade with the dominions and colonies. There had been a 33 to 15 vote in support of free trade as 'the soundest way to extend and consolidate trade relations.' The Chamber had also opposed the repeal of the Imprisonment for Debt law on the grounds that it had 'a salutary effect on those with debts and would destroy the retail credit system which the working class in times of necessity require to obtain food.' 1882 was a year in which the improvement of trade had been 'only partially maintained.' The productive powers of this and other countries 'was increasing so rapidly and consequent rivalry was so keen that there had been great and increasing difficulty in finding remunerative markets.' In 1883 there had been some prospects of developing trade; in the staple trades the volume of business had increased but competition had reduced profits. 1884 was another bad year there being 'no improvement in trade whatever.' 1885 was the year of the Royal Commission. Support for free trade was beginning to crumble and the idea of an Imperial Federation had been supported, although in the following year a motion demanding retaliation against those who refused to grant Britain 'most favoured nation' status in trade had been defeated. No improvement in trade was reported in that year, 'the staple industries being impaired and destroyed by internal and external competition.' Improvement in 1887 was recorded cautiously:

> The time has not yet arrived to congratulate traders on the return of that prosperity so long delayed and so anxiously hoped for.

1888 saw a 'gratifying increase in the volume of trade but prices were so low that there were very small profit margins. 1889 was much better 'a very considerable and profitable increase in trade' being reported. The improvement continued into the following year but 'increased wages had restrained output and reduced employment in some important trades'. The boom was faltering. In 1891 there had been 'a probable increase in home trade but a fall in foreign,' whilst the next year 'trade was most unsatisfactory'. The report for 1893 was pessimistic 'having regard for the increase in population the steady and alarming decrease in the volume of trade was detrimental.' In 1894 trade was unsatisfactory. 1895 was a mixed year 'opinions being so various it is difficult to come to a conclusion.' The boom was resumed in 1896 and reached its peak in 1899. In 1900 'weaknesses had developed during the year' and by 1901 'the great prosperity of 1899 was passing away. This was the last year in which the Birmingham Chamber of Commerce annual report gave a state of trade summary.

This year by year account suggests that from mid-1875 to 1880 trade was almost universally acutely depressed. From 1881 to 1886 trade was better, but at a plateau much lower than the 1870–74 boom period; 1887–1890 saw a mini-boom; 1891–95 was another depressed plateau; 1896–99 were years of increasing trade raising hopes that the Great Depression was over. Perhaps it was, but depression returned in 1900. All this suggests not only that the Great Depression was very real in Birmingham, but raises the question of when it ended, if indeed it did end before 1914.

Royal Commission on the Depression of Trade — Written Questions.

We can next turn to the Birmingham Chamber of Commerce response to the questions posed by the Royal Commission on Trade and Industry.

Nationally the Great Depression had been a prolonged period of depressed trade with horrific troughs in 1876–79 and again in 1884–85. But in the immense length of time that 'bad trade' had existed, the break with the periodicity of the trade cycles of 1850–75, the obvious restructuring of industry that was then proceeding, the emergence of new industries and the enormous increase in foreign competition raised very sharply the question of what sort of Depression there was and very specific series of questions were addressed to both trade societies and to the trade unions. At least the Birmingham Chamber of Commerce grappled with its questions, whereas the response of the trade unions in Birmingham was poor.

The first two questions asked what area was covered and what were the trades of particular importance. The Chamber replied that their area was that of Birmingham borough and the important trades were iron, metals, hardware, jewellery, gun, leather, glass and coal trades. The next question asked how the market divided into Home and Foreign. This question the Chamber was unable to answer because no statistics were available.

Question 4 was very detailed requesting comparison with five-yearly periods from 1865 regarding volume of trade, its value and profitability, capital invested and quantity of labour employed. Again, the Chamber was unable to give the details requested, but answered as follows:

> Trade received a great impulse during the periods 1870 to 1875, partly through the Franco-German war, which threw the bulk of the carrying trade into the hands of England, and increased greatly the demand for goods for foreign markets. The volume of trade, the value, the net profit, the amount of capital invested and the labour employed being largely increased.
>
> The trade and industry of the district has been much depressed during the years 1880 to 1885 and before, but the extent of such depression, the loss of profit, the diminution of capital and decreased demand for labour, can only be guessed at, the necessary factors for making any accurate or reliable estimate not being available.

Question 5 stated that 'depression of trade' seemed to imply some norm of trade and asked during which recent years trade had been at, below, or above that level. Again the Chamber could not answer the question and replied:

> There is no normal level of trade. There was great and unusual activity from 1870 to 1875, and great and almost continual depression (with one or two intervals) since 1875.

Question 6 asked, judged by the 'normal' level of trade, what special trades and industries could fairly be described at that time as 'depressed'. The answer was short and not very sweet:

> Every trade, special and ordinary, can only be described as depressed.

Question 7 asked when the depression began, when it reached its lowest point, and its most prominent symptoms. The answer was that distinct depression began in 1876–7 and the lowest point was reached in the present year (1885). The answer with regard to the lowest point is surprising and important to the question of the nature of the depression. For if the Great Depression in Birmingham is to be written off as a myth it would seem to be necessary to find some turning point in the early 1880s which would keep the trough of 1885 higher than the trough of the disaster years 1879 – 80. The Chamber of Commerce finds no such turning point.

Questions 8 and 9 asked whether the depression had been uniform or irregular and what was thought likely to be its subsequent course. These questions also probed deeper into those effects on different trades. Again, the Chamber was stumped:

8. Irregular. The Council have no means at their disposal to judge of the immediate future.

9. On the whole uniform in duration and intensity, with occasional, short periods of activity in special trades, arising from recent Government requirements, and other exceptional causes.

Question 10 asked whether there were any special circumstances in the area. The Chamber was more at home with this and answered:

1. German and Belgian competition.

2. Foreign import duties on home manufactured goods exported abroad.

3. The exorbitant cost of carriage of goods from Birmingham to the sea board, which has placed inland districts at a great disadvantage compared with maritime towns.

Question 11 asked whether the demand for, supply of and return to capital was above or below the average of the last twenty years. This was a matter of crucial importance to the debate, but, again, the Chamber could not answer it:

The Council consider this question, in its present form, is too ambiguous to be dealt with.

The Commissioners then turned to wages and Question 12 asked whether wages for skilled and unskilled workers were above or below the average of the last twenty years. The Chamber replied that skilled wages had been maintained but unskilled wages were below that average.

The last two questions concerned remedies for and causes of the depression. Question 13 asked what measures could be adopted to improve trade both by legislative and other means. The Chamber replied:

1. Fresh legislation on the regulation of railways and railway rates, making minimum rates charged for foreign goods the maximum for home goods, and including the emancipation of canals from the control of the railway companies.

2. The imposition of an import duty on foreign manufactured goods in all cases where the same class of goods are manufactured in this country.

3. The formation of a trading union between the mother country and her colonies and dependencies.

4.   The establishment of an international bi-metallic currency.

Question 14 was very detailed, asking to what extent the depression in Birmingham was due to all the various causes which had been put forward such as changes in the relation between labour, capital, producers, distributors and consumers; changes in hours of labour, appreciation of the standard of value, currency and banking laws; conditions of credit; over-production; foreign competition, tariffs and bounties; taxation; transport; legislation affecting trade and land. The replies were:

> This question demand so large an amount of labour and so much statistical information, which the Council have no means of obtaining in their collective capacity, that they can only briefly summarise what are in their opinion some of the principal causes of the present depression.
>
> 1.   Legislative interference with the hours of labour by Factory & Workshop Acts.
> 2.   Foreign competition in neutral markets, the rate of wages and hours of labour in Germany, France, Belgium and all other manufacturing countries being lower and longer than in this country, except in America.
> 3.   The influence of trade unions limiting, if not destroying, freedom of contract between masters and men.
> 4.   The better technical education of the foreign workman.
> 5.   The demonetarisation of silver by Germany and the consequent disturbance of the 15.5 to 1 of silver and gold. This has operated most injuriously upon our commercial interests with all countries having a silver currency, India, China, Japan, South America and others.
> 6.   The great agricultural depression caused by the long series of bad seasons and foreign competition, resulting in diminished purchasing powers.

Thirteen was unlucky for the Council as the answer to the question repudiated free trade and opted for protection. This roused a storm of protest, and a well-attended full Chamber meeting of 113 members passed a resolution regretting that the Council should have answered the question without previously submitting the answers to the Chamber for its approval and, without expressing an opinion on the other answers, strongly disapproved answer No 2. to question 13. Thus the Chamber confirmed its age long adhesion to free trade.

The Royal Commission — Oral Evidence

The representatives deputed to give oral evidence to the Commission on behalf of the Chamber of Commerce were Mr. Henry Z. Muller and Mr. Wyley Lord. Neither were manufacturers. They were both general merchants and exporters. They were closely questioned on most of their answers to the written questions.

Regarding the proportions of trade between home and foreign markets they reiterated that there were no statistics enabling them to be answered.

There were Board of Trade figures showing that Birmingham foreign trade had fallen, but the delegates differed concerning the volume of home trade, Muller thinking it 'much the same' in recent years whilst Lord thought that it had fallen and both agreed that the profit was less.

Manufacturers sometimes worked on exports and at other times for the home market; in the absence of figures for the total produce of Birmingham nothing further could be said. Where profits had been reduced, the Commissioners asked, were these the profits of the manufacturers, merchants or retailers? Principally manufacturers, said Muller; also merchants added Lord. If lower profits came from greater competition could the delegates pinpoint whether the competition came from foreign or home manufacturers? 'Both' they replied. Does the home competition arise from Birmingham or from other parts of the kingdom? Again the reply was 'both'. The Commissioners probed even further, 'Do you mean that in spite of the Depression more have come to the place that is depressed to compete with those whose profits are less than formerly? 'Yes'. Is the competition from individuals who have entered or from limited liability companies? The latter, said Muller, both said Lord. They agreed that the aggregate capital of private firms was distinctly larger than twenty years before, that the capital of limited liability companies was large and increasing, but profits levels were lower for both. Did the increasing number of limited liability companies represent the intrusion into Birmingham of new trades or were they formerly Birmingham firms? The latter, the delegates agreed; only the Compressed Air Company could be thought of as representing a new trade without a large number of private firms.

The gun trade, as one of the most seriously depressed, gave rise to much discussion. The general conclusion was that the military gun trade had fallen very low due to lessened demand, other countries making their own guns, and even exporting them, and domestic competition from the large Enfield factory. The sporting gun trade was much reduced from foreign, mainly Belgian, competition.

The discussion then turned to the question of why foreign trade was so much reduced. Muller and Lord answered (a) because foreigners were receiving less for their goods due to the devaluation of silver and so could not afford to buy as much from Britain as before (b) countries formerly buying from Britain were now making their own goods (c) foreign competition from France, Belgium, Germany, USA and even Norway and Italy decreased our share of the market and (d) tariffs on our exports.

Jewellery, together with iron, were considered to be two of the most depressed trades and at least one of the reasons for this was common to both, there had been a very large increase in capacity during the years of the boom 1870 – 75 and thereafter because of lack of demand there was 'overproduction'. But what was overproduction and who was responsible for it? Was it the large limited liability companies which had gone on producing after private traders had ceased to find this possible? 'Yes' was the answer. Can you give an example? 'No', said the witnesses. How is this overproduction evinced? 'By the enormous stocks they have.' But no examples could be quoted, although the two delegates later spoke of engineering firms and lamp makers as holding large stocks.

Still the Commissioners were not satisfied:

Q. If in the boom years capital had entered into trade more than it could bear at the moment, do you think that was because business was not increasing as fast as capital, and employment is not increasing as fast as population?

A.   Capital must be increasing to enable people to put down the
      stocks they do.
Q.   Is there anything particularly favourable which would attract
      greater capital to Birmingham?
A.   No.
Q.   Then what you call overproduction may in fact be the want of
      a legitimate increase in demand either in the home or the
      foreign market?
A.   Yes. Overproduction is want of demand.

We may leave these exchanges at this point with Muller and Lord
sticking to their guns and no one raising the question of Underconsumption.

The witnesses were also quizzed on their advocacy of bimetallism. This
was the policy of the Birmingham Chamber of Commerce, continuing the
tradition of unorthodoxy in monetary theory dating back to Thomas
Attwood and Robert Owen. Lord was the expert on bimetallism. His
main argument was that the demonetarisation of silver by Germany had
led to a depreciation of the value of that metal compared with gold. This
decreased the value of the exports of all those countries still on a silver
standard such as China, India, Japan, South America etc. and these
countries were consequently not able to buy as much from Britain as
before.

When the question of lack of technical education was raised, it was
largely confined to its effect on design and fashion. It arose in connection
with sporting guns and the 'vulgarity' of the ornamentation of Belgian
guns. This ensured that they could not capture the British market
irrespective of their price or quality, because British buyers considered
the ornamentation 'not in good taste'. In view of the fact that many goods
which were fashionable and popular could be considered 'vulgar', while
goods that were 'tasteful' were neglected, it was suggested by the
Commissioners that raising standards through better technical education
would not necessarily lead to greater demand for our goods. This the
witnesses agreed to. It was pointed out, however, that Elkington's were
noted artistic manufacturers in Birmingham, but their principal designers
were French.

Finally, the discussion turned to worker/employer relationships and the
alleged effects of trade unionism on the Depression. High wages and
restrictive practices allegedly caused by the trade unions have always held
a high place in the demonology of the employers. Usually these are
discussed by the employers more in sorrow than in anger. But sometimes
the venom shows through. It began with unemployment. 'There are very
large numbers of persons out of employment in Birmingham now, are
there not?' was the first question. 'It is stated so' replied Muller. 'From
your own experience would you say that it is the fact? 'Yes. . . but
whether there are quite as many as they want to make out is the question.'
Lord broke in to assert that the unemployment was 'chiefly in the inferior
class of workmen'. Does the fact of large numbers out of employment
tend to keep up or diminish the average rate of wages, was the next
question. Muller said that it did not make much difference because there
are those unions of artisans who will not reduce their wages; there was
a fixed scale all through.

Q.   But were not earnings generally lessened by deficiency and
     irregularity of employment?
A.   Yes.
Q.   So that upon the whole you would say that wages in
     Birmingham have very greatly fallen off, although the rate for
     piecework may not have diminished.
A.   Yes.

The discussion then moved on to the alleged restrictive practices said to
have been affecting our ability to compete with the Germans. Muller had
said that it was difficult to get workmen to change the pattern of products.
Pressed for a case in point Muller said that if it was desired to make an
improvement in an article which had been made at a certain rate of wages
a workman, perhaps, would not give a price without consulting his union
or trade society. Muller was then questioned on his 'perhaps' and asked
whether workmen had absolutely refused or thrown obstacles in the way
of improvement in manufactures generally. Very frequently, insisted
Muller. Lord then chipped in:

> Most people would find it so, because we found that when our workmen
> had been gorged with plenty the wants of buyers and suggestions for
> improvement were not cheerfully received; in fact they were difficult to
> enforce. This arose partly from the inconvenience of altering machinery,
> dies, patterns etc and partly from unwillingness to change. There is a
> very strong feeling against making changes, and it is very intelligible in
> some respects. What has been done before, the workmen knows the
> result of and any changes in the manufacture may lead him into
> difficulties that he does not know.

At a later stage, Lord attacked the principle of trade unions suggesting
that it would be better if manufacturers and workmen were able to make
their own arrangements without the interference of trade unions. 'Better
for whom?' he was asked, 'the manufacturers or the men?' For both, he
replied. Very often both are willing to agree, but the trade union
intervenes. Asked if he had any direct knowledge of this, Lord replied
that he had. Asked if he had ever had dealings with trade unions or their
officers, Lord had to admit that he had not. Muller came to his rescue
by relating his experience with gas engines (the only branch of
manufacture he was connected with). The price for one machine having
been established, the next week another size would have to be made and
the men would not give a price without consulting the trade union. When
Muller wanted a reduction in the price proposed, they would not reduce
it, although the non-union men would have been willing. Asked whether
prices were fixed between unions and employers, Muller said it was fixed
by the unions alone. 'But were not prices in many trades fixed by
employers and workmen', he was pressed. 'Yes', he replied. 'Were not
prices often fixed by employers alone without any consultation with the
workmen?' 'I do not know, I am speaking only from my own experience,'
said Muller.

The gruelling session continued, often returning to topics already
discussed as each Commissioner pursued his special interest. In all, over
1,900 questions were asked. It is a great pity that Birmingham trade
union representatives did not give evidence to the Commission, neither

answering the questions addressed to them nor appearing to give oral evidence.

Factory Inspectors and the Great Depression.

At this time, the Birmingham district had two Factory Inspectors. Sub-Inspector Bowling serviced north Birmingham and sub-Inspector Johnston the south. One of the effects of the 1870 – 75 boom was an increase in the demand for child labour. Because of the demands of the 1870 Education Act, this manifested itself in an increase in the number of Birmingham children attending school part-time and in October 1875 Bowling reported nearly 3000 half-timers in Birmingham schools, whereas there had only been about 200 in 1871. The demand for male young workers had completely outstripped demand and the position would worsen, Bowling said. Part-timers did indeed increase to 3872 in May 1876, but a year later they were down to about 3300.

In April 1876, Robert Baker, the Inspector for the area, commented on the Birmingham trade position. He said that the general state of trade had for some time appeared to have been worsening and was then worse than at any other time that he could remember. Baker had been an inspector in the west midlands since at least 1864. Johnston offered the opinion that it was not until May 1876 that 'the town began to feel the general depression of trade which had not much affected its industries (with the exception of the gun trade) up to that time.'

In his annual report for the year ending October 1879, the Chief Inspector dealt with the Birmingham area. During the winter the depression had reached a very serious state and had 'rendered a public fund for the relief of distress necessary.' He went on:

> I cannot report any material increase in the various industries up to the present, half or three quarters time being the rule in most.

The flint glass industry had not expanded since 1868, he claimed, and the building trade was then much depressed 'after having been greatly overdone during the last two or three years.

In October 1880 Bowling reported 'a steady but not largely developed improvement in almost all branches of trade in the district'. In the brass trade, chandeliers and lamp fittings were well supplied with orders, but cabinet and building brass foundries were quieter owing to the dullness in the building trade. Engineers and ironfounders had had a bad year, flint glass was suffering from much foreign competition, but the button trade had seen a general improvement.

Bowling made his last report in October 1883 and it was a eulogy of improvements in Birmingham worthy of the most enthusiastic Chamberlainite civic gospeller:

> On quitting a district in which I have had charge of the Factory & Workshops Act for 13 years, I feel it to be alike a pleasure and a duty to bear testimony to the great steps which have been taken during that time by the whole community of the large and important town of

Birmingham to improve in every possible way the conditions under which its thousands of toiling people will perform their daily round of work, and to brighten their social life.

There is much more in the same vein, but Bowling then goes on to repeat what he wrote in 1872:

There is another cause which I think goes a long way to account for much that one sees to deplore in the moral and physical condition . . . of a large number employed in Birmingham factories and workshops. I refer to the wretched condition of the factories themselves. You know, Sir, there are many such places in Birmingham which are a disgrace to a civilised country. Low, dirty and dark, cramped up in back courts, half a dozen factories, perhaps, converted into a factory, or I might more properly say, a kind of human warren, in and out of which you see men, women and children burrowing their way to their appointed holes.

Bowling goes on to claim that there had been great improvements in the thirteen years since 1872 but adds, 'there are still too many places which should be improved off the face of the earth.' He then makes a proposal:

So much has been done in Birmingham by a combination of philanthropic and commercial enterprise to provide for the working classes scientific and literary institutes, public libraries, hospitals, provident dispensaries, coffee palaces, parks and recreation grounds, that I sometimes wonder that the idea has not entered the heads of some of the public-minded and large-hearted citizens of this great town to form a company for the creation of model workshops to be let out to the thousands of small masters who are found now to carry on their handicrafts under very wretched and insanitary conditions. I feel sure that such an enterprise could be made a commercial success and would result in a vast benefit to the community. Some of the so-called 'mills' in Birmingham, which perhaps hold from 20 to 40 tenants, are hopelessly miserable places and must exercise a very depressing and demoralising influence on the poor people who have to work in them.

Before taking Bowling's glowing report of progress in Birmingham during the Great Depression at its face value one can turn to another matter involving this inspector. One of the cases against Depression in Birmingham is that certain trades, for instance the brass trade, undoubtedly expanded very considerably during the years 1875 – 95. When he left Birmingham Bowling became an inspector in the East End of London. In his report for 1887 he wrote:

It is a remarkable fact that although the amount of distress from want of employment in the East End is undoubtedly large, manufacturing industry continues to increase and I should judge that the volume of production is greater than it has ever been.

I was told of one firm which took over an adjacent works which closed. Both works now turn out twice the amount of products but the receipts are now £5000 a year less than when it occupied only one factory.

It is likely that such a state of affairs was not uncommon in Birmingham as well as the east end of London.

The local factory inspector's reports from 1884 to 1887 have not been found, but in 1888 S.H. Knyvett, who was Bowling's replacement, reported a marked advance in the prospects for trade. He linked this with the number of notifications he had received of overtime working:

1882 — 420 notices from 48 different firms.
1883 — 422 notices from 43 different firms.
1884 — 515 notices from 52 different firms.
1885 — 714 notices from 68 different firms.
1886 — 515 notices from 47 different firms.
1887 — 771 notices from 72 different firms.

Knyvett reported a continuing marked improvement of trade in 1887 instancing the jewellery trade.

	1887	1888
Gold wares assayed and marked (ozs)	108,233	122,743
Silver wares assayed and marked (ozs)	858,662	775,901

The local factory inspectors' reports for 1889–95 have also not been found, but when they reappear in 1896 cautious use is still being made of overtime notifications as an indicator of prosperity. One of the limitations of this use is that the notifications could come from a restricted number of industries. For instance, of 684 notifications from factories in Birmingham 1 District in 1896, 200 came from printing, 156 from box making and 187 from warehousing leaving only 141 from all other industries; the vast majority of notifications from Workshops came from wearing apparel. The figures, for what they are worth, are as follows:

Notifications of Overtime in Birmingham.

	Birmingham 1 District		Birmingham 2 District	
	Factories	*Workshops*	*Factories*	*Workshops*
1896	684	1807	722	1031
1897	451	1529	657	912
1898	335	337	420	440
1899	158	1882	100	1318
1900	306	3435		

The single figure for 1900 is given with the additional information that overtime had largely increased owing to the war, but whether the figure is for District 1 or District 2 or even both together, is not known. Knyvett's general comments on conditions in Birmingham work places at the end of the century may be gleaned for his 1898 report:

> I always feel that we are marking time until that happy time comes when all premises have to be licenced. But when that time comes I hope we shall be dealing with the landlord and not the occupier. Abominable privies, dilapidated roofs and premises, unsafe stairways, badly lighted courts and alleys, why should these continue to be leased out to employers of labour?

Chapter Thirteen

TRADE UNION RESPONSE TO THE GREAT DEPRESSION
1874 – 1884

Trade Unions 1870 – 74
The boom years of 1870 – 74, brought a surge of trade union membership as the struggle to raise wages and decrease hours brought considerable improvements in conditions. New unions such as the Birmingham branch of the Amalgamated Society of Railway Servants emerged, skilled workers such as engineers in the new large-scale factories assumed greater importance, glass workers were still more numerous in Birmingham than in Stourbridge and the Birmingham trade union movement was developing in ways unique to the town which conditioned their response to the Great Depression when it came.

One of these developments was the emergence of the local Tinplate Society as the largest branch outside London. In the past, each local Society had been independent and when the Birmingham society was negotiating a 10% increase in wages they were told that this was impossible because of competition from the Wolverhampton area. So the Birmingham branch merged with the powerful Wolverhampton branch. Not only was the increase granted in both towns, but a price list for government work was produced in conjunction with the Employers Association consisting of 135 pages. When tenders were invited there were meetings of workers and employers to determine prices and no final decisions were made until actual samples had been produced; all this was done with government co-operation.

Another development was even more significant for Birmingham. In 1872 a twenty-three-years-old trade unionist, W.J. Davis, had the audacious plan of organising the myriad branched, notoriously sweated brass trades into a National Society of Amalgamated Brassworkers. The results brought national notoriety to both Davis and his union.

Davis was born in 1848 into a family of Birmingham brass makers. His only 'formal' education was two years and a half at a dame school. In 1860 he began to attend George Dawson's Church of the Saviour Sunday School. After two or three years he became a teacher at the Sunday afternoon school. He also attended Sunday morning training classes in grammar and composition. Later he attended Arts & Science classes and was awarded a Queen's Prize under the South Kensington Science and Art Department. He then joined YMCA classes in drawing, geometry etc. and was attending these when he became secretary of the Brassworkers. He also attended Barr Street Improvement Society and took classes in oratory and essay writing.

Davis' tactics were to make a virtue of necessity, isolate groups of employers and attack them singly before moving on to the next group. Thus he first attacked the Cabinet brass founders making hinges, handles and drawer furniture. These were the most prosperous employers. An initial meeting requested a 15% advance which the employers ignored.

The Union was then inaugurated at a mass Town Hall meeting in April 1872. Davis was elected secretary and his first step was to start branches at Wolverhampton, Walsall, Stourbridge, London, Sheffield and other brass centres. The demand was repeated and the employers conceded the 15% advance in August. This created a national sensation. Advances could be achieved without strikes. Davis became a national figure. After organising workers, he next turned to organising the employers. This was less popular, but by 1874 Davis had reached an understanding with the Gas Fitting and Chandelier employers that all disputes should be referred to the Employers' and Workmen's Associations. If no agreement could be reached there would be a joint meeting of the two Associations. If there was still not agreement a further joint conference would be called with an umpire mutually agreed. The findings of this Conference would be final and binding for the next twelve months. Davis went on to another remarkable success with the Hinge Dressers. In this trade there was no uniform price paid. Within six months prices were levelled up and an average 22.5% rise gained. The resultant list was still in operation nearly forty years later at the outbreak of the First World War.

Davis' first annual report for 1872 – 73 stated that the Society had been started at a time when the 'state of trade so well sustained and so rapidly improving to the employer offered but slight encouragement to the artizan. Exorbitant increases in the price of provisions and the common necessities of life have reduced workmen's wages at least 20%.' In addition, 'a general decline in piece prices, dearness of underhand labour and the contemptuous manner in which a pacific approach was rejected led to the inauguration of the Society.' Prompt action secured a 15% advance and the power of the Society had rapidly been increasing. Total membership at the end of the year was 5,700 and income was £4,691.

Over the period 1874 – 76 Davis improved the system of Conciliation and Arbitration which was to be the main initial response of the Birmingham Trades Council and trade union movement in general to the Great Depression. But this response cannot be entirely written off as one of class collaboration. The main characteristics of the schemes were as follows, some of which were also applicable to periods of more open class conflict:

1. The iron fist in the velvet glove by the use of the strike weapon only when all other methods of conciliation had been exploited and such overwhelming power could be brought to bear that a strike became either unnecessary or could be won in the shortest possible time.
2. 100% trade unionism in each trade buttressed by the payment of the higher trade union rate only to union members.
3. Minimum wage rates negotiated nationally, maximum rates negotiated locally.
4. Recognition of trade unionism by 100% of employers through 100% of them belonging to their trade association and thus eliminating price cutting.

These early Birimingham experiments in Conciliation and Arbitration took their inspiration from the Black Country where similar schemes in the coal and iron industries originated in the late sixties. The early Birmingham schemes were inaugurated during the prosperous years of the early 1870s and tended to founder during the Depression years. The hey-day of the famous Birmingham Alliances was the decade 1890 – 1900 when the worst years of the Great Depression were over. The system was almost totally dependent on the existence of arbitrators with the confidence of both employers and trade unionists. Such arbitrators were produced, Rupert Kettle and Joseph Chamberlain on the employers' side, but more remarkable, W.J. Davis and Richard Juggins on the trade union side.

Both the course and the principles of Conciliation and Arbitration are so well documented for Birmingham and the Black Country that they will subsequently be dealt with here only in the context in which they arise, but a general judgement can be made. The 'heroic' periods of trade union development in Birmingham when not only membership has advanced rapidly, but developments of national significance have occurred are 1779 – 82, 1824 – 26, 1830 – 34, 1870 – 74, 1890 – 95, 1910 – 1914 and 1934 – 39. In this town of reputed employer/employee common interests only one of these periods — 1870/74 — has been one of close class collaboration and this might well be deemed the least productive and least significant of these periods.

Depression and Retreat

With the ending of this period of good trade and the onset of the Great Depression all hatches had to be battened down.

Like the Chamber of Trade, but with better reason, the Trades Council was slow to acknowledge better times and quick to stress the unlikelihood of their long continuation. The sixth annual report of 1872 stated:

> There has been a prosperous state of trade and many advances have been obtained, but hope for a very long continuance of such prosperity does not appear to be sanctioned by the experience of the past. Calling to mind like years in times gone by with succeeding relapses, panics and starving thousands seems rather to point to the necessity for all societies to husband their resources, perfect their organisations and prepare themselves for more adverse times which, perhaps, the not far distant future must bring.

Meanwhile projects for advance were put in hand which the Depression was to cut short. In 1874 a letter from the then rural area of Stirchley asked the trades council to provide a speaker on political-social questions and to help secure the vote for the rural population. The trades council had already involved itself from 1872 in rural affairs by its support for Joseph Arch's Agricultural Workers' Union. by September 1874 nearly £356 had been collected, but that union was already being overwhelmed by the agricultural depression. Such solidarity and assistance had urban repercussions in the demand for land nationalisation and the growth of Republicanism, as we have seen. Another trades council intitiative which had to be abandoned with the onset of the Depression was a project to build in Birmingham a trades' hall.

As with the subsequent Great Depression of the 1930s and the on-going one of 1974, the first reaction to mass unemployment was not increased militancy and solidarity but a reversion to the more primitive instinct of individual self-preservation, a desperate struggle to protect gains already made and an employer counter-offensive on the trade unions as scape-goats for the existence of the Depression when, in fact, slump and mass unemployment is a recurring and necessary condition for the continuance of the capitalist system and any subsequent expansion.

It is indicative of the problems of the Trades Council in the years 1875–85 that its records are badly kept, that its minutes are difficult to read and the records from August 1879 to October 1881 are missing altogether. The political philosophy of the skilled trade unionists dominating the Council was a cloth-capped Chamberlainism of Lib/Labism and in fact the Trades Council lagged behind the Radical (indeed socialist) Programme of 1885 which was to be the high point of Chamberlain's radicalism before he changed the political geology of Britain in the following years by his defection to the Tories with his Liberal Unionists over Home Rule in Ireland.

The Chamber of Commerce records can again be reverted to to chart the course of unemployment from the mid 1870s: Considerable depression of some trades was reported from the first half of 1874; the Depression widened during 1875 and 1876 and brought no relief from the depression affecting the staple trades in general industries of the town. By 1877 the depression was great and almost universal and in 1878 had still not reached its depth. For 1879 the Chamber of Commerce records are deficient, but in 1880 there was no change in the almost universal depression.

These comments can be supplemented from the two trade unions whose records are available for this period. These are the brass workers and glass makers. As early as his third annual report for 1874–75 Davis was reporting 'trade unionism through the depression of trade is becoming somewhat unpopular.' In the next year, however, the Out of Work benefit paid out by the union declined from £2763 to £1487. In 1876 Davis reported the year as active as the previous ones but, 'much trade unionism in other trades where organisation is less efficient or through unusual depression have suffered and you may be congratulated on the strength of your organisation. It is numerically weaker, but financially stronger'. In 1877 Davis made a spirited defence of trade unionism:

> Times are bad. There is a general impression among the upper and middle classes that trade unionists are responsible. This we deny. Our hours were 54 (a week) long before the 8-hour Movement. Our 15% increase had been the first for one hundred years and put 4% on the selling price. We are told we are draining the trade from this country. To what country? Germany is loudly complaining of the badness of trade. France and America are just as bad. The trouble began from the Franco-German War when output expanded and joint stock companies increased. It is this glut which is now being worked off.

Out of Work pay was 'very heavy' that year at £1792. In 1878 Davis reported 'the opponents of trade unions have taken the opportunity to reduce wages and tens of thousands of workers are in a state of semi-starvation.' 1879 was probably the worst year of all. 'The depression continued with ever greater intensity. Reductions (of wages) made impossible the purchase of more than the necessities of life. Out of Work benefit had leaped from £5305 to £8861 compared with total union income of only £5971. 1880 brought improved trade but was 'far from satisfactory'. Out of Work payments fell to £4128 and the union's losses were reduced to £636. Out of Work benefits could be continued at the existing level, but if the funds fell below £1,500 there would have to be a levy on all members — a solution which seemed to work well in other unions, Davis noted.

The years 1881 – 83 were years of better trade. In each year the Union reported a surplus of income over expenditure:

Year	Income	Expenditure	of which	Out of Work Benefit	Surplus.
1881	£4932	£4796		£3366	£136
1882	£5284	£4430		£2757	£954
1883	£6356	£6320		£3847	£36

In 1883 Davis ceased to be secretary of the union and became one of the first working men factory inspectors. He occupied this post until 1889 when he returned as secretary of the Brassworkers. During Davis' absence the union became very weak and his return was accompanied by another spectacular period of growth. The whole of this gain should not necessarily be attributed to Davis' personality and dynamism, since the years of his absence were years of bad trade during which the union would have been likely to decline whoever had led it.

The annual reports from 1882 to 1888 were written by Edward Lilly and these tended to be fuller than those of Davis. Lilly's 1884 report philosophised on slumps and class collaboration. The past year had been a most taxing one to trade societies generally. The long prevailing depression had been the signal for taking advantage of workmen. There had been an amazing accumulation of capital and an increasing aggressiveness of capitalists against labour, 'what is there in competition or human nature likely to prevent employers taking advantage and decreasing wages at each recurring period of trade depression?' Lilly asked. The great evil in the brass trade was the Slaughter Shops paying starvation wages and cutting prices. Without apathy and weakness among workers these shops would have been compelled to pay reasonable prices or close altogether and the better class of employer would have been able to pay higher wages. Many brassworkers were being compelled to seek relief and break stone who should have been in the union, Lilly concluded.

1885 was a year of 'exceptional severity of depression' and 1886 'the most trying the society had ever experienced' In both years the union made financial losses and membership fell.

In 1887 there was 'a limited revival of trade'. This report also commented on the fact that the brass trade was an expanding one as new uses for brass were found. As early as 1881 Davis had reported going to the Crystal Palace to see whether the new fashion of internal electric lighting would injure the chandelier trade and had concluded that the extra lights used would ensure that there would be no injury. Trade continued to improve in 1888 but 'competition was more severe.' Membership plummeted badly in those two years of improved trade.

Davis returned and his report for 1889 was a full one, although his subsequent ones were brief and discontinued the valuable practice of giving financial information and membership figures. From this 1889 Report, however, we can trace both the fortunes of the union and the expansion of the trade. In Davis' first spell as secretary membership had peaked at 5271 in 1875. It subsequently declined to 4149 in 1883 when Davis left, down to 2243 in 1888. With Davis' return membership was hoisted to 7625 in a single year and by 1891 Davis claimed that every known brassworker was in the union with a total membership of 7958. The dominance of Birmingham in the brass trade can be seen from the fact that 6891 members in 1889 were in the Birmingham central branch. Wolverhampton came next with 340 members and Manchester was third with 97.

Depression returned in 1893 and 'most brassworkers have more or less felt the bitterness of short employment.' In 1884 it was reported, 'we can make some small provision — if sadly inadequate — for members deprived of their means of livelihood.' 1895 was 'a year of unusual depression. A terrible distress fell on the community like a blight in the past winter.' There was severe depression in the first quarter of 1896, but 1897 was 'one of labour's fat years. There was plenty of work and a great number of our comrades obtained better pay.'

The boom lasted until the end of the century. Such are the seductions of a few years of regular pay packets that in 1899 Davis could write, 'acute observers believe a great future is opening up for the working classes and the whole human race.' At this stage Davis was concentrating on achieving a minimum wage for his members ranging from 25/-d. to 30/-d. a week. His 1900 Report estimated that of 8,500 members, 2,500 were already receiving this minimum. For the remainder:

> 1000 required a 30% advance to get to 25/-d.
> 1000 required a 25% advance to get to 26/-d.
> 1000 required a 20% advance to get to 27/-d.
> 1000 required a 15% advance to get to 28/-d.
> 1000 required a 10% advance to get to 29/-d.
> 1000 required a 5% advance to get to 30/-d.

Davis' faith in the future was based on imperialism. 'Western civilisation is overspreading the earth. In another generation or two millions of savages and semi-savages will be exchanging commodities with us.' Alas for such illusions. Trade gradually declined in 1901 and by 1904 and 1905 'the shortage of work was very marked.' The laws of capitalist development were not to be denied.

The other trade union for which we have detailed reports and accounts is the Flint Glassmakers Union. This is due to the survival of the Glass Makers' Magazine from 1860. The flint glass trade can, for our present purpose, be roughly equated with blown glass as distinct from sheet glass which is machine manufactured. The flint glass trade then, as now, was highly localised. In the 1870s there were roughly the same number of glass workers in Birmingham as there were in the main glass centre of Stourbridge (more properly Brierley Hill) with membership of over 300 each. The only other 300 plus branch was Manchester and in Lancashire as a whole there were about 500 members. This included 100 at Warrington. The only other 100 plus branch was Newcastle-on-Tyne. National membership was about 1900. Both the trade and the union were dominated by the west midlands. The union, which still survives, has never been affiliated to the TUC. Glassmaking is carried on by a 'chair' of four people. A Boy (apprentice) prepares the materials, a Footmaker gathers the glass and blows the bulb, this is passed on to the Servitor who puts on the leg and foot and it is finally passed on the the Gaffer (Maker) who is the Master of the Chair and designated the Workman. Within a working life one would expect to progress from Apprentice to Workman. The wage structure was such that the Workman was quite well paid and might be regarded as an aristocrat of labour, the Servitor was reasonably well paid, but the Footmaker was abominably paid at an unskilled rate even though he had served an apprenticeship and was a glassblower.

The affairs of the union can conveniently be taken up in 1871 with the appointment of Joseph Rudge as Central Secretary (i.e. General Secretary) at a time when the trade boom was developing. In his first report for the June-August quarter Rudge states that when he took over many men were unemployed (calculations from the report suggest that this was about 7% of the membership) and it had been a heavy quarter on the funds of the union. Trade was now prospering, however, and if men wanted to change their employers it was a good time to do so as this would help to raise wages. Vacancies would first be filled from the union members who were unemployed. The following quarter Rudge was complaining that brisk trade was being met by employers working extra turns. This kept wages down as it meant that extra hands were employed only by new employers setting up. Birmingham wages were raised to between 24/-d. and 40/-d. a week. Trade continued good in the following years and the sensation of 1874 was the embezzlement of union funds by Rudge. He was prosecuted and received eighteen months hard labour.

Once the Great Depression began to bite, the union complained that instead of spreading the work (i.e. short-time working), the employers were discharging whole chairs. This was contrary to practice and so serious a matter that it was regarded as victimisation. In 1877 both the Birmingham and Stourbridge branches had assets exceeding £1000. Before the year was out, the union was reporting losses of £840 in six months and the depression was reported as the worst since 1851 and union contributions were raised. One of the problems of the union was that dues were paid quarterly and there were always large numbers of members in arrears who were disqualified from benefits.

A conference was organised with the employers regarding the 'best means of removing the present Depression of Trade', but it broke up without agreement. One of the issues highlighted by the Depression was that of the older worker. When is a man too old to work? it was asked. The union replied that it was at the age of 45; the employers, on the other hand, said that the age was 50. In fact, trade union superannuation schemes recognised this grim reality of working life in the nineteenth century and both the glass union and the Amalgamated Society of Engineers allowed superannuation at the age of 45. The lack of agreement with the employers led the glassworkers to publicise the views of John Ruskin, the famous art critic and sociologist, on the causes of the Great Depression which he claimed were:

1. The separation of Master and Men which was the fault of the masters.
2. Loss of custom from bad workmanship.

3.   The substitution of machinery for labour which produces a
      glut.
4.   Foreigners realising that they had hands and brains like us.

This was part of a general discussion on the causes of the Depression
sparked off by Crawshay's decision to close the Cyfarthfa iron works.
Crawshay had amassed £7million, it was said, and could well afford to
retire. All aspects of the trade came under consideration. The market for
glass was an expanding one, but the flint glass trade had not been affected
by labour saving machinery. In Staffordshire the number of glass workers
had almost doubled between 1850 and 1878. In Birmingham, at the latter
date the trade was said to be 'all tumblers and chimneys' (i.e. cheap table
glasses and glass covers for oil lamps).

In 1878 'the shadow over the trade grows darker and darker' and the
drain on the funds of the union worsened. It was agreed to take action
against those members 'who were incapacitated, but go through the
unemployment scales before declaring themselves superannuated.' Unemployment benefit was, of course, higher than superannuation. From
December 1878 union contributions were raised to 3/-d. a week for
Workmen and Servitors and 2/-d. for Footmakers. This was at a time
when employers in Birmingham, Stourbridge and Dudley were giving
notice of a 15% reduction in wages. The reduction eventually accepted
by the union was 7.5%. In 1879 the funds of the society reached crisis
point. It would be bankrupt within twelve months at existing scales of
expenditure; stoppage of all benefits for one year would save £9,000.
Such a draconian solution was not applied, however. Levies were called
for, conditions for benefits were tightened and the union survived one of
the worst years of the Great Depression. An analysis of Birmingham
membership in 1879 showed total membership of 351 which was probably
the highest number reached by the branch. Of these, 26 were superannuated, 62 were unemployed, 3 were honorary, and 8 were permanently sick, giving a total paying membership of 252. This
unemployment rate was therefore 18% to which should be added
members out of benefit and those on short-time working.

By the mid 1880s T.C. Barnes was the central secretary; he was also
an unsuccessful parliamentary condidate for East Birmingham in the
1885 elections. Over the previous 20 years the market for glass had
increased by 500% but membership of the union had remained almost
the same, Barnes reported. The increased trade had chiefly been supplied
by Germany, he claimed. Discussion on the causes of the Great Depression quickened with the proposal to appoint the Royal Commission on the
Depression of Trade. The union rejected the explanation of
Overproduction, preferring the term Underconsumption. In November
1887 it was suggested that the existing Depression would have been
regarded as real prosperity half a century before; but a letter in the same
issue reported Birmingham unemployment in the trade at 22%. In
August 1888 it was reported that 22% of the total union membership was
unemployed. This at a time when nearly one third of Birmingham and
Stourbridge members were in arrears of payment and not entitled to any
benefits until four weeks after the arrears had been paid.

In 1888 the age for receipt of superannuation benefit was raised to 56.
Most of the superannuation claimants were out of work men over 40 who

would not have retired so early if work had been available it, was stated, During the Depression both contributions and benefits changed frequently in response to the financial position of the union. It was not only unemployment benefit that fluctuated widely; in 1886 it was reported that sickness benefit had been particuarly heavy due to the long and severe winter of 1886. By 1890 trade had 'much improved' and contributions were reduced. In September 1891 a Birmingham proposition that superannuated and unemployed members be paid an extra 1/-d. a week through the three winter months 'met with almost unanimous approval.' A similar increase the following winter was also approved unanimously. By 1889 contributions were down to 2/3d. a week and in 1893 were reduced again to 2/-d.

The McKinley tariff was a blow to the glass trade at a time when the Great Depression was lifting. It brought discussion on methods of work as well as comparison of wages. In September 1891 it was reported that U.S. methods of arranging pay were much the same as the British i.e. each 3 hours work was called a 'move' and there were two moves to each 'turn' or 'shift'. Eighteen moves represented a week's work and all hours beyond this was overtime paid at ordinary rates. English weekly wage rates at the time were given as Workmen 36/-d. Servitors 26/-d. Footmakers 17/-d. Boys 6/-d.

Clarification of the conditions for claiming unemployment benefit was sought in 1894 by men in the Hunslet district who asked whether they were entitled to claim when they had only worked three moves in a week due to the furnaces not being fit to work at. They were told that they could not claim unemployment benefit. An address of the central committee at this time stated:

> It is a sad fact to record that although there is a far greater demand for glass in this country than at any previous time it is still continuously becoming more difficult to find employment for our members.
> This fact is proved by the long list of unemployed that we constantly have before us, many of them good and industrious workers who are spending the best of their days in enforced idleness and consequently have no opportunity of making any provision for the time when they will be incapable of working at the trade except through the superannuated funds of our society the benefits of which are kept miserably low by the vast amount of money we are compelled to pay in providing for our unemployed.

In 1895 the scandal of footmakers' wages was discussed at a conference in Dudley. The central secretary said:

> Never before had it fallen to my lot to listen to such miserable conditions of labour as they suffer under ... the wages they get are a lasting disgrace to us unionists.

Two resolutions were passed. One was to the Midland Association of Employers requesting a meeting to discuss minimum wage rates for footmakers. The other was that in future no footmakers be supplied in the Midland district at less than 18/-d. or 19/-d. a week. This minimum wage was conceded by the midland employers the same year.

In 1895 trade was still depressed. In July 1897 'another quarter had passed without any change for the better in trade'. But by the end of the year it was reported that 'nearly all factories are now fully employed.'

The above material has illustrated both the reality and the depth of the Great Depression in Birmingham. It has also shown that the initial reaction to slump, as in our present Great Depression, was not an increased hostility to capitalism as the source of the slump and an increased militancy among working people, but a considerable weakening of the ability of trade union and militants to maintain organisation and living standards. With this went an ideological onslaught by the employers, through their control of the press, to blame workers for the crisis, to destroy the gains made in working class organisation in the earlier, more prosperous years of 1870 – 74 and to advocate the bankrupt but beguiling solution of a low wage economy. It was under these circumstances that in the first decade of the Great Depression so many trade unionists sought salvation and prosperity in class collaboration and the fixing of prices.

It took ten years for these primitive reactions to work their way through the system and for the alternative of Socialism, firmly based on the ideology of Marxism, to surface. Before this later reaction is outlined, however, it is necessary to deal more fully with that phenomenon which makes Birmingham so singular and interesting an area to trace the rises and falls of working class consciousness, namely Chamberlainism.

Chapter Fourteen

JOSEPH CHAMBERLAIN — THE RADICAL LIBERAL

Building a Base

The remarkable career of Joseph Chamberlain can, for our purposes, be divided into three phases. The first is from his birth in 1836 to 1867 when he first bursts onto the Birmingham political scene. This period is dominated by his business achievement in building one of the first British monopoly businesses in the screw trade and making his personal fortune. The second period is from 1868 to 1885 when Chamberlain dominates first Birmingham Liberal politics and then national Liberal politics as a genuine progressive radical espousing both socialism and republicanism. The third is from 1885 when in opposition to Gladstone's Home Rule for Ireland policy he uproots Birmingham and national Liberalism from the Liberal Party and engrafts it as Liberal Unionism on to the Tory Party. It is with the first two stages that we shall be concerned here.

Joseph Chamberlain was born in London into a family which for four generations had been in business as boot and shoe manufacturers and wholesalers. He was educated at a private church of England school from the ages of 10 to 14 and then spent two years at University College School. This was the leading public school for dissenters at this time and here he mixed with leading Birmingham families including Kenricks and Nettlefolds who would later be his associates in Birmingham. He left school at sixteen to enter the family business. In 1854 one of Chamberlain's uncles, J.S. Nettlefold, who had a screw manufactory in Birmingham, purchased the English rights to a U.S.A. patent for the production of screws by new, improved machinery. Nettlefold acquired the additional capital necessary for him to develop this patent from Joseph Chamberlain's father and at the age of eighteen Joseph moved to Birmingham to work in the firm. Twenty years later Chamberlain's financial and administrative manipulations had given the firm of Nettlefold and Chamberlain a virtual monopoly of the screw trade in Britain. Chamberlain then retired from business in 1874 taking about £120,000 of the £600,000 for which the three Chamberlain brothers sold their interest in the firm. Henceforth he devoted all his time to radical political activities and the augmentation of his invested fortune.

The latter soared throughout the 1880s, but a disastrous investment in sisal growing in the Bahamas together with lower dividends made such inroads into his income that by the mid-1890s he briefly contemplated withdrawing from public life.

When Chamberlain came to Birmingham he was a Unitarian in religion. He thus absorbed the democratic radical traditions of Joseph Priestley the scientist and the entrepreneurial pioneers of the Industrial Revolution in the West Midlands such as Boulton, Wedgwood, Watt, Wilkinson and others who had been connected with the Lunar Society. Like many of them, this democratic outlook was constantly warring with the class conflict and ruthlessness necessary to succeed in business. One of the ways that this contradiction shows in Chamberlain is that while he was one of the great communicators of the world, he was also a non-communicator. His speeches and written works are magnificently constructed; always allowing his opponents' arguments the full weight of their strengths; invariably courteous and never descending to the abuse and misrepresentation to which he was constantly subject, he countered his opponents with a mass of statistics and a devastating display of logic.

On the other hand, most of his important business and political decisions were conveyed by third parties or by word of mouth and find no reflection in Chamberlain's papers. This is true of both Chamberlain's business methods and the political decisions of the famous Caucus. His business activities are only now being extensively researched by, a Canadian scholar, Peter T. Marsh. Since these occupied most of his time during the first twenty years of his working life and culminated, as with Robert Owen, in a fortune sufficient to allow him to devote the rest of his life to radical and political activity, a study of Chamberlain's business methods are relevant to this study.

Chamberlain was not a scientist or technical innovator. He was a financial and commercial expert, the take-over whiz-kid of his day pioneering monopoly almost two decades before monopolies were to dominate the industrial scene in Britain.

Chamberlain's first step was to integrate backwards into firms manufacturing wire and then to buy the iron making facility for the iron rods from which the wire was manufactured. Coincidently, through contacts with his wife's family (the Kenricks), Chamberlain played a leading role in transforming the Birmingham private bank of Lloyds into a public joint stock company, thus ensuring access to capital. With a dominant position in domestic sales from near-monopoly and technical innovation, which reduced the price of screws ten fold compared with the beginning of the century, Chamberlain turned to the export market. By personal contact and close attention to the requirements of the market, he greatly extended sales in Europe. Where local competition could not be entirely overcome, as in France, Chamberlain formed an early cartel with one of the two main French producers to divide the European market between them; the rival French firm succumbed when the Paris Commune cut off the firm from its markets.

Pioneering techniques later to be used by Rockefeller, Carnegie and other USA monopolists, he negotiated preferential rates with railway and canal companies. When the Nettlefold and Chamberlain monopoly was threatened by the formation of the Birmingham Screw Co. in 1870, Chamberlain resolved to use every method to smash the opposition. Consulting friends and contacts he gathered information on his rival's methods and intentions in ways which today would be considered 'industrial espionage'. Chamberlain's master plan was to raise his prices until the rival monopoly was in action and then use the extra profits to subsidise prices and under-cut the rival. Chamberlain was doubly fortunate in his circumstances. The great trade boom of 1870 – 74 was just beginning, raising his profits even higher than expected; also the Franco-Prussian war ended the Birmingham Screw Co's co-operation with Japy, the French rival firm, which was vital to the success of the rival monopoly. Such were the business methods that Chamberlain was to bring to his radicalism and politics.

Basic to Chamberlain's radicalism was his religion and education. As a Unitarian he was at the radical end of the almost unbroken chain which stretched from right to left beginning with Evangelicalism and the High Churches through the varying shades of Nonconformism through to secularism and atheism. The Unitarian belief that the kingdom of God is within you leads on to the conclusion that the fatherhood of God implies the brotherhood of man. When Chamberlain came to Birmingham he entered the living circle of that tradition carried on by the great christian divines Dr. Dale, Dr. Crosskey, Charles Vince and, above all, George Dawson. Chamberlain worshipped first at New Meeting and then with George Dawson at the Church of the Saviour. He became a Sunday school teacher with classes in history, literature and arithmetic. He also participated in educational activities at his Smethwick works. Such work brought him into contact with more working people than most industrialists of the time, but his circle of personal friends was drawn from the wealthy families of Martineau, Ryland, Russell, Matthews, Nettlefold and Kenrick who were the nucleus of the Birmingham and Edgbaston Debating Society. It was here that from 1854 Chamberlain learned and practised his speaking skills. This debating society was extremely important playing a role in the town somewhat between that of a Lunar Society and an Oxford Union. Here the limitation of Chamberlain's radicalism is displayed quite early. Speaking against the motion 'That the character and conduct of Oliver Cromwell do not entitle him to the admiration of posterity', it was, no doubt, the foreign and Irish policies that Chamberlain stressed. Four years later Chamberlain opposed John Bright in support of the motion, 'That this Society strongly condemns the principles enunciated in the speeches recently made by John Bright in Birmingham, and also the spirit in which these speeches were delivered.' The debate lasted two evenings and was lost by only one vote. This emphasises that while John Bright was the greatest of contemporary radicals, his Quaker, pacifist anti-war stance was opposed by many, especially in a town where war meant trade. C. B. Adderley, an MP, later commented on this debate 'among the skilled artisans of Birmingham'; he was sharply reminded that the Birmingham and Edgbaston Debating Society 'is in no sense a working man's institution, but comprises among its nearly two hundred members many graduates of both Universities, physicians, surgeons, architects, lawyers, manufacturers and tradesmen'.

Municipal Socialism

From this background, it was the educational issue that was to launch Joseph Chamberlain on his public career. In February 1867 the Birmingham Education Society was formed with Chamberlain as its driving force. This was also the year of the Second Reform Act which gave the vote to many working people in towns. Two years later he became a town councillor, returned unopposed at a by-election in St. Paul's ward. His leadership of the struggle for the 1870 Education Act made him a national figure almost overnight. The details of that struggle need not detain us here, but as chairman of the National Education League, Chamberlain led the 'whole hog' party, uniting the disparate strands of Nonconformism and the working class movement to demand 'immediate provision of free, unsectarian, compulsory education, supported by local rates supplemented by Government grants, under local representative management and Government inspection, and sufficient for the requirements of all children in the country.'

1873 – 75 were the three years of Chamberlain's mayorality. It is instructive to turn to a speech made by Chamberlain in November 1874 at the Severn Street school annual meeting to see both the educational background from which Chamberlain operated and his view of the problems then existing. Severn Street was a voluntary, Quaker founded, British school. After outlining the numerous calls made on the time of the mayor he says:

> But I felt that this institution had a special claim on me and that I could not refuse myself the pleasure of coming among you ... Now although this is my first visit to you I have long been aware of the existence of the Severn Street school and have looked upon it as one of the peculiar institutions of Birmingham. For more than twenty-eight years you have been working supplementing the labours of educationalists by doing what no one else attempted to do ... Mr. White told me that you have already in connection with your schools over two thousand scholars, all of them over fifteen years of age, and of that large number more than half have passed the age of twenty. Your scholars and teachers do not occupy the ordinary positions which scholars take towards their masters, but you are rather a great association of friends mutually aiding one another ... Well now, setting aside all the good which may be effected by your religious and social work, putting out of count the kindred organisations, the temperance societies, the savings banks, and so on, which are connected with the schools, what marvellous good has been effected simply by your educational work. It is not too much to say that you have in the long course of years of which I have spoken endowed multitudes of your fellow townsmen with a new sense, with a sense that has thus enabled them to appreciate the works of others and to communicate their own ideas.

Chamberlain then discussed the achievements of the Birmingham School Board and the need of institutions such as Severn Street to change:

> Well, when I am able to say so much for your work, it may appear strange that I should wish to see that work shortly coming to an end ... It must be evident that changes are imminent. It must be evident that schoolmasters are abroad with a vengeance, and there are buildings rising up which to my mind are the most splendid of all the buildings in Birmingham — great schools for your children, provided lavishly with every appliance for education, provided with ground for the recreation of the children so that their physical as well as their mental health is cared for; and these schools I firmly believe will effect a wonderful change in a few years in the character of our population ... These schools upon which I have spoken are filling almost as fast as they are erected. Already the average attendance in this town is increased by twelve thousand children ... And this additional attendance is not the only thing. Besides those in regular attendance, there are an enormous number who are irregular attendants, and although they make very unsatisfactory scholars at present, yet their presence in the school familiarises them and their parents with the idea of the school as a necessity in the life of a child and that must bear fruit in a future when the children of this town will be in a position of the children of every great German city and will leave school knowing at that time all that you now attempt to teach their seniors.
> And under these circumstances you will have to ask yourselves what will become of your work. Is it possible that you will then no longer have anything to do? Well, I don't think you need be afraid of idleness.

Chamberlain then goes on to suggest that while the religious and moral work of the school will still go on, it should widen its curriculum 'beyond mere reading and writing'. He goes on to urge the support of such causes as the sanitary improvement of the town:

> It seems to me to be ridiculous to talk of temperance to men who have every reason to leave their homes and are driven thereby to the public house. It seems to me monstrous to preach thrift to those whose whole lives are wasted in a perpetual struggle with disease and death. I think you could do much to remedy this state of things.

In this way Chamberlain linked education with the civic gospel of town improvement. In furtherance of this end, he convened a conference of civic authorities in Birmingham in January 1875. Again, it is only in the words of Chamberlain that an adequate idea of the scope of his ideas can be conveyed. In his opening address he explained that his first intention had been a gathering of one hundred or so practical sanitarians willing to confer with their fellow workers in Birmingham, but between eight and nine hundred mayors, chairmen of health committees, medical officers of health, and other sanitary workers were in attendance. He went on to explain that the purpose of the conference was to rouse public opinion to the importance of the issue. Concern was expressed only at times of exceptional catastrophe when the usual reaction:

> . . . is to throw the blame upon local authorities — to say it is owing to our stupidity, selfishness or indifference. I do not think any argument can be more unfair or foolish; more foolish because if we are to do anything radical in the way of sanitary reform, it must be by means of our local government bodies. It is only through them that we can act upon the population in this matter. It seems to me, therefore, suicidal to bring into contempt and to depreciate the only machinery by which we can efficiently secure our needs. It is unfair because it ought to be remembered that local bodies cannot be much wiser than the constituencies they represent; and were they wiser than the constituencies that elect them, and did they attempt to put their wisdom into practice, we know that all legislation which is in advance of the sentiments of the people is nearly always a failure.

Chamberlain then outlined the problems that arose when each emergency had to be tackled on an ad hoc basis and cited the Birmingham example of attempting to open an isolation hospital during a small pox epidemic:

> We were met by clamour of all kinds from property owners and from the inhabitants of the neighbourhood who said we were unjustifiably bringing pestilence in their midst. While all admitted such a hospital to be eminently desirable, they were all of opinion that the place selected was the worst that could possibly be chosen . . . But this opposition did not proceed merely from people who had a pecuniary interest in the matter. When the town council finally selected a site, upon the recommendation of our medical officer of health, a memorial was presented signed by one half of the medical staff of the town protesting against the undertaking as being fraught with serious danger to the neighbouring population.

Chamberlain then quoted national figures of mortality from preventable diseases and went on to a typically thorough outline of the local situation and its consequences:

Coming to the town in which I now address you, I have calculated that the preventable deaths in Birmingham are something like 3000 a year ... I find that the annual loss from this cause is £54,000 per annum. I think that if only we could induce our population to make these calculations for themselves, we should have very little to complain of as to ill-judged parsimony, which saves hundreds of pounds in sanitary precautions in order to lose tens of thousands in the death and ill-health of our population ... local governing bodies have not merely to consider questions affecting the lives and the health of the people entrusted to their charge we have to consider also their happiness and morality. The circumstances of which I have spoken are fruitful occasions of misery, pauperism, intemperance and crime. It is usual to say that these results are due to the ignorance of the people. That is true; but would it be almost truer to say that this ignorance in its turn is the result of the conditions amid which people live. What can the schoolmaster or minister do when the influences of home undo all he does? We find bad air, polluted water, crowded and filthy homes and ill-ventilated courts prevailing in the midst of our boasted wealth, luxury and civilisation. A paternal Government provides for our criminals in gaol 1000 cubic feet of air as a minimum, and those criminals, after their confinement is terminated, go back to their homes in which 300, 200 and even 100 cubic feet of air is the maximum. Even the air they have is contaminated by unmentionable impurities and filth. Hardly a gleam of sunshine ever comes into the dark and dreary courts. The dead and the living lie together in the same room for days; all reverence is blotted out from the minds of people subjected to such conditions; as for common decency, it is an empty name; it is obliterated from the category of virtues; and when these people whom we have suffered to grow up like beasts behave like brutes, we rush to the Home Secretary in a blind paroxysm of terror and ask him to give us the humanising influence of 'the lash'...

Something must be done, and that quickly to make life a little brighter and easier for those who now groan under its burden, if our boasted prosperity is to rest upon its only sure foundation — the happiness, the welfare and the contentment of the whole community.

The conference proved a powerful influence on the Artisans' Dwellings Act passed the next year in 1875.

Participation in local and national politics brought Chamberlain immediately to the problems of political management. The first problem was the organisation of the Liberal Party against the Tories. This involved the registration and control of the voters. The second problem was the organising of radical Liberal opinion against the Whigs within the party. The third problem was to manipulate voting against the specific provisions made with the intention of seeing that minority interests were protected and represented. Thus the 1867 Reform Act had increased Birmingham representation from a two-member one constituency town with two votes to a three-member single constituency where each voter continued to have only two votes in the hope that the third seat would go to a Tory. The 1870 Education Act had gone further by providing that School Boards should be elected with each voter having the same number of votes as representatives to be elected, but with a system of 'plumping' whereby an individual could cast all his votes for a single candidate. Most Roman Catholics plumped all their votes on a single candidate, usually their local priest, who often headed their poll, but having used all their votes these Catholics could have no further influence on the composition of the Board. At the first School Board election in Birmingham the Liberal non-conformists made the mistake of fielding as many candidates as there were vacancies with the result that the Tories, plumping their votes on a lesser number of candidates ended with a majority of the Board. This was a mistake never to be repeated.

But the solution had already been found in 1868 when the Liberal vote in Birmingham was organised by William Harris, secretary of the Birmingham Liberal Association to return three Liberals at the general election. This was done by 'directing' Liberals how to vote. Some were to vote for Liberal candidates A and B, some were to vote for Liberal candidates A and C and the remainder were to vote for candidates B and C. In this way, no votes were wasted in majorities larger than necessary and the Tories were kept out. From these beginnings, later extended to other towns, under the guidance of Francis Schnadhorst, the famous, or infamous, Caucus arose. The name was at first a term of abuse used by Disraeli, but later accepted (as had the labels Whig and Tory) as convenient terms and thus losing their opprobrium.

The first great principle of the Caucus was that all Liberals, voters and non-voters alike, should be organised in their wards. The subscription was 1/-d. a year which could be waived if the member were too poor provided he supported the aims and organisation of the party. Each ward elected a committee of unlimited numbers. Above the ward committee was an Executive Committee consisting of the chairman and secretary of the ward plus three other elected delegates. In the sixteen then existing wards of the town this made a total of 80. This eighty had the right of adding thirty to their number. As well as this Executive Committee of one hundred and ten there was a General Committee composed of all the members of the executive committee plus thirty members from each ward elected at public meetings plus a Managing Sub-Committee of four persons appointed by the general committee plus seven members nominated by the executive committee. This body of 594 people became celebrated under the name of 'the Six Hundred', later the Eight Hundred and eventually the Two Thousand as the city grew.

The Six Hundred met eight or nine times a year, chose candidates for parliament and public bodies in the town and discussed local policies. It could be summoned by any two ward committees or twenty members. Birmingham liberals claimed that this organisation represented the highest form of local democracy; the Six Hundred were the cadres who mobilised the members of each ward and controlled the policy of the party; they in turn were controlled by the rank and file who ultimately elected the Six Hundred. With this organisation Chamberlain and the radical Liberals rallied the enthusiastic support of the people for the ambitious schemes of social improvement in the town represented by the civic gospel of Municipal Socialism; as the Birmingham organisation was widely adopted by the National Liberal Federation after 1879 it went on to organise the ultimate radicalism of the National Socialism of the Radical Programme of 1884.

Asa Briggs aptly applies the description of 'democratic centralism' to the Caucus system. It indeed resembles the form of democracy operated in the Soviet Union and claimed to be the highest form of democracy, a claim later endorsed by Beatrice and Sidney Webb in the second edition of their mammoth work *Soviet Communism, a New Civilisation*. The criticisms of the Caucus, as of the Soviet system, must centre on the manipulation of the organisation rather than on the organisation itself.

Critics of the Caucus maintained that ultimate control was not with the Six Hundred or the ward committees but the Managing Sub-Committee of eleven who consisted of Chamberlain and his close associates. The decisions of the eleven were invariably word of mouth and rarely published or recorded; the eleven took such far reaching decisions as the appointment of the architects of the famed Board schools without consultation; large contracts were placed without tender and preferment depended on large public subscriptions to local liberal causes; freedom to vote was supplanted by direction to vote; democracy was interpreted as 'the life of the people as an organised whole' and the organiser was the Liberal Association. To achieve this, the Tories had to be driven from public life — first from the town council and then from any other organisation that they controlled — Midland Institute, King Edward Grammar Schools etc. It became almost impossible to distinguish between the powers and duties of the town council and other public bodies, and those of the Liberal Association. Government by Caucus left no 'space' for an opposition party to play a role in affairs. Such were the more temperate and theoretical criticisms of the Caucus. The less temperate criticisms ranged from the unceasing flood of vituperation and personal abuse of Chamberlain to charges of corruption, bribery, nepotism and Tammany Hall politics.

During these years 1867 – 85, however, Chamberlain's radicalism continued and expanded many of the best democratic traditions of Birmingham inherited from the Lunar Society, the Corresponding Societies of the 1890s, the Political Unions of 1815 – 32. Civic pride was to be joined with greatly needed civic improvement to provide control of natural monopolies, and to generate profits for the people. Municipal enterprise would also provide the town with additional sources of revenue besides rates. Other town owned docks or landed estates, Chamberlain pointed out. Birmingham had nothing.

Chamberlain's first great municipal venture was the purchase of the gas supply of the town. It was fitting that an industry which had seen pioneer developments in Birmingham when William Murdock had lighted the Soho factory of Boulton & Watt by gas in 1798 should be publicly owned. Here Chamberlain's motives were to control a natural monopoly and by more efficient management to control the price and make profits for the town. Negotiations began in January 1874 and royal assent to the Gas Bill was given in August 1875. The total purchase price was almost £2 million. In the first ten years the price of gas was reduced from 3/3d. to 2/3d. and net profits totalled almost £500,000.

Next came the water supply. Here the motive was different. Water was to be acquired to safeguard the health of the town. The profits would accrue in the form of the improved health and welfare of the people. The purchase of the water supply had been projected but blocked as early as 1851. In December 1874 Chamberlain put forward new proposals and the bill received royal assent at the same time as the Gas Bill. The total purchase price was £1,350,000. The daily supply of water in 1873 was 15.25 million gallons per day; by 1884 it was 26.5 million gallons per day. Water rents were successively reduced in subsequent years particularly for houses of the lowest rateable value and small net profits were made.

These schemes were enthusiastically supported by the town's people and the campaigns sustained by public meetings and consultation.

The project which had greatest national impact, however, was the Birmingham Improvement Scheme. This had been made possible by the Artisans' Dwellings Act of 1875 over which, as we have seen, Chamberlain's influence was considerable. The Act conferred on towns power of compulsory purchase to clear unhealthy areas and erect working class housing. The Birmingham scheme as the largest and most publicised scheme in the country need not be followed in detail here. The driving through the centre of Birimingham of a great new thoroughfare, Corporation Street, and the clearance of the slums was spectacular. But the landlords who extorted exorbitant prices for their properties were the principal beneficiaries. The cleared sites were difficult to dispose of and eventually sold for less than their value. Chamberlain's greatest miscalculation, however, was in his belief that municipal enterprise was necessary only to purchase and clear sites; private speculative builders would then move in to build dwellings and let at 'economic rents' which working people could afford. It is not true now and it was not true then. So houses were not built and the poor were dispersed outside the city centre to create slums elsewhere. In addition, Chamberlain's luck was beginning to run out. The gas and water schemes took place at a time when trade was still brisk when capital was cheap and plentiful. The Improvement Scheme began in 1876 and dragged on through the worst years of the Depression resulting in a large increase in the town's debt and charges on the rates.

The Improvement Scheme ended the phase of municipal socialism in Birmingham. It was superseded by Chamberlain's increasing absorption in schemes of national socialism. If this had not been the case, however, he would undoubtedly have gone on to challenge the formidable drink interest in the town. Chamberlain was no teetotaler. He ate and drank well and early in life contracted the scourge he associated with Tory and Whig gluttony — gout. Chamberlain knew that drink — perhaps more than religion — was the opium of the people; necessary to most to make poverty bearable, but in turn making poverty permanent. He advocated and spoke in Parliament in favour of the Gothenberg system under which town or county councils bought out the liquor interests and managed the retail trade in the interests of the public. But Chamberlain became an MP and the matter was taken no further in Birmingham. Beyond drink there would have been other schemes of municipal enterprise. Perhaps banking, as it was Chamberlain's son, Neville, who in 1916 when he was mayor of Birmingham, strongly advocated a Birmingham Municipal Bank which was set up in 1919.

Joseph Chamberlain's views and motives during these years of municipal socialism can perhaps be best summed up in a speech he made in October 1874 on the Task of Birmingham Corporation:

> The Corporation of Birmingham is engaged in a great struggle to promote the welfare, health and happiness of the population over which it rules ... In the course of the last thirty years Birmingham has made marvellous progress. The population has more than doubled, its wealth has greatly increased, its public buildings have multiplied, its institutions have been enlarged ... Yet there still remains untouched a great

plague-spot of ignorance and vice. We have multiplied our churches and chapels, but unfortunately the public houses seem to grow even quicker. We have increased our school accommodation and at the same time find it necessary to enlarge the workhouse and gaol. What are we do to? Are we to fold our hands and say, the poor we have always with us? No man with any sense of his duties and responsibilities but will scorn to act on such a principle. Well then, we may go on multiplying private charities and increasing subscriptions and we shall do well; but I do not believe that by any amount of private or individual effort we shall really and thoroughly grasp the evils and difficulties which confront us. People call me a very advanced Liberal politician — I am an extreme Radical and I don't know what that is terrible besides. Well, if I am an advanced politician and all the rest, it is because I don't believe that any means but political means deal effectively with these evils. They have their origin in bad legislation and nothing, I believe, but good legislation will reform and remove them. Therefore I am not ashamed to be called an advanced Liberal. I am a Radical Reformer because I would reform and remove ignorance, poverty, intemperance and crime from their very roots ...

During these years of municipal socialism Chamberlain was also an important radical figure in the national struggle to maintain liberties and free trade unions in the period of reaction that followed the onset of the Great Depression. His views at the time were made clear in a speech he made on Class Legislation to a meeting of the Sheffield Reform Association in September 1873. Chamberlain began by saying that he had intended to confine himself exclusively to 'certain phases of class legislation by which capital has from time to time sought to restrain the freedom of labour and by which the working classes allege, and I think justly, that they have been grievously injured.' But he had been publicly challenged by the editor of the *Sheffield Daily Telegraph* to deal with other instances of class legislation 'by which he thinks the middle class have shown their magnanimity, their self-denial and their generosity, while the working class have made for this exercise of virtue only an ungrateful return.' Chamberlain could not resist such a challenge. In sarcastic vein he said that as a member of the middle class he also was 'proud of the ability, shrewdness, the industry, the providence and the thrift' which distinguished them, but he did not know 'that to these virtues we added ... this generous self-sacrificing spirit, the entire ignoring of our own interests which the Sheffield editor attributes to us.' Far from this being the case, '... the British tradesman well knows how to take care of No.1; he knows that charity begins at home and preaching that principle is careful to practise it.' It was perfectly true that the middle class had 'relieved the working class of a great load of taxation, yet they have not altogether forgotten themselves in the process'. But if the middle class had taken the taxation off, they had been the ones who put it on in the first place and it was agreed that the working class still pay more than their fair share of taxation. It the working class had been represented in Parliament such taxes would never have been put on, or they would have been taken off sooner and the present inequality would not now exist:

> ... this argument is only the old Tory cry which has been furbished up for this occasion. It is the argument that is always brought forward to oppose claims for the redress of grievances ... It is the argument that because an instalment of the debt has been paid, therefore the creditors should not demand the remainder.

Other arguments put forward by the editor of the *Sheffield Telegraph* did not merit lengthy debate:

> Certainly it shows great hardihood in a man who lives in the middle of a coal district to tell you that the enormous increase in the price of coal is due to the rise in the rate of wages. When I know, as I do know, that collieries which were for a long time unprofitable are now paying 50 and 100 and even 150% dividend to their shareholders, I think I can form a shrewd guess who are those who be benefitted by these advantages. It seems to me that the coal owners ... have persuaded an innocent Sheffield editor that they have been obliged to double the price of coal because they have added a few shillings a week to the wages of their workpeople.
>
> Before I leave this subject there is one illustration of class legislation I would not willingly forget. There is one class in this country who have never had any voice in the work of government. They have been wholly dependent upon the beneficient legislation of the class above them; and this class, mark you, has never suffered from the baneful results which your editor appears to consider must follow the establishment of trade unions. They have never known what it is to combine until very recently; and what has been the result? Why, this, that the agricultural labourers in this country are the worst paid, the worst fed, the worst clothed and the worst housed peasantry in the civilised world. It is not I who say this alone It is stated upon the evidence of Royal Commissioners; upon the testimony of clergymen, ministers of religion and travellers of undoubted impartiality and intelligence. And what have the upper classes done for these men? How have they benefitted from remission of taxes? I thank God that at last they have been driven by terrible wrong to combine in their own defence. They have done more in one twelvemonth by organisation for themselves than all other classes have done for them in thirty years of previous legislation.

Turning next to a general review of existing labour laws Chamberlain continued:

> There are two objects, as it seems to me, which underlie all this legislation. One of these objects is concealed — the other is avowed and legitimate. The first object is to repress trade unions; to have labour without organisation in the struggle which it must occasionally be called upon to maintain against capital. The other object is to protect persons and property from violence ... I feel that the second of these objects — which is legitimate — can never be secured until the first is entirely abandoned. Just so long as masters refuse to admit that their men have just as great a right to combine for their own object as the masters have to combine in order to arrange the terms upon which they will sell their products ... so long they may expect to hear of strikes ... One thing is quite certain, whatever employers may think upon this subject, trade unionism is inevitable. You may as well expect in the present day to repress combinations as Mrs Partington could hope to sweep out the Atlantic with a mop.

The question of restrictive practices of trade unions was another that enraged the middle class. Here Chamberlain drew attention to the fact that such restrictions were widely practised by the professions. Architects fixed wages at a five per cent commission whether the man could design a cathedral or whether he could only design a barn; 'any physician who should presume to do the work of an apothecary by dispensing his own medicines would never again be met in consultation with any member of that learned body; if I employ a counsel to defend me and I want to see him, I am not allowed to do so without the intervention of an attorney, whether I want the man or not. However much he may be in my way, he must be employed and must be paid, or else I cannot see my counsel. What is that but the rule that requires that the bricklayer or the mason should invariably be attended by his labourer?'

Having enjoyed himself at the expense of the editor of the *Sheffield Telegraph*, Chamberlain turned to an examination of the 1871 Criminal Law Amendment Act which had been the subject he had originally been invited to speak on. First there were the prosecutions for Conspiracy under which then, as now, savage sentences had been passed. There was the case of gas stokers who had been sentenced to twelve months' hard labour and when the law officers of the Crown had admitted they had been unjustly convicted, the sentence had been reduced to four months! If two or more people combine together to commit an offence however trivial, conspiracy can be alleged. Chamberlain suggested that two children recently charged with skipping in a park contrary to the bye-laws could have been indicted for conspiracy and would then have faced an automatic sentence of two years' imprisonment. Secondly there were the injustices of the Master & Servant Acts under which 17,000 had been prosecuted in a single year. Accused workers were subject to criminal law and imprisonment but masters only to civil action brought by workers. How would masters fare, asked Chamberlain, if the positions were reversed and all cases heard by a bench of footmen? Chamberlain summed up as follows:

> In conclusion let me say that I yield to no man in my desire that the law and its administration should be respected in this country . . . I believe that this is the distinguishing mark of a civilised and enlightened community. But the law must be impartial to gain respect. I dread more than I dread the possibility of violence from trade unions, I fear infinitely more than I fear the evil results of restrictive combinations, the growing conviction on the part of the great mass of the people that 'laws grind the poor and rich men rule the laws', and that the sacred name of justice is invoked to perpetuate class distinctions and to protect class interests. I know perfectly well that in stating frankly my convictions on this subject, I lay myself open to the usual reward of those who strive to separate themselves from the unfounded prejudices of the society in which they move. We are relegated at once to the rank of agitators; we are charged with setting class against class . . . But I say it is no use preaching a peace which is no peace. There is no patriotism or wisdom in ignoring a patent danger and self-evident wrong. There is no folly more stupendous than that which refuses to consider the just claims temperately urged by great masses of people. There is no crime so base as that of those self-styled instructors of public opinion who pander to selfish prejudices and intolerant assumptions, while they ignore the irrefutable evidence of injustice and wrong. Such men may stay for the moment the settlement of these questions, but they cannot stave it off. The time will come when the solution will be obtained with or without them; and according to their conduct now will they then be consulted or entirely set aside.

National Socialism.

Joseph Chamberlain appeared to sweep effortlessly from municipal to national politics. Returned, unopposed, to Parliament in 1876 for a seat vacated, not entirely willingly, by George Dixon; in virtual control of the national party electoral machine through the National Liberal Association centred on Birmingham from 1877, by 1880 he had forced his way into the Cabinet. In fact, however, Chamberlain had considerable qualms about moving on to the national scene and it was a period of personal unhappiness for him.

Finding Radicals in Parliament with neither organisation nor programme, Chamberlain set about providing both in partnership with Sir Charles Dilke. Once within the Cabinet as President of the Board of Trade, Chamberlain carried through a series of radical reforms in the merchant navy, the bankruptcy law and the patent law. In the teeth of the most ferocious opposition from ship owners, he attempted to carry the Merchant Shipping Bill into law. From statistics he showed that over a working life of 24 years, one seaman in three would be killed. That overloading accompanied by over-insuring of ships was the rule and not the exception, to the extent that the loss of a ship led to a rise in the value of the shares on the stock exchange. The worst cases were 'single ship companies' buying up unseaworthy vessels and issuing prospectuses guaranteeing dividends of 20% to 40% per annum without risk, since even if the ship were lost its value would more than be recovered from over-insurance. Such was the opposition aroused by the ship owners to this 'coffin ship bill' that Gladstone withdrew it and an outraged Chamberlain offered to resign. The following year a Royal Commission on loss of life at sea was set up and this resulted in an Act of 1888 and other Acts of 1892 and 1894 which greatly improved conditions at sea, but did not encompass all the reforms in Chamberlain's bill of 1884.

The culmination of Chamberlain's radicalism came with the Radical Programme designed for the election of 1885. This election took place against the background of the 1884 Reform Act which had greatly increased the electorate, introduced single member constituencies in the larger towns such as Birmingham, and enfranchised large numbers of rural voters who, the radicals confidently expected, would greatly weaken Tory representation in the shires. These factors would, at last, undermine aristocratic Whig influence in the Liberal Party and require the socialist measures which would cement and perpetuate middle class control of and working class adhesion to, the Liberal Party. The abiding importance of the Radical Programme is that it is the first political party programme ever produced. Before this, parties studiously avoided producing 'programmes' and elections were fought on single, or a number of, current issues expounded by the leader in his election speech.

The Radical Programme developed as a number of anonymous articles published in the *Fortnightly Review*. An essay on *Housing of the Poor in Towns* (known to have been written by Frank Harris) advocated an extension of compulsory purchase and expropriation of the unearned increment of the value of land.

> The expense of making towns habitable for the toilers who dwell in them must be thrown on the land which their toil makes valuable without any effort on the part of its owners.

This was taken further in a contribution by Jesse Collings on *The Agricultural Labourer* demanding provision of cheap housing in the

countryside, the elimination of the vast landed estates by the development
of small holdings and the restitution of common rights illegally taken by
enclosure. *Religious Equality* by John Morley argued for disestablishment
and a Free Church. *Free Schools* by Francis Adams argued the case for
abolition of fees with its corollary of the end of sectarian schools and
complete control of education by the School Boards. *Taxation and Finance*,
also by Francis Adams, argued the case for direct taxes and graduated
income tax against the existing preponderance of indirect taxes which
threw the weight of national taxation onto the poor. The final essay on
Local Government and Ireland argued for the extension of local democracy
and

> to entrust to Wales, Scotland and Ireland the free and full administration
> of their internal affairs which do not involve the Imperial interest.

These articles were later published in book form. T.H.S. Escott wrote an
introduction taking on himself to agree that much of the proposed
legislation was Socialist which was both necessary and desirable, but not
Communist which was unnecessary and undesirable:

> If it be said that it is legislation of a socialist tendency, the impeachment
> may be readily admitted. Between such legislation and communism
> there is all the difference in the world. Communism means the reduction
> of everything to a dead level, the destruction of private adventure, the
> paralysis of private industry, the atrophy of private effort. The socialistic
> measures now contemplated would preserve in their normal vigour and
> freshness all the individual activities of English citizenship, and would do
> nothing more spoliatory than tax — if and in what degree necessary —
> aggregations of wealth for the good of the community.

Chamberlain's contribution was limited to a preface dated July 1885:

> The Reform Acts of 1885 have set the seal on the great change which the
> Reform Act of 1832 inaugurated . . .
>   At last the majority of the nation will be represented by a majority of
> the House of Commons, and ideas and wants and claims which have
> hitherto been ignored in legislation will find a voice in Parliament, and
> will compel the attention of statesmen.
>   Radicalism, which has been the creed of the most numerous section
> of the Liberal Party outside the House of Commons, will henceforth be
> a powerful factor inside the walls of the popular Chamber.
>   The stage of agitation has passed, and the time for action has come.
>   There is need, therefore, for the attempt which is made in the
> following pages to compile a definite and practical Programme for the
> Radical Party.
>   It is a mistake to suppose that the objects of the advanced Liberals are
> simply destructive, for although the ground has been cleared in many
> places, the new necessities of the time can only be met by constructive
> legislation.
>   New conceptions of public duty, new developments of public
> enterprise, new estimates of the natural obligations of the members of the
> community to one another, have come into view, and demand
> consideration.
>   On this account, and not pledging myself to all the proposals
> contained in the following articles, I welcome their appearance, and
> commend them to the careful and impartial judgement of my fellow
> Radicals.

Joseph Chamberlain's actions were never guided by any coherent system of ideas, but his Socialism rested on the principle of natural right, the basic philosophy behind the American revolution and the Rights of Man. This idea of natural right was developed in the most famous radical speech that Chamberlain ever made. This was the Doctrine of Ransom expounded at a meeting in Birmingham in January 1885, to an audience of working men:

> If you will go back to the early history of our social system, you will find that when our social arrangements first began to shape themselves, every man was born into the world with natural rights, with a right to share in the great inheritance of the community, with a right to part of the land of his birth.
>
> But all these rights have passed away. The common rights of owner-ship have disappeared. Some of them have been sold, some of them have been given away by people who had not right to dispose of them; some of them have been lost through apathy and ignorance; some have been destroyed by fraud; and some have been acquired by violence. Private ownership has taken the place of these communal rights, and this system has become so interwoven with our habits and usages, it has been so sanctioned by law and protected by custom, that it might be very difficult and perhaps impossible to reverse it. BUT THEN I ASK, WHAT RANSOM WILL PROPERTY PAY FOR THE SECURITY WHICH IT ENJOYS?

Such was the Socialism of Chamberlain and the ideas underpinning it. But within a year radicalism and the Radical Programme were in ruins. In the election of 1885 Tories continued to be returned in the shires in large numbers. The following year Chamberlain resigned over Gladstone's Home Rule for Ireland proposals, the Liberal Unionists were formed and the transfer of capitalist interests from the Liberal Party to the Conservative party was to usher in the classical stage of imperialism. Municipal gas and water Socialism passed to the Fabians. National socialism re-emerged within the scientific framework of Marxism but developed from 1900 through the mass working class, reformist Labour Party. Liberal radicalism was eclipsed until it surfaced once again in 1905 with Lloyd George playing the role of Chamberlain in a last desperate attempt to retain working class support under middle class control within the Liberal Party. Like Chamberlain, Lloyd George was eventually des-troyed by his jingoism and support for imperialist war.

How can one summarise this radical phase of Joseph Chamberlain's career? It could be said that he rose above his bourgeois origins, but not far enough. He saw that Landed Capital was theft, but he could not take the final step of seeing that all Capital was theft. Capital was and is labour converted into a commodity bought and sold like any other commodity; profit arises from the necessity of the labourer to sell his labour power and in the process create a surplus which is appropriated by the capitalist. Chamberlain could go no further than suggest that the expropriators give up some of these ill-gotten gains as ransom for the right to continue to expropriate. It took another bourgeois, Marx, to penetrate to the heart of the matter and show that the expropriators should be expropriated. Of George Bernard Shaw, who also could not take this final step, it is said that he was a good man fallen among Fabians; of Chamberlain it might be said that he was a good man fallen among Imperialists.

Chapter Fifteen

THE RE-EMERGENCE OF SOCIALISM 1884 – 1900
The Political Parties

Introduction.

Socialism in Birmingham, as in Britain as a whole, emerged, like its catalyst, the Great Depression, almost as a bolt from the blue. Yet the preceding pages have shown that the bases of Socialism had been firmly laid. These bases included the ideology and organisation of Secularism which had been continuous since the 1850s with the decline of Chartism and Owenite Socialism; the numerous political and social movements peripheral to Secularism, but in which there was a Secularist presence; the development and consolidation of the trade union movement; and the inevitable but unstable lurch towards socialism by radical-Liberalism as it faced up to the problems of (a) analysing and countering the Great Depression and (b) cementing the connection of the newly franchised and better educated working people to the Liberal Party and heading off the development of a working class party.

But the re-emergence of Socialism in a Marxist dimension posed a potentially fatal challenge to the capitalist system and it is worth recapitulating the key elements of Marxism which either appealed directly to masses of people, or were in fact Marxist, although those holding such views were not necessarily aware that this was the case. In some respects this understanding was deeper than at the present time, when Marxist works are freely available and Marxist concepts, particularly in sociology and history, are widely accepted.

1. The economic base of capitalism was under attack. This showed itself in the existence of the Great Depression and the widespread belief that it was caused by Underconsumption which led directly to Marx' trade cycle theory. To this was allied traditional beliefs based on classical political economy that value was created by labour. There was also wide understanding of the class position of working people. This surfaced particularly in the trade union movement, and ensured that these unions never became solely associations for the protection of narrow craft interests, protectors of skilled workers' interests alone or completely class collaborationist. This is particularly important to stress in the case of Birmingham where the reverse has so often been claimed.

2. There was a deep and abiding hostility to the landed interest. This was partly fanned by the radical Liberals in their struggle against the Whigs within the Liberal Party, but also in the realisation that land monopoly was at the root of the vile housing and social conditions. In addition there was widespread support for that section of working people which was perhaps the most atrociously exploited by capitalism, namely the agricultural labourers. This detestation of the landed interest at a time when it was claimed that only 710 persons owned 25% of the land area of England and Wales had ideological spin-offs. It led to the development

of concepts of primitive Communism and the understanding that private property and class society occupied little more than 10,000 of the two million or so years that mankind had existed; it led on to a re-examination of socialism in ancient Greece and Rome together with the role of the Hebrew prophets in advocating a return to the simplicities of the primitive Communism from which these tribes had emerged as the only remedy for the evils of the Sodoms and Gomorrahs resulting from commerce, trade, wealth and capital; also the Socialism of the Essenes and other sects as well as primitive Christianity itself. This further fuelled an interest in our own history leading either to the direct acceptance of the principles of historical materialism or a pragmatic radicalism of historians such as Thorold Rogers exposing class oppression through the ages and the study of prices which led to conclusions on living standards far from favourable to existing capitalism. It also led to an examination of the communal roots of the ancient English village by Seebohm, Gomme and others — studies long overdue to be re-opened after the long preoccupation of progressive historians with seventeenth century class struggles and the Industrial Revolution.

3. The fact that the transition from Chartism to Socialism was bridged by Secularism meant that there was always a healthy materialist opposition to the vast pretensions of organised religion. Again, Birmingham occupied a special position, with its unbroken spectrum from the darkest reaction through to the 'natural' religion of the Unitarians and Owenites, softening the conflicts and usually managing to avoid the worst excesses of religious bigotry. This at a time when the ancient obscurantism of conservative theology was reeling from the blows of Darwin and Huxley.

4. This hostility to the landed interest and the critique of religion was joined with an anti-Royalist and republicanism stretching back to the seventeenth century and the obscenities of the Prince Regent.

All of these factors meant that Marxism fell on ground better prepared to receive it than is generally acknowledged. Where Marxism led, however, reformism and social democracy were not far behind. The Fabian Society was also founded in 1884, although its first local Branch, which was in Birmingham, was not formed until 1890.

The conflicts of the period after 1884 centred on the economic question of whether British capitalism, deprived of its world monopoly, could generate sufficient resources to renew itself and enter another period of expansion. In the field of ideas it was a struggle between the ideologues of capitalism attempting to prevent working class consciousness from growing and the efforts of the working class and its class conscious, but divided, vanguard to develop the struggle for better conditions and the replacement of capitalism by socialism.

The Social Democratic Federation in Birmingham 1884 – 1900.

H.M. Hyndman formed the Democratic Federation in 1881 and it became the Social Democratic Federation in 1883. Its weekly journal *Justice* first appeared in January 1884.

The first report of a Birmingham branch was in June of that year when it was announced that Taylor, Sketchley and other members of the Birmingham Democratic Federation would hold meetings in West

Bromwich. The meeting place is significant, for it was the Black Country which was at that time suffering some of the worst effects of the Great Depression and where militancy was widespread.

The local speaker at that first meeting was John Sketchley who was a much respected old Chartist, still with years of service to give the midlands movement. The national speaker was either Helen Taylor, step-daughter of John Stuart Mill, or Jonathan Taylor of Sheffield, both of whom were in the Black Country at that time.

This meeting was duly held and it was announced that another meeting would be held the next week dealing with Giffen's statement on the welfare of the working classes. This is indicative of the indignation caused by people such as Giffen and Bowley who were then laying the basis for the all too easily accepted belief that living standards for working people rose throughout the second half of the nineteenth century.

The beginning of Socialism 'as an organised force with a definite militant policy' is set by Arthur Burns as November 1886 when Tom Mann came to Birmingham for six weeks with a brief to organise the SDF in Birmingham and the Black Country. Mann formed a stable branch in Birmingham, but in the militant but more volatile Black Country he was less successful.

The new Birmingham branch immediately plunged into its main activities which were to be open-air agitation, organisational and educational branch metings, trade union and workshop organisation, and the taking up of social issues including contesting local elections. From 1886 to 1890 the branch was particularly active and successful.

By February 1887 the local branch was meeting weekly at the Hope Street Board School listening to lectures by local comrades on such subjects as Socialism and Trade Depression, How the Poor are Robbed, The Wants of the Age and the Remedy of Socialism, The Gospel of Socialism etc. In March the Queen visited 'loyal Birmingham'. The comrades complained in *Justice* that the visit cost £10,000 'although £500 could not be found a few weeks ago for starving children'. It was admitted that the branch was not strong enough to mount a really effective protest, but Hyndman was brought to the city and held large open-air meetings at which resolutions, presumably pointing these contrasts, were largely carried.

In the summer of 1887 an extended campaign of open-air meetings was launched. The main Sunday morning meeting was held at Gosta Green. In May a good meeting of 200 was reported and in June a meeting of 600. Afternoon meetings were held outside the Council House, and in the evenings after experimenting with Hockley, regular meetings were held at the Sturge Monument, Five Ways. In September 'an immense meeting' was reported there. In July open-air activity was extended to a regular meeting on Wednesdays at Smithfield market.

From August open-air meetings were combined with electoral activity. John Haddon was adopted as a candidate for St. Mary's Ward. He held large open-air meetings, including one at the Bull Ring with 1,000 present. In October the campaign was continued indoors. A meeting at Dartmouth Street board School was considered 'unique in municipal contests in Birmingham. Not only was the audience unanimous, but on the word of a police officer it was the most orderly and enthusiastic he had ever attended.' The SDF also packed meetings of their opponents and at one meeting where Councillor Pollack asked Haddon to withdraw his supporters 'five sixths of the audience adjourned to Gosta Green.'

The campaign was going so well that it was decided to run Joe Tanner at Ladywood Green. In the last days before the election large meetings continued. A 'magnificent meeting' at Gosta Green collected £1-17-0d. for Haddon. At a Bull Ring meeting on Unemployment a 3,000 crowd was claimed to be the biggest Socialist meeting ever to be held at the Bull Ring.

Haddon's election result was magnificient. He polled 759 to the Liberal victor's 1016. Tanner did less well polling 232 against 1558 for a Liberal/Unionist, although it was claimed that Tanner had been put up for purely tactical reasons and he had polled more than any other labour candidate despite the fact that not a single vote had been solicited.

Election campaigning seems to have given a fillip to recruiting and a No.2 Branch of the S.D.F. was set up meeting at the Squirrel, Moland Street. From June No.1. Branch met at Bell Street Coffee House every Friday at 7.30 p.m.

Open-air meetings continued into the winter. In late November rain drove the comrades under the portico of the Council House whereupon half a dozen constables called on Tanner to move off. 'Haddon then mounted the rostrum and called for three cheers for the social revolution. Names and addresses of member were taken.'

1888 was another good year. Two Birmingham branches were maintained. No. 1. moved to Baskerville Hall. This was where a Secular Society Sunday School had been started in 1886 which had provided eight or nine young people to the SDF when Tom Mann had started the branch.

The branches were getting out to other institutions. A discussion with the Ashted Assembly Rooms Debating Society which had been started in December on 'Is Socialism Sound?' was still continuing in February 1888. In March there was a discussion on Socialism at the Bishop Rider's Mutual Improvement Society.

Open-air activity continued at the regular sites of Gosta Green, the Council House and Five Ways, but constant attempts were made to develop new pitches. New ground was broken in May at Small Heath, in June at Bordesley and Saltley and July at Nechells Green.

In November 1888 Haddon and Tanner contested the same wards as before at the municipal elections. This time results were less satisfactory. Haddon polled a creditable 519 against a Liberal/Unionist's 1206 while Tanner had 123 votes against 1672 for the successful Liberal/Unionist.

In assessing the Federation's presence in Birmingham compared with the SDF elsewhere in the country it can be noted that there were regular reports of Birmingham activity in *Justice* during this year when only ten other provincial branches were regularly reporting. But one can never be sure to what extent this reflects a lively reporter rather than greater activity compared with other branches.

At the beginning of 1889 there were still two SDF branches. The propaganda was divided between No.1. Branch which was responsible for the Council House meetings on Sunday afternoons and Five Ways in the evening as well as a lecture at Oozell Street Board Schools the same evening. No.2. Branch was responsible for the Gosta Green Sunday morning meeting and a Wednesday meeting at Nechells Green.

Electoral activity was stepped up in 1889. In June Rotton Park Ward was contested for the first time and Joe Tanner polled 160 against the victor's 729. At the November elections Tanner stood again at Nechells and got 437 votes. The *Justice* report stated:

> The indefatigable Birmingham comrades are pushing on with ever greater vigour. No stauncher SDer ever stood than Joe Tanner and the fact that he polled 437 against 1059 for the 'philanthropist' Middlemore was little short of a triumph. Every effort was made to bribe Tanner off.

At the end of November there was another bye-election at Rotton Park and Tanner stood. This time he polled 356 votes to the Liberal/Unionists 1568, claiming a 125% increase in his vote. Tanner had now stood five times in two years. The bourgeois parties were rather annoyed at all this SDF activity. Alderman Pollock said that Tanner was abusing public privileges by saddling the corporation with these election expenses. Tanner replied, however, that with 300 or more burgesses behind him he had the right to contest any election in the city.

In August 1889 the SDF held its national annual conference in Birmingham. In June Harry Quelch had been in the city addressing public meetings and also, apparently, negotiating with the authorities, for it was reported that the SDF had gained free use of the Town Hall for its Conference. During the period of the Conference the usual mass public meeting was held while all the national leaders were assembled. Herbert Burrows presided at this Town Hall meeting. One of the local speakers was Joe Tanner who said that 'Tears rolled down his cheeks for the deplorable conditions of the mass of ordinary workers in St. Mary's Ward which he found when canvassing for John Haddon.' Sentimental, no doubt, but a salutary reminder both of the depth and extent of late nineteenth century poverty and also the motivation of those who risked livelihood and liberty as activists in the SDF.

1889 was the year of the national Dock Strike and the gains of the Gas Workers. In September (London gas workers had gained the 8-hour day in May), Will Thorne was in Birmingham organising the gas workers. At a large meeting and march of 5,000 it was reported that 'The weather beaten banner of the SDF was carried calling for 'Work for All: Overwork for none'.' John Haddon said that the 8-hour day had been conceded. But it applied only to those permanently employed and cost only £1,500 whereas if it had applied also to the casual workers (800 carboniers in winter and only 300 in the summer) it would have cost £15,000.

Further light on the 8-hour day campaign is shed in Arthur Burns' third article on the Twentieth Anniversary of the Socialist Movement in Birmingham in the *Labour Mail*. He says that before 1889 the gasworkers of Birmingham were unorganised with low wages and long hours. These conditions had not improved after the Corporation took over the gasworks. One Sunday morning several gas workers had attended the open-air meeting at Gosta Green and explained their grievances to Joe Tanner. Plans were then laid to gain first hand knowledge of these conditions:

One morning a party of gasworkers entered the gates at the Saltley gasworks. There was apparently nothing unusual about this ... but one of that party was a stranger to the calling and that stranger was Joe Tanner ... First he assisted in the stoking, then he tried the job of a labourer, wheeling a barrow of hot coke ... It was the hardest work he had ever experienced. After this experience the agitation for shorter hours and better wages commenced in real earnest; meeting after meeting was held addressed by John Haddon and Joe Tanner causing the gasworkers to organise and arousing public feeling on their behalf. On the emblem of that trade union are the photographs of two labour leaders — Councillor Eli Bloor and Allan Granger — two good men in their way. But the initiation in the organising of that trade union was the work of John Haddon and Joe Tanner. The two Labour councillors appeared on the scene when the union had become a success. I do not wish to depreciate their actions or in any way belittle their work ... but it is simply stating a fact when I say that the founders of that trade union were not Bloor and Granger, but Haddon and Tanner.

So the 1880s ended with another full year for the Birmingham Social democracy; but there was probably only one Birmingham branch at the end of the year. In the next decade the branch was to have many ups and downs. A number of leading cadres disappear at this point and others take their place.

It seems appropriate here, therefore, to quote Arthur Burns' account of the establishment and subsequent fluctuations of the branch. This illustrates the general problem of branches established by leading figures of the party.

As soon as he arrived at New Street Railway Station he went straight to the office of each of the local daily newspapers and told them 'I am Tom Mann, I have come to Birmingham on a mission to form a branch of the Social Democratic Federation ... I shall be pleased to see one of your reporters present at each of my meetings.'

Tom Mann set to work in real earnest, almost every night he was holding meetings either indoors among the trade unionists or outdoors at the Bull Ring. As a man of eloquence and of endurance there were few in the whole country his equal. He possessed a fund of energy which awakened the whole town. In three weeks when he held a meeting at the Temperance Hall he had a following of over 60 members. At the end of six weeks he left an organisation in Birmingham of about 150 strong. Men dressed in top hats, frock coats and wearing gold-rimmed eye-glasses gave the membership of the branch quite a respectable appearance.

But alas! When Tom Mann left us, the supply of eloquence was not forthcoming to satisfy the appetite of the emotional Socialist and there was a sudden falling off of membership. The Alexandra Hall which previously was packed every Sunday and had been too small for us became deserted and much too large, and we removed our meeting place to Hope Street Board Schools opposite. Out of the 150 membership only about twelve remained true to the cause ... Our meetings were dull and uninteresting; lectures were delivered to a scanty audience by Joe Tanner, John Haddon, Mrs. Thomas and Mr. Lloyd. The same faces week after week, indeed it needed the heart of a true Briton to deliver those lectures.

The only hope of living to maturity lay in Joe Tanner, he was the only man who had had any previous experience in organisation. His knowledge of the work was crude, but it was backed up with unbounding zeal. Of that gallant band of Socialists only two remain to continue in the work with the new large band of today (1906 – GB) — Councillor John Haddon of Aston and myself.

1890 – 1900.

1890 does not seem to have been a very productive year. It was not until August that a report from Birmingham appeared in *Justice* when Joe Tanner wrote, 'Many may think the Soclialist cause in Birmingham extinct, but our members are more of the working than the writing type.' He went on to say that he had polled 214 votes in Rotton Park and that they were having trouble with the police at Five Ways. In October the branch moved from Baskerville Hall to the Social Democratic Club at 2 Stafford Street. The branch meetings were still held on Mondays and the discussion classes on Thursdays, but an innovation was a Speaking and Reading Class on Wednesdays.

1891 was a better year. In March the branch was not only advertising more open-air meetings than before, but also announcing the speakers. For instance, the report of 21st March in *Justice* gave:

11.a.m.	Gosta Green — Rooke, Milner, Holloway.
	Nechells' Green — Tooth, Riley, Brown.
	Belmont Row/Lawley St. — Smetham, Ellis.
3 p.m.	Bull Ring — Tooth, Milner.
7 p.m.	Bull Ring — Tooth, Riley, Babbington.
	Paradise St/Suffolk St. — Smetham, Ellis, Thomas.
	Sturges Monument — Rook, Milner, Brown.

This is a remarkable number of meetings to be sustaining as early in the year as March and was a much more detailed list than any other branch, either London or provincial, could produce.

During the 1890s May Day developed both as a specific platform for the 8-hour day world wide agitation and as a Labour Festival. In 1891 a 'Monster 8-Hour Day Demonstration under the auspices of the S.D.F.' was announced with local SDF and trades council speakers. It was the SDF which had inaugurated May Day the previous year when 2,000 were said to have attended a demonstration at Gosta Green in support of the 8-Hour bill.

At the November municipal elections John Haddon stood and polled the splendid vote of 763 against his Tory opponent's 1128.

S.D.F. reports for 1892 are very meagre. In January the branch moved to McCullogh's Temperance Hall, Gosta Green. By July this was called McCullogh's Social Democratic Hall, 47 Aston Road.

1893 saw a Socialist revival in Birmingham. May Day was fairly successful. There was only one platform at Gosta Green, but it was a good example of unity, we are told. The resolution (on the 8-Hour Day?) was moved by an independent Labour man, seconded by the S.D.F. and supported by a Fabian.

District organisation was discussed for the first time in June. At that time there were SDF branches in Birmingham, Coventry, Dudley, Hanley, Leicester, Nottingham (two), Northampton and West Bromwich. In December the Midlands District council of the SDF was formed, but its first centre was at Northampton rather than Birmingham. This was Bradlaugh territory and suggests that the SDF developed best where there were traditions of secularism, republicanism and land agitation. The East Midlands seem to be stronger in these traditions than Birmingham or the Black Country.

1894 was another quiet year. J. Bland of Northampton visited the city in February. He reported two good out-door meetings 'despite windy weather' and also recorded that the Birmingham Trades Council had called for the collective ownership of the means of production. He ends on a familiar note:

> This Chamberlain stronghold is one of the worst places for Socialist propaganda. But I believe that when Socialism takes firm root it will spread rapidly through the district.

In June the formation of a Birmingham SDF brass band was announced and an appeal made for money to buy instruments. The band Secretary was C.Smith.

By July the SDF branch had moved again. This time to the Trades Hall, Wrottesley Street. Open-air meetings were at Gosta Green on Sunday mornings and the Bull Ring in the evening.

1895 saw some progress. In June the SDF general council approved an additional Birmingham branch at Nechells. All east Birmingham comrades were asked to join the branch which was then meeting at the home of comrade Riley. In August, however, at the height of the open-air meeting season, it was reported that meetings at Gosta Green and the Bull Ring had not done very well during the previous fortnight due to speakers not turning up. 'If it had not been for the old SDF war-horses Riley and Thomas these meeting would have fallen through.'

The 15th annual conference of the SDF was held in Birmingham in August at the Labour Church, Bond Street. At the public Town Hall meetings it was estimated that the hall was full and the gallery three quarters full and this was reckoned satisfactory. George Tooth took the chair.

The highlight of 1896 was a three months' stay in Birmingham by George Lansbury. Another Town Hall meeting addressed by Hyndman and Lansbury took place in February, but Lansbury's final report in March was one of only guarded optimism:

> There is a much more hopeful spirit in Birmingham than there was three months ago, but it is necessary to remind some members that hopelessness is no earthly use in a movement like ours. I am convinced that all our comrades in Birmingham need is the energy and determination to go up and possess the land; I am also convinced that there are sufficient Social Democrats in Birmingham to do this.'

In March 1896 the movement celebrated the 25th Anniversary of the Paris Commune. This commemoration was to become an annual event observed until the 1917 Russian Revolution made greater celebration possible. In Birmingham the SDF organised a tea and social meeting at the Labour Church attended by about 100 people. After the concert there were short speeches by Lansbury, Tooth and Crease. Another new SDF branch was also announced at Bordesley.

In April there was a long report in jocular style signed by the pseudonym Looker-On which reflected the growing Clarion influence.

> 'Notwithstanding the appointment of two correspondence secretaries there has been an entire lack of notes of work in this city of His

Mightiness Joseph of the Coloured Coat. Let me state that the SDF in
Birmingham is not doomed to an ignominious death as our temperance
friends seem to think.'

Looker-On then went on to say that about twelve months ago there was
one branch with about 20-30 comrades. Now there were four branches
each with an average of 20 members. Looker-On brings to his report an
unaccustomed spirit of criticism of some of his comrades. He notes, for
instance, that at a lecture on Bax' Ethics of Socialism a clergyman had
objected:

> I agree with him. We must not let religion come into our movement or
> the SDF will commence to fall to pieces. Last Saturday our comrade E.
> Sale gave a lecture on the Economic Basis of Socialism. He no doubt
> delivered a splendid lecture but it should have been given, in my
> opinion, under another title. It should not have dealt so much with
> Fabian papers as the land question. I can assure comrade Sale and others
> that they are entirely mistaken if they believe we will have capital in a
> Social Democratic state. What is looked on as Capital today will be
> Wealth under Socialism.
> On Sunday April 5th our comrade, Frank Milliner, had a debate with
> our temperance friend, Lovesay. Milliner had the best of the debate, but
> he could have done better.

By October, there were only three branches in Birmingham. Another
wag, Lucifer, reports that the East Birmingham branch in reply to a
Chamberlainite claim that workers were spending too much, were getting
up a petition asking capitalists to *reduce* wages, 'relieving the workers of
the necessity for spending so much and thus giving them time for study!'

1897 began with a report from another anonymous scribe, Eye-On.
Birmingham had just been through a period of depression in 'suspended
animation' from which they were being slowly roused by one or two
energetic comrades. Propaganda had been carried on in a very slipshod
fashion for some time and the whole work thrown on the shoulders of a
few. East Birmingham had commenced indoor lectures and Birmingham
Central, which had been languishing for some time, was about to open
a club for all members. In March the Central branch organised the Paris
Commune anniversary celebration which took the usual form of a tea and
social at the Labour Church. The main speaker was John Chatterton,
who was the midlands organiser at that time.

In June, Birmingham East was meeting regularly each Monday at a
Coffee House at the corner of Duddeston Mill Road and Great Francis
Street. The branch had an important new secretary in Mrs. L. Vernon.
A woman SDF secretary was almost unique and Mrs. Vernon played an
important part until her tragic early death a few years later. Birmingham
Central branch at this time changed their venue to the Bell Hotel, Colehill
Street. The secretary was V. Davies. There was a considerable body of
opinion in the SDF nationally opposed to the use of licensed premises for
branch meetings, and although there is no explicit discussion of these
views in Birmingham, it is noticeable that, up to this point, the SDF had
avoided public houses as meeting places.

Also in June, the SDF branches combined for a social visit to Sutton
Park on the occasion of Queen Victoria's jubilee. Again, the Clarion
influence appears.

In August, John Chatterton stayed in Birmingham for ten days. He outlined a first, full week. On Sunday he had spoken at good Outdoor meetings at Gosta Green and Five Ways. On Monday he visited the Nechells branch and was successful in persuading them to arrange a programme of outdoor meetings for the next two months. On Tuesday he seems to have been less successful in reviving the St. George's branch which he visited with George Tooth. 'All members visited expressed a desire to continue the propaganda, but because of overtime etc. they could not get together.' A Bull Ring meeting was scheduled for the Wednesday, but it rained so heavily that no meeting was possible. Chatterton was given a night off on Thursday, so he went to Coventry and reported 'a lively and cheerful branch despite recent problems.' On Friday there was an aggregate meeting of all Birmingham members at the Bell Hotel. On Sunday he had two exceedingly good meetings at Gosta Green and Five Ways. 'From the standpoint of numbers it was all that could be desired. The sale of literature was quite remarkable. Rarely have I had the pleasure of addressing a better audience.' Chatterton's final report was rather different from George Lansbury's a year earlier:

> I'm bound to say I have been most encouraged by my visit. I have visited Birmingham many times before, but never have I had such good meetings.

In October 1897 another national organiser, G. Green, visited the city briefly. He held a good meeting at Gosta Green 'despite constant drizzle.' In the evening he was 'at the more aristocratic part of the city known as Five Ways.' With the help of two local comrades 'the meeting was kept going until a late hour.'

November brought an interesting report from George Tooth. The branch had come to the end of a most successful open-air campaign which had left it in a much better position than for some time. The winter indoor programme included an economics class to which Tooth had been appointed instructor. He goes on to give his method of taking the class 'which may be useful to other branches'. A week ahead of the class, all the economic terms to be defined are listed. The members of the class are then arranged in alphabetical order and allocated a term which, at the next meeting, they have to explain urging the arguments and the authorities in its favour. They go round the class until everyone present has spoken. The job of the instructor, Tooth continues, is to take each definition and argument, pointing out its strengths and weaknesses:

> As it is a Socialist class, mind you, the Instructor comes in for a general volley of criticism. This method makes each one take an intelligent interest in economics and increases his knowledge of the same. The classes are never dull, always interesting, bright and attractive.

Perhaps so, but by 1899 Tooth is admitting that the class which had been successful for two years 'had fallen on very hard times indeed'.

At the beginning of 1898 the SDF Directory in *Justice* showed two Birmingham branches. The secretary of Central was Fred Hanks and the Birmingham East secretary was still Mrs. Vernon.

Hanks was an energetic new secretary. In January he was complaining that the Birmingham Central Library was refusing to take copies of *Justice* for its Reading Room, and in view of the part the SDF had played in getting Clarion into that library, he appealed for a united effort for *Justice* complaining that many branches did not advertise themselves in the paper. This should be rectified not only to support *Justice* but also for the convenience of other branches, he claimed.

1898 is officially designated an economically prosperous year, although before its end there were reports of the starving unemployed in Coventry. In February, a report by George Tooth on Central branch stated that its financial membership had trebled in the previous twelve months. Tooth also makes some interesting comments on the efficacy of winter open-air propaganda at the time when this was so important for every active branch:

> Outdoor work has been abandoned for the present as little use to the movement and even less to the active members whom we are in no hurry to kill off.

Many members were keeping in training, Tooth claimed, by attending local debating societies, one of which had been debating Socialism for two months.

Lantern slide lectures were popular in the winter. Three hundred people attended a lecture by John Chatterton at Bristol Street Schools. 'His droll wit and apposite criticism did much to impress on the audience the cruel injustice being perpetrated.'

The Commune celebration took place at the Victoria Hotel, John Bright Street, 'The annual gatherings bring many old faces together and many older comrades will come back and take their rightful place in the movement,' George Tooth reported.

In April 1898 there was a long report on the activities of Birmingham East. Beginning with the customary disclaimer ... 'We may have appeared on the surface asleep, but our pile of letters would require the space of the whole paper to report' ... It went on to detail the campaigns the branch was engaged in. Firstly, it had taken up the defence of the women employed in the slaughterhouses of the city who worked 70 hours per week. Secondly the issue of public parks was taken up in a part of the city where there was only one park and a gas works was being built in that. Thirdly the scandal of child labour was being taken up. Finally 5,000 manifestos had been issued calling for municipal dwellings.

Another issue raised by the East branch later in the year was the shoddy clothing issued to the city scavengers. Dye from new overalls and overcoats was working through to the men's skin and seventy were off work with skin complaints.

By the end of the year two other notable events had taken place. In December a new branch was started at Handsworth and in October we have the first mention of Billy Holliday as having taken over the secretaryship of Central branch from Fred Hanks. Of Holliday, who can be considered one of the martyrs of the Birmingham movement and who was to die in jail, much more will be heard.

The last year of the century produces rather less material on the branch. In January, Holliday was pursuing the question of *Justice* being

placed in the city library by enquiring in *Justice* of all SDF branches which
have the paper in their local libraries. Birmingham East had congratulated the city School Board on raising the school leaving age.

In February Hanks and Clapshaw had gone from Birmingham to
Oldbury to speak at an open-air meeting. They had been arrested and
given 14 days in prison. A national appeal was set up for funds. In
March, the annual Commune Celebration again took place at the
Victoria Hotel and in April, Central branch reported increased member-
ship 'even in these dull times'.

By June, the Central branch was holding its regular meetings at the
Victoria Hotel and Fred Hanks had resumed the secretaryship. There
was social activity in September when the Birmingham and Coventry
branches joined forces for an outing to Hampton. Tea was at the Ring
of Bells and consisted of roast beef, boiled ham, bread and butter,
preserves, cake, salad etc. for 1/6d. In October Central branch held a
Grand Smoking Concert at Victoria Hotel. By the end of the year there
had been a Birmingham Socialist SWARRY (again the *Clarion* influence) and plans were afoot for a Birmingham Socialist Club.

So the century closed quietly for the Birmingham Social Democracy
and we might mark the fourteenth year of the revival of Socialism in
Birmingham by referring again to the 1907 articles of Arthur Burns to
remind ourselves of what it meant to be one of those pioneers:

> To be a Socialist in those days was like unto being a member of a
> desperado party, and we were described as such; it was to be
> contaminated with a dreadful social disease, and people would look upon
> you with contempt and reproach, and shun one as a social leper.
> Relations and associates when they heard that you had become a
> Socialist would lift up their hands in horror and exclaim, 'Oh, dear!'
> with a deep sigh, as if he, or she, had met with a terrible misfortune.

Clarion in Birmingham 1891 – 1900.

Any analysis of the contribution of Robert Blatchford and the *Clarion*
to British socialism invites such nationalistic comments as 'typically
British' or 'could not have occurred anywhere else in the world'. Such
nationalism easily spilled over to jingoism and it was indeed such
jingoism which led to the downfall of Blatchford, as of Hyndman.
Nevertheless *Clarion* brought a mass, social element to Socialism which
has never been regained and without which we may never· achieve
Socialism. *Clarion* became the centre of Cheerful Socialism and around it
the paper wove a web of political and social clubs covering every cultural
and recreational requirement of working class life, combining it always
with the sharp, cutting edge of Socialist politics.

Robert Blatchford was the son of a strolling player. Margaret Cole says
that no one except Keir Hardie knew more about poverty. At twenty,
Blatchford became a soldier for seven years and then turned himself into
a brilliant journalist, eventually earning £1,000 a year with the *Sunday
Chronicle*. He was converted to Socialism through bitter opposition to a
pamphlet by Hyndman and Morris, which he subsequently retracted.
When he proposed to open the columns of the *Chronicle* to the Socialists
he was forced to resign and brought out the *Clarion* in December 1891.

Clarionettes, as supporters of the paper quickly acknowledged themselves, were much given to the use of pseudonyms. Blatchford himself wrote as Nunquam and he brought with him to the paper other fine journalists such as Alex Thompson (Dangle), his brother Montague (Mong Blong) and Edward Fay (the Bounder). The *Clarion* really took off in 1893 and became a weekly feast of fun reporting and supporting all Socialist and labour organisations — the I.L.P., S.D.F. Socialist League, Socialist Centres, Labour Churches and trade union struggles. *Clarion* also initiated and fostered social clubs and activities. Finally it made an independent contribution to Socialism with its pamphlets and books, the most incredible of which was Merrie England.

1893 brought a new Socialist impetus to Birmingham. It was the year of the founding of the Independent Labour Party and branches were quickly formed in Birmingham. 1893 was also the inaugural year of the Labour Church in Birmingham.

From these events, others flowed. Blatchford had started a Cinderella Club in Manchester as early as 1886 to provide treats for poor children; through the influence of the *Clarion* it spread to Birmingham in 1893 and soon became the largest Cinderella in the country. In February 1894 seven Birmingham men on the initiative of Tom Groom met to form the first Clarion Cycling Club in the country. From the Cycling Club followed the Clarion Fellowships which, like the Cycling Club, spread across the country. The Clarionettes not only made Socialism respectable and popular, they also made it enjoyable.

Clarion influence grew in Birmingham from 1894. It was an 8-page, penny newspaper with plenty of comic verse and line drawings. Readers were intrigued with such cryptic messages as 'Did the Bounder get the hamper?' and reports such as 'a very jolly social at Bond Street Labour Church' were signed with such pseudonyms as Arturo or Q.E.D. There was always some commercial advertising such as 'Dunn's hats made by TU labour at TU rates' and as the cycling clubs grew the advertisements of the cycle industry (largely from Birmingham) virtually subsidised the paper.

Attempts were made at the beginning of the year to establish a Democratic Club in Birmingham. Arturo declared that if every Birmingham Clarionette did his or her duty this would soon be established even in backward Birmingham. Later in January, a well attended meeting at the Cobden Hotel elected a provisional committee of the proposed Democratic Club. In May it was reported that the inaugural meeting of the Club had been held at the Kensington Restaurant where the Clubroom was situated.

In March, the column *Notes to Clarionettes*, Aston Clarionettes wishing to form an Aston I.L.P. were invited to contact J. Haddon.

In April the famous seven of the Birmingham Clarion Cycling Club took to the road for their Easter tour travelling by train to Wolverhampton and then cycling to Bridgnorth & Bewdley. The next day they travelled to Evesham noting on the way that there was 'hope for Worcester because the *Clarion* is sold here'.

In May 1894 *Clarion* announced that the I.L.P. had opened a trading shop at 82 Dale End where it was hoped that 'all Socialists, Clarionettes and other advanced thinkers would repair'. The reporter had just filled his ILP pipe with ILP tobacco and lit it with an ILP match.

The first meeting of the Nunquam Scouts took place in July. Despite glorious weather fifty young people turned up, it was reported. The secretary was Tom Groom. At a second meeting the same month seventy-one youngsters turned up. George Richards was appointed secretary in place of Tom Groom 'who has more to do than any good Socialist believing in the 8-hour day would wish.' The Scouts met at the Labour Church where good work was also being done by Mrs. Norman, Miss Davies and Mr. & Mrs. Carlile with a children's drum and fife band. Soon the Scouts were distributing *Clarion* literature — leaflets such as *Practical Politics* and *What is Socialism?*

The early Birmingham reports of 1895 came from the unknown Arturo. In February he wrote that things were quiet in the Socialist camp. The Scouts were rather quiet. The movement to start the Democratic Club 'on the ashes of the old' were thought at the Labour Church to be premature. Later in the month Arturo said that he had no heart to write because of the terrible distress in Birmingham:

> The poor would rather starve — ay, and die — rather than subject themselves to the brow beating of the cast iron Poor Law. Hundreds and hundreds of half starved creatures beseige the offices of the Charity Organisation. Yet there is no exceptional distress.

May Day, however, was very successful, with six or seven thousand people at Gosta Green to hear Tom Mann.

Evidence of apathy comes from an October report of open-air ILP meetings:

> The great socialist virtue of punctuality is not present in Birmingham. The secretary of the Propaganda Committee says to a speaker 'Go ye to Bordesley, or Nechells or Smethwick and be there at 11 a.m.' And the Speaker goeth. At 11.30 one of the local comrades turns up. At 11.45 the chairman turns up and the meeting probably begins at 12. Again, Committee meetings are called for 8 o'clock sharp at a quarter to nine. Now this isn't good enough. Let's have some personal honesty in engagements. If speakers who have gulped their breakfast down and hurried to the other side of town to be in time gets to the meeting place, don't keep him waiting three quarters of an hour before turning up. One good position was lost on several occasions and almost for good through this. Tom Mann gave it to our men strong for lack of organisation in the midlands. I understand that unless we get to work quickly we will not be represented at the next Conference.

In September it was deemed a sign of progress that J.A. Hobson M.A. a socialist, should open the winter programme of the Midlands Institute. Hobson traced political economy from the old Manchester School to the more humane teachings of John Ruskin. In November there was a plea to feed 4,000 Cinderellas during the winter, subscriptions to be sent to Frank Matthews or Herbert Everitt.

Only the Cycling Club flourished, it seemed. The energetic Tom Groom had been transformed into O Groomie O and there was much good natured banter and rivalry between the cycling clubs, particularly those in the West Midlands and Manchester.

Arising from a general meet, Manchester were chided with not being able to win prizes at dances. S. McSprinter of Manchester CCC replied that they were better at mustering than winning prizes. O Groomie O described the revelries at the Coventry dance in October. Birmingham had won six prizes in all. At 4 a.m. Poet was discovered trying to inflate his tyre with the valve out. 'We climbed into Birmingham at 7 a.m. a weary, wan-eyed miserable lot of dejected perishers. We don't turn out a hundred. But the quality!'

All reports so far quoted would lead us to write off 1895 as a poor to average year for Socialism in Birmingham; and yet it was the year of that minor miracle — *Merrie England*.

This originated as a series of articles by Robert Blatchford in *Clarion*. These were quickly published in book form, first at 1/-d. but as sales sky rocketed the price was reduced to an incredible 1d. The book sold one million copies! and was translated into many languages.

Modern socialists turn to this book to see what lessons it can teach present day propagandists. It is, of course, well written, but it is not an easy read. It assumes an intelligent reader, and the arguments for socialism are closely reasoned. The success of the book was not therefore due to its author having discovered a magical formula for the presentation of socialist ideas. Nor can its success be explained by its appearance when the movement was at a flood; the reverse was the case. Its massive sales appear explicable only in the enthusiasm, intelligence and organisation with which it was sold.

The first mention of the book in Birmingham was a notice in October 1894 which said that the book of the century had arrived! Already it was selling like hot cakes. A joint organisation of all socialists in Birmingham was proposed to ensure a proper distribution and to see that not more than one copy was sent to each public man. By December there were Merrie England classes at the Labour Church and also at Little Green Lane Board School. These classes were said to be very popular. During the winter sales were organised through such classes and the normal channels of socialist literature.

In April Kryptos, who appears to have been in charge of sales, announced that classes would be suspended for the summer months in favour of open-air propaganda. Hostilities would commence with a march to Sutton Park and sales of Merrie England. At the successful May Day meeting with Tom Mann 'sales of literature were immense, including 500 copies of Merrie England.'

Kryptos continued his reports through May and June. On another ramble to Sutton Park the three dozen copies they had brought with them were sold out before they got to the park. A good, socialist vicar was said to be selling the book at 1/-d. a copy instead of 1d. because he considered this its true value. The next Sunday two people sold three dozen copies before they were half way to Sutton Park. They aimed to sell half a gross the following Sunday.

The Clarion Scouts sold large numbers of the book:

> What a glutton for work is Comrade J. Sayers. To see him set out for Sutton Park on Sunday mornings with six dozen Merrie Englands on his person and return home empty handed is a sight for Scouts and men.

The Scouts had a regular stall in the Bull Ring. 'Last Saturday they sold 50.' The markets committee objected to sales in the Bull Ring, so the

Scouts changed their pitch to the Rag Market.

By August it had been decided to run an enormous Merrie England Fayre. This seems to have overstretched socialist resources in Birmingham for a November report states:

> The Merrie England Fayre is a thing of the past. It accomplished its mission and the Labour church debt is cleared. The clear profit will be about £50. Consequently bright, smiling faces abound. But let no villain propose another Fayre! Part of the £50 will be spent on a meat chopper, so let the rash take warning.

By the end of the year we hear no more of sales of the book. How many thousand of copies were sold in Birmingham? How many people were first introduced to socialism through Merrie England? What, if any, were the long-term effects of this remarkable socialist campaign?. Unfortunately, the answers to these questions are not known.

Clarion continued in 1896 to report the wide (if not deep) spectrum of socialist activities in Birmingham.

In January the indefatigable Frank Matthews had started another Cinderella at Gem Street School. A long report in February noted numerous events including the opening of fine new public buildings for Handsworth I.L.P., socialist lecturers 'cornering business' at the Cobden Hotel, Ben Tillett speaking at the Labour Church, Hyndman at the Town Hall for the SDF, a Ladywood ILP social and Aston ILP moving to larger premises:

> 'Pon my word, I'm out of breath and sure I've missed a few items and shan't get another chance. Still, the fiat hath gone forth and so I make my bow.

In March Kryptos reappeared, this time as reporter for Aston ILP stating that with a view to increasing the circulation and usefulness of the *Clarion* he proposed that the front page of the paper be cut off and posted on suitable walls where it would catch the public eye.

By May, a Clarion Field Club was operating in Birmingham. Field Clubs were another brain child of the paper. These flourished elsewhere, notably in North Staffs, but never really caught on in Birmingham and the Black Country.

The rest of 1896 yields only routine announcements of meetings, except for the Cycling Club. The second annual soirée took place on Wednesday 22nd January at Wretham Road Assembly Rooms with dancing from 8 p.m. to 2 a.m. Tickets 2/-d. or double 3/6d. O Groomie O pronounced the 'swarry' a great success, although 'In point of numbers we were few, but oh! so very select.' A smoking concert the next Saturday with Whiffly Puncto and Clarionette was 'a wonderful success'.

Clarion was now carrying a weekly advertisement for the Clarion Cycle Company of Birmingham 'made by TU labour with an 8-hour day'. Advertisements for Birmingham-made accessories quickly followed such as Searchlight Smokeless Oil for cycle lamps and Special Lubricant. An advanced product was the tubeless tyre advertised for a number of years' which then abruptly disappeared. The longest lived was the Fleuss Tubeless Tire. 'A Child can Detach it, Record Breakers ride it', it was claimed. At the national Cycle Show at Birmingham in December the tyre 'was a great attraction and very successful'.

At the end of February O Groomie O was outlining the activities of the Birmingham CCC in the paper. The subscription for the season was 3/6d. Intending new members must take a preliminary run with the club before being proposed for membership. The opening run was to be an easy sixteen miles to Wishaw. The club had a special greetings card designed for it by 'that clever artist J. Cruwys Richards which was a thing of beauty and a joy for all time.'

Typical of subsequent reports was one of the Smoking Concert at Kinver:

> This was held under difficulties. We had a tough struggle with a tough tea. We played football afterwards. Our regular pianist failed to turn up. He hasn't done this for years. But we drank each others health. The Perishing Bounder with the india-rubber face sang Perhaps, the Merry Widow and other songs until our sides ached. On Sunday morning we climbed Kinver Edge — well worth doing. Then through Bewdley, Ombersly and home. The McSpatkinson and Edgbastonia Edwards hunted up Dowlais Bank and have since been over to Horsehay ... Next Saturday is an inter-Midlands run to Burton. And Wolverhampton, don't leave that Perhaps Not perisher behind.
>
> O'Groomie O

1897 produced several new social developments. In March a Clarion Glee Club was announced. Clarion Vocal Unions had flourished in the north for a number of years, but Birmingham has rarely been a leading musical centre:

> There *is* a Clarion Glee Club in Birmingham. We have pretended to sing at Labour Church socials etc., but our singing is all bass (very). We have good teachers and if we had sopranos and tenors we could *shine*. Will sopranos please note and turn up in hundreds at the Labour Church on Monday nights.

Also in the north and down as far as North Staffs there were successful Clarion Field Clubs, but again, Birmingham was backward. In April, however, a brief notice announced that Aston I.L.P. had formed a Field Club.

Birmingham's strength was in Cinderella work. A request from the *Clarion* in May for Cinderella secretaries to report their activity in the paper brought responses only from Birmingham, Hanley, Hull, Liverpool and Stalybridge. By September, however, there were nineteen Cinderellas including one at Walsall.

In December there was a further progress report on the Glee Club:

> Birmingham choir was started four months ago by the Clarion Cycling Club. It has nine members and rehearses once a week, twice if possible. It gave *the Hunter's Farewell* and *'Tis the Song whose Spirit* (both by Mendelssohn) at the Club dinner. Early in the new year it will be able to assist local Socialist societies giving concerts. They have a rule of collecting 2d. per head for the Cinderella Fund at each rehearsal. They want a few recruits, altos and tenors, with some knowledge either of staff notation or tonic sol fa. Postcards to E. Garbutt 108 New Street.

During 1898 reports of socialist activity in Birmingham continued to be sparse. The usual Cinderella report at the beginning of the year stated that 3,200 poor children had been fed at Christmas. Advertisements appeared for a Birmingham Spiritual Fellowship, which held a special service in April for the Unemployed in connection with the Central Labour Bureau. 1898, incidentally, was reckoned to be a year of good trade.

In May, Frank Mathers of Cinderella was appealing for wild flowers on behalf of the Domestic Mission and People's Hall at Hurst Street. Mathers offered to distribute any weight of flowers sent to invalids, slum children and the poorest Board Schools of Birmingham. In June he gratefully acknowledged flowers from the scholars of an Ipswich Board School, from donors in Banbury, Haverford West, Shields, Kilchutton Bay and several anonymous parcels.

There is very little else in 1898, and nothing of the Cycling Club.

In 1899 the Cinderella report was delayed until February, but was more detailed than usual:

> The Christmas feasts went off splendidly. A capital staff of helpers who worked with true esprit-de-corps did an overworked, underpaid Secretary proud. Friends were very generous with gifts of puddings, fruit, toys etc. We entertained 2,500 children including 300 infants. It is impossible to thank personally the School Board teachers for their careful distribution of tickets. Great schemes are simmering in our busy brains. The principal one is the building of a Convalescent Cottage on freehold land. £300 will be wanted for this.

Also in February in connection with a Clarion circulation drive a correspondent complained:

> Clarionettes in Birmingham bristle as thickly as thorns on a bush. Yet a certain trade unionist went into six newsagents without being able to obtain a copy or see a bill. What is the Brum Contents Bill Brigade doing

The annual Grand Plain and Fancy Dress Ball of the Birmingham Clarion Cycling Club was at the Drill Hall Assembly Rooms on Monday February 27th with dancing from 8 p.m. until 3 a.m. Tickets were only 1/6d each or 2/6d. double.

In April the Birmingham Crippled Children's Union advertised ladies' cycle baskets made by crippled children at 1/9d. They were available from Frank Mathews at the People's Hall, Hurst Street. Mathews also appealed for wild flowers for these crippled children.

The Birmingham May Day event was reported as a joint Socialist platform and the speakers had included P.J. King, George Tooth, John Davies, Ernest Wright etc. The affair was modest, it would seem, without big-name national speakers.

In June a meeting was called at the Trades Hall, Hurst Street to inaugurate a Birmingham and District Socialist Federation.

It had become a tradition for the Clarion Cycling Club to meet each summer in Shrewsbury as the heart of England; 1899 was the first year of the Clarion Van and the event was improved by the Van being in Shrewsbury over the August holiday.

In the autumn, Birmingham CCC started a Book Club and opened with a reading from Silas Marner. In November they announced the annual dinner of the Dejected Perishers at the Metropole Hotel.

At the end of the year, Nunquam raised in the paper the question of starting Clarion Social Clubs. This evoked a large correspondence including a letter from F.E. Baker of Birmingham. He claimed that Birmingham CCC had laid the basis for such a club over a long period. In the summer they had runs, meets, holiday tours and socials. They also have a nice Clubroom with a piano which is available every night. In the winter they have their book club every Saturday night when members read papers on books and discussion followed. Their headquarters was the Crown Hotel, Ludgate Hill. Clarion Fellowships were to flourish in the new century not least of all in Birmingham.

But the nineteenth century died unspectacularly for *Clarion* and its activities in Birmingham.

The Fabians.

There was never a very active organised presence of Fabianism in Birmingham. The national society emerged as a Socialist body in 1884, but it was not until 1890 with the first publication of Fabian Essays that it launched itself into the provinces. This was supported in 1891 by the publication of *Fabian News* which reported at the end of that year that membership had risen from 173 to 361, the majority of whom were organised outside London.

The Birmingham society was formed on 20th October 1890 and, according to Margaret Cole, it was the first provincial society formed. In its first eight months it was recorded, in typical Fabian detail, that it had enrolled 100 members, organised seventeen public lectures with an average attendance of over 200 people, sold 200 copies of Fabian Essays and raised £83. Beatrice Potter had some contact with Birmingham through a romantic attachment with Joseph Chamberlain before she married Sidney Webb.

Subsequent progress of the Society can be traced through *Fabian News*. The first two weekly lectures in February 1893 were on *Christian Socialism* by the Rev. Stewart Headlam and on *Home Colonisation* by the Rev. H.V. Mills. In November the Society announced its winter programme. Circulars had been issued to the various literary and debating societies in the city offering to lecture or debate on Socialism. The secretary was anxious to obtain as complete a list as possible of those societies and members were urged to let him know of any society likely to respond to such an invitation. There was also to be a class for the systematic study of Socialism every Tuesday evening at the Cobden Hotel (Room 5). This was intended to replace the previous method of public lectures and the Committee earnestly desired that members should endeavour to make it a success.

In 1894 the Society was participating in the local election, a joint committee having been formed consisting of three delegates each from the Fabian Society, the S.D.F., the I.L.P., and the Labour church, for common action in this matter. The fourth annual general meeting took place in September at the Cobden Hotel. By this time membership was falling, it being down to sixty-four compared with eighty for the previous year. Eighteen lectures on Socialism had been delivered. Expenses were £30 and there was a good balance.

By March 1895 the Society seems to have reverted to the weekly lecture. John Lawson was speaking on *Temperance*, Miss A.L. Goyne on the *Ethics of State Interference*, the Rev Todd on *Old Age Pensions* and A.K. Constantine on *Socialism and Evolution*.

The Birmingham Fabian branch disappeared sometime in 1895, but instead of being absorbed into the I.L.P., as happened to many Fabian branches at this time, it merged with the Birmingham Labour Church. This is perhaps not surprising, since the Secretary of both the Labour Church and the Fabian Society at that time was Tom Groom.

The Socialist League

The Socialist League was established nationally in December 1884 as a breakaway group from the S.D.F. because of the alleged intolerance and sectarianism of Hyndman. Its leadership included William Morris, Belfort Bax, Eleanor Marx, and the personality-flawed socialist she lived with, Dr. Edward Aveling.

The Socialist League appeared in Birmingham in 1886 about the same time that the Social Democratic Federation was establishing itself in the city; and the cause was the same. Both organisations were attracted to the west Midlands by the epic eighteen-month strike of the Black Country chainmakers and the shocking revelations of starvation wages and sweating which aroused national concern.

In February 1886, John Sketchley of 348 Cheapside (The Chartist veteran) advertised himself as the Birmingham agent for the League's newspaper *Commonweal*. By May 1886 a Birmingham branch was established, meeting at Bell Street Coffee House every Monday at 7.30 p.m. William Morris had visited the branch in May speaking on the *Aims of Art* in the afternoon and on *Socialism* in the evening. From August the branch met at Carrs Lane Coffee House at 8 p.m. every Monday.

At the end of August 1886 A.K. Donald, a national lecturer, held a large meeting outside the Council House, while Sanders and Weaver, both Walsall activists held a good meeting at the Bull Ring. This report was signed 'J.B.'.

In May 1887, Donald was again in the area on an extended tour. In August he was still addressing meetings and at Spring Hill the police 'again intervened'. In September Sanders also held meetings in Birmingham. In October 1887 Donald made a report on Socialism in the midlands in which he claimed that there were Socialist League branches in Birmingham and Walsall, both of which had carried out a 'vigorous propaganda' in the three months of his tour.

Advertisements for the activity of the Birmingham branch continued to appear in *Commonweal* until March 1888, although John Sketchley claimed that the branch had been dissolved as early as November 1886 'through indifference within and bitter opposition without'. With its small numbers and its early tendencies towards anarchism, the Socialist League took root in the west midlands only in Walsall and the Walsall Bomb Plot of 1892 was central to the national demise of the organisation.

The Birmingham Labour Church

Making a unique contribution and acting as a co-ordinating body to the multifarious political and social organisations making up Socialism in Birmingham, was the Labour church founded in 1893.

Birmingham has a long tradition of Christian participation in the labour movement dating back at least to the Christian Chartism of Arthur O'Neil and the Chartist Churches. The Labour Church accommodated both practising Christians and non-Christians in the 'religion of Socialism'. The Labour church was an ideal vehicle for the development of the various Clarion social activites. The Church acted as a co-ordinating body for the activities of all other existing Socialist bodies in the city. Its outlook was entirely unsectarian and it co-operated equally well with the S.D.F. as with the I.L.P. and the Fabians. Only very occasionally did the differences between the orthodox Christians and the non-Christians obtrude.

A very full history of the Birmingham Labour church should be possible as its minutes have survived. Unfortunately, at the time of writing the early minute books at the Birmingham Central Library have disappeared or been misplaced and the minutes are available only from 1903. The problem is minimised however, by the fact that from 1892 until 1897 the Labour churches had their own monthly journal, the *Labour Prophet*, containing fairly full reports on the activities of the Birmingham Labour Church. From the beginning, the Labour Church movement nationally was dominated by the strongly nonconformist north of England. But the development of the movement was disappointing. At the Fourth Labour Church National Conference which was held in Birmingham in December 1895 there were only 24 delegates representing 19 Labour churches. At the Sixth Annual Conference two years later only seven Churches, all in Lancashire and Yorkshire, sent delegates, although there were said to be twenty-seven churches in existence. By then the movement was incapable of supporting its monthly journal. It is against this background that the longevity and vigour of the Birmingham Church should be judged.

In the absence of the minute books it is impossible to discuss the initiatives which gave rise to the Church, but it was inaugurated on New Year's Day 1893. The original premises were probably at Frederick Street, but in October 1894 a former Wesleyan chapel capable of holding 500 people was acquired in Bond Street. The Church operated from here until the middle of 1897 when problems with the lease forced it to leave and operate from Oozell Street Board Schools. It remained here for about a year and in June 1898 it moved to Bristol Street Board Schools which it continued to occupy for most of its remaining life.

The opening was deemed a great success and the address was given by Fred Brocklehurst, a national speaker, who explained the Five Principles of the Movement. These were:

1.   The Labour Movement is a Religious movement.
2.   The Religion of the Labour Movement is not a class religion, but unites all members of all classes in working for the abolition of Commercial Slavery.
3.   The Religion of the Labour Movement is not Sectarian or Dogmatic but a Free Religion allowing every man to develop his own relation with the Power that brought him into being.
4.   The Emancipation of Labour will only be realised inso far as men learn to obey the Economic and Moral laws of God.

5.   The development of Personal Character and the improvement
     of Social Conditions are both essential to man's emancipation
     from Moral and Social Bondage.

Progress was slow and in May the secretary pro-tem, A.G. Humphries, reported that the Labour Church 'had not yet caught on in Birmingham among the workers. Audiences were small.' In February 1894 attendances were again deemed 'still not good', although the average attendance at the Sunday meetings was 120. Membership, which was 45 when the Church was formed, had grown to 130 by the end of the year.

During the early days at Bond Street the main activity was the Sunday evening service. There was also a meeting in the afternoon when a short paper was read followed by discussion. These were encouraging, it was said, although attendances at 30 to 40 were small. Tea was provided as such people came from a distance and stayed for the evening service. No weekly night class was held as all the active Church members were attending the Fabian class for the study of Socialism. The 'few of our friends who form the choir' usually met on Fridays after the Committee meeting, for practice. A few members were also about to start a class for instruction in reading and speaking. It became the practice for the Church to have a national speaker on one Sunday of each month for a 'public meeting'. In March 1893, for instance, Fred Brocklehurst who was in the district for four days 'addressed us on *Socialism and Character* in grand style.' Before the meeting they had a social, tea and chat. A string band played two selections of music, and a choir 'which was a strong one, sang Labour songs splendidly.' Other national speakers during 1894 included Halliday Sparling, Margaret McMillan and Leonard Hall. Most national speakers addressed the Sunday service at some time or other including the popular Enid Stacy and George Lansbury. On the other Sundays of the month speakers from Birmingham and the surrounding areas such as Tom Groom, Arthur Fallows and George Whittaker filled the bill adequately. Sometimes experts on matters of national or local interest spoke on such subjects as *Our National Food Supply, Lead Poisoning in the Potteries*, or *Landlordism in the Limelight*. Sometimes the subject veered towards the religious such as *Paul the Enthusiast* or *Religion and Socialism*. Cultural matters such as Socialism and Art were also dealt with.

An early priority was a Labour church Hymnbook specially commissioned by the Birmingham Church, a copy of which has survived at the Birmingham Central Library. None of the fifty 'hymns' appears to be Christian. Longfellow has four 'hymns', James Russell Lowell has three. Enid Nesbit has two. William Morris is represented with 'What is this, the Sound and Rumour', 'Saith Man to Man' and 'Each Eve Earth falleth down the Dark'. Shelley has 'The World's Great Work Begins Anew' and 'Men of England wherefor Plough?' Others represented are Ebenezer Elliot, Havelock Ellis, Charles Kingsley, Harriet Martineau, R.W. Emerson and Oliver Wendell Holmes. Judging solely from the hymnbook it would appear that the 'religion of Socialism' in Birmingham was entirely secular, although Christian members and visiting speakers would introduce their own faiths. The hymnbook was ready for distribution by the autumn of 1894 and at the November Town Hall meetings 1,000 copies were sold.

Besides the monthly national speaker at the Church, a tradition was established of beginning the winter programme with a Town Hall meeting. These meetings were usually extremely successful. At the best of times, however, they usually ended with a financial deficit, but this was deemed well worth while as a platform for socialist ideas in the city. In October 1893 'the great town hall was crammed for the reopening of the Labour Church by Keir Hardie.' In October 1894 Keir Hardie again packed the town hall and the *Clarion* reporter complained that the police had refused to allow another 600 into the hall, although at a recent Joseph Chamberlain meeting the police had allowed another 1,000 people to cram the gangways. The next October the town hall was 'not quite so crowded' for Tom Mann.

Cinderella activity found a natural focus in the Labour church and it is from reports in the *Labour Prophet* that we have the fullest reports of these activities. In September 1896 the following report appeared concerning activity:

> The Cinderella Club in Birmingham. There are excursions every Saturday afternoon from Bond Street to Sutton Park. Six helpers and fifty children usually get there from 3.30 to 4 p.m. It takes a long time because the children travel in furniture vans. On arrival the girls loll about or play with skipping ropes or balls. The boys, no matter how hot the weather, play football almost to a man. Sutton is eight miles away from Birmingham. It is not a conventional park but a great tract of moorland with pools and woods abounding with wild flowers and everything calculated to delight the hearts of town dwellers. About five or half-past tea consists of three *big* slices of cake and lots of tea. Then comes the great event of the afternoon — a long ramble through the woods, past the pools, sometimes stopping by little streams to paddle, then back to the camping place but *not* ready to go home. 'We don't want to go', they say. 'We want to stay all night.' But alas, we can't. So about half past seven we start home, the children singing choruses and cheering nearly all the way. This is a very bare description, but you must imagine for yourself the shouts of joy and delight at the various sights of the country. But better than imagining, collect 3-/-d. (for that is what it costs) and take a party of slum bairns to the country.
>
> Our Cottage Home at Kingswood started last April and was kept going until the end of July. It is a picturesque 4-roomed cottage covered with honeysuckle almost from top to bottom and a pretty little garden in front. We are able to send 33 of the poorest little invalids we could find in the Birmingham schools for a fortnight each, four at a time. To emphasise the need we should mention that in selecting the children we found cases where these became imbeciles temporarily from want of fresh air and good food. The cottage was lent to us by Arthur Holden free of rent, firing and lighting. The children are clothed throughout by the Police-aided Clothing Association. Our caretaker lent us part of his furniture and other friends gave blankets and all sorts of things. The total cost is less than 25/-d. a week inclusive of the caretaker's wages. We are proud to be the first Cinderella in the country to start this work.
>
> Winter entertainment is from the first Thursday in October to the last Thursday in March. It is the same on Saturdays except that there are two parties — one for infants from 3 to 6 years. On Thursdays we entertain 100 children who come at 7.30. I ought to say are let in at 7.30 for they come at 5 o'clock and some before. We begin with a good feed of cocoa and cake. Then comes the entertainment. If it is a magic lantern show, we frequently put the slides in and let the children sing anything they think appropriate. Some are most apt. Sometimes there is a conjurer or nigger minstrels. Or a comic concert with fairy tales in

between songs. Or failing organised entertainment the children have 'one on their own', singing comic choruses, giving recitations, step dances etc. These are often more enjoyable than the most elaborate entertainment we can get. We finish about 9 p.m. and the youngsters then have another hunk of cake and an orange and bustle off home thoroughly happy for once. On Saturdays the entertainment lasts from 3 to 5 and 7 to 9 respectively,

Frank Matthews, Market St. Lichfield.

In December 1897 the *Labour Prophet* again gave pride of place to a long Birmingham Cinderella report stating that it was the largest Club in the country. Frank Matthews gave some comparative figures:

	Winter	*Summer*
1893/4	Fed and amused about 1000 children.	Took 100 children to the country
1894/5	Fed and amused about 2000 children.	Took 400 children to the country
1895/6	Fed and amused about 5200 children.	Took 400 children to the country
1896/7	Fed and amused about 7000 children	

In his report for 1897 Frank Matthews reported an innovation:

Finding that, as a rule, the children came to the entertainments in a condition the reverse of clean, we instituted prizes for cleanliness, a doll for the girls and a ball for the boys. This has effected an improvement, although not such a great one as we hoped for, but it has given *great* pleasure to all the children, especially the prize winners.

Matthews, in the same report, stresses the need for this work. After stating that at Christmas they had entertained at the Labour church in three evenings 1,750 children, he goes on to say:

The extent to which the bairns appreciate these entertainments will be understood when we state that although admission is only by ticket, over 1,000 children came on the chance of getting in, and *ten days after*, when we resumed our ordinary weekly entertainments, in addition to the 100 children who had tickets, there were between 200 and 300 waiting and hoping for admission. Alas! this will always be so until our subscribers assist us to give 20,000 meals a season.

Other social activities which involved the Labour church such as the development of the Clarion Scouts, the Glee Club, co-operation in selling Merrie England and the Merrie England Fayre which paid off the Church debt have already been dealt with. The Church's part in trying to develop One Socialist Party in Birmingham and united action to stand labour candidates in elections will be dealt with later.

The administration of the Church was simple and democratic. The annual general meeting elected an executive committee which arranged lectures, hired halls and carried out the administration of the Church. In addition there was a monthly meeting of all members which appointed sub-Committees to consider special matters, decided on policy questions and heard progress reports from the secretary.

The Birmingham Socialist Centre.

The Birmingham Socialist Centre began in 1897 and ended in 1915 when its secretary volunteered for the army. Most of its history, therefore, lies outside the period dealt with here. Moreover, annual reports giving full details of its activities each year are only available from 1901. Something must be said here, however, of its origins and early activities.

The Labour church evidently did not fully fulfil a role of co-ordinating Socialist activity in the city. In the latter half of the 1890s co-ordination became even more essential due to a number of factors. One was the growth of the Independent Labour Party carrying out activities similar to those of the S.D.F. Another large and complex area was the endorsement of a single 'labour' candidate for elections to parliament and local bodies. A third factor was the co-ordination of the increasing number of political campaigns around such local issues as school meals for children, relief works for the unemployed, the provision of municipal housing, etc. In addition there was the widespread desire for One Socialist Party instead of the existing competing factions.

The Socialist Centre came into existence at the end of July or the beginning of August 1897. One advantage of the Centre was that it had a permanent office in the city centre at 76 Corporation Street, although its secretary, Joseph T. Gumersall, was not employed full time. J.A. Fallows soon became secretary, a post he held until 1902. The chairman was changed annually and those who held the post in the early years were S.G. Hobson, Tom Bond and Joseph Gumersall. Others, who were either on the executive committee, or played an important part in setting up the Centre were the Rev. Arnold Pinchard, P. Galloway, Frank Matthews, Tom Groom and Max Sturge. The Centre therefore relied heavily on the middle class elements associated with the Fabians, Labour church and I.L.P. rather than the proletarian core of the S.D.F. and trade unions.

In 1899 a small, eight-page monthly journal called the *Pioneer* was started which lasted until 1902. The editor of the journal was J.A. Fallows, M.A. who was also secretary of the Socialist Centre. The aim of the journal was to unite all midland socialists and, apart from reporting the activities of the various socialist bodies, it issued comprehensive directories of organisations and their secretaries in Birmingham and the Black Country.

The Independent Labour Party
The tangled web of organisations and parties set up to promote candidates to parliament and local bodies who were independent of the Liberals and Tories, who genuinely represented the interests of labour and who were themselves working men, will be traced in the next chapter on the trades council and labour representation. However, the formation of the Independent Labour Party was an important step in that direction and from 1895 until after 1918 when the Labour Party opened its ranks to individual members, the I.L.P. was the largest labour political organisation in Birmingham. It was from the beginning a proletarian, socialist organisation, but it also continued the ethical socialists and middle class liberals associated with the centre and right-wing of the present Labour Party.

From 1890 with the development of the New Unionism and the U.S. McKinley tariff which created so much unemployment both in the northern textile towns and the metal-using industries of Birmingham and the Black Country, a rash of new working class newspapers appeared. One of these was the *Labour Leader* started in October 1891 and folding two months later, which was subsequently to reappear in March 1894 as the organ of the Independent Labour Party. In those first two months however, a David Miller of Aston announced that an Aston Labour League had been set up. Meanwhile, a more robust paper, the *Workman's Times* edited by Joseph Burgess appeared. This followed the setting up in 1890 of the Bradford Labour Union which subsequently became the Bradford Independent Labour Party. Inspired by the Bradford example, Burgess doggedly persevered with a campaign in his newspaper requesting all readers who wanted to set up an Independent Labour Party to send their names to him. By June 1892 Burgess could announce that Independent Labour Party branches were functioning in at least seven towns and these included Birmingham and Stafford.

The historic, inaugural conference founding the Independent Labour Party subsequently took place in Bradford in January 1893. Among the 125 delegates representing trades councils, SDFs, Fabians and other organisations was David Miller of Birmingham and J.W. Buttery of Stafford. Buttery was subsequently to play a leading part in Birmingham politics.

A year later, the Birmingham I.L.P. branch was reported as contemplating setting up a Co-operative Trading Association on the lines of the Manchester Assocation. The I.L.P. trading shop at 82 Dale End mentioned earlier was presumably the result of this.

In June 1894 the ILP was giving advice to the local SDF regarding meetings:

> An idea! Why don't the local SDF use their talents in the direction of back street lecturing on Sundays instead of sticking to the dismal and often forlorn statue of Nelson in the Bull Ring (Oh, shades of Tom M..n). The enthusiasm their meetings arouse is small like the crowd which seem to remain about the same number and character as of years past. Birmingham people as a rule are a cold blooded lot.

The first conference of midland I.L.Ps took place in October 1894. Eleven towns were represented including Birmingham, Hanley, Stafford and Wolverhampton in the west midlands. An executive committee was appointed. No Birmingham delegate attended the 1894 national I.L.P. conference and the only west midlands delegate was J.W. Buttery, still of Stafford.

In March 1895 a progress report in the *Labour Leader* claimed that socialism was making great progress in the 'proprietory' city of Birmingham. A propagandist committee had been set up with the brief of establishing I.L.P. branches in all parliamentary divisions of the city. Two new branches had already been formed at Bordesley and West Birmingham. It had also been decided to form branches in East Birmingham. A *Clarion* report the same month was more detailed. I.L.P. branches had been opened at Bordesley and Ladywood. Negotiations were proceeding to open branches at Nechells, Aston and Handsworth. This recruitment had arisen from the activities of national speakers Leonard Hall and Enid Stacy. Fred Brocklehurst was also in Birmingham at the People's Hall, Hurst Street on Monday 25th March answering

Joseph Chamberlain's 'alleged Social Scheme'. J. Whiteley of 8 Arthur Place, Summer Hill was the secretary of the Birmingham I.L.P. branch and also secretary of the proposed Democratic Club.

In May, Tom Mann, the national secretary of the I.L.P., toured the midlands and was the main speaker at the highly successful Gosta Green May Day meeting at which 'sales of literature were immense, including 500 copies of Merrie England,'

At the 1895 national I.L.P. conference there were 85 delegates including J.W. Buttery now representing Birmingham Central and William J. Buckler of the Midlands I.L.P. Federation.

1896 opened with a report in the *Labour Leader* concerning the suicide of a former comrade:

> Birmingham regret to announce the suicide, or rather the hounding to death of Comrade Herman Severing. Exiled from Germany and persecuted in England because of his lack of understanding of English, Socialists of Birmingham decided to keep his body from Bumble. About fifty comrades followed him to his grave. There were several wreaths including one from Smethwick socialists.

Aston I.L.P. dominated Clarion reports in the early part of the year. The branch had been meeting every Thursday at Burlington Hall, High Street, but after February 6th they would be meeting on the same night at St. Stephen's Schools, New Town Row. The opening lecture was to be by the Rev. Arnold Pinchard. In March, Drypta was writing of Aston I.L.Ps intention to increase the circulation of *Clarion* by fly-posting the front page on walls in the area.

At the annual conference Bordesley was represented by Edward J. Sale and Birmingham Central by A.J. Remdale. Each branch was registered as having 25 members. Sale reported back to his branch which was then meeting at the Dolphin Inn, Coventry Road.

The activities of Bordesley branch were regularly advertised in the *Clarion* at this time. Thus we know that in August the branch organised a picnic to Hampton-in-Arden. Rail fare plus a big tea cost 2/9d. In November, Birmingham I.L.P. was claiming that among its members was the only Socialist parson of Birmingham, Arnold Pinchard, who was vicar of St. Jude's.

From 1897 as well as reports in *Labour Leader* and *Clarion*, an organisational paper, *I.L.P. News*, was started. This gave publicity to activities, considerable information on finance and membership and also collated election material in a very useful way.

In January 1897 a South Birmingham I.L.P. branch was formed which met at the Crown, St. Paul's Road, every Thursday. The secretary was David Miller. In April, Aston I.L.P. formed its celebrated Field Club and in July the I.L.P. was trying to form a band. By October, Aston I.L.P. had moved again and was meeting on Mondays at Gower Street Board Schools. But despite this activity, only Bordesley with 32 members was represented at the annual Easter Conference, Edward J. Sale again being the delegate.

There are virtually no reports of I.L.P. activity in 1898. The one highlight was that the national Easter conference was in Birmingham. It was held at the Priory Rooms, Upper Priory on April 11th and 12th.

There was a reception for delegates at the Metropole Hotel on Saturday evening. The next day there was the usual mass demonstration at the Town Hall, the main speaker being Keir Hardie. In the evening there was a Grand Soirée at the Assembly Rooms, Hurst Street, with dancing from 8 until 2 a.m.

The main item at the Conference was the attempt to form a single Socialist party by joining with the S.D.F. But after three previous years of discussion, the only contribution of this Conference was to set up a Committee to define the implications of either 'federation' or 'fusion' between the two organisations. The two Birmingham delegates, neither of whom spoke in this debate, were both new to Conference. They were Samuel H. Morgan representing 41 members from Bordesley and Frank Spires representing 27 members in West Birmingham.

The century closed with the I.L.P. still in the doldrums. In January, *I.L.P. News* reported membership at Bordesley as 89 and Birmingham West was 40. A full report from Birmingham West the same month reported a soirée attracting 200 people and making a profit of £3 which had been the first of its kind. Forty-five ordinary branch meetings had been held the previous year, there had been a debate on Trades Federations between comrades Fey and Spires; ten meetings of impromptu answers to written questions had been held for speaking practice; three social events had been held and it was regretted that Frank Spires had been forced to resign as secretary.

In the autumn, attempts were made to improve the position. A Birmingham and District I.L.P. Federation was formed and in November, *I.L.P. News* printed a full report of the state of the branches:

Birmingham I.L.P. movement has been reorganised and shows signs of renewed activity. The West Birmingham branch has continued to make progress. It has 50 members and during the year it raised £86-7-0d. most of which was spent on indoor meetings. A series of socials last winter made the branch better known. The formation of a Cinderella Committee has brought several women members into the branch.

As a result of organising expensive indoor lectures last winter, the Bordesley branch is in debt.

Attention has lately been paid to the voters lists as this branch will probably be the first to run candidates for one of the local public bodies. Two members are on the Birmingham Co-operative Committee and have done good work.

Aston branch after a period of dormancy has been reorganised and is making its views known in the local press.

On October 1st a new Central branch was started. It already has several members. Four branches are now federated. Comrade Shallard will be a lecturer under the auspices of the federation and in conjunction with the Socialist Centre during January and other central meetings are contemplated.

Efforts will be made to resuscitate several branches which formerly existed in the district, the eventual aim being a branch in each of the eight constituencies.

A strong central committee has been formed. The chairman is Robert McDonald, the treasurer Alf Hunt and the secretary Frank Spires.

Chapter Sixteen

THE RE-EMERGENCE OF SOCIALISM:
THE TRADE UNIONS
1884–1900

The Assault on Liberalism

We have seen that the period of retreat which began with the Great Depression from 1874 ended ten years later with the re-emergence of Socialism in 1884. The later 1880s saw the vast upsurge in trade union activity organising many unskilled and semi-skilled workers in the New Unionism of 1888–92. Class collaboration between unions and employers did not end; indeed the hey-dey of the Birmingham Alliances was still to come. But within the Birmingham Trades Council, as in other parts of the country, a fundamental struggle for leadership developed between the militant, socialist outlook of the new unions together with changing trends in the older unions, and the domination of the Liberal hegemony, and the Lib-Labism that followed. This struggle reached a climax in 1900 with the setting-up of the Labour Representation Committee which, by 1906 had become the Labour Party.

The turn of the century also marks a period in which the worst effects of the Great Depression had ended temporarily: imperialism as a basic ruling class strategy to ward off foreign competition was developed and the jingoism of the Boer War which, briefly, threatened to destroy the whole labour movement both industrial and political brought the century to a close.

The unique feature in Birmingham was the apostasy of Joseph Chamberlain in 1886 on the Irish question which created Liberal-Unionism and enormously strengthened the existing national trend of the change of allegiance of capitalist interests from the Liberal Party to the Conservatives.

Such developments increased the urgency of developing Independent labour representation. In discussing this, attention is usually focussed on parliamentary representation, and this was supported by the popular saying 'we want not only representation where laws are administered but above all, where laws are made.' True as this is, there is a case for arguing that working class representation on local bodies had a more immediate impact on the lives of working people. These local bodies, to be discussed below, were the ad hoc authorities of the Poor Law and Education Boards as well as city and other local councils. Also included is the struggle to obtain justice for working people through the appointment of working class magistrates.

Representation on town councils and poor law boards depended on the extension of the franchise and the abolition of property qualifications for candidates. The former was achieved partially in 1867 and more substantially in 1884. High property qualifications tended to linger longer in local than in parliamentary affairs, since working class representation in Parliament was made almost impossible until the payment of MPs which came only in 1911. From the beginning, there was no property qualification for the householder franchise of School Boards and a special clause allowed women to be elected. Property qualification for Poor Law Boards was always high. Agitation to reduce it was strong in the 1890s, but only in 1894 was it eventually abolished. Women's disabilities were particularly great. Wolverhampton's first woman Guardian was elected in 1876 on her own property qualification. Two years later she married and lost her property qualification; legally she became a chattel of her husband and was forced to resign.

With regard to the political stance of the Trades Council, this was first clarified in the year of its foundation, 1866, when in reply to a Conservative demand for no politics in the trade unions, the trades council circularised all societies in the town:

> We shall be found following and supporting those advanced and independent Liberals who believe that the broader the basis of our institutions the firmer they will stand.

The first steps towards labour representation in Parliament was taken in 1873 when a large committee was appointed and William Gilliver, the secretary of the trades council, was adopted as a candidate. A £1000 fund was to be raised of which £500 would be spent on the election and £500 to pay him, if elected. The fund was to be raised and invested in the names of five trustees, three of whom were to be members of the trades council and two 'gentlemen of position from outside.' For these two latter posts the nominations were Councillor Joseph Chamberlain, Alderman Thomas Avery, Dr.J.A.Langford, Councillors Jesse Collings, William White and Alderman G.B. Lloyd, in that order of preference. All of these were, of course, prominent members of the Birmingham liberal establishment. In February 1874 Gilliver reported that his nomination had been withdrawn because the shortness of notice of the election had deprived the Committee of the possibility of raising the necessary funds. In truth, however, the difficulties were more fundamental. A one thousand pound fund was very ambitious for the trades council and a working class candidate could only be successful if the Liberals approved of him, and either adopted him as their candidate or refrained from standing against him. Neither of these was likely in Birmingham in the early 1870s.

One of the first problems was to define what a working class man was. The trades council definition was eminently sensible:

> One who earns his living from his own hand labour without receiving benefit from the labour of others.

Such progress as was made in the late 1870s and early 1880s in working class representation was made by men who were Liberals and who were beholdened to the Liberal Party for their election. The first was W.J.Davis who was incorporated into the Caucus 'slate' for the 1876 Birmingham School Board election. In 1880, Davis became the first Labour representative on the town council, but with the support of the Liberal Federation. The Liberal ascendency was ending and the age of Lib-Labism began in Birmingham. Davis was joined by Allan Granger, the trades council president, in 1882 and Eli Bloor, the glass workers' leader, in 1883. All of these men were Liberals supported by the Caucus, but all rendered conspicuous service to the working class movement and Davis was, of course, a national figure.

1886 was a key year. It saw the end of a rule which had prevented the Amalgamated Society of Engineers from affiliating to the trades council. The ASE affiliated two branches. The delegate from No.1. was A.R.Jephcott, a notable Liberal, and from No.2. Branch Joseph Tanner the Marxist of the Social Democratic Federation. 1886 was also the year when Joseph Chamberlain split the Liberal party and with it the Liberal town councillors in Birmingham. Finally 1886 was the year of Tom Mann's visit to Birmingham which led to the consolidation of the SDF. From this time the initiative in standing working class candidates passed to the Marxists. As we have seen (section on the Social Democratic Federation) although they did not win any seats, some of their votes were remarkable for men who stood openly as revolutionary Socialists. These results, in a period of growing militancy, stimulated both Lib-Labs and socialists to further efforts for independent working class representation. In 1889 John Valentine Stevens, the tin plate workers' secretary, was elected to the city council as a Lib-Lab and Eli Bloor, although not a nominee of the trades council, had been re-elected. After the election, the trades council considered its position. A.R.Jephcott proposed a motion congratulating the two members of the trades council elected and hoped 'that these victories would lead to further efforts in the same direction.' He said that up to then the trades council's electoral efforts had been 'pooh-hooed' but they had now shown their strength and did not intend to stand still now they had made a start. F.Favell (glass workers) seconded the motion and thought that if they had had a larger number of labour candidates their success would have been even greater. He regretted that the trades council had not given Joe Tanner some support ('Hear, hear' and 'No') and reminded them of a previous resolution to support all labour representatives. Gilliver (Lib-Lab) supporting the motion said that they deserved better representation on the city council and if a political party assisted them to get it so much the better for that party. So long as they got labour representation he did not care who were the people who helped them get it ('Hear, hear'.) The resolution was passed.

In May 1890 the trades council returned to the subject of labour representation with a motion that three candidates for the Labour interest should contest the November city council elections. Gilliver moved a second motion that a sub-committee of five be appointed to 'select the names of such as may be able and willing to undertake labour representation on either national or local assemblies.' W.F.Hill (Silversmiths) moving the first motion said that Gilliver's was not antagonistic to his. Personally he was sick of politics, for all political parties seemed to ignore the question of labour. He thought it was not the political element but the labour element only that had secured the victory of Stevens. This resolution was agreed to. Gilliver's resolution introduced the question of the next general election. He said that the Liberal Committee at Bordesley had challenged the trades council to produce a parliamentary labour candidate in whom they had confidence. Working men wanted direct representation, Gilliver continued, and if they could get it through any political party, they were entitled to do so. He regarded it of much more importance that they got representation in Parliament where laws were made than in assemblies where law was administered. There were several political parties anxious to secure the support of working men and he would take the assistance of either the Liberal or the Conservative parties to get representation in Parliament, he concluded. Here was the classic case not only for Lib-Labism but for Tory-Labism as well at a time when Tory radicalism under Randolph Churchill was savaging the traditional Liberal hegemony in Birmingham weakened by the Chamberlain split. It also suggests that there might be different arguments for local and national elections. Working men might win independent local representation, but could they win Parliamentary elections without the support of one or other of the two main parties? Clarke ASE said he could not see why the matter was brought forward again. If politics were to enter the trades council then all harmony would leave ('hear, hear' and a voice 'Nonsense') Joe Tanner said that Gilliver stated that any candidate in Bordesley must be a Liberal. In matters of political parties he thought it was only a question of dealing with the alligator on the one hand and the crocodile on the other. Tanner's was the straight case for labour representation independent of the two main political parties. Councillor Stevens put a third position. He thought they were trade unionists first and politicans afterwards ('Hear, hear') it would be a long time before the trades council could nominate candidates by themselves, and in the meantime they should welcome the support of any political party.

When the general election did occur, in 1892, Davis and Bloor both stood, but were unsuccessful. They were both given a clear field by the Liberals. W.J.Davis called himself 'the friend of the Oppressed and champion of Labour'. he polled 2,658 votes to Jesse Collings 6,380. Eli Bloor was 'the Liberal and labour candidate'. He polled 2.089 votes to W.Kenrick's 4,814. A Labour Representation Workingmen's Committee was set up to organise the campaign.

These contests, however, caused further heart searchings in the trades council. In July 1892, T.J.Henson (Cabinet maker) moved a resolution 'That in future the name of the Birmingham Trades Council be not used by its officers and members for political purposes except by special resolution of the Council'. Henson said that the name of the trades council had played a prominent part on every political platform where there had been a contest and this was becoming intolerable. Not only had support been given to members of the capitalist class, but to workmen who had no connection whatever with the council. Neither W.J.Davis nor Councillor Bloor would recognise the trades council as being the labour parliament of Birmingham. The members and officers were working for their own pecuniary interests ('Shame'.) Within the last two months prominent members of the trades council had signed articles to speak for certain gentlemen. Such articles suggested that there must be payment (Cries of 'Name'.) One member who went on his own account stated that he came representing the trades council ('Name') and it was only through the press that they learned of such things. The name of the trades council should not be used unless the members had been asked for consent. Gilliver, the veteran honorary member of the trades council, reminded the members that this was not the first time this issue had been raised. He would be sorry to see officers tied down by a resolution preventing them from saying that they were officers. What they needed was a resolution stating that the council was not responsible for what its officers said outside the trades council. ('Hear, hear'). A.R.Jephcott (Liberal-Unionist) thought that trade unionists should support anyone prepared to defend labour against capital. He had stood on Mr Bloor's platform. Bloor might not be a delegate to the trades council, but his society was affiliated to it and no one was more representative of his society than Bloor. The resolution was directed against Mr. Davis (Cries of 'No' and 'Yes'). Although Mr. Davis' society was not represented on the trades council, he would be recreant to his principles as a trade unionist if he refused to go on his platform, because Davis had done as much for trade unionism as any man in the town. There was no disguising the fact that the trades council was not the power in the town that it should be and this could only be remedied by taking part in every contest in Birmingham by ascertaining the opinions of all who stood and then deciding whether to support or not to support them.

S.G.Middleton (Schoolworkers' Union) thought the motion was an attempt to curtail the liberty of the individual. Every member of the trades council had the liberty to say so and this would suffer if the public saw that they were so narrow as to curtail its members' liberties.

Councillor Granger (Gladstonian Liberal) opened a great onslaught on the Liberal-Unionists. He said there was no doubt that some of the officers had given the trades council a blow from which it would not soon recover. Labour representation was now more discredited than it had been for twenty years. Mr. Jephcott was perhaps the greatest sinner in this respect. There had recently been appointed a number of new magistrates and none of them was of their number. He believed this was partly because he (Jephcott) had been present at a meeting where the Stipendiary, falsely, Granger thought, had been libelled as partial in his judgements and Jephcott had not protested at that libel. The president of the trades council, C.C.Cooke, and other officials were placarded around the town to show that the trades council was supporting the party politics of certain individuals. The resolution was not directed against Davis, but such men as Jephcott. Strange to say, Granger continued, there were officials of the trades council who had given the warmest support to men who had attempted, not once, but twice and thrice to crush it, because they could not control it ('Hear, hear' and 'No'). He appealed to Mr. Gilliver to say if attempts had not been made to crush the trades council out of existence because it could not be handled for party purposes. These attempts had been made to make them mere disciples of what had once been the Great Caucus, but was now the small Caucus. No party could expect the blessing of God or man that was controlled by such a person as Mr.Schnadhorst ('Laughter' and 'Shame') who was the man who wanted to control the trades council ('Bosh'). Granger protested at being dragged at the heel of any party whether Conservative or Liberal.

F.Favell (Plate Glass Bevellers) said he was sorry that Mr. Henson had been made a tool of a small clique inside the trades council ('Hear, hear'). Henson had made two astounding charges and the trades council should demand from him the names of the men he had accused of signing an agreement for pecuniary considerations. At this point, the discussion was adjourned for a fortnight.

When the trades council reconvened, standing orders were unanimously suspended first to discuss the labour laws of the time. E.Fookes (Tin Plate Worker) said that two respectable trade unionists picketing one of the few and insignificant firms in the iron and tin-plate trade maintaining a 10% reduction in wages, had been fined £5 and costs for calling the non-unionists 'black-legs.' It was a gross and unjust sentence showing that it was impossible in Birmingham to get justice for trade unionists. The same deputy stipendiary, on the same day, had fined a prize-fighter only 10/-d. for physically assaulting a tramway worker. Jephcott moved the appointment of a deputation to the mayor with a view to reopening the case complained of. Tanner said it would be a waste of time because the mayor had no authority to reopen the case. They should determine on an appeal to the court of Queen's Bench and begin to collect money for it. The resolution was carried, however, amid applause and a deputation was appointed of the secretaries of the two societies involved, the chairman of the trades council and Jephcott. After this, several members wanted to move resolutions reflecting on the general partiality of the stipendiary and deputy-stipendiary, but the chairman (C.C.Cooke) 'strongly discountenanced such evidence as biased and prejudiced.' The meeting then turned to further discussion on Henson's motion.

G.Copham, a typographical society delegate, said that unless there was an end of the endeavours to make the trades council a political body, his society would disaffiliate from the council. Tanner, while agreeing with the spirit of the motion, thought it was superflous since there was already a resolution on the books stating that no member had the right to use the name of the trades council for political purposes. Alfred Keegan (Carpenters and Joiners) said it was ridiculous to suggest that because a man was described on a bill as a member of the trades council that the public would jump to the conclusion that he spoke as the mouthpiece of that body. The resolution was childish in the face of such great questions as were at stake ('Hear, hear'). At this point the chairman intervened to say that he had been using his influence to get the resolution withdrawn, but before this could be done, the accusation that some officials had used the name of the trades council for pecuniary purposes should be substantiated or withdrawn. A delegate then moved 'Next Business'. The chairman said that he would not accept that, but would close the discussion after Henson had replied. This did not suit the delegates, next business was defeated and the discussion continued.

'R.Hine (ASE) said he was opposed to the resolution because it could not be carried out. But the council should know that a member who had spoken to the resolution a fortnight ago had, ever since the Labour party had put him in the position of a representative, done his utmost to prevent anyone else occupying a similar position. Yet he had spoken in the name of the Liberal Association many times in opposition to Labour candidates who had fought on independent grounds. This person had never been a true friend of labour and had always been animated by personal spite. Whenever in the city council another member had taken the initiative he had opposed it, unless he had been in at the planning of it. At this point the chairman called the speaker to the question, but Hines said that he was trying to get to the bottom of the motion. He believed that gentleman had prompted Henson to move his motion ('No, no' and 'Hear, hear') just because certain members had given their support to Bloor and Davis ('No' and 'Yes') as to whom he appealed to anyone in the room to say whether they were true and honest representatives of labour. D.Byfield (Tin Plate Workers) thought the supporters of the motion were trying to get more out of it than there was in it. Its purpose was not to maintain a principle, but to curtail personal liberty. Councillor Granger had made it a personal peg on which to hang an attack on Jephcott, but forgot to remind delegates that he owed his position to the same political party.

Councillor Stevens pressed for a clearing up of the accusation referred to by the chairman. The offenders should be named, and as to the general principles of the discussion, the trades council, like the great friendly societies, should know no creed in religion and no code in politics.

H.J.Devolle (printer) shed some light on the origins opf the motion. He said it had resulted from a conversation between himself, Henson and Baker about the conduct of F.Perrin (who became president of the trades council in 1893), Perrin had told them that he had signed articles to take the chair at one of Mr.Browning's open-air meetings, but they did not know whether any pecuniary interest was involved. After several delegates had averred that their societies had only affiliated to the trades council on the understanding that there would be no politics and would withdraw if it were used for political purposes, Jephcott spoke. He said that he had never used the name of the trades council at a political meeting and was unaware that his name and that of the trades council had been associated on any bill. After this, Henson replied. There was no intention of preventing members from announcing that they were members of the trades council, only making it impossible for them to speak in its name unless authorised to do so, he declared. Perrin had taken the chair the other week at a meeting of Oscar Browning, who was not a working man, and had said that he came representing the trades council. Favell too, during his term of office had addressed a meeting in Walsall where he had been described as the president of the trades council. Pass the resolution and they would have labour representation pure and simple. Moreover, they would be under the obligation to find the funds to fight elections with their own candidates. The resolution was carried with a large majority, but some abstentions.

This discussion revealed the main cross currents within the trades council, in the period of the dissolution of the Lib-Lab consensus, between Gladstonian Liberals, Liberal-Unionists, Conservatives, those who wanted no politics at all (following the friendly society tradition which ideologically tied that movement to capitalist politics) and the 'no politics' of the socialists which meant no support for liberals or tories but led to a separate labour party.

Effects of Labour Representation

At this point we can turn to the beneficial effects of Labour represen-tation on the city council and the increased strength and influence of the trades council arising from the new unionism and increasing militancy generally. In 1885 there were 25 affiliated societies sending 64 delegates to the trades council. By 1893, 56 societies sent 186 delegates.

Early in 1889 the trades council passed the first resolution on fair wage clauses in local contracts. The ultimate adoption of this resolution by both the city council and the school board was moved by Councillor J.V.Stevens. The first fruits of this was a deputation to the Watch Committee regarding the low prices paid for the making of police uniforms which resulted in a promise of a 'fair wage' clause in all future tenders. In the same year Tanner and others helped organise women in the tailoring trade, and exposed the system of fines on female workers in the pen, printing and other industries. Joe Tanner was congratulated for giving up his job to help organise the pen workers. Such activities were part of the never-ending campaign against sweating in Birmingham trades.

The 25th. Anniversary of the trades council was celebrated in 1891 in considerable style. Celebrations began with a procession of hundreds of trade unionists led by one hundred members of the Lampmen's Union with lighted torches and two bands. They marched from the Bull Ring watched by thousands of people to a crowded meeting at the Town Hall. William Gilliver as a founder member and the first president moved a motion inviting congratulations over twenty-five years of existence and confidence in present policies. Allan Granger seconded the motion saying that when the trades council was founded trade unionists were looked upon as Nihilists and revolutionists, but now they were able to crowd the town hall with trade unionists who believed in organisation. During the years of its existence the trades council had done incalculable good to the working classes and in no case had injury been done to employers. C.C.Cooke supported the resolution remarking that they had not met to threaten or destroy the good relations that existed in many instances between masters and men, but to cement the present good feeling. He denied that the trades council was a political organisation and thought they could do much more as a non-political body than as one constantly clinging to the neck of a political organisation (Applause). A.W.Haddleton, however, struck a different note. Capitalists had never done anything for working men and if they were to secure anything, it must be by their own efforts (Applause.) The resolution was unanimously accepted, as was another inviting all non-unionists in the town to join their trade union. The meeting ended with votes of thanks, including one to the mayor for the free use of the town hall.

The growth of the trades council exacerbated the question of accommodation. It had met for a number of years at the Public Office, Moor Street. In the anniversary year a committee was set up which opened negotiations with the trustees of the schools attached to the Curcis Chapel in Bradford Street and Sherlock St. East. Here, with considerable voluntary labour, rooms were divided to accommodate committees and small meetings and opened as the Trades' Hall. In the meantime, the council had been meeting at the Oddfellows Hall, Temple Street. The Trades' Hall, though not all that could be desired, allowed for such activity as a base from which considerable sums were collected during the Miners' Lock-out of 1893. Unfortunately, the site of the building was shortly afterwards taken over and the trades council moved to rooms attached to the People's Hall, Hurst Street. For about ten years careful management and the subletting of rooms to various societies enabled the trades council to show a substantial profit, but as trade societies became stronger they set up their own offices, and eventually the hall became a financial burden and was given up.

In 1894, resulting from a stream of resolutions to their M.Ps., Joseph Chamberlain suggested a conference between the trades council and the city's M.Ps. An agenda was agreed of: Employers' Liability for Accidents without Contracting Out; The Eight Hour Day; The Housing of the Poor; Foreign-Made Prison Goods; Pauper Immigration. Debate went on for three hours and Chamberlain was subjected to 'some fierce but good-humoured heckling'. The debate helped to clarify outlooks rather than leading to tangible results. But it was clear that the old Chamberlain magic still exercised much of its spell.

1895 was the year in which the council decided to publish the *Birmingham and District Trades Journal*. It ran from March 1896 to March 1899. The project arose from general dissatisfaction with the treatment of the council by the Birmingham capitalist press. Here it must be said however, that much of the foregoing has been taken from detailed press reports stuck into the trades council minute books and these are an indispensable supplement to the brief, hand-written and often barely legible minutes of the secretary. However, for these three years the council published its own reports under the editorship of the secretary of the trades council. *The Trades Journal* also published an almost continuous series of biographies of leading local trade unionists, together with portraits. An oddity is that virtually the only advertiser was the Bi-Metallic League. Bi-Metallism was, as we have seen, part of the policy of the Birmingham Chamber of Commerce, but there is no evidence that it cut much ice with the trades council. Weekly full-page, small print advertisements on such subjects as 'Why Working Men should support Bimetallism', 'How Bimetallism came to be Abandoned' 'Consequences of its Abandonment' etc. must have helped considerably in paying the bills.

In 1896 much time was taken up with discussion of the superannuation of public servants and a committee produced a useful report on how the matter affected employees of the Birmingham council. This considerably increased the influence of the trades council with council employees even if it had little effect on the city council.

1897 was the year of the second visit of the T.U.C. to Birmingham. It nearly didn't take place, a resolution being passed by the trades council against inviting the TUC to Birmingham. But the matter was taken out of their hands by the local delegates at the 1896 T.U.C. convening a conference of all trade societies in the city which enthusiastically set about organising the event. It began with a procession displaying local manufactures *on lorries* provided by the various unions. It was 'one of the most imposing sights that had up to that time ever paraded the streets of Birmingham', according to Dalley. Like the first TUC in Birmingham, it was a herculean feat, showing the organising ability of working people at their best and undoubtedly increased the influence of trade unions and the trades council in the city.

Two other events ensured that the influence of the trades council at the end of the century stood at, probably, its highest point. The first was the Engineers' Lock-out of 1897. Birmingham was not directly involved, a wage increase having been conceded the previous year after a short strike. The lock-out was seen, however, as a deliberate attempt by the newly-federated Engineering Employers to break the power of one of the strongest unions in the country. Birmingham's role was to collect money. In all, more than £3,000 was raised, mainly from the new, large factories of Birmingham. Despite this, the Engineers suffered a humiliating defeat. But as is so often the case, industrial defeat was the springboard for political advance and the fate of the engineers was a key factor turning Lib-Labs into supporters of an independent Labour Party.

The third event was a decision in July 1899 to subscribe to the fund for scholarships for working people at the new University of Birmingham. This culminated in the magnificient industrial exhibition of 1901.

At this point we must record the struggles to obtain working class representation on other public bodies in the town, notably the School Boards, Boards of Guardians and the magistracy, during the period 1884–1900.

The first successes were in the three-yearly elections for the Birmingham School Board. As we have seen, at the elections to the first Board in 1870, David Kirkwood, the Secularist, was the only working class candidate and he polled 7,095 votes. This was the famous occasion when the Liberal fifteen were beaten by the Church eight due to the 'plumping' system. This defeat was an important factor in the development of the Caucus and the mistake was not repeated. For the second Board in 1873, the Liberals stood only eight candidates who were all elected. After this the Radical and Church parties co-existed in acceptance of the facts of life and elections were few and far between. In 1875 there was a by-election at which W.J.Davis stood as a Labour candidate. He polled 9,951 votes to the successful Liberal's 26,000 and the unsuccessful Church candidate's 10,500. In 1876 when the third Board was due for election the Church party agreed to field only five candidates, the Liberals put up eight and between them they allowed two Independents. This totalled fifteen candidates for fifteen places and meant that no election took place. One of the Independents was a Roman Catholic priest guaranteed a place because of the plumping system whereby each elector was able to give all his fifteen votes to one candidate. The other was W.J.Davis 'a trade union official'. According to Dalley, Davis was the first national trade union secretary ever to serve on a School Board. Davis also served on the fourth Board, which was again returned without an election. The second School Board had abolished all religious teaching in Board schools in accord with the principle of secular education. This proved highly controversial and the fourth Board voted by 7 to 1 to restore the bible to the schools. The one vote against was that of W.J.Davis; the seven votes for were the Church party; there were seven abstentions including the Roman Catholic priest, Father O'Hanlon.

There was not another election until 1888 when the cause of the contest was again the bible issue. Nineteen candidates went to the poll. The Caucus 'instructed' its supporters whose surnames began with the letters A to F to give five votes to each of three named candidates. Surnames G to O were to vote similarly for a different three named candidates and P to Z for yet another three. The policy was successful overall, but the pattern of results indicated some personal influences. Top of the poll, of course, was the Catholic. George Dixon, one of the two Liberals who had voted to restore the bible came next. Then came an Independent followed by a Churchman; then two Liberals followed by two Church; then six Liberals and one Church. Among the successful Liberals was J.V.Stevens of the trades council. Joe Tanner, the SDF socialist, stood and polled a creditable 7,281 compared with the lowest successful vote of 16,000.

In 1891 there was another contested election for the ninth Board. Again the Caucus swept the field. John Haddon, the SDFer, stood and polled 7,281 compared with the lowest successful vote of 29,000.

The 1894 election was sensational. W.Ansell (Independent) had been the headmaster at Bristol Street Schools and had resigned to stand as a nominee of the Birmingham Teachers' Association expressing the 'seething discontent of teachers over low salaries, too much inspection and the educational fads of the Board.' George Dixon expressed surprise and said that if the Board had been approached a seat would have been found for him and if he withdrew now and prevented a contest he would be given the next vacant seat. Ansell replied that he preferred the judgement of the electors to the favours of the Board. Ansell came top of the poll with 146,000 votes, forcing even the Catholic into second place. Third was David Miller, a Labour candidate and trades council delegate. George Dixon had to be content with fourth place. Ansell polled more votes than all the Liberals put together. The writing was on the wall for the Liberals.

In 1897 Ansell discredited himself by standing as a Liberal. A Roman Catholic layman topped the poll followed by two Churchmen. Ansell was the top Liberal with 31,832 votes, but an Independent and another Churchman separated him from the next Liberal followed by another Independent and another Churchman before another six Liberals overcame three more churchmen. Two trades council candidates stood at this election — J.Millington polled 17,606 and Arthur Eades 15,747 compared with the lowest successful vote of 27,092.

At the 12th and last School Board elections in 1900 control passed from the Liberals to the Church. J.Millington again stood as a trades council delegate polling 22,934 votes to the least successful candidate's 27,586.

The appointment of working class magistrates constituted a small break in the social control over working people, but one the capitalist class was loathe to make. This social control is not traced in detail here and it is a major gap in the narrative, but the main links of the chain of social control can be indicated. They include absolute control of the national and local legislatures, control of administration, and control of the coercive apparatus of the state — the judiciary. Even more important was (and is) capitalist economic control at the workplace involving the determination of prices, wages and behaviour at work with the ultimate sanction of being able to grant or withold the means of livelihood of working people. The necessary complement to this iron fist of control is the velvet glove of ideology involving control of education and information to persuade working people that they like what they are getting, or when that fails, that any possible alternative could only be worse. The working class movements seeks to break this chain with the inter-related forces of its trade unions and political parties.

It was not until the 1880s that the demand that employers locally should no longer be both accusers and judges of their own cases began to be met. At the December 1890 trades council meeting, Gilliver proposed the following:

> That this Council observes with regret that while in many of the larger towns of the Country, one or more working men have been raised to the Magisterial Bench, no similar appointment has yet been made for this City, and therefore considers it desirable to approach the Lord Chancellor on the subject, and hereby instructs the Officers to prepare a Memorial asking that such an appointment may be made.

After rejecting an amendment by Cooke that the City Council and not the Chancellor be approached on the matter, the motion was passed and referred to the Standing Orders Committee to prepare the memorial and suggest names of working men.

The matter was again raised in July 1892. Cooke, the chairman, stated that fifteen months had elapsed since their approach to the Lord Chancellor and their Memorial had not even been acknowledged. Since then Jephcott had sent two letters, Favell one and now Perrins had taken up the matter. Favell said that his letter had been acknowledged and he had been told that the matter would be placed before his lordship, but there the matter seemed to have ended.

It was at this meeting, during the subsequent discussion on politics and the trades council, that Granger had fiercely attacked Jephcott for remaining silent at a meeting where the Stipendiary had, libellously in Granger's view, been accused of unfairness and partiality. Perhaps this was the reason why, although there had been recent new appointments to the magistracy no working men were included, Granger concluded.

Eventually William Gilliver and Eli Bloor became the first Birmingham working class magistrates, appointed probably in early 1893.

This was far from being the end of the matter, however; Bloor died in 1895 and Gilliver in 1898 and neither was replaced by a working man. There is a vast trades council correspondence with the Lord Chancellor's office stretching into the 1920s and 1930s on this question of working class magistrates.

The Birmingham Trade Unions and The T.U.C.

Against the background of trade union activity in Birmingham already sketched, we can turn to the parallel, national struggle to change the ideology of the movement from Liberalism to Lib-Labism and then to Labourism and Socialism.

Birmingham trade unionism was an important influence in the formation and sustaining of the annual gatherings of trade unionists which developed into the Trades Union Congress and this influence has remained. The first TUC was at Manchester in 1868 and two delegates from Birmingham Trades Council, A.Wood and T.Wilkinson, attended.

When choosing a venue for the Second Congress, Birmingham was one of the few centres capable of adequately hosting such an event. Of the 48 delegates representing 250,000 trade unionists, seventeen were from

Birmingham. These were J.Loughton (Carpenters & Joiners), G.Badger (Basket Makers), H.Lerwill (Carpenters & Joiners), J.Taylor (Wire Drawers), Hunter and Summers (Bricklayers), H.Gaunt (Coopers), C.Williams (Plasterers), C.Blakemore (Nail Casters), J.Doody (Glass Cutters) F.Cox & T.Wilkinson (Glass Makers), C.Hibbs (National Education League), W.J.Davis (Barr Street Reform Association) G.J.Holyoake (by invitation). The Trades Council delegates were T.Green and the secretary R.McRae.

But during the 1870s the Trades Council ceased to send delegates and it was left to the trade societies to represent Birmingham. Foremost among these unions was the Brassworkers whose secretary, W.J.Davis, attended regularly from 1875 and who was to become the 'father' of the TUC. In 1876 Davis moved a resolution on returning working men to parliament and in 1877 he moved a resolution on the control of female labour through the Factory Acts. The latter was vehemently opposed by Marie Patterson representing the feminist view of women's right to jobs however deplorable the wages. In 1878 Davis first stood as a candidate for the TUC Parliamentary Committee but received only 13 votes. Davis was elected for the first of his three stints on the Parliamentary Committee in 1881; this lasted until 1883. Another regular Birmingham delegate to the TUC was C.Williams of the National Association of Operative Plasterers, representing 8,000 members in 1878, but only 4580 in 1880.

A Birmingham Trades Council delegate appeared in 1878 when J.J.Lewis represented 4,000 affiliated members, but there were no TUC delegates in 1879 and 1880. When two trades council delegates appeared at the 1881 London Congress they were involved in a fierce controversy which threatened the free trade, Liberal hegemony of the TUC at a point in the Great Depression where protectionist views were gaining some ground. The two Birmingham delegates were J.T. Harlow who was secretary of the trades council and S.W.Maddocks who was president of the Brassworkers. Congress started with a change in standing orders passed by a large majority. This was:

> That, in the opinion of Congress, no one should be eligible as a delegate
> to Congress whose expenses are paid by private individuals or by any
> institution not bona fide Trade Unions or Trades Councils.

Congress then turned to offending delegates. It was alleged that at least seven had been paid for by the 'sugar interests'. This was a body of 'fair-traders' demanding countervailing duties against countries which subsidised their sugar exports by bounties. It was found that among those whose expenses had not been paid by the trade organisations they represented were the two Birmingham delegates. Harlow tried to brazen it out. Birmingham Trades Council had not been able to bear the costs of representation and he had undertaken to pay his own expenses while the trades council paid the affiliation fee, he claimed. He had been a member of the trades council for three years and a trade unionist all his life, he continued. Was Congress going to throw him out? This seems to have mollified delegates and Harlow was allowed to remain. But the debate was resumed the next day when John Burnett of the Parliamentary

Committee stated that there had been a Fair Trade Conference in London earlier in the week and the delegates to it had had their fares paid. Williams, one of the culprits, admittted that he had been at the Fair Trade Conference, but claimed that any action under the revised standings orders should have been taken on the first day. Would other delegates say that their hands were clean from accepting aid from organisations outside their trade societies? Maddocks, the other Birmingham delegate, then challenged Congress to answer these points; but the main offenders, Williams, Kelly, Peters and Kenny were removed and Congress turned to the Birmingham delegates. W.J. Davis said he was reluctant to intervene since Maddocks was the president of his union, but being challenged by Kelly to defend a comrade, he was bound to protest at the violation of the representative principle. He knew that efforts were being made to pack the Congress with delegates paid to advocate certain principles and who were not there to further the principles of trade unionism. Maddocks had misled the trades council by stating that he would pay his own expenses and not revealing that they would be paid by an outside body. Maddocks was expelled. When it came to Harlow's turn, he was defended by no less a person than Henry Broadhurst, but even this did not save him and he was expelled on a vote of 80 to 21. After the Congress the trades council affirmed its support for the decision, and at a special meeting reiterated its support for free trade. Harlow was replaced as trades council secretary by Ben Church. But not only is the influence of Joseph Chamberlain clear in this matter, but also his direct hand.

There was no other trades council representation until 1888 when J.V.Stevens was the delegate representing 3,100 members. W.J.Davis attended for the Brassworkers in 1882 and moved a resolution on protecting working men by changes in the patent law. When Davis became a Factory Inspector, E. Lilly, the new secretary, attended in 1883, but thereafter Brassworker representation disappeared until Davis' return. At the 1883 Congress, Ben Church appeared, but not as a delegate from the trades council nor from his own society, the printers, but as a delegate for 350 Bone and Ivory Workers and 650 members of the National Society of Nail Casters. At this Congress, Church stood for the Parliamentary Committee, but received only two votes. Church also attended the 1884 Congress representing the same two societies and the 1885 Congress as a delegate for the Nail Casters alone.

The most persistent and vocal Birmingham delegate of these years was C.O.Williams. He attended regularly from at least 1878 to 1882 as the delegate for the National Association of Operative Plasterers. In 1882 Williams stood unsuccessfully for the Parliamentary Committee, but he polled the respectable vote of 36. At this Congress he seconded an amendment demanding that labour representatives on national and local bodies should be paid by the state, remarking that they should not have to run to the Carlton or Cobden Clubs. He also seconded a motion on the federation of trades. This motion was withdrawn after criticism that this matter was continually being brought before the TUC, but there was little they could do apart from urging all societies to affiliate to their trades council. But the issue of federation, both for trade unionists and employers was already looming large. The first federation to appear at the TUC was the Nottingham Federation of Trades from 1879, and from 1886 the Midland Counties Federation of

Trades with 2,000 workers, mainly in the Black Country, was regularly represented by the redoubtable Richard Juggins.

In 1889, the only Birmingham delegate at the TUC was A.W.Haddleton of the trades council, but with the development of the New Unionism representation grew. In 1890 the trades council delegate was Councillor Allan Granger. W.J.Davis also reappeared for the Brassworkers, E.Fookes represented the Tin Plate Workers, and another regular attender, W.Mills, representing 2540 Bedstead Workers appeared. In 1891 Mills, Fookes and Haddleton were again delegates for their respective societies, T.Poole represented Boot and Shoe operatives and J.McHugh 1,400 Iron & Tinplate Workers. In 1892 attendance fell sharply, only Mills attending. Davis was back again in 1893 with Mills, Fookes and Haddleton. In 1894 Mills and Davis attended and the trades council delegate was C.C.Cooke. In 1895 it was again Mills and Davis, but this was the year when the new standing orders were operated and the trades councils were excluded.

In 1896 Davis and Mills were joined by C.Gibbs of Bakers and Confectioners and R.Hawkes was one of 17 delegates from the Amalgamated Society of Carpenters and Joiners.

The 1897 TUC was held in Birmingham and is dealt with more fully later. What is significant, however, is that this Congress gave a fillip to Congress attendance which continued to the end of the century, of greater representation of general unions. The general unions in Birmingham were represented for the first time, as were the newer Birmingham trades. Thus, at the 1897 Congress Sam Lakin and Robert Toller represented the two General Labourers' unions and, with larger numbers of delegates from the societies regularly represented there were also delegates from Cycle makers, Electro-Platers, Musicians, Coachmakers, Guns, Tailors and Printers.

The T.U.C. And Labour Representation

With regard to Labour representation, the second TUC at Birmingham in 1869 had voted to support the labour Representation League which had been set up following the dissolution of the National Reform league. Its terms of reference were:

> ... to secure the return to Parliament of qualified working men ... (and) ... where deemed necessary, recommend and support as candidates from among the other classes such persons as have studied the great labour problems and have proved themselves friendly to an equitable settlement of the many difficult points which it involves.

But the Labour Representation League quickly became an appendage of the Liberal Party.

Between 1869 and 1885 when the TUC formed the labour Electoral Association, there had been progress in electing working men to Parliament and to local bodies but they were either Liberal or Conservative working men assisted by those parties. In 1873 Alexander McDonald and Thomas Burt, both miners, had been elected on the Liberal ticket. In 1885 eleven Lib-Labs were elected and Henry Broadhurst, stone-mason and secretary of the TUC Parliamentary Committee briefly became an Under-Secretary at the Home Office.

The 1885 TUC resolution seeking greater Labour representation consequent upon the 1884 Reform Act was followed the next year by more positive action. It proposed an annual conference of delegates from the labour Electoral Association with a subscription of 5/-d per annum per society. According to W.J.Davis it was envisaged that it would come under the control of the TUC Parliamentary Committee, but like its predecessor, the Association soon became another appendage of the Liberal Party.

The deepening depression and large-scale unemployment was reflected in the 1886 Hull TUC Congress which saw a militant presidential address from F.Maddison the local trades council man attacking the Parliamentary Committee and advocating the nationalisation of the land as well as the legal 8-hour Day. The 1887 Congress was the first attended by Keir Hardie. He demanded the 8-hour Day and fiercely attacked Henry Broadhurst for supporting Liberal anti-trade union employers. Broadhurst replied defending his actions and counter-attacking Hardie. He was not aware that Mr. Hardie and the men he represented (1,000 Ayrshire miners - GB) had made sacrifices in the great Labour movement. He did not remember that Mr.Hardie until that year had taken part in the great struggles which had lifted labour up from the position it was 50 years ago ... And so the rhetoric went on. Hardie protested that 50 years before he had not been born, but he was heavily out-voted and the Lib-Labs remained in control.

The Birmingham Trades Council equivalent to Keir Hardie at the TUC was Joe Tanner. Linked to the question of independent Labour representation was the 8-hour Day. Everyone supported the 8-hour Day, but most miners and the socialists wanted it enacted by Parliament, whereas most of the Lib-Labs wanted to obtain it through trade union action. Tanner forced a discussion on the trades council in 1887 that lasted several weeks and it was decided to hold a plebiscite of affiliated societies on the question.

1888 was the first year of the New unionism with the Bryant & May's match girls' strike. J.V.Stevens attended as the Birmingham Trades Council delegate. Keir Hardie again attacked Broadhurst and the Parliamentary Committee for their lack of activity, but again the Lib-Labs triumphed. Also in 1888 the TUC rather reluctantly called an International Trades Union Congress in London which was well attended by New Unionists and socialists. George Shipton of the Parliamentary Committee gave an interminable and patronising chairman's address covering British trade unionism from Edward III together with a lecture on laissez-faire economics and monetary policy. This safely occupied much of the first day. Birmingham Trades Council had agreed to attend this International TUC and had elected Allan Granger as their delegate. But Granger excused himself and Joe Tanner went in his place armed with a mandate to vote for international regulation of the working day.

1889 saw the full flowering of the New Unionism with the Dock Strike and the Gas Stokers' successes. Again Keir Hardie fought a lonely battle against Broadhurst and the Parliamentary Committee. So little were they in sympathy with the Dock Strike that it was referred to in their report as 'this lamentable dispute.' Alfred Haddleton attended as the Birmingham Trades Council delegate. Again, the Lib-Labs swept the board.

In Birmingham the clash had come before the TUC met. In January

1889 Joe Tanner successfully argued that at least the Corporation should institute an 8-hour day and pay trade union rates. The following month the trades council demanded a 10-hour day for the tramwaymen. At this meeting Tanner called Broadhurst a traitor (echoing Keir Hardie at the TUC) and accused J.V.Stevens of voting against the legal 8-hour Day at the previous TUC. Stevens was in the chair and called Tanner to order, but Tanner refused to stop talking and challenged the meeting to talk him down if they could. The meeting had to be adjourned. Tanner's ASE branch was asked to elect another delegate, but they re-elected Tanner. The trades council refused to hear him until he apologised. This he refused to do. Eventually, by the casting vote of the chairman, Tanner was allowed to return to the Council. Lib-Lab domination had been challenged and J.V.Stevens did not subsequently stand as president.

When the 1890 Liverpool TUC convened in September the position was transformed. No longer was Keir Hardie a lone voice in opposition to the Parliamentary Committee. The new unions of Coal Porters, Dock and General Labourers, Gas Workers, Match Makers (with a female delegate) etc. were represented by such militants as Ben Tillett, John Burns and Tom Mann. Also the Congress was much larger. In 1889 there had been 211 delegates representing 885,000 trade unionists. In 1890 it was 457 delegates representing 1,470,000 members. Birmingham Trades Council was represented by the Lib-Lab Allan Granger; Birmingham membership registered at the TUC had risen from 3,000 in 1889 to 4,400 in 1890.

Again, the local TUC president was a New Unionist. He spoke of the great labour revival at home which had also inspired the continental labour movement. He saw this as the forerunner of the national organisation of industry. 'So long as the working classes are kept in uncertainty as to their present subsistence and future security.' they would use the power of the state for the benefit of the labouring multitudes. Their immediate demands would include an 8-Hour Bill, direct Labour representation, nationalisation of the land and mines, federation of trades etc. So the scene was set for the historic 1890 TUC.

On the Parliamentary Committee's report an amendment of protest was moved on their failure to carry out the definite instructions given them on the Miners' Eight Hour Bill. Both John Burns and Tom Mann supported the amendment, and Ben Pickard, a mining MP, reckoned that 11 of the 12 members of the Parliamentary Committee were opposed to the Bill. But Broadhurst, in a masterly reply, had the amendment defeated by 258 votes to 92.

With regard to Labour representation, an innocuous resolution was moved on the desirability of increased representation of labour and urging all trades and industries to do their utmost to effect this. It was strengthened by an amendment requiring the Parliamentary Committee to sponsor a joint conference of all kindred organisations to ensure payment of M.Ps and place local and board elections on a popular basis. To this, James McDonald proposed an addendum:

> ... that no candidate shall receive the support of working men unless they declare in favour of the nationalisation of the land, shipping, railways and all other means of production.

On this addendum, John Burns, already showing the ambivalence which was to be a feature of his future political position, said that he would rather go to prison a dozen times than parliament once for the cause of workmen, but they should vote for labour candidates irrespective of party politics. With this latter sentiment, Granger, the Birmingham delegate, was quick to agree. McDonald's addendum was lost 363 votes to 55 and the main resolution, with amendment, was passed with only one dissentient.

W.J.Davis, utilising his experience as a factory inspector moved a resolution requiring that factory and workshop disciplinary fines be made illegal and the necessary amendments to the Truck Acts be made. This was passed unanimously. Davis also spoke to a motion calling for considerably more factory inspectors. He said the district for which he had been responsible stretched from Grimsby to Barnsley and contained upwards of 14,000 factories and workshops.

The great debate on the 8 Hours' question in 1890 revolved round a resolution and an amendment. The resolution was:

> ... the time has arrived when steps should be taken to reduce the working hours in all trades to eight per day, or a maximum of forty-eight per week and while recognising the power and influence of trade organisations, it is of the opinion that the speediest and best method to obtain this reduction ... is by Parliamentary enactment. This Congress therefore instructs the Parliamentary Committee to take immediate steps for the furtherance of this object.

The amendment, moved by W.H.Patterson a Durham Miners' delegate showed not only the differing principles, but also some of the practical problems involved. It read:

> That in the opinion of this Congress, it is of the utmost importance that an eight hour day should be secured at once by such trades as may desire it, or for whom it may be made to apply without injury to the workmen employed in such trades; further, it considers that to relegate this important question to the Imperial Parliament, which is necessarily, from its position, antagonistic to the rights of labour, will only indefinitely delay this much needed reform.

Patterson argued that they were the Labour Parliament and to turn the matter over to the Landlords' Parliament would delay the matter for another 40 years. The amendment was supported by most of the miners and cotton workers. The motion was supported by most of the new unions. Allan Granger spoke to the amendment, contending that the 8-Hours Movement was being used as a lever for the engineers' movement; this was to get him in hot water when he returned to Birmingham. T.Threlfall, John Burns and Keir Hardie made the most powerful cases for Parliamentary action. The debate, in the main, seems to have been conducted in a serious way, each side recognising the opposed principles of the other. When the vote was taken on Patterson's amendment the result was:

For the Amendment	173
Against Amendment	181
Majority against	8

When the original resolution was put the majority in favour was 38. This historic result, which of course, greatly strengthened the case for independent Labour representation in Parliament, proved to be Henry Broadhurst's swan-song, if not the end of his era. The final irony was that he was instructed by his society, the Stone Masons, to vote for the resolution; Broadhurst resigned, on the grounds of health, as secretary of the Parliamentary Committee.

For the vacant secretary's position the three nominations were Charles Fenwick, a miners' MP, George Shipton of the London Trades Council and T.R.Threlfall of Southport Trades Council. After a second ballot, the Lib-Lab Fenwick won by 197 to Shipton's 181. But the New Unionists found themselves with one representative, John Burns, on the Parliamentary Committee by the following accident of circumstances. T.Birtwistle with the second highest vote refused to sit on a Parliamentary Committee that was mandated to support the legal 8-hour Day. Slatten, the first unsuccessful candidate, refused to serve and so John Burns the second of the unsuccessful candidates with the next highest vote found himself a member. So the New Unionists had made significant, but limited gains. There was to be a reaction in the following years as depression returned, trade union membership dropped below one million and the old guard counter-attacked.

The Socialist Attack on The Lib/Labs

Back in Birmingham, Granger reported to the trades council in October 1890 the proceedings of the TUC the previous month. Again, the confrontation of the New Unionists and the Lib-Labs at the TUC was replicated with the clash between Joe Tanner and the Birmingham TUC delegate. Granger summed up the Congress by saying that it had been a trial of strength between the old trade unionists and the new. The old school had had the best of it, but the new school had obtained a foothold within the Parliamentary Committee. They had no doubt read pessimistic accounts of the Congress, but he was more cheerful. The new would give a necessary widening impulse to the old and the old would moderate the youthful enthusiasm of the new.

Such rhetoric did not suit Tanner. He demanded to know whether it was true that Granger had said at the TUC that Birmingham Trades Council was not in favour of the 8-Hour Day, and that it was an engineering question. Granger replied that he had, as a debating point against John Burns, used the engineering question, but he had also read the resolution passed by the Trades council on the 8-hour question. Tanner accused Granger of prevaricating and demanded a straight 'yes' or 'no' to the question of whether he had said that the trades council was not in favour of the 8-hour Day. This brought hisses and cries of 'Shame'. Tanner retorted that they could react as they liked, he wanted a straight answer. Jephcott, the chairman, then asked the council not to get into a heat over the question. Councillor Stevens said they didn't want more headlines in the newspapers, 'Another scene at the Trades Council'. He considered that Granger had answered Tanner fairly. The chairman then asked Granger if he had anything to add. Granger replied that he did not know what he could add. He didn't think he had used the words that the trades council was opposed to the 8-hours movement, but he had read the resolution condemning eight hours. After more uproar, John Erskine, a Conservative, asked the secretary to read the actual resolution passed at the trades council. Haddleton replied that he did not have the book containing the resolution with him. The chairman then said that Granger had answered the question and they must take it that he had said that the trades council had passed a resolution against the 8-hour Day. A motion to move to next business was not seconded and the heated exchanges continued. Tanner then moved that the discussion be adjourned to the next meeting. This was lost by 19 votes to 21 and the TUC Report was approved.

But what had been the original decision of the trades council on the 8-hour Question? To find the answer to this we must go back to March 1890. The 8-hour Day was not only linked with independent labour representation, but also with the international movement. The foundation Congress of the Second International took place in Paris in 1889. Its principal immediate decision was to establish an international day of working class demonstrations in all countries for the aims of the 8-hour day and other resolutions of the Congress. Since the American Federation of Labour had already decided on a similar demonstration on May 1st. 1890 it was decided to adopt this date. Thus labour May Day was born.

The question came before the Birmingham Trades Council in March 1890 with a resolution in the name of A.V.Haddleton, the secretary:

> That this Council communicate with the various trade societies in order to consider the advisability of organising a demonstration in favour of the 8-hour working day.

The resolution gave rise to the first full-scale debate on the question. Councillor Stevens began the objections. Nine or ten hours a day was the rule on the continent, he said, and it would subject our trade to unfair competition if adopted here before other nations did the same. But if the time were ripe, he would be prepared to support legislation for an 8-hour day. Gilliver spoke at length against a legislated 8-hour day. He considered that it would be impossible to enforce. J.Allen, a tailor objected on the grounds that he knew many trades where piece-workers could not earn a living wage in eight hours. F.Favell, a glassworker, supported the motion saying that the 9-hours movement had led to wage increases for nearly everyone and he thought the 8-hour movement would have the same result. D.Dobson, stonemason, also supported the motion arguing that there had been an enormous fall in the death rate following the 9-hour day. Joe Tanner explained that the resolution arose from the Paris Congress decision that working men all over the world should demonstrate in favour of 8-hours on May Day. He attacked Gilliver for voicing middle class ideas and said that in a town like Birmingham with hundreds out of work and thousands on the brink of starvation something was radically wrong with society and an 8-hour day would give work to numbers who now have none. Gilliver had talked of the manhood of the country being able to take care of itself, but what about the womanhood? Not long before, hundreds of women pen workers had promised him that they would join a trade union, but when the meeting was called no one came. The employers had told the women that if they went to a meeting they would be discharged. Was their manhood content to see their wives and daughters domineered over in this way? Councillor Granger then asked Tanner to name the firms and he gave the names of Perry & Co. Josiah Mason and Gillots. Tanner was then reminded by the chair that the discussion was on the 8-hour day. Mouncey, another tailor, said that restriction of hours would lead to trade going elsewhere, as in slack times, men often worked only 5 hours a day.

Councillor Granger then enlarged on the point he was to make at the TUC. A reduction of hours led to the introduction of machinery. Engineering, Mr.Tanner's trade, was like Aaron's rod swallowing up all the others. Men had been replaced in thousands to make way for girls with a few members of the ASE superintending them.

Haddleton in reply said working men wanted their fair share of labour saving, but he was prepared to leave out the question of a demonstration and make his resolution simply a declaration in favour of the 8-hour day. This amendment was moved by Councillor Stevens and seconded by Councillor Granger and then passed unanimously. So Birmingham Trades Council was clearly committed to an 8-hour Day, but it had not pronounced on the key issue of whether by legislation or trade union action. The very successful first May Day demonstration in 1890 was, it will be recalled, organised by the SDF in Birmingham

The old unionists were not to leave the 8-hours' question in the uncertain state of the March 1890 decision and, in January 1891, Gilliver proposed the following resolution:

> That this Council, while recognising the desirability of reducing the hours of labour in some of our National industries, and willing to render assistance to all sections of workmen in any proper effort to secure for themselves such a limitation of the hours as may be needful in their case and agreed upon by those engaged in the Trade or Industry records its opinion that such changes as may be found necessary, will be soonest and safest brought about by Organisation, and the legitimate Agitation of the workers engaged therein. And this Council is further of opinion that any compulsory limitation of the hours of labour applied to the adult manhood of this country, must prove subversive of all true freedom, extinguishing the rights and individual liberty of its citizens.

Gilliver said that he had no objection to the 8-hour day, but it was difficult to apply a cast-iron rule to every trade. He had a strong objection to over-legislation. People seemed to want acts of Parliament for every little thing. The public generally were not prepared to accept the 8-hour day for every trade, especially those who were piece-workers. Even the miners were divided on the subject. A.Beeman of the House Decorators & Painters seconding the motion said his trade was done largely in the summer and to restrict hours to eight in their busy season would be hard on the workmen. D.Dobson of the Stonemasons said his society took the opposite view from that of Beeman and moved the following amendment:

> That this Council seeing that Labour is unable to raise itself from the thraldom of capital by means of trade organisation only, considers that any trade which requires a limitation of the hours of labour is justified in demanding the Government of this country to give effect to its wishes.

F.Perrin then suggested that Dobson should alter his amendment as follows:

> That this Council hereby records its opinion that an eight hours day is desirable; and that such day can best be secured by Act of Parliament.

Dobson agreed to accept this as his amendment, and Perrin, seconding the amendment said that no man should be compelled to work more than eight hours a day for his living. Parsons supported the original resolution on the grounds of foreign competition from countries where wages were lower and hours longer. Castle also supported the resolution on the grounds that an eight-hour day would enable employers to introduce three shift working. Erskine said the 8-hour day may be good for miners and some other trades, but it would be detrimental to introduce it for all trades. W.F.Hill, an influential old unionist delegate from the Silversmiths and Electro-platers, made what must have been a telling point when he said that he could not commit himself to the 8-hour movement, but he would support the amendment because his trade had long been unsuccessfully struggling to obtain a uniform system of working hours. The Lib-Lab heavy-weights then had their say. Granger said the 8-hour day was impracticable and would bring disaster to those it was intended to benefit. But Stevens was a Lib-Lab changing his mind. He supported the amendment saying he had been convinced by the railway struggle in Scotland that the only way of securing legitimate hours for workmen was by Act of Parliament. After Gilliver had replied, the amendment was voted on. The result was 27 for and 13 against. Thus all ambiguity was removed and the influence of the Birmingham Trades Council from then on, both locally and nationally, was for a legal 8-hour day. The New Unionists had won a decisive victory, but in such a way that it left a minimum of bitterness and rancour.

An impending election brought the question of working class representation to the fore, but nationally, the increased strength of the Lib-Labs at the 1891 TUC ensured that little was done. When the election came in July 1892 the Gladstonian Liberals were returned as prisoners of the Irish nationalists. Only ten of the twenty Lib-Lab candidates were returned and only Keir Hardie, John Burns and J.Havelock Wilson as Independent Labour. This led to renewed attention to the question at the 1892 TUC and again it centred on the 8-hour issue. Fenwick, the secretary of the Parliamentary Committee had voted against an 8-hour Bill on the grounds that he was a Liberal and most of his constituents were opposed to the 8-hour Bill. Keir Hardie moved a successful amendment requesting that the Parliamentary Committee be required to produce a scheme for labour representation which dealt particularly with the financial problems. This to be produced in time to be circulated and delegates mandated for the next TUC. The Birmingham Trades Council delegate at the 1891 and 1893 TUCs (there was no delegate in 1892) was Alfred Haddleton, the secretary, who was not a Lib-Lab and could be depended on to vote according to the policy of the trades council.

At the 1893 TUC the Labour representation issue was duly put on behalf of the Parliamentary committee by a resolution in the name of J.Wilson M.P. who had delegated his duty to Ben Tillett. It was in three parts:

1. That a fund be established to assist Independent Labour candidates in local and Parliamentary elections.
2. That societies desiring to participate should subscribe 5/-d p.a. per 100 members. That the fund be administered by a Committee of thirteen elected annually at the TUC from delegates representing contributing societies.
3. Candidates should be selected locally, but if there was no suitable local candidate, selection could be made from a list approved by the committee. All candidates selected must pledge themselves to support the labour programme *as approved from time to time.*

The latter clause was so vague as to invite amendment, and James McDonald (the Socialist tailor from London and not J.Ramsey Macdonald with whom he was often confused) duly moved to remove the last sentence and substitute:

> All candidates selected must pledge themselves to support the principles of collective ownership and control of the means of production and distribution and the Labour programme as approved from time to time by Congress.

The main opposition to the amendment came from Robert Knight of the Boilermakers. Like many Lib-Labs, his attack on Socialism was not direct, but oblique and subtle. The amendment was not complete, he thought, since it did not say into whose hands the means of production etc were to pass. Knight was not prepared to hand them over to the present Government. They would have to get a new House of Commons and do away with the House of Lords before they could do anything. He suggested they set about getting a new House of Commons rather than go in for such a visionary scheme. John Burns supported the amendment, but voiced the alarm felt by some at the growth of the ILP set up earlier in the year. Burns wanted the Independent Labour Party put out of existence and the blending of the trade union movement with a Socialist labour party set up by the TUC. When voted on, this historic amendment of James McDonald was passed by 137 votes to 97 and the amended resolution approved 150 to 52.

The national organisational, financial and political problems of obtaining independent Labour representation were compounded by local conditions as can be seen by returning to this problem in Birmingham.

In September 1893 T.Henson presented the report of the trades council's Independent labour Committee appointed to carry out the resolution of a special meeting to bring forward purely Labour candidates for the November municipal elections. Their first recommendation was that candidates be provided for St. Martin's and Ladywood wards on the grounds that the retiring councillors were not seeking re-election and the seats were therefore 'open'. But it had been decided to leave that matter over until the next point had been considered. This was that 'no candidate be accepted who retains his connection with any political party.' When put to the meeting Middleton denounced this as the most absurd he had ever heard. W.Hill, the Electro-plater, said that he had been thought fit to be nominated as a candidate, but when he appeared before the committee he had been insulted by being asked to forgo his politics. Erskine, the Tory, had another dig at Tanner by asking why members should give up their parties any more than Joe Tanner, who presided over the committee, should give up his red flag. ('Laughter.') Were they to lose such Labour representatives as Allan Granger because he associated with a political party. Gilliver said he had always advocated the thorough independence of the trades council, but he did not mean they all were to sacrifice their individual liberty. He would not make such a sacrifice. Alfred Keegan said he had been invited to put his name forward, but when the condition of political effacement had been put, he had declined. Were the Council prepared to put Councillor Stevens on one side? Arthur Eades thought the only way to have an independent labour party was to put their labour above their politics. It was no good having as their leaders men before whose eyes politicians were dangling factory inspectorships or political agencies ('Laughter', 'Applause' and 'Oh! oh!'). Councillor Stevens thought the resolution from the special meeting had been misinterpreted. He admitted that he was the nominee of a political party and he would not, as such, ask trades council's support. The object of the special meeting had been to get a nominee of the trades council, and if they got a good man to run solely as their nominee, what more could they ask? The chairman of the trades council, C.C.Cooke, could win the St. Martin's seat, Stevens continued, and if he was prepared to come out solely as a Labour candidate, what did it matter if he belonged to a political association? Cooke supported this view, saying that when his society sent him as a delegate to the trades council, he was not asked to forsake his political party, so why should the trades council expect him to sacrifice his manhood? After further 'excited discussion', the resolution that 'No candidate be accepted who retains his connection with any political party' was carried by a large majority and the consideration of candidates was deferred to a special meeting. At this meeting Arthur Eades was selected to contest St. Martin's and Joe Tanner, Ladywood. It would seem that the New Unionists had won that round, but the Lib-Labs were to take their revenge by failing to support the two Labour candidates and Eades polled 540 votes and Joe Tanner 110.

An inquest on the election was held at the November trades council. Henson reported and said that if they looked at the election from the standpoint of having the support of the whole of the council, then the result was a disgrace. But if they took into consideration the fact that only six of the 240 members of the trades council participated in their work, then they had something to show for their labours. In St. Martin's, the committee had worked night and day for the movement. The ward Liberal Association had offered to work four of the districts, but under the terms of the resolution this had been declined. The committee had done its work and it was now up to the delegates to pay the piper. Henson concluded on an optimistic note saying that if only all members would put their shoulder to the wheel, they would come out on top. Fookes said that the committee had done what it could and the best thing the council could do was to thank the two gentlemen for fighting their battle. R.Peck, a printer, who said he did not believe in direct labour representation, asked how the election could be considered a success when Tanner had only got his proverbial hundred and Councillor Granger had been ousted through the machinations of the council. (Granger had resigned from the city council just before the election - G.B.) Joe Tanner was stung by the reference to his 'proverbial hundred'. Once in a lifetime did not make it 'proverbial', he said. Those gentlemen who were not prepared to work for labour representation should at least not work against it. But they had done nothing of the sort. Eli Bloor had presided over a meeting to assist capitalists against working men, Bloor had said that he (Tanner) had only been selected by a minority (quite right). Bloor also said that only 32 voted for Tanner and 18 against. Was that right? ('No'.) He (Tanner) found representatives of labour recording their votes for his opponent and members of that Council were driving vehicles for the middle class men ('Hear, hear' and 'Laughter'). He was not ashamed but proud that there were 110 strongbacked men in Ladywood when they could not find that many on the trades council. Eades said that he was not disappointed and would be prepared to stand again. He thought they ought to adhere to the resolution of the trades council, majority or minority. The discussion concluded with the acceptance of Henson's report, thanks to the two candidates and instructions for the election committee to continue its work.

The electoral question was moved forward a stage the very next month when Henson reported a by-election in St.George's ward and asked the council to consider naming a candidate. Tanner said that the Independent Labour Party in Birmingham had decided to run a candidate at this election and if they supported him they would not be put to the trouble and expense of running their own candidate. He therefore proposed that they endorse the ILP candidate, G.H.Humphries. David Miller seconded the motion saying that Humphries was a good, staunch trade unionists who had been a delegate to the trades council for a long time. The opponents of independent labour representation then put an amendment 'That we do not contest the ward.' This was defeated and the resolution supporting the ILP candidate was approved. So another piece was fitted into the jig-saw of working class representation with the acceptance of a candidate from the newly-formed working class party, the I.L.P. Humphries was not elected, however.

The trades council then turned to the unpaid November election expenses. The two elections had cost £43 and the amount raised was only £15. The council had authorised the expenditure and they would have to pay. C.C.Cooke, the chairman, thought that those who had voted for the candidates should pay. Granger also was prepared to take advantage of the discomforture of the New Unionists. He said that the candidates had incurred the expenditure and were no doubt ready to meet their responsibilities in this regard ('Laughter'). But this would be unfair and those who had voted for the elections should pay. This was carried, the secretary being instructed to bring the matter before the various trades represented on the trades council.

The trades council meeting in February 1894 followed up the resolution at the TUC the previous September regarding the acceptance of a socialist policy. David Miller, who like Henson and Eades was a Cabinet Maker, moved:

> That this Council views with satisfaction the acceptance by the recent
> Trades Union Congress held in Belfast, of the principle of collective

ownership and control of all the means of production and distribution;
and further records its opinion that in the realisation of such principle
lies the only real and permanent solution of the Labour problem.

In moving the motion Miller said the theories might sound fantastic, but
they were gradually coming into force. E.Luck of the Amalgamated
Carpenters & Joiners seconded the motion. Ward, an ASE delegate,
opposed it and thought the system advocated was a disgrace to trade
unionism. A good and honest trade unionist had never been an agitator.
It was through these men that trade unionism was going down. Agitators
were doing a great deal of harm and his own society had made a grant
to one of these agitators. Jephcott said that he belonged to the same
society and whatever money had been given to John Burns had been
freely voted by their members from a levy to provide such funds. If any
other member of the society got into Parliament, he too would receive
payment. Eades spoke in support of the Co-operative movement as a
means to the end in view. Haddleton, the secretary, said that they should
have control of the whole of manufacturing trade so that the profits should
go to the working classes. All land owners should pay rent for the land
they possess and those who had stolen land by Act of Parliament should
hand it back. The resolution was voted on and passed.

E.Grist (Carpenters & Joiners) then moved:

> That this Council heartily approves of the introduction into the House
> of Commons of the Bill for the Nationalisation of Mines and Minerals,
> believing such a measure to be the only reliable preventative against such
> another calamity as the late Lock-out in the coal-mining industry.

Grist said that he would not be unwilling to take the mines from the
owners, but it would perhaps be cheaper to buy them out than to fight
for them. Gilliver then suggested that 'Land' be put before 'Mines'. No
one seems to have opposed this resolution and it was passed. It sealed the
night when the trades council adopted Socialism as its programme in a
city where the Lib-Labs remained deeply embedded.

Socialism And The TUC

The struggle for Socialist policies was carried over into the 1894 TUC in
September. John Burns was chairman of the Congress when it opened
and reported that of the 380 delegates, at least 100 were members of
parliament, members of town or county councils, School or Poor Law
boards or magistrates. The Birmingham Trades Council delegate was the
Unionist Lib-Lab president, C.C.Cooke. An attempt was made at this
Congress to remove 'Clause 4'. It was done by J.J.Rudge of the Flint
Glassworkers moving a resolution supporting nationalisation of the land,
mines and mineral rents only. This was scotched by Keir Hardie moving
that 'and the whole means of production, distribution and exchange' be
substituted for 'mines and royalty rents'. This amendment was passed by
the decisive vote of 219 to 61. But another Lib-Lab, Sam Woods, was
elected as secretary of the Parliamentary Committee against Fenwick, the
previous secretary and the intervention of Tom Mann. Will Thorne
caused uproar by requesting that each candidate state how much time he

was willing to devote to the office for the £200 per year salary. Tom Mann, of course, stated that he was prepared to spend all his time, but the other two candidates were outraged, holding their rights and privileges as individuals inviolable, not surrendering other official connections and stating that they would give as much time to the Parliamentary Committee 'as was necessary'. The change from a North East miner M.P. to a Lancashire miner M.P. reflected the growth of the Miners' Federation, strongly represented at the Congress for the first time, against the old Miners' National Union.

The issue of federation was again exercising the minds of trade unionists and a fraternal delegate from the American Federation of Labour was another first at this Congress. A committee of fifteen was also appointed to pursue the question of federation.

John Burns again topped the poll for the Parliamentary Committee and was joined by Ben Tillett and Will Thorne. W.J.Davis was third among the unsuccessful candidates with 88 votes.

The 1894 TUC ended with an innocuous sounding resolution that was to have very large effects. It was moved by John Burns and proposed a committee to review standing orders.

When the 1895 TUC convened, it operated under these new standing orders. One of the main changes was that trades councils were effectively excluded by a provision that no trade unionists could be represented twice, and trades councils could attend representing only those trade unions not directly represented at Congress. The other two main changes were that no delegate could be appointed who was not working at his trade or an official of his union; these standing orders also introduced for the first time the card vote with one vote for every thousand members affiliated to the TUC. There was uproar at the first session as the chairman operated the new standing orders without the prior approval of Congress, but these were eventually accepted. The result was that people like Keir Hardie ceased to be eligible as delegates (Hardie had already in fact absented himself by being in America on a speaking tour and was more concerned with the I.L.P. and the next election rather than the TUC.) Another result was that no Birmingham trades council attended either in 1895 or subsequently.

The 1896 TUC met in pessimistic mood. Membership had been static for some years at around one million. In the Parliamentary elections the year before none of the 28 ILP candidates had been elected and only nine Lib-Labs. Joseph Chamberlain was passing 'progressive' measures such as his Workmen's Compensation Act and a Conciliation Act. These tended to strengthen Lib-Lab views, but nothing much was expected from the Conservative government. In addition, a most determined attack on trade union rights by employers had been under way since the early 1890s. Yet another attempt was made to remove 'Clause 4' by the Power Loom Overlookers. It asked that all previous motions on nationalisation of all the means of production etc. be rescinded and in their place the nationalisation of the land, mines, mineral royalties, and railways, together with the municipalisation of water, artificial light and tramways substituted. This misfired when the chairman ruled that previous decisions of Congress could not be rescinded. The movers then argued for the second part of the motion as being more realistic than the millenial schemes of socialism. Opposition this time was led by Pete Curran, the militant London gas worker, who argued that anyone who thought it was possible to reconcile the interests of the labourer and the capitalist ought to be in a lunatic asylum; but it was perfectly possible to reconcile the claims of labour and capital by nationalisation of the means of production. The motion was carried, but when Curran asked whether it did in fact rescind previous motions of Congress he received the ambiguous reply from the chair that each Congress legislated for the following Parliamentary Committee and that alone.

At this 1896 Congress J.Holmes of the National Hosiery Federation moved that the Industrial Union (of which W.J.Davis was secretary) representing organised workers and federated employers was a step in the right direction as a means of preventing disputes and promoting good feeling between employers and workers. Both Davis and J.Taylor of Dudley, representing the Midland Counties Trades Federation spoke in favour of the motion, but it was defeated. At this Congress W.J.Davis was returned to the Parliamentary Committee for his second stint, which was to last from 1896 to 1901. This Congress welcomed a fraternal delegate from Australia where state Labour governments were enacting 8-Hours Bills. It also accepted by a large majority an invitation to attend the next American Federation of Labour convention, despite objections of 'costly junketings'. But there was no discussion of Labour representation at the 1896 TUC.

The Trades Council And Labour Representation

Returning once again to Birmingham to review events between the 1894 TUC and the 1897 TUC in Birmingham, the arguments concerning Labour representation were again raised at the TUC report back meeting at the trades council, in October 1894. Again it was an SDF delegate who raised the issue. On the agenda, in the name of Arthur Burns, was the motion:

> That the motion with reference to the Labour Representation Committee now standing on the Minute Book be rescinded, and the following substituted in its stead:- That the different Trades Unions and branches of Trades Unions in Birmingham, who are in favour of Direct Labour Representation, be requested to appoint a delegate to form an Independent Labour Representation Committee, and that this Council appoints one delegate to represent them as a separate organisation.

Before the motion was put, A.Keegan explained the existing position of the trades council. Labour representation had been referred to the Standing Orders committee who had referred it to a separate committee which had recommended, 'That an independent Labour candidate shall be regarded as such who receives the support of the Trades Council irrespective of his political opinions.' Keegan then moved the acceptance of this committee's recommendation. This, of course, was a retreat from the previous position and put the whole question back into the melting pot. W.J.Davis, naturally, supported the recommendation. Burns was put on the defensive. He thought there was danger in allying themselves with any political party. If they made conditions with one party, they were defeated by the other. R.Hine, the ASE socialist, thought it was time they shook off the shackles of party. They were strong enough to return their own candidate. Gilliver did not see why they should not work with parties for the benefit of labour. Granger agreed with the recommendation. Their experience the previous year showed that the course then pursued distracted them from their trade union influence; besides, advocacy of so-called 'independent' representation coming from well-known party men tainted the movement with suspicion, Granger argued. T.Henson opposed the recommendation in a long speech as did Joe Tanner, but we are not given their arguments. Councillor Stevens did not think that a man's trade unionism should be shaken because he belonged to a political party. It was asking too much of a man to deprive himself of his political opinions. When the recommendation was put to the vote it was approved by 45 votes to 30. Another round had gone to the Lib-Labs.

Burns' motion was deferred to a special meeting on October 20th at which Keir Hardie was a special guest. E.Luck seconded the motion arguing that only independent labour representation would secure the adoption of a programme that would emancipate their class. Gilliver opposed. They all wanted *direct* Labour representation; they differed with regard to the attainment of it. Anything done would come with greatest force from the trades council and not from a separate organisation. He thought, therefore, that the recommendation passed at the last trades council meeting was far better than the one now proposed. Grist then asked what that recommendation had been and after the secretary had read it, Grist asked if the resolution had been submitted to the various unions and branches who proposed to contribute to independent Labour representation. He believed that several societies had agreed to double their subscriptions, giving half to the trades council and half to the proposed committee. C.C.Cooke, the chairman, then said that a circular had been sent to every society, but they did not yet know the results. A motion by Granger and Ramsden to adjourn the debate until this information was known was defeated by 50 votes to 44. Keegan explained that any candidate nominated by the trades council and receiving its full support would have his expenses paid by the council if he did not claim political support. Haddleton, the trades council secretary, spoke in favour of the motion and then Granger, remarking that the secretary had spoken 'a tremendous amount of rubbish', again suggested adjourning the debate. But it was decided to put the matter to the vote. The resolution was lost by 49 or 53 (the tellers could not agree which) to 46. Another round to the Lib-Labs.

When Keir Hardie rose to speak he was circumspect, but outspoken regarding socialism. He had listened to the preceding debate with interest, and if the discussion had been planned for his benefit it could not have been better planned. Looking back over TUC reports he had noticed that the second TUC had been held in Birmingham and he was struck by the similarities with many of the issues raised twenty-five years before. But then the talk had been of profit sharing. Since then ideas had broadened and workers now took the position that there is no one with whom to share the profits. Workers did not admit the right of any able-bodied idler, whether he called himself a duke or a capitalist, to share with him, the wealth that he (the worker) had created. The Birmingham TUC was the first at which Labour representation had been mooted. Hardie felt that the reason why they had not a larger number of Labour men in Parliament was because their forces were divided. They should see how important it was to wean the mind of the honest, straightforward, susceptible working man from his allegiance to his party; for if the trades council gave countenance to party politics municipally, they bound the tie imperially, and made it all the more difficult to break it asunder. He was convinced that ere three years had elapsed, the trifling differences which separated the Independent Labour Party from the Labour men would have disappeared. They were at present in a transition stage between old ideas and new ones. Hard words would be said on both sides which neither would care to justify in calmer moments. But as long as they admitted that each was honestly endeavouring to do what they could, they would achieve their aims, Hardie concluded.

The Election Committee of the Trades Council continued to meet and recommend Labour candidates, but its recommendations continued to provoke controversy. In February 1895 W.J.Davis, then chairman of the Committee, reported that it had considered candidates for the Board of Guardians, but as they had no money, they had decided to nominate 'friends of labour.' Two Trades Council members, however had been elected to the Aston Board of Guardians. These were C.C.Cooke and G.H.Humphreys. The election expenses of the former were £13-6-6d. and of the latter 4d. These expenses had been defrayed by various societies and friends of labour. With regard to the School Board contest, the Labour candidate had headed the Liberal eight. His expenses were only £34-10-0d. whereas 'one of the political parties' had spent £200 on polling cards alone. In consequence of the lamented death of Eli Bloor a vacancy had occurred on the City council. He (Davis) had been approached by members of the Liberal Association, but he was not prepared to stand unless his name was submitted to the verdict of the trades council. The election committee considered that the vacant seat belonged to Labour and therefore they had nominated C.C.Cooke, whose adoption he now recommended. Haddleton seconded the motion. L.Gascoigne then proposed an amendment, 'Seeing that there is already a labour candidate who is also a member of the trades council in the field at Bordesley, we do not deem it advisable to run a candidate in oppostion to him.' ('Oh! oh!' and 'Hear, hear') Much as he admired Cooke, he did not think he would stand a chance in these circumstances. Middleton then expressed the hope that Jephcott (the Labour candidate in question) would show his loyalty to the trades council by refusing the nomination of a party and leaving the choice to the trades council. Alfred Keegan (who had taken over the chair from Cooke for this discussion) said he should not really accept Gascoigne's amendment as the trades council had previously resolved to choose Labour candidates 'irrespective of parties.'. N.Donovan objected to the selection of men intimately connected with political parties and nominated Alfred Bigby of ASE no.3 branch. This amendment was seconded. Cooke was asked whether if selected by the trades council he would also be the candidate of a political party. He replied ambiguously that the Unionists had selected their candidate (Jephcott) and he did not anticipate that the Liberal Party would ask him to stand. A long and confused discussion then ensued. W.J.Davis in reply regretted that there would be two labour candidates and if Mr. Jephcott had done what he and Mr.Cooke had done, he would have been accepted as the trades council's nominee. Davis appealed for Bigby's nomination to be withdrawn, but it was not and Cooke was accepted by 57 votes to 17. Cooke then stated that £50 had already been promised and he could say that no cost for the contest would fall on the trades council. He regretted, however, that he was in opposition to Mr. Jephcott, for whom he had the greatest regard. For his part, Jephcott said he reciprocated the feelings of Cooke and his intention was to conduct the contest in a gentlemanly manner. So the dilemmas of the trades council had landed it with two Labour candidates for the same election.

But Cooke did not stand at this election. Jephcott was elected and there was uproar at the next trades council meeting, which was 'well attended by both delegates and the public.' The main item at this meeting was the relations of the president (C.C.Cooke) to the Election Committee, both Cooke and the election Committee having resigned. Keegan, the vice-president, occupied the chair, but after a great deal of confusion regarding the order of business, Haddleton, the secretary, took over the chair, as Keegan was a member of the Election Committee.

Davis said he rose with considerable reluctance to perform a very grave duty. He recalled how Cooke had been chosen as candidate at the meeting on Saturday 2nd. February and how emphatic Cooke had been in accepting their nomination. But the following Wednesday Cooke had waited on the election committee and informed them that he wished to be relieved of the candidature and suggested that Jephcott might be allowed a walk-over. Cooke had given a number of reasons for standing down, including one which was very weighty with him (Davis.) The committee told Cooke that he had had three weeks to consider whether to stand and if there were any doubt in his mind he should not have accepted the nomination. They were a poor body and could not afford to convene a special meeting to elect another candidate. (Nor would there have been much time, for the election was on February 16th, — G.B.) Under these circumstances the election committee would have been deficient in pluck and principle if they did not tender their resignation on such a vital issue ('Applause'). Cooke was a staunch advocate of labour representation, and his conduct as president of the trades council had been all that could be desired. Therefore, for such a man to trip us ('Sell us') and throw us overboard ruthlessly was a betrayal of the Labour party in Birmingham. If the council thought Cooke had been right, they would reinstate him as president, but if they thought the cause of labour had been hurt or betrayed, they would support the action of the election committee.

Middleton, another member of the election committee, supported everything that Davis had said. He added the vital piece of information that prior to the Saturday night when he was nominated Cooke had said to a friend, who had then told Councillor Stevens, that if a Gladstonian were put in the field against Jephcott, he (Cooke) would not go to the poll. They had been given an object lesson in favour of the principles of the Independent Labour party. It was absolutely necessary to demand from persons selected to represent them they they wipe their hands, for the time being at any rate, of their political association.

In fact, Jephcott had been opposed by a Gladstonian, the result being:

A.R.Jephcott (Liberal Unionist) 1805
C.Smith (Gladstonian Association) 1044

The election had obviously caused problems for both the political parties. The Unionists eventually chose Jephcott, because the seat had previously been a Labour one and James Moffatt, who had expected to receive the nomination, stood down. It would also seem that the Gladstonian candidate was a late choice if there had been no nomination at the time of Cooke's endorsement by the trades council. Only 36% of the electorate had gone to the poll and this was considered a very apathetic response accounted for by the fact that the Unionists had been confident of taking the seat and only the Gladstonians had put any effort into the campaign.

Returning to the trades council meeting, the next speaker was Alan Granger, himself a Gladstonian Liberal, who challenged Middleton's statement saying that the whole discussion now depended on whether it was true or not. This brought the response from Keegan that Councillor Stevens told him what Middleton had said and Davis confirmed that Councillor Stevens had told him. Davis had then said to Stevens 'You had better come and make that statement to the trades council yourself.'

Cooke then denied that he had made the statement attributed to him, saying that it was positively untrue and a wicked lie. Robert Toller, the secretary of the Gasworkers, who was also a member of the election committee then confused matters further by saying that he had advised Cooke to withdraw from Bordesley as he (Toller?) was not going to be placed in the position which he found some of the committee wished to place his society in. He had not been present when Cooke was nominated and if he had been present he would have opposed the nomination.

Gascoigne then moved that the resignation of the Election Committee be accepted and W.F.Hill of the electro-platers said, 'I will second that with pleasure.' The chairman, however, moved this out of order on the grounds that the election committee had been appointed by the Standing Orders committee which had refused to accept their resignation. Several other delegates spoke in favour of accepting the resignation of the election committee, but ultimately a resolution moved by Wilkinson and seconded by Bigby that the action of the Standing Orders committee in not accepting the resignation of the election committee be approved was carried with only four dissentients.

Wilkinson next moved the acceptance of Cooke's resignation. Cooke then addressed the meeting. He said that he really had nothing to add to what Davis had told them. Many circumstances had brought about his decision to withdraw. There was the urging of friends — trades council friends, not political friends, there had been no wire-pulling. That he had lost the confidence of the trades council went without saying and he thought it advisable to resign.

Clifton then put yet a different face on the matter by saying that he was a delegate of the same society as Cooke (the city Lampmen) and he could assure the trades council that his decision to withdraw was made not by the influence of any political party, but more through the influence of Cooke's own society. They had recommended his withdrawal because of the impossibility of their being able to go out and assist him because of pressure of work and they knew that if Cooke's own society could not work for him, no other society would.

The socialists, Burns and Donovan, then spoke against Cooke, Donovan's speech, we are told, being interrupted by outbursts of impatience 'as no coherence could be perceived in his remarks.'

Jephcott then asked the council to exercise some liberality towards Cooke. He (Jephcott) was sorry if he had been the cause of storms in the trades council, but while he was a city Councillor he would consider it his duty to further the interests of the class he belonged to and trade unionism in particular.

By now it was getting late and, amid considerable confusion, the chairman moved a resolution that the motion be now put and this was carried. Hill, Granger and Davis, among others, objected to this procedure, Davis saying that where the honour of an individual was affected, it was wrong to put the question. The chairman said he had sympathy with Davis, but he must be guided by the majority. Dawson angrily exclaimed that a resolution on Cooke's resignation was being put without an opportunity for amendments and Hill interposed to say that he had an amendment to put. Amid further confusion, Wilkinson, the mover of the resolution against Cooke, said the chairman ought to take amendments. But the resolution was put and carried, amid a general exodus of delegates for the door. Within two years of this resignation, Cooke was president of the trades council Election Committee.

The next major trades council debate on labour representation took place later in 1895. In the afternoon of July 6th. a delegate conference with 260 delegates approved an extremely detailed programme and the setting up of a Birmingham United Labour Federation. The Programme was in four parts:

Constitutional Reform

1. Adult Suffrage.
2. Each elector to have one vote only.
3. State payment of Returning Officers' fees.
4. State payment of members.
5. State ownership of the land, and all instruments of wealth production, distribution and exchange.
6. The abolition of the House of Lords.

Legislative Reform.

1. A general 8-hours day with trade exemption.
2. No contracting-out of Employers' Liability.
3. The extension of the Factory & Workshops Act to all trades, with an increase of workmen inspectors.
4. Reform of the Poor Laws by which ready help could be given to deserving poor without the present degrading conditions.

Taxation Reform.

1. An Act to empower local authorities to rate ground values.
2. Abolition of all duties on food.
3. A substantial reduction in Tobacco duties.
4. An extension of the graduated Income Tax so as to lighten the burden on those least able to bear it.

Muncipal Reform.

1. Evening meetings for all representative bodies, so as to assist intelligent workers employed during the day to take part in civil work, and to enable those to attend who desire to see how public promises are broken.
2. The Fair Contract clause to be rigidly enforced, with a penalty for violation.
3. Labour Representatives to be appointed on all public charities and institutions.
4. The erection of Workmen's Dwellings at fair rents covering costs of erection and maintenance only.
5. Municipal ownership of the tram systems.
6. The 8-hour day for all municipal employees.
7. Municipal responsibility for the increasing (numbers) of the unemployed.
8. Each applicant's claim for public work shall be considered on its merits and age to be no bar to employment.

In the evening the trades council met to consider the programme and discuss Labour representation. Davis, as chairman of the Election Committee and who had also chaired the afternoon proceedings, reported. He said he had rather a large order for them. A great deal of the programme was contentious and they had so little time. He then outlined the programme and said that a number of gentlemen had been invited to co-operate with the election Committee to consider the present crisis (the pending general election — G.B.) and whether they should invite a Labour representative to stand or whether they had the means of paying his election expenses. Programme and representation went together, Davis explained, because it was necessary to have a programme that was agreed for Labour representatives whether they be for MPs, city council, or local Boards. The Birmingham United Labour Federation would not fuse the organisations in the town, but federate them so that when they came together to choose representatives, they knew the outlines of the programme they were supporting.

Davis received general support from Middleton, Hodenot, Keegan, Donovan and Pritchard. Criticism came from Gamble, a Prudential Insurance agent, who said he was sorry that the programme had been passed in the afternoon because they had been twitted that the trades council had been captured by the Independent Labour Party and he strongly objected to choosing representatives on the grounds laid down. Cooke also, of course, was critical. He did not think that the afternoon conference had done much harm, but he was satisfied that it would do no good. A great deal of the programme would never be realised in his lifetime. They should tackle the questions most affecting them and get them settled, never mind by which party. It was a harebrained movement, bringing the trades council into contempt, Cooke considered. He did not wish to say anything disrespectful of the gentlemen who had enjoyed three hours talk, but the apathy remarked on by Davis which showed itself in the smallest meeting the trades council had had on the eve of a great crisis was an illustration of the lack of enthusiasm. He protested at being dragged at the heels of the Independent Labour Party.

Davis in reply admitted that there was lukewarmness to the scheme, but said the history of political movements showed that there had always been an advanced guard and Cooke should be joining with them and not providing the hostile Birmingham press with good copy. The report was adopted with only two dissentients.

The lack of enthusiasm seemed justified. At the 1895 general election the Conservatives were returned to power, none of the 28 ILP candidates was elected and only nine Lib-Labs. The pessimism still existed in the autumn of the next year when the 1896 TUC met, as we have seen.

The Birmingham 1897 TUC

But the 1897 TUC was held in Birmingham and by then confidence was returning, the Congress was slickly and colourfully organised, and gave a fillip to the local movement. As was usual at the time, the host city provided a larger number of delegates than usually attended. The representation from Birmingham was:

Union	No. of Delegates	TUC Reg. Members.	Names of Delegates
Nat. Amalg. Society of Brassworkers	5	12,000	W.J.Davis, J.Ramsden, W.,McStocker, A.Cashmore, G.Benwell.
Bedstead Workers Assn	2	2,800	W.Mills, J.Wolverson.
Nat.Society Cycle Makers	1	1,647	J.Ward
U.K.Society of Coach Makers	1	6,500	W.Robin
Alliance of Cabinet Makers & Furnishing Trades	2	4,000	A.Eades
Amalg. electro-Platers Union	1	463	R.Ricketts.
Birmingham & Dist. File Smiths Assn	1	90	W.R.Tubb.
B'ham Dist.Nat.Union Gas Workers and General Labourers	–	–	S.Lakin
Gas Workers, Brick Makers & Gen. Labs.	2	3,500	R.Toller,J.Floyd.
Nat. Union Metal wire & Tube Makers	1	1,700	J.Cuthbertson
Amalg. Musicians Union	2	3,340	J.Ward.
United Operative Plumbers Assn G.G.	2	9,173	W.H.Gilbert.
Sporting & Military Gun Makers	1	–	S.G.Middleton
Amalg.Society Tailors	4	16,000	M.Byrne.
Amalg.Toolmakers, Engineers and Machinists	1	2,372	A.H.Betts.
Amalg.Assn Tramway, Hackney Carriage etc. Employees	2	6,000	A.Jones
Nat.amalg. Tinplate Workers	2	3,287	Councillor J.V.Stevens. A.Harvey
Typographical Association	4	14,000	A.Granger.
United Assn Patternmakers	1	3,781	D.Jones

Some of these are local societies; others are national unions which did not usually send Birmingham delegates, notably the Tinplate Workers and the Typographical Assn. The Birmingham Filesmiths was the smallest organisation represented at the Congress.

By a long-standing precedent (soon to be broken), a local man was voted president and became chairman of the Congress. One might have expected this to be W.J.Davis (his turn was to come in 1913), but the honour fell to J.V.Stevens who had previously attended only one TUC as a delegate, although he was a local councillor (which was important in this context) and his name was well known as he had recently been arrested in a campaign for free speech in Birmingham. Again by precedent (again soon to be broken) the president was allowed a Presidential Address which generally took up a considerable part of the second morning's proceedings. Stevens seems to have been relatively brief. His main theme was federation. This was topical in view of the movement of employers to federate; this had resulted in the powerful Engineering Employers' Federation which had declared war on the engineering unions and locked them out. Stevens reckoned that if one million of the two million existing trade unionists federated and levied themselves 6d. a week, a fund of £25,000 a week would be available. The best way to preserve peace was to prepare for war, he maintained. Stevens' other main theme was the 8-hour Day, the case for the legal enactment of which had been strengthened by the Engineers' Lock-out. Stevens ended with the following lines and sat down to loud applause:

> No great deed is done by falterers who ask for certainty,
> No good is certain but the steadfast mind;
> The undivided will to seek the good,
> 'Tis that compels the elements, and wrings
> A human music from the indifferent air.

The vote of thanks to Stevens was moved by Betts.

The most important result of the 1897 TUC was the decision to elect a committee to promote Federation. This led to a special TUC in 1899 which set up a General Federation of Trade Unions separate from the TUC.

The impetus to Birmingham representation at the TUC given by the 1897 Congress continued to the Bristol Congress in 1898 where Bedstead Workers, Brass Workers, Tramway etc. Employees, Toolmakers and electro-plate Operatives continued to send delegates. In addition the Flint Glassmakers were, rather unusually, represented. W.J.Davis had been chairman of the Parliamentary Committee again in the previous year. Again, the Congress did little but bemoan the ineffectiveness of the Parliamentary Committee and the annual TUC deputation to the Home Secretary and President of the Board of Trade. Local participation took the form of a successful motion by Davis to amend the ambiguities of the 1896 Truck Act and Sam Lakin's seconding of a motion regretting the limited number of workers covered by the Workmen's Compensation Act.

It was the 1899 TUC which decisively moved forward the question of Labour representation. But with the employers' offensive still under way and the looming jingoism of the Boer War, the debate stirred little heat or enthusiasm. J.H.Holmes, the secretary of the Amalgamated Society of Railway Servants moved:

> That this Congress having regard to its decisions in previous years, and with a view to securing a better representation of the interests of Labour in the House of Commons, hereby instructs the Parliamentary Committee to invite the co-operation of all Co-operatives, Socialistic, Trade Unions and other working class organisations to jointly co-operate on lines mutually agreed upon, in convening a Special Congress of representatives from such of the above named organisations as may be willing to take part, to devise ways and means for securing the return of an increased number of Labour members to the next Parliament.

The motion was supported by a succession of speakers mainly from the general unions, and opposed mainly by some miners and most textile workers. The last speaker in the debate was a Birmingham man, W.J.Simmonds of the Cabinet Makers and Furnishing Trades Alliance. He supported the motion, saying that there was direct antagonism between the two main political parties and the Labour party. It was their duty to utilise the powerful weapon of independent political action in the interests of the working classes in the same way that the Liberal and Conservative parties did on behalf of their adherents. At this stage the chairman suggested that the matter had been sufficiently discussed and nothing further could be said with advantage. A show of hands showed a majority in favour of closing the debate and when this was challenged a card vote showed 688,000 to 273,000 for closure. The motion was then voted on and passed by the narrow margin of 546,000 votes to 434,000. Thus was the historic decision taken that was to bring into existence the Labour Representation Committee, which in 1906 became the Labour Party.

Origins of Birmingham Labour Party

So we can return once again to Birmingham to see how the Labour Party finally came into existence in the town. The Birmingham United Labour Federation set up in July 1895 does not appear to have taken off and at the trades council meeting of December 1896 A.C.Lloyd of the electro-Plate workers moved:

> That for the purpose of effectually organising the labour interest, the Executive Committee be instructed to take steps to form Labour Electoral Associations in each ward of Birmingham and Aston; and that societies affiliated to the Trades Council be asked to guarantee definite annual subscriptions to a fund for the payment of election expenses, and for the remuneration of labour representatives on public bodies.

The subsequent discussion showed both how actual experience of labour representation was shaping new demands and also interesting shifts of emphasis of the Lib-Labs. Lloyd said that it was imperative that they should follow the lines of the other political parties to form Labour Electoral Associations and also canvass. William Hill, another electro-plater, seconded the motion but said he was inclined to think that the scheme was too advanced. They had been told over and over again that the labour party had no standing in the town, but it was his firm conviction that if they could band themselves together in the different wards they would cast off that stigma. John Erskine, the Tory brush-maker, took exception altogether to the resolution as a matter particularly foreign to their meeting. He believed there was a grander motive in federation in every society and community than in any political action by liberal or any other denomination. Gilliver, the old Lib-Lab, was in retreat. He considered that the resolution 'from its comprehensiveness was not within their grasp, but that was nothing against it.' Certainly if they wished for Labour representation they must send their own men, despite the fact that those outside their class were willing to help them. Politics were in existence. He did not say it was their duty to support these political associations,but he did not see why they should not have one working man representative in each ward of the City council.

Henson, who had been the staunchest advocate of labour representation, rather surprisingly said he thought the resolution went a little too far. He moved an amendment that 'Aston' be removed from the resolution. Toller was strongly in favour of the principle of the resolution, but he thought it should be referred back to the Election Committee for presentation in a way which would be acceptable to the trades council. From his own experience on the Board of Guardians, where nearly the whole of the clerical work passed through his hands, he thought it would be a great help. Allan Granger was also being forced from his Lib-Lab stance. He thought that for 'all wards' they might substitute 'some convenient wards'. He would not discuss the question on its merits, but the one thing they all wanted was representation. But were they prepared to pay for it? He found, as a rule, that the great bulk of societies affiliated to the trades council were not prepared to do so. They should remember that election expenses were a costly affair to the individual who stood. Other speakers in suport of the resolution were Middleton, Tooth, Bingley and O'Connor. When Lloyd replied he said that he accepted the verbal alteration suggested by Granger, and the resolution, in that weakened form, was passed with three dissentients.

In 1897 there was a triumph for Labour representation. Robert Toller stood at a by-election at Saltley as a candidate of the Labour Association of that ward. Toller was a leading trade unionist in the town, general secretary of the Birmingham based Amalg. Society of Gas-workers, Brickmakers & General Labourers as well as being a delegate to the trades council. But he was not nominated by the election Committee of the trades council. Toller, however, was the first Labour councillor on the city council who did not owe his seat to Liberal organised support.

Two candidates for the School Board elections of 1897 were nominated by the trades council Election Committee. They were Arthur Eades and Joseph Millington of the Amalg. Society of Railway Servants. Neither was successful, but at the December 1897 trades council 'inquest' it was considered that if only one candidate had stood, he might have been successful. Against this, however, must be set the fact that the Rev. Pinchard, an avowed Socialist, had also stood.

In the atmosphere of increasing attacks on trade unions in the later 1890s further progress was difficult. In October 1898 the trades council Election Committee surrendered abjectly to the Lib-Labs. It thanked Stevens and Jephcott for what they had done for working people and requested that they allow themselves to be renominated. Again the resistance was led by the SDF. George Tooth opposed the resolution saying that if Stevens and Jephcott really sided with Labour their place was within the ranks of Labour without the aid of the political parties to which they belonged. The Election Committee's recommendations were approved, however.

But the next month, November 1898, circumstances forced another approach to the matter. G.Pinson reported that there were pending retirements from the city council. Because of the differing views of members and their being allied with different parties, the Election Committee had refrained from opposing sitting members of the city council. But where there was a vacancy in a ward with large numbers of trade unionists, the Committee felt justified in nominating a candidate for the vacancy. They therefore unanimously recommended that Arthur Eades, secretary of the trades council, be nominated for the next vacancy in Deritend ward. Further, that a committee be formed in the ward immediately and that a public meeting be called in the ward as soon as possible after the declaration of the vacancy. Hill seconded the resolution saying he regretted they had not been prepared with a candidate in any of the wards at the recent local elections and he thought it showed lack of energy on the part of the Committee. Redmond was also pleased that the Election Committee was at last doing something to justify its existence. Tooth said he would oppose the report unless their candidate was absolutely free from party trammels. Eades assured Tooth that he was unconnected with any political party. He (Eades) fully recognised that the only way to get trade unionist work done was to have representatives free from party ties and the trades council was the body from which labour candidates should emanate.

Dobson strongly deprecated the idea of the trades council nominating a candidate when they had no chance whatever of winning. In the case of Deritend, three candidates had been run at various times and had made an ignominious show. The discussion was prolonged, but the eventual decision was to endorse the Election Committee's recommendation to run Eades.

At the December trades council, the Election Committee reported. Eades had been the first candidate nominated and conditions appeared favourable. The Liberal Association had decided not to stand. George Jackson had declined to oppose a Labour candidate and was publicly supporting Eades. The one other opponent nominated, Ellaway, appeared not to be a strong candidate. But disaster struck. Another working class candidate appeared and split the Labour vote. In addition, the weather on polling day was unfavourable and the other two candidates were well supplied with vehicles. The result was: Ellaway 842: Eades 679: Pentland 649.

Many more active workers would be needed if seats were going to be won, the Election Committee warned. Expenses had been £45 of which £16 was in hand and £9 promised. Delegates were asked to appeal to their societies to cover the deficit and the trades council voted £10 towards this.

The Birmingham Trades Journal for December 1898 also carried a long and revealing editorial, presumably written by Allan Granger, the Gladstonian Lib-Lab, who was the editor. He first pointed out that nearly

5,000 electors voted at Deritend, but 2,700 did not, and most of these were working men. This demonstrated the degree of apathy to be overcome. Was it possible to run candidates independent of party? Granger asked. Elections were casual affairs for trade societies and other labour organisations, but for Political Associations they were the one object of their existence. Men living by their daily toil had little leisure to devote to the necessary work of canvassing and bringing up votes. In addition, many of the more enthusiastic workers lived at considerable distances and it was difficult after a day's labour to walk miles to the scene of action and then canvass on dark, wintry evenings in courts of an unknown district. Granger then went on to hint at more sinister matters. Instances in Birmingham were not unknown where independent action was strongly resented by political associations. The burden of implicit obedience was sometimes too heavy to bear especially when such obedience was demanded by underlings and hirelings of these associations, always on tap to pour forth their foul and false accusations and inventions. These disreputable methods nowadays were within the knowledge of the people, hence the prevalent hatred towards political parties. Upon this difficult question he was not disposed to enlarge, they were dangerous questions to discuss in the paper, and were best left alone.

The December 1898 *Trades Journal* also gave a breakdown (with portraits) of the meagre working class representation in Birmingham and Aston at that time:

City Council
1. Councillor J.V.Stevens (Gladstonian Lib/Lab) St.Thomas' Ward.
2. Councillor A.R.Jephcott (Unionist Lib/Lab) Bordesley Ward.
3. Councillor Robert Toller (Labour Association) Saltley Ward.

W.J.Davis who had been the first Labour representative in 1880 had resigned three years later when he became a Factory Inspector. Allan Granger, the second Labour representative elected in 1882, had resigned in 1893 and Eli Bloor, elected in 1883 had died in 1895. There was no Labour representation at all at that time on the Birmingham School Board or the Board of Guardians and, of course, there were no members of Parliament. With regard to Aston, C.C.Cooke, Joseph Floyd, Edward Bentley and John Millington were on the Aston Poor Law Board of Guardians and S.G.Middleton, the recently resigned secretary of the trades council and a member of the School Workers' Union, was on the Aston School Board.

In February 1899, events were again forcing the trades council's Election Committee's hand. It was reported that there were plans to stand Richard Bell, general secretary of the Amalgamated Society of Railway Servants as an independent Labour parliamentary candidate in East Birmingham. There was a large population of railway workers in that area, and a prime attraction was that the ASRS was willing to pay a large slice of the election expenses. The proposal was unanimously endorsed and members turned to the vexed question of an election fund. One proposal was that the affiliation fee be raised, the extra going to the election fund. The problem here was that some societies could approve higher contributions, but others could only vote a lump sum from their funds. Other societies could find funds, but only when the candidate was one of their own union. Another question was how many societies were actually in favour of independent labour representation; a recent appeal for funds for the purpose had not been encouraging, it was stated. Lastly, there were reports that the National Federation of Employers intended to take political action to cripple the funds of trade unions. (This anticipated both the final Taff Vale decision and the Osborne Judgement of 1906 — G.B.) In view of all these difficulties, the Election Committee had resolved to send a questionnaire to all societies, bearing in mind that a similar exercise two years before had elicited replies from only three or four societies. The questionnaire read:

1.   Are you in favour of Direct Labour Representation on all Public Bodies?
2.   What amount are you prepared to subscribe per annum towards an Election Fund?
3.   By what method are you prepared to subscribe, either (a) by a donation from your General, or Local or Management Fund (b) by increasing your subscription to the Trades Council and stipulating the amount for election purposes or (c) will your members agree to levy themselves a small amount each quarter for such a purpose.

The report was accepted and replies to the questionnaire requested within three months.

1900 saw two key developments. One was the first Labour man standing for Parliament. It was J.V.Stevens, the local man and not Bell. He stood as a Liberal and was endorsed by the trades council and therefore was a Lib-Lab candidate. He polled 2,835 votes to the Conservative J.E.Stone's 4,989. Fought in the jingoist Boer War period, it was a notable result.

The second event was that in February 1900 the Special Conference of Labour Representatives called by the TUC met at the Memorial Hall, London and set up the Labour Representation Committee, which became the Labour Party. 129 delegates representing 568,000 trade unionists and socialist societies took this historic decision. Birmingham was strongly represented at this Conference by W.J.Davis and W.C.McStocker of the Brassworkers, Sam Lakin, one of thirteen delegates of the Gas Workers, Robert Toller representing the local Gasworkers etc. and J.Cuthbertson of the Wire and Tube Makers.

The final shape of independent Labour representation had emerged. Such candidates were not to be chosen and financed by the TUC or local trades councils, but by local federations of trade unionists, socialists, Co-operators, radical religionists and independents. The logic of policy and discipline dictated that such MPs should be bound together in *the* Labour Party and the logic of organisational support and finance eventually showed that local Labour Parties, to which all participating bodies would affiliate, was the best way of achieving these aims.

The above narrative has shown the important part that Birmingham working people played in helping to solve the complex political and organisational problems involved in the creation of *the* Labour Party. The cross the Birmingham movement carried, in contrast to the rest of the country, was the baneful Chamberlain interest which held back Labour control of the City council and any Labour representation in Parliament until 1945 and has, quite wrongly, given rise to legends of the 'backwardness' of the Birmingham working class.

Chapter Seventeen

VERDICT ON THE GREAT DEPRESSION

The first question to pose, of course, is whether or not there was a Great Depression in Birmingham. S.B.Saul published his influential booklet *The Myth of the Great Depression* in 1969 and since then the Depression has been down-graded to a non-event like the Hungry Forties; terms, if they are used at all, to appear between inverted commas. For those who have thrown in their lot with Saul, Birmingham as already stated, is the jewel in their crown — the city of a thousand trades where depression in one trade was offset by prosperity in others, the city where unemployment was low, the city of greatest structural change with workshop and handicraft production giving way to new industries and the primacy of large-scale factory production. Much of the preceding evidence, however, has shown that the Myth is itself a myth for Birmingham, and additional examples will be used in this summing-up.

The most important requirement, however, is a theoretical structure which will define, measure and explain the Great Depression. Contemporary economics had nothing to offer in this regard any more than modern, bourgeois theory today. The main characteristic of the time was that the old labour theory of value accepted by classical economists from Petty to Adam Smith and Ricardo and being given a new, dangerous twist by Marx, was rapidly giving way to Marginal analysis. This assumed that prices were determined subjectively by peoples preferences. It was allied with an almost universal acceptance of Say's law which stated that since every sale was at the same time a purchase, general crises of overproduction were impossible and Depressions therefore could not and did not exist! If the facts contradicted the theory, so much the worse for the facts, and temporary, partial disequilibrium was looked for, not in the mechanism of capitalism itself, but by factors outside or peripheral to the system. So, the most searching economic examination of the period, the Royal Commission on Trade & Industry of 1885, probed relentlessly into the questions of markets, capital, prices, wages etc, but because it specifically refuted the idea that there could be general overproduction produced no overall explanation and could suggest only the most elementary causes of partial 'over-production' and a few, equally simplistic remedies. Unfortunately, as we have seen, the Birmingham business community was not even equal to participating in the enquiry at that elementary level, being able to articulate only its own immediate, particular problems.

From a theoretical point of view, the working class movement was not much better off. Liberal doctrines of laissez-faire, free trade and cloth-capped Chamberlainism dominated the movement, particularly in Birmingham. Experience in the workshop taught many the reality of class struggle, which was stiffened by historic reading and folk-lore stemming from the Peasants' Revolt, the struggles of the English Revolution of the seventeenth century, the Utopian socialism of Robert Owen, Chartism,

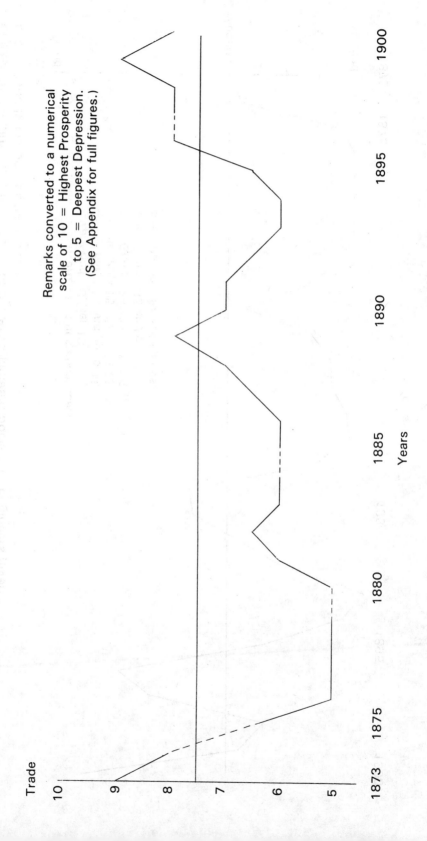

Profile of the Great Depression constructed from the Annual Report remarks of the Birmingham Chamber of Commerce. 1873–1900

Graph 1

Trade

Remarks converted to a numerical scale of 10 = Highest Prosperity to 5 = Deepest Depression. (See Appendix for full figures.)

Years

Graph 2

Profile of the Great Depression constructed from the remarks on the state of Trade of each of the Birmingham Branches of the Amalgamated Society of Engineers given in the Monthly Report of each branch.

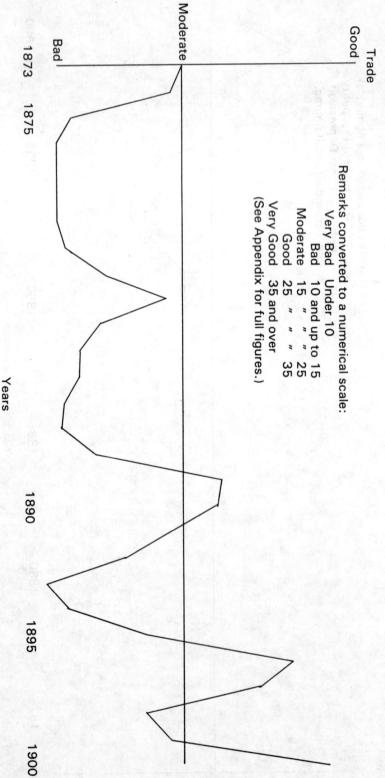

Remarks converted to a numerical scale:

Very Bad	Under 10	
Bad	10 and up to 15	
Moderate	15 " " " 25	
Good	25 " " " 35	
Very Good	35 and over	

(See Appendix for full figures.)

Trade

Good

Moderate

Bad

Years

1873   1875   1890   1895   1900

and an elementary labour theory of value asserting, without being able to prove, that all value was created by labour and deductions from this for profit, rent and interest was robbery of working people. Into this was injected the heady doctrines of Henry George with its trenchant criticism of landed and capitalist society. But George's remedy — the Single Tax on land — harked back to the French physiocratic belief that value arose from land.

The basic cause of the Depression was therefore contended to be partial Overproduction by bourgeois authorities to which the working class counter-poised Underconsumption. As we have seen, there was a fundamental difference between the two. Overproduction was a passive concept requiring no action and waiting for low prices and profits to eliminate surplus capacity and restore equilibrium. This looked backward to Adam Smith's hidden hand and the self-regulating economy. Underconsumption, on the other hand, as popularised by J.A.Hobson was an active concept, requiring state and local action to increase demand. This looked forward to the modern, demand economics of Keynes which, in its turn, was to prove inadequate to cope with the later Great Depression of the 1970s.

The marginal analysis, pioneered by Jevons, Menger and Walrus was being refined in Britain by the Rev. Philip Wicksteed. The result was to remove any lingering trace of the classical labour theory of value wrestled with by Smith and Ricardo and Marx. This elevated capitalism to the only natural order of society, maximising benefits to all classes at all historic periods, so long as the laws of competition were respected and not interfered with. Such generalisations were heartily welcomed by the middle class as banishing any concept of exploitation or any close inspection of the origins and development of class society and its resultant inequalities. Unfortunately, however, by its very generalities, it banished its conclusions from the realms of reality, reducing it to an irrational ideology incapable of answering the questions posed by the real world.

Marx, on the other hand, whose political influence we have traced on every aspect of working class activity from 1848, was re-shaping the labour theory of value and advancing a theory of value which, although in all its complexities is difficult to grasp and easy to criticise kept in touch with reality to the extent that it stands today as the only coherent theory of historic, political and economic development.

Two basic clashes between the developing schools of Marginalism and Marxism occurred during the Great Depression and must be dealt with here. The first was H.M.Hyndman's tilt at Jevons in his lecture *The Final Futility of Final Utility*. Hyndman began by quoting Jevons' opening statement in his *Theory of Political Economy:*

> Repeated reflections and enquiries have led me to the somewhat novel conclusion that value depends entirely on utility.

With heavy sarcasm on 'repeated reflection and enquiry', Hyndman had no difficulty in refuting the statement as it stands by showing that decades before, Ricardo had rejected that position when he wrote:

> When I give 2,000 times more cloth for a pound of gold than I give for

a pound of iron, does it prove that I attach 2,000 times more value to
gold than I do to iron? Certainly not; it proves only that the cost of
production of gold is 2,000 times greater than the production of iron.

Hyndman was on weak ground here, however, because although at that
time Jevons was using the term 'degree of utility' he clearly understood
that value was determined by what was later to be called 'marginal
utility'. Hyndman's second thrust was to show that Jevons' theory of
value was really a cost of production theory and again quoted Jevons'
own words to prove it:

> Cost of production determines supply, Supply determines final degree of
> utility, Final degree of utility determines value.

If the second proposition is correct, the above can be simplified to

> Cost of production determines value.

This left the cost of production to be explained. Until the Marginalists
could formally demonstrate that costs of production were subjective and
also determined by marginal utility instead of more satisfactorily
explained as the expenditure of a part of society's total labour, this
remained the Achilles heel of the Marginalists.

Hyndman's lecture had other merits, besides attacking the heart of
marginal theory. It questioned the ambiguity surrounding the term
'utility'; that under capitalism production was determined not by
'wants', 'necessities' nor even 'satisfactions', but by the social position
and wealth of its members. That 'cost of production' begged the question
of monopoly ownership of the means of production and whether those
who received the rewards accruing to land and capital were entitled to
receive them.

Turning to the practical aspects of Utility, Hyndman poured scorn on
Jevons' other concepts. His view that the 'wages of a working man are
ultimately coincident with what he produces after the deductions of rent,
taxes and the interest on capital', Hyndman said amounted to what a
working man can get after landlord government and banker have
scrambled for their portions. There was also the inability of Utility to
throw any light on the trade cycle and Jevons' own unfortunate theory
that they could be attributable to sun-spots. Above all, Hyndman was
able correctly to state Marx' theory of value, which, as we shall see,
eluded Wicksteed.

The other great confrontation between the Marxist theory of value and
Marginialism was an article in *Today*, the Socialist journal, in October
1884 by Philip Wicksteed, with a famous reply by George Bernard Shaw,
which played an important role in determining that the Social Democratic
Federation would continue to be based on Marxism and the Labour
theory of value, and that the Fabian Society would finally accept the
bourgeois Marginalist theory.

Ironically, Wicksteed was a Unitarian minister and Christian Socialist
with a high regard for Marx. Wicksteed's contribution to marginal
analysis is considered by Lord Robbins to have been crucial.

Wicksteed begins by setting out Marx' main proposition, namely, that capitalists buy labour at its value (i.e. its cost of production, maintenance and reproduction), but what they have in fact purchased is the workers' labour power. It it takes, say, five hours for the worker to produce his value, the other, say, five hours of the working day produces surplus value, which is appropriated by the capitalist as profit, although he might subsequently have to share it with landlord and moneylender.

Wicksteed goes on to say that in support of these propositions Marx states that commodities to be saleable must possess both Use Value and Exchange value. In use value, the commodities — cotton, iron, coal etc — are entirely different, but to exchange with each other in any given ratio they must possess something in common. This cannot be Use value, nor have such dissimilar commodities any physical, chemical or other natural properties. Their only common property is that they are products of labour — abstract, general, undifferentiated labour. Wicksteed then summarises this proposition:

> The Gleichheit (common something) of several wares consists in the fact that they are all products of abstract human labour and the equation x of ware A equals y of ware B holds in view of the fact that it requires the same amount of human labour to produce x of ware A as y of ware B.

Wicksteed goes on:

> Now the leap by which this reasoning lands us in labour as the sole constituent element of value appears to me so surprising that I am prepared to learn that the yet unpublished portions of Das Capital contains supplementary or elucidatory matter which may set it in a new light.

This was indeed to be the case. The complexities of the transformation of Values into Prices of Production and the latter into Market Prices are the arenas in which demand and supply fight the battle to realise the Values created and where Use value and marginal analysis plays a legitimate role.

But Wicksteed wanted it both ways, and his crowning criticism of Marx was that in claiming that only socially necessary labour created value and it was not the case that the longer and more inefficient the labour the greater the value, Marx had given away his whole case:

> A few pages, then, after we have been told that wares regarded as 'valuables' must be stripped of all their physical attributes, ie. of everything that gives them their value in use, and reduced to one identical, spectral objectivity, as mere jellies of undistinguishable abstract human labour, and that it is this abstract human labour which constitutes them valuables, we find the important statement that *the labour does not count unless it is useful*. Simple and obvious as this seems, it in reality surrenders the whole of the previous analysis, for if it is only useful labour that counts, then in stripping the wares of all the specific properties conferred upon them by specific kinds of useful work, we must not be supposed to have stripped them of the abstract utility, conferred upon them by abstractly useful work. If only useful labour counts, then when the wares are reduced to mere indifferent products of such labour in the abstract, they are still *useful* in the abstract, and therefore it is not true that 'nothing remains to them but the one attribute of being

products of labour' for the attribute of being useful also remains to them. In this all wares are alike.

Here, Wicksteed is misrepresenting Marx in two ways. Marx does not speak of *useful labour* he speaks of *socially necessary labour* creating *value;* also Marx is concerned solely with those commodities which are produced under capitalism and must be brought to the market to have their values realised in exchange between the competing forces of supply and demand. Wicksteed passes on, however, to bolster his case by turning to monopoly prices and the hoary examples of paintings by old masters etc. which have ever since been the stock-in-trade of the legion of lesser critics who consider that they have confuted Marx.

Having 'demolished' Marx, Wicksteed then turned to elaborate the now familiar marginal analysis that the only common product of comodities is subjective utility, and price is determined at the margin. This, of course, not only removes the argument from the sphere of capitalist reality where men contend in class struggle for the main revenues of society, not only excludes the questions of the origins and development of this system, but denies the ultimate reality that whatever part Use value plays in the determination of prices and production, the ultimate reality is that the total output of society is the total of present labour and past labour (depreciation of plant and machinery) acting upon nature.

Wicksteed was replied to by George Bernard Shaw:

> The October number of *Today* is memorable for containing an attack by a Socialist on the theory of value held by the late Karl Marx. A Roman Catholic impugning the infallibility of the Pope could have created no greater scandal. Sentence of excommunication was pronounced by *Justice. The Enquirer* and other papers well affected to the cause demanded impatiently, as the months passed, why the heretic remained unanswered. That he can easily be answered, refuted, exposed, smashed, pulverised and economically annihilated, appears to be patent to many able Socialists. Without adding such an atrocious comment as that I am glad to hear it, I do not mind admitting that a certain weight will be removed from my mind when the attack is repulsed, and the formerly pellucid stream of the Ricardian labour theory of value has deposited the mud which the late Stanley Jevons stirred up in quantities which, though expressed by differentials, were anything but infinitely small.

Shaw then puts 'my own complexities with regard to 'final utility'. He quotes the case of a community where the utility of beef consumed in a single meal varies from infinity to zero only to rise and fall to the same extent within six hours, but the cost remains the same, because the cost of production has not changed. Or the case of drinking water in a desert controlled by a monopolist who, having extracted the total, differentiated income of half a dozen travellers dying of thirst is unable to extract anymore after 24 hours when the situation recurs because all their means are already spent. Shaw says he quotes these two examples 'to illustrate the ordinary economist's habit of regarding the value of a thing as the maximum which its possessor can extract from the person who desires to consume it.'

One other of Shaw's examples deserves quoting: 'At present a middle class man furnishes himself with commodities in a certain order, as, for instance, wife, house, furniture, piano-forte, horse and trap. The satisfaction of each desire leaves the mind free to entertain the next . . . Let the cost of a piano-forte suddenly rise above that of a horse and trap and the conventional order of furnishing will be altered.' Shaw suggests that this would be used by a Socialist administration 'since the comparative utility of things is of far greater moment to the community than their ratio of exchange, to which our social system has given a factitious importance.' Wicksteed's reply to what he calls Shaw's 'brilliant, but good natured comments' is not entirely convincing even to the monopolist examples which, of course, in no way contradict Marx' theory of value.

Cost of production on the supply side continued to disturb the elegance and logical construction of Marginalism even when it was contended that the supply curve really only represented the sellers 'demand' for his own product. It did not finally disappear until it was declared that the latter conclusion did away with the necessity for a supply curve, leaving only the demand curve, which was then transformed into an 'indifference curve'.

The whole edifice was finally crowned by Lionel Robbins' definition of economics as 'the science which studies human behaviour as a relationship between ends and scarce means which have alternative uses.' By this time, however, marginal analysis was so remote and so assailed by the reality of the second Great Depression of the nineteen thirties, that bourgeois economics had to be rescued by the partial realities of Keynesianism. The result has been that orthodox economics now limps along with no theory of value, bravely contending that none is necessary, while semi-Marxists like Mrs. Joan Robinson urge those of us who continue to hold to the labour theory of value to abandon it because of its complexities.

In concluding the Wicksteed-Shaw exchange one might repeat Shaw's query and ask why Wicksteed was not refuted, especially as the article appeared in a socialist publication. Engels could have answered it, as could Eleanor Marx or her consort Edward Aveling, or Hyndman. Were they all too busy? Or did they take the view that the old and hallowed academic tradition of ignoring what is inconvenient to bourgeois prejudices and interests while dashing precipitately to embrace anything that confirms them, did not make it worth their while to reply?

Before attempting to analyse the Great Depression in Birmingham in Marxist terms, a few words on Marx' method are necessary. With regard to the labour theory of value, Marx traces the 'atom' of capitalist production e.g. the 'commodity' through various metamorphoses whereby value is created by labour. But profit has to be equalised through prices of production which themselves are established and changed by market prices. At all these stages Use value, interacts with exchange value. It is the contradiction between the *production* of value and surplus value and its *realisation* through prices which gives rise to the *possibilities* of crisis. Marx goes no further than this and insists that each crisis arises from specific causes which must be investigated and not one general cause which can be invoked as a talisman, although the overall development of capitalism takes place in cycles of expansion and depression.

The Marxist analysis, to which the labour theory of value is integral, is a theory of devlopment exposing four potentially fatal flaws of capitalism (a) that it is a system of exploitation and robbery and thus immoral (b) that it is cyclical by its nature and periods of mass unemployment, poverty and hardship are inseparable from it (c) that in its development it moves from competition to monopoly on a national scale and from thence to competition and monopoly on an international scale (d) that capitalist struggle for world markets, sources of raw materials etc. is the main factor in generating wars.

Utilising this Marxist analysis, one can return to Birmingham and finalise a verdict on the existence, causes and consequences of the Great Depression.

In the first place, the period can be almost exactly located as between 1875 and 1895. As additional evidence for this, two 'profiles' of the Great Depression are offered. The first is from the assessments offered, and already discussed, by the Birmingham Chamber of Commerce (see Graph 1) These comments are given in full in appendix 1. The comments themselves are subjective varying from estimates of the period of greatest depression to estimates of the years of greatest prosperity. A mid-point between these two has been taken as representing 'normal trade'. The results show 1872 (off the graph) as the year of greatest propery and the years 1876–80 as those of greatest depression. There is a rise in 1881 which is not sustained and a plateau of depression until 1886. There is another climb from 1887 to 1889 which just breaks through to 'prosperity' in 1889. Then descent again into depression from 1890 to another trough at 1893–94. Another climb then begins into prosperity in 1897 to high prosperity in 1899. But this is a peak; by 1901, the last year reported by the Chamber of Trade, it is stated that 'the great prosperity of 1899 is passing away.'

Another, more detailed profile has been constructed from the monthly returns of the Birmingham branches of the Amalgamated Society of Engineers. Each branch made a monthly statement of the state of trade as it affected employment in terms of 'bad', 'moderate' and 'good'. To these comments I have given numerical values of 10, 20 and 30 respectively and averaged among the branches for each month, the monthly totals finally being averaged for the year. The number of ASE branches varied from three in 1873–74 to seven in 1898–1900 as the union grew. The resultant 'profile' is shown as Graph 2. It will be seen that it is very similar to the profile of the Chamber of Commerce. The 1873 peak of trade as being only 'moderate' is an interesting comment on the Great Boom as experienced by engineering workers. Between 1874–75 trade in the engineering industry seems to have plummeted with the years of greatest depression being 1876–79. 1880–82 gives a break from 'deepest depression' but then descends to another trough to 1887. The climb rises to 'prosperity' for the latter part of 1888 to the first half of 1891 and then descends to the very deepest depression in 1893. Prosperity returns in the final quarter of 1895 and lasts until the second half of 1897. The profile differs most widely from that of the Chamber of Commerce for the years 1898–99 which shows slight depression, but trade booms in 1900.

From these two profiles, despite legitimate criticism which can be made of the way that they are constructed, there is no doubt that the Great

Depression was a reality in Birmingham for the years 1875 – 95. From both 'profiles' it could be argued that the period sub-divides into at least three distinct cycles. The Chamber of Commerce graph suggests that the depth of depression in 1876 – 80 was never again plumbed, but the peaks of these sub-cycles are still in the zone of depression. The reality of the Great Depression in Birmingham cannot be wished away.

Unemployment

The most crucial factor in denying Depression in Birmingham is an alleged low level of unemployment. As Marx points out, the fetishism of commodities leads to a representation between individuals being interpreted as relations between things, and such abstractions as 'a buoyant economy' can have no validity if the reality is large scale unemployment. A Reserve Army of Labour has been a normal feature of capitalism, sometimes depleted, but rarely completely disappearing even at the height of a boom. This reserve army has been a notable feature of the Birmingham employment scene drawn on for the characteristic seasonal nature of much of the industrial output of the city.

With regard to total employment we first set out the most widely accepted national measure which comes from the Returns of Trade Unions. These give average quinquennial percentage levels of unemployment as follows:

1875 – 79	*1880 – 84*	*1885 – 89*	*1890 – 94*	*1895 – 99*
5.8	4.4	6.8	3.8	3.4

Such levels of unemployment are quite unrealistic. They have often been criticised, but gratefully utilised by all those wishing to contend that mass unemployment is a modern phenomenon. Alternative quantitative indexes are not easy to find. I have made a rough calculation from the answers of those trade union branches which replied to a specific question requesting the numbers of their members unemployed in the questionnaire of the Royal Commission on Trade & Industry for 1885. This random sample (in the dictionary sense of 'haphazard', not the statistical sense) ranged from 'all members out of work, the trade having completely deserted the town' to naval dockyards where unemployment was nil. It gives national unemployment at 11.3%. A basic weakness of the Returns of Trade Unions is that they comprise almost entirely skilled workers less liable to unemployment than the mass of unskilled and semi-skilled comprising the bulk of the reserve army of labour. For these, and other reasons, I have suggested that the national trade union index of un-employment be accepted as an indicator of *relative* levels of unemploy-ment, but the given percentage should be doubled when estimating *actual* unemployment.

Unfortunately, as we have seen, no Birmingham trade union completed the questionnaire or gave evidence to the Royal Commission of 1885. Apart from the Amalgamated Society of Engineers, the only Birmingham trade unions from whom we have sufficient material to estimate levels of unemployment are the Flint Glass Workers and the Brassworkers. For the former there is the *Flint Glassworkers Magazine* running from 1860 to 1898. The unions' two main branches,

Birmingham and Stourbridge, had almost the same number of members for most of this period. Each quarterly magazine gave the names of all those in receipt of benefits, including unemployment benefit and the number of days in each quarter for which the benefit was paid. By complex calculations multiplying the number of days of unemployment benefit paid divided by the man-days of the total membership, one can arrive at the percentage of the membership receiving out-of-work benefit. When these four quarters are averaged for the year and the annual percentages averaged for five years, the quinquennial average unemployment figures for the Birmingham branch of the Flint Glassmakers are:

1875 – 79	1880 – 84	1885 – 89	1890 – 94	1895 – 98
5.3%	6.4%	5.2%	6.3%	7.5%

The much higher percentage figures than the national average for the 1890s partly reflect local problems when the membership was falling and the relative strength of the Stourbridge branch was rising, but all the figures reflect other problems. Subscriptions were payable quarterly, which resulted in large numbers of members being out of benefit at all times. Benefits were payable only four weeks after these arrears had been paid off. In addition, unknown numbers had exhausted their unemployment benefit, while others who were in reality unemployed, were in receipt of sickness benefit. The result was that when a breakdown of membership was occasionally given in the Magazine, much higher levels of unemployment were revealed. For instance, an analysis of members of the Birmingham branch in 1878 – 79 at the depth of the depression gave:

Total Membership	Superannuated	Unemployed	Honorary Members	Permanently Sick	Paying Members
351	26	62	3	8	252

This gives an unemployment level of total members of 18% and paying members of 25%. A similar analysis in August 1888, a year of improved trade gave an unemployment rate of 22% ot total membership.

The Brassworkers' Union also gave regular information on unemployment expenditure. Its presentation, however, does not allow us to quantify unemployment among Brassworkers to the same extent as for the Glassworkers. But the information does show other problems illustrating the general difficulties faced by even the financially strongest unions in sustaining unemployment pay and suggesting that percentages of unemployment revealed would be gross underestimates. The Brassworkers' Union gives unemployment benefit as benefit per head per member. Expenditure on selected dates was as follows:

1872	1874	1876	1877	1879	1881	1883	1885	1890	1896	1900
6/10d	11/-d	6/7d	13/8d	34/4d	15/3d	10/1d	19/4d	15/6d	7/3d	14/-d

The 1872 figure would be expected to reflect 'normal expenditure' in a year of prosperity. The 1874 figures suggests an early onset of the

Depression in the Brass trade, but expenditure was cut back in 1876, a depressed year. Expenditure then climbs to a peak in 1879 when it was 146% of each member's contributions. Payments at this level were ruinous and the amount per week paid, or the period of payment, or non-qualification for benefit had to be lowered. All three were tried by most unions during the Depression. Subsequent Brassworkers' payments at about half the highest level of 1879 reflect, therefore, not a halving of unemployment but an increasingly realistic disbursement of funds. Expenditures did not fall proportionately to unemployment in more prosperous years because rules regarding benefits tended to be relaxed at such times. The glassworkers, for instance, had the endearing habit of voting the unemployed 1/-d. per week extra during the winter quarter, when funds permitted. Unfortunately, for the Brassworkers we do not have either scales of payment or duration of payment for most of the Great Depression; we only know that when funds were depleted below certain levels, the Brassworkers, as did other unions, had recourse to additional levies on the whole of the membership to restore funds, but these were draconian methods at times when unemployment was at its highest, and even when most members could respond resulted in members dropping out of the union. If we take the peak 1879 figure and assume that out-of-work benefit was 10/-d. this would mean that every member was unemployed for nearly 3½ weeks in that year. This gives an average unemployment rate of 7% of membership. But in 1884 the annual report states that 'many brassworkers have been compelled to seek relief and break stones who should have been in the union.' When a scale of benefits and contributions is available dating from about 1906 it shows unemployment benefit at 10/-d. a week for general section adult members paying 9d. per week contributions, but no unemployment benefit for trade members paying 6d. per week. We return to the conclusion that not all union members were in benefit and not all brassworkers were in the union. This lifted levels of unemployment much above those stated by trade union returns.

To these levels of mass unemployment must be added short-time working which was endemic to Birmingham, because of the seasonal nature and marketing problems of the trades. Responsible estimates of under-employment in the city come from the authoritative series of reports on Birmingham industries issued after the Great Depression. The Report on the Jewellery Trade, for instance, stated that 'Long-term under-employment was characteristic of Edwardian Birmingham' and the Report on the Brass Trade did not hesitate to put a figure to it stating that seasonal unemployment averaged 25% in Birmingham before the 1st World War.

High levels of unemployment and chronic levels of short-time working were present throughout the Great Depression and · the consequent fluctuations of income were probably the key factor in perpetuating the mass poverty that characterised Birmingham throughout the nineteenth century.

The last objection to the reality of the Great Depression is that output increased throughout the period. If we start with the national figures, the Hoffman Index (itself highly speculative) shows an increase of total industrial production including building of 40% between 1875 and 1895.

During the same period the population of the U.K. increased by 19%, so the increase of production per head was 34%.

As far as Birmingham is concerned, it is undoubtedly true that the demand for some products expanded throughout the period 1875–95. Brass and glass are two examples. Yet, as we have seen, increased output of brass goods brought static or even lower profits, while glass production was contracting in Birmingham. The bulk of increased domestic and export demand was being met by Germany and other competitors. The jewellery trade increased after being depressed during 1885–86. Gold and silver ware marked at the Assay Office in Birmingham was:

	1887	1895	1900
Gold (ozs)	108,233	239,872	371,433
Silver (ozs)	858,662	1,796,056	2,957,679

The silver figures are markedly affected by the fall in the price of the metal. The number of male workers in jewellery decreased over the period, and the number of women rose markedly, suggesting a growth of mass production.

Another expanding trade throughout the Depression was the pen trade, based on increasing world literacy. But the low wages, poor conditions and hostility to trade unions recorded earlier make the contribution of the largest firms such as Gillott and Jos. Mason a less than glorious page in the history of Birmingham's industrial history, however much these employers might plead squeezed profit levels and foreign competition in mitigation of their misdeeds.

Did the new, developing, manufacturing industries make a significant contribution to arresting Depression? The only new industry that did expand throughout the Great Depression was the cycle industry, and even here, the industry remained in the luxury class until the invention of the safety cycle in 1885 began to end the reign of the penny-farthing. And it was to be not cycle manufacturers but the parts' suppliers, such as Dunlops and Lucas who were to develop factory production in Birmingham. It is said that Joseph Lucas and the bicycle grew up together, and it is through a study of the firm that we can study that rare phenomenon — a manufacturing firm that developed throughout the Great Depression.

When Lucas finished his apprenticeship at Elkington's, he worked for a carriage-lamp maker and first branched out to selling paraffin which, as a recently invented process, greatly extended the lamp trade. By 1872 he is listed in the Birmingham post office directory as an Oil and Colourman. He began manufacturing ships' lamps, made his first cycle lamp in 1878 and patented his King of the Road Lamp, which was to make his fortune two years later. By 1880 he was employing 58 people. By 1885 it was 150. In 1888 Dunlop's pneumatic tyre appeared. By 1890 the Lucas work force was 300 and by 1897 700. Joesph Lucas was therefore fortunate in all his circumstances, apart from his own initiative and energy, as his son was not slow to remind him in 1880, 'We have such splendid business prospects, such capital chances, as few people in these times of bad trade have got.'

Where technical change brought large new investment prospects,

Birmingham seems to have had little share. Thus steel output increased by about 360% over the 20 years of the Great Depression and coal output by 42%, but Black Country output of coal declined and its output of steel was negligible, thus depriving Birmingham even of advantages of carriage of these commodities or marketing. In other words, there is little to suggest that Birmingham industrial output kept pace with the national growth.

If we look to trade rather than manufacturing for rapid growth, we are again disappointed. We have already commented on the slow growth of agents, brokers, factors, merchants, etc and the moderate growth of clerks and commercial travellers over the Census periods 1871 – 1891.

Employment on roads and railways did increase over this period, thus boosting the carriage manufacturing trade in Birmingham. But railways showed small profits on heavily watered stock.

Even the service industries of food, drink and lodging failed to provide greatly increased employment for either men or women.

Our final verdict can only be that the evidence would have to be pushed very hard to claim that Birmingham achieved even the national rate of growth in the period 1875 – 95, and, as we have seen, expansion of output is no criterion of prosperity, if profit margins are low. The Great Depression was a grim reality in Birmingham.

Having established the reality of the Great Depression, an attempt will now be made to provide a framework within which it can be analysed, with particular reference to factors which might have applied to Birmingham.

Marx stresses that the *possibility* of crises occurs within the actual process of capitalist production, but that each crisis has specific causes which must be investigated and established. Clearly, the anarchy of capitalist production is one which was a powerful factor in the Birmingham case. The contrast between the efficiency, discipline and planning within the workshop and the hopeful placing of that product on a market whose size and whereabouts were quite unknown, has been sufficiently posited in the previous pages as to need no further comment. The wonder is not that capitalism is so often in crisis, but rather that it is ever out of it.

The seeds of the slump are sown in the previous period of expansion. Again, the example of Birmingham is instructive. The vast inequalities of income generated from the boom led to the popular belief that nine tenths of the wealth of Birmingham found its way to Edgbaston and the other one tenth to the rest of the city. This was perhaps an exaggeration, but the process was a real and inevitable one. A realistic politician such as Joseph Chamberlain articulated this with his 'doctrine of ransom', telling his fellow-exploiters that if they wished to continue the enjoy the fruits of their ill-gotten gains, it would be advisable to part with some of it in alleviating poverty and providing elementary social services to those whose labour produced the wealth. Unfortunately, while there was always a small proportion of the middle class who recognised this and while there was always a small section who recognised the moral dimension of this unfair income distribution, neither was able or willing to recognise that the actual operation of the system itself generating even greater wealth at one pole and poverty and misery at the other, could not be removed while the system itself continued. Thus Marx leads us deeper into the reality of capitalist production. Competition dictates that Capital (i.e. the bringing of labour into relation with raw materials, machines, buildings etc. in the process of production) must be turned over continuously, on pain of the owner of capital ceasing to be a capitalist. Moreover, the increased value at the end of each turnover of capital demands not simply reproduction, but extended reproduction (i.e. increased output). Finally, such expanded reproduction must take place at the level of socially necessary labour when the means of production are constantly being refined and improved. All this creates a further range of *possibilities* of crises.

In Marxist notation, the value and surplus value created (v + s) must be realised in the market together with the constant capital (c) of raw materials, depreciation of machinery etc whose value passes unchanged into the finished commodity. The ceaseless imperative to produce more efficiently, dictates the necessity to raise the rate of exploitation (s) either through longer hours or greater intensity of work or to substitute constant capital (c) for labour (v). This latter course increases the *organic composition of capital* (c + v + s) and because this decreases the value creating component of capital (v) brings into play the *tendency of the rate of profit to fall*. At the same time, the increasing organic composition of capital increases inequality of incomes by decreasing the proportion going to labour. Thus the possibilities of crisis aggregate themselves into the certainty of crisis.

This progression seems to be a realistic account of what occurred in Birmingham during the years of expansion from the 1850s to 1875 and showed themselves in the unemployment, low wages and general failure of working class living standards to rise substantially during these years, despite the enormously increased amounts of wealth created in those years.

Before tracing this progression further, account must be taken of the main critique of the Marxist theory of value made by the Marginalists. The fact that the increasing organic composition of capital leads to a lesser use of the value and surplus value creating element of capital has been held to invalidate the labour theory because it would suggest that a gang of navvies working with picks and shovels produce more value than an automated plant using virtually no labour. This is not the case. Apart from the fact that the navvies would produce no value at all as they would be working at a lower level of socially necessary labour than was required to produce any value, Marx showed how the aggregate value produced by society is transformed into *prices of production* by the requirement that all capitals must compete against each other whatever their extent or their periods of turnover to establish an average rate of profit; furthermore, that prices of production and the average rate of profit are themselves established and changed through the day-to-day competition of market conditions. Most important of all, it is within this transformation process that the class struggle takes place and also the sources of crisis come into operation. This is the ultimate reality of capitalist production — the necessity to *realise* the value created by actually selling the goods. Far from these realities discrediting the labour theory of value, they bring into full play the dialectical unity of opposites of the necessity of a commodity to contain not only abstract exchange value, but also concrete Use value. The error of the Marginalists was in the mistaking of the *partial* process of subjective evaluation of Use value of a commodity for the *total* process of capitalist production with its self-evident truth that whatever subjective forces determine the commodities actually produced, *total* production will always be the objective process of present labour and past labour (capital assets) operating upon nature.

The above processes can be demonstrated from the example of Birmingham. Profit is determined by the ratio $\frac{s}{c+v}$ The aim of the capitalist is to increase s by longer hours or greater exploitation. This is resisted by workers. Alternatively, the capitalist can hope that the cost of v (the production of labour) will fall, by a fall in the cost of living or forcing down v by persuading workers to accept a lower standard of living. During the expansion such draconian methods are less necessary, but once the Depression began in 1875, the employers immediately intensifed the class struggle with their attacks on wages resulting in the rapid growth of 'sweating', and the drive to cancel the previous gains of the trade unions by lengthening hours, lowering safety standards etc. As we have seen, this process was successful for ten years under the beguiling slogans of costs must be reduced and the trade unions are 'too powerful.' With the re-surfacing of Socialism from 1884 this phase ended and the fight-back began.

The last alternative for increasing surplus value was the dangerous one of increasing the organic composition of capital and thus invoking the tendency for the rate of profit to fall. But the mechanics of capitalism give no choice. Capitalists must modernise because the first to do so will reap profits above the average rate due to producing at a lower cost than the socially necessary level of labour. Even when competitors also modernise and this source of extra profit disappears, an increase in the *mass* of profit may hide a fall in the *rate* of profit; a return of 10% on a capital of £10,000 is greater than a 12% return on a capital of £8,000. Another incentive to increase the organic composition of capital is to establish a monopoly position of some sort to escape the consequences of the averaging of the rate of profit; although this in itself will bring adverse consequences by lowering the share of profit available in the non-monopoly sector. The crisis was deepened and prolonged into the Great Depression by the fact that the possibilities of crisis matured in the main industrialising countries at about the same time that they did in Britain with the result that it became the first genuinely world depression. Competitors using modern capitals of higher organic composition kept the rate of profit low and temporary expedients which had been successful in previous crises, such as lowering the cost of v below its value were insufficient. Drastic new measures were necessary; the old order had come to an end; Britain's world industrial monopoly was at end. These measures, characterised first by J.A.Hobson and then Lenin, as Imperialism, included the jettisoning of free trade and the development of colonies as markets and new sources of raw materials. A leading role in this came, of course, from Joseph Chamberlain backed by the slavish support of the Birmingham business community performing the sharpest of U-turns on all their previous principles and policies.

What brought the eventual upturn and the end of the Great Depression in the later 1890s? An important, fortuitous event was the lowering of the value of v. The cost of living between 1875 – 79 and 1895 – 99 (measured by my cost of food and rent index for the adjacent Black Country) fell by 30%. The bulk of this fall, nearly 20% came between 1880 – 84 and 1885 – 89, a factor determining that the second phase of the Great Depression was probably not quite so severe as the first. This lowering of the cost of v was accompanied by successful attempts to push v below its value by low wages, and the substitution of women for men in the labour force. This is indicated by the special importance of sweated industries and the growing importance of women in the subsequent phase of class struggle in Birmingham after 1895. In addition, there were the first stirrings of the new, manufacturing industries which were ultimately to transform Birmingham from a predominantly craft to an overwhelmingly mass manufacturing town calling for large capital outlays and raising the beleaguered rate of profit. But in 1895 it is likely to have been forces outside Birmingham leading the city out of slump rather than the local contribution.

PART 4

IMPERIALISM TO WORLD WAR

'Children of the Poor' photographed in Sutton Park during the summer outing provided for them by the Birmingham Cinderella Club, *c.* 1898

Chapter Eighteen

TOWARDS SOCIALIST UNITY
1900 – 1910

Introduction

The period begins with the almost total collapse and paralysis of the labour movement arising largely from the jingoism of the Boer War. December 1899 had brought the Black Weeks when Kimberley, Mafeking and Ladysmith were all besieged. May 1900 brought the delirium of their relief and in September the Khaki Election had returned the Tories, but with a reduced majority. Chamberlain's Liberal Unionists, however, retained all the seven Birmingham seats. In 1901 came the disgraceful incident when, egged on by the Unionist press, the Birmingham jingoes attacked the Town Hall meeting of Lloyd George whose life was nearly lost.

But this jingoism was not long-lived. It was most marked in the very poorest wards of the centre and in the more affluent areas of the city. But there was always a very considerable minority who recognised from the beginning that the war was an unjust one waged for the benefit of the gold and diamond interests represented by Cecil Rhodes and supported by Joseph Chamberlain. The two years of guerilla war waged by the Boers which was combatted by the British concentration camps brought disillusion. Unemployment began to grow and was particularly severe in the period 1905 – 08. By that time, Chamberlain had performed his U-turn on free trade and in 1903 he resigned from the government on the issue of Tariff Reform.

1904 brought the defeat of the Tsarist world centre of reaction in the Russo-Japenese War; and a year later, the first Russian Revolution. The 1906 general election gave a landslide victory to the Liberals and twenty nine Labour Representation Committee candidates were elected who turned themselves into the Labour Party.

But disgust with the rapid degeneration of the ILP leaders of the Labour Party from Socialist militants to parliamentary 'statesmen' in the House of Commons quickly brought further disillusion with Lib-Lab politics. The result was the twin reaction of the growth of the demand for Socialist unity which led to the formation of the British Socialist Party in 1911 and the growth of Syndicalism from 1910. The following chapter traces these developments in Birmingham.

The S.D.F.

In June 1899, the *Pioneer,* newspaper of the Birmingham Socialist Centre, reported that Birmingham Central branch of the S.D.F. had never been in a better position either numerically or financially. It met every Friday at 8.30 p.m. at the Victoria Hotel on the corner of John Bright Street and Station Street. The secretary was V.Davies. At the 1900 May Day demonstration at Gosta Green, a platform was occupied jointly by the S.D.F., the Labour Church and the Socialist Centre.

The summer open-air campaign began with Sunday meetings at 11.30

a.m. and 7 p.m. at Gosta Green. By September two further meeting places, at Easy Row and the Bull Ring, were being serviced both morning and evening, each Sunday. In September T.H.Griffin, a member of the Bakers' and Confectioners' Union, stood for the party at the School Board elections and his campaign opened with a large Sunday open-air meeting where he was supported by two S.D.F. comrades, W.Simmonds of the Birmingham branch who was also a trades council delegate, and H. Brockhouse, a member of the West Bromwich School Board. Griffin claimed that the policy of the Liberal Eight was now no different from that of the Clerical party and the trades council had dropped their demands for state maintained schools with secular education. This was truly pitiful after the splendid example set by Birmingham in education matters in the past twenty years, Griffin declared. He was the only Socialist standing, he was adopted by the Labour Church and Griffin asked everyone to plump all their fifteen votes for him.

1901 opened with the redoubtable W.F. (Billy) Holliday recorded as secretary. Much more will be heard of Holliday. In March the Paris Commune was celebrated with a meeting at the Victoria Hotel.

In April, a real tragedy struck the branch. George Tooth recorded the death of Mrs. Vernon at the early age of thirty. She would be remembered as the intelligent and enthusiastic secretary of Birmingham East branch. Several of the comrades had paid their last respects at the funeral and the branch contributed a handsome wreath. At the last branch meeting 'the feeble band and few' passed a resolution of sympathy and condolence to her husband, Sam Vernon, and the bereaved relations. Tooth ended by saying that her death was a distinct loss, for active and enthusiastic women were too few in their ranks.

The jingoism of the Boer War was evident in the problems of the branch at that time. There were no regular meetings advertised in *Justice* in May, although the Chartist veteran, John Sketchley was undertaking lecture engagements. There was also one of those prime indicators of a lack of branch activity — a suggestion book was available at Birmingham S.D.F. headquarters!

However, Harry Quelch was moving into South Staffordshire for an extended organising and political campaign and he reported from Wolverhampton that 'war fever was subsiding.' This was to be tested in August when the S.D.F. Annual Conference was held in Birmingham. In July, Birmingham S.D.F. was advertising arrangements for this. There would be a concert and reception for the delegates on Saturday August 3rd at the Colonade Hotel, New Street and delegates were asked to contact Sam Vernon at 53 Sutton Street, Aston. The Conference would be held in a committee room of the Town Hall from 10 a.m. on the Sunday and that evening there would be a 'great Socialist demonstration' with Dan Irving, Billy Gee, Harry Quelch, C.L.Buzza, and of course, the star turn, H.M.Hyndman. This report was signed by E.E.H. The report of the Conference showed that George Tooth had been elected to the SDF executive committee. The town hall was said to be full for the public meeting which had been chaired by the local comrade John Haddon and Simmonds had spoken. The eventual national speakers had been Quelch, Gee, Irving and Burrows.

But the Conference and meeting do not seem to have given the necessary fillip to the branch. At the end of August it was reported that the Central branch had no regular meeting place. Outdoor lecturing was continuing, but only at Gosta Green. However, at the end of September, Sam Vernon was reporting attempts to develop a Birmingham East S.D.F. branch at St. Saviours school, Saltley, meeting every Tuesday at 8 p.m. and Birmingham Central were meeting regularly at the Coffee House at the corner of Carrs Lane and High Street. Billy Holliday of 124 Garrison Street was the secretary.

By March 1902, Birmingham SDF meetings were being held at a grandly named Marxian Club, Swan Buildings, Albert Street, and in April the branch was contributing to the Dues, the Central Election, and the Political Secretaries Wages Funds.

In May 1902, the SDF comrades were talking socialist unity with the ILP. After a discussion on 'Is a United Socialist Party Possible?', a resolution had been moved by Comrade Simpson of the ILP and seconded by Comrade Partridge of the SDF that 'in the opinion of this meeting it is desirable in the interests of Socialism that arrangements be made to bring about a more united Socialist effort on the part of socialist organisations in Birmingham.'

In February 1903 a celebration of the first anniversary of the Marxian Club was advertised. Tea at five and entertainment at seven. Anyone willing to help was asked to contact William Hanks. But there was no public activity of the SDF advertised during the summer.

However, the retreat of jingoism, the development of the labour movement and the growth of Socialist consciousness were real. At Aston, in the municipal elections of November, the Unionists had won with votes of 990, 982 and 952. But Berry of the ILP had polled 900 votes, John Haddon of the SDF 893 and R.Hine, standing as an Independent Socialist, had polled 820. Elections were now being co-ordinated by the Socialist Centre and its annual report of May 1904 stated that these three had stood as labour candidates for Brook Ward. At a subsequent by-election for two vacancies in this same ward Berry and Haddon had again stood and this time were successful the results being:

Berry 931: Haddon 900: Towle (Conservative) 704: Wakley (Lib/Union) 697.

John Haddon thus became the first Marxist socialist to win a seat on a municipal body in the Birmingham area.

From 1905 political activity clearly revived. *Justice* was enlarged and Birmingham reappeared in that paper's Directory with B.J.Rowlands as secretary at 217 Bell Barn Road, In the middle of January there are hints of the problems which invariably accompany the falling off of political activity. It was reported that the branch continues to grow and 'those driven away by the insults and intrigues of wreckers are coming back. George Tooth is the latest. No one worked harder than he in days past.' Readers of *Justice* in Stourbridge, Dudley, West Bromwich, Walsall, Smethwick etc. were asked to communicate with W.J.Russell of 270 Broad Street. Russell reported that Birmingham was still progressing in August and there had been activity at Camp Hill, the camp formed by Prince Rupert when he came to sack Birmingham in April 1643.

In August a great demonstration in the Bull Ring was planned on the visit of the SDF executive committee to the city; also a concert on Saturday August 26th. at the Hotel Metropole, High Street, to meet members of the EC. The demonstration was subsequently reported as not being as large as expected because of rain. In September a United Socialist Winter Campaign was inaugurated at the Alhambra Hall, Hope St. The ambitious programme was to include meetings, demonstrations, visiting committees, distribution and sale of literature, a children's school teaching the elements of socialism, socials, entertainments, men's and women's clubs with singing, dancing, physical development etc. a men's brass and reed band, and a boys' drum and fife band.

Early in 1906 Birmingham Central Branch was meeting every Tuesday evening at 7-30 p.m. at Reade's Coffee House in the Bull Ring. Rowlands was still the secretary. In March the SDF initiated a meeting on Education which was reckoned to be the largest Socialist gathering ever seen in Birmingham. Socialists of all types had loyally co-operated with Mrs. Bridget Adams in organising it. Dan Irving had moved a resolution for free and secular education and the Countess of Warwick had seconded it.

In April John Sketchley was advertising his 80 page pamphlet *Crimes of Government* at 6d and another, *The General Outlook,* of 40 pages for 3d. In June the famous Sweating Exhibition organised by Cadbury's newspaper, the *Daily News,* opened in Birmingham. It brought the wrath of Hyndman on the head of Cadbury. In a letter to the paper Hyndman said that the Liberals and radicals in Birmingham were anxious to divert attention from the capitalists to the landlords. Sweating would always exist while capitalism existed. Where did Cadbury think his money came from? At least the Roman slave owners had no illusion on this point. Even if the land were in the possession of the people they would be little better off. He (Hyndman) had proved this conclusively many years before in his debates with Henry George. A copy of this letter had been sent to Cadbury who subsequently replied that his hands were very full and he could not enter into controversy with Hyndman, but he enclosed a leaflet of which 1.8 million had been distributed during the recent election. Hyndman replied that he too was busy as an active member of the largest and fastest growing international party in the world, but he would never allow honest criticism of his views by any person of reputation to go unchallenged. It was a pity Cadbury had no time to defend erroneous views when he had time to make them, Hyndman concluded.

By the summer of 1906 the fortunes of the branch were still in the ascendancy. Central branch comrades were asked to note a new meeting place at Reade's Coffee House on Tuesdays at 7-30 p.m. Rowlands was still the secretary. There was a Birmingham East Branch with D.Dunbar of 109 Philippines Rd. Aston as secretary. A report in September stated that after years of active propaganda in Birmingham comrades Joe Tanner, George Tooth, W.Simmonds and John Haddon had been lost to activity. In spite of obstacles, younger members, with the assistance of the veteran Comrade Thomas had carried on. Now the situation had changed. A district committee was in existence with four branches from the Birmingham area. They had held at least four meetings in the previous three months and they had drawn up a list of speakers most of whom had never taken a platform before. A quarterly district council was to be held the following Saturday at the the Red Lion Hotel, Bull Ring. This report was signed by Frank Barker and the *Justice* Directory showed that the secretary of Central branch was A.Cuin of Handsworth. In October another report from Frank Barker said that Birmingham was waking up. For the first time for some years there had been a gathering of Birmingham and Coventry comrades at Hampton-in-Arden and fifty comrades had sat down to tea. Barker suggested an even wider, regional organisation with a Midland Federation.

On November 26th. the labour movement suffered the grievous loss of the death of Joe Tanner, Birmingham's greatest Marxian Socialist pioneer. Tanner died of consumpton at the age of fifty five. Symptoms of this disease would seem to have appeared as early as 1890. In that year Tanner was on the executive of the Trades Council and attended thirteen of a possible fifteen meetings. From 1891 he was off the Trades Council E.C. and in 1893 attended Trades Council only once. At the end of 1894 the *Labour Leader* reported that 'Joe Tanner had fallen on evil days' without giving further details. By 1896 his ASE branch was no longer affiliated to the Trades Council. In 1899 Tanner was a delegate from No.1. ASE branch, but managed only one attendance against Jephcott's ten. In 1903 Tanner became a delegate for No.4. branch but managed only three attendances in that year, none at all in 1905 and only one in the year of his death.

An obituary appeared in the *Labour Mail* of December 1906 under the initials R.R.B. It said that Joe Tanner joined the SDF in November 1886 when Tom Mann organised the Birmingham branch. He was 'a thorough revolutionist which some people call extremist and he never wavered an inch'. He was 'a hard worker for the cause for which he made great sacrifices and suffered for his principles . . . for energy and thoroughness he was a monument of strength and never recognised defeat.' It went on to remember his part in the formation of the Gas Workers' Union and the organisation of women in the pen trade.

> On behalf of women workers he sacrificed time and means trying to organise a union for them; a hopeless task.

The obituary ended, 'Those who did not know him ten or twenty years ago can scarcely know what the movement owes to our deceased comrade.'

The next month, Arthur Burns in the second of his series of articles on the twentieth anniversary of the Socialist movement in Birmingham added his tribute. After echoing the last sentence of RRB's tribute he went on:

> As a trade unionist and as Socialist he played an important part in the struggle for the Rights of Labour. He had his faults, like most men, some of them grievous faults . . . (these) were often magnified as is often the case with Labour men and Socialists; his virtues were often lost sight of, even by his fellow workers. The self-sacrifices he made for the cause from time to time he bore alone, without praise. Whenever there was work to be done he was prepared to perform the most difficult part. He had a rough and ready way of doing and speaking, but he was always actuated with an honest conviction of what he believed to be right.

These remarks brought comments from both Joe Tanner's sister and his wife. His sister objected to the words 'grievous faults'. Burns apologised and said the expression referred to his political work and not his personal life. Joe's wife asked if Burns had forgotten to mention in his first article the midnight bill-posting expeditions; those who sat up all night making paste for us and the hot coffee to warm us on our return. Burns replied:

> I hope Mrs. Tanner will excuse the omission. You know, we men are so selfish and want all the credit; we forget about all the labour we impose on our sisters and our wives.

In 1907, *Justice* was enlarged from eight to twelve pages. An early January Directory shows four Birmingham Branches. Birmingham Central whose secretary was A.Corbet of 9 Duke Street met Monday evenings at 8 p.m. at the Herb Beer Shop, 5 Moat Row near Bradford Street. The Birmingham East branch secretary was still D.Dunbar. Kings Norton was the third Birmingham branch, secretary H.Gilbert of 61 Linden Road, Bournville. The fourth branch was Smethwick, secretary Charles Harris of 44 Windsor Green Road. The SDF continued to prosper throughout the West Midlands and in August a second meeting of the Midland District Council had taken place at Leamington. A branch had been formed at Worcester and the Coventry branch, which had been active throughout the jingoist years of 1900–02 under the leadership of comrade Bannington, had started a Socialist Sunday School

1908 opened with the announcement of an important meeting at the Red Lion Hotel, but the Directory advertised only one branch whose secretary was Charles Riley of 20 Hutton Road, Saltley and an organiser F.W.Latham of 71 Barford Road. Lectures were being held outside the Sir John Falstaff in Monument Road at 11-15 a.m. on Sundays and the branch met the same evening at 7-30. The first SDF Red Van was on the road in May and the Birmingham branch had a new secretary, W.J.Salmon. In August the branch was holding open-air meetings on Sunday mornings at 11-30 a.m. and Thursday evenings at 8-30 p.m. on the corner of Peel Street and Windsor Green Road. Comrades were urged to turn up early to form a nucleus, to sell literature and take a collection. The previous Sunday there had been a good meeting but a poor show of supporters. Comrades Latham and Salmon had made a good impression. There was to be a branch meeting at the Rotton Park ILP Club, Dudley Road. This report, signed by G.F.Millington ended with the clarion cry 'Sleepers awake, the voice of the Revolution is calling'. In October the branch was still holding open-air meetings, still meeting at the ILP Club and Millington was the secretary. A Speakers' Class was being organised for the winter.

1909 opened with only Birmingham (Rotton Park) branch advertising in the Directory. The secretary was W.J.Salmon and organiser F.W.Latham. The branch met on Tuesdays at the Labour Club, Dudley Road. In March the Rotton Park ILP had to give up their Labour Club and the S.D.P. (as the Federation was now becoming known) transferred its headquarters to the Birmingham Clarion Scouts premises at 65, Stafford Street. The new secretary was F.B.Silvester, a comrade destined to influence the socialist movement in Birmingham for many years. As an enthusiastic newcomer, his report was characteristically militant. As the SDP would now be meeting both in the city centre and at Rotton Park he hoped that all unattached comrades would rally round. 'We want to make Birmingham, once the hot bed of Chartism and radicalism a storm centre of Social Democracy. Come along and help keep the Red Flag flying in the Mecca of Tariff Reform.' In April Silvester reported that the branch had fourteen members and they had helped the Clarion Scouts to distribute anti-militarist leaflets. Silvester reported that the May Day demonstration 'was not impressive to the man in the street, being local, scattered and sectarian.' The movement was now strong enough to mount a united demonstration, he claimed. Central branch had supported the Aston Labour Club demonstration. The speakers had been Alderman Hartley, ex-Councillors Parkes and Haddon, George Tooth and the Clarion Vanner, Drysdale. They had addressed an enthusiastic crowd. Silvester went on to say that the branch had begun its open-air propaganda at Nechells Green, where veteran comrade Thomas was the chairman and Frank Barker 'had made a rattling good speech.' Silvester, who lived at 12 Majuba Street continued as secretary of the growing Central branch and Salmon as the Rotton Park secretary.

In June, A.E.Mabbs, an SDP full-time worker who had been in the Black Country, began a week's mission in Birmingham. In August Central branch was holding open-air meetings at the Park Gates, Golden Hillock Road, Small Heath. It was a fine pitch with big crowds. B.Rowlands and R.Clements were good speakers and Comrade John Haddon was making exellent progress in Aston. Regular reports continued from Central branch. On September 26th. a demonstration had been 'a decided success' and they were then actively working for a great Town Hall meeting with Hyndman and Blatchford on 14th. October.

Reports for the early months of 1910 were sparse. J.Fisher had become Rotton Park secretary. The first full report gave news of May Day. Councillor Jack Jones and Comrades Latham, Dr.Scott, Haddon, Tooth, Griffin, Clements, Salmon and Rowlands had helped make the SDP May Day 'the finest for many a long day.' A concert held on the eve of May Day 'was enjoyed by a large and enthusiastic gathering.' Silvester, who took to signing himself SYL reported that in addition to the Park Gates meetings another pitch opposite the Ship Hotel, Camp Hill 'had lately shown some improvement following good work by Rowlands and Podesta.' In August the branch was supporting agitation for the over-worked and under-paid bakers. Their trade union in Birmingham had recently grown from 200 to 600. The Sunday pitches had been used to organise demonstrations for the bakers. In the morning John Haddon had taken the chair for J.E.Berry, the Trades Council secretary, and in the evening J.Bath had taken the chair for Julia Varley, W.Bamfield and Cde R.Clements. There was a fine crowd. The bakers were demanding a 54 hour week and 28/-d.

In October the Church Socialist League had held a well attended Labour Conference at S.Judes School, Hill Street. Comrades R.Jeff and F.Silvester represented Birmingham Central SDP branch. The Rev. Pinchard had opened a discussion on the Osborne Judgement, and a lengthy resolution, which had been carried unanimously had been moved by Fred Hughes of the Socialist Centre. The next day there had been a debate 'Can a Christian be a Socialist?' Father Adderley had taken the chair and Comrades Silvester and Norman Tiptaft of the ILP had taken opposite sides.

In November the issue of Syndicalism, which was eventually to split the movement, arose. Birmingham Central SDP branch organised a debate on Political Action and Industrial Unionism.G.H.Hill of the Wobblies (Industrial Workers of the World) had defended political unionism and George Tooth had defended political action.

In December Silvester raised the other issue which was profoundly agitating the movement. His report said that the year had ended, as it had begun, with a general election and for a second time Asquith and Balfour were running neck and neck. The Labour Party, increased by two seats, had managed to limp back to Parliament with the aid of the right hand crutch of Liberalism and the left hand crutch of Nonconformity. While the Labour Party goes on crutches, it behoves Socialists to be up and doing. Silvester appealed all Socialists in Birmingham to join the S.D.P. They would have membership cards for 1911 at 65 Stafford Street the following Thursday.

Clarion 1900 – 1910

Clarion throughout this period continued to be the voice of cheerful, non-sectarian Socialism, reporting all Labour movement activities and injecting its own campaigning ideas.

The January 1900 Birmingham report gave details of the Cinderella Christmas activities. The Clarion Scouts had helped entertain 2,000 children on five nights. Thirty women had helped. Marie Corelli, the famous novelist, had provided for one evening's entertainment, and each child had been given a doll at her expense. She regretted that she could not be there personally. Smoking concerts were being arranged to raise funds for the summer outings. The book club was still flourishing.

In March, a notice of the SDF advertised the annual Paris Commune celebration at Victoria Hall and a meeting on the South African War at Bristol Street Schools with George Tooth as the speaker. One of the smoking concerts with Tom Groom in the chair had raised £2-4-0d. for the Cinderellas.

In June there is the first notice I have found of Dr.Robert Dunstan who was to play an important part in Birmingham socialist politics for many years. He described himself as a medical student and Clarionette socialist. His letter defended Vivisection against What Not's statement that it was useless and cruel. Dunstan also defied another correspondent to prove his contention that children were experimented on in our hospitals.

In October, Birmingham Clarion Debating Society reported meetings being held in Room 65, Lincolns Inn. The secretary was D.Cole. In November the Birmingham Clarion Vocal Union was being formed. 'All those who wish to shake Birmingham to its foundations' were invited to apply to Dennis Cole at 84 Brunswick Road, Balsall Heath. In November a Clarion Fellowship dinner had been a great success with 200 diners.

At the end of December a report of the West Birmingham Cinderella stated that 700 children from the slums had been fed and entertained. 200 had been given a Christmas dinner and twelve children had been sent to the Cottage Home for a fortnight. In January 1901 the Labour Church

Cinderella said that reporting so early in the year they were still in the middle of their Christmas festivities, but already they had given enjoyment to 1,500 children. A sumptious meal of beef sandwiches, tea and plum pudding had been provided. 'You should have heard the cheers when the plum pudding appeared.' Entertainment had been provided by the Black and White Minstrels.

Birmingham Clarion Vocal Union again reported in February:

> We are going along pretty well for a baby, but the vagaries of the task are causing the conductor to tear his hair a bit. We started with a fine, able-bodied set of men, but only one lady. We then moved heaven and earth to get more ladies and they seem to have frightened the men away. We have commenced with the *Comrades' Song of Hope* and *Awake Aeolian Lyre* from Oberon. By the time of the first meet we hope to be sufficiently advanced to take our proper place as the most progressive c — in the kingdom. Better leave that blank for fear of exciting jealousies in other CVU centres.

The next month they gave their first concert at the People's Hall, Hurst Street. A belated report in June gave the additional information that:

> On March 31st. we gave a grand concert at the People's Hall just to show those northern people that they are not the only ones who can sing. Five glees astonished all those who heard them and resulted in at least one favourable press notice.

In July the choir reported a series of *professional* engagements in Victoria, Cannon Hill and Summerfield Parks. In August the choir reported performances at picnics and open-air concerts being supplemented by one organised by the Court and Alley Concert Association at the Court at the back of 43 Aberdeen Street. A report of the autumn activity of the choir stated that the conductor was E.W.Beadwell and the secretary was Dennis Cole. Rehearsals were at Bristol Hall, Bristol Street but:

> What with holidays, marriages etc. rehearsals were sparsely attended and we had to cry off the Town Hall meeting (ILP speaker Snowden, chairman Blatchford, 8000 present). We are booked for Leicester in October and the ILP bazaar and December for the Cinderellas.

The 1902 surge of Socialist activity replacing the jingoism of the war found its reflection in the pages of *Clarion*. The Birmingham Clarion Fellowship held its AGM on Saturday January 4th. at the Crown Hotel, Ludgate Hill. A Fellowship Tribute 1/-d. Fund was formed with a committee of nineteen mainly from the midlands, but whose treasurer was the Rev. Cartnel-Robinson the vicar of Holy Trinity Church, Hoxton in London. The chairman was Harry Atkinson of Birmingham and other Birmingham members were J.A.Sayers, W.E.Baker and C.R.Coop.

The cyclists were also expanding their activities. A resolution from the South London C.C.C. suggested regional groupings of the cycling clubs including a midland region stretching from Yorkshire through Notts. Derby and Leicestershire to Wolverhampton, West Bromwich, Birmingham, Coventry and Northampton, the idea being to arrange Meets where no club travelled more than 50 miles.

Under *Handicraft Guild Notes* it was recorded that:

> At Birmingham, Chief Baker has a dozen names of energetic
> Fellowshippers who have promised to do things at home for the Easter
> Exhibition and he wants to hear from more, especially women.

Also in January 1902, H.L.Barrett, a Clarion full-timer was planning a
different sort of lecture tour which instead of taking him to different towns
for a certain number of days, would keep him in town A, say, for three
consecutive Sundays. From February 1st to 28th centred on Stourbridge
he would work some of the Black Country towns as well as Kidderminster
and Worcester. From March 1st. to 28th with Birmingham as the centre,
he would work the city and the rest of the Black Country. In April he
would be centred on Coventry. Barrett said he would be particularly
pleased to hear from towns where there was no socialist organisation.

Still more events were advertised for January. Keir Hardie's week-end
visit to Birmingham and district ILP would include a Tea and Social at
Bristol Street schools on Saturday January 25th and a Town Hall meeting
the next day. Birmingham Clarion Fellowship Cycling Club had a
Smoking Concert. Tickets were available from Chief Baker, W.Field,
J.Taylor, J.A.Sayers, Tom Groom, E.Garbett etc. On Tuesday January
28th. Birmingham South ILP had a meeting at Friends Institute,
Moseley road to discuss 'Is Keir Hardie a desirable Socialist leader?'

February *Clarions* reported activities past and future. There had been
150 at the Keir Hardie social. The concert at the Metropole Hotel had
been a *huge* success. There was to be a meeting to form a Birmingham
East ILP. The Fellowship Tribute Fund had reached £1000 and lists of
contributors included many from Birmingham. Tom Groom was
operating from the *Edgbastonia* office, Five Ways. Birmingham CCC had
opened their season with a run to Solihull.

In March, George Tooth was opening a discussion at the Marxian
Club, Sawn Buildings, Albert Street on Is a United Socialist Party
Possible? The next week the SDF were holding the annual Paris
Commune celebration at the Marxian Club and all socialists were urged
to celebrate this 'epoch making event.' SDF events continued to
dominate the Birmingham notices in *Clarion*. In April it was announced
that George Tooth had become a provincial member of the SDF
executive. The SDF Labour Day Celebrations would be in the Bull Ring
on Sunday 4th May. John Haddon would be in the chair and the
speakers, George Tooth, W.J.Simmonds and T.Partridge would take as
their text 'Workers of the World Unite.' The Birmingham Joint May
Day demonstration was to be held at Victoria Park gates, Small Heath
when the speakers would be J.A.Fallows, Halstead, Tom Groom and
Frank Spires. The chairman would be Hallam.

In May a Birmingham Clarion Cricket Club was announced meeting
Wednesdays and Saturdays at the Athletic Union Field, Pershore Road.
Ellis Richards was the secretary. There was to be a conference of
Birmingham and Black Country ILP branches at Bournville to consider
Socialist and Labour Unity. S.D.Shallard of the NEC would be in the
chair and Frank Spires was the convenor of the conference. Birmingham
Fellowship Club was holding a Joint Coronation Picnic. The first meeting

of the newly formed Handsworth branch of the ILP was held at the YMCA Rooms, Soho Road.

Reports of summer activity for 1902 were sparse. There was to be a Great Socialist Picnic in Sutton Park on June 21st. Birmingham Selly Oak ILP was organising an outdoor meeting opposite the Workhouse Infirmary.

By the autumn, the municipalisation of the Birmingham trams was the key political issue.

At the November municipal elections:

> Bordesley ward was fought and won for Socialism by our comrade J.A.Fallows M.A. the result is staggering to the opponents of municpal trams, workmen's houses etc. and it has been brought about by the most energetic work of the Clarionettes.

The next week a long leader in *Clarion* celebrated 'A great triumph in electing a Socialist and getting the bill through':

> It was a heavy defeat for the British-American Pierpoint-Morgan Trust. Also enormous opposition from the British Electric Trust, Industrial Freedom League, Property Owners' Association, City Association and the whole press except the *Birmingham Gazette*. For the Bill 15,139 voted, a majority of 6,581. All voters *had to come to the Town Hall*. The riff-raff were brought in by the Property Owners . . .

The year ended, however, with sadder news from the Birmingham Choral Vocal Union:

> We can hardly call this a report of our 'doings'. Mr.Beadnell has resigned his conductorship, presumably through the members failing to attend. The secretary has also been conspicuous by his absence. A few members who have continued to attend have started an elementary tonic sol-fa singing class with myself as instructor and we invite all previous members to attend on Thursday at 8-15 at the Marxian Club. It is hoped that all who can attend will do so to encourage the few who have stuck and to —
>
> A.Bayliss.

Also in December a special Cinderella night at the Metropole Hotel was announced because funds were low.

The report of Cinderella activity at the end of January 1903 stated that the feeding of the poor had started on New Year's Eve. Over 1,000 children had been fed and regaled with Punch and Judy etc. Later in the month, 500 children had been fed at the Rea Street Schools on the Wednesday and Thursday and 350-400 on the Saturday. The report was signed T.Groom, secretary, and T.Bond, treasurer.

Birmingham Clarion Fellowship announced that Joseph Crouch had accepted presidency of the Birmingham Guild of Handicrafts.

In March 1903, the Birmingham New Age Debating Society operating from 26 Smallbrook Street advertised in the paper and the formation of a Birmingham (Aston) ILP was announced.

In May, for the third year running, the existence of the Birmingham Clarion Cricket Club was announced, but again we learn nothing of their matches apart from September when there was a Great Cricket Match between the Cricketers and the Cyclists. The same month the Birmingham CCC were going to Sutton Park 'where the Wolves are coming over.' There was much good humoured rivalry between Birmingham Clarion Cyclists and those of Wolverhampton, who had a strong Club at this time.

In October, the Labour parliamentary candidates were announced. These were James Holmes for Birmingham East, W.J.Davis for Birmingham West and S.D.Shallard for Bordesley. In an important year for municipal electoral advance Alf Hunt won All Saints Ward with a vote of 1878 and a majority of 50 and at Aston there were the important bye-election victories of Berry and Haddon already discussed under S.D.F. activity.

December emphasised the up-turn in political activity. The Birmingham Labour Church inaugurated a Sunday School and the SDF announced that Hyndman would be in Birmingham talking about Chamberlain's Fiscal Policy. At the International Club, Ball Tavern, Ken Street, Comrade Gisbourne spoke on the 'Philosophy of Anarchism' on Sunday 6th. and the next week John Sketchley, the indestructible ex-Chartist spoke at the same club on 'Crimes of Governments'. Even the Clarion Vocal Union revived with a meeting at the Bull's Head where intending members were invited to attend by T.Gill, hon. sec. pro. tem.

Clarion flourished in 1904 and the paper reached its highest national circulation in March at 53,500 copies. In January the Birmingham CVU announced that a 'goodly number' had assembled on December 3rd. and they had decided to make a fresh start. There was plenty of room for more singers and a hearty welcome was extended to Fellowhippers, ILpers, SDFers and others. A Clarion Cycling Club at Small Heath was announced. They had started the previous June with 6 members and now had sixteen. In April a Birmingham Clarion Field Club was announced.

In April the paper carried a letter from John Sketchley stating that he intended bringing out his book on *Labour Movements since 1816* and personal recollections from 1838. It must come out as a subscription at a cost of 1/-d. and cloth gilt 1/6d. After publication the prices would be 1/6d. and 2/6. Intending subscribers were asked to forward their money to John Sketchley at 84, Dale end. In June a letter from a Fleet Street Clarionette supported Sketchley's book and gave the following short biography. He had been born nearly 82 years ago. From 1839 he had been secretary of the South Leicester Chartist Association. In 1851 he organised a strong Republican group connected with W.J.Linton.

In 1847 he was attached to the Socialist and Free Thought movement of Robert Owen. In 1859 his pamphlet on *Popery* led to his excommunication from the Roman Catholic church. He was a victim of the bitterest persecution and excluded from his own home. In 1872 – 73 he was the chief contributor to the *International Herald*. He settled in Birmingham in 1870. There he founded the Birmingham Republican Association on a broad Socialist platform in 1875 which became the Midland Social Democratic Association in 1878. Of late he had suffered severe losses. For 64 years he had worked well and nobly for Freedom. He was still full of energy and looked forward to still more public work. Many of Sketchley's written works were quoted in this biography.

The Cinderella work was expanding at this time and in June it was announced that it had been divided into Summer Outings, Cottage Homes, Winter Evenings and Christmas Treats, each with its own Committee.

In July a Birmingham, Coventry and Midlands Great Socialist Picnic was announced 'A brilliant programme of sports has been arranged and no speeches!' This was later said to have been 'A great success and Captain wants to give a better report', but this report has not been found.

Birmingham Labour Church announced its list of winter speakers in September. These included Mr. & Mrs. Bruce Glasier, Pete Curran, J.A.Fallows, Gustav Spiller and J.Seebohm Rowntree. The last named would speak at the Town Hall on the occasion of the Church's 12th. AGM.

1905 started with a letter from J.Simpson secretary of the B'ham ILP Federation headed 'Wake up Birmingham'. He complained that people who were Socialists were not in any organisation and he offered to compile a list of them and supply them with copies of *Clarion* for a month.

In April, the Cricket Club announced its existence again. In May there was a report of the Socialist Sunday School at the Labour Church. It had started in the previous October. The general aim was to give moral instruction irrespective of theology — 'To do good is our Religion.' There were 57 children on the books and eight adults. The average attendance was 31 and there were six classes. They were mixed boys and girls and there were no punishments or rewards. The hymn books used were 'Hymns of Love and Duty' compiled by Gustave Spiller, and 'Hymns of Modern Thought.' There was a Savings Bank and an Annual Treat. The school was financed by subscriptions from adults. They had started with a donation of £20 from John Fallows MA. The adult members all in turn became teachers and chairman. Examples of the Syllabus were given:

Class I (Big boys and girls) Dicken's Christmas Carol, Tennyson's Idylls of the Kings, Olympic Games of Greece, Music, Singing, Bible Stories, History of all Religions etc.

Class II. Kindness, Courage, Order, Mother and Father, Peace and War etc. Guided by Gould's *Book of Ethical Instruction.*

Class III. Stories — Alice in Wonderland, Stories from the Greeks, Stories from Real Life. Kindness to Old People, Unfortunates, Sick Animals etc.

Class IV. (Very Small children) Stories of animals, pictures, kindergarten work etc.

In October 1905 the Birmingham Clarion Fellowship announced its 12th. Anniversary Dinner and in November the Clarion Cyclists advertised the resumption of their winter Book Club at Knapp's Hotel, High Street. Tom Groom would kick-off dealing with H.G.Wells' *Modern Utopia*. In December the existence of the Selly Oak Labour Church was announced under the auspices of the North Worcestershire I.L.P. with lectures by 'Fred Hughes of the Socialist Centre and Tom Groom of Cinderella fame.' Their own Cinderella was also said to be flourishing.

By 1906 the national circulation of Clarion had risen even higher to 72,000. In Birmingham, artistes from the pantomime were coming to help at a concert for Cinderella funds.

In April, Fred Bramley started work in the area and was 'doing well.'

but, he reported, 'Never have I seen meaner streets or more miserable looking men and women. And this in Imperial Birmingham!'

There were few Birmingham reports for the rest of the year, but in December Bramley, who had been in the West Midlands since April, was said to have brought a two months mission in Birmingham to a close with 'good results.' Birmingham was to have its own *Clarion* van.

In February 1907 it was announced that the Birmingham van would be ready to go onto the road on May 1st. Fred Hughes, who would be in charge, was appealing for funds for the Van saying that apart from the Birmingham Fellowship organising a concert, only two Clarionettes in the whole of the midlands had subscribed. 'Would the other 498 for whom collecting sheets are waiting wake up and apply for them at the Socialist Centre.' Such financial considerations, no doubt, played a large part in the final preparations for the Van, which by April was being called the Midland Van with C.D. Drysdale in charge of it.

Again, there are few accounts of Birmingham activity in 1907, but at the end of the year the Cyclists had joined the Women's Labour League at a social and dance and the Birmingham Clarion Scouts had been re-formed.

The object of the Scouts was 'to propagate Socialism by all legal means.' The entrance fee was 1/-d. and the weekly contribution 1d. Members four weeks in arrears would be lapsed. A Board of Directors was to consist of captains, secretary, chairman, literature secretary and rank and file members. It was the duty of members to inform the secretary of anything anti-Socialist in his zone. This latter requirement was the subject matter of the first report of the Scouts in January 1908.

> On the 20th. last a regrettable incident occurred when Tory Van No. 9 came and held a meeting at Gosta Green and we never noticed it. My word, if we had only caught it!

A second report the same month was more positive. The Scouts had attended twenty four churches to date and had distributed hundreds of *Clarions* and *Labour Leaders*.

Also in January it was announced that an Unemployed Association had been recently formed in Birmingham, but its work had been frustrated by its leaders being sent to jail for varying periods. In February the Scouts went to Lozells Hall where the Christian Investigation Society had held a lecture on *Socialism*. The Scouts also appealed for any news of the Tory vans to be reported to them.

In April the Labour Church had a social to bid farewell to Tom Groom. By the middle of the year national *Clarion* circulation had climbed to 81,400, there was mention of an Aston Socialist Party choir and the clarion Scouts had been at an Asquith meeting. Police had been present in their hundreds to protect him and they had distributed about one thousand *Clarions, Leaders* and leaflets.

Summer Cinderella activity was reported by P.Banner. The work flourished in all departments, he reported, but they had to close their home this year. It was hoped to reopen it next spring. Two brake loads of children went every other Saturday to Sutton Park. The Clarion Scouts remained active, reported secretary J.Savrin Hill.

In September the Cyclists reported only a small turn-out. In October the Women's Labour League held a Sale of Work. In November members of Birmingham Cinderella were taking up Blatchford's call for Loaves for Hungry Children during the winter.

1909 saw a Bread Fund in the paper. Birmingham was distributing 700 loaves a week in January increasing to 850 the next month. In May a final Birmingham report said that all the money provided had been spent and they were satisfied that they had 'kept many starving people just alive.'

By May, the Clarion Cyclists had recovered sufficiently to muster sixty cyclists and distribute 500 *Clarions* and *Women Workers*.

Again, Birmingham reports for the year are sparse. The Midland Van was experiencing problems. Much of its activity had been in the surrounding Black Country and other parts of the midlands and not in Birmingham. The deficit for the first year had been about £12. This seems to have been paid off by a Birmingham Clarion Scouts social. But in November 1909 there was a Midlands Van Conference at the Clarion rooms, Stafford Street, Birmingham where the deficit for the second year was reported at £33. They could not consider another year's activity until this deficit was cleared.

The Van did, however, take the road again in 1910 even though it was reported in April that a Guarantee Fund was insufficient. By September Drysdale was owed £20 in wages, but he reported it the most successful season for propaganda most of which had been in the north midland counties.

When the cycling season began in the spring of 1910 there were Clarion Scouts reported at Aston Manor, Birmingham Central, Harborne and Selly Oak. The Birmingham Scouts continued active and provided good reports to the paper for most of the year. •

The Independent Labour Party 1900 – 1910.

At the turn of the century, before the jingoism of the Boer War began to bite, the Birmingham ILP showed renewed signs of vigour. A report in *ILP News* in November 1899 stated that the West Birmingham branch had 50 members and continued to make progress. A series of socials the previous winter had made the branch better known and the formation of a Cinderella had brought several women into the branch. Attention was being paid to voting lists as this branch would probably be the first to run candidates for local public bodies. Two members were already on the Birmingham Co-operative committee and doing good work. A series of indoor meetings organised jointly with the Bordesley branch had led to a debt.

Aston branch, after a period of dormancy, had been reorganised and was beginning to make its views felt in the local press. In October a new Central branch had been set up. The four branches were now federated. Comrade Shallard would be the lecturer in January under the auspices of the federation in conjunction with the Socialist Centre. Efforts were being made to resuscitate further branches which had previously existed with the eventual aim of a branch in each of the eight parliamentary constituencies. A strong central council had been formed with Robert McDonald as chairman, Alf Hunt treasurer and Frank Spires secretary. Reports of activity in 1900 are sparse however, although there were

reports of a Selly Oak branch early in the year and in November Frank
Spires had moved a successful resolution at the Trades Council affiliating
them to the Labour Representation Committee. In 1901 a South
Birmingham ILP branch was formed in July with S.F.Williams as
secretary. R.Rankin became secretary of Birmingham central. In
October, Selly Oak was recorded as a new branch with Frank Spires, who
had recently been chairman of Birmingham Central, as secretary.

In January 1902 *ILP News* was noting the proposed Home Office
enquiry into the 'disgraceful rioting at the Lloyd George meeting at the
Town Hall', commenting that few people expected anything from it,
since it was prominent members of the government who had virtually
incited the rioting, suppressed free speech and destroyed the property of
those opposed to the war. 'That the local Chamberlainite press did its best
to suggest and organise the disturbance is hardly possible of denial.'
There was still some prospect of forcing the town council to make an
investigation of some sort, but it was unlikely that anything would be
done to implicate those principally responsible for the outbreak. They
were glad to notice that Birmingham Trades Council had unanimously
passed a resolution condemning the disgraceful affair and urging the town
council to hold an enquiry, the report concluded.

From this point, jingoism in Birmingham was on the wane and political
activity rose to the peak marked by the Russian revolution of 1905 and
the general election of 1906. This was helped by S.D.Shallard settling in
Birmingham and becoming secretary of the Socialist Centre in June 1902,
the month the Boer War officially ended.

By the autumn of 1902 the Birmingham working class movement was
locked in battle with another manifestation of monopoly capital in
Birmingham. *ILP News* called this Municipalisation v Millionaires and
Monopolists and it raged round the new municipal General Powers Bill
to run trams, compel landlord improvements and regulate certain
industries:

> British Electric Traction Co. and the Property Owners' Association are
> uniting their forces for the fray. Hoardings are covered with mendacious
> statements such as municipal trams in Newcastle, Leeds, Sheffield etc.
> run at a loss and Municipal Socialism spells ruin. It is understood that
> Pierrepoint Morgan (who holds £400,000 of shares in BETC) and other
> American speculators are deeply interested in this anti-municipal
> campaign. It is rumoured that these gentlemen are hatching a scheme to
> obtain a monopoly over all the non-municipal trams in the country.
>   The appearance on a British platform of Hon.Robert Porter of
> Standard Oil Trust as an advocate of private monopoly is not
> insignificant.
>   Meanwhile the Birmingham Trades Council, ILP and Socialist
> Centre together with many progressive Liberals enthusiastically organise
> for Municipalisation.
>   A feature is the part that Arthur Chamberlain and son-in-law of
> J.S.Nettlefold is taking in support of private monopoly.
>   Shallard, referred to as 'a man of facts and figures' is organising the
> campaign for Municipalisation from the Socialist Centre.

Meanwhile J.A.Fallows was 'alarming friend and foe by the amazing
candour of his utterances during his election campaign. He had never in
his life been discreet and never intended to be. His only qualification was

his youth. He was 39 years 9 months old whereas most Liberals on the council had one foot in the grave and it would be better if both feet were there. He found another qualification however. This was that he did not drop as many 'h's' as many Labour representatives did.' Such tactics seem to have paid off; Fallows was elected as an ILP candidate by 2666 votes to the Conservative's 2485.

At the annual meeting of the Birmingham ILP Federation the same month, Fallows was congratulated, more contests promised for the coming year and an increased number of officers elected to deal with an increasing work load. These were Fallows (president), Frank Spires (chairman), T.Clay (treasurer), Alf Hunt (secretary) F.Rudland (assistant secretary) with Tom Groom and F.Broadhurst (auditors).

In January 1903 *ILP News* reported:

> S.D.Shallard may be found any day as secretary of state in the office of the Birmingham Socialist Centre and Town Crier dictating the municipal policies of the city. BETC have not sent him a card wishing him a Happy New Year.

In June a new branch was formed in East Birmingham with E.J.Simpson as secretary. In September Alfred Hunt 'a one-time student of Ruskin Hall' was nominated as municipal candidate. *ILP News* later reported this election as follows:

> We award the palm of electoral victories to Alf Hunt who won All Saints ward in the heart of Chamberlain's constituency despite a fulsome letter sent to the Unionist candidate stressing his support for Tariff Reform. The defeat of their candidate who was a popular man and chairman of the Guardians caused great chagrin.

1903 was a temporary high spot for municipal electoral success. The annual report of the Socialist Centre summarised the position as follows. Alf Hunt in a well-organised campaign won with a majority of 50. In St. Bartholomews ward J.G.Speake opposed Pentland at about a week's notice and was defeated by a large majority. At a bye-election three weeks later, however, Speake again contested the ward against a Unionist and won by 67 votes. This made the fourth member returned to the City council under the Labour Representation Committee, these being Keegan (1901) Fellows (1902) Hunt & Speake (1903). With Stevens and Toller previously elected this made a Labour group of six who were now taking concerted action which was proving effective.

There were also the successes for the new Aston Town Council to report of J.E.Berry and John Haddon. Frank Spires and T.Father representing the Sparkhill Labour Representation Committee had won the Greets ward of Yardley District Council and in the only contest in Kings Norton 'Bednall with the support of all the progressive and labour forces was successful in securing the seat by a handsome majority.'

Despite the lack of further immediate electoral success 1903 can be seen as a turning point in the Birmingham labour movement. With jingoism in temporary retreat, political activity developed to another peak in 1905–06 with the effects of the Russian revolution and the landslide Liberal victory of 1906 which brought twenty nine Labour MPs into parliament, although none of these was in Birmingham. The result was the formation of *the* Labour Party. Disillusion with the Labour leaders was quick to follow, however, and resulted in the Great Labour Unrest of 1910 – 14. This, together with the parallel growth of the women's Suffrage Movement with all their revolutionary potential, were to collapse ignominiously in the even greater jingoism of the Great War of 1914 – 18.

In Birmingham, despite the Unionist iron control, ILP branches proliferated in the city, as elsewhere, in the first decade of the new century. They had a dual but uneasy role of upholders of Socialist principles and also developers of ward organisation which tended to turn them into purely electoral machines. This led to the growing importance of the Birmingham ILP Federation co-ordinating the work of these branches. But as the Trades Council relaxed its prerogative in determining what was a Labour candidate and who would stand by disbanding its Electoral Committee, the Finance Committee of the ILP grew in importance, solving (or not solving) the key question of finding the money necessary to fund electoral activity. Co-ordination of the activity between the ILP, the other political parties (SDF and Fabians), the social and political groups around Clarion, the Labour Churches and the Trades Council, became increasingly the function of the Socialist Centre. The number of ILP branches in Birmingham eventually reached twenty five in 1910. It is impossible to trace the fortunes of all these branches as many of them were ephemeral, the minimum number necessary to set up such a branch being six members. Here there was a potential source of conflict between the Birmingham ILP Federation (or Council as it came to be known) which wanted to see the maximum number of branches, and the Finance Committee whose concern was that each branch set up was able to pay its quota of finance to support electoral activity and the wages of full-time organisers. Thus the Finance Committee tended to become the arbiter on matters beyond those purely financial.

It seems best, therefore, to temporarily leave the Birmingham ILP and deal with the Labour Churches and the Socialist Centre, both of which were closely linked with the ILP before dealing with trade union activity and bringing this section on 1900 to 1910 to a close.

Labour Churches in Birmingham.

Nationally, the Labour Church movement peaked before 1900 at about 54 such Churches. But in Birmingham the movement enjoyed a modest prosperity in the twentieth century, and at least three Churches survived until 1914.

The minutes of the main Labour Church enable us to take up the narrative again at the end of 1903. At this time John Davies was the secretary and leading EC members were Tom Groom, S.D.Shallard, J.A.Fallows and Archie Lacon. The form of leadership was under discussion, however, some members favouring a return to the old organisation of a monthly business meeting of the whole Church membership and the abolition of the EC, a proposal that the EC members opposed. Bordesley Labour Church was being asked to return 300 hymn books which had been lent to them. This is an interesting item as it is the only reference to a Labour Church at Bordesley and the number of hymn books involved suggests a not insignificant congregation. The perennial question of music at Bristol Street schools was brought up by Frank Roscoe who recommended a Mr.T.Eldridge as capable and willing to instruct the choir and take the organ at services, a proposal that was remitted to the Annual Meeting.

On the 12th. November a combined Quarterly and Annual meeting was held with Tom Groom in the chair and twenty five members present. Frank Hardie undertook to report activities to the press. G.F.Berry was elected reporter and delegate to the Labour Representation Committee. Max Sturge moved that Mr. Eldridge be engaged for three months to instruct the choir from 4-30 to 5.30 on Sunday evenings and play the organ at the subsequent evening service for a remuneration of 6/-d. for each Sunday. This was discussed briefly and passed nem. con. Then it was heartily and unanimously decided to thank comrades T.Bone and E.T.Westley for their services gratuitously rendered for so long in playing the organ. G.F.Berry reported that the Sunday school was an accomplished fact and, giving satisfaction with 13 children and five adults in average attendance. John Davies was to be paid 10/-d. per week for his services to the Church, which included the preparation of two posters per week and responsibility for seeing that all newspaper advertisements were made.

Max Sturge was thanked for long, devoted and valuable services to the Church. Membership of the Church was 86. Income for the year had been £122, although subscriptions and collections had amounted to only £57. Expenditure had been £77 including £10 rent, £6 caretaker, £40 lecturer's expenses and £21 printing and advertising. This left a healthy balance of £33, but this was due only to a large donation from Fallows of £48. Average attendances at Sunday services throughout the year had been 90. This represented a steady improvement which the EC report attributed to better lecturers ('we seldom or never have unsatisfactory lecturers, whereas this was frequent in the past'), the sound financial position ('through the generosity of comrade Councillor Fallows') and greater and more regular advertising.

The last monthly EC meeting of 1903, in December, presented the programme of Sunday lectures for the following quarter. These included, in January, lectures on the 'Economic Side of Social Reform', the 'History of Licensing in England', 'Self Sacrifice', as well as Bruce Glasier on the 'Theory of Socialism' and Shallard on 'Heinrich Heine'. February's lectures were Fallows on 'Lessons from Denmark', Cohen, the rationalist on 'Herbert Spencer', H. Snell of the Ethical Society on 'Jesus as a Social Reformer', and Councillor Morley from Halifax on the 'Moral Necesity for Socialism'. In March Denis Hird was to lecture on 'Ethics and Revolution', Prof. Muirhead from Birmingham University was to lecture on a subject to be announced and there was to be a lecture on 'Re-afforestation.' Again it can be seen that there is no religious speaker.

The December EC also discussed a proposal to amalgamate the Labour Church with the Socialist Centre and a sub-committee of Lacon, Davies, Groom, Shallard and Hardie was appointed to go into the matter.

Early in 1904 it was discovered that the appointment of Mr.Eldrige had been a mistake. He had been absent for three Sundays in November and he was written to terminating his employment. But expansion was in the air and the proposal to build a joint Trades and Socialist Hall was under active consideration. By June it was announced that the Socialist Centre and Labour church between them had taken up £350 in shares for the Hall.

The 1904 AGM in November confirmed this growth. Membership had risen from 86 to 106. Average attendance at services had risen from 90 to 117 ('although many came late, some even after the lecture had started'). The EC reported that the improved attendance made it imperative to find larger rooms, and it was desirable to hold a Reading Class to bring out younger members.

The end of 1904 brought a farewell social for Tom Bond and his family who moved to London.

Early in 1905 there was another celebration. This time it was the marriage of A.J.Fallows to fellow church member Miss Busek.

In February 1905 the annual Labour Church Conference was held at Watford. It discussed basic issues concerning which the Birmingham church was to be at odds with the majority of churches for a number of years. The two Birmingham delegates, J.H.Shaw and Lacon reported back to the Quarterly Meeting in April. There had been only 13 delegates from churches at Ashton, Birmingham, Bradford, Hyde, Leek, Nottingham, Stockport, Watford and West Bromwich. Reports from each church were read. 'None appear in a flourishing state, but all were hopeful for the future', was the verdict of the Birmingham delegates. There was a motion of several clauses defining the purpose and nature of the Church. The first, which was passed unanimously was:

> The Labour Church exists to give expression to the Religion of the Labour Movement.

The second clause was the controversial one involving the Birmingham Church:

> That the religion of the Labour Movement is not sectarian or necessarily theological, but respects each indivdual's personal convictions.

This was opposed by no less than four separate amendments from the Birmingham Church. The first was to reframe the clause to read:

> The Labour Church neither denies nor confirms life after death or a reality beyond experience, but respects each individual opinion on these matters.

This was defeated and Birmingham delegates then moved the deletion of the whole clause. This also was defeated as was their third amendment, which was to removed the words 'or necessarily theological' Their fourth amendment was finally carried so that the final version read:

> The religion of the Labour Movement is not necessarily theological, but respects each individual's personal conviction on this question.

Although the argumentation behind these amendments is nowhere given, the intention appears to prevent any direct association of the Labour Churches with theological churches, but if this is the case, one is surprised by the opposition from a majority of the other labour Churches. The next clause was also amended by the Birmingham delegate and lost by one vote. This was to be an annual amendment which was finally carried in 1909. The original clause was:

> The Religion of the Labour Movement seeks the realisation of universal well-being by the establishment of a Co-operative Commonwealth founded upon Justice and Love.

The lost Birmingham amendment was to delete 'a Co-operative Commonwealth' and substitute 'Socialism'. Another Birmingham proposal was also defeated. This concerned a Report by the Hymn Book Committee which was charged with the duty of preparing a new hymn book. The Birmingham proposal was that all hymns containing theological words should be deleted from the new book. This was lost by several votes.

The intent of the Birmingham resolutions and the reason for their defeat was given by the Birmingham delegates:

> We must complain at the chairmanship of J.H.Belcher. He was unfair in carrying out his duties; he often spoke on amendments immediately preceding the vote. He was entirely responsible for the narrow defeat of the Birmingham Agnostic and Socialist amendments.

Other motions at the Conference had been less controversial. Birmingham had proposed a motion for the preparation of ceremonies for Labour Churches on the occasion of Births, Marriages, Burials or Cremations. This was carried nem.con. But the actual forms of ceremonial were to generate much controversy in the future. A West Bromwich motion asking for 'whole-hearted support for the Labour Representation Movement' was passed. The Birmingham delegates thought the 'most up-to-date and vital question raised at the Conference was the one raised by the Watford delegates that the Government take immediate steps to carry out the recommendations of the Inter-Departmental Committee on Physical Deterioration, in particular those dealing with the care of infants and children. This had been 'passed with acclamation.' Finally, the national standing of the Birmingham Church at this time was emphasised by the final matter:

> Your delegates invited the Conference to Birmingham next year. This was accepted.

The Annual Business Meeting of November 1905 reported mixed fortunes for the Birmingham Church. Average attendances were down to 114, but forty new members had meant a net growth of eleven. The problem of late arrivals had been solved by closing the doors when the lecturer commenced. The financial position was 'by no means satisfactory.' A finance sub-committee had been appointed which had issued a circular asking for increased contributions, but it had met with a poor response. A one shilling fund to pay off a £10 debt had raised only £3 and the deficit on the town Hall meeting could not be met so a Guarantee Fund had been promoted to which it was hoped all members would respond.

Cinderella work does not figure in the Labour Church minutes, but a letter head affixed to the minutes is a reminder of how dependent this was on Church members, the secretary being Tom Groom, the Cottage Home organiser Percy Banner, and the treasurer Max Sturge.

The annual conference of Labour Churches was held in Birmingham in March 1906. Arrangements for Birmingham's annual motion changing the aims from Co-operative Commonwealth to Socialism were finalised, but a written report by Miss Margaret Smith said to be affixed to the minutes, has not been found.

The proposed programme of weekly lectures on Sunday evenings at Bristol Street Schools showed the usual non-theological mix. J.A.Dale, secretary of the Ruskin Society spoke on the 'History of Popular Education'. Two London speakers from the Ethical Society were Dr. Oakeshott on the 'Ethics of Natural Beauty' and Harry Snell on the 'Captive City of God'. Dennis Hird from Ruskin lectured on 'the Struggle with the Dead'. The only topical lecture was by Aylmer Maude, the translator of Tolstoy, on the 'Crisis in Russia'. Women lecturers were prominent, Margaret Bondfield speaking on the 'General Election', Mrs. Despard on the 'Child Under Socialism' and Charles Bradlaugh's daughter, Mrs.Bradlaugh-Bonner on the 'New Index'. The only local lecturer was A.J.Fallows on 'Wells' Kipps'.

In March a Labour church delegate attended the AGM of the Birmingham Labour Representation Committee and pronounced himself 'not impressed':

> The business was mainly routine; the reading of the annual report (which had already been printed) and the election of officers. Personally I was not much impressed by the methods pursued by the late officer, but as our friend Fred Hughes is elected as Secretary and, as a point of departure, is to be supported by an E.C. it is most likely that there will be a great improvement in the future.

May Day brought a plethora of demonstrations, all of which were supported by the Labour Church. Aston Manor received support for their demonstration at Whitehead Road at 11 am and a donation of 10/-d was granted. The ILP Federation and Socialist Centre received support for their demonstration at 3 p.m. on the 6th. May at Small Heath Park Gates and were granted £1. The Trades Council sought co-operation for their Town Hall meeting at 7 p.m. on the same day. Literature at both the afternoon and evening meetings was provided by the Labour Church.

The November 1906 annual meeting elected the following officers. Percy Broadhurst (secretary), Frank Bradshaw (assistant-secretary), Archie Lacon (treasurer), Arthur Wilson and Amy Bishton (collectors), Frank Knibb (literature secretary), and Victor Norman (asst.lit sec.). The Committee consisted of these officers plus the Misses Ethel Lewis, Constance Prior and Connie B.Taylor, together with Max Sturge, Herbert Shaw and R. Sewell. At this AGM the EC wanted to abandon the quarterly general members meetings and this was proposed by Lacon and supported by Tom Groom. It was opposed by Percy Broadhurst and Frank Hardie. With its usual independence of mind, the meeting defeated the proposal by a large majority.

The report of the EC showed average attendances at lectures up to a healthy 130, but membership had slipped, 28 joining and 31 leaving, giving a total membership of 116. There had been three Birmingham delegates at the annual conference of Labour Churches and Max Sturge had represented the Church at the Third National Peace Congress of Great Britain which had been held in Birmingham. The deficit on the Town Hall meeting had been £8-11-0d.

A decision which was inevitably to cause problems was the charitable one to pay John Davies 2/6d. a week. Davies, who had given many years service to the Church and who had latterly been secretary, had been taken ill and spent several months in hospital. He had now been discharged, but was a permanent invalid. A sub-committee of Tom Groom, J.A.Sayers and the Church treasurer had been set up to supervise a fund.

Archie Lacon ended his secretary's report with an all-too-rare reference to other Labour Churches in Birmingham looking forward to the time 'when there would be Labour Churches in all parts of the City.'

The annual demonstration which opened the Church year in the autumn was another outstanding success. Philip Snowden was the speaker. The Town Hall had been crowded in all parts and the doors had been closed half an hour before the meeting started.

1907 opened with further indications of progress. A branch of the Women's Labour League had been started in Birmingham with Mrs.Fiorci, a Labour Church activist for many years, as secretary. A recruitment drive for trade unionists had been supported with the proposal for a Trades Exchange. The *Birmingham Weekly Mercury* had offered one page each week to the Labour movement and the Church discussed whether this offer should be taken up. But the *Labour Mail* was being published at this time and some thought that this should be their priority. Fred Hughes, however, thought that the offer might not be repeated and it would be given to 'more dubious Labour men.' This matter was left to the next meeting.

Hughes had found premises at the corner of Edmund Street and Easy Row at a rent of £50 p.a. which he thought would be suitable for permanent Church premises and a sub-committee was set up to pursue this matter. This was subsequently overtaken by a proposal for a Labour Institute in Bristol Street, which in turn came to nothing.

A written report of the annual conference of Labour Churches held in Stockport in March is in the Church minute book, signed by the delegates Archie and Annie Lacon. They reported that the national hymn book had been discussed and Birmingham had supported the Hyde delegates in objecting to too many theological hymns being included. The form of a burial service presented to the delegates was also opposed by Birmingham. Birmingham and West Bromwich had joined in objections to their Churches being described as 'Atheistic.' Finally, Birmingham had moved their annual motion on 'Socialism' and had again been defeated. Archie Lacon had relieved some of his frustrations when, in seconding the Vote of Thanks he had said that since no matter of public concern had been voiced and the question of the Emancipation of women had not been raised, the delegates could not congratulate themselves on this year's Conference.

At the quarterly meeting in June 1907 the national draft of a burial service was approved. The E.C. also drew attention to the steadily decreasing number of members which was only partially accounted for by the growth of other Labour churches in the city. These Labour Churches were not named, however.

In November there was an indication of the thoroughness with which the EC prepared for the AGM when they drew up a complete list of officers to recommend to the general meeting plus a slate of twelve other prospective committee members from whom six were to be elected.

In 1908 the EC made early preparations for the Labour Church Union AGM held at Bradford in March. Tom Groom and Percy Broadhurst were recommended as delegates. Birmingham's usual resolutions were drafted. The first requested the removal of all thological hymns from the national hymn book. The second was the clause on 'Socialism' to be strengthened this year by the more radical demand that the name of the organisation be changed from Labour Church to Socialist Church. These proposals met with opposition from the members at the quarterly Meeting in February. Frank Knibb and Percy Broadhurst moved that the first resolution on theological hymns 'be expunged.' This was lost and Broadhurst then asked not to be sent as a delegate, and Percy Banner was elected instead. Fred Bradshaw then moved that in future resolutions for the Labour Church Union conference be considered at the Birmingham Church AGM in November.

The whole Birmingham labour movement suffered a severe loss in 1909 when Tom Groom and his family moved to London. Groom deserves recognition as a local leader of equal stature with national leaders of the time. At a farewell social in April he was presented with a revolving bookcase and some books. This left an unspent balance of £2-18-0d. from £7 collected. The EC suggested to Groom that he purchase further books with this sum. But photographs at the social had turned out badly and Groom insisted, from motives unlikely to have been egotistical, on the purchase of one dozen cabinet photographs of himself from which postcards would be made which would be sold to raise funds for the Cinderella. Groom and his wife were subsequently elected Honorary Life Members of the Church, as were Mr. & Mrs. Sayers, who also left Birmingham about the same time after many years service to the Church.

The loss of Tom Groom was at least partially offset by a new member. At the February EC Percy Banner reported that a recently joined member, Mr. Pascoe, was prepared to attempt to form a Labour Church choir. The matter was referred to the quarterly meeting. The next month it was decided to hire a room for choir practice at 2/6d. per night and the harmonium at Bristol Street Schools for 10/-d. per annum. One dozen tune hymn books were also to be purchased, half of which were to be placed at Mr. Pascoe's disposal and the other half sold to members. Non-church members were to be admitted to the choir at the discretion of Mr. Pascoe. Pascoe's more abiding service, however, was to take over much of the Cinderella activity previously performed by Tom Groom.

1908 brought a break with the London based Ethical Union. The Birmingham church was affiliated to the Ethical Union and, as we have seen, its speakers from London were popular at the church. But the affiliation fee was a drain on scarce funds, and this was made the excuse for the eventual break, although the increasingly Socialist tendencies of the church and the movement at this time, may have been the predominant motive. In December 1906 a letter had been read from the Ethical Society Union asking that each Labour Church member take the four-page monthly journal which was to replace Ethical Review. The Church replied that it could not accede to this request. A year later there was an appeal for funds from the Union; this was deferred. In April 1908 it was resolved to cease affiliation to the Union. The grounds given were that there was a resolution before the annual conference of the Union to increase subscriptions and the Church could not afford this. In addition, Birmingham's remoteness from the Ethical Union's centre of activities made it difficult to take any active part in the affairs of the organisation. Subsequently a letter was received from Harry Snell, the secretary, asking the Church to reconsider its decision, but the members remained adamant.

At the April quarterly meeting, membership of .the church was reported as down to 77. This was because of the effects of a previous resolution to remove from the membership all who failed to renew their subscriptions after being personally visited. Eleven new members had been made, but twenty six had been struck off. The same meeting heard a full report of the Labour Church annual conference. Twelve churches had been represented, all of which seemed to be thriving. Hyde church had abandoned the national hymn book because of its theological content. The proposed burial service had been remitted to the branches and information was to be sought concerning Consecrated Ground. Birmingham's usual two resolutions had again been put and lost, the deletion of theological hymns by 13 votes to 7 and the change of name by 12 to 8. But Lacon's strictures of the previous year had not applied, for three resolutions on matters of national concern had been passed. The first stated that as the capitalist sytem was unable to prevent unemployment, the time had come for the state to provide work for all the unemployed. The second said that as the land and all the instruments of production were in private hands for individual profit and workers were unable to secure a fair return for their labour when employed, and were often unemployed, the time had come to provide Old Age Pensions on a non-contributing basis and free from the taint of the Poor Law. The third resolution demanded full and free education for every child to the age of sixteen and state measures to ensure adequate food, clothing and housing for all children.

At the November AGM, attended by twenty six members, the EC reported average attendances for the year down from 130 to 112. The highest attendance had been 213 for Mrs. Bruce Glasier in September and the lowest 62 for Fred Hicks in December, when there had been a snow storm. But the committee had taken strong measures to maintain attendances, including a special 'whip' for all members in August preparatory to the new season. 'These efforts seem not to have been without avail.'

The Labour Church was now entering a stormy period. The euphoria of Labour successes at the 1906 general election was fading fast into a disillusionment with the new Labour Party leadership and the right-ward drift of its two best known leaders, Philip Snowden and Ramsay Macdonald. Lloyd George and the new Liberal radicals were putting forward their package of social reforms, aspects of which were opposed by militants in the labour movement, particularly as the main purpose of the reforms were seen to be the retention of working class support for the Liberals and not the ending of the capitalist system. Mass unemployment was again a main issue. The constitutional struggle with the Lords culminating in the two general elections in 1910 lay ahead.

The surfacing of all these trends within the Labour Church can best be exemplified by the problems of the annual Town Hall public meeting that opened each Labour Church year in September, and especially the problems of the 1908 meeting.

Preparations for these meetings had to be made early in each year. The first step was to draw up a list of the crowd pullers such as Keir Hardie, Snowden, Ramsay Macdonald, Bruce Glasier, H.M.Hyndman, George Bernard Shaw etc. and hope that at least one of these would be available and willing. In July 1907 two uncompromising and very controversial Socialists had won sensational parliamentary by-election victories. These were Pete Curran at Jarrow and Victor Grayson at Colne Valley. The preferred candidates for the Town Hall meeting in Birmingham for that year having failed to materialise, it was proposed by the EC that Pete Curran be invited as the town Hall speaker. This was passed, but a motion by Herbert Shaw that Grayson be invited to chair the meeting was lost in favour of one of three local speakers, Fred Hughes, Frank Spires or Miss Margaret Smith. It was later reported that the Town Hall had been crowded in all parts, but unfortunately, Pete Curran's vocal powers had not been at their best! A deficit of £6 had been incurred.

In 1908 the preferred list had been drawn up in January and consisted of Ramsay Macdonald, Victor Grayson and the chairman of the Labour Party. By February it was known that Macdonald had refused on the grounds that he was already booked for one Birmingham meeting during that year, the chairman of the Labour Party had refused on the grounds that he never accepted engagements on Sundays and Grayson had been written to twice, without response, and a wire had now been sent to him at the House of Commons. By March, Grayson had consented to be the speaker and Robert Blatchford was to be the chairman. Having netted two such large fish it was decided to investigate the costs of hiring the Grand Theatre or the Hippodrome, the advantage being that whilst there would be costs for hiring the theatre whereas the Town Hall was granted free, a charge could be made for the theatre and the possibility arose of lifting the burden of the annual deficit of the town hall meeting. By May the Hippodrome had been booked at a cost of £12 which included all facilities and the attendants.

Victor Grayson was a spell-binder of a speaker. He had in fact once spoken at a Sunday lecture of the Birmingham Labour Church before being catapulted to national fame. This had been in December 1906. Attendances that month showed that Aylmer Maude had attracted 117 people, a session of Readings and Music 84, Victor Grayson 83 and Fred

Hicks 62. But it was stressed that the low average attendance of 84 that month had been due to extremely inclement weather.

Before the Hippodrome meeting took place there were to be other developments. In October a letter was received from the Clarion Scouts asking support for their Town Hall meeting on the 29th. at which Blatchford was to be chairman. The church wrote back, more in sorrow than anger, pointing out that in view of the nearness of the date to the Hippodrome meeting the Scouts meeting could only prejudice the success of the labour Church meeting. They suggested that in future the Scouts consult with other Socialist organisations before arranging their meetings. However, with a magnanimity which was to pay rich dividends, the Church went on to say:

> We will have great pleasure in assisting you as the Labour Church has always endeavoured to act as a unifying influence and we hope that the Scouts will work for our Hippodrome meeting.

Very detailed arrangments were made for the Hippodrome meeting:

1. *Posters.* 100 black on yellow 90" × 60" to be posted a fortnight immediately prior to the date of the meeting and to be kept on the walls until Sunday November 19th. The wording to be on the same lines as last year with the addition of the following places for the purchase of tickets ILP Publications Society, John Bright St. F.A.Lacon 24 Grosvenor Rd. F.Hughes, Socialist Centre, and The Secretary, 47 Bishopton road Bearwood.
2. *Handbills.* 10,000 with list of lectures on back. Colour — black on yellow. Question of distribution to be left to the Sub-Committee.
3. *(a) Tickets.* Orchestra stalls (reserved and numbered price 1/6d. (Settee at back of stalls to be numbered also.) Circle, unreserved 1/-d. Pit 6d. Gallery free — but Collection. Note to be put on 'Reserved' tickets that no seats reserved after 6-45.
(b) *Quantities* Orchestra stalls in accordance with number of seats. Circle 800, Pit 1000, Gallery 1500 Platform 200 — 'admit bearer and friend.'
(c) *Distribution of tickets.* Reserved seats — in the hands of the persons named on the posters. Gallery tickets — some to ILP secretaries Platform by C.Brown in conference with F.Hughes, secy Socialist Centre.
4. *Hymns.* 4000 Hymn Sheets. Hymns selected 1. 9. 6. offer of help from West Bromwich and Aston choirs (jointly) accepted. Expenses abour £1. Choir to give a few glees prior to commencement of meeting. Pianist to be arranged for by Choirmaster of W.B. & Aston choirs — Mr.Nicholas.
5. *Stewards.* For Orchestra Stalls 15, Circle 10, Pit 6, Platform 2, Gallery 15. Organiser on night — Tom Groom, if possible. Literature stewards to be in addition and selected byFrank Knibb.
6. *Advertisements.* Labour Leader 2-6d, Clarion 5-0d, Justice 1-0d, Woman Worker 1-0d, Daily Mail 10-0d. to be inserted week before.

Meanwhile, Grayson's reputation for militancy was growing as he raised the question of unemployment in the House of Commons and incurred the wrath of the Labour Party leaders who he castigated as traitors for not bringing the House of Commons to a halt on the question. Eventually Grayson was suspended from the House. The fact that this 'trouble maker' was to appear at the Hippodrome came to the ears of the

Birmingham Tory and Unionist mafia who began to spread rumours that there would be violence at the meeting. What actually occurred appears in two reports to the Labour Church. The first was an EC report of the 5th. December:

> The Hippodrome meeting was a great success. It was crowded in all parts and almost as many were turned away. In spite of fears to the contrary, the meeting was entirely peaceful, thanks no doubt to 200 stewards. There was trouble with a license for music for a piano. The licensing authorities refused to license a piano, but stated that they did not think anyone would object if a piano was used. But the management refused to allow a piano. The hymns were sung, however, thanks to the assistance of Mr.Nicholas' Socialist Choir. When the Secretary of the Hippodrome found that Grayson and Blatchford were to be the speakers he expressed his indignation that the Hall should be used by two such firebrands and stated that if he had known he doubted whether the Directors would have let the håll. PHB was of the opinion that we would not get the Hippodrome again.

The second report was given to the quarterly meeting in January 1909:

> There was widespread interest in Grayson due to his suspension from the Commons on unemployment, but there was some criticism of the chairmanship of Blatchford. An agenda was prepared for him but he did not adhere to it omitting the second hymn and omitting to announce the collection in the gallery. There had been disquieting rumours of violence, but the meeting was entirely orderly, thanks to the stewards under Tom Groom. There was valuable co-operation from the Clarion Scouts with stewarding and the sale of literature.

And the Hippodrome meeting was not only a political success, but a financial one as well, the profit being no less thatn £32-2-9-d.

Predictions proved to be true. No private venue was available for the 1909 meeting and preparations began normally enough. In February the preferred panel of speakers was George Bernard Shaw, Keir Hardie, Philip Snowden and G.N.Barnes. The next month it was known that Keir Hardie could not come and Philip Snowden was therefore booked for the Town Hall

Before proceeding to the sequel it would be better to back-track to the other activities of the Church in 1908 – 09 to provide the background for what was to come.

At this time Percy Broadhurst was secretary. It was he who produced what has become a classic statement of the function of a Labour Church at a time when its role was changing and its useful existence was under challenge. The Labour Church exists:

> As the common meeting ground of men and women of all sections of the Socialist movement and where the SDF lion may lie down with the ILP lamb and receive the benediction of the Fabians.

Broadhurst was involved in an incident which throws some light on Church proceedings while he was secretary. In September 1908 Fred Hughes was giving the Sunday lecture at Bristol Street when he was heckled by a Communist Anarchist, C.Kean. Broadhurst then invited Kean to lecture at the church and proposed a motion to that effect, which was passed. For these actions Broadhurst was criticised at the next EC. In·his defence, Broadhurst admitted that his action was 'technically unconstitutional' but he pleaded that the circumstances were special and that it was 'active democracy.' The secretary's action was strongly condemned, although the EC agreed that Kean should speak. The EC then passed a motion adding Kean's name to the list of speakers.

Early in 1909 the EC considered their usual motions for the annual Labour Church Conference. They also recommended C.Brown and Mrs. Fiorci as the two delegates. At the quarterly meeting, the members, however, rejected the deletion of all theological hymns by 11 votes to 9, but agreed that the name should be changed to Socialist Church with the necessary constitutional changes that this would involve. A resolution to publish 'the form of Burial service submitted to the Churches for their approval in 1907' was amended to 'publish *some* form of Burial Service . . .'

At this time Max Sturge resigned from the Church for reasons that were not given. It was acknowledged that 'he had made a large contribution to the success of the Church and his services would be greatly missed.'

In March, the event occurred which was to affect the Snowden town hall meeting. Arthur Wilson reported that a Joint Socialist Committee had been formed which had resolved to hold four large meetings in Birmingham in 1909, one of which would be the Labour Church meeting.

The issue of theological hymns was becoming complicated by the fact that the old hymn books (presumably the local one discussed above) were wearing out and it had been agreed that they be replaced by the national hymn book. A Hymn Book Sub-Committee had been set up which, in April, had declared that no less than 75 of the hymns were 'unfit for use.'

The April quarterly meeting of the Church was notable for two events. The first was the report of the annual Labour Church Union Conference. At this Conference the Birmingham proposal that the name be changed from Labour Church to Socialist Church had at last been accepted. In the new hymn book there was a number of printing errors and these had been pointed out by the Birmingham delegates. Nine churches had been represented at the Conference.Hyde with 150 had the highest number of members and Hanley with 75 the lowest. Watford appeared to be the most active church; Longton now had a weekly newspaper and Stockport had the largest Sunday School with 150 pupils and 15 teachers. Nearly all the Churches had such Sunday schools and these were now becoming more popular than the Churches themselves. The report ended by saying that but for Victor Grayson many of these Labour Churches would be penniless. So it was not only Birmingham that was benefitting from Grayson's oratory and popularity.

The other item discussed at the April Quarterly was an attack by the Birmingham ILP Federation on the decision to change the name from Labour to Socialist Church The Federation had passed the following motion which was sent to the Church:

> Seeing that the term 'Church' is understood to apply to ecclesiastical bodies and religious sects, this Conference hereby deprecates the decision arrived at by a section of the Movement to establish a Socialist

Church as envincing a narrow sectarian spirit and likely to create an erroneous impression that Socialism is a new religious Sect; and further, extends to all men and women who desire a juster social order a hearty welcome to its ranks and leaves all questions to the private judgment of individuals.

To this, a spirited reply was sent:

Resolved that the Birmingham ILP Federation be informed that whilst the members of the Socialist Church accept in a friendly spirit the criticism of their comrades, they feel bound to point out that as the Church is, and always has been, a separate body from the ILP the criticism either of its name or methods hardly comes within the province of the Federation.

That it be further pointed out to the Federation that their deprecation of the use of the word 'Church' is rather belated having regard to the fact that this organisation was founded, under the name of the Labour *Church* as long ago as 1892 (before the formation of the ILP) and that while the adjective was changed by the Union of Labour Churches at their recent Conference, the noun has not been altered. The members of the Birmingham Socialist Church are, therefore, at a loss to understand why this word should so suddenly appear objectionable to the ILP.

It is noticed that the ILP deprecate the decision to establish a Socialist Church as 'evincing a narrow sectarian spirit' and that their resolution goes on to state that they 'leave all questions of religion to the private judgement of individuals.' In reply to this charge of 'narrow sectarianism' and the implication contained in the latter part of the resolution that the Socialist Church attempts to interfere with the private judgment of the individual on matters of theological or religious belief, the following Aims and Principles are quoted:-

The Socialist Church exists to give expression to the religion of the Labour Movement.

The religion of the Labour Movement is not theological but respects each individual's personal convictions on this question.

The religion of the Labour Movement seeks the realisation of universal well-being by the establishment of Socialism: a Commonwealth founded upon Justice and Love.

The religion of the Labour Movement declares that the improvement of social conditions and the development of personal character are both essential in emancipation from social and moral bondage; and to that end insists upon the duty of studying the economic and moral forces of society.

As a proof, if such be needed, that the Church is neither narrow nor sectarian in its methods, the attention of the ILP is drawn to the following facts:

1.   That the Church maintains a broad platform open alike to representatives of the ILP,SDP, Fabian Society, Church Socialist League, Clarion Scouts, Women's Suffrage Movement (all sections) and social Reformers generally — the only test being the one of ability — and that quite recently a Christian was allowed to deliver an address in reply to a critical lecture delivered by Mr.Dennis Hird having reference to Christianity.

2.   That the Church has always been pleased to render help to any local Labour or Socialist organisation.

3.   That it is affiliated to the Labour Representation Council.

Having regard to the foregoing circumstances and to the fact that the Church affords a common meeting ground for socialists of all shades of opinion, where they may forget for a time their differences as to mere matters of policy or procedure in their agreement upon the great social ideal towards which we are all working, the Members claim that, so far from being a disintegrating force, the Socialist Church is working to attain that unity which is so much desired in the Socialist ranks.

Further light was also shed on the formation of the Joint Socialist Committee which suggests that the ILP Federation attack on the Church was the result of a split between the Birmingham ILP Federation and its branches since the Committee had been formed on a proposal by the ILP, the SDP, the Socialist Centre, the Clarion Scouts and the Labour Church.

These events now lead back to Snowden and his proposed Town Hall meeting. In May 1909 Snowden wrote asking under whose auspices his meeting would be held. He was told that it was organised by the Labour Church, but was part of a series of meetings organised by the Joint Socialist Committee. Snowden then cancelled the engagement on the grounds that he was associating with other organisations with which he had no sympathy. The Church was in no mood to kow-tow to such views. Snowden was no longer the young, slightly deformed enthusiast traipsing the country in all weathers and preaching the gospel of Socialism to all who would listen. Snowden, together with his wife Ethel, was now an Important Figure in the Labour Party, acquiring the 'statesmanlike qualities' that were to mark his right-ward march to eventual betrayal of the Party in 1931. The Church wrote back to Snowden expressing their surprise that he had *no* sympathy with some Socialist organisations and telling him that his action would cause disaffection and disappointment among rank and file Socialists. The cancellation would be accepted, however, and Leonard Hall had been engaged to speak in his place. Leonard Hall was already a well-known militant and he was destined to play an important role in the formation of the British Socialist Party in Birmingham.

This dispute reached down to the Joint Socialist Committee, and in July it was reported that the Birmingham ILP Federation had resigned from the Committee on the grounds that 'some object to Hyndman and others to Chiozza Money M.P. being on the list of speakers, but we will stand by any financial obligation undertaken.'

In October the church suffered another severe loss when Archie and Annie Lacon resigned. A letter of regret was sent thanking the Lacons and stating that the success of the Church had been largely due to their continuous, enthusiastic and self-sacrificing labours. The Committee was glad to learn that they would continue their work for the same Cause in their new home.

In December 1909 the EC was putting proposals to the membership for the first of the Socialist Church Union Annual Conferences. These included the compulsory change of name from Labour to Socialist Church, but if that failed the name shouild be Socialist and Labour Church Union. They also wanted a revision of the aims and principles of the organisation. Whether the members accepted these resolutions, we cannot say as the available minutes of the Birmingham Socialist Church end in December 1909.

We can close by showing the state of the Church as reported to the

AGM in October 1909. Forty two members were present. The officers elected were A.Williams and Dolly Parkes (secretaries), Mr.Sewell (treasurer), Mr. & Mrs Knibbs (collectors) C.Walton & F.Pascoe (literature secretaries), F.Pascoe (choirmaster). As the choir had not grown as expected the office of choir secretary was dispensed with. The commitment to Cinderella remained strong with Percy Banner as secretary, C.E.Smith as treasurer, and ten Socialist Church representatives on the committee. The treasurer reported that with income at £76-15-11 and expenditure at £76-19-7d, the balance of 10/3d. which had been brought forward was reduced to 3/8d. Average attendances had been up at 145 compared with 112 the previous year, but the number of paying members was down from 99 to 87. The secretary's conclusion was that it had been another year of useful work, but the number of members was disappointing and far too few for the needs of the Church.

Other Labour Churches in Birmingham

We have already mentioned three other Labour Churches in Birmingham, Bordesley, Erdington and Selly Oak. No other references to these have, however, been found and one must therefore conclude that all were short lived. But the records of two others have survived; the first is Stirchley Labour Church and the other is King's Heath Labour Church.

The Stirchley records take the form of two printed syllabuses for the Church years October to March 1911 – 12 and 1913 – 14. These syllabuses include a large number of commercial advertisements and valuable photographs and potted biographies of speakers. There is also additional information to be gleaned indirectly. For instance, the 1913 – 14 syllabus states that after holding its meetings for five sessions in Council schools, the current session would be held at the Institute, Stirchley. So from this it is to be inferred that this church was founded in 1908.

In 1911 – 12 the Sunday lectures were in the Stirchley Council Schools at 6-30 p.m. and branch meetings were held every Thursday at the Clarion Club 13a, Bournville Lane, Stirchley at 8 p.m. There were also frequent social events. Socialists desirous of joining were asked to apply to the secretary, Wilfred Brookes, at 58 Bournville Lane or the chairman, Cyril Harding, at 10, Victoria Road, Stirchley.

It is noticeable that all the speakers advertised were local people. The session was opened by Julia Varley, the organiser of the Women Workers' Union, speaking on 'Sweated Industries'. Other lectures in October were Kneeshaw on 'Socialism and the Railways', Professor Muirhead on 'Methods of Social Democracy', R.Clements (advertised as 'a young man who is going far') on the 'Life of William Morris.' Among other speakers that year were Philip Durant, who had been a member of the Socialist Centre for four years, was the founder of the *Commercial Traveller*, of the Commercial Travellers' Socialist Society and a member of Carrs Lane Church; Tom Bryan, who was warden of Fircroft College and who had been the mayor of Southwark in 1902, speaking on 'Walt Whitman; Bertram Ladkin ,who was the grandson of a Chartist and had served as a sergeant throughout the Boer War on 'A Night with the Poets'; Dorothy Evans, who was the organiser of the WSPU and who had served seven days in Winson Green jail as a tax resister, speaking on 'Votes for Women' and Beatrice Orange, who was ex-Cheltenham Ladies' College and Girton College and currently sub-Warden of the Women's Hostel at Birmingham University, speaking on 'A Greek Socialist'.

The lack of theological content in the programme is marked. This could also be said for the session two years later, but the 1913 – 14 syllabus does seem to have been a more ambitious one, reflecting no doubt, the hopes of moving from the council school to Stirchley Insitute. It included many local speakers such as George Shann, Eldred Hallas, Jack Beard, Frank Spires etc. but also national speakers. Among these were Keir Hardie, J.C.Wedgwood M.P., J.Walton Newbold M.P., who was to become the first Communist M.P., and Katherine Glasier.

The 1913 – 14 Syllabus also advertised the Stirchley Men's A.B.C. This organisation met from 2-45 to 4 p.m. presumably every Sunday, at the Stirchley Council Schools. whether this organisation was an integral part of the Stirchley Labour Church or whether it was a separate organisation cannot be deduced, but its aims are worth quoting in full, both because the secular ones would be fully in accord with the aims of the Labour Church, but also because they include a specific commitment to Christianity which would differentiate it from the Labour Church:

1. To study the bible frankly, freely, reverently, and without prejudice.
2. To encourage International Brotherhood.
3. To advance Equality of Opportunity.
4. In short, to help men and women to understand the life of Jesus Christ and encourage them in their personal allegiance to Him.

The other Labour Church in Birmingham for which there are records is the King's Heath Church. It lives, however, only in the minutes of the Kings Heath Independent Labour Party. These minutes have survived for the period October 1906 to December 1911. All the main decisions regarding the church seem to have been made by the ILP and it is difficult to regard the Church as a separate or independent organisation.

Kings Heath ILP branch was inaugurated in October 1906. The next month the minutes reveal that for music at their meetings the secretary was to acquire two dozen Labour Church hymn books and the formation of a choir and the appointment of a choirmaster was discussed and had been deferred. The next month the hymn book purchase was rescinded for lack of funds. In August 1907 it was resolved to introduce Labour Hymns at meetings and a Choir Committee of Comrades Ballard, Robinson, Mullins, Read, Viney and Harper were to organise musical items. In August 1908 Comrades Harper and Price were delegated to attend the Church Socialist League Conference. In November 1908 a sub-Committee had resolved to *re-start* the Labour Church on the second Sunday in January the next year. In March 1909 it was resolved that the Labour Church be run, until further notice, from the ILP branch. The same month a letter of condolence was to be sent to the wife of the late Comrade David Read and an offering of £1 made at the Labour Church was to be handed informally to the widow. At this meeting it was also agreed to raise the question of a Socialist Sunday School. In June it was agreed that 'Comrade Hallas' generous offer to give four lectures at the Labour Church next session be accepted,' and the secretary was to be furnished with a list of the speakers at the previous session of the Labour Church to see who should be invited again. At the same meeting arrangements were to be made for an open-air meeting to be held with the Rev.G.H.Davis on 'Socialism and the Bible.' The seriousness with which such an open-air meeting was approached is shown by the fact that 4,000 'bills' were to be distributed and Comrade Hallas had the printing in hand.

In August Hallas reported that the Labour Church meetings would commence on 26th. September and the administration of the session was outlined with considerable detail by the ILP branch. Comrades Francis, Bengough, Sharpe, Roberts, Hanbrook and Ballard were to be chairman for one month in turn. Church stewards were to be chosen from Hanbrook, Francis, Clarke, Price, Harris and Smith. Music was to be arranged by Ballard. Two thousand Syllabuses were to be printed on post cards and a large poster made. Bengough undertook to sell literature at the meetings. C.D.Drysdale, the Clarion Vanner, was to be booked for one evening at the Church and a further four dozen hymn books were to be ordered at at cost of 3/-d. There are no other important references to the Church until March, when it was resolved to end the current session on the 10th. April.

Preparations for the 1910 – 11 session began in July, but again, only administrative details were discussed: A suitable person must be appointed for proper readings. The collection was to be made without announcements from the chairman; instead, a voluntary was to be played by the organist. Final arrangements were to be made by the ILP EC. The desirability of a choir should again be discussed by the branch.

The choir came into existence in September when it met at Comrade Sharpe's house, 184 Addison Road. A week later the choir was being asked to attend for a short practice at 5-45 pm before the Church opened. In February 1911 a special branch meeting with Edward Sharpe in the chair was called to discuss the financial position of the branch. A crisis had occurred because of the activities of the Labour Church, the meeting was told. It was, however, known that this problem would occur and the position was not particularly serious. The remedies agreed on did not involve any particular contribution from the Church. There was to be Co-operative Tobacco Trading among members, the Women's Section was to be asked to give 30/-d and provide a further £5; further collections were to be made at all ILP meetings. The financial position was again raised in July 1911 when it was asked whether Fred Hughes could be paid 7/6d. for a lecture at the Labour Church, but it was resolved to offer him only 5/-d. as 'they could pay no more.'

Arrangements for the 1911 – 12 session were also in the hands of the ILP EC. In September it was recorded that the reading and singing was to be arranged by Mr.Hallas and the pianist was to be Mr.Haldane Hallas. Mr.Arrowsmith was the Chief Steward. Larger hymn books were necessary, but this was a question of cost. Bengough agreed to investigate the possiblity of hymn sheets as an alternative and Eldred Hallas suggested that these might be combined with propaganda matter and 'scattered broadsheet'. In September C.Arrowsmith was elected treasurer of the Labour Church alone, whereas before he had been treasurer both of the ILP branch and the Church.

The only other reference to the Church is in the October 1911 minutes when a minor contretemps led to Comrade Arrowsmith being deputed to explain to Mr.Allen why his daughter had been called upon to sing only one song at the Labour Church instead of two. This was due to the belief that she had only one song to sing! It was explained.

The Kings Heath ILP minutes end in December 1911 and nothing more is known of Kings Heath Labour Church.

The Birmingham Socialist Centre

The Centre was set up in 1897 as a co-ordinating centre for electoral and political activity in the city. The electoral work overlapped, to a large extent, with the functions of the ILP Federation and the Labour Representation Committee; the co-ordination of the political work overlapped with the function of the Labour Church. But despite strains and differences, the Socialist Centre survived until 1915 and made, if not a unique, then a noteworthy and unusual contribution to the development of Socialism in Britain. Up to 1910, with the sole exception of 1904 – 05, the growth of the Socialist Centre was unbroken. Starting with thirty seven members, it had doubled its membership to 75 by 1900, doubled it again to 144 in 1906 and reached its maximum of 200 in 1908 – 09. This number then steadily declined to 120 in the year before the outbreak of war and in 1915 the secretary, Richard Clements, announced that he was joining the Army Service Corps and the Centre was suspended for the duration.

The secretary from 1897 to 1902 was J.A.Fallows MA, from 1902 to 1905 it was S.D.Shallard, from 1905 to 1913 Fred Hughes and from 1913 John Clements. The centre elected other officers — a chairman who changed each year, a treasurer, and an executive committee. Members met monthly.

The great advantage of the Centre was that it employed a full-time secretary with an office in the centre of the city. From June 1899 to February 1902 Fallows edited a monthly paper, *The Pioneer,* which provided reports of Socialist activity and a directory of Labour organisations not only in Birmingham, but also further afield. Its declared aim was 'to unite all Midland Socialists.' The paper could not be sustained, however, and it is to the annual reports of the Centre that we owe most of our knowledge of its activities.

The fifth annual report for the year 1901 – 02 records as the key events of the year the housing campaign of the *Daily Gazette,* the formation of the city Housing Committee and the disgraceful riots on the occasion of Lloyd George's town hall meeting.

The sixth report speaks of a great extension of the work. The Centre had joined with the ILP, Labour Church and Trades Council in forming a Citizen's Committee to support the British Electric Traction Company's purchase of a controlling interest in the anarchic Birmingham tramway system, as a step towards municipalising it. 120,000 leaflets had been distributed. *The Town Crier* had been purchased by several members of the Socialist Centre to further this end. During the year the Centre affiliated to the Labour Representation Committee and took part in the

most successful April Conference which had decided to contest the East
Birmingham and Bordesley seats at the next general election; Fallows and
Shallard had been elected to the Birmingham Central Literary
Association; the secretary had lectured at Labour Churches and ILP
branches throughout the year; there had been debates with the Central
Literary Association , Carrs Lane Literary & Debating Society, and the
New Age and Cosmopolitan Debating Societies. Income for the year was
£207 with a favourable balance of £32.

The report for 1903 – 04 records even greater activity. The city council
had voted 50 to 15 to municipalise the tramways. 'Thus came to a
successful end the agitation initiated and practically engineered by the
Socialist Centre the members of which had laboured so enthusiastically
in this matter.' The outstanding successes at the municipal election of
1903 were enumerated. The *Town Crier,* having fulfilled the main purpose
for which it had been purchased, ceased publication

The Centre characterised as the most important event of the year, the
Chamberlain speech in May which foreshadowed his campaign for
Protection. Several members of the Centre had spoken against Protection
and the Centre itself had organised a successful meeting at the New
Temperance Hall in November when the secretary had spoken on 'the
Socialist View of the Tariff Question.' A statement of these principles had
also been distributed.

Early in 1904 the fiscal problem had been overshadowed by the
controversy of the Chinese Labour Ordinance which introduced
conditions of near slavery into southern Africa. The Centre had discussed
organising protests itself, but this was eventually undertaken by the
Citizens' Committee located at the offices of the Centre with Fallows as
secretary.

The 1903 – 04 Report noted not only an increase in activity of the
Centre, but also of the Labour Church and ILP. Both in West and East
Birmingham the ILP branches had held a series of Sunday night meetings
similar to those of the Labour Church, so that there had often been four
Sunday night Socialist meetings held in the city.

In March 1904 the Centre had moved into a new office at Coleridge
Chambers, Corporation Street, beside the Law Courts, and the venue of
monthly meetings had been changed to Hughes' Restaurant in the Great
Western Arcade where meetings had been 'well attended.'

Although 'space would not allow the recording of the various activities
of all our members' the report gives an impressive list of the work of the
leading figures. J.A.Fallows as a city councillor served on the School of
Art, Proof House, Education, and Library Committees; as a Kings
Norton Poor Law Guardian be also served on the Cottage Homes and
Out-Relief Committees. He also served on the Committees of the Peace
Society and the Midlands Education League; in addition to his trade
union work, Fallows had also lectured at most of the Labour Churches
and Ethical Societies in the country. Other members of the Centre whose
similarly large range of commitments were recorded were H.T.Hallam,
J.A.Sayers, Tom Groom and F.A.Lacon.

In the interests of Socialist unity, the possibility of an amalgamation of
the Socialist Centre and the Labour Church had been discussed by a Joint
Committee and also common action with the ILP.

The eighth annual report for 1904 – 05 reported that the work had been interrupted by the illness and eventual resignation of the secretary, Shallard. This had forced forward the proposals for a merger of the Centre with the Labour Church. The result had been 'an emphatic expression that the independent existence of both organisations was decidedly justified and their respective spheres of influence capable of considerable expansion. The new secretary, Fred Hughes, had been appointed in March and the office was once again available to all Socialists in the city during normal business hours.

The issue of the year had been Unemployment and a special committee of the Centre had been set up to consider proposals for Labour colonies, bureaux etc. and it will visit the Poplar Union Colony in Essex. Efforts were being made to get the local Poor Law Guardians to accept an offer of land made by J.Fels for an experiment on the same lines as Poplar.

Other matters taken up during the year had been housing and the feeding of school children.

Unemployment and its resultant destitution continued to occupy the Centre the following year. The Citizens' Committee had organised a meeting at which George Lansbury had spoken on the Labour Colony established for all able-bodied unemployed in Poplar. A petition had been handed to the Lord Mayor asking for a similar Colony for Birmingham and this had been handed on to the Distress Committee.

In July there had been a great Bull Ring demonstration organised with the ILP, Trades Council and other bodies supporting Labour Colonies. This had been one of a series of demonstrations throughout the country which had led to the passing of the 1905 Unemployed Workmen's Act. This Act sanctioned the setting up of Labour Colonies. The Socialist Centre called the Act 'very unsatisfactory, but it can be a lever for further activities.' That activity had already begun; a National Right to Work Committee had been formed and also a local one on the initiative of the SDF which had the 'hearty support' of the Socialist Centre, one of whose members (Miss Evans) was secretary.

On school meals, a Labour Party bill had received a second reading 'but even if it is successful it will only transfer activity to the local arena, since the Bill is permissive.'

The centre had also been associated with the SDF in organising a most successful meeting at the Hippodrome on School Meals and Secular Education. On the Housing Question, no progress had been made.

Other activities reported by the Centre were, a 'much appreciated' list of lectures circularised to all Literary, Political and Religious associations in the city; the formation of a mock Parliament providing 'a sphere of public propaganda not neglected by the Centre,' whose secretary acted as leader of the Labour Party and half a dozen members regularly attended; the important book *Women's Work and Wages,* whose joint authors E.Cadbury & G.Shann were members of the Centre, was announced.

The tenth annual report spoke of a gratifying growth of Labour representation on various bodies and a consequent extension of Socialist Centre influence. The main campaigns of the year had been for the medical inspection of school children, a conference on Land nationalisation and protests at the maladministration of the Congo Free State.

On working class housing there had been a meeting with Nettlefold, the chairman of the Housing Committee, but his proposal to lease a site at Bordesley Green for private and philanthropic enterprises to build houses was opposed by the Centre who wanted the Council to build the houses.

The success of the Centre as a co-ordingating and research centre for the local labour movement, seems, however, to be beginning to conflict with its role as a propaganda agency, and for the second year running it reported poorly attended members' meetings.

The 11th. Annual Report for 1907–08 reported a 'notable and steady increase in Socialist activity in the past year, partly due to the election of Victor Grayson and the growth in activity of the Fabian Society and other Socialist bodies.'

A prominent feature of the year's activity had been the Clarion Van with Charles D.Drysdale in charge. Two Centre members were 'generously guaranteeing the undertaking against financial loss.'

Local parliaments and debating societies were proliferating and R.J. Bailey had been elected Labour prime minister in the main local mock Parliament.

An important departure had been a Centre sponsored Town Hall meeting where 2,000 people had heard George Bernard Shaw speak on 'Socialism and the Political Situation.' Monthly meetings had been better attended and there had been a public debate on 'Financial Reform' when Leonard Hall had represented the Centre.

Unemployed agitation had continued with meetings at the Bull Ring and a town hall meeting with George Lansbury. Sweated Labour had been the main issue, however. The Centre had taken an active part in the convening and conduct of the Midlands Conference on Sweating in the spring. Canon Masterman had presided and addresses given by Mary McArthur, Chiozza Money MP and others. Resolutions had been passed demanding a minimum wage, the stringent inspection of home industries and the further restriction of child labour. Edward Cadbury and George Shann had published a *Handbook on Sweating* and Shann had been closely connected with the Sweated Industries Exhibition at Bingley Hall.

Work on the Labour Representation Committee had occupied much time; a new Committee had been set up in Edgbaston and, as well as the existing Committee, the Centre was helping in East Worcestershire, Aston, Handsworth and other places.

The 12th. Annual Report for 1908–09 reported 'an increase in members surpassing any previous record.' The most important event had been the Report of the Royal Commission on the Poor Law; the evidence of the secretary of the Centre had been incorporated into the famous Minority Report. The Unemployment agitation continued and 'scenes of a disorderly nature had taken place in the city.'

The Centre had again been responsible for the Clarion Van. There had been two nights of debate at the Town Hall with Leonard Hall opposing the representatives of the Unionist Association. Other town hall meetings during the year had been two by the ILP, one in June with the Rev.R.J.Campbell and the other in December with Ramsay Macdonald; a Clarion meeting in October with Blatchford, Hyndman, Hall and Margaret Bondfield; a Right to Work meeting in October with Frank

Smith from the London County Council, Hall, Stevens, the Rev. Pinchard and Fred Hughes; and the Labour Church meeting in November with Blatchford, Grayson and Hall. There had also been large Cinderella meetings during the year at the Central Hall, Digbeth Hall and other places. The Socialist Joint Propaganda Committee was co-ordinating the town hall meetings.

Good educational work was being done among Adult Schools, Literary Societies etc. But ground had been lost in municipal representation and the organisation of an Anti-Socialist Union 'will create plenty of opportunities for propaganda work in the coming year.'

The 13th Annual Report of the Socialist Centre for the year 1909 – 10 was the harbinger of stormy times ahead. For the first time in five years membership had decreased; the untimely death of Francis Arthur Lacon from a railway accident was recorded; for the first time a telephone number is given — Central 5315.

The Poor Law Report and the general election had made the year a particularly busy one. In May there had been a Poor law Conference at Digbeth. In September George Lansbury had spoken on the 'Break-up of the Poor Law' at a Town Hall meeting. The Socialist Centre together with the University Sociological Society arranged a Town Hall meeting in December chaired by Sir Oliver Lodge at which Sidney & Beatrice Webb, two of the main architects of the massive Minority Report, had spoken on the Poor Law Commission. A series of smaller meetings had also discussed the findings of the Royal Commission. As a result of all this activity, it was proposed to turn the influential Citizens' Committee into a permanent, non-partisan organisation for the discussion of Poor Law Reform.

With regard to the general election, Fred Hughes had stood as Labour candidate for Bordesley and polled 3453 votes to Jesse Collings, the successful Unionist candidate's 9201. J.J.Stephenson, a land values expert, had been the Labour candidate in East Birmingham and polled 3958 votes against Steel-Maitland the successful Tory, who polled 8460. In summing up these results the report said that the Socialist Centre had always supported those members of the Labour Party who advocated an independent fighting policy. The existing political situation was delicate and another early appeal to the country was possible. Under such circumstances it might be well to concentrate on those consituencies where Socialist candidates were likely to be selected. The electoral organisation of the Labour Party in Birmingham was faulty and the Centre thought this was a field of activity in which it could be helpful, particularly since Quinton had been annexed to the city and the progress of the Greater Birmingham scheme which proposed to include the districts of Erdington, Handsworth, Kings Norton and Yardley. This scheme was supported by the Centre.

The Tory Lords' opposition to the Liberal budget had brought the question of national finances to the fore and the Socialist Centre report considered that some uncertainty on this question had been revealed by the budget discussion. The Labour Party had taken some steps towards defining a Socialist finance policy, but many Socialists had adopted different views. In September the Centre had participated in a Church Socialist League conference which had discussed national and local finance, and the land and income tax proposals of the budget had received general consent. But the same subject had been dealt with at the October Town Hall meeting of the SDP and the Labour Church at which both Hyndman and Leonard Hall had criticised the Finance Bill.

The 'political unrest' had raised a number of difficult problems for the centre. At the October members' meeting a resolution had been passed for the preparation of a definite Municipal Programme before next Autumn. In November there had been a discussion on Proportional Representation; this had not been endorsed by the meeting. In February a meeting had discussed the relationship of the Centre with other Socialist organisations in the city and it had been decided that no alteration or change of attitude was necessary.

On Unemployment it was stated that the Centre remained affiliated to the Right to Work committee, but not much progress had been made that year.

The budget had increased interest in the land question and there had been a visit of the Land Nationalisation Van in July. This had been followed in November by debates with the United Irish League on 'Land Nationalisation vs Peasant proprietorship' and another with the Young British Liberal Society.

The Clarion Van had had a successful tour organised by Leonard Hall, Fred Hughes and C. Brown, but a cold, wet season had led to another financial deficit. In July, the annual picnic had been to Warwick Castle by courtesy of the countess. The report summarised matters as follows. 'The year may be considered one of useful activity in spite of unusual financial difficulties.'

The last report dealt with here is that for 1910 – 11. It showed a greatly increased level of political activity, although the worst fears of the centre were realised at the December general election which 'had followed so closely' the one in January that Labour had been unable to contest any of the Birmingham seats. Despite this, the summer and autumn had been a period of exceptional Socialist activity in Birmingham and the Centre had been busier than ever before. In September the Centre had been responsible for one week for the Clarion Van in Small Heath. In October four public meetings had been organised; C.E.Smith had spoken on 'Birmingham Municipal Finance' and there had been three lectures at Birchfield Library on 'Socialism'. There had also been a meeting at the Central Hall with J.R.Clynes. In October there had been a debate at the Midland Institute between G.K.Chesterton and Capt. Parsons organised by the Church Socialist League and the Anti-Socialist Union. There had been a number of Town Hall meetings. In June Tom Mann had been the main speaker for the SDP and the Socialist Church. In September Grayson, Hall and the Rev. Pinchard had spoken for the Clarion Scouts and the Scouts had organised a lantern lecture by H.F.Northcote. Finally, Keir Hardie and W.C.Anderson had been the speakers at a town hall meeting organised by the Clarion Scouts.

Members of the Centre had addressed 'innumerable meetings' and thirty members were engaged in correspondence with the press. A number of pamphlets had been produced; Walter Jones on *Finance & Unemployment*, Leonard Hall on *The Next Thing to Do* and also *Socialism, Tariffism and Free Trade*, A.J.Fallows on *British German Relations* and Fred

Hughes on *Old Laws and New Prophets.*

At the March business meeting the following programme of Electoral Reform had been passed:

> Payment of MPs: Adult Suffrage : Abolition of Plural Voting. Elections to be on one day and that to be a Public Holiday. The closing of public houses during polling hours. Three months residential qualification for automatic registration. the issue of Polling Cards by the Returning Officer only. Prohibition of conveyance to the Polls by vehicles. More Polling Booths. Single member constituencies and the Alternative Vote in three-cornered contests. Payment of the Returning Officers' expenses by the Exchequer.

The imminent application of the Greater Birmingham Bill had stimulated political activity. The Town Planning and Tramways Extension Bill made more urgent the question of municipal land ownership; every member of the Health Committee had been given a copy of the Fabian pamphlet *What a Health Committee can Do;* assistance had been rendered to the Operative Bakers in their efforts to abolish their scandalous sweating conditions, and the Health Committee had been induced to take the same action on public contracts for bread; the establishment of a Municipal Milk Depot had been agreed.

The administration of school meals had been criticised for the last three years and after Unemployment and Sweating, this matter had received most attention. There had been deputations and correspondence, a Trades Council resolution and Town Hall meetings. The result was 'some slight improvement.' The neighbouring authority of Kings Norton proposed to introduce a dental clinic and a superior system of School Meals and it was hoped that one of the first fruits of the Greater Birmingham Bill would be reforms in this direction.

The Centre had consistently supported the local branch of the Committee for the Prevention of Destitution. It had actively assisted with the Arts and Crafts Exhibition in the town hall in the autumn; this had been a complete artistic success, although a financial failure. Music all the week had been provided by Rutland Boughton and there had been lectures by Holbrook Jackson, Joseph Crouch and the Revs. James Addersley and Arnold Pinchard, among others. A specially interesting item to Socialists was a one-act play by George Bernard Shaw called *Press Cuttings.*

In January there had been proposals to establish a Socialist Representation Committee in Birmingham, but the chairman, who had attended as delegate for the Socialist Centre had deemed it inadvisable to support a proposal for a conference on this subject in view of the satisfactory working of the Labour Representation Committee in Birmingham.

With regard to social functions, there had been a change of policy. In place of the annual picnic, the Centre had joined with the ILP in organising a United Garden Party and Sports Day at Harborne Hill House which had been kindly placed a their disposal by C.E.Innes. Large numbers had attended despite torrential rain in the afternoon.

The Reports summed up the work for the year 1910 – 11 as follows:

> The work of the office as a unifying centre and information bureau increases year by year and it is not too much to say that it is

indispensable to the efficient conduct of Socialist propaganda in
Birmingham. With the enlargement of the city it will be necessary to face
the problems of providing further clerical assistance to the secretary.

The Socialist Labour Party.

Last, but not least, among the working class political organisations in
Birmingham to be considered is the Socialist Labour Party. It has been
left to last because it was the most uncompromising body in the search
for Socialism. It wanted unity — but only Socialist unity. It was at once
the conscience of all Socialists, but opposed to the compromises which all
socialists were forced to face in widening support for the achievement of
a Labour government and socialism. Thus the SLP were the most
vehement in criticising the 'opportunist' and Liberal elements within the
Socialist Centre, Labour Church and all the other political parties, but
they were also the most vocal in denouncing the welfare measures such
as old age pensions and labour exchanges as plots to strengthen capitalist
control and the attachment of the working class to the Liberal Party.

The formation of the SLP was preceded by the publication of its
monthly newspaper *The Socialist*. The paper first appeared in August 1902
and the SLP was formed in August 1903. *The Socialist* was published by
dissidents within the Social Democratic Federation, mainly from
Scotland.

The split can be traced back to at least the Paris Congress of the Second
International in 1900. Here, Kautsky had moved a successful resolution
excusing the action of Millerand in entering a French government which
also included Gallifet, the butcher of the Paris Communards. The
resolution, condemned by Lenin, was the origin of the subsequent
dubbing of those who favoured entry into capitalist governments as
Possibilists and those who opposed such participation as Impossibilists. In
Britain, this split was also connected with the wider issue of the attitude
of the SDF to the new Labour Party. Critics within the SDF took the line
that the LRC and ILP bureaucracies were anti-Marxists who were
opposed to class struggle and revolutionary mass action. Macdonald,
Snowden, Keir Hardie, Bruce Glasier and the rest were characterised as
a 'gang of fakirs' who were betraying the movement by holding back
revolutionary action. The SDF leadership then called their critics
Impossibilists and refused to print their criticism in *Justice*. The
opposition then had its criticism published in the New York *Weekly People,*
the newspaper of the Socialist Labour Party of America. Later, *The
Socialist* was printed in Dublin by the Irish Socialist Workers' Republican
Party led by James Connolly. Before the Easter Conference of the SDF
an article severely critical of SDF policy by George S. Yates was
published in *The Socialist*. For this, Yates was expelled and the
Impossibilist delegates withdrew from the conference to form the Socialist
Labour Party in Edinburgh in August 1903.

In October 1903 there were only seven branches — five in Scotland and
the other two in East London and Southampton. By December 1903 a
Birmingham branch had been formed whose secretary was W.F. (Billy)
Holliday of 74 Wolseley Street; this was the eighth branch recorded in *The
Socialist's* Directory. In the summer of 1904 the Birmingham branch was
advertising Sunday meetings in the Bull Ring at 11 am and 7 pm. In

September the branch reported writing to L.Cotton, the full-time organiser, to speak at a May Day meeting, but he had been unable to come. He did come on Sunday July 31st where he held a meeting in the Bull Ring with Billy Holliday in the chair:

> He delivered a speech to a fair audience for upwards of an hour pointing out that they were working class slaves and the only hope of emancipating themselves was by joining the SLP which was the only Socialist Party in Britain.

Cotton's visit had been preceded by one from J.S.Grose from London

> . . . and this, together with the propaganda of the Birmingham comrades was beginning to make the Labour fakirs in Birmingham sit up. We have a city council with what is called a Labour caucus. This consists of J.A.Fallows (Socialist Centre and ILP) A.Hurst (ILP) G. Speake (ILP & Bricklayers' Society) with the support of Liberal members A.Keegan (USL) J.V.Stevens (Tinplate Union secretary and prominent member of the Liberal Association) and Richard Toller (Secretary of the Gas Workers). All these spoke recently and voted in favour of increases in city official's salaries.

In October 1904 there was an interesting article on the conduct of open-air meetings in Birmingham. It was useless going to slum areas as 'people there seem to be hopeless.' An elected propaganda committee of from three to five members was necessary. Meetings should be regular and start on time. They had a little wooden platform 18 inches long by 11 inches broad and 12 inches high with hinged legs. It had formerly been the practice to start with a song, but unless members had a knowledge of harmony this was no good. From start to finish literature should be pressed vigorously both inside and outside the ring of listeners because, 'men may listen for hours, but one who buys *The Socialist* or a pamphlet will read it at some time.'

The branch reported a busy time from September 4th to 12th. when Grose had been with them. On Sunday 4th. there had been a good meeting at the Park Gates, Small Heath, the constituency Shallard was contesting.

> It is now reported that he has withdrawn from the contest. The ILP usually hold meetings here, but this is the first time for the SLP.

In the evening there was a good meeting at the Bull Ring where D.Dunbar reported seventeen pamphlets sold and a collection of 3/4½ d. On Monday the 5th. the SLP had opened a new pitch at Nechells Green in the constituency James Holmes of the Railway Servants was contesting. On Wednesday, Friday and Saturday they had again been at the Bull Ring:

> On Friday we spoke after a religious meeting and had opposition from that sect. Grose answered in fine style. The meeting carried on until the police called attention to the time. (Police rules stop all meetings at 10 pm.) The Saturday meeting had some opposition from the ILP who stated that Socialism was best got by reforms, and by Clarionettes who objected to our preaching the class war.

On Sunday 11th. we were at the Park Gates in the morning and the Bull Ring in the evening. We sold all our *Socialists* (fifty two) and during the week sold 35 pamphlets and also one copy of Das Capital. We held nine meetings during the week and it was most successful.

The October issue of *The Socialist* reported these activities and also printed the results of the efforts of a reporter of the *Evening Despatch* to track down 'this new Socialist organisation in Birmingham.' After failing at the Trades Hall, he eventually went to the Bull Ring and asked about the Birmingham Socialist Centre. Whereupon the following dialogue occurred:

> There is no Socialist Centre.
>   But I thought it was in Livery Street.
> No, the people who go there are not Socialists but Opportunists.
>   The SDF is a socialist body isn't it?
> No, the SDFers are Opportunists.
>   The ILP then?
> They are weak Opportunists.
>   Then who are the Socialists?
> The new Socialist Labour Party.
>   Dear me, I never heard of them.
> It is a new organisation and comprises the forward elements of the SDP and the ILP.

Propaganda continued into the winter opposing the 'political jugglers and tariff reformers':

> Birmingham being the land of the birth of protectionism most people expect to find economic salvation dancing to the trumpet of protection. We point out that in the USA, Germany etc. where there is Protection, these have their starving millions and unemployed.

By the end of 1904 the Birmingham branch was of sufficient importance for the national leadership to investigate the possibility of holding the 1905 national conference in Birmingham, but this proved impossible.

In June 1905 Holliday was excusing the lack of reports on SLP activity in Birmingham by saying that a decision had been made suggesting that members took it in turn to make reports, 'but this has not been done and, as usual, it has fallen on the person who led the work, namely the secretary, to make reports.' Holliday went on to report scornfully a recent Labour Church meeting at which Pete Curran had spoken on 'A Socialist View of Unemployment.' Curran had suggested land reclamation and reafforestation as means of solving the problems! Halliday also reported that, at a Bull Ring meeting, comrades Dunbar and Robertson had shared a platform to debate with the Hybrid Party (Liberal Unionists) and the SLP had been given a fair hearing.

In August there were Birmingham Notes in the paper written by James Stewart, the national SLP organiser. Stewart reported active propaganda in Birmingham with three meetings a week and a regular distribution of leaflets. A feature had been the exposure of the Labour Group by comrade Holliday. The SDF had brought a West Ham councillor into the district and on the Tory Gold allegations (SDF candidates had been accused of taking money from Tories to finance election contests — GB);

local SDFers had declared that they would accept more, if it was offered. The Birmingham Labour Party was organising demonstrations against the government's Unemployment Bill, but admitted that these would have little effect. George Cadbury had invited Honest John Burns to Bournville along with Will Crooks. 'Socialists will be surprised to learn that the home of Socialism is at Bournville according to Cadbury. The ILP says it is a step in that direction; but Cadbury gives money to them.' Aston Labour Party was holding indignant meetings protesting at the failure of the government to appoint working class magistrates. 'This shows their willingness to administer capitalist law.' A debate had been fixed with the Temperance Party. 'It speaks well for their intelligence that they can distinguish between the SLP and the ILP.' Stewart ends his report by saying 'the Birmingham branch is doing its utmost to expose the Freaks, Frauds and Fakirs of which Birmingham can boast many.'

The Birmingham SLP continued its propaganda activities. While Stewart was still in the city a debate was held with the Birmingham Temperance Society. Stewart told the audience that they lived in a class society divided in two and temperance therefore did not reach to the heart of the problem; the sums spent in drink were nothing compared with the robbery perpetrated by the master class, many of whom supported temperance. His opponent, J.H.Lear Caton was not prepared to deny the evils outlined by Stewart, but these could not all be put down to the single cause of the economic state of society. The Brewers' Almanac showed 395 MPs supporting the liquor trade and these MPs were only put there by working class votes. 75% of trade union branches met in public houses. Stewart also reported a debate between the SLP and 'an individual calling himself Prof. William Fautham.' At that debate, Jack Beard, Editor of *East Birmingham Forward*

> ... demanded that our platform refute the charge that the Labour Representation Committee wanted only part of labour reperesentation. He accused us of being 'brick-slingers' (what's wrong with mud?). He looked rather sad.

1905 started with a comforting maxim: 'Remember, the more you work for Socialism today by selling *The Socialist* the less you will have to do in the future'. But the January 1906 Directory in *The Socialist* listed only nine branches; five of these were in Scotland and the four English branches were East London, Southampton, Oxford and Birmingham. From this time, the paper became deeply involved in Industrial Unionism which was to be of wider significance in Birmingham in the stormy 1910–14 period. The paper was printing long articles on this question, later destined to be influential pamphlets issued by the SLP Press. The only item of local interest in the paper during 1906 was that information on Industrial Unionism was available from A.Leflock of 3, Salford Road, Sparkbrook.

1907 began with a financial crisis for *The Socialist* and the all too familiar call for an increased circulation of 5,000, but more local activity was recorded in that year. In July, Holliday reported that

> Like other towns, Birmingham has its freak fakirs. One of these is Councillor J.E.Pentland who calls himself Conservative-Labour. He

always takes collections to feed children at Christmas and bills himself
as 'the children's friend.' His audience being diminished (he holds
meetings every week) by the successful propaganda of the A of IU
(Association of Industrial Unionism — GB) he talks of comrades as
being 'Weary Willies who get their living by rubbing the paint off lamp
posts' or makes such remarks as 'I was responsible for keeping another
comrade's father out of the workhouse.'

On June 2nd he challenged the Socialists, and the writer debated with
him and called him a traitor to the working class. He lost his temper and
practically called on Joseph the Great's friends to do their worst for me.
The meeting closed at 10-20 pm.

Holliday's report went on to record events the next Sunday when
Pentland and the SLP were both holding meetings. In St. Stephens ward
in the forthcoming municipal elections the candidates were Haslam
(Independent) and Newey (Conservative) who was a large manufacturer
of hooks and eyes which was one of the worse sweated trades in the city:

> . . . and the greatest sweater was Pentland. Pentland made a mad rush
> for our platform and Comrade Williams was arrested but later released.

On August 3rd and 4th. the A of IU held a conference at the Trades Hall,
Hurst Street. Eleven clubs were represented and the delegates were
welcomed by Billy Holliday who was elected the chairman. James Stewart
and James Holmes were the national speakers and Leflock also spoke.

The January 1908 Directory showed an increase of SLP branches to
fifteen and there was a long article on SLP activity in Coventry. But the
Branch Activity column was disappearing from the paper and we learn
nothing of SLP activity in Birmingham during 1908 – 09. A Special Press
Fund Appeal, however, allows us to identify those who were probably the
leading members at that time. W.F.Holliday sent in a collecting sheet
with 3/6d. and others who sent in 6d. each were Charles Riley,
H.Williams, C.Hawthorne, W.Lane and R.Rutherford.

Chapter Nineteen

THE LIBERAL DIMENSION — IMPS, LIMPS, NEW RADICALS AND LIB-LABS.

Joseph Chamberlain — from Radical to Imperialist.

The battle for the minds of Birmingham working people in the early years of the twentieth century embraced a wide spectrum of ideologies ranging from jingo imperialism, through social imperialism (attractive to many Fabians), to a re-built Liberal radicalism, and on to the various brands of Socialism offered. The scales were heavily weighted against the latter.

Above all in Birmingham towered the ubiquitous influence of Joseph Chamberlain, the development of whose political ideas must be briefly summarised here. When Chamberlain resigned from the government in 1886 in opposition to Gladstone's proposed Home Rule for Ireland bill one of his first and characteristic acts was to call a Town Hall meeting and force a vote of confidence in himself, despite the plea of the chairman and many others for a compromise solution that would not split the Liberal party. Then in June 1886 Chamberlain led 92 Liberals into the lobby to oppose the second reading of Gladstone's bill and irrevocably split the Liberals. Chamberlain however, retained the vast majority of his support in Birmingham. In reply, Schnadhorst, one of the real architects of the Caucus but by then opposed to Chamberlain, who was secretary of the National Liberal Federation, then had the headquarters of that organisation removed from Birmingham and Chamberlain formed his own National Radical Union. From this organisation the Liberal Unionists were born. Chamberlain then sought to take up the mantle of Lord Randolph Churchill and make the Tories appear the radical party and the Conservative government did, indeed, pass progressive measures such as reforms in local government (Chamberlain's solution to the Irish question), free education in Scotland and increased death duties. Chamberlain continued to advocate radical measures such as old age pensions and land reform. From 1890, however, Chamberlain's momentous conversion from free trade to protection began, and his final break in Birmingham with the Liberal Party came at a joint conference of Tories and Liberals at a town hall meeting in 1891.

Chamberlain was moving in the direction that capitalist development was dictating. The Tories were fast becoming the representatives of big business and the new monopolies. Already in Birmingham the Liberal hegemony was being undermined by the reorganisation of the Tories under J.B. Stone in the 1880s and later by Satchell Hopkins along lines pioneered by the Caucus; also the Tories were winning seats on the municipal council. Monopoly capital in Britain required not the free trade panacea of laissez-faire, appropriate to small scale capitalism, but Protection against new and formidable foreign competitors. By his break with Gladstone Chamberlain forfeited his certain and imminent elevation to the leadership of the Liberal Party, but he gained the undisputed leadership of the British business class, a position he held until his stroke in 1906.

In 1895 after a general election had given the Tories a majority of 152, thanks largely to the Unionists, Chamberlain entered the Cabinet as Secretary of State for the Colonies. From this time Chamberlain became the most important figure in the advocacy of the two main prongs of British imperialist policy — the racist, social imperialism which fuelled the jingoism of large sections of the working class, and the transition from free trade to protection.

The immediate issue was South Africa. In the self-governing Boer colony of the Transvaal the discovery of gold was transforming it from a farming to an industrial state dominated by the Uitlanders of British monopoly capital origin. The Boers, under Kruger, denied the arrogant Uitlanders the means to dominate the state, whilst taxing more heavily than the monopolists were prepared to tolerate, the enormous profits they were making. Masterminding monopoly capital interests was Cecil Rhodes, prime minister of Cape Colony and chairman of the British South Africa Company. In 1895 Rhodes demanded the annexation of Bechuanaland to the Company in pursuit of his dream of a Cape to Cairo railway which would run along the border between the Transvaal and Bechuanaland. Kruger objected to this and penalised goods from the Cape passing through the Transvaal. British interests by then were busy organising an uprising against Kruger to annex the Transvaal, but in December the insurgents thought better of it and Rhodes was forced to disown the plot. Despite this, the infamous Jameson Raid which was to have linked with the uprising, went ahead and failed miserably. Few people now doubt that Chamberlain knew the substance of the plot, although he denied it. From this time, Boer suspicions and British imperial interests made the Boer War all but inevitable.

Birmingham and the Boer War.

Birmingham suffered more than most areas of Britain from the rival imperialist powers such as Germany and the USA who had arisen during the period of the Great Depression. This, together with the development of new industries and the large monopoly firms such as Dunlops, BSA, the Chamberlain family empire etc. led to a struggle for markets and sources of raw materials in which a very largely expanded empire formed a most important part. This process included the important dimension of convincing large sections of the working class of the desirability of imperial expansion and also Protection. The memory of the mass unemployment of the Great Depression made this easier and when this was allied to the latent racism of so many people of all classes, 'social imperialism' carried the field.

Britain was 'over-populated' it was claimed and colonial development would help cure unemployment. Chamberlain's speeches of the time continually harped on the themes that our standards could not be applied to races which were centuries behind in the process of national evolution; that native populations must be provided with white superintendance from the experiences of a higher civilisation; that our colonies were undeveloped estates; or the rhetorical question, 'Who will take up the burden of Empire?' Such propaganda, enthusiastically taken up by the local press, was reinforced by the fact that Birmingham had always produced armaments and this trade flourished in times of war.

The course of events after 1895 strengthened imperial sentiment further. The Kaiser's letter to Kruger congratulating him on the crushing of the Jameson Raid was used to relieve some of the pressure on Rhodes and Chamberlain. The conflict with British imperialism strengthened Boer ties with German, Belgian and Dutch imperial interests. When the war broke out in October 1899 accompanied by the usual initial military disasters, national feeling rallied and the relief of Mafeking and Ladysmith in May 1900 raised national jingoism to unprecedented heights. In June, the Transvaal capital was occupied and Kruger fled to Holland. In September 1900 a Khaki Election returned the Tories to power with a thumping majority of 134.

Working class jingoism in Birmingham has been dealt with by Michael Blanch in an important and comprehensive thesis *Nation, Empire and the Birmingham Working Class 1899–1914*. Blanch concludes that the propaganda of nationalism and imperialism was systematically inculcated through schools, youth movements, many of which were of a quasi-military nature such as the Scouts (originating in Birmingham), boys brigades etc, local and national politics, newspapers, military support movements, cinemas, music halls and theatres. The process began in schools and Blanch points the irony of masses of deprived children subjected to grand bourgeois and aristocratic notions of honour, glory, duty and Empire. The dominant thread of jingoism is an all embracing threat. There were the external threats of foreigners, not only blacks and Chinese, to whom it was our duty to bring 'civilisation', but also Jews, French, Germans, and indeed anyone else so unfortunate as to not have been born British. Then there were the internal threats of 'pro-Boers', 'pro-Irish' 'socialists' and all other radicals.

The war began to rapturous applause from the whole Birmingham press. Some sections of the press had even welcomed the Jameson Raid and castigated the cowards who had called off the uprising and thus prevented the annexation of the Boer republics at that time. But in December 1899 came the Black Week with defeats at Colenso, Stormberg and Magarafontein with 3,000 dead. The foreign press reported these Boer victories and the *Birmingham Daily Mail* commented:

> It is a wonder that half a dozen stalwart Englishmen with horsewhips do not go to Paris and adminster a severe castigation to these vulgar cowards.

Then came victories, each greeted with greater crowd enthusiasm than the last. After Ladysmith:

> Khaki clad Imperial Yeomanry troopers were carried shoulder high up and down the streets amid shouts and a pandemonium of cheers and songs.

The occupation of Pretoria saw scenes of unrestrained joy. The departure of volunteers to the colours in Handsworth were speeded by crowds singing *Soldiers of the Queen* and gifts of khaki covered bibles were given to every man by a chaplain. So eagerly was the relief of Mafeking anticipated in Lozells that it was celebrated two days before the official dispatch:

The streets were filled with staid citizens whose severe respectability and decorum were usually beyond question or reproach, singing patriotic songs with the full force of their lungs, dancing, jumping and screaming in deliriums of unrestrained joy.

It was in this atmosphere that the Khaki Election was held. In fact, only one of the seven Birmingham seats were contested. This was in Birmingham East where J.V. Stevens, the Lib-Lab trade union leader opposed J.B. Stone, the leading Birmingham Conservative. Stevens thus faced the full force not only of Tory jingoism, but also the Unionist press which supported five unopposed Unionists in the city, including Joseph Chamberlain himself in Birmingham West. Chamberlain, speaking at an election meeting in a council school ended by inciting the crowd to sing *Rule Britannia* in the school playground. Stone had posters:

Don't vote for pro-Boers, Little Englanders, Krugerites and Home Rulers. Vote for Stone and the Unity of the Empire.

Stevens was forced to join in the myth that 'the nation rose as one man and by gigantic effort and unstinted sacrifice of life and money and by the heroic gallantry of its soldiers and sailors saved the situation and converted defeat into victory.' By and large Labour neither contested the legitimacy of the war nor the courage of its soldiers, it attacked only the conduct of the war by the government. Principled opposition to the war was maintained only by Socialists and pacifists. Stevens used the patriotic card and had posters flanked by the union jack and the royal standard with:

Who imported Swedish workmen to take the place of Englishmen? (this was a reference to Stone's strike breaking activities a few years earlier — GB) Vote for Stevens and British Labour and Stevens the True Patriot.

Stevens lost to Stone by 4989 votes to 2835.

But the confident expectations of victory gave way to the reality of two more years of guerilla warfare, and it is perhaps noteworthy, that no other major outburst of jingoism can be recorded until December 1901 when Lloyd George held his famous meeting at the Birmingham Town Hall. This visit can be viewed either as one of supreme courage or of considerable foolhardiness. Lloyd George had relentlessly pursued Joseph Chamberlain and the Tory government first on the principle that the war was being fought to enrich the gold and diamond monopolists of the Rand and, by 1901, on concentration camp atrocities. Lloyd George had faced some very nasty opposition in other towns, but when he proposed to say such things in Chamberlain's home town, the wisdom of such a decision was questioned. Lloyd George, however, insisted that the visit take place.

The whole Birmingham press denounced Lloyd George as a traitor and his visit as an insult to the city which every patriot should resist. If the editors shrank from direct incitement to violence, they opened their correspondence columns to those without such inhibitions and the final thrust of the *Birmingham Daily Mail* on the eve of the meeting was:

There is every reason to believe that Birmingham is menaced by the prospect of serious rioting.

In addition, the Tory working man Councillor J.G. Pentland and Councillor William Lovesey hired sandwichmen to parade through the town proclaiming:

Come and Demonstrate. For King. For Country. Birmingham wants no traitors.

By mid-afternoon Victoria Square was packed. Lloyd George had arrived in Birmingham earlier than expected and thus avoided a 'welcoming party' at the station. In the evening he arrived at the Town Hall at 6.15 for the 7.30pm meeting having taken a local train to the city centre and then, disguised with a peaked cap and a rough overcoat, a closed carriage to the hall, thus avoiding an even larger 'reception committee' intent on preventing his entrance to the town hall. When it became known that he was in the hall pandemonium broke out, four brass bands were posted at the outside corners of the hall playing patriotic airs and men were doing a roaring trade selling half bricks from a piece of waste land in Edmund Street.

Inside the hall was a packed, ticket only audience of Lloyd George supporters, forged tickets having been quickly recognised. But about 7 p.m. there was a great crash as a scaffold pole was used to break down a door and within a few seconds about 7,000 people were jammed in the hall.

Lloyd George appeared on the platform to roars of 'Pro-Boer! Traitor! Kill him!' Not a word of his speech could be heard. Then there was a noise like hailstones as the brickbats were hurled through the town hall windows. Later, the Liberal Association paid for 1,198 windows to be replaced. Then the jingoes burst through the police cordon protecting the platform and Lloyd George was clearly in danger of losing his life. He consented to be barricaded in a committee room where, by the order of the chief constable, he and his party sat in darkness for two hours. At the end of this time, the mood of the crowd was as bad as ever and the police insisted that at all costs he must be got away. So, in a police cape and helmet Lloyd George went out of the town hall in a long file of policemen. They marched for two miles to Ladywood police station and safety. By other ruses, the rest of the party were rescued just before the crowd finally smashed everything else in the town hall.

Then the Riot Act was said to have been read, the police drew their truncheons and charged the crowd. In an excess of zeal one man was killed, many badly injured and nearly forty detained in hospital. Some police were also hurt and one subsequently died.

The inquest on the dead man returned a verdict of manslaughter by a police constable unknown, adding a double rider of censure that some policemen had been guilty of culpable excess of duty and also that no evidence was forthcoming from the police who knew who had struck the blow that killed Harold Curtin.

The Watch Committee then invited the Home Secretary to set up an independent enquiry and in the event of his refusal, agreed that the City Council should conduct its own enquiry. The Home Secretary refused this request, as did the city Council, but it instructed the Watch Committee to continue its own investigations. After hearing evidence from 48 police officers and 66 others their report concluded:

(a)   that the baton charge had begun without orders, but was justified by the aggresive temper of the crowd.
(b)   that no evidence had been obtained identifying the policemen who had lost their self-control and committed unjustifiable assaults.
(c)   that certain police officers had committed errors of judgement, but not such as to deserve censure.

This report was then debated and accepted by the Council by 38 votes to 17. The disgust of the Labour movement at the whitewash of the report, coupled with the universal opinion that nothing else was to be expected from the Unionist controlled council has already been recorded.

Opinions were divided in the city as to whether this outburst represented genuine pro-war jingoism and how much it was local pro-Joe patriotism. Certainly jingoism was on the wane from 1900 and was further temporarily douched by the subsequent protracted guerilla struggle which ended with 22,000 British dead, a bill for £205m and the odour of concentration camps in which thousands of Boer women and children perished. Perhaps the most bizarre statistic of the war is that no less than 518,000 horses died as a result of the war.

By 1906 the patriotic Tory government was completely discredited and the landslide Liberal victory occurred, although in Birmingham Joseph Chamberlain's Unionist empire survived.

Birmingham Business and the Boer War.

The economic exploitation of the South African market from the end of the 1880s with the development of gold mining at Witwatersrand united Unionists, Gladstonians and Conservatives. The heavy capital outlay involved in equipping the mines at first formed the most significant segment of the market and Birmingham took its full share. Tangyes provided hydraulic presses, pumping engines, lifts etc. and had a virtual monopoly, through a world patent, of winding machinery. Many other Birmingham firms supplied mining equipment as well as harbour and lighthouse material and also railway rolling stock.

Cadbury's, together with Fry's dominated the consumer market for confectionary and Cadbury's tried to monopolise supplies of cocoa, but this failed. Birmingham carriage and cycle trades catered for the wealthier consumers and the whole vast range of cheap jewellery and other 'Brummagem goods' supplied the 'native' market. This enormous volume of trade was organised by the great Birmingham merchant firms such as Kannreuthers, Keep Brothers etc. usually with their own agents on the spot. With trade opportunities on this scale it is scarcely surprising that the Birmingham business community were hot for military intervention and 'Man in the Street' in the *Birmingham Financial Times* in 1898 at the time of the Jameson Raid could write:

Truly we have had a repetition of the bounce and bluster of that sanctimonious old humbug Oom Paul, and although there has been a revival in Kaffirs I don't think it will be maintained until the ignorant bombastic crew who 'rule the roost' in the Transvaal have been cleared out. Ten thousand pities that Dr. Jim's bold efforts were frustrated by the weak-kneedness of the Uitlanders. How different things might have been!

Direct British government intervention increased from the election of the Tory government in 1895 and Joesph Chamberlain's appointment to the Colonial Office. When war did break out, Chamberlain sat on top of a vast pyramid of interconnecting interests controlling strategic development. Chamberlain himself was virtual Minister of the British Empire. Also in the government was J. Powell Williams an old Caucus crony, M.P. for Birmingham South as Financial Secretary to the War Office, and his own son, Austen, who sat as M.P. for East Worcestershire was briefly in the government. Powell Williams was also a director of the Midland Railway Carriage & Wagon Co. with large export interests in South Africa, as was J.S. Keep whose interests, besides the great merchant firm included Lloyd and Lloyd supplying the Rand with tubes and Elliots Metal Co. controlled by the Birmingham Trust Co., a creation of the Chamberlains. Next came Joseph Chamberlain's business interests through his marriages and the activities of his brothers. He was nephew to the Nettlefolds, to whom his screw monopoly, operating also in South Africa, had passed. His first marriage was to Harriet Kenrick and when she died, to her cousin Florence, who in turn, based on the hollow-ware business in West Bromwich were connected by marriage and business to other large sections of the Birmingham business community.

Chamberlain's brother Herbert was chairman of B.S.A. which dominated the gun trade and Joseph had been a substantial shareholder until he sold out only about 1900.

Joseph's son, Neville, was a director of Elliotts Metal, as was Joseph's brother Walter, who was also chairman of W.T. Avery, another large participant in the South Africa trade. Birmingham Metal & Munitions Co., a subsidiary of the Nobel explosives empire connected itself to B.S.A. about 1900; three directors of B.S.A. were also directors of B'ham Metal & Munitions, one of whom, T.F. Walker, was chairman of the latter and thus personally linked BSA and Nobels. Kynoch's manufactured explosives and munitions and had set up a dynamite factory in S.Africa before the war to supply explosives to the Rand. The Chamberlains acquired decisive interests in Kynochs and its associated firms which included Nobel.

The Chamberlains, Kenricks and Keeps were also associated with Lloyd's Bank and other large banks which, as well as their direct financial interest in the S.Africa trade, also had interests in Mitchell & Butlers, large suppliers of beer and spirits to S.Africa.

Such business interconnections, webs of influences, and sources of nepotism and corruption operated discreetly in Britain. But in S.Africa they were open and blatant. These same business interests marshalled in S.Africa by Cecil Rhodes and through him to the government of the South Africa Company fuelled the increasing racism and brutality which marked the later stages of the war creating the modern problems of that beautiful but unhappy land.

After the war, Chamberlain and other imperialists were convinced that a new era of opportunity was opening out with further intensive development of deep mining, vast investment opportunities in the superstructure of railways, roads, communications etc as well as a mass market for consumer goods.

Alas for Chamberlain, he was wrong, as he was so often, in his expectations of capitalism. The costs of the war, the fact that not all Birmingham industries benefitted from the war, and the development of another slump with its mass unemployment from 1903, led to a resurgence of the Liberals as a political force and the further development of Socialism.

But the South African dream was a chimera mainly because the capitalist development of the country on the basis of the single, foreign owned, non-productive commodity of gold retarded balanced, local industrial development, led to the impoverishment of the work-force both black and white at that time and permanently limited the market for consumer goods.

As for the British soldier who did the actual fighting making the imperial dream a reality, we learn very little from Rhodes, Chamberlain and the like. The army rank and file were, in the main, the sons of those who had borne the brunt of the unemployment of the Great Depression forced into the army as the best option of job security. Their pay was meagre, and in misfortune they were dependent on the cold hand of charity. At the 1901 annual general meeting of the B.S.A. Co. which revealed record profits and the payment of a 40% dividend we read:

> As showing that the employees at the BSA are not unmindful of the adverse affects of the South African war, they are found to be the largest contributors to the *Birmingham Daily Mail* Reservists Fund, having sent in over £1,200; while the Company have given almost as much in sums of 10/-d. a week to the wives of reservists who had to leave the works and go to the war, and £100 to a special appeal.

Such a contribution of about £2000 illustrates well the old adage that the rich will do anything for the poor — except get off their backs.

Gladstonian Liberalism and Lib-Labism.

The three pillars of Gladstonian Liberalism after 1886 were the Cadburys, the Tangyes and Arthur Chamberlain, who broke ranks from the family.

The most important Cadbury — George — was a reluctant politican. Endowed, like Chamberlain with a ruthless business organising ability, he combined it with a paternalism which was made to further his business ends. If his labour was paid slightly more than the average, it had to be justified by a higher productivity; insistence of cleanliness, neatness of person, good manners etc. which were essential in the building of a food monopoly in an industrial area:

> The entire policy depends on the supreme economic value of quick, clean work. Behind all the athletics, the dentistry, the swimming baths, the doctoring, the arrangements for meals, lies a supreme commericial objective — speed of hand coupled with accuracy of eye. These are the qualities which in the workers make the business pay. The wages may be high, the various benefits costly, the hours may be short, but the

labour is concentrated, eager, effective. It does not last long, but it accomplishes much while it does last.

This is the description of the Cadbury philosophy by his biographer A.G. Gardiner.

Cadbury, like Robert Owen had discovered that efficient labour is the cheapest labour. Unfortunately, employees not only enjoyed his welfare, they had to suffer his prejudices. The chief of these were no married women employees, no drink and no betting.

George Cadbury at the age of 14 and his brother Richard had inherited from their mother £5,000 each and an ailing chocolate business. Within a decade the business was made profitable on the basis of an improved formula for cocoa. By the 1880s Cadbury held first position in the trade and used one third of the cocoa imported into Britain. The need for expansion led to the crucial decision to start a green fields factory at Bournville in 1879 which developed into a garden suburb employing thousands of girls whose labour created the vast wealth of the two Cadbury brothers.

Cadbury's stake in the consumer trade made him, like the Manchester cotton men, a natural advocate of free trade at the time when Chamberlain was leading national imperialist and Birmingham hardware interests on their U-turn to Protection. Cadbury was also the implacable enemy of two interests which flourished under the umbrella of the Caucus — the jerry-builder and the drink trade. So when Chamberlain broke the Liberal Party in 1886, Cadbury found himself the richest and most influential Gladstonian in Birmingham. By the 1890s Cadbury was sympathetic to many Labour causes and his patronage and largesse was diverted from the Liberal Party machine to specific causes which he supported. For instance, he was a warm supporter of John Burns, helped him in his election and contributed £50 a week to the funds of the A.S.E. during the great engineering dispute of 1897. He supported the Independent Labour Party and the Labour Representation Committee, believing that a House of Commons dominated by land, liquor and other monopolies, militarism, finance and the law required one hundred working men in Parliament to achieve any real social reform. Cadbury also found that the Labour Party at that time, best expressed his general support for peace, taxation of land values, housing reform, the feeding of hungry children, old age pensions, national insurance against sickness and unemployment and municipalisation of the drink trade. When the Boer War broke out, Cadbury had no doubt where he stood:

> This war seems the most diabolical ever waged. It is so evidently a speculators' war and no one else can derive any benefit from it. Just now it seems to me that speculators, trust-mongers and owners of enormous wealth are the great cause of most of its poverty ... There are three families drawing from land values in Birmingham alone, without contributing to local taxation, at least £150,000 a year, made by the industrial classes of the city.

Because the jingoist national and provincial press was almost unanimously pro-war, Cadbury became involved not only in Richard Tangye's control of the *Birmingham Daily Argus*, but also Lloyd George's wider scheme of acquiring a national newspaper. This involved the purchase of the *Daily News* which, despite the boycott of advertisers and the self-inflicted handicap of excluding all horse racing intelligence and advertisements from brewers, became an influential, if costly, vehicle for the propagating of Cadbury's principles.

From 1902, Liberal fortunes revived with nonconformist opposition to the 1902 Education Act which supported Church of England schools from the rates and further Liberals returned to the fold as Chamberlain led his tortuous way through the semantics of Fair Trade, Reciprocal Duties, Empire Preference and the rest to Protection.

Most importantly, however, the war again demonstrated that the problems of capitalism were structural and not peripheral with the onset of another capitalist slump and mass unemployment. To this employers responded with their invariable but suicidal panacea of low wages, and once again the 'sweating' issue surfaced. In May 1906 the *Daily News* organised an exhibition of Sweated Industries in London for which George Cadbury undertook to defray the whole cost. The Handbook of the exhibition contained articles on Birmingham Hook and Eye Carders and also Button Carders, by George Shann. Shann also wrote on Cradley Chainmakers and Florence Rine wrote on Bromsgrove Nailmakers. The unique feature of the exhibition was stalls at which sweated workers actually carried on their trade. The Hook and Eye Carders and the Button Carders both had stalls and the following facts were disclosed:

The Hook and Eye Carders were mainly married women, widows or elderly spinsters. A random count among the married women disclosed that the average wage of their husbands was 19/6d. a week; so it was clearly family poverty that drove the women into this sweated trade. The processes were that, first the eyes were stitched to the cards, then the hooks attached to the eyes, and finally the hooks stitched to the card. The rate of pay varied from 9d per pack to 1/4d for the smallest items. A pack consisted of 144 completed cards with two dozen hooks and eyes on each card. This meant 384 hooks and 384 eyes linked together and stitched on a card for 1d! No wonder that children from the age of five, with their deft fingers, were introduced to this home, family labour. Workers provided their own needles and thread amounting to about 1d for every 1/-d. earned. Average earnings for an average weekly day of 14 hours was 3/4d. Each card sold in the shops for 1d. a mark-up of 900% on the cost of labour. The woman who worked the stall at the exhibition had a husband who had worked for the Midland Railway for 33 years. At the age of 54 he sustained a fall at work which he failed to report, thinking it was not serious. The next day he lost the use of his right arm. He was dismissed and told that he had no claim on the company for either compensation or a pension.

As we have seen, the efforts of Cadbury and Birmingham Lib/Labs like George Shann were not universally appreciated, both Hyndman of the SDF and the SLP condemning Cadbury for offering palliatives for capitalism instead of advocating its extirpation, root and branch.

George Cadbury also played a significant part in the negotiations which led to the national Lib/Lab pact giving the Labour candidates of 1906 a clear field. Cadbury supported the Labour Representation Committee from the beginning. Through his political adviser and agent,

Robert Waite, he contributed generously to Labour Party funds. He supported the candidacy of John Holmes in East Birmingham from his nomination in 1903. Waite became the recognised but unauthorised link between Liberal Central Office and the leaders of the Labour movement. With the landslide victory of 1906 under the semi-radical Liberal Campbell-Bannerman, Cadbury foresaw a long period of fruitful collaboration between the Liberal and Labour parties around a programme of free trade, land reform, poor law reform, old age pensions, trade union reform, sickness and unemployment insurance and municipalisation, especially of the drink trade. In one sense, his hopes might be said to have been realised; certainly much of the programme was carried out, but the growing strength of the Labour Party meant that these reforms were carried through in changing political conditions which perhaps, could better be expressed by transposing the terms and referring to the strength of LAB/LIBism.

Joseph Chamberlain

Chapter Twenty

BIRMINGHAM TRADE UNIONISM & LABOUR POLITICS
1900 – 1910

The main Birmingham Trade Unions and their Structure.

The contribution of Birmingham trade unions and their leaders has usually been understated and undervalued, often deliberately, in the effort to create and preserve the myth of a city of social harmony. It is not intended here to move to the opposite extreme, but an important survey of trade unionism in the city by the *Birmingham Evening Despatch* in 1908 together with other evidence of the growing importance of the Amalgamated Society of Engineers in the new, large scale factories which were transforming conditions of labour in Birmingham, and the emergence of new craft unions such as the Electrical Trades Union, require that the structure and practice of trade unions at this time be more closely examined.

The *Evening Despatch* series of articles began, naturally enough with the National Society of Amalgamated Brassworkers because:

> . . . it is one of the oldest and largest in the country, because it has its headquarters in Birmingham and because it is managed by a gentleman whose name is a household word.

The brassworkers epitomised many of the characteristics of Birmingham trade unionism at the time. The first was that of the Birmingham Alliances, which only a shallow analysis will write off as entirely an exercise in class collaboration. The principles of Alliance were as follows:

> All masters must be organised into an employers' federation.
> All men working at the trade must be organised into the trade union.
> All masters must employ only trade unionists.
> All men must work only for federated firms.
> Wages to be based on movements of prices around a published Price List.
> Wage increases negotiated to be paid only to trade unionists.
> Wages and conditions to be conciliated between trade unions and employers' federations.
> Differences to be settled by a named, agreed, permanent arbitrator whose decisions were binding on both sides.

W.J. Davis had pioneered this system from the boom years of the early 1870s, although a case can be made that the real pioneer was Richard Juggins in the Black Country. These Alliances were always beset by the problems that in good times, workers felt they were not maximising their opportunities, and in bad times the lower wages offered by sweating employers were difficult to resist by workers who would otherwise be unemployed.

The most celebrated alliance was the Bedstead Alliance organised by an employer, Walter Mills, which lasted from 1893 to 1901, roughly, the period of renewed capitalist expansion in Birmingham. Other Alliances covered spring mattresses, cased tubes and stair rods, spun brass bedstead and fender mounts, rolled metal, tubes and wire, fenders, china door furniture, china electrical fittings, earthenware, coffin furniture, pins, bricks and jet ware. By 1899 500 masters and 20,000 men were said to be involved in Alliances, almost all of them centred on Birmingham.

The theoretician of the Alliance system was E.J. Smith, a prominent bedstead manufacturer who extolled not only the benefits but the virtues of the system in an article in the *Economic Review* of 1898. One of the main criticisms of the alliances was that they were monopolies which maintained artificially high prices. To this Smith replied that collaboration not only ensured that costs were covered, but that competition was maintained and increased. Taking the argument to the opposition he maintained:

> . . . that the liberty to ruin honest competition by price cutting is a blot on the laws of a free country.

Some of these alliances remained operating until World War I, but most perished or could not be revived in the slump of 1903 – 09.

The influence of W.J. Davis was at its height in the period 1900 – 10, and a catalogue of his activities demonstrates his centrality to Birmingham labour history and also his national importance. Although an advanced liberal, Davis insisted on standing as a Labour candidate for Birmingham School Board. He was unsuccessful, but was elected unopposed in 1876 by being included in the Birmingham Liberal Caucus slate. In 1880 he became the first labour town councillor, elected as a nominee of the Labour Association, with Liberal support. He resigned three years later on leaving for Sheffield to become one of the first working men factory inspectors on the recommendation of the TUC. Davis eventually became the 'father' of the Trades Union Congress, first attending as a delegate at the Birmingham Congress of 1869 and as a trade union delegate from 1875 until his appointment as a factory inspector. When this ended in 1889 and Davis returned to Birmingham to re-build the Brassworkers Union, he resumed his regular TUC attendance. In 1896 he was elected to the Parliamentry Committee and in 1898 was chairman of the TUC. Davis supported the Boer War and lost some support, but continued to be elected to the Parliamentary Committee up to 1914, when again he supported the war. Electorally, Davis unsuccessfully contested the Bordesley seat in the parliamentary election of 1895 as a Gladstonian Liberal against the Liberal Unionist, Jesse Collings, one of Chamberlain's closest allies. In 1906 Davis was prepared to fight Chamberlain himself in Birmingham West on the issue of free trade, but he did not receive the support of trade unionists which would have enabled him to stand as Labour, so he withdrew.

On old age pensions, Davis was elected on to the TUC National Committee of Organised Labour, became the unofficial spokesman for the trade union movement, and ranks with George Cadbury as both a Birmingham and national figure in the pensions fight. Davis was active in the crusade against sweating which overlapped with the question of conciliation and arbitration in industry and when in 1909 the government appointed a National Board of Arbitration consisting of two employees, two employers and a neutral chairman, Davis was appointed.

Davis consistently clashed with feminists over the statutory control of labour in dangerous or 'degrading' trades such as chainmaking. The women argued that (a) this restricted opportunities for women and (b) men like Davis opposed it to protect male wages. In the 1870s he clashed with Emma Patterson, the pioneer woman delegate to the TUC and maintained his position into the 1900s when he clashed with Mary McArthur.

In the long, drawn out struggle for working class J.Ps. Davis' name was first put forward in 1892 and he was finally appointed in 1903.

As one of the most distinguished trade unionists of his time Davis was appointed, among many other things, a life governor of the Imperial Institute in London and in that capacity was one of the first two trade unionists ever to be invited to a coronation — that of George V.

In 1908 such was the power and prestige of Davis that the *Evening Dispatch* could end its article:

> The Brassworkers Society is managed, so far as it seems fit to Mr. Davis to allow it to be managed, by a president (Mr. W.C. McStocker) a vice president (Mr. John Ramsden) by seven trustees and by an executive council comprised of representatives from the various brass works in Birmingham.

The second local society dealt with by the *Evening Despatch* was the Tin Plate Workers Society with a Birmingham membership of 1650. A short-lived Birmingham society had been formed in 1812, but the existing society had been formed in 1857 and in 1874 had come the merger with the Wolverhampton society which made it the largest outside London. The outcome had been a price list of 135 pages for government work agreed with by the employers. Collaboration with the government went even further and the society was provided with a list of all firms tendering for government contracts in order that the society could ascertain that all firms were conforming to the Fair Wages resolution of the House of Commons. In 1890 a minimum rate per hour for each class of work had been agreed with the Birmingham employers. The pride of the society was its superannuation scheme paying a pension to members at age 60 on a sliding scale from 3/-d. a week for 7 years membership to 10/-d. a week after 25 years membership. Other benefits were £1 a week dispute pay, 12/-d. unemployment benefit, 8/-d. sickness pay with an £8 death benefit.

The general secretary was J.V. Stevens who, together with Davis, was the most prestigious Lib-Lab in Birmingham. Stevens had been born in Bristol in 1852 and came to Birmingham to find work. In 1874 he had joined the Tinplate Society and became president in 1880. In that year he had initiated the society superannuation scheme and as a result had been elected president of the National Committee of Organised Labour representing about 1.5 million workers formed to obtain old age pensions. He had been appointed general secretary of the Tinplate society in 1894. Like so many of the trade union leaders of the day he had for many years been associated with friendly societies, in this case Court No 1601 of the

Order of Foresters. Stevens entered the wider public life of Birmingham by being elected to the School Board in 1887 and was active in advocating a fair wages clause for all Board contractors and school caretakers. In 1889 he became a city councillor, beating Austen Chamberlain in St. Thomas' ward, remained until ousted by Rudland in 1907, but returned in 1911. Stevens unsuccessfully contested Birmingham East in the 1906 and the December 1911 general elections. He was (in 1908) the only working man who had ever been a governor of King Edward's School.

The next union dealt with by the *Evening Despatch* was the best known of the Amalgamated Societies operating on the opposite principle to that of the Tinmakers, namely centralisation instead of autonomy of branches. The eight Birmingham branches of the Amalgamated Society of Engineers had well over 2,000 members. The benefit scheme of the union was outlined with the additional information of the subscription. For 1/6d. per week (a very considerable sum) the following benefits were paid. 10/-d. a week sickness benefit, 20/-d. a week dispute benefit and £12 funeral benefit. Superannuation began at 55. This reflects the early wage at which men became unfit for work. Glassworkers, for instance argued that this age was 50 whereas their employers argued that it was 55. W.J. Davis estimated that only one worker in thirteen in Birmingham lived long enough to collect an old age pension at age 65. The ASE pension ranged from 7/-d. to 10/-d. a week and to collect the higher amount 45 years membership of the union was necessary. In fact, calculations from the national figures given in the *Despatch* showed that current average pension being paid by the ASE was 3/-d. a week.

The Society of National Toolmakers was then dealt with as a union originating in Birmingham in 1882. It was not a craft union of skilled workers but catered for all those in the engineering trades who were ineligible for membership of the ASE because they earned less than the standard rate of pay for skilled workers. In 1908 there was fifty five branches of the Toolmakers with a national executive committee and a local executive drawn from branches within a sixty five mile radius of Birmingham. The general secretary was William F. Beston who had been associated with the union from the beginning. The society paid sickness, unemployment and dispute benefit. The noteworthy feature of its scheme was a Travelling Benefit for members moving from one town to another for work. Another was the Holiday and Exception Benefit whereby during the normal unpaid holidays such as Christmas, Easter etc. a benefit was paid provided that the 'holiday' lasted more than six days. From each branch of the fund members could receive a total benefit of £10, but only £6 in any one year.

The *Evening Despatch* next dealt with the two Gasworkers unions. The Amalgamated Society of Gasworkers, Brickmakers and General Labourers was the society which had originally organised the Birmingham gas workers and had then spread to become a national union with its headquarters in Birmingham. The society's first secretary had been Beston of the Toolmakers. He was followed by Robert Toller until 1907 when Henry Simpson was appointed. Simpson had worked at Saltley Gas Works and was the first general labourer to become president of Birmingham Trades Council. He had been an Aston Poor Law Guardian since 1901. National membership of the union was between four and five thousands. Contributions were 3d. a week and benefits appear to be generous for this comparatively small sum. Unemployment pay was 6/-d. a week and dispute pay 12/-d. augmented by an amount from the Federation of Trade Unions to which the union was affiliated. 10/-d. a week injury benefit was paid and this was said to be a large drain on the funds. All classes of workers catered for by this union were subjected to large fluctuations of trade. The gasworkers suffered from the fact that large numbers were laid off in the summer when the demand for gas fell. For this the union had negotiated an agreement of last in, first out. The society's history showed no serious dispute and grievances had been 'invariably rectified by conciliatory negotiations.'

The other gas workers' union was the National Union of Gas Workers and General Labourers which claimed to be the largest such union with 40,000 members. This national union had organised the London gasworkers and the spread of this union to Birmingham was through recruiting non-gas workers, mainly in the engineering trades. Birmingham comprised a district of 3,500 men and Sam Lakin was the district secretary. The union subscription was 3d. and for this there was a 12/6d. dispute benefit augmented by 2/6d. from the National Federation of Trade Unions. For a contribution of 4d. a week additional benefits of 10/-d. a week sickness and accident benefit was payable for 13 weeks and 5/-d. for a further 13 weeks. A death grant of £8 for members and £4 for their wives was also paid. There was no unemployment pay but a Contingency Fund could be used to relieve distress. The 'considerable success' of the union was attributed to its diverse membership, which ensured that when some members were in dispute, enough were at work to support them.

The *Evening Despatch* next turned to the Amalgamated Society of Railway Servants, remarking that however ignorant the man in the street might be about trade unionism he had certainly heard of the ASRS and it was the great public interest in the recent threatened strike of railwaymen which had led to the present series of articles. This was a reference to the celebrated All Grades Movement directed against grade elitism and demanding an 8-hour day for all men engaged in the manipulation of traffic, a maximum of a 10-hour day for all railwaymen, and immediate increases of pay for Sunday and overtime working. Above all, the action was for recognition of the union, which the military minded railway employers had vowed they would never do. This threat of a national stoppage brought Lloyd George, then President of the Board of Trade into negotiations and great, momentary glory by his negotiation of the settlement of 1907. This left the union unrecognised and the railwaymen enmeshed in a web of Conciliation Boards separately set up for each railway company and final, binding arbitration for a period of six years. The results showed railwaymen's earnings even lower by 1910 than they had been in 1907. Dissatisfaction led to the emergence of the National Union of Railwaymen and repudiation of the agreement in 1911.

There were 600,000 railway workers in Britain of whom 100,000 belonged to the ASRS, while many others were organised in the Engine Drivers and Firemen's Society and others in the Railway Clerks Society. The ASRS organised 2,000 of Birmingham's 5401 railwaymen. The society had been started in 1871 not at a great railway centre, but at Worcester, by a clerk in the clearing house there. The grievances giving rise to organisation were 'well nigh incredible.' Drivers, guards, signalmen as well as all other employees could be called upon to work a twenty four hour stretch and after three hours sleep, start again, refusal leading to instant dismissal. The working week was one of seven days, railwaymen were subjected to a military discipline and wages were very low.

The first Birmingham branch had been formed in 1872. As in the coalmining industry, the initial impetus to organisation had not been wages, but safety and conditions of work and the union 'was only now turning to the question of higher wages'. A survey of over 250,000 men covering all grades had shown that nearly two thirds of railwaymen were paid between 17/-d. and 25/-d., the largest group earning 21/-d. and the average for the whole UK was 23/2d. These were earnings for a 12-hour day for almost half the workers in Scotland and Ireland and one quarter for the whole of the U.K. Two thirds of all U.K. railwaymen worked a ten hour day. Speed-up on the railways was another major grievance. Between 1895 and 1900 freight traffic had increased by more than 25% and passenger traffic almost as much. From 1900 to 1913 freight traffic increased by 11% and passenger traffic by 9%.

The low wages and bad conditions tolerated by the railwaymen suggest the very high premium placed on regularity of earnings and security of employment. This, again, emphasises the existence of the high rates of unemployment and short-time working prevalent in Birmingham, as elsewhere.

The next union profiled was the Bedstead Workmen's Association beginning with the celebrated statistic that 30,000 bedsteads were produced every week in Britain, of which 75% were made in Birmingham with price tags varying from £1,000 for an eastern potentate to a few shillings for Workhouse beds. The society had been set up in 1889 by Walter Mills, a bedstead manufacturer, who was also the existing secretary of the union. A successful fifteen day strike had brought a 15% pay increases. This had been negotiated between a hastily initiated Masters' Association and final arbitration by Judge Chalmers, then Birmingham County Court judge. By 1893 when almost all men were trade union members, the masters suggested working together on Alliance principles. This Alliance had existed until 1899 when it broke up through a Manchester strike and the secession of one of the leading firms. Ever since then, Mills had been trying to renew the Alliance and his most powerful weapon was the celebrated Passport System. This was made possible by the fact that most men belonged to the union and most masters still recognised the Alliance. Such masters requiring men notified the union of their requirements and men needing employment had to apply to the union. Each man sent to a firm was provided with a Passport certifying that he was a society man. From the men's point of view it ensured that no employer undercut the agreed wage and it provided an efficient labour bureau. From the masters' point of view it enabled prices to be maintained and sweating employers were deprived of labour. The 1889 settlement which had been an advance of 15% rose to 40% in subsequent years, but the mass unemployment of the mid 1900s had reduced that to 7.5% in 1908.

Ninth in the *Evening Despatch* series was the old, strong, craft union of the printers, with traditions mythologically going back to Caxton, but whose antiquity was attested to by the fact that their branches were called chapels, and their shop-stewards fathers. Organisation was always strongest in London, however, and Birmingham printers were first associated with the Provincial Typographical Association in 1856, seven years after its formation. Early efforts to improve conditions in Birmingham were dogged by the two competing societies. The economic boom of the early 1870s had brought stable membership and a demand for a minimum wage of 30/-d. a week for jobbing printers, a 56-hour week and 8d. per hour overtime. Since then there had been three wage increases bringing the rate up to 36/-d. a week.

The tenth union dealt with was the white-collar National Union of Clerks. The difficulties of such organisation were stressed — the 'genteel' nature of the occupation which generated snobbery and hostility to trade union organisation; the small numbers in offices and the ease with which trade unionists could be victimised. The union had originated in London in 1890, but the Birmingham branch was not formed until 1905. The leading Birmingham figure was Fred Hughes, who initiated the Birmingham branch and continued to be its secretary; he was also national president in 1907, represented his branch on the trades council and was secretary of the Birmingham and District Labour Representation Committee.

The eleventh union dealt with was the Workmen's Union. Its special characteristics were that, with its comprehensive title, it catered for all workers without a specific union and also meant that into whatever industry the mobile general labourer of Birmingham moved, he retained membership of the same union. In addition, generous benefits for 3d. a week (including unemployment pay) meant that the union catered for both employed and unemployed members. Further, it accepted, and welcomed, women members who, for a half subscription received half benefits. Finally, it was a political union from the beginning with a Socialist programme of nationalisation and the aim of political representation on local bodies and in parliament. This type of union reflected the views of such men as Tom Mann who had been its first general secretary.

The Workers' Union began in 1878, but the Birmingham branch was not formed until 1905. It was organised by Jack Beard who resigned the district secretaryship of the ASE in Shropshire to do this. Beard had originally gone to Shropshire to organise the Agricultural Workers Union which had collapsed with the Great Depression. Birmingham membership of the Workers' Union in 1908 was just over 1,000.

The last union dealt with was another old craft amalgamated society, that of the Carpenters & Joiners. The society dated from 1860 and a Birmingham branch had been started three years later. One existing union, the General Union of Carpenters and Joiners had not joined the Amalgamation and had about 120 members in Birmingham. The Amalgamated Society was divided into districts of trades within five miles of a given point and no branch could consist of more that 250 workers. In the Birmingham district there were sixteen branches with over 1,800 members. Contributions were high and dues were about to be raised from

1/-d. to 1/3d. a week. Unemployment benefit was 10/-d. for twelve weeks and 6/-d. for another twelve. Sick pay was 12/-d. for twenty six weeks and 6/-d. thereafter indefinitely. Superannuation was 8/-d. a week after 25 years membership if over 50 or if disabled or sick. Relations between employers and union had usually been good in Birmingham and many members regarded the society more of a benefit society than a trade union.

Finally, the *Despatch* dealt with the Birmingham Trades Council, outlining its development already given in the foregoing pages and it is to the records of the trades council that we now turn to complete the picture of trade union spread in the period 1900 – 1910.

If one takes regularity of attendance as a criterion, delegates of the following unions, not covered by the *Despatch* made the greatest contribution to the trades council in 1901: Bookbinders, brushmakers, bakers, basketmakers, bricklayers, city park men, cabinet makers, coach makers, coopers, farriers, glass workers, insurance agents, lampmen, Britannia and other metal workers, plumbers, pattern makers, painters and decorators, stonemasons, shop assistants, and silversmiths. But the spread of trades was wider even than this and included such interesting examples as artists, Jewish tailors, musicians, and theatrical and music hall workers.

Birmingham Trades Council, the Right to Work and the Origins of the Welfare State.

The above survey of Birmingham Trades Council begins to point its centrality and importance in the struggle to improve working class living standards and promote changes in the organisation of society. By 1900 it had already been the key organising factor in bringing the Labour Party into existence and through its election committee was still the determining influence on what was a working class candidate and who stood.

In the next decade it was to play an equally decisive part in two wide-ranging complexes of activity which can be brought under the umbrellas of the campaign for the Right to Work and another campaign through which the demolition of the Poor Law was to lay the basis for the Welfare State.

The Right to Work Campaign had two dimensions. The first was the ideological concept that capitalism was a system of organised, legalised robbery of the surplus value created by labour over and above its cost of maintenance and renewal; that periodic mass unemployment was inevitable while this system existed and that it ought to be replaced by Socialism. The second was the practical dimension of exploring the various forms of municipal and state aid that could create work and livelihood during periods when the normal processes of capitalist realisation of profit broke down and mass unemployment occurred.

The other complex of campaigns was the wide ranging social agitations to extort from the authorities the services such as health, education and welfare which were necessary to the survival and development of working people. Where such embryo services had been forced, their adminstration had been embodied in the hated Poor Law. The main event of the decade here was the Royal Commission on the Poor Law and the subsequent Minority Report with its proposal to demolish both Poor Law philosophy and practice. The two campaigns finally coalesce in Birmingham with the merging of the Right to Work Committee with the Committee for the Break-up of the Poor Law.

It is to these two main campaigns, therefore, we now turn.

The Right to Work.

There are three basic positions which can be taken up on the question of the Right to Work. The first is that of the political and economic Conservatives who deny that any such right exists, that employment is regulated by market forces, that unemployment is a signal that workers are demanding too high a wage and that a lower wage would enable goods to be sold at a lower price which would increase demand and enable those currently unemployed to be re-employed. The second might be termed the Reformist view. This acknowledges that capitalism moves in cycles of Overproduction resulting in mass unemployment, but that this can be corrected by limited controls of the system ensuring that Investment and Savings are kept in step. This was the conclusion of J.H. Hobson which developed into Keynesianism. The third basic position is the Radical one that only labour can create value, that capitalism is a system of exploitation whereby the surplus the labourer creates over his 'cost of production' and reproduction is appropriated by the capitalist who employs him. It is in the attempt of the employer to realise that 'surplus value' that the causes of crises must be sought. Crises therefore, are integral to the process of production and can only be removed by the ending of the class system of exploitation and its replacement by Socialism.

During the expansionist phase of capitalism 1845 – 75, the ideologues of the system had established capitalism as the eternal 'natural' order of society which had, and always would, exist. The mass unemployment of the Great Depression saw the re-birth of Socialism and the blight of mass unemployment again in the 1900s challenged capitalist assumptions.

The relief of distress was traditionally viewed to be the province of (a) private charity and (b) the poor law. So that when mass unemployment occurred something had to be done, or civil disorder would result. When normal channels of philanthropy were exhausted, therefore, there was usually a town appeal for charitable aid. If this were exhausted the unemployed were forced into the Poor Law. But the 1834 Poor Law Act had been constructed on the philosophy that poverty was the consequence of the improvidence of the poor themselves. Relief should therefore be given only to the 'deserving poor' and that only on a scale of 'least eligibility' meaning that relief must be lower than the lowest possible wage available, in order to ensure that relief did not become an alternative to work. If the unemployed sought relief through the Poor Law, they would be 'offered the House'. This meant that they would be accepted as inmates of the Workhouse, provided that they were destitute i.e. all their possessions had been sold and that husband was separated from wife and children in segregated quarters.

Working class agitation against these barbarities led to the next stage; that of Outdoor Relief. But this was only given to the Able Bodied in return for work; so for the unemployed the Stone Yard was opened and the 'lucky' ones were paid about 1/6d. for a day spent breaking stones;

the 'luckier' ones (usually those with the largest families) might even get two such days work. Pressure from the labour movement had created a third channel of relief whereby the local authority provided a limited amount of work for the unemployed. This work was limited by the fact that the local authority was not able to raise a rate for such work, and when the extremely limited funds provided from the Mayor's Fund, or other Funds, were exhausted no further work could be provided: This was the general position that had prevailed during the Great Depression. A detailed examination of the Birmingham position is not possible because of the absence of a comprehensive study of the Poor Law. But the position after 1905 can be fully explored, and has been by Cyril Collard.

Its starting point is the 1905 Unemployed Workmen Act. This required that all towns of population of 500,000 and above were obliged to set up Distress Committees consisting of local councillors, Poor Law Guardians and 'persons experienced in the relief of distress' including at least one woman. The Birmingham Distress Committee was set up in October incorporating Guardians from the various Poor Law Unions covering the city and also a representative of the trades council. The duties of the Committee consisted of the maximum of 'investigation' and the minimum of action. It was to enquire into the applications made by unemployed persons; to endeavour to find work for the applicant if satified that the case was more suited under the Act than under the Poor Law; to establish or assist Labour Exchanges, to assist emigration or removal to another area; to provide or contribute to the provision of temporary work; to administer a fund provided partly by voluntary contributions and partly by a contribution from the rates provided that this did not exceed the product of ½d. rate, or 1d. if approved by the Local Government Board. The core of 'persons experienced in the relief of distress' was the odious C.O.S. (Charity Organisation Society). This originated in Birmingham as the West Birmingham Relief Fund founded by Chamberlain in 1891, and other similar Funds in other parts of the city. These came together in 1906 as the City Aid Society.

The working class in Birmingham organised themselves around two main bodies to assert the Right to Work and the lesser claim that when work was not available the unemployed and their families should have the right to maintenance on a humane scale exceeding that of the Poor Law. The first body was the Right to Work Committee. This was initiated by the SDF through the Socialist Centre in November 1905 and quickly became representative of the whole movement. John Beard of the ILP and organiser of the Workers' Union became chairman; Annie Evans, feminist and member of the Socialist Centre was secretary and John Berry, the secretary of the trades council was the organiser. The aims of the Committee were to organise the unemployed, to publicise their condition, to gain recognition of the right of the unemployed to work and to bring pressure on Parliament and local authorities to enforce and improve the new unemployment legislation.

The second working class organisation appeared only at a later stage, during the period 1908–09, when unemployment was particularly severe. This was an organisation of the unemployed themselves, the Birmingham Unemployed Association which seems to have been formed in 1907 and whose leaders had either not before been connected with the labour movement in the city, or, where they were socialists, their previous links with the movement had been tenuous.

The unemployed agitation which occurred during the years 1903 – 1910, can best be viewed against the background of national agitation and the many social issues which became entwined with the concept of the Right to Work, including the right of free speech.

The brunt of the first wave of unemployment protest 1903 – 06 fell on a Tory government. Their main aim was to head off the ideological challenge of the Right to Work, while doing as little as possible, since whatever they did would be regarded as a concession to that principle. If that was their Scylla they were acutely aware of their Charybdis. This was the power of the unemployed if they took to the streets and repeated the agitation of the 1880s when they had marched through clubland and the west end of London. One result of this was that heavy policing was the order of the day throughout the period both in London and the provinces, (including Birmingham). Both the ubiquity and overaction of the police throughout the country points to tacit agreement between the Home Office and chief constables in the localities.

London remained central to the Right to Work campaign, largely because of the huge mass of festering poverty, unemployment and casual employment of the east-end, but also because the SDF in London was stronger than the ILP and therefore the main political ideology of the capital was Marxist and militant.

From early 1903 the SDF was organising processions of the unemployed through the west-end, culminating in a mass rally in Trafalgar Square on the eve of the reassembly of Parliament. Reactions were various. The Mansion House Fund, in abeyance since 1895 was resurrected; the broad labour movement set up a National Unemployed Committee, partly to pursue more effectively the cause of the unemployed, and partly to limit the influence of the SDF. By such means the government was enabled to avoid taking any action until the Unemployed Workmen Act of 1905.

Birmingham Trades Council was active on the unemployment issue from the beginning. In 1904 it supported the national call for a special autumn session of parliament to deal with unemployment through relief work. Towards the end of the year a deputation met the General Purposes Committee of the city Council to stress the gravity of the situation and the need for council provided work. Berry, the secretary, put forward a series of proposals. He suggested that the river Rea improvement scheme be started, the Balsall Heath baths built, that public buildings be painted, courts and alleys cleaned and roads laid with Rowley Rag be re-laid with flagstones. The cost of these schemes should be subsidised by a £10,000 grant from the profits of the Gas Committee. In December the mayor launched a Distress Fund, but public works expenditure rose only minimally from £224,000 in 1900 – 01 to £257,000 in 1909 – 10.

The Birmingham Right to Work Committee began to operate in November 1905. John Beard, on behalf of the Birmingham Right to Work Committee, organised midday meetings in Victoria Square as the Birmingham equivalent of the London marches. Deputations of the unemployed waited on the Distress Committee to demand that work be provided. Police instructions at that time were to tolerate the thrice-weekly meetings in the square, but on no account to allow the unemployed to march through the streets because they would then be liable to produce collecting boxes and this was a considerable incentive for the unemployed to join such marches.

In December 1905 the general election produced not only the land-slide Liberal victory, but also the return of 29 Labour members and the conversion of the Labour Representation Committee into the Labour Party. Another effect was the appointment of the first working man to cabinet office, namely, John Burns, the Independent Labour M.P. for Battersea, as secretary to the Local Government Board. The appointment of Burns brought some illusions, but not many, for it was by then widely acknowledged that John Burns had moved very far to the right since the Dock Strike of the 1880s. Burns proved to be a ferocious opponent of the right to work principle as well as a master of inactivity and delaying action in assisting the unemployed. On the other hand, the emergence of a block of Labour MPs relieved Keir Hardie of the pressure of being virtually the sole Member of the Unemployed, and made possible the drafting and introduction, although not the passing, of legislation in favour of labour.

The Right to Work agitation continued throughout 1906 and 1907, but was hampered by problems of staffing and financing the Committee. John Berry resigned in 1906 and it was found impossible to replace him, so John Beard became both organiser and secretary; affiliated organisations such as the Labour Church found difficulty in providing representation on the Committee. But the greatest weakness was the inability to draw the unemployed themselves into activity. This was to be overcome in 1908. In addition, the attacks on the principle of the Right to Work and the possibility of various reforms mitigating some of the consequences of unemployment, meant that the only coherent strategy could be that of the militants who proclaimed that reforms were only palliatives and Socialism was the only answer to the problems. Such a strategy attracted only minority support. The trades council continued to exert pressure, but its failure to endorse the principle of the Right to Work weakened its action to demanding such minor measures as the ending of all overtime and the setting up of farm colonies.

The most important stalling action against measures for dealing with unemployment was the setting up in August 1905 of the Royal Commission of the Poor Laws which reported in 1909; but Chamberlain's Tariff Reform campaign which attracted working class support outside the organised Labour movement was also influential in diverting attention from immediate measures to relieve unemployment.

The severity of unemployment in Birmingham is unquestioned; what is more difficult is to assess the actual amount. In 1906 J.V. Stevens had estimated that 10,000 were out of work in the city. This would be about 6% of the male employed population. The next year unemployment rose further. In 1908 unemployment nationally was double that of 1806 and if Birmingham unemployment had increased in the same proportion, about 21,000 would have been out of work. This led to the next surge of unemployment agitation, this time led by the unemployed themselves.

Nationally, John Burns continued to oppose all proposals to find work for the unemployed including refusal to sanction the setting up of land colonies. In Manchester in 1906 church lands had been occupied and the unemployed set to work cultivating them and this spread to other parts of the country. In January 1907, a Hunger March from Manchester en route to London clashed violently with the police in Birmingham. In July 1907 the two sensational bye-elections brought Pete Curran and Victor Grayson into parliament. In the same month, Ramsay Macdonald introduced a Labour Bill in the House of Commons with the radical Right to Work demands of (a) a Central Unemployment Committee to plan national works (b) the appointment of local commissioners to develop local works and (c) registration of the unemployed and subsequent provision of work or adequate maintenance for all those on the registers.

At the end of 1907 the Birmingham unemployed took matters into their own hands. A deputation visited the chief constable and informed him that they would resort to self-help by taking to the streets and collecting money. Permission was refused and they were told thay anyone found collecting would have their names taken and told to desist, but they would not be arrested. In January 1908 the press reported an attempt by the unemployed to 'storm' the Council House after failing to obtain a meeting with the Lord Mayor whom they accused of failing to implement the Unemployed Workmen Act and the failure of the Distress Committee to act. The protestors then held a meeting in Victoria Square where H.T. Williams, W.H. Skett and Satchwell were arrested. Undeterred by this, the unemployed planned further meetings at the week-end and police instructions were issued that under no circumstances were the unemployed to be allowed to hold meetings or march about the streets. Skett was charged with obstruction. He defended the right of the unemployed to hold meetings and put their case to the public, to which the magistrates claimed, quite wrongly, that such meetings were held only on sufferance and if the police put an end to a meeting they were carrying out the law of the land. Skett refused to gave an unconditional undertaking not to engage in further agitation until the local authorities implemented the Unemployed Workmen's Act and promoted special measures for the unemployed. He said he 'would risk imprisonment rather than see his fellows starving.' Skett was fined 40/-d. and costs; on refusing to pay he was 'sent down' for a month. Further attempts were made to organise meetings in Victoria Square and all were prevented by the police with further arrests being made.

The normal, insolent attitude of the Unionist press to the unemployed began to change. *The Birmingham Mail*, while continuing to be critical and patronising regarding 'self-constituted leaders of the unemployed and the considerable number of loafers and undesirables gathered around them', conceded that something must be done and on the very day of Skett's trial, the Distress Committee in conjunction with the City Aid Society issued an appeal for funds to relieve 'all cases of distress arising from temporary unemployment' provided that the recipients were 'of good character.' They denied that this action had anything to do with the agitation of the unemployed!

Also in January 1908 Jack Williams, the SDFer, led another march from Manchester bound for London with a petition to the king and Local

Government Board. The Birmingham police were instructed to meet the men at the city boundary, escort them to the Salvation Army hall where food and lodging was to be provided and see them off to Coventry the next day. But after an appeal by local socialists the police reluctantly allowed a meeting the next day (Friday) in the Bull Ring, which was addressed by Fred Hughes. An unemployed demonstration for the Sunday was banned by the police, however, and the marchers were bundled out of the city.

The actions of the unemployed stimulated the Labour movement. In February 1908, the trades council expressed 'deep concern' regarding the plight of the unemployed and how little was being done. Both the trades council and the Socialist Centre appointed delegations to wait on the Watch Committee regarding the right of the unemployed to demonstrate, but it seems that these protests were not even discussed. On 9 February a town hall meeting to publicise the Labour Party's Right to Work Bill was organised.

Meanwhile the Liberal government was shuffling its pack of cards. Winston Churchill was sent to the Board of Trade to work on Labour Exchanges and Masterman was appointed under-secretary at the Local Government Board to try to prod John Burns into action. Burns was now using the excuse that he was waiting for the findings of the Poor Law Commission.

The Labour Party's Right to Work Bill was rejected in March 1908. This led to the resuscitation of the National Right to Work Council. Their first decisions were to collect reliable unemployment statistics and also to activate local Right to Work Committees. The Birmingham result of these decisions was a trades council resolution asking all affiliated societies to provide details of unemployment and short-time working among their members and asking them whether they would be prepared to support a Right to Work demonstration. Nationally, unemployment had been growing throughout the summer and some Birmingham societies' Out of Work funds were so depleted that special levies were being made on members.

By October the Commissioner of the Metropolitan Police in London was complaining of the strain on police resources with hunger marches, church parades and suffragette agitation. In Birmingham the autumn campaign began with two superintendents and 25 constables on daily call at the Council House to prevent demonstrations in Victoria Square, and by September this force had been increased to 55 men. The police maintained, however, that the unemployed had been allowed meetings in the Bull Ring 'without let or hindrance.'

The Birmingham Right to Work Committee announced a Victoria Square meeting of the unemployed at noon on Monday 28th September. Since such meetings were prohibited by the chief constable a confrontation became inevitable. The *Birmingham Gazette* estimated that a crowd of between 4,000 and 5,000 gathered on the day, so the true attendance was bound to have been greater than that. The two Socialist speakers, Fred Hughes and Margaret Smith, were both arrested as also was Skett who was charged with being disorderly and causing an obstruction — although not before he had managed to accuse the Distress Committee, the Boards of Guardians and the Lord Mayor of neglecting their duty to the unemployed.

The issues now became not only the Right to Work, but the right of free speech and demonstration. The Right to Work Committee therefore announced another demonstration in Victoria Square for the following Monday 5th October. The unemployed themselves declared that they would have to show themselves on the streets if they were to bring the question of unemployment home to the rulers of the city and on Wednesday 30th September they organised a meeting at Five Ways. Again, the police arrested the speaker, Mr. Edwards, which, according to the *Birmingham Gazette* left the crowd 'on the brink of a great riot.' Police provocation increased even further in October when 150 police officers, including detectives and plain clothes men (16% of the police force) were wholly employed in the prevention of unemployed meetings in the vicinity of the Town Hall.

A large police presence was mobilised for Skett's trial on Friday 2nd October. Skett argued that he had not been an organiser of the 28th September demonstration and had only spoken because an advertised speaker had failed to appear; but Skett was considered the instigator of the 'disturbances' and was again fined 40/-d. plus costs, or one month. Knowing that Skett would not pay the fine and wishing to avoid making him a martyr to the cause of unemployment, the magistrate then, with dubious legality, levied a distress warrant on his goods. Three articles of his furniture were seized and subsequently sold, but were bought by the Right to Work Committee and returned to Skett.

A deputation from the Right to Work Committee met the Watch Committee who professed sympathy with the 'genuine unemployed' and a desire to help them; the deputation left with the impression that orderly processions would be allowed provided that due notice of the time and route was given. The same day the Birmingham and District Unemployed Association organised a large meeting at Gosta Green where 50 police were present, but kept a low profile. Speakers pointed out the inadequacies of relief agencies in the city and urged the promotion of relief works and the provision of meals for necessitious children by the city council. But by now there was growing agreement that the 1905 Act was inadequate, and it was the duty of the state, as well as the local authority to provide work or maintenance.

The police continued to violate the right to demonstrate. Another large demonstration planned for October in Victoria Square was eventually called off because the unemployed thought that their need for relief would be overshadowed by the principle of free speech. In addition, agitation was taking a different direction.

We have seen that the Right to Work Committee depended heavily for its personnel on the Labour Church; by the autumn of 1908 the wider church communities were showing concern. A meeting of the National Right to Work Committee had asked local committees to organise Church Parades on Sunday October 11th 1908 on the eve of the reassembling of Parliament. This was to serve the two-fold purpose of overcoming the prohibition of demonstrations, which applied not only in Birmingham, but was widespread throughout the country, and also as a new and novel way of presenting the case of the unemployed to a wider public.

The local Right to Work Committee had anticipated the national decision and organised its first Church Parade on the Sunday before the 11th. This was to the parish church of St. Martin's in the Bull Ring, when 400 unemployed attended and Canon Denton Thompson, a Liberal Unionist, conceded that it was both a national and municipal duty to give the unemployed 'the opportunity of earning their daily bread.' The next week the Right to Work Committee organised an initial gathering in the Bull Ring and a march, albeit a short one, to Carrs Lane chapel, where a sympathetic audience could be expected. The chief constable was informed and promised a quite unnecessary 'escort' from the Bull Ring to Carrs Lane. Perhaps predictably, the second Parade was less successful than the first, only about forty unemployed being 'escorted' from the Bull Ring, although about 100 attended the service.

The following day the unemployed gathered in much greater numbers in the Bull Ring and, accompanied by the police, marched, 'in the utmost orderliness', through the main thoroughfares of middle class Edgbaston. So, as unemployment in Birmingham rose to its peak, some concession had been wrung from the police.

This was partly because national concern had been aroused and John Burns had been told that he must do something. The only result was an increase in the Exchequer grant to £300,000 and certain relaxations of restrictive provisions of the 1905 Act. Locally, middle class concern was expressed by the Birmingham Aid Society opening several branches around the city and a joint appeal by the Lord Mayor and the Bishop of Birmingham for a Relief Fund. This had a modest target of £5,000, but eventually realised £7,800. Also in October 1908 the city council announced that 150-200 extra men had been given employment for parks improvements. Before the end of the year 2,200 unemployed men were registered with the Distress Committee and 6,645 during the winter of 1908 – 09, of which only one third were provided with any relief work.

The Unemployed Association continued with Church Parades well into 1909 and the Right to Work Committee functioned throughout 1909. By the end of the year, unemployment was beginning to fall, the Poor Law report had finally appeared and the Right to Work Committees found themselves with a series of propositions which addressed the various elements of the problems of unemployment and poverty which merged into the campaign to break up the detested Poor Law system.

The fragmented statistical material shows the total inadequacy of the 1905 Unemploymed Workmen Act and local charity to touch even the fringe of the poverty created by unemployment. The £7,800 raised by the 1908 – 09 Relief Fund would have provided the *registered* unemployed (which by no means measured total unemployment) with a single payment of just over £1 per family. The municipal contribution to the expenses of the Distress Committee were as follows:

    1905 – 06 £300
    1906 – 07 £700
    1907 – 08 £1,700
    1908 – 09 £1,000
    1909 – 10 £2,000

Never did these paltry contributions approach the product of the ½ d. rate permitted, and such sums were for highly dubious administrative expenses and not for relief of the unemployed.

The questions of the actual number of unemployed and their 'relief' will be discussed in Chapter 21.

The Trade Unions and the Origins of the Welfare State.

Parallel with the ideology and politics of the Right to Work ran a vast amount of activity on the social issues eventually aimed at that security from the cradle to the grave for working people to which the rich are born and the affluent hasten to purchase.

First, however, the establishment of Labour Exchanges which might more properly be considered one of those measures necessary to implementing the Right to Work can be dealt with.

To some extent, most trade unions performed the functions of Labour Exchanges and some, such as the glassworkers and the Alliance trades operated a monopoly, or near monopoly of the supply of labour. It should, perhaps, be remarked that the use of the expression 'Labour Exchange' as a mart to which employers and employees came to match the supply of and demand for labour is at a distinctly lower level of ideology and usage than the original Owenite Labour Exchanges to which workers brought the products of their labour to directly exchange with the products of other labourers, of which the Birmingham Labour Exchange of 1834 was the outstanding example in Britain.

Whilst agreeing that these new Labour Exchanges would be useful in facilitating job information, there was deep suspicion within the working class movement as to other effects and the motives of those introducing such an organisation. One fear was that they would offer jobs at less than trade union rates of pay; another was that they would be used to recruit blacklegs during strikes or lock-outs; others saw them as deliberate attempts to destroy trade unionism by removing one of their basic functions. For all these reasons, the trade unions demanded that these exchanges be adminstered by committees consisting of equal numbers of employers and trade unionists with a neutral chairman. It is interesting that this was one of the few working class demands that was not bitterly resisted to the last.

In Birmingham there had been attempts to set up private labour exchanges. This, together with the fear that if the trade unions were not co-operative, a large part in their adminstration might be played by the recently formed anti-trade union body, the National Free Labour Association, ensured that, although all of the foregoing criticisms were found locally, the Trades Council, after a discussion in June 1909 welcomed the Exchanges. They began operating on 31st January 1910, and W.J. Morgan, an ex-president of the Birmingham Trades Council, was appointed manager of the Bury labour exchange.

Another grave social evil was the housing question in Birmingham. Again, the lack of an adequate study for the city inhibits comment, but it can be said that the improvement of the situation (it is not likely that a *solution* can ever be found under capitalism) was hampered by the influence of the erroneous ideas of Joseph Chamberlain that state interference should be limited to compulsory purchase of land, and that private enterprise could then be safely left to develop the area. Even this limited amount of interference was opposed by the important slum landlord interests represented on the city council.

As a result of the Artizans Dwellings Act of 1870, the celebrated Birmingham Improvement Scheme cut a wide swathe through some of the worst slum areas of the city which led to the civic dignity of Corporation Street but not to the rehousing of the slum dwellers who created further slums elsewhere in the city. The Housing of the Working Classes Act of 1890 gave powers for local authorities to clear smaller areas and build houses. Some authorities such as London built on a wide scale, but the only council houses built in Birmingham before World War I were sixty one tenements in Milk Street let in 1901 – 02 at an average rent of nearly 4/-d. a week which was too high for slum dwellers. At such rent levels these houses made "losses" every year; although no one calculated the social gain from improved health and living conditions. The subsequent history in Birmingham to 1914 is of the appointment of a Housing Committee which distinguished itself by never building a house.

The trades council pursued the city authorities through all their prevarications. For instance in 1901 when a proposal to build 631 houses at Bordesley Green at rents between 3/9d. and 5/-d. was lost by two votes in favour of referring the matter to the Housing Committee to be appointed in November of that year, the trades council protested. This was followed by the creation of its own Housing Committee by the trades council. This was hastened by an increased shortage of working class housing and a sharp rise in rents at the beginning of the century. The 1904 report of the trades council Housing Committee surveyed rents in the city and concluded that working people were paying 20% of their incomes in rent. It also commented on the fact that the city Housing Committee was not only not building houses, but was closing and demolishing unfit houses (instead of making them fit for habitation) which decreased the housing stock and was a cause of rent rises. In this, the law was the submissive agent of the landlord, who after thirty days residence could eject a tenant or double his rent. Neither private landlords nor the municipality could house workers with money borrowed at 3.5% or 4%, but the trades council committee pointed out that the municipality had monies lying idle in the banks earning only 1¾% and recommended:

> That the City Council be asked to borrow money at 2½% from its trading committees for the purpose of housing the workers . . .

The trades council continued to harry the city Housing Committee. In 1906 the trades council report commented that they had 'devoted considerable time to the question of housing'. In that year they were making the opposite criticism that local magistrates were opposing closing orders obtained by the Housing Committee and sanctioned by the medical officer of health, thus enabling slum landlords to continue in their nefarious trade. A petition of protest had gone to the Local Government Board, but John Burns had stated that he could do nothing. There was a close connection between better housing and land reform, it was noted, and the trades council Housing Committee had been closely associated with a well attended Midland Conference on Land Nationalisation.

In 1907 the trades council was exasperated that the land at Bordesley earmarked for council houses had been let for other purposes. Enquiries into working class rents and agitation against the property interests which dominated the city council continued, but nothing could shift the council from its posture that 'public money could be used to much greater advantage than in building houses.'

The other two main social issues, that of old age pensions and national insurance were directly related to the Poor Law and its future. The fear of old people dying in the Workhouse has been the longest lasting memory of the detested Poor Law after 1834 which, in general, might be described as a vast, centralised bureaucractic apparatus for the systematic violation of the human rights of the poor. Theoretically, there was no way of relieving old people except by the process of sale of all their possessions and when they were completely destitute applying for admission to the Workhouse. If they were a couple, they would be admitted to separate wings of the Workhouse and their life together, would effectively be at an end. In practice, some poor law authorities after 1834 did pay out-relief to some old people, averaging perhaps, 1/-d. or 2/-d. per week; in the absence of an adequate study of the poor law in Birmingham, we do not know to what extent this applied to the city.

It was in 1896 that serious discussion opened, on Joseph Chamberlain's scheme for old age pensions which were to be paid for by voluntary contributions of 3d. per fortnight for forty years through Friendly Societies after which a pension of 2/6d. a week would be payable which the state would then double. This scheme competed with that of Charles Booth who advocated a free pension for all at age 65. The trades council became actively involved in the pensions issue with the demand that corporation manual workers should be entitled to join a corporation Superannuation Fund which, up to that time, had been confined to salaried officials of the council.

The campaign for old age pensions over the next ten years was spear-headed mainly by George Cadbury, with the support of the trades council. In March 1899, Cadbury sponsored and financed a conference in Birmingham. Stevens and Eades, prominent members of the trades council, were members of the organising committee, which invited Charles Booth to put forward his ideas. The conference was an outstanding success and Allan Granger, David Jones and Arthur Eades were appointed chairman, treasurer and secretary of a local Campaigning Committee. The trades council consistently promoted the cause of old age pensions from that time. A year after the Liberal victory of 1906 at a town hall meeting called by the trades council they expressed regret that no bill had been introduced and demanded a non-contributory pension of 5/-d. for all at 65 years of age. The Old Age Pension Act was finally passed in 1908. It granted 5/-d. a week to all whose incomes were below £26 a year, with a downward sliding scale for those who earned more. But the pension was not payable until the age of 70, and few working people lived to reach that age. The trades council also accepted representation on the Pensions Committees of both Birmingham and Aston. These committees dealt with the complex questions of the eligibility of old people for the pension. The trades council welcomed the concession of the principle of old age pensions, while regretting that the existing scheme fell short of trades council demands.

The other main social issue to concern the trade union and labour movement was that of national sickness and unemployment benefit. Lloyd George's radical budget of 1909 proposed increases in income tax and death duties. These might have been swallowed by the House of Lords, but Lloyd George had also included land taxes which proposed a 20% tax on the increased value of land when that increase was due solely to the community and not to investment. This was held to be the 'revolutionary' demand which either replaced or presaged the age-long demand of the radical movement for land nationalisation. The issue of increased taxes therefore became entangled with the constitutional issue of the rejection of the budget by the House of Lords, which, in turn, was further complicated by the death of Edward VII in 1910 and the necessity to allow a 'decent' interval of time to elapse before pressurising George V to create, if necessary, the large number of new peers necessary to overcome the resistance of the Lords.

The immediate financial commitments of Lloyd George in 1909 was £6m required to pay for old age pensions and also an enlarged navy, but he already had in mind a limited health and unemployment insurance scheme which he was trying to sell to working people under the slogan of 9d. for 4d. viz. a contributory scheme under which workers paid 4d. a week, employers 3d. and the government 2d. The principle of national insurance divided working people in much the same way as other social reforms. Many working class leaders were officials of the powerful Friendly Societies or agents of the insurance companies, largely because such employment gave the flexibility of hours which enabled them to attend to voluntary labour movement activity during the day and the business of earning a living in the evening. Others were deeply suspicious of contributory schemes which smacked too much of Bismarck's schemes in Germany which ran parallel with the anti-Socialist laws which outlawed the Socialist Party. Others felt that schemes of state welfare entangled working class organisations in a web of commitments to the maintenance of capitalism rather than its replacement by Socialism. In addition, the principle of self-help which maintained that working people, like others, should maintain themselves without the intervention of the state, was still widespread.

In Birmingham, trades council officials in the 1890s such as A.R. Jephcott, C.C. Cooke and S.G. Middleton had been pillars of the two main sections of the Oddfellows and the Ancient Order of Foresters. This influence was less in the first decade of the twentieth century, but still strong enough to dictate that national insurance, when it came, should be both contributed through and paid out by friendly societies and insurance companies instead of through the post office, as old age pensions were paid.

The National Insurance Bill was put to parliament by Lloyd George in 1911. In July of that year the trades council discussed the bill. The vice-president G.B. Spray represented strong minority opposition which united two opposing principles; the first was opposition to the contributory principle by those who wanted a comprehensive, free service, and others who thought that adequate insurance was available through joining a trade union. The resolution eventually passed stated that, while adhering to the non-contributory principle, it approved the action of the Labour Party in parliament in its endeavours to eliminate the many features inimical to Labour interests and resolved that the whole case for Labour could, with confidence, be left in their hands. The trades council reinforced its opposition to the contributory principle by a statement of the subsistence theory of wages:

> Public health must be damaged by any deductions, whatever their object, from wages that do not afford the workers more than mere subsistence, and that in such cases, contributions under this measure, apart from the contribution of the state, should be taken solely from the employer . . .

The final result of the debate was very close, the Bill being approved by a margin of only two votes (31-29). The annual report added to this the hope that every trade society should become an Approved Society under the Act. The 1912 annual report had further information to add. A representative of the Commissioners appointed under the Insurance Act had addressed the trades council, and in May affiliated societies had been invited to a series of lectures on Part I of the Act, which concerned health insurance. Kesterton, the president of the trades council, and Julia Varley had accompanied the Lord Mayor and two other delegates to interview the Commissioners in London with regard to the appointment of a Provisional Committee in Birmingham. The secretary of state had also called together the representatives of societies affected by Part II of the Act, which dealt with unemployment insurance, to elect the Workmen's Panels of Referees for Birmingham, which resulted in trade unionists only being elected to these posts. The trades council also took a strong stand against the attempts of Chambers of Commerce (including Birmingham's) to promote Employers' Works Clubs as approved societies and it had issued posters in the city warning wage earners to avoid these and join approved societies connected with the trade union movement in which full and real power of control would be exercised by the members themselves. There was evidence, it was claimed, that these posters had resulted in many trade unionists making their trade union their approved society. The trades council had also passed a resolution condemning the doctors:

> This Council protests against the selfish and over-reaching demands of the medical profession under the National Insurance Act; declares their attitude merits strong public condemnation and repudiation, and calls for decisive Government action. This Council calls upon the Government to inaugurate without delay a National State Medical Service for all as the only satisfactory solution of the present difficulty, and the sole means of guaranteeing efficient treatment of illness and disease, without regard to the financial resources of the sufferer.

The annual report went on to say:

> In view of the selfish and extravagent demands of the doctors, it is to be hoped that the insignificant demands of the workers for a living wage will meet with less condemnation from the professional classes, and less talk about the leaders exploiting the movement for their own ends. The doctors would appear to have overthrown their leaders just in time to prevent the establishment of a State Medical Service.

The doctors had not only sabotaged a national health service, but they also wanted the panel system limited to those below a certain income and greater 'freedom of choice of doctor' both of which would have limited the amount of time doctors spent under 'contract' and increased the time available for private practice. They achieved some concessions on the contract. Sickness benefit under the scheme which came into operation in January 1913 was 10/-d. a week. Unemployment insurance under the Act was limited to about 2¼ million workers in those trades where the risk of unemployment was particularly high whose incomes were below £160 a year.

George Cadbury

Chapter Twenty One

POVERTY AND SLUMP
1900 – 1910

Some analysis

The measurement of poverty in Birmingham was never attempted on the systematic scale of London by Booth or York by Rowntree. These surveys established levels of poverty and deprivation affecting almost 40% of the population and both were conducted in years of 'good' trade. My own studies of the Black Country conclude that 40% of the population was unable, over its life-span, to provide at all times, for its basic needs of food, shelter, food and clothing. Such an average implies much greater poverty in periods of mass unemployment.

Nor have the causes of poverty been satisfactorily quantified. My categories would be: fluctuations of income (none with unemployment and greatly reduced during short-time working); low wages; sickness, disability and reduced capacity to earn; large families; old age. Bottom of my list would be 'improvidence'. For the middle classes, however, whether it was the relatively enlightened Joseph Chamberlain or the bigoted majority, the 'self-inflicted' poverty of 'improvidence' was at the top of their list providing them with a comforting illusion in their affluence and a warming glow for their niggardly charity.

The present study will not, therefore, start from the prejudices of the middle class, but from the belief that the statements of the poor themselves were of greater validity than the generalisations of the affluent. Other main assumptions made here are also set out:

1. That the national Index of Unemployment most widely used, namely the return of trade unions paying unemployment benefit, is not only wrong, but pernicious. Wrong because it considerably under-estimates unemployment and pernicious because it perpetuates a myth that levels of unemployment in the nineteenth century were much lower than they have been since World War I. This existing index should be doubled as a more realistic percentage figure of unemployment plus short-time working.

2. The main estimates made by working men in Birmingham regarding poverty were:
(a) Councillor J.V. Stevens' estimate that unemployment in Birmingham in 1906 was 10,000.
(b) Glassworkers and brassworkers generalisations, supported by the practices of their unions, that the average man's working life was finished at age 50.
(c) J.W. Davis' estimate that only one in thirteen working men lived to the age of 65.

3. That the normal terms of discourse were usually prejudicial to working class interests and should be abandoned in labour studies where possible. An outstanding example is 'Guardians of the Poor' who were in fact the Guardians of the Ratepayers and Oppressors of the Poor.

The problem of poverty in Birmingham was forced to the top of the agenda by the growing power of the labour movement and the reappearance of mass unemployment after 1902 and the challenge of the Right to Work. The middle-classes in Birmingham therefore produced studies to try to substantiate their basic propositions (a) that poverty was caused by improvidence and ignorance (b) that it was possible and necessary to distinguish between the 'deserving' and the 'undeserving' poor.

The studies can be followed from the statistical material attached to the Reports. of the Birmingham City Distress Committee and the City of Birmingham Aid Societies. Both of these societies were mis-named; their function was not to relieve distress, but to relieve as little as possible.

The City of Birmingham Aid Society annual reports are available from 1907. The first report shows that the Lord Mayor was president and the Bishop of Birmingham vice-president of the Society. It consisted of eight branches throughout the city which before 1906 had been separate societies, originating from the 1890 Charity Organisation Society.

The main categories of cases dealt with were: those out of work where this had not been due to 'moral defect' and the Distress Committee had not found them work; sickness of the bread winner; old age or other unavoidable incapacity; and 'cases of the inability of the breadwinner to meet the requirements of the household' (e.g. widowhood). The number of applicants during the year had been 2,413. Of these 1,545 had been given help and 858 had been refused aid. These decisions had been reached at 319 meetings with the aid of 808 voluntary helpers. The total of aid granted had been £1,234. This averaged less than £1 per person over 52 weeks. But the actual income of the Society had been £2,055, so that 40% of their income had been spent on the administrative expenses of salaries (£261), office rent, heating and cleaning (£105) and stationery, printing, advertising, postage etc. (£286).

In true Caucus fashion, all donations to the funds of the Society were listed. The *Birmingham Daily Mail* Christmas Fund had yielded the largest donation of £106. There had been two individual donations of £100, one from Barrow Cadbury and the other from Cregol Colmore of Cheltenham. There were several donations of £25-£30 including the chairman of the Society, Sir Hallewell Rogers, and such well-known names as Kenricks, Lloyd and Hollinsworth. Joseph Chamberlain, Neville, a Chance and a Nettlefold gave £10 each.

The next year's report, 1908, showed an increase of applicants to nearly 3,000 with about 1,800 assisted to the total amount of £1182. A 'striking increase' in the number of unemployed applicants was reported and all the indications were 'that the coming winter would be a period of exceptional distress'. The outlook was 'grave and serious' and fellow citizens were appealed to to enable the Society to expand its work. But what work was it actually doing? Well, one of its most important activities was its Thrift Section. The report recorded a more systematic re-visitation of aided cases. In fact the secretary of the Thrift Section had personally visited 1,682 cases previously helped 'to encourage them to save when they had the means.' In spite of bad trade, 149 of these families 'had become depositors and 31 ladies were calling regularly to collect pence and give hints on household management etc.'! Nor were these beneficient visitations confined to those who had been aided:

> We hope gradually to train at least some of our citizens in habits of thrift
> and not only lessen the need for charity, but to foster a greater spirit of
> self-respecting independence. The movement is growing and it is one of
> the most hopeful features of our constructive work.

Middle class patronising, ignorance and misdirected application of wholly
insufficient funds could hardly have been better expressed.

The 1909' Report summarised some of the results of the severe
unemployment of the winter of 1908 – 09. Applications as early as
October had totalled 819 as against 62 in the same month of the previous
year. During the winter months the rule relating to 'prospects of
employment' had been relaxed (thus revealing another large category of
unfortunates who had not been previously assisted — GB) and all
unemployed 'of good industrial and moral character' had been assisted.
But it was made clear that nothing else had been relaxed and 'no case had
been helped without rigorous examination.' The Thrift Section reported
an expansion of its work. £92 had been collected in savings and £46
withdrawn. These sums were paid into savings accounts administered by
City Aid, but when deposits reached £2, savers were recommended to
transfer the money to the post office savings bank, and City Aid would
not pay interest on sums higher than £2. The Mutual Registration of
Assistance had also been improved; every aid organisation in the city
filled in forms for every case helped. This 'eradicates overlapping and
imposture', it was claimed, thus revealing one of the main presumptions
and purposes of the Charity Aid Society.

Some of the results of the 'rigorous examination' and form filling of
City Aid can be seen from the Statistical Summary which provides hard
facts on 4,623 applicants:

Marital Status	4086 married men (88%), 140 widowers, 263 widows (6%) 115 single men (2%), 13 single women.
Ages of Men	Under 25 — 6%, 25-35 36%, 35-45 29%,45-55 17%, 55-65 9%, 65 and over 3%.

Number of Children

1	2	3	4	5	6	7	8	9	10 or More
17%	21%	19%	17%	11%	7%	4%	2%	1.5%	1%

Maximum Wages Stated to have
been received at last place of
employment.

Under 20/-d.	20-d. to 25/-d.	25/-d. to 30/-d.
17%	37%	24%

30/-d. and over.
22%

Rents per Week.

Under 4/-d.	4/-d. to 6/6d.	6/6d. and over.
15%	53%	27%

Period of Unemployment before
applying for Relief.

1-4 weeks	1-3 months	3-6 months	6-12 months
27%	32%	20%	14%

Over 12 months
7%

Analysis of these figures show that applicants were overwhelming married
men between the ages of 25 and 65 with an average of 3-4 children, whose
previous wage had been 25/-d. a week, paying rent of 5/-d. a week. The

average duration of unemployment before applying to the Society had been 4 months.

Why had these men become unemployed? 70% said it was from 'shortness of work' 8% said it was because of the 'failure of the firm,' and 16% said 'illness'. Of the remainder, 2% gave 'dispute' as the cause and 4% 'various'. It is from this 6% that one would have to look for those who had 'sacked themselves' or left employment without 'good cause.'

To what extent were these unemployed 'shiftless' people moving from job to job? Well, 4% had been in their last position for 20 years or more, 23% for more than 5 years, 20% over 2 years, 28% for six months, 22% for only one month and 3% were 'hawkers etc.'

With regard to stability of residence, over the previous two years about one third had had only one address, one third two addresses, and one third three or more.

Had the poverty of the applicants been induced by early and reckless marriages? The ages of men at marriage were as follows (women married at a slightly earlier age):

15	16	17	18	19	20	21
0.3%	0.4%	1.1%	2%	5.5%	7¼%	10½%

So only 2% married below the age of 18, but by 21 a quarter of the applicants were married. Marriage, however, tended to be late for both men and women. Another 28% married between the ages of 21 and 25 and a further 27% between 25 and 30. The remainder married after the age of 30 or remained single.

If the above facts had not convinced even the most bigoted investigator that those they were dealing with were over-whelmingly the category they patronised under the nomenclature of 'deserving poor', they should have been convinced by the 'characters' which City Aid obtained from the previous employer of all those they were considering for aid. These were:

Good	Fair	Moderate	Bad
89%	7%	3%	1%

The last useful exercise was an attempt to identify unemployment through five of the most important groups of employment in the city. These gave the Census figure of total employment provided and the applicants who were unemployed:

Occupation Group.	Conveyance of Men & Goods.	Metals, Machines and Implements	Precious Metals & Jewellery	Building & Works of Construction	Food & Drink.
% total adult employment	10½%	35%	5%	10%	7%
% applicants to City Aid.	8%	46½%	3¼%	20%	3¼%

The aggregation of these groups showed that they provided 67.5% of male employment in the city, but were responsible for 81% of the unemployment. One would expect that the 'metal bashing' trades providing 35% of employment in Birmingham would be responsible for nearly 50% of the unemployment, or that the building trades employing 10% of the city's male workforce should contribute 20% of the unemployment; but the fact that such groups of employment as Transport and Food and Drink which would be expected to provide much greater continuation of employment, show considerable numbers of unemployed, is important in assessing how widespread unemployment was in Birmingham.

From the activities of the voluntary middle-class organisation of City Aid, we can turn to the statutory middle class provision through the City council. The annual Reports of the Birmingham City Distress Committee run from 1905 – 06 to 1920 – 21. Once again, the emphasis is not on aid, but on investigation and finding reasons not to give aid. The Distress Committee was appointed in October 1905 and at the end of December 774 persons were registered with it as unemployed. A policy of visiting the houses of all applicants had been adopted as well as communicating with the previous employer; about 18% of employers ignored these communications. From 12 January to 14 April 1906, 1705 applications had been received, of whom 1364 had been registered. The average period of unemployment before registration had been 15 weeks.

Great difficulty had been found in providing work. 150-200 men per week had been taken on by the Public Works Committee for street cleaning, but the Estates Committee had been the only other to respond.

Street sweeping had taken place from 16 January to 26 April. Men had been offered three days work and, if satisfactory, further blocks of three days' work. 1046 men had been thus provided with work averaging 15/10¼d. at an hourly rate of 5d. Further analysis of these figures show:

Relief given over 14 Weeks.

Number of Men	344	755	180	61	24
Total Relief each	12/6d.	25/-d.	37/6d.	50/-d.	62/6d.
Relief per week	10½d.	1/9½d.	2/7½d.	3/6d.	4/6d.

Such amounts of relief were derisory, and where they constituted the only means of subsistence, can only be viewed as prolonging the period of death by starvation.

The income of the Distress Fund had totalled £1,867 of which over £1,200 had come from the national Queen's Unemployment Fund. Locally, £250 came from the Lord Mayor's Fund and £300 from rate aided Borough funds. Total expenditure was £1,485 of which just over £1,100 went on relief and the rest on administrative expenses.

Such a scandalous ratio of expenses to aid at least had the advantage of providing the future historian with further information for estimating standards of living and levels of poverty.

The first figures concern the contribution of children's earnings to family budgets. Of 1705 applicants, 262 had one or more children working. Most earned between 1/-d. and 15/-d. with an average of 9/-d. Averaging this over the total number of applicants, the average amount added to all families by children working was 1/4d. a week.

Similar calculations can be made of the earnings of wives. In 371 cases the wife was earning. In nearly 60% of these cases earnings were between 1/-d. and 5/-d; about 36% earned between 5/-d. and 10/-d. and only 5%

earned over 10/6d. the highest being 18/6d. This gives an average of where the wife was earning of an additional 5/-d. a week to the family budget, but contribution averaged over all applicants' families' incomes of only just over 1/-d. a week since only about one fifth of applicants' wives worked.

The period of each year during which the Distress Committee functioned is something else to be noted. For 1905 – 06 it was effectively fourteen weeks from October. In 1906 – 07 no applications were taken until November, but the 'season' was extended to the beginning of May. The number of applicants at 707 was less than half those for the previous year. The reasons given were an improvement of trade and stricter examination of applicants. Of the 707 applicants, 330 were selected for work but 51 failed to appear. The Committee had tried to distinguish between skilled and unskilled labour; in the building trades there were 49 skilled men to 90 unskilled; in brass there were 91 and in metals 148 skilled men. Other statistics showed that fourteen were in benefit with trade societies, ex-servicemen numbered 76 or 11% of applicants and the average period of unemployment before application to the Committee was fourteen weeks.

In 1906 – 07, as always, there was the greatest difficulty in finding work for the unemployed. Baths and Parks were the best providers for which work the city Council allocated £640 from the rates. The drainage Board wanted to use unemployed men 'in view of the satisfactory results the previous year', but the work was done cheaper by steam ploughing and the Local Government Board refused to give a grant for the manual work. There was a sequel to this the next year.

The Committee had changed its work policy and given continuous employment for the maximum 16 weeks permitted under the Act, rather than in three day blocks, which, it was admitted, gave little relief. The week consisted of 4½ days work at 4/-d. a day; in the remaining day and a half the men were requested to search for work. The average amount earned had been £6-5-10d. by the 299 men who eventually worked or 7/10½d. per week.

The Committee had also concerned itself with emigration to Canada. There had been 65 applicants, 31 had been accepted and 154 persons (30 men, 27 wives and 97 children) eventually left at a cost to the Committee of £1,112. This included the cost of rail and sea fare from Birmingham to Canada, provision of outfits (or portions thereof), insurance, contingencies and £1 for each adult and 10/-d. for each child required by the Canadian authorities on landing. In case hawk-eyed Guardians of the Rich gained the impression that the Committee was going soft and actually giving something away to the poor, reassurance was given that these were only loans and agreements to repay had been entered into by all applicants. Ten of those emigrating had been ex-service, for whom preference had been shown.

Removals had also been another concern of the Committee and 9 people had been assisted to move to other towns at a total cost of £2-8-8d.

A Labour Exchange had also been established in July in Great Charles Street, 2,909 had registered at this bureau, 374 remained on the register at the end of May and work had been found for 107 men.

The accounts for 1906 – 07 showed income at £1,790. Of this the rates had contributed £700, the Local Government Board £800, the Lord Mayor's Fund £250 and the Baths and Parks Committee £380. Expenditure had been £1,574 on providing work, £228 on establishing the Labour Exchange and £300 on administration, giving a better ratio of aid to administration.

The 1907 – 08 'season' lasted from 1 Nov. to 31 March. 1,195 persons applied of whom 1069 had not previously been on the register.

Baths and Parks had again been the main source of work, providing 169 men with an average of 13.4 days work at 3/4d. a day. The Health Committee also provided work at the Emergency Hospital, Yardley, for 85 men.

Men had also been re-employed by the Drainage Board doing work at Water Orton. The engineer's report gives important evidence of the effects of poverty and unemployment:

> When the men started work on 2nd December they were not in the best condition to perform work and it was costing 2/-d. a cubic yard. This cost gradually fell to 1/3d. as the men became fitter and used to navvying.
>
> None of the 97 had to be discharged and they were a most respectable squad.
>
> The work performed by the unemployed was the most satisfactory ever done on the Drainage Board's Works.

There is also an indication of how cold public charity really is. The report states that an appeal for funds had produced £938, but despite wide advertising, 4,000 circulars and the amount of distress in the city, only 230 private persons had subscribed. So much for the famed middle-class conscience which, we are so often assured, was a prime mover in the change from a brutalised to a more humane society.

1908 – 09 was the worst year for unemployment in Birmingham. Applicants soared to 6,645 of whom 3,428 were recorded. But 1,220 single men applied and were not registered. The Local Government Board ruling that only two winters' work could be provided was relaxed, so that one hundred men were receiving work for the third successive winter, 480 had been found work the previous winter and 2,984 received their first winters' work.

On the semi-starved state of applicants the Report said:

> The condition of applicants was even worse then last winter and poverty more widespread, but children had been improved by school breakfasts.

Baths and Parks were again the main provider of work. But the total inadequacy of this sort of work provision is revealed in the accounts. These showed that income had risen to approximately £4,000 provided, roughly, by £1,000 from the rates, £2,000 from the Local Government Board and £1,000 by public charity. Only £1,500, however, was spent on the provision of work and £2,500 was not spent.

By the next year, 1909 – 10, the worst of the unemployment was over. Registration did not start until 13th. December and closed at the end of January with 1,573 registered.

The Labour Bureau closed when the Board of Trade official Labour

Exchange was opened on 1st. February 1910. The previous year nearly 12,000 had registered at the Distress Committee's bureau, 11,000 of whom had been removed at the end of the year either through having found a job or having their application cancelled or refused, leaving nearly 1,000 on the books at 31st May 1909.

From a total budget of £5,250 the rate contribution of £2,000 was spent entirely on the inquisitorial function of collecting information. The 'voluntary contribution account' of £3,200 included the £2,500 unspent the previous year, £350 from the Local Government Board and only £21 from public subscriptions. £2,600 was spent on providing work, leaving an under spent balance of nearly £600. Nearly £2,000 of this work expenditure was paid to the Baths and Parks Committee, who thereby reaped a well-deserved reward for the support they had provided in previous years. The £2,000 contributed from the rates was, therefore, more than offset by a total of £2,237 being returned to their committees.

This was effectively the end of the work of the Distress Committee, although it remained in existence. No public work was provided in the years 1910 to 1914 nor, of course, during the War. The last report was in 1919 – 20 when mass unemployment had again returned.

Conclusions scarcely need to be drawn from the above material; the facts have spoken for themselves. For the 'deserving' poor of Birmingham there were depths of poverty, destitution and semi-starvation, only the surface of which have been touched on here. As for the 'undeserving' poor, their fate remains unknown until the records of Birmingham's poor law, hospitals and asylums, drink trade etc. are systematically researched.

What has been revealed is the ignorance, callousness and indifference of the large majority of the middle class and the institutionalised barbarity of measures allegedly concerned with the welfare of the poor. The so-called provision of work for the unemployed was at the best totally inadequate and at worst, sheer pretence.

Present day academic apologists usually come from the same middle-class tradition and, if forced to concede that such unspeakable levels of poverty existed in Birmingham, their first line of defence is that it applied only to a small minority of working people. So it is in that field that enquiry must be made.

The actual numbers of unemployed in Birmingham can only be assessed by taking an intelligent and informed estimate and testing it against such other evidence as may be available. The figure I want to take is the 10,000 in 1906 estimated by Councillor J.V. Stevens (see Corbett p.83). This is about 6% of the males ten years of age and over employed in Birmingham, (see Table 35, 1901 Census). The only national Index of Unemployment is that compiled from returns of trade unions paying out of work benefit to members (see British Historical Statistics pp 64-65). This gives a national unemployed figure of 3.6% in 1906. This Index, for many reasons, is deficient, and I have argued elsewhere that the percentages given should be doubled, although the index can be taken as a more reasonable index of *relative changes* in unemployment (see my Standard of Living in England pp 39-42). If the national percentage of unemployment figure was doubled for 1906 it would show 7%. This would compare with the 6% estimates for Birmingham. This suggests either that Birmingham unemployment was a little below the national average, or that J.V. Stevens figure is not exaggerated.

If the trade union percentages are indexed and the numbers of unemployed in Birmingham calculated from the index we get the following:

	1900	1906	1907	1908	1909	1910	1911
National TU Index of Unemployment	100	144	148	312	308	188	120
Numbers Unemployed in Birmingham	6950	10000	10275	21650	21400	13050	8325
Percentage Unemployed in Birmingham	4%	6%	6%	13%	13%	8%	5%

It is unwise to push the figures further, because 1912 was the year of the extension of Birmingham and the bases for the figures change. If it is questioned whether unemployment more than doubled in Birmingham during the years 1908 and 1909, the figures of applicants to both the Distress Committee and City Aid suggest they did. One further piece of information can be introduced here, since it affects the numbers of unemployed who received some aid. These are the figures of Poor Law Relief. These were given weekly in the Labour Gazette from 1907. They showed both the numbers in the Workhouse and the Outdoor Relief. The numbers in the Workhouse varied very little, since the Workhouse was always full; when unemployment was high rules for 'offering the House' had to be relaxed and some people given Out Relief; when unemployment was low rules were more strictly adhered to, so the Workhouse remained full. The numbers receiving Out Relief I have calculated roughly by taking a representative week in winter (the second week in January) and an average summer week (second week in July) and averaging them. The results are:

	1907	1908	1909	1910	1911
Numbers Receiving Weekly Outdoor Relief in Birmingham District (av)	3522	3525	5485	4836	4822

The figures show a large jump in 1909. My main conclusions would be:

1. That Birmingham unemployment followed much the same pattern as national trends in the period 1900–1910. This unemployment was both severe and prolonged.
2. That under conditions of flourishing trade the Birmingham Reserve Army of Labour (i.e. 'normal' unemployment) was between 4% and 5% (7,000 to 8,000 men).
3. That this unemployment rose to a peak of 13% in 1908 and 1909 (about 21,500 men).
4. That female and juvenile unemployment virtually 'disappeared' in times of mass unemployment, because there was nowhere it could register and certainly no agency that would grant relief, except to women without husbands who had dependent children.
5. That the mass of unemployed received no relief whatsoever and were thus dependent on their savings (if any) or their families for survival. A small number received benefit from a trade union or friendly society for a limited period. Some of the 3,500 or so who received Out Relief from the Poor Law may have been the

unemployed, but, if so, they shared the beggarly amounts of 2/-d. to 3/-d. a week which was usually doled out to the sick, disabled and aged poor. After about three months unemployment without relief, an unemployed working man with children might apply to register with the Distress Committee for relief work. He had a 50%-70% chance of being registered, a lesser chance of actually being offered work and if he was granted work he received an average 'wage' little above the Poor Law standard. Failing this, the family man could apply to City Aid where he would be processed, inquisitioned, and patronised with the hope of equally miserly financial relief.

Finally, the depression of 1902 – 10 should be put into the context of general trade cycle history. Was this Depression a continuation of the Great Depression of 1875 – 95? If so it would extend the Great Depression from 1875 to 1910 with three serious troughs of 1878 – 90, 1884 – 86 and 1907 – 09. Or can it be regarded as a separate cycle extending from the 'full' employment of 1895 – 1900 continued for a couple of years by the Boer War, followed by large-scale unemployment 1903 – 10 and ending with 'full' employment again from 1910 to 1914?

Whatever its context, the following years 1910 – 14 were some of the stormiest since the 1840s as the semi-skilled and unskilled organised themselves and gained large increases in wages. This, together with the revolt of the women and trouble in Ireland brought Britain to the verge of revolution and a belief that the country was becoming ungovernable. This was ended with the outbreak of World War I and it is to this Big Bang that we will eventually turn.

Mary MacArthur

Chapter Twenty Two

THE BRITISH SOCIALIST PARTY

The British Socialist Party was formed in 1911 as a fusion of the Social Democratic Party with the left-wing of the ILP and various other Socialist groups. Initial high hopes for the party were not realised as the clash with Syndicalists, and later pro-war factions, split the party. It remained in existence, however, to be merged in the Communist Party after World War I.

A seminal influence on the rise and decline of the BSP in Birmingham was Leonard Hall. Hall was born at Windermere in 1866 one of a family of six children. His father was a compositor, who became editor and poet and later embarked on a medical career becoming a homeopathic doctor. But non-recognition in Britain of his Tubingen and Cincinnati degrees led to a precarious existence and Leonard Hall left school at thirteen. Three years later he became a seaman and emigrated to the United States. Here he encountered the working class movement and became connected with the Knights of Labour. At the age of twenty he returned to England, took part in the London dock strike of 1889, settled as a journalist in Manchester and became secretary of the Socialist League there. Leonard Hall was one of the founders of the Independent Labour Party in Manchester. About 1890 he became editor of the Eccles Advertiser and one of his most notable achievements was the organisation of the navvies working on the Manchester Ship Canal. Hall became Lancashire district secretary of the Navvies, Bricklayers and General Labourers Union and active on the Manchester and Salford Trades Council. He also became president of the influential Lancashire and Cheshire Federation of ILP branches from 1893 and was the district representative on the National Administrative Council from 1894 to 1896. Adopted as parliamentary candidate for Manchester NE for the 1895 election, Hall was slandered regarding union funds. He was cleared by an ILP NAC enquiry, but shortage of funds and, no doubt, the humiliating strain of such an enquiry, led to his withdrawal from the election.

In 1893 Hall was involved, together with Mrs. Emmeline Pankhurst in the celebrated Boggart Hole Clough free speech agitation when Manchester City Council refused to allow meetings in this public park. Hall was sent to Strangeways Jail for one month, suffering severely from the barbarous conditions there while his family suffered equally severely from financial difficulties.

Hall's activities in the intervening period before he came to Birmingham are more difficult to trace. A long illness after his release from prison and difficulty in maintaining himself and his family by journalism led to a withdrawal from politics and consideration of emigration, but his most prolific period as a writer was between 1899 and 1901 when he published *Man and Microcosm, Land Labour and Liberty* and *The Evolution of Consciousness*.

Hall left Eccles for Stoke-on-Trent in 1902 and a gap in his life

continues until 1907. During this period it is said that he was head
traveller for an oil firm and travelled extensively abroad.

He re-emerged as a political figure in 1907, the year of the election of
Victor Grayson, when he came to live at 42, Kingscote Road, Kings
Heath.

In the meantime, however, his family was politically active. His wife,
Pattie, was one of the group of women, who, together with Emmeline
Pankhurst formed the Women's Social and Political Union in 1903.
Hall's elder daughter, Nellie, became a full-time WSPU organiser and
suffered imprisonment and forced feeding. Pattie was carrying their
second daughter during Leonard's imprisonment in 1893; she was named
Emmeline after Mrs. Pankhurst, and she also became a Suffragist.

Leonard Hall immediately established himself with the Birmingham
ILP and in 1909 he was again elected to the NAC. From 1908 to 1913
Hall was also an executive committee member of the Birmingham
Socialist Centre. In 1910 Hall produced two pamphlets. The first, *The
Next Thing to Do* was published as Midland Socialist Pamphlet No 1. *The
Next Step*, according to Hall was Land Nationalisation. Labour and Land
were father and mother of all wealth creation. Land monpoly was the
stem from which all other monopolies flowed.

Hall confessed that he had entertained some hopes of the Small
Holdings Act of 1907, but only 2,400 of the 30,000 applicants had been
granted land. Moreover there would have been ten times the number of
applicants if those knowing that the authorities would put every
conceivable obstacle in the way, and those who objected to paying from
twice to five times the legitimate value of the land, and the multitude of
labourers in the villages who knew that they would be sacked from their
jobs and evicted from their cottages if they had the impudence to incur
the displeasure of the local squirearchy, had applied for land.

With regard to means of acquiring the land there were a dozen
practical ways, according to Hall. There was the budget method of
collecting both tax revenue and death duties from landowners in kind.
There was the time limit method of announcing that after twenty years
all land would revert to the state. There was also the Single Tax proposal.
Hall's objection to the latter was that if land was taxed at 20/-d. in the
£ it was bald confiscation, but if tax began at, say 1/-d. in the £, the battle
for nationalisation would have to be fought all over again every time it
was proposed to raise the tax. Hall's solution was therefore state purchase
as in New Zealand and Ireland by Land Courts fixing the value of the
land and Government Land Bonds paying, say, 3% per annum which
would be called in and settled within 20 years by means of a Sinking
Fund. Hall's justification for his emphasis on Land Nationalisation was
that it was the "main plank":

> The more I see of it the more I am convinced that without Land
> Nationalisation, no other reforms can have any but a tinkering,
> superficial, artifical, disappointing and proportionately reactionary
> effect.

Hall's other pamphlet was published in London, probably by the Fabian
Society. It was entitled *Socialism, Tariffism and Free (?) Trade* and was in

reply to R.B. Suthers in a *Clarion* article who espoused Protection as part
of the socialist answer to poverty. Hall's first line of attack was that "free
trade" did not and never had existed:

> . . . our entire conditions of production, transportation and exchange are
> everything except free and all our trade is under the stranglehold of the
> landowner and financier from the first step in extraction to the last step
> in consumption.

Mere 'freedom of imports no more constitutes free trade than chimney
pots constitute houses'. It is tempting to follow Hall through this hard-
hitting and often witty pamphlet, but Hall provides his own summary
which we will quote.

1. Tariff Reform is a red herring that protects only the buyers of
   labour and not the sellers.
2. That countries 'protected to the eye balls' suffer as severe or worse
   unemployment and poverty as those with 'free trade.'
3. The true cause of poverty is the legalised plundering of the poor
   by the rich and the only remedy is public control over public
   necessities.

While both of these pamphlets deal with fundamental policy questions
relevant to both Birmingham and Manchester, neither gives more than
a hint of the policy and organisational questions in which Hall was to play
such an important part in forming, and subsequently splitting the British
Socialist Party. These were Industrial Unionism, and political action.

Dissatisfaction with the performance of the Labour Party in Parliament
brought Grayson, Blatchford and his Clarion organisations, the SDP and
the left-wing of the ILP together in a project to form a united Socialist
Party.

In the summer of 1910 four members of the ILP NAC broke ranks and
published a pamphlet *Let us Reform the Labour Party* more popularly known,
from the colour of the cover, as the Green Manifesto. The authors were
C.T. Douthwaite, J.M. McLachlan, the Rev. J.H. Belcher and Leonard
Hall. Hall's contribution was a hard hitting introduction in which he
accused the leaders of the Labour Party (who were also the leaders of the
ILP) of 'a fatal obsession that the retention of their own seats is in itself
the first importance in the life and destiny of the Labour world.'

At the Easter Conference of the ILP the Green Manifesto was
discussed. George Lansbury said that the complaint of the majority of the
NAC was not that the pamphlet had been published, but that it had been
issued to the branches before being discussed by the NAC despite the fact
that it contained serious charges against that majority. Also, the matters
discussed in the Green Manifesto had all been discussed and accepted at
the last ILP Conference. MacLachlan, for the minority, denied that the
unanimous vote of confidence at the Labour Party Conference in 1910
meant that all who voted for it were satisfied with the parliamentary
policy. Leonard Hall finally moved the reference back of that part of the
report dealing with the Manifesto, saying that talk of the way the
pamphlet was produced was only rhetoric. The charge was the serious
one, Hall went on, of criticism of the carrying out of Labour policy, and
the majority of the ILP NAC did not like it. They had funked a

referendum of the membership on the issue. *The Labour Leader* and *Socialist Review* had been disgracefully biased and Hall regarded the editor of the latter journal as the leader of the defence; he had done more that Winston Churchill, Lloyd George and Asquith to wet blanket the militant Socialist movement. At this point Hall was called to order for not speaking to the subject which was the way the pamphlet had been produced. Hall objected to this and wanted to read extracts from a document that he had specially prepared for the Conference, but the chairman ruled him out of order. Douthwaite then got up and said that he had fought for the question of policy to be brought before the Conference for four years and had accepted nomination to the NAC when he found criticism impossible.

Dr. M.Eden Paul then formally moved the 'reference back' and W.C. Anderson stepped down from the chair to reply on behalf of the NAC. He contended that the NAC was not concerned with Labour Party policy, so why had the four signed the manifesto as members of the NAC? Charges had been made that a caucus had been formed to control what appeared in the *Labour Leader*, but no justification of this had been submitted. Hall and MacLachlan then immediately demanded the right to reply to this new point. A card vote was taken, however, and the reference back was lost by 39 votes to 283.

The question of the policy of the Labour Party, and thus the matter of the Green Manfesto was, however, discussed later at the Conference. A motion on this question in the name of the Bradford branch was called. But when the chairman announced that he proposed to close the debate at 5 p.m. or 5-30 thus allowing only one hour for discussion the Bradford delegate said he wished to formally withdraw the motion as he was not going to be bludgeoned in this way. Since the Harborne branch appeared next on the agenda in support of the motion, Leonard Hall found himself with the 'unexpected honour' as he termed it of moving the motion. Hall then moved:

> That in order to establish the authority of the elected representatives of the people in Parliament, as against the overpowering political influence now exercised by Ministers, who treat nearly every important decision of the House of Commons as a vote of confidence, on the refusal of which a Dissolution may follow as a penalty, the Labour Group in the House of Commons be requested to ignore all such possible consequences and declare their intention to force their own issues and to vote steadfastly on the merits of the questions brought before them.

Hall said, that in his opinion, the Labour Party in the past three years had been pursuing the same kind of policy as the old Labour Electoral Association which the ILP in 1892 had been formed to kill. He felt proud to say in passing that he was one of the half-dozen who founded the ILP. It was against the policy of the present leaders of the Labour Party that this resolution was aimed. The resolution was said to be nebulous, but it was only nebulous to those who had nebulous political brains. An amendment was then moved summing up the dilemma that faced the Labour MPs and the whole gamut of well known arguments was then heard from both the mighty and the lowly. Ramsay Macdonald made a typical mystifying speech: He was not going to say that he was in favour of putting on govt. whips on every occasion; he was not going to say that the people should not have control over the administration and the executive; he was not going to say that the people should not determine the programme of the Government ... but holding such beliefs he did say that the resolution was meaningless. Were they to turn out a Liberal government to put in a Tariff Reform one and call that raising their own issues?

The argument did spill over to the next day. George Lansbury admitted that during his short period in the House it was becoming increasingly difficult to differentiate his actions from those of the Radicals. They were constantly taking into account 'all the merits of a question' as demanded by the resolution, but when Keir Hardie raised the question of the treatment of the Welsh miners by the police and soldiers only 17 Labour members had voted for it, the others feeling that they must not endanger the government.

MacLachlan attacked Macdonald. First he had said that to vote on the merits of a question was a meaningless phrase and then he had said that the Labour Party was what it must be and not necessarily what he would like it to be. MacLachlan thought it perfectly possible to vote on the merits of a question.

Keir Hardie said that he was delighted that the ILP Conference was finding its real function in discussing the policy of the Labour Party. He took the two speeches of Macdonald and Lansbury as representing two types of mind. From Macdonald they had had an intellectual treat and he was the greatest intellectual asset in the movement. In Lansbury they had a big, capable man who, fortunately, allowed his heart to rule his head. They could not make Macdonald into Lansbury nor Lansbury into Macdonald. The Party must be big enough to offer room for both types. Hardie concluded by making an earnest appeal not to press the discussion to a definite conclusion. When he sat down 'the previous question' was at once moved and carried 'by a large majority.' Thus stood the matter of general attitudes to the Labour Party in parliament as Victor Grayson, Leonard Hall and others pressed on with the project for a United Socialist Party.

At the SDP Conference in April 1911 a resolution had been passed calling for the establishment of a United British Socialist Party. In early August the Party executive, in conjunction with other Socialist bodies issued a circular to all other Socialist organisations asking whether they would participate in a Unity Conference. The local groups associated with this appeal were the Birmingham Socialist Representation Committee, Birmingham Clarion Scouts and, possibly, the Birmingham branch of the Church Socialist League.

By this time, Victor Grayson, who had lost his parliamentary seat in 1910, was ensconced in the *Clarion* offices editing the paper and using all the resources of the Clarion organisation to mobilise support for the new Party. Grayson had resigned from the ILP in August and Leonard Hall followed suit.

For the subsequent activity of Leonard Hall and the birth of the BSP in Birmingham we must leave John Smethurst's biography of Hall and consult the BSP papers in the library of the London School of Economics. The first sign of the new Party in Birmingham is a letter from Victor

Grayson to H.B. Williams, the secretary of the SDP, on the 15th. August. This is on notepaper with the typed heading 'BSP' at 44a, Worship St., London (a Clarion address). It thanked Williams for his proffered assistance in the formation of the BSP and suggesting that, pending further correspondence between them, Williams should distribute a four-paged leaflet, and collect as many signed declaration forms as possible.

On the 26th. August Leonard Hall sent a letter to Williams suggesting that Williams call a meeting for Monday 11th September to consider the organisation of Socialists and asking him particularly to get in touch with Smethwick Socialist Society as 'there were a lot of 'em and they seem keen.' A further letter from Hall to Williams of 2 September stated that the Smethwick Socialists had not heard from him. It also made the important point that he noted that Williams had invited the SDP. "This will (one word illegible — GB) if you don't keep it clear that the meeting is to organise a new Party — not, at present, to consider the unification of existing Socialist parties."

From a subsequent newspaper cutting (probably from Clarion) it seems that this arranged meeting did take place on 11th September at the People's Hall, Hurst Street and it was here that the British Socialist Party (Birmingham Section) was formed.

Hall's next step was to get a Birmingham Manifesto in print. This embodied Hall's ideas with regard to the organisation and activities of the new Party and was to be of national importance. An acknowledgement from the printers, Utopia Press, to Hall for 1,000 copies of the Manifesto at £1-17-6d. or 500 copies at £1.1.6d. dated September 21st suggests that the Manifesto was not printed at that time, and an important letter from J(?).A. Jackson of 22nd. September regrets 'that the Manifesto is not available to put through the door as it gives Kneeshaw (who took Hall's place as the leader of Birmingham ILP) the chance to say that the new party only talks at times of elections.' Whatever the date of printing of the Manifesto, it was certainly in print before the inaugural conference of the new national party at the end of September 1911 and when it appeared it bore the date of 16th September and was issued in the name of the Committee of the Birmingham Section of the British Socialist Party. The salient points were as follows:

Addressed to Fellow Citizens it states that the unexampled labour revolts of 1911 prove the growing sense of 'one-ness' of all workers and demands from all earnest Socialists greater concentration than ever before on agitating and organising 'on those straight, unequivocal, revolutionary lines off which the Labour movement has been so cunningly side-tracked during the past four years by the political fakirs and the 'rest-and-be-thankful job limpets'. The object of the B.S.P. was therefore the 'Socialisation of the means of livelihood, administered by a free democracy. Land and capital must be collectively owned and used BY THE WORKERS FOR THE WORKERS.'

The methods to be employed in the impending transition to Socialism would be:

1. General and combined Strikes developing towards the final Lock-out by the nation of its exploiters.

2.   The placing, whenever opportunity offers, of militant Socialists in
        Parliament and other public bodies . . . to eventually take charge
        of the national and local administrations and co-ordinate them
        with the industrial revolution which it is our first and vital business
        to develop OUTSIDE them.

This was to be the blue print for the new Party as projected from
Birmingham.

The Correspondence reveals further details of the developments in
Birmingham. Leonard Hall's relations with H.B. Williams go back to
December 1910 when he asks Williams if he could let him have some of
Williams' material on early Socialists and Socialism in Birmingham
which Hall could use for a brief introduction to the delegates to the ILP
Conference being held in Birmingham the following year. The only
known work of Williams' is newspaper cuttings catalogued under
"Syndicalism" in the Birmingham Reference Library but it is in fact on
Owenite Socialism in the city.

The meeting that had set up the BSP in Birmingham had clearly been
organised by some form of Committee and confirmation of this comes
from the letter of Jackson of September 1911 already quoted addressed
'Dear Comrade' (presumably either Hall or Williams — GB) suggesting
that the three Birmingham delegates to the founding conference of the
new party should be Hall, Smith (of the Smethwick Socialist Society) and
Whittingham 'as the three that had been at all the Committees'.

The Socialist Unity Conference took place at the Caxton Hall, Chapel
Street. Salford on Saturday 30th September and Sunday 1st October
1911. 220 delegates attended and it was roughly calculated that they
represented 35,000 members. 85 of the delegates came from SDP
branches, 50 from Socialist Societies and Socialist Representation
Committees, 41 from ILP branches, 32 from Clarion Clubs and
Fellowships and 12 from already formed branches of the BSP. There were
four delegates from Birmingham: Leonard Hall, J. Smith and Eli
Stephens represented the Birmingham BSP and Richard Clements
attended from the Birmingham Socialist Representation Committee. In
addition E. Wenlock attended from Smethwick ILP.

Leonard Hall made his presence felt immediately by proposing H.M.
Hyndman as chairman of the Conference and this was agreed
unanimously. The Conference then discussed the following motion
standing in the name of the EC of the SDP:

This Conference of Socialist organisations, believing that the difference
of opinion and the adoption of dissimilar tactics which have hitherto
characterised the various sections of the British Socialist movement, have
arisen from circumstances peculiar to its initial stages, is convinced that
the time is now ripe for the formation of a United Socialist Party, and
the delegates pledge their organisations to co-operate in the unification
of their forces on the following basis of common agreement:

The Socialist Party is the political expression of the working-class
movement, acting in the closest co-operation with industrial organisation
for the socialisation of the means of production and distribution — that
is to say, the transformation of capitalist society into a collectivist or
communist society. Alike in its objects, its ideals, and in the means
employed, the Socialist Party though striving for the realisation of
immediate social reforms demanded by the working class, is not a

reformist but a revolutionary party, which recognises that social freedom
and equality can only be won by fighting the class war through to the
finish, and thus abolishing for ever all class distinctions.

The delegates to this Conference therefore appoint a Committee of
- - - - - - to draw up a constitution in accord with this common basis,
a draft of which shall be submitted to the bodies here represented, who
pledge themselves on ratification of that constitution to cease their
existence as separate organisations and to amalgamate in a united
Socialist Party.

Discussion and amendments centred around the second paragraph of the
resolution.

Tom Groom, in the name of the EC of the National Clarion Cycling
Club moved:

This Conference is of the opinion that societies and individuals pledging
themselves to the Socialist principle of the ownership and control of the
means of life, and the establishment of an independent political party to
further this object shall be entitled to membership.

This was the first major principle of the resolution and was opposed by
Leonard Hall. He testified to the good work done for Socialism by the
movers of the amendment but it 'left open the door to every jelly-fish in
Great Britain' and it leaned too much on the political side without even
mentioning industrial activities. This amendment was lost 'by a large
majority.'

The next crucial amendment moved to delete the words 'though
striving for the realisation of the immediate social reforms demanded by
the working class.' J. Hunter Watts of the SDP represented the
opposition to this amendment. He said it was time they nailed the lie that
only those who advocated wresting nothing from the foe until they could
demand all, were revolutionarists. It was possible to distinguish between
reforms that were palliatives and those which advanced the cause of
Socialism, Watts maintained.

Opponents of this amendment claimed that they did not want to enter
into competition with Lloyd George on the question of reforms; that they
opposed advocating social reforms that the capitalist class would have to
concede anyway; that they knew the deterioration that went on within an
organisation when they advocated social reforms and forgot their
revolutionary ideals. The deep split among the delegates was made clear
when the amendment was declared carried by 85 votes to 77.

At the evening session of the first day Leonard Hall moved the next
crucial amendment on behalf of the Birmingham BSP. This was to delete
the words after 'a revolutionary party which', and insert 'working by
revolutionary industrial tactics supplemented by political action for the
abolition of class distinctions and the establishment of freedom and
equality.'

Hall argued that the resolution did not take account of the industrial
upheavals of 1911 and gave the impression of a lop-sided reliance on
parliamentary methods; that the most valuable work they could do during
the next few years was to popularise the idea of sympathetic and general
strikes. He did not think that the general strike could be made the 'whole
suit of trumps', but if they frittered away their enthusiasm and money on

parliamentary action, the response from a large number of their members would be unwilling and unconvinced. Except perhaps in four constituencies they could not expect to win seats or even to poll respectably unless they were prepared to trim and hedge their policies as did candidates of other parties. Far better to remain in the wilderness for another five or ten years than to compromise their revolutionary principles and become a second edition of the so-called Labour Party.

Opponents of the amendment argued that trade unions were not socialist organisations and would not strike for political objectives. Dan Irving reminded delegates that the International had recently discussed these problems and made a clear distinction between the Socialist objectives of political parties and the industrial activity of Socialists within trade unions.

When Hall's amendment was put to the vote it was lost by 62 votes to 92 and the original resolution, with the single successful amendment, was then passed unanimously.

On the second day of the Conference the issue of political versus industrial action was again raised under the question of the policy of the united party. Again Hall intervened, claiming that it was not fair to hurl the epithet 'anarchism' at a proposal for closer Labour unionism. If they could 'biff' the devil in the eye with their political left, there was no reason why they should not prod him in the stomach with their industrial right. Again, Dan Irving was the main opponent. Their job at the Conference was to constitute a political party to work primarily in the political field; they were not a trade union party. The previous question was then moved and, again, carried by 'a large majority'.

Despite Hall's defeats in the debates, when it came to the election of a Provisional Committee for the new Party, Hall's standing both as a previous ILP NAC member and as pioneer of this new Party was recognised by his receiving the largest number of votes — 171. The others elected were E.C. Fairchild 161, Victor Grayson 161, H. Russell Smart 156, Dan Irving 143, F.C. Hagger 142, Tom Groom 130, T. Kennedy 115, J. Hunter Watts 102 and George Simpson 95.

The BSP in Birmingham got off to an enthusiastic start. An initial Fellowship Concert was held on December 9th. at the Colonnade Hotel, New Street, with Victor Grayson booked to appear. There was a second Fellowship Concert and reception to H.M. Hyndman on Monday 12th. February at the same hotel. A draft programme of this concert has survived. It lists twelve musical and comedy items ranging from piano, violin and mandolin pieces, through mezzo-soprano, baritone and bass solos to a local comedian and a ventriloquist act:

> The evening will conclude with the singing of the Internationale sung with that spirit and fervour which is a sign that the singers are fully resolved to break the fetters that bind them.

— NE PLUS ULTRA —

The programme continues in the best *CLARION* style:

> A silver collection will be taken to help defray the expenses of this concert.

We earnèstly request comrades not to put buttons, old trademen's tokens discs etc. on the plate. We have a large stock left over from the last concert.

As a portion of the collection is devoted to the waiters, it is not necessary that they should be tipped as they will be Tiptaft(ed) later.

The programme contained advertisements for cycles, trade union labour built boats, for Hallas' coal and the following:

The Pill with a Reputation
Try Hall's Pills. Invaluable for Tariff Reform and the Insurance trouble.
GOES STRAIGHT TO THE SEAT OF THE DISEASE AND STICKS THERE.

Besides these concerts an initial Town Hall meeting had been arranged. This had to be cancelled 'owing to the intervention of the authorities,' but another was arranged for 13th. February 1912. Hyndman was the main speaker on the 'Revolt of Labour'. Councillor Eldred Hallas was the local speaker with Leonard Hall in the chair. The West Bromwich Socialist Choir were to 'render selections'. The comrades seemed confident enough of a good turn-out both to hold the meeting on a Tuesday evening and also to charge admission fees of 3d and 6d with reserved seats 1/-d.

The 1st Annual Conference of the BSP was held at the Lesser Free Trade Hall, Manchester from 5-7 April 1912 and found the new Party at the peak of its numerical strength with 250 delegates representing 186 branches. The Birmingham delegation consisted of E.Moorby from Aston Manor branch, Leonard Hall from Birmingham Central, Councillor Eldred Hallas from Kings Heath, Ralph Parr from Northfield, D.E. Davies from Sparkfield and George Simpson from Smethwick branches.

Hyndman, the chairman, gave an optimistic assessment of the past transition period and said they were now entering upon 'a full and active life as a healthy, vigorous and determined organisation'.

The main business of the Conference was to be to discuss the proposed constitution of the party under the two contentious issues of its formation, namely the Objectives of the Party and its Methods. The Rules of the Party were also to be determined.

The Birmingham branches had devoted considerable time to these questions and numerous proposals had been tabled by them.

Problems were first revealed when a Rochdale delegate raised from the Report of the Provisional Executive Committee the fact that Victor Grayson had attended only two and Tom Groom only three of the seven meetings of this EC. Grayson's absences were explained as being due to speaking engagements. But neither was nominated to the new EC and in Grayson's case this was clearly connected with his political waywardness and increasing unreliability through drinking. Tom Groom probably gave up because of increasing Syndicalist influence.

Also on the Report Hall raised the question of a proposed monthly journal and was told that 'as it contained a considerable amount of contentious matter, the Committee had decided that it should not be brought before the Conference'. The Report and Accounts being accepted the Conference moved on to a motion on the Women Suffragists in the name of the Provisional E.C. and this was moved by Leonard Hall:

> That this Conference ... strenuously protests against the shameful betrayal of the Women Suffragists by the Cabinet's proposal to give more votes to men whilst refusing to include in the Government's measure the enfranchisement of women; it heartily congratulates the women upon their unbroken courage and thanks them for the personal sacrifices they are making for the cause of equal freedom; bitterly denounces the vindictive prosecution of the women's leaders for conspiracy and the savage sentences of from two to six months' hard labour upon suffragist prisoners; and this Conference further demands the immediate introduction of such legislation for the enfranchisement of women as will remove the national scandal of their great grievance.

Immediately the Conference erupted in controversy, led by the women. Mrs. Victor Fisher opposed the resolution. It was couched in the language of hysteria, she claimed. They must beware of rich women who pour thousands of pounds into the coffers of the WSPU. The Conciliation Bill was based on a property qualification. It was no business of the BSP to fritter its power on Votes for Women. It would mean a large addition of reactionary votes, she concluded. Mrs. Boyce (Central London) said that whatever admiration they had for the leaders of the movement, it would not help Socialism to get votes for women. She would rather live under the domination of a man than under the thumb of some of the ladies who were asking for the vote.

Harry Quelch also opposed the motion. They could not support a middle-class, reactionary, anti-Socialist movement because of sentimental regard for women in prison for doing what they had no right to do and for which severer punishment would have been imposed if it had been done by men. It was absurd to think that they were going to intimidate a government by breaking windows in the Strand.

H. Russell Smart supported the women. He could not get to the bottom of Qelch's objections, he said. Did he want the women's punishment to be severer and so equal to that of men? If Quelch had brought himself up to date he would know that the women had abandoned the Conciliation Bill directly the Government brought in Manhood Suffrage, which meant that the women now demanded Adult Suffrage.

The Conference Report notes, 'There were several interruptions of speakers during the course of the discussion and several delegates were on their feet at once, some wishing to address the Conference, others raising points of order, most of which could not be heard.'

F. Victor Fisher then spoke in favour of Adult Suffrage and urged that some reference to it should be made in the resolution. However, 'next business' was moved and this was accepted by 92 to 58. So support for the Suffragists seemed to have been rejected. But peace was made with the women later in the Conference when a motion was passed making Adult Suffrage the policy of the party and protesting against the savage sentences on the women and the tortures of forced feeding; it also demanded that political offences should not suffer the penalties of the criminal code.

The whole discussion on the Constitution and Rules to which the branches had devoted so much time and tabled so many proposals was then pre-empted by a resolution from the Provisional EC stating that 'it had been drafted by two of the most experienced trade unionists in the country who were also Socialists'. The first paragraph welcomed the exisiting industrial discontent and said that the BSP stood for the most complete industrial organisation by means, wherever possible, of amalgamations or federations of existing trade unions 'and the strengthening of these bodies in every possible way in order to fit themselves more thoroughly for the administration of production in the Socialist community'. The key paragraph was the second one which read:

> The main function of the Socialist Party however, is the organisation of an independent political party of the working class, aiming at the conquest of political power by that class as the political expression of the working class movement, and as a means to its final emancipation.

The third paragraph of the resolution stated that the political and industrial organisations of the working class should complement each other. 'It is idle for workers to strike for better conditions of life unless they are prepared to take steps for the holding and working of the common means of life by and for the workers collectively.' All trade unionists were therefore urged to join the BSP and all eligible BSP members were urged to join and work in their trade unions.

The fourth paragraph pointed out that only 25% of the labour force was organised in trade unions and stated that it was the obvious duty of the BSP to help organise the remaining 75%. The last paragraph set the final objective:

> Then in co-operation with the political organisation of the British Socialist Party, the whole movement may march forward to the complete emancipation of Labour by the abolition of the class ownership of the great means of production, distribution and exchange, and the establishment of the Co-operative Commonwealth.

Leonard Hall was the first speaker in the debate. He moved to delete in the second paragraph the words ... 'the main function' and substitute '... one of the main functions.' It was neither principle nor tactics to treat industrial organisation and action as secondary matters, he declared. Their business was to link up with the industrial movement. They must avoid falling in line with the political Labour people 'who now use the trade unions as warming pans for politicians, damning with faint praise militant industrial organisation and action'. Their main function in the Socialist movement was the education of the people in the principles of Socialism, not to make it an electioneering party.

The Conference Report then notes, 'A large number of delegates now rose to speak and numbers proceeded to talk all at the same time. It was suggested that those wishing to speak ... should hand in their names in writing and for a few seconds there was a rush for the platform to hand in the slips.'

Harry Quelch opposed the amendment arguing that the main function of the BSP was to organise as the political expression of the working class. The TUC was the expression of their industrial organisation and it would be a gross impertinence to say that the main function of the Socialist party was to organise and conduct industrial operations.

J. Sheppard opposed both the resolution and the amendment. A more jumbled up affair would be hard to find. Trade unionism was played out. he. went on, because of the introduction of machinery. The Socialist movement must advocate industrial organisation.

Most of the ensuing discussion centred around the above opposing views. George Simpson of Smethwick opposed Hall's views, but seemed to concede most of Hall's case. Simpson argued that the functions of the Socialist Party and the functions of the trade unions were two totally different things. As a member of his trade union he was already engaged in industrial organisation. But trade unionists were disgusted with the Labour Party leaders who were now a failure because they had no economic basis. As Socialist Party members they should concern themselves with mainly political activities while assisting the trade unions all they could in their work of industrial organisation.

Hyndman then vacated the chair to contribute to the debate. He submitted that the resolution did not depreciate in any degree the value of industrial organisation. Socialists supported trade union action, but considered that political action was a more excellent way. The worse the Labour Party were in Parliament, the greater the need for Socialists to be there. Industrial organisation without political power was of little use. As long as their actions were confined to starving themselves and their families it was the duty of Socialists to organise. 'Organise, forget your petty differences and remember you have 75% of men and women to organise. Bring them in and bring them in as Socialists. Organise politically, organise industrially and sweep away the classes that rob you today.' After this exhortation, the vote was taken, the amendment was lost by 100 votes to 46 and the original resolution carried by an overwhelming majority.

Leonard Hall was more successful when he raised the question of the *Daily Herald* later in the proceedings. A motion was passed welcoming the first Socialist-Labour daily newspaper and urging BSP members to buy and support it.

Regarding political action, an omnibus resolution was eventually carried which supported Proportional Representation, the Referendum, Single Chamber government and Home Rule for Ireland.

It was agreed that the Executive Committee should continue to be elected on a regional grouping of branches, so the eventual result may not entirely represent personal popularity, but it may be significant that Harry Quelch topped the poll with 161 votes and Leonard Hall came second with 159. The others elected were:Ben Tillett 153, Councillor Dan Irving 148, E.C. Fairchild 143, H. Russell Smart 130, Miss Zelda Khan 96, Rev. Conrad Noel 81 and F. Victor Fisher 79.

George Tooth had also been nominated for the EC by Birmingham branch, Councillor Eldred Hallas by Northfield and J. Smith by Birmingham and Smethwick. They received respectively 5, 3, and 2 votes. The Conference was closed by Hyndman. The Report records:

> Then came a scene that was really affecting. The delegates all rose and the cheering and waving of handkerchiefs was continued until it became

painful. It was a personal tribute to the chairman, and more than that — it was a tribute to the life-long devotion to the cause of Socialism which his personality carries with it.

This first annual conference was a high point of the BSP, but not even the tidal wave of militant industrial action which followed could solve the problems of the differing priorities of Party members and these problems were as difficult in Birmingham as they were elsewhere.

The first post-formation document of the Birmingham BSP is a circular dated October 5th. 1911 on printed paper headed British Socialist Party (Birmingham Section) with headquarters at City Coffee Rooms, 15 Spiceal Street. It was addressed to all members of the Party and signed by W. Williams (not to be confused with H.B. Williams — GB). This circular stated that the Birmingham Manifesto of the party had been unanimously approved at a meeting on 18th September at the People's Hall where the delegates to the Unity Conference had been elected. This conference had been a 'triumphant success' and the new party 'is now nationally connected with the brightest prospects'. The Birmingham meeting of 18th. September had also decided that the dues for the party should be 2/-d. per annum payable quarterly to the treasurer, W. Parkes of 253 Birchfield Road, Handsworth. This low figure had been decided upon 'so that no comrade should be prevented from joining'. (A quarterly fee seems most unproletarian, even though it was only ½d. a week; a paid-up card of an unknown Birmingham member showed spaces covered with 60 stamps printed 'BSP 1912' — GB)

The circular went on to explain that meetings would be advertised 'in our official organ the *Clarion* which it is expected you will constantly peruse.' Then followed a questionaire asking whether members were prepared to 1. Distribute literature. 2. To speak for the Party at outdoor or indoor meetings 3. Could oblige with any Vocal or Instrumental item at any Fellowship Concert 4. Act as Stewards at meetings. 5. Offer hospitality to visiting speakers. The Circular ended:

> The Progress of the British Socialist Party, and in particular the Birmingham Section, has exceeded our most sanguine expectations. The membership grows by leaps and bounds, and with all our members strenuously pushing forward our propaganda and a reawakening of the old spirit, a brilliant future is assured.

This prematurely formed Birmingham Section of the BSP had its last meeting in June 1912 and duly merged itself into the general body of the BSP. The accounts showed a favourable balance of £5-14-2d and it was agreed that £1 of this should be sent to the BSP Central Election Fund and the remainder should be handed over to the Birmingham Federation of the Party. The report stated: 'It will be remembered that Birmingham was one of the earliest to respond to the *Clarion* appeal for the formation of the BSP the initiation of which was due to two youthful comrades'. Votes of thanks were made to W. Williams, the initial secretary, and Whittingham who replaced him pro. tem. Parkes the treasurer was presented with a gold mounted umbrella and the secretary with a fountain pen 'as small tokens of appreciation of the BSP now strongly established in Birmingham, a one-time stronghold of Owenite Rational Religionists, whose Socialistic work in pre-Marxist days has yet to be understood and appreciated by a later generation, and when coupled with the present activities of Birmingham BSP is destined to make history.' This report is signed 'HBW' and reflects H.B. Williams interest in the history of Socialism in Birmingham, noted already.

On July 5th 1912 the Birmingham District Federation held its monthly meeting at Spiceal Street with 'a good muster of delegates from nine branches.' It was decided to form a Propaganda Committee to meet on the last Friday of each month. Proposals to form an Industrial Committee and a Political Committee were referred back to the branches. It was suggested that educational classes the following winter should be under the Central Labour College, London. Local comrades interested in forming a local branch of the Plebs League in association with ex-students and supporters of the Central Labour College were asked to communicate with the Federation secretary, F.B. Silvester of 29 Stanmore Road, Edgbaston. The Federation also announced that 'to stimulate the local movement', a monthly journal the *Torch* was being produced by Kings Heath branch.

Four numbers of the *Torch* appeared. The first, in July 1912, presents the Birmingham BSP at the peak of its membership and influence. It listed nine branches. These were, with their secretaries: Central (T. Flowers at Spiceal Street), Smethwick (J. Smith, Clarion Cottage, Warley), Walsall (Wm. Buck), Handsworth (Mrs. J. Wright), Aston (H. Watts), Sparkhill (T.W. Blunt), Selly Oak (J. Daniel), Kings Heath (Ralph Parr, Hollywood), Northfield (P.W. Roberts). These branches were linked into a Birmingham BSP Federation with an executive of branch delegates which met on the first Friday of each month. Its officers were: C.J. Griffith, Selly Oak (Chairman), J. Silvester, Central (Secretary), J. Smith, Smethwick (Propaganda Sec), and R. Parr, Kings Heath (Treasurer).

The paper represented the combined journalistic talents and temporarily united ideologies of Eldred Hallas, Leonard Hall, Norman Tiptaft and Fred Silvester. Their unity was not to last, but while it did it was a formidable force.

Hallas, the editor, set out these united views as follows. The value of the present strikes were not so much in what the working class gained, but what they were learning. Never before had workers been awakened to the comparative futility of sectional trade unionism and sectional strikes. When the employing class deal with their wage slaves in detail they can beat them and laugh at them. But it will be another story when the Sympathetic Strike becomes an accomplished fact. When a nation of workers put down their tools, the strike will be swift and sure.

Better conditions, shorter hours and better pay were the immediate objects of Industrial Unionism. The fighting aim was Socialism. On the political plane there must be educational propaganda and the gradual capture of the reins of local and national government. The one is the complement of the other. The Syndicalists had probably laid too much stress on mines for the miners and the railways for railwaymen, without explaining sufficiently the meaning of the terms used. If it meant the body politic relegating the management of the mines to the miners for the good of the community by whom, in the ultimate analysis, they would be controlled who could complain? Surely one could not expect mines to be managed by dentists and railways by tailors? Industrial Unionism points to Socialism, the primary objective of which is the abolition of the private possession and control of the means of life.

The first issue of *The Torch* also contained an article by Leonard Hall called Practical Lessons from Italy. Hall recalls that the last newspaper headline that caught his eye before the boat train left Dover was A Bill for the Feeble-Minded of Great Britain. 'Ah, thought I, the most reasonable motion we have had lately. Very urgently needed. But how on earth will they house them all? Are they going to fence and roof over half the island to asylum the poor things? For indeed the twin troubles afflicting the masses in Britain — their ugly poverty and their sickening servitude — are wholly due to their own feebleness of mind and poverty of spirit.

'Workers can scrap their chains by gaining control (through their Industrial Unions) of the practical management of their industries and adminster them co-operatively in the common interest. In the case of the great public services — railways, canals, shipping and mines — ownership should be national and the actual working management should be in the hands of the workers engaged in those departments.

'. . . The doubtful part in my mind is whether the working people of Britain have imagination enough to be practical. Italian workers are showing that they have. Their bottle blowers fought their Employers' Syndicate. When they looked like losing the strike they started their own Co-operative Trade Union Bottle Works, and out of the profits a second factory and a third until all the men on strike employed themselves. Now they have taken three quarters of the entire trade out of the hands of the Capitalist Trust.

'Land cultivators are moving on similar lines. The state railways have been badly mismanaged by an incompetent government . . . Well, the Railway Workers Labour Union have now offered to take over the management leaving the general policy in the hands of the government . . . The government is considering the offer.

'But have the workers of Britain enough intelligence and spirit to convert their Labour Movement on to similar hopeful and businesslike policies? I leave you with that query.'

Another feature of the first issue of the *Torch* is worth quoting as reflecting on the modern problems of Birmingham. It was a reply by 'Uncle' to 'Young Socialist' who was worried by 'imagining a state of society in which every man and woman who wants a motor car can have one.'

> You have conjured up the vision of a population driven frantic with confusion, collisions and death. Of highways presenting the appearance of battlefields. If this is Socialism, you say, let me get back to the simple life.
>
> But motor cars have no greater complexity than walking-sticks. Complexity and simplicity are states of mind. Think of every dwelling house having its own motor-house; fine, broad roads devoid of dust, providing ample room for every kind of traffic without confusion or danger.

> Life's complexities are balanced by its simplicities. An artisan is not
> so skilled as his forbears. But the complete product of numbers of
> artisans may be beyond anything conceived by his forbears.

Whether Uncle was the editor or not, the author of City Council column
·by "Insider" certainly was. Hallas said that City Councillors showed an
overwhelming desire to help the poor *in* their poverty but were staggered
at the very notion of being required to help them *out* of it. They were very
decent fellows according to their lights, though there were differing
opinions regarding the candle power of those lights. These good
gentlemen were prepared to alleviate, tinker. repair. patch and palliate
social evils. But they were opposed to wage increases of public employees
because this would increase the rates. The fact that it would stimulate
increases elsewhere — more food, better housing, better health and
morality; less Workhouses, prisons, hospitals etc. and ultimately reduce
rates, they did not appear to comprehend.

Hallas also called attention to the rate of interest paid on Corporation
loans and advocated a higher initial rate to pay for capital projects out of
current expenditure and thus, eventually, to save on the rates. Hallas also
advocated a local income tax instead of rates on property.

The nearest *Torch* No.1. came to an extremist was "Willie" who said:

> Those of us who see further than the Academic Vapourings of the
> Westminster Charnel House realise the great and potential power of
> Direct Action ... which will cripple the system by years of General
> Strikes, culminating in a total collapse of the Capitalist System.

Another feature in *Torch* No 1. was An Open letter to Lord Charnwood
by Fred Silvester. The noble lord had offended by stating at a
Wolverhampton Conference on Labour Unrest that one of the causes
was, 'the unbalanced character and very pardonable conceit of ambitious
young fellows who succeed in penetrating the regions of higher
intellectual study.' Charnwood was read a lecture by Silvester on Marx'
theory of value, and he ended, 'Just as a prostitute sells her body to
gratify the carnal lusts of young gentlemen of your class, so workers are
forced to sell their labour to satisfy the venal lust for rent, interest and
profit.'

The second issue of *The Torch* was in August 1912. An article by
Norman Tiptaft, 'Is Birmingham Barmy?' carried on the Leonard Hall
theme of the previous issue. Tiptaft's main reason for thinking people
barmy was the very fact that they themselves did not think they were, 'yet
they live in poverty and semi-starvation when they know that there is
sufficient wealth in Birmingham for everyone to live in comfort. They
also know that the rich have so arranged the laws that things always
remain the same and yet they insist on returning these very same rich
people to Parliament and local government.'

A column called Sparks and Splutterings by SYL, who was Fred
Silvester, lamented that: 'The great Strike is ended. The men have been
defeated. Direct Action has failed. Honour to the strikers who honourably
and bravely fought. Shame on the unions which failed to come to their
assistance. Sectional unionism is played out. It cannot succeed against the

Federations of masters. Urgently needed is the amalgamation of unions on the basis of one union for one industry. Industrial Unionism plus Social Democratic political action is the workers' only hope.' Whether the strike referred to was the miners' strike or the strike of London transport workers is not clear, but Silvester's 'line' was still fairly close to Leonard Hall's in advocating both Industrial Unionism and political action. Both were also close to the views of the U.S. Socialist Party and an article in this issue of *Torch* by Eugene V. Debs, the leader of the US Socialist Party which was having considerable success in 1912, brought a theoretical dimension to the discussion on the Growth of Socialism. According to Debs, industrial forces were making for the maturing of Socialism; Capitalists were centralising and combining instead of competing and the working class was organising. This process was perfectly peaceful and orderly; workers must be taught to vote Socialist and then the Government and Capitalism would pass into their hands.

Silvester's great interest at that time was the conflict on the teaching of Marxism which had led to the break with Ruskin College and the setting up of the Central Labour College. In *Torch* No 2. Silvester had a piece hoping that Birmingham BSPers were seriously considering the claims of the CLC to be the only genuine workers' educational institution in the country and that the Socialist movement would avail itself of the scientific teachings in economics, sociology and ethics given by the CLC; comrades who would like to promote the interests of the CLC were invited to contact Silvester.

The main feature of *Torch* No 3. was an extremely detailed national Socialist Municipal Policy set out by G.H. Russell Smart. Smart explained that this differed fundamentally from the policy of the ILP. The ILP wanted an industrial society under the bureaucratic administration of the state. Agriculture and Industry would be conducted as national monopolies controlled by Government officials. Workers were to be regimented and the production of wealth regulated by a Board of Statisticians in Whitehall. Prior to this, destitution was to be abolished by social reforms such as National Insurance, Relief Works, Old Age Pensions etc. to mitigate the worst effects of capitalism. These reforms would whet workers' appetites for more, and they would vote in Socialist majorities. The BSP, on the other hand, Smart went on, hates the idea of bureaucracy and does not believe in state organised industry except in such matters as postage. Production was best conducted by free association. Those engaged in production were those best qualified to organise it. Exchange would be a free and automatic process. This view shows Socialism as a revolutionary movement achieving itself through working class institutions instead of a series of mechanical measures bestowed by political elites on an acquiescent population.

The chief weapon of revolution, Smart went on, was strikes. Municipal gas, water, trams etc. was no solution to poverty. But a free supply of bread for all and free milk was revolutionary; but only as a product of revolutionary method. Otherwise it was only a subsidy to lower wages.

Torch No 4. appeared in November 1912. Like the previous issues, it reported municipal matters but it was notably short on reports of BSP political activity. At the end of the file containing the paper is a post-card from H.B. Williams addressed to the Librarian at Birmingham Library and says:

Dear Sir,
    This is to confirm that *The Torch*, (which I promised to present monthly to the Library) has extinguished itself as from No 4.
                    Yours faithfully,
                    H.B. Williams.

The political differences that split the BSP and led to the demise of the *Torch* can be followed by returning to the BSP (Birmingham) Section documents previously quoted. The first is a letter from Leonard Hall to Harry Williams. This is undated, but pre-dates the formation of the BSP nationally:

> Thanks for the Agendas. Yes, I know that you must have your hands full. Its no light job starting a new Party and keeping it going. You were plucky to tackle it but I don't know anyone else in Birmingham who would or could. I'm afraid some (a few) of our people are shy about taking any local initiative and they want to hang on to the coat tails of some Central Mahatma. This is a fatal mistake. Neither us nor the rest of the movement do anything or get anywhere on these lines. Either we have an idea and purpose and therefore the work to do, or we haven't and if we have to be 'led' along by others are only a burden to the others.
>
> At any rate, I know very definitely and clearly what it is I want to do and see done and I've said it in the Manifesto unanimously carried by the local party, and unless they repudiate it, that is our 'platform'. Do you agree or do you see it differently? I think you seem pretty much of the same mind and I know several others of the Committee are. If, however, the majority are against let them produce their alternative programme and let's get it out and decide. I myself am convinced that the far most valuable service the Socialists can do is to propagandise and push for all we're worth the idea and organisation of the combined and General Strike as the most potent lever of the Social Revolution. Other lines will be a waste of time and opportunity for some years ahead yet. And house to house distribution of leaflets and pamphlets (the right ones) is the only way of getting at the citizens. Yrs hopefully L. Hall.

There is a note in the margin of this letter: 'And you have now an opportunity to mark Birmingham and the Midlands with a new idea that will have permanent force.'

    Thomas Whittingham, on the other hand, although one of pioneers of the BSP in Birmingham, held strong views that were not likely for long to coincide with those of Hall. A letter of his dated 15 November 1911 states:

> My dear Williams,
>   I have not been able to locate the Graysonian (slot ?) to which you refer. But I may perhaps be pardoned for being aware of what Socialism is and what it is not and I prefer to place Industrial Unionism in the latter category. Grayson is not a god or fetish with me as you seem to suppose. On the contrary I am able to detect qualities in Grayson which are quite human. I think his "obituary" of Stolypin, for instance, would have better been left unwritten.
>   I consider Grayson should be asked to speak (at the Town Hall meeting? — GB) because as Founder of the BSP he can most clearly demonstrate what the policy of the BSP is.
>   I am fully aware of your countrymen's religious enthusiam for Lloyd George. But is it to be wondered at? The career of the Limehouse Orator is perhaps the most romantic in the annals of Welsh political history. And are not the Welsh a romantic people whose imaginations fall an easy

prey to the men from Manchester — Lloyd George, Blatchford, Grayson, Hall and others?

I adhere to my statement as to Grayson not being asked to speak for the *Birmingham Section* of the BSP. I am aware he has been asked to attend the musical evening. You say he has been asked three times by 'our' Smethwick organiser. I did not know we had a Smethwick organiser but if you refer to Comrade Smith, I shrewdly suspect the invitation was extended to Grayson on behalf of the Smethwick Socialist Society and not from the Birmingham Section of the BSP.

Our orginal obligation, in my opinion, consisted of firmly establishing the BSP on BSP lines and not to establish the BSP on lines advocated by Strike Agitators who may or may not be members of the BSP.

> Yours for democracy,
> T.R. Whittingham.

Leonard Hall continued to defend and try to develop his views. In April or May of 1912 he was preparing a four page leaflet to present at the Whitsun BSP Conference, based on Industrial Unionism. His argument is too complex to do justice to here, but the following mix of old and new points is a reasonable summary. Hall reiterated the need for both political and industrial action. But until a strong political presence had been established the industrial weapon was the more important. The capitalist class would not allow the establishment of working class power and workers would be confronted with the military. Socialism could not be established without destroying capitalism. The General Holiday must establish Socialism. Craft Unionism could not do that, only Industrial Unionism.

By the autumn of 1912 the differences in the Party could no longer be hidden. From the *Socialist Record* (a monthly record of the internal affairs of the BSP published from 1912 to 1916) we learn that in October the Birmingham and District Federation 'is not progressing here as we should like. Members seem more inclined to criticise than to work.' This report was, presumably from Silvester.

Also in the autumn of 1912 dissatisfaction with the views of Leonard Hall was growing and seems to have crystalised around a 'left' and 'right' criticism. On the 'left' Ralph Parr and Harry Williams came together. On 23 September 1912 Parr wrote to 'Dear Harry' from Drakeness Cottage, Hollywood, near Birmingham. Parr had recently returned from a holiday at Aberdovey where he had 'forgotten everything except the joy of being alive.' Parr went on:

> And now to direct action and the (damned rat race ?) once more. Have you taken any steps with regard to the ISEL (Industrial Syndicalist Education League — GB) yet? I have very little hope of the BSP doing anything to further the revolution, and I feel like diverting such coppers as I can spare to the Syndicalist Cause. What say you? Can we talk together? The wife says will you spend a week-end with us before the leaves are off the trees. Ever. Ralph.

On 27th. October 1912 Parr wrote another letter to Harry (Williams ?):

> I have only tonight received a reply from Silvester to matters I wrote to him about. His letter is very unsatisfactory. He says the principal items on the Federation agenda will be the Tom Mann meeting and the election of the secretary and chairman. Try to be there, there may be fun.

He has cancelled the order with the Twentieth Century Press, but says
the Federation must decide as to handing over the literature department
to the Syndicalist Group. If they agree, have we anyone who could take
charge of the thing and see it through? ...
    L. Hall thinks the Fabians are doing the best work in the movement
now and he has increased his subscription! Well, its a merry world!

As we shall see, the Fabians were indeed engaged on valuable
'educational' work, some of which was eventually to surface as Guild
Socialism.

On the 'right' Fred Silvester was clarifying his position in a long letter
in *Justice* of 2 November 1912 which covered so much of the disputed
ground that it must be quoted fairly fully:

I have been not a little interested in the controversy inasmuch as there
is more Syndicalism in the movement here than Social Democrcy. The
effect, to say the least, is deplorable. Although we have amongst us a
member of the Executive and a Councillor, the Birmingham BSP is
being rapidly disintegrated over the miserable question of Direct Action
v Political Action. The curious thing is that the members who are most
in favour of Syndicalism are not trade unionists at all, but are either
middle class people who would not be seriously put about by strikes or
are clerks or shop assistants who are too indifferent to join a trade union.
In discussions in which I have taken part some of our local Syndicalists
seem to think ... that Syndicalism is not necessarily antagonistic to
Social Democracy or political action. Surely they are speaking without
their book. In the *Syndicalist* for October ... the view is expressed (by
one writer) that 'he would not bother to discuss Syndicalism with a Social
Democrat,' for Social Democracy is 'the apotheosis of the weak, the
exaltation of the defeated, the enthronement of the inefficient and the
survival of the unfitted.' This absurd, but grossly insulting depreciation
of the greatest political movement the world has ever known is endorsed
by the president of the ISEL, who, by the way, is not above receiving
heavy lecture fees from Social Democrats.
    From the foregoing it ought to be clear to the dullest intellect that the
Syndicalists are as violently against political action as they are against
Social Democracy.
    That being so, am I wrong in assuming that the Syndicalist movement
is nothing more nor less than a recrudescence of Anarchism?
    Whether that is so or not, it is evidently so hostile to Social Democracy
that no member of our party could support the Syndicalist movement
and remain loyal to the BSP.
    It is, of course, quite a different matter to endeavour to promote
solidarity in the trade unions, to advocate the amalgamation of the
unions on the basis of one union, one industry, and to urge the trade
unions to back up political action, when crises arise, by political mass
strikes. This course is strongly recommended by Kautsy in his pamphlet
The Social Revolution and I consider it should be our policy to advocate
such tactics.
    Is this line of action what Leonard Hall and Simpson really desire the
trade unions to pursue, or are they endeavouring to get the BSP
committed to the heretical principles and the impossibilist tactics
advocated by Tom Mann and Guy Bowman? If the former, I and many
others in the party are with them. If the latter, they are in honour bound
to retire from the BSP, or should be compelled to do so.

By this time the national executive of the BSP was beginning to consider
firm action against the 'Syndicalists' and Leonard Hall and Smart were
rather desperately trying to maintain their position. The *Daily Herald* of

1 November 1912 stated that the previous day it had published a statement by the executive of the BSP concerning the future of Socialism and its opposition to Syndicalism. Now it was printing a declaration by Messrs Hall and H. Russell Smart both members of the EC expressing their individual views.

> As members of the EC we protest against the unauthorised and premature publication of the Manifesto which appeared in yesterday's *Herald*. A draft on similar lines but much more uncompromisingly anti-industrialist was submitted to a recent meeting but was referred to a sub-committee.
>
> (The present) publication does not represent the views of the EC. (It attacks) Direct Economic Action under the name of Syndicalism, which is not so much a theory of society as a movement of revolt. It is not our business to oppose any movement fighting for the freedom of the working class. We are not therefore inclined to denounce methods of revolt whether strikes or even sabotage of Syndicalism or militant action of Suffragists. The formalists are too much obssessed with dry theory. In revolutionary movements what matters is the revolutionary spirit.
>
> There should not be two armies but one fighting with foot, horse and artillery with the common objective of overthrowing capitalism. Long May the *Daily Herald* flourish to voice the interests of Labour and the spirit of revolt.
>
> Hall, Russell. 31 Oct.

During this period, public BSP work was proceeding in Birmingham. On Tuesday 12th. November there was a public rally at the Town Hall. Tom Mann was the main speaker on the subject of the 'Doom of Capitalism' with Leonard Hall as supporting speaker and Eldred Hallas in the chair. Trade unionists were especially urged to 'come and hear the world famous Agitator on revolutionary Industrial Unionism.' Quick on its heels came a Sunday town hall meeting on 30th. November on the theme of 'The Turn of the Tide — Birmingham for Socialism.' The main speaker was Ben Tillett of the Dockers' Union supported by John Stokes of the Glass Blowers. Local speakers were R. Clements of the Socialist Centre and Norman Tiptaft with Councillor J. Kesterton the secretary of the Trades Council, in the chair.

But the splits rending the BSP nationally could not be avoided in Birmingham and at the end of December 1912 it was announced in *Clarion* that the Birmingham and District BSP Federation had been disbanded 'as serving no practical purpose.' The weaker branches intended to amalgamate. The balance in the funds was to be donated, not to the BSP branches, but to the *Daily Herald* fund. So the Birmingham BSP reverted to the SDP writ slightly larger.

Meetings of the BSP continued. In January 1913 *Clarion* reported that 'a meeting was held of lively BSPers at our Central Club Room, 15, Spiceal Street.' This was evidently an AGM as officers were elected, although no details are given. The branch met every Monday at 8 pm. The next month a BSP class on Economics and Industrial History taken by William Paul on Sundays at 11-30 am was advertised.

In March, Blatchford aired his views on Socialism in a *Clarion* article written, he admitted, when he was 'a bit down in the dumps.' It reflected both the current and looming problems of the movement:

> So you still believe in Socialism? If you mean you think it would be a
> good idea if mankind were fit to rule itself and accept partage of the
> world's goods according to individual needs, so am I. But if Socialism
> means trade union organisation for the government of Mr. Balfour; if
> it means exploitation by bureaucratic Labour leaders instead of
> exploitation by Pierpoint Morgan and the Rothschilds; if it means a
> model state with morals enforced by the Pleasant Sunday Afternoon
> Society; if it means a Christian foreign policy of handing over the cloak
> if another nation pinches the coat, then I go groggy at the knees.

In May 1913 the Second Annual Conference of the BSP took place at
Blackpool. The number of delegates had fallen to 106 representing 85
branches. Birmingham was represented by the Handsworth branch
(H.Parke) and Smethwick (W.J. Salmon). From the Report it appears
that the only Birmingham input into the Conference came from Salmon.
He proposed the acceptance of the Agenda. He also opposed a criticism
of the EC that it had not taken up the question of Universal Suffrage
vigorously enough, saying that he failed to see why an executive elected
to organise the BSP should trouble themselves with problems of 'high
politics.' It was a red herring to draw them off questions of more
importance to the workers, he claimed. Salmon also opposed a Self-
Denial Fund, saying that he did not consider that the idea would catch
on and their lives were already too much of a self-denial.

When it came to elections to the EC for Group 9 (Midlands and
Eastern Counties) no Birmingham nomination was made and A.C.
Bannington the very active Coventry member, who in November was to
become a local Councillor, was elected.

What had happened to Leonard Hall? It would seem that he withdrew
from BSP politics in disgust. He did not join the Syndicalists, nor did he
join the SLP. He remained a member of the executive of Birmingham
Socialist Centre for 1912 – 13, but not for the next year. If he was active
in the Birmingham Fabian Society, it does not show up on the record. It
was likely that he became more supportive of his wife and daughters in
the Suffragist movement, but they were active nationally and such
support does not register in the Birmingham movement. He remained in
residence in Birmingham. We do not know what his attitude to the War
was.

Tragically, Leonard Hall died in a street accident in Birmingham on
29th. June 1916 when he was knocked down by a bus and died in
Birmingham General Hospital at the age of 49.

An obituary appeared in *Justice* 6 July 1916 written by his friend H.
Russell Smart:

> (He was) a doctor's son, journalist, orator, adventurer. A restless will
> would not allow him to settle for any length of time. He found outlets
> for his energy in the Socialist movement. He fought for the ILP and
> stayed with it until it surrendered its soul. He played a large part in the
> formation of the BSP. His speeches were marked with distinction in a
> movement famed for its oratory. The polished scorn and sarcasm with
> which he withered the arguments of his opponents delighted his hearers
> and reduced his opponents to limp and rageful silence.
>   He was always a fighter and had little regard for theory. This led him
> to support both the Syndicalist and the Women's movements.
>   In the last few years he achieved a considerable degree of prosperity.

Perhaps his moderate fortune came more from speculation than from legitimate business.

He was fond of gambling, and I have known him to lose thousands with no more disturbance than a shrug of the shoulders.

Socialism has lost an earnest, strenuous agitator.

Returning to Birmingham BSP, in August 1913 Thomas Kennedy, the national organiser was in the midlands and he reported that he had spent a week in Birmingham. He had a feeling that 'the days for street meetings are over.' The movement was marking time. At a meeting it had been decided to re-form the District Committee. He was due back in Birmingham in September to address a series of meetings. Kennedy then reported again: Handsworth had completed its outdoor programme. Meetings had been good and members had been made at most. He had spoken at the Midland Institute under the auspices of local Socialist and Labour bodies on the Dublin Outrages. Birmingham had more than its share of sectionalism, but he missed entirely the bad feeling usually associated with such divisions. At Aston, the BSP and the ILP lived at peace under the hospitable roof of the Aston Labour .Club. At Handsworth the BSP, ILP and LRC were busy promoting Norman Tiptaft in Soho Ward. He (Kennedy) had received every assistance from Richard Clemence the secretary of the Socialist Centre. In view of this feeling and the large number of Socialist organisations in Birmingham (BSP, ILP, Socialist Centre, Socialist Church, SLP, SPGB and goodness knows how many others) he felt that Birmingham would not be far behind when the day of Socialist Unity came. At the BSP District Council, Buckeridge of Central branch had been elected secretary and Burden of Handsworth assistant secretary, but Smethwick 'had not yet fallen in line.' The District Council had agreed on a Christmas Bazaar at Aston and were looking for central premises for the BSP.

In 1914 Birmingham BSP continued at this lower level of activity. Of the leading spirits who set up the party only Fred Silvester can be identified and he by his role as supporter of the Central Labour College against Ruskin College and the WEA rather than by his general political activity. So that, for instance, he had a letter in *Justice* in March in which he deplored Ben Tillett's support for Ruskin College, which had been taken over by the University and 'was as unsound as the WEA which is patronised by the nobility, prominent Liberal and Tory politicians and members of the Anti-Socialist Union.' This Marxist educational interest brought Silvester within the ideological ambit of both the 'Syndicalists' and the SLP and the fact that he did not hold a prominent office in the BSP may indicate that he did not continue in membership at this time, although his antipathy to the non-political stance of both the former organisations ensured that he did not join them.

The third annual conference of the BSP took place at the Cannon Street Hotel, London in April 1914. There were more delegates at this Conference, 140 representing 97 branches. The only Birmingham delegate was Richard Clements from Handsworth branch, but he made no recorded political input to the conference. Bannington, by now a councillor, was the unopposed choice of EC delegate for No.IX District.

There is no sense of impending catastrophe in any of the working class newspapers as the outbreak of World War 1 approached, except for such

occasional patriotic outbursts by Blatchford, Hyndman and others as
quoted above. Coming as it did at the beginning of August, the event is
all but unrecorded and it was not until 20 August that Silvester gave a
'war report' in *Justice* in which he comments that 'Imperial Brummagem
has not yet become infected with war fever.' In September the BSP
officially announced its support for the war and permission was given to
members, with provisos, to take part in a recruiting campaign. The
notice was signed by the entire executive including Bannington.

Thus ended all the high hopes of Socialist Unity aroused by the
formation of the BSP in 1911. By 1914 there was even greater
fragmentation and the war brought the complete restructuring of the
political scene.

Chapter Twenty-Three

SYNDICALISM, THE ILP AND OTHER PARTIES AND TRENDS 1910 TO 1914.

Syndicalism

'Syndicalism' has consistently appeared here between inverted commas because the reality defies political definition. Leonard Hall called it 'not so much a theory of society as a movement of revolt.' Perhaps it is best described as a spectrum of attitudes and policies ranging from concepts of violent direct action usually attributed to anarchism, through to Industrial Unionism with, or without, accompanying political action. There was also a highly sophisticated, middle class version of syndicalism — Guild Socialism.

The roots of the movement were in the USA and France. The former from the Industrial Workers of the World (the Wobblies) together with the Socialism of Daniel de Leon (Dandelion). The French influence ranged from the name, coupled with the general revolutionary tradition, and the specific disgust with the political corruption of the Second French Republic. Stirred into this brew was the English Catholic contribution of Hilaire Belloc and G.K. Chesterton prophesying the inevitable degener- ation of state power, whether capitalist or socialist, into the Servile State.

The British architect of 'Syndicalism' is recognised to be Tom Mann. Mann had spent eight years in Australia and New Zealand organising workers under conditions of Labour state and provincial legislatures with industrial policies of conciliation and arbitration. He had not thought much of what he had seen. On his return to England, via South Africa in May 1910, Mann joined the SDF and teamed up with Guy Bowman, the ex-manager of the SDF's Twentieth Century Press. Mann is alleged to have said to him, 'Let's go and see the men of direct action,' and Bowman took him to meet the revolutionary syndicalist leaders of the French GCT. From July 1910 to May 1911 Bowman and Mann produced the highly influential monthly paper the *Industrial Syndicalist* and during that period Mann formed the Industrial Syndicalist Education League. Mann resigned from the SDP in May 1911 and therefore had no part in the formation of the BSP.

With regard to Syndicalism in Birmingham we can start with what might be called the 'main stream' Syndicalism associated directly with Tom Mann. Neither the *Industrial Syndicalist* which ran from July 1910 to May 1911 nor the Industrial Syndicalist Education League, founded in December 1910 had much initial response in Birmingham. In January 1912 a new monthly paper *The Syndicalist* appeared as the official organ of the ISEL. The July issue advertised the paper as being available at the National Labour Press 100 John Bright Street, Birmingham. This was the general bookshop of the Labour movement in Birmingham at that time. It was not until October 1912 that Harry Williams took the first step towards establishing an organised syndicalist presence in the city by advertising in *The Syndicalist* a preliminary meeting to consider the formation of a Syndicalist group. Unusually, prior application was to be made to Williams and admission was to be by ticket only. I have not found a report of that meeting and there was no Birmingham representative at the ISEL Conferences in Manchester and London in November 1912. But a Group was set up and the paper, by then called *The Syndicalist & Amalgamated News*, in its January 1913 issue reported on its activity. Members had visited Saltley branch of the Workers Union and a National Union of Clerks meeting at Smethwick Town Hall. Comrade Hawey (?) had opened a discussion on Syndicalism on both occasions. The Group met at the Coffee House, 15 Spiceal Street on alternate Saturdays. The secretary was E. Robinson of 31, Ashmore Road, Cotteridge, Birmingham.

There are no other reports of Birmingham activity and ISEL itself split in the autumn of 1912 along the divide of those working in what might be called the British tradition of attempting to revolutionise existing trade unions, and those supporting the policy of setting up new, separate, revolutionary trade unions. The latter trend was more logical for countries of later industrial development and trade union formation. This formed a link with continental anarchism and the *Wobblies*. All of these trends grouped themselves around the *Daily Herald* and the local support groups which sprung up, the Herald Leagues. The pot was kept boiling by the continuing industrial upheavals of 1913 – 1914, particularly the Black Country and Birmingham strikes of those years. Thus, instead of unity, there came an unprecedent fragmentation of the labour movement bringing in new elements, previously of little or no importance, such as anarchism. It seems best to consider these new elements before returning to the older, established political organisations in Birmingham.

Anarchism.

Like Syndicalism, Anarchism also defies definition, ranging through another spectrum of ideas from pacifist repudiation of all social organisations through to the media concept of cloaked, bomb-throwing immigrants.

As far as organised anarchist activity in Birmingham and the Black Country is concerned it can be asserted with considerable confidence that anarchism rooted itself only in Walsall from the period of the split in William Morris's Socialist League in the 1880s; it found notoriety in the so-called Walsall Bomb Plot of the 1890s and tenaciously continued in Walsall thereafter with occasional forays into Birmingham. But of anarchism in Birmingham until the growth of the Syndicalist movement there is virtually no trace, and not much thereafter. It continued a fragmented existence through the war and up to the great realignment of the Labour movement in the early 1920s.

Anarchism developed in Britain from the 1880s with the influx of European refugees. This coincided with the reappearance of Socialism in Britain and German refugees from Bismarck's anti-Socialist Laws. This orientated anarchism towards Socialism and the development of Anarcho-Communism.

John Quail, the historian of British anarchism, states that there was a revival of anarchist propaganda in 1903 – 05 in which Birmingham shared and a local group was set up. Again, in 1908, a group 'was being set up', the leading figure being Charles Kean.

The main anarchist newspaper from 1903 was *Freedom* and from the September 1912 issue we learn that the paper was available from the National Labour Press, 100 John Bright Street, but I have found no reports of anarchist activity in *Freedom*. On the other hand, Guy Aldred, who was a prolific Anarchist publicist for many years published the *Herald of Revolt* from 1910. It was not until November 1912 that there is any evidence of Birmingham activity from the paper. In that month there was a letter from 'Seagon' of Birmingham stating that he had never before seen the paper, but congratulating those concerned for the 'high merits of that issue.' In February 1913 there was a letter from C. Martens of Birmingham explaining in no uncertain terms what anarchism stood for. It stood for Direct Action. Martens was equally sure what it did not stand for: 'Not strikes, nor trade unionism, nor the present damnable system, nor society, nor leadership.' On Syndicalism he was equally clear — 'Anarchists do not accept Syndicalism.' At the beginning of 1913 Martens was running an Anarchist bookstall in Smithfield Market. In July 1913 'Birmingham is active', *Freedom* tells us. Guy Aldred visited us and there was ' a good meeting in the Bull Ring on June 15th, on Trade Unionism and Revolution with Comrade Pollard in the chair.' In the evening Aldred debated with William Paul, 'Is the SLP worthy of Working Class Support?

Miss Shaw of the SLP ably presided. Comrade W.G.E. Smith of Coventry had also visited them. This is the only report found of Anarchist activity and was signed by R. Poole.

Daily Herald Leagues

The first daily working class newspaper in Britain flourished in the general industrial upheavals of the period 1910 – 14. The *Daily Herald* first appeared as a strike sheet produced by London compositors after they had been locked-out in retaliation for their demand for a 48-hour week. The paper rapidly became the focus for the Left, especially as the TUC and Labour Party moderates backed the alternative *Daily Citizen*. In particular, under its editor George Lansbury, the *Daily Herald* became the unofficial paper of the Syndicalists as they broke with the BSP. The paper quickly developed support groups, and these Daily Herald Leagues developed rapidly. By December 1912 there were three of these Leagues in Birmingham. The *Daily Herald* was supported not only by the Syndicalists such as Williams and Parr, but by the Industrial Unionists such as Leonard Hall, because the *Daily Herald* also supported the Suffragists. In December there was a mass Herald League meeting at the Birmingham Town Hall. The main speakers were George Lansbury and Leonard Hall (who was billed in type as large as that for Lansbury). Other speakers were Gladys Hazell (the Birmingham ·leader of the WSPU), Councillor Hallas of the BSP, Councillor Beard of the Workers' Union, Fred Hughes of the Socialist Centre and John Simpson of the ILP.

With the outbreak of war, the *Daily Herald* became a weekly, but the paper and the Leagues survived the war to become a significant part of the post-war political reorganisation of the Labour movement.

The Church Socialist League.

Although not a direct product of Syndicalism or the Great Unrest of the period 1910 – 14, the Christian Socialist League played a not inconsiderable part in the development of the BSP. It was also connected with Syndicalism by its opposition to bureaucratic Socialism and the arguments concerning the Servile State, injected by the two Roman Catholic publicists, Hilaire Belloc and G.K. Chesterton, who also influenced the development of Guild Socialism.

Another reason for dealing with the Church Socialist League separately and at this point, is that it was a specifically Church of England organisation, which whilst collaborating with other Christian denominations in the mainstream development of Socialist Churches, was not absorbed into them. The last reason is that it was unusual for the established Church to make a direct input into the Socialist movement in Birmingham and this was probably for the fortuitous reason that two of the leading national figures of the organisation were centred on Birmingham.

The main sources of information on the Church Socialist League are the Birmingham ILP .Federation Handbook of 1908 and the auto-biography of Conrad Noel; this latter source, however, is rather thin on dates and it is not always possible to pin down exactly when some events occurred.

The Church Socialist League was formed in 1906 by Conrad Noel and both the Hon. Rev. J.G. Adderley, who was Vicar of Saltley, and the Rev. Arnold Pinchard, vicar of St. Judes, were connected with him. The Birmingham branch was formed in January 1907 and covered the new diocese of Birmingham. In the Autumn of 1907 the branch organised what it described as 'a very successful' Labour Conference at Saltley to discuss points of common interests to all Socialists and trade unionists.

The League's ordinary activities consisted of monthly meetings. The chairman of the branch was Arnold Pinchard, who was also chairman of the national organisation for the year 1909 – 10. The local secretary was the Rev. C.H. Davies of 67 Wheeleys Road. The principles of the organisation were

1. The Church has a mission to the whole of human life, Social and Individual, Material and Spiritual.
2. The Church can best fulfil its social mission by acting in its corporate capacity.
3. To this end the members of the League accept the principle of Socialism.
4. Socialism is the fixed principle, according to which the community should own the land and capital collectively and use them co-operatively for the good of all.

The following Christian Socialist books by the Rev. James Adderley were advertised in the 1908 Birmingham ILP Federation Handbook. *The Socialist Churchman* (3d.) *Stephen Remarx* (3d) *Behold the Days Come* (1/-d) *A Piece of Cloth* (2/-d) and *Little Primer of Christian Socialism* (3d.) The Handbook's list of speakers gave two other clergymen who were probably members of the League. These were the Rev. E. Chambers of the Parsonage, Saltley, and Rev. J. Lopes of 178 High Street.

Conrad Noel tells us that Arnold Pinchard was a leading supporter of Barry Jackson when he formed the Birmingham Repertory Theatre.

Adderley became a member of the Committee of the Birmingham and

Midland Women's Suffrage Society in 1906 – 07 at a time of renewed militancy when a greatly enlarged committee, including men, was elected. In 1908 Arnold Pinchard supported the formation of a Domestic Servants branch of the National Federation of Women Workers when it was set up in Birmingham.

Conrad Noel tells us that there was a stormy AGM of the League in Birmingham at which he (Noel) resigned. Dates fail him at this point, but it was probably 1910 – 11. Much remains to research on the CSL in Birmingham.

The SLP and SPGB.

I group together here the two 'impossibilist' parties, but their contributions to Birmingham politics were very different. The Socialist Labour Party had a real presence in Birmingham during the period 1910 – 14 and the Party became important during the war when the BSP split again. In addition, the SLP had a leading activist in Birmingham, Billy Holliday, who died in prison and can properly be counted as one of the victims of the class war. The Socialist Party of Great Britain, on the other hand, never secured more than a toehold in Birmingham and its story is soon told.

The activity of the SLP for the period 1900 – 1910 has already been outlined and it remains to clarify the relationship of the party with Syndicalism in Birmingham from the few remaining references for the period 1910 – 14. In general, the SLP differed from Tom Mann and the Industrial Unionists in refusing to work with the existing trade unions. The SLP aimed at creating separate Socialist industrial trade unions, but insisted on the primacy of political propaganda for Socialism.

The branch directory in *The Socialist* showed that in 1910 the secretary of the branch was F.W. Holliday of 74 Wolseley Street who had held that office since the formation of the branch in 1903. During the winter, open-air meetings at the Bull Ring were advertised for Sunday evenings at 7-30.

The attitude of the SLP to the women's suffrage movement was that the main struggle was the class struggle and not one of sex. Whilst paying tribute to the courage of the women, and indeed asking the rhetorical question of whether Socialists would do as much, *The Socialist*, in a number of interventions in 1910 appealed to the women to weigh carefully the claims of Socialism before devoting themselves to 'a sectional and partial movement obviously being manipulated in the interests of the propertied classes.'

In 1910 Billy Holliday joined in the Birmingham Sweated Trades agitation as a member of the Cabinet Makers No. 1 Branch. He said that there were 3,000 employed in the furnishing trades. Hundreds of men worked from 8am to 7pm with a twenty minute dinner break for 18/-d. to 22/-d. a week. The union was fighting for 8½d. an hour and a 54 hour week. The cream of the trade was emigrating to Australia and New Zealand and this was another example where machines had become a curse to the workers, Holliday concluded.

In February 1911 the Branch Directory showed that the branch met at the Coffee House in the Bull Ring every second Sunday in the month and held outdoor meetings in the Bull Ring every Sunday at 7 pm. There is no other report from Birmingham until the end of the year, when in November, as well as a general comment that neither the SLP nor the SPGB had been invited to the BSP Unity Conference, there was a report from the SLP national organiser of a tour of the Birmingham area. He stated that as there were several local speakers in Birmingham he had addressed only two meetings in the city. One was a very large meeting in the Bull Ring at which a collection of 20/-d. had been taken which, he claimed, was a record for the town. Birmingham comrades had also assisted him with meetings in Walsall, where considerable opposition was being encountered.

At the beginning of 1912 availability of *The Socialist,* which was a monthly paper of 8 large pages costing 1d. seems to have improved. Besides being available at the John Bright Street bookshop, it could also be bought from E. Fagg at Yardley, Mackenzie at Handsworth and Muir at Hurst Street (opposite the Empire). But if this can be seen as an indication of growth, proceedings at the 1912 Conference were calculated to end such progress. At this annual conference a motion was moved that 'to support reforms . . . is inconsistent with the revolutionary character of the SLP'. This was supported by the Birmingham delegate at the Conference. The motion was eventually lost by 14 votes to 12, which gives some indication of the tiny membership of the SLP, but the motion also indicates the sectarianism and impossibilism of 'keeping principles intact.' The sequel brought an even clearer example. The defeat of the motion led to the resignation from the party of the Ashton branch which had tabled the resolution, and also four other Lancashire branches, which together formed the majority of the members throughout the country; this was on the grounds that the party had become reformist. The result was that by 1914 the party was reduced from 28 branches to 15 and total membership fell to around 300.

But in 1913 the Birmingham SLP was still functioning and the branch directory in *The Socialist* showed, for the first time, a change of secretary. This was J. Donaldson of 213 Deakin Road, Hay Mills. The branch met every alternate Thursday at the Coffee House, Spiceal Street, and an outdoor meeting was held every Sunday at 7pm in the Bull Ring. 'Members receive no other notice than this,' the paper announced.

There are no other reports of branch activity for 1913, nor for 1914 except for the branch directory which showed another change of secretary to G. Melbourne of 70 Blythe Street, Ladywood. The branch met on the first Sunday of each month at Spiceal Street and the Bull Ring meetings continued every Sunday at 7pm.

The SLP unwaveringly opposed the war from the very beginning in 1914 and it was on this basis that the party was to grow in Birmingham subsequently.

The sectarianism and impossibilism of the Socialist Party of Great Britain was of a rather different character from that of the SLP.

Like the SLP, it arose as a breakaway from the SDF, but a year later in 1904. Although its criticisms of the SDF were of the same nature as those of the SLP — the alleged reformism of the SDF and its Hyndmanite leadership — the SPGB was London orientated from the beginning and its criticisms included complaints of the behaviour of the predominantly Scottish leadership of the SLP. In addition, the SPGB laid great stress on electoral struggle and purity of Socialist doctrine, whereas the SLP stressed industrial organisation.

The SPGB paper was a monthly called *Socialist Standard*. Only two references have been found on Birmingham. In 1906 it was stated that information concerning the party could be obtained from H. Oldknow of 227 St. Saviour's Road, Saltley, and in 1914 the branch directory showed E. Jesper of 74 Murdock Road, Handsworth as secretary of the branch which met at the invariable venue — 15, Spiceal Street.

The Fabians.

The first period of growth of the Fabian Society, from 1890, was connected with the national development of the New Unionism. In Birmingham, one of the results of this was the formation of the first provincial society on 20th October 1890. The history of this development has already been traced up to 1895 when the branch merged with the Birmingham Labour Church.

The second period was from 1908 when the Society's annual report recorded 'unprecedented growth', but it was not until 1911 that the setting up of a new society at Birmingham University is recorded. In the 1908 Birmingham Fed. ILP Handbook Sir Oliver Lodge is recorded as representative of the Fabian Society under 'Workers in Reform Movements etc.' and his address is given as The University, Birmingham. The following year, 1912, another Fabian branch was set up in S.W. Birmingham and a joint committee with the ILP was formed. It was about this time that the University Fabians were reported to be engaged on 'important work' on Industrial Unionism, and it was probably this which was attracting Leonard Hall as disillusion with the BSP spread, and which aroused the scorn of Ralph Parr.

In 1913 the Fabians joined in a joint War against Poverty Campaign and held a conference in Birmingham with the ILP. The membership of the University Society in 1913 was given as 26 members and 14 associates. The secretary was F. Knowles. In 1914 membership had grown to 32 with 11 associates and the secretary was Miss Joan Edghill. National membership in this period had grown from 784 in 1905 to 2015 in 1908 and 2627 in 1910. It continued to increase up to 1914 when it stood at 2786.

Clarion.

The importance of the weekly newspaper *Clarion* as an organising focus of social groups, dispenser of 'cheerful Socialism' and reporter of all aspects of the movement continued unabated until 1914.

The core of such activity was the cycling clubs and scouts for outdoor activity in the summer and the Social Club in the winter. In January 1911 a report from the Kings Norton Social Club stated that the movement there was spreading. The Clubhouse at 13a, Bournville Road was 'cosy' The Reading Circle re-commenced at 8pm on Saturday January 15th. with a lecture on *Political Economy for Plain People*. 'Chairs and other furniture, including members, are still wanted.' The same month the Birmingham Clarion Fellowship celebrated its tenth anniversary under the chairmanship of its fund secretary, Walter Field. Mrs. Gladys Ashton with her 'exquisite rendering of the songs she chose created a furore and took the honours. Mrs. Olive Kneeshaw was a good second.' In March 1911 a Bearwood Clarion Social Club was formed. 'All good Socialists in Smethwick, Harborne and Bearwood desirous of good fellowship' were invited to apply to G.H. Parker at St. Marys Road, Bearwood. The Kings Norton Social Club had closed during the summer, but in October it was announced that 'the re-decorated Club Room is now open.'

The Clarion Scouts in March 1911 were 'hard pressed financially'. They had considered taking a smaller room to leave more money for propaganda. They appealed to all Birmingham comrades for 'members and finance.' But this does not appear to have prevented the work going ahead. In the same month they reported outdoor meetings every Monday at 8pm at the corner of Steelhouse Lane and Corporation Street. They were 'not letting the agitation for school feeding rest' and promised 'some startling new moves soon.' In May the Scouts announced the availability of a new leaflet on the feeding of school children. In the same month they announced that all the money available in Birmingham had been spent and they were satisfied that 'they had kept many starving people just alive.' In June the Scouts announced that they were abandoning their headquarters at Stafford Street for the People's Hall in Hurst Street and that they were continuing with the feeding of school children agitation. The Scouts included girls as well as boys.

The success of the Clarion Van was greatly dependent on the support of the Scouts and the Cycling Clubs. In June 1911 Tom Groom had been present at a delegate meeting of Midland and Birmingham Unions for Clarion Cycling Clubs at Burton-on-Trent to discuss the Midland Clarion Van. It was decided that the Van should begin its mission in August. despite considerable financial arrears, under the auspices of the CCC's. A Committee of nine (three from each of the Unions) had been appointed and all secretaries were called on to inform the Committee of the amounts of their weekly guarantee.

The Van eventually got under way in July. In August it was reported that it had been a good month for the Van and in September that 'all debts to Clarion were cleared and the Midland van is now clear of debts.' By October there was a surplus of £15 which was going towards the cost of a new van and there was talk now of a Motor Van.

Of other matters receiving considerable coverage in *Clarion* during 1911, one was the amendment of the constitution of the Birmingham and District Socialist Representation Committee. Another was the great Easter Sunday demonstration in the Bull Ring on Votes for Women. In the summer and autumn there was much coverage of the formation and development of the BSP and the Birmingham Manifesto, which has already been discussed in the section on the BSP.

Clarion reports on activity in Birmingham during 1912 are unusually sparse. The Midland Clarion Van took the road in May and it was the 'much discussed' Motor Van, which all Clarionettes were invited to make their way to Burton-on-Trent to see opened by Leonard Hall. But, as in 1911, much of the Van's activity seems to have been in N. Staffs, Coventry and the Black Country.

The slump in Clarion activity seems to have been general, but in 1913, *Clarion* pronounced a revival. The Birmingham and District Union and the Aston CCC were active and there were now Motor Cycle

Notes in the paper as well as cycling news.

In April 1913 there were advertisements for a series of Clarion pamphlets such as *Socialism and the Poor, Socialism and the Middle Classes, Socialism and the Christian Tradition* (by Conrad Noel), *Why Women need Socialism* (by Julia Dawson) and two others which had particular application to Birmingham. One was *Socialism for Commercial Travellers* written by Norman Tiptaft and the other was *Socialism for Clerks*. In the 1908 Birmingham ILP Federation Handbook there was notice of a Commercial Travellers Socialist Society in Birmingham and also a Civil Service Socialist Society as well as a Caxton Socialist Fellowship. Tiptaft probably had a hand in the development of the Commercial Travellers Socialist Society as well as producing the pamphlet and it is a pleasure to record this pioneering Socialist activity by Tiptaft, since his later writings reveal no trace of his Socialist beginnings. Birmingham Socialists such as Hallas and Silvester were active in developing trade unionism among clerks and Hallas probably played an as yet unrecorded part in the development of this activity nationally. For instance, the Planet Insurance was advertised nationally in Clarion as a friendly society run by socialists. Its trustees included Tom Groom, Henry Brockhouse and H.T. Hallas of the ILP and Birmingham Socialist Centre. It was from the Planet offices that Eldred Hallas edited the Birmingham paper *The Torch* in 1912.

1913 brought news of the Birmingham Clarion Choral and Operatic Society whose director was George Painter and secretary Will Garman. They reported a most successful winter season with average attendance at rehearsals of about 50. But they would welcome more, particularly basses, tenors and contraltos. Rehearsals were at Murdock's Rooms, Carpenter Street. A matter relevant to the choir was the influence of Rutland Boughton. In August 1911 there had been a notice in *Clarion* from him stating that he was opposed to the Songs of Mary and since he had accepted the conductorship of the Clarion Vocal Union on condition that he chose the music, he asked Vocal Unions to drop these Songs. The basis of his objection was not given. Boughton, in 1911, left a post at the Birmingham School of Music, victimised, it seems, for his progressive political views. Boughton continued to live in, or near, Birmingham as he was a celebrity speaker for the Socialist Church in the 1913 season. But his connection with the Birmingham choir remains unclear. In September 1913 the Birmingham Clarion Choral and Operatic Society announced that rehearsals for the new winter season had begun and that it had an engagement for October. In December there was a call for all Clarionettes to be at the Fellowship of Musicians, Riley Hall, Constitution Hill on the 13th. when there would be a performance of *King Estmere* by Von Holst.

1913 was also a year in which Clarion Clubhouses were being widely discussed and this extended to both Birmingham and the Black Country. A Birmingham Clubhouse scheme was said to be 'proceeding space' in July with a provisional committee operating from the Aston Labour Club. A further report in September stated that the committee had had a busy time considering all the schemes submitted to it. They wanted a Clubhouse where they could spend Christmas. Readers were invited to send for shares either to Arthur Radford of Aston or to T.W. Stevens at Bearwood.

Birmingham continued to have music in 1914. A notice in January stated that the Birmingham Clarion Choir had had 'an accession of several new members, but, like Oliver Twist, we want more.' The concert on 13th. December had been 'enjoyable'. *King Estmere* and *Minnehaha* had been the two main pieces performed. Rutland Boughton's *Skeleton in Armour* was next on the board, 'so come and enjoy the feast.' Both the conductor and secretary remained the same, and it was, no doubt, this continuity of leadership which accounted for a relatively protracted period of musical activity in the Birmingham labour movement.

Problems were looming, however. In February, Walter Southgate, editing the *Clarion Yearbook*, complained that he had not received reports from the Birmingham or West Bromwich choirs. A further notice in April reported another concert at Riley Hall. The choir had also been invited to amalgamate with the Co-operative Choir in singing at the South African Deportees Demonstration at the Town Hall on the 23rd ... 'but owing to the short notice, members had other appointments and had to decline.'

> Why were we shelved until the last minute? The choir was formed to help the local Socialist movement let me impress on the Boot and Spur brigade. Do they want us or are we ever to rest and rust?

These dissatisfactions seem to have brought about a reorganisation in the summer. In August it was announced that the Birmingham CVU had secured new quarters at Priory Rooms, Old Square. The autumn session would open on 16th September. There was a new conductor, George Paritis (?) of 213 Galton Way, Warley. There was also a Concert Organiser, Miss C.J. Musgrove of 16 Lonsdale Road, Harborne, as well as a secretary, Bert Webber of 47 Durham Road, Sparkhill.

In November another change of conductor was announced. The new appointment was W.L. Nicholas of 86 Antrobus Road Handsworth and a meeting was being called for November 25th at Aston Labour Church for 'important business.' There were no other reports in 1914, however.

Fellowship, the Clarion Van and the Cycling Clubs occupied considerable space in *Clarion* during 1914. In January the annual Fellowship Reunion of the Birmingham CCC was announced with a list of the artists appearing. In February, cyclists from Hednesford, Wolverhampton, Coventry and thirty from Birmingham enjoyed a concert in Walsall organised by the Birmingham and District CCC.

In late February the Birmingham Clarion Fellowship, which Tom Groom had been actively promoting on a national scale, 'was duly launched.' They had 'met in the Cinderella Room at John Bright Street with a few veterans of the Clarion Fellowship Movement to revive that once glittering Fellowship.'

Also in February, preparations began for the Van season. A 'most representative meeting' had been held in Birmingham. The Vanner, Tom Jones, was congratulated on his report and engaged for the ensuing season. The secretary was changed from J. Hobson of Stoke to Tom Stevens of Bearwood. In March, the financial position was stated to be satisfactory and the season was to begin in April.

In March the Fellowship spirit was said to be 'forging ahead.' The Birmingham headquarters for Social Clubs was at County Chambers, Martineau Street and all organisations were entitled to send two delegates.

A rash of cycling notices appeared in March. The Birmingham CCC had met two of the deported South Africans at the Town Hall meeting. Aston asked, 'Is your cycle ready? Next week we hie to the lanes and fields.' Harborne CC reported a successful whist drive. Premier CC asked, 'Have you made up your mind about Shrewsbury?' Selly Oak asked, 'Whose for Shrewsbury?

Shrewsbury was a favourite national meeting point for Easter rallies to start off the cycling season, it being the town reckoned to be the nearest to the centre of England. Elaborate programmes were laid on. Tom Groom explained in his national cycling Notes that the first Shrewsbury Meet had been in 1900 when 200 – 300 had attended. The next had been 1908 when 1,080 had signed the Muster Roll. 1914 would be the biggest Meet ever. Cyclists would first go to Uriconium, the Roman city, near Shrewsbury.

The meet was duly held at Shrewsbury, but *Clarion* pictorial interest was in the Clarion Motor Cycling Club and the new national Clarion Van which was launched at Shrewsbury. A rather indistinct picture of the Van suggests that this was also a horse-drawn one and not a Motor Van.

At a subsequent meeting of the midlands Van committee, some dissatisfaction was expressed that the Van was not scheduled to visit the South Midlands that year. It was explained that last year the Van had covered 524 miles and experience had conclusively confirmed that the longer the Van stayed at a particular location, the greater the interest it aroused, and so a considerable amount of haulage was going to be avoided by covering only two Unions during 1914.

In the middle of May the last week of the Birmingham campaign of the Midland Van was reported. It began at the Blue Gates, Smethwick in wintry weather and was rained off altogether during the day. But in the evening 'a good crowd listened attentively, though the night was cold and cheerless. Collections and sales were poor and might have been better if the local comrades had turned up.' We hear much of the lovely summer weather in 1914, but the unusually wide coverage of the Midland Van in 1914 across the Black Country, into the Potteries and on to Derby, suggests that the wet and the cold played havoc with the programme that year.

The war brought the Van to a halt, although by then the season was nearing its end. Early in September, the Van Committee considered:

> '. . . it was futile to continue the propaganda work. It was agreed that the Vanner's services be utilised by his visiting the larger towns and helping the circulation of *Clarion*. But this he refuses to do. Clarionettes must therefore do it themselves. We have tried it in Birmingham and the results are worthwhile.'

So it looks as if the Vanner was anti-war, but the committee pro-war.

With the outbreak of war *Clarion* was reduced to twelve small pages with half front page advertisements 'Your King and Country Need You.' In the following weeks there were pages of letters both pro- and anti-war.

The movement nationally, as in Birmingham, split. Blatchford and most of the leading figures of the paper were pro-war, but although the paper continued throughout the war and after, its period of unique importance in the working class movement was at an end.

Socialist and Labour Churches.

The minutes of the main Birmingham Church end in 1909 virtually at the point when it was transformed into the Socialist Church; the Stirchley Labour Church programmes for 1912 – 14 have been dealt with in the previous section. There remains therefore only limited references in *Clarion* etc. with regard to the continuance of these Churches.

Aston Socialist Church met in Ruskin Hall, 145 Victoria Road during the 1911 – 12 season. It had met there since at least 1908. The Hall was the premises of the Aston Labour Club and Institute, advertised in the 1908 Birmingham ILP Handbook as 'lit with electricity and well heated.'

Birmingham Socialist Church continued to meet at Bristol Street Schools where, in November 1911, Julia Varley spoke on Feeding Destitute Children. Notices for the Socialist Church appeared regularly in *Justice* during 1912, but disappeared in 1913. But if there was a lull in 1913, revival took place in the 1913 – 14 season when the Church took over the Birmingham Repertory Theatre for its lectures. In October Eldred Hallas spoke on 'Social Righteousness;' in November, Dr. Marion Phillips, secretary of the Women's Labour League, spoke on 'Patriotism and International Relations,' and in December Norman Tiptaft was the speaker on 'What to do with Agitators.' The policy of getting away from Bristol Street seems to have paid off and the Repertory Theatre was still being used in April 1914 when the young G.D.H. Cole was the speaker on 'The Greater Unionism', developing the early elements of Guild Socialism.

After the outbreak of war *Clarion* carried notices for Aston Labour and Socialist Church and for the Birmingham Socialist Church at Bristol Street schools.

The main Birmingham Socialist Church came to an end in 1915 when it became – or merged with – the Birmingham Socialist Society. A notice in *Clarion* of 1st October advertised that the Winter Session of the Birmingham Socialist Society (late Socialist Church) would open on October 3rd. and a fortnight later stated that its meetings were at Bristol Street schools with Fred Hughes speaking on 'Looking Forward.'

Aston Socialist Church continued until at least March 1915, but that is the last notice of it found in *Clarion*.

Birmingham Socialist Centre

The Report for 1911 – 12 gave pride of place to the Socialist representation on the enlarged City Council. Seven members of the Centre had been nominated and Harrison Barrow (St. Martins and Deritend), George Shann (Selly Oak), and Eldred Hallas (Duddeston and Nechells) had been successful. The four unsuccessful candidates had been T.F. Fathers (Acocks Green), A.J. Smith (Aston) and Leonard Hall and Fred Hughes (Small Heath). Three other labour members had been elected so that the Labour group on the Council now totalled six. The first fruits of this increased Socialist representation and the current industrial movement had been wage increases for the lower paid municipal workers in health, parks, tramways, gas, public works etc. The railway and transport strikes of the summer of 1911 and the coal strike of the spring of 1912 had also been symptomatic of these two advances in politics and industrial organisation.

The Socialist Centre had joined with the Citizen's Committee to protest against arrests under the Mutiny Act of 1797 over the employment of troops to 'maintain order' during industrial disputes.

The Bread Fund, which had been so beneficial in the depression three or four years previously, had been revived.

Under 'Literary and the Press,' the Centre recorded a notable contribution of leaflets and posters on the maldistribution of the national income with special emphasis on the rise in the cost of living while wages remained stable. There had been a large number of leaflets on School Clinics. Eldred Hallas' pamphlet *Is Socialism Possible?* had been published and Leonard Hall's broadsheet on *Industrial Unionism*. Some members, notably Hubert Humphreys, had done good work through the playgoers club connected with the WEA.

There had been five ordinary meetings of the Centre all of which had been badly attended, but well reported. There had been two national conferences in Birmingham — The ILP at Easter and the Labour Party in January. There had been public demonstrations at each. Other town hall meetings had been the annual demonstration of the LRC with George Lansbury and Leonard Hall and a BSP rally in February with Hyndman, Hallas and Hall. There had also been the annual demonstration of the Socialist Church at the Hippodrome with George Lansbury, Fred Hughes and the Rev. Arnold Pinchard. Support for the Suffragists was carefully phrased. 'The Centre has consistently supported the removal of sexual disability from the Parliamentary franchise.'

The strain of maintaining its traditional co-ordinating role in this period of rapid development and conflict is made clear in the conclusions of the report which had begun by noting a serious decline in membership of the Centre which was put down to abnormal causes and a larger than usual number of members moving to other districts; it ended by reporting a financial shortfall:

> This, together with decreased membership is not due to the lack of progress of Socialism, but to diversion of effort to other organisations, especially the new party with branches in the city (the BSP — GB). It is short sighted as well as futile to deplore this. It is obvious that for some time to come there will be two more or less definitely opposed methods of expressing Socialist principles and it is probably as well that each has its organised force.
>
> It may be timely to reaffirm the principles of the Centre which is purely a local body to assist, organise and focus the energies of all Socialists in the common propaganda of principles and securing representation of those principles especially in our local administration. For fifteen years we have rendered this assistance by maintaining a permanent, central office open to all seeking information on Labour and Socialist questions., and never has there been more scope for activities such as ours.

The 16th. Annual Report for 1912 – 13 began by noting that the membership decline had continued in the early part of the year, but this had been reversed and the year ended with an increased membership of fourteen to 168.

The previous AGM had laid down a programme of activities which included lectures on *Syndicalism* and the *Socialisation of Land, Mines and Railways*; special Hoarding Advertisements; an exhaustive discussion on alternative policies open to Socialists; and a series of Tutorial Lectures on Socialism. The hoarding advertisements had not materialised because of lack of funds and the lectures had been abandoned from lack of support. The rest of the programme had been carried out. The lecture on Syndicalism had been delivered at the Midland Institute by Tom Mann, with Rev. Pinchard in the chair, to 'a large and interested audience.' But the expenses of the meeting had been very heavy. The lecture on 'Land, Mines and the Railways' had, after several delays, been given at the Town Hall by L.G. Chiozza Money M.P. on 1st April 1913 with the Rev. James Adderley in the chair. The Discussions on Socialist Policy were reported as follows:

> . . . although only moderately attended (these) have been of considerable interest and value. They opened with a two-nights debate between Mr. Leonard Hall and Mr. C.E. Smith in which were reviewed the respective merits of (A) industrial and political action and (B) reformist and revolutionist politics. The debate disclosed wide divergences as to tactics, but a large measure of agreement on fundamental principles. The publication of Mr. Hilaire Belloc's book — 'The Servile State' — emphasised some of Mr. Hall's contentions, and also opened new controversial issues; and two evenings in December were devoted to an examination of Mr. Belloc's case. The discussion showed that our members are very little perturbed by this new attack on our position.

Other Special Propaganda Efforts in which the Centre had co-operated with other Labour organisations in promoting had been: the Protest against Mutiny Act Prosecutions in April 1912 at which J.C. Wedgwood MP had been the principal speaker and a meeting in the Bull Ring in consequence of the Lord Mayor's refusal to allow the town hall to be used for that meeting; a May Day demonstration in the town hall addressed by George Lansbury MP; a Trade Union demonstration in July in favour of the Eight Hour Day; a BSP town hall meeting in November with Tom Mann; a War against Poverty Conference in the Association Hall during the same month with Sidney Webb under the joint auspices of the ILP and the Fabian Society.

The Centre had waged a steady campaign against existing methods of Municipal Financing. A pamphlet by C.E. Smith — *Municipal Socialism and the Rates* had been issued and a special committee appointed at the previous AGM had submitted a report in October which had been extensively reported in the Labour press and also the *Birmingham News*; the digest in the latter had been reprinted and circulated among city councillors and had been a major topic of the local elections in November.

Press controversies had been provoked, and the discussions on the Earnings of Capital, Municipal Music, Municipal Hostels for Women, Railway Nationalisation, and Co-Partnership and Industrial War, stood out. W.E. Merry had conducted 'with marked ability', a little paper circulating in the ward called *Rotton Park Forward*; Eldred Hallas had edited *The Torch* but had been obliged to relinquish it 'for financial reasons', and R.C. Woodward had edited the Soho Co-operative *Wheatsheaf* throughout the year. Edward Cadbury had published his account of the Bournville business as 'An experiment in Industrial Organisation', and Norman Tiptaft had published a volume of short stories and sketches entitled '*God's Englishman*'.

The report stressed the attention paid to Registration work during the previous year and the dividends it had paid at the local elections. Three members of the Centre had contested these elections, but failed narrowly, as had other Labour candidates. But Councillor Kneeshaw had been re-elected in Rotton Park with a majority increased from 12 to 599. C.E. Smith had again been appointed City Auditor without opposition.

The most notable achievement in Administrative Work was recorded as the revised system of school meals and a really adequate beginning to school clinics. Improvements in school breakfasts were 'satisfactory'; but these limited improvements had led to a rise in the rates which had been an issue in the local elections when the Unionists had tried to create a panic. On the Council, Harrison Barrow had opposed a proposal to vest the Finance Committee with a practical veto on the expenditure of other committees. Eldred Hallas had carried a resolution instructing all employing committees to prepare returns showing how many of their employees received less than 26/-d. a week and why. Hallas and George Shann had supported the claims of teachers and school caretakers to increased remuneration, but had been unsuccessful.

The 1913 Report had a special section on Research Work. It reported the secretary, Fred Hughes, with other members engaged in 'important research work' with the Fabian Society's Committee on the Control of Industry and 'valuable information had been gathered with reference to Co-operative and Municipal Management.' The Report stressed the increasing efficiency of the Centre as a reference library with its system of press cuttings, and the increasing use being made of these facilities by the Labour movement. The Centre had been especially useful to the trade unions during the year in explaining the National Insurance Act and inducing workers to select their trade unions as Approved Societies under the Act, combining this with a demand for improved wages and conditions. George Shann and Julia Varley were mentioned as 'exceedingly active' in these matters.

The April 1914 Report stated that the year 1913–14 had been extremely difficult and membership had dropped to 110. Fred Hughes had resigned as secretary to become assistant secretary of the National Union of Clerks and he had moved to London. The new secretary of the Centre was Richard Clemence.

On Press and Literary Propaganda there had been 'a steady and persistent campaign waged in the local press'. W.E. Merry continued to edit *Rotton Row Forward* and had been joined by Norman Tiptaft with *Soho Forward* and George Shann's *Selly Oak Forward*.

Three membership meetings had been held. The first was a lecture by F.E. Sandbach, president of the University Fabian Society, on 'Socialism in Germany'; the second had considered Fred Hughes' resignation and appointed his successor; the third had discussed the desirability of continued affiliation to the Labour Representation Committee and had decided to defer the matter for six months.

A series of meetings had been held in the central area of the city consequent upon a motion moved by Councillor Hallas at a Centre meeting. Meetings with other Socialist and Labour organisations had included a meeting at the Midland Institute protesting at police brutality in Dublin and Cornwall; a BSP meeting with Ben Tillett; a demonstration at the town hall addressed by two of the South African deportees; a town hall meeting of the LRC protesting against Conscription and increasing expenditure on Naval Armaments; and another town hall meeting in support of the victims of the Dublin Lock-out at which George Lansbury, James Larkin and William Haywood were the main speakers.

At the municipal elections George Shann retained his seat at Selly Oak; Tom Hackett won a seat from the Unionists in Rotton Park and J. Kesterton secured a seat on Smethwick Borough Council. Norman Tiptaft, however, had been defeated in Soho ward by 235 votes and T.F. Fathers had again been unsuccessful in Acocks Green.

The outstanding municipal achievement had been the extension of the School Clinics. The Labour demand for free dental and medical treatment had been defeated, however, and a scale of charges imposed to conform with the provisions of the Medical Treatment Act of 1909. 'But in spite of this formal compliance with the Act, it may be claimed that no one in future will be debarred from treatment because of these charges.' This had justified the anticipation in last year's Centre Report that 'Birmingham will shortly have one of the best systems for dealing with the ailments of children at school.' This Report had also said 'This is a result of Socialist propaganda of which we may well be proud.'

The accounts showed a deficit of £10, due not to the falling off of income at £203, but a failure of it to keep pace with growing expenditure.

The 18th. Annual Report for 1914 – 15 was the last. It reported serious curtailment of the work due to the war. Richard Clements, the secretary, had resigned to join the Army Service Corps. He wrote that 'he was proud to think that he could take such a step and carry with him the best wishes of all the members.' The Committee had therefore recommended the suspension of activities during the war due to a lack of public interest in propaganda work and also a lack of finance. The three main political parties had decided that there should be no local elections during the war and 'Labour and Socialists were loyally abiding by the agreement.'

The Independent Labour Party

From the Labour revival after the Boer War, the ILP established itself in Birmingham, as in many other parts of the country, as the main Labour/Socialist organisation. Rent almost asunder by the violent controversies that would have committed the party to Marxist-Socialist theory and practice, the Fabian-Socialist leadership and the left-centre majority of the rank and file managed to retain sufficient cohesion to build an impressively wide and stable working class presence in the city. This is demonstrated by the 1908 *Birmingham and District ILP Federation Handbook*, which was either the only yearbook printed, or the only one to survive.

From the annual report by the secretary, John Beard, in the *Handbook*, we learn that at the beginning of 1908 the Federation had 20 branches affiliated to it with 939 members and at the end of the year the branches had increased to 22 and total membership was almost 1,300. *The Handbook* listed the meetings of every ILP branch from May to September 1909. Smaller branches, such as All Saints, which met every other Friday at The Flat at the corner of Lodge Road and Icknield Street, met indoors, but one is astonished at the number of branches which maintained the tradition of open-air public meetings, many of them throught the year. Such branches, and their meeting points, where given, were: Aston & N. Birmingham (Gosta Green), Bordesley (Bordesley Green), Central (Six Ways, Cregoe Street), East (Tram Terminus, Alum Rock Road), Erdington, Handsworth (corner of Whitehall Road and Soho Road), Harborne (the Junction, Harborne), Kings Heath, Kings Norton and Stirchley, Murdock (Cable Tram Terminus), Nechells (Nechells Green), Rotton Park (corner of Aberdeen Street and Dudley Road), Selly Oak, Sparkhill, Small Heath (Park Gates, Golden Hillock Road), Smethwick and S. Birmingham. So important was this out-of-door speaking that a section of the annual report brought this advice:

> Another innovation introduced into our propagandist methods was continuous outdoor meetings sustained for the week. These meetings resulted in larger crowds, better collections and sales of literature, and from every point of view can be generally recommended in preference to weekly meetings.

This advice was given at a time when Weekly Missions were being experimented with; branches participating in these Missions of nightly meetings included Aston, N. Birmingham, Bordesley Green, E. Birmingham, Sparkbrook and Sparkhill. Most of the speakers were local ones, the names recurring most frequently being Leonard Hall, Fred Hughes and G.R. Shepherd, but every local councillor and party activist appears somewhere in the speakers lists. There was a smattering of ouside speakers such as Kenneth Holden (Labour & Socialist candidate for Stratford-on-Avon), and Sydney Stranks (late Parliamentary candidate for Croydon). There is a lack of women speakers, Miss M. Smith BA being the only local one, although Margaret Bondfield and Mrs. Bruce Glazier appear under Smethwick's list at Town Hall meetings. A separate list of speakers available gives 65 local names and addresses, and it is clear that every party activist was expected to take his place on the hustings.

The activity of the ILP after 1908 is recorded from the Federation Minutes of 1909 to 1912 and the Federation Finance Committee Minutes from 1912 to 1915. Officers of the Federation in 1909 were Councillor Frank Spires (chairman), John Beard (secretary), A.J. Smith (propaganda secretary), Councillor Fathers (minute secretary), and W. Shirley (treasurer). In addition there was a Council, which included Leonard Hall. The Federation held quarterly Conferences and an AGM, the decisions of which the Council was expected to carry out. The first quarterly Conference of 1909 was held in April. Predictable policy motions were passed — from Smethwick supporting the Minority Report of the Royal Commission on the Poor Laws, and from Small Heath regretting that Birmingham Council had not take up the provisions of the 1906 Education (Provisions of School Meals) Act, and protests that some employers were demanding compulsory military service as a condition of employment. There were also two internal movement matters. The first was a motion from E. Birmingham stating that 'it was not desirable that ILP members be members of any other political organisations admitting Liberals, Liberal-Unionists or Conservatives.' By 32 votes to 9 this was amended to read 'It is advisable that any member of the ILP strictly reserves his political independence if he joins any organisation that admits members of the Liberal, Liberal-Unionist or Conservative parties.' The second was a 29 – 18 vote deprecating the decision of the newly-named Socialist Church to use the word 'Church' in relation to Socialism.

The quarterly and special conferences were largely concerned with electoral work and influencing the LRC in the city. For instance, a special conference had endorsed Fred Hughes as Parliamentary candidate for Bordesley and an ILP National Administrative Council decision not to accept this, was deplored in December 1909. The same month there was an annual conference of Midland ILP branches where it was 'noted' that a decision to boycott Leonard Hall at a demonstration in December 1909 had been 'due to a misunderstanding and this had now been cleared up.'

In 1910 the vexed question of the actions of the Labour MPs in Parliament was raised with regard to the abolition of the veto of the House of Lords. Here it was resolved that if this matter was not pressed by the Liberal government then the Labour MPs 'shall take steps to force the question to an early and vital issue.' In July 1910 a quarterly conference gave a 'cautious welcome to the Greater Birmingham Bill', and, after an 'interesting discussion' an amendment requesting that Proportional Representation be embodied in the Bill was lost.

In September 1910 a Special Conference of the Birmingham Federation had been held to discuss a very detailed programme of Municipal Socialism to present to the new, enlarged city council. This had been drafted by the local LRC. It was:

1. Land to be acquired by the Corporation to (a) carry out Housing Schemes on the lines of a Garden City with plots of land for allotments to be let at rents to cover costs of construction and maintenance only.
   (b) the erection of Municipal Common Lodging Houses and
   (c) for the establishment of a Municipal Farm, Allotments and Small Holdings.
   (d) to hold against future needs thus ensuring that the increased values created by the growth of the city shall be secured to the people.
2. The extension of the Tramway system to all the suburbs. Workmen's cars to run until 9 am, the blind to travel free and children of school age at half price.
3. Enforcement of the provisions of Acts of Parliament in favour of the people which the present authorities have failed to carry out.
4. Municipal Employment — A maximum working week of 54 hours at trade union rates of pay for all Municipal employees and the Direct Employment of Labour wherever possible. Where work is done by contract the Fair Wages clause to be strictly complied with. One day's holiday a week for all Police and Asylum attendants. Maintenance of the Right of Appeal of all corporation workmen to the Committees.
   Opposition to all unreasonable and excessive advances of salaries to highly paid officials.
5. Comprehensive Superannuation Schemes for all municipal employees.

6. Extension of Municipal Trading: — Milk, Bread, Meat, Coal, Laundries etc. etc. this being the only guarantee of purity and quality and of prices which will bring these services within the reach of the people.

7. Provision of Public Lavatories.

8. Hospitals, Blind, and Deaf & Dumb Institutions to be taken over and conducted by the Municipality.

9. The establishment of a Municipal Bank.

10. Poor Law Administration. The General Mixed Workhouse and the existing Board of Guardians should be abolished and the power and responsibility should be imposed on:

(a) The local health authority for the searching out and necessary treatment of all forms of sickness.

(b) The local educational authority for all children of school age needing public provision of maintenance.

(c) The Asylum Committee for the charge of the weakminded and imbeciles.

(d) The local Pensions Committee for all the necessitous aged and invalided.

(e) Grants in aid to be paid out of the national funds for all these services and allocated in such a manner as to secure the most efficient and uptodate service from every authority.

(f) All local services under the full control, not of any nominated or co-opted bodies, but of the directly elected representatives of the people.

11. Education. Ability to learn being dependent on physique, the school should be in the first place a health centre.

Provision of a midday meal per day for every school child when required, at cost price . . .

Provision of baths and gymnasiums . . .

. . . Immediate provision of School Clinics.

Mental training on a scientific basis of individual development.

12. Abolition of the Aldermanic Bench.

13. Prohibition of street trading by children.

14. Finance. All municipal enterprise to be conducted on the basis of use rather than profit . . . Where profits are made, such profits to be used to further the foregoing proposals, not for the reduction of rates.

The ILP Federation AGM in March 1911 called on the Lord Mayor of Birmingham to arrange a town hall meeting to 'Promote the Peace of the World by the future policy of the English speaking peoples and to approve a policy of International Arbitration.' Mrs. Arnot Robinson addressed this AGM on Women's Enfranchisement and Adult Suffrage; we learn only that 'this was followed by a lengthy and interesting discussion.'

The quarterly conference in May 1911 favoured the principle of State Insurance but 'deplored the contributory basis of the bill and the exclusion of widows and orphans.'

In December 1911, Comrade Fathers had his knuckles rapped for 'accepting nomination at Handsworth without consulting the Handsworth branch.'

In February 1912 the Federation Council was instructed to attempt to organise summer outdoor meetings at Northfield, Sparkhill, Bordesley Green, Aston, Selly Oak, Smethwick, Balsall Heath and Small Heath. Other branches, such as Kings Norton were 'making their own arrangements.'

The coal strike in the winter of 1912 led to a rise in coal prices and a Harborne resolution demanded that 'in view of the unscrupulous manipulation of the prices of coal and the bare-faced robbery of the poor, that Birmingham City Council should establish a municipal coal supply.'

At the AGM in March 1912 it was reported that the Rev. R.W. Cummings was hoping to conduct a Socialist Crusade in Birmingham in July and Mr. Garman requested assistance in forming a Socialist choir for Birmingham and district. The increasing militancy of women was reflected at this AGM and continued throughout the year. There were two resolutions on this subject by Fred Hughes. The first condemned the refusal of the government to 'concede the demand of the Labour Party to enfranchise all men and women.' The second attacked the Labour MPs:

> As the government brought forward proposals applying to men only and afforded no guarantee that women would receive the vote, the Parliamentary Labour Party should vote against the government until women are included and, if necessary institute a policy of relentless opposition to the government with the object of forcing them from office.

In April 1912 a Federation Council meeting expressed sorrow at the death of Comrade Berry, the Trades Council secretary. A letter from Handsworth branch requested that the ILP co-operate with other bodies in opposing the 'Don't Shoot' prosecutions. It was also reported that the Federation had joined the Citizens' Committee which had prompted a successful 'Don't Shoot' protest, but this had been held in the Bull Ring because the Lord Mayor had refused to allow the town hall to be used. In connection with the coal strike, 3,000 loaves had been distributed by joint Socialist effort to raise a bread fund.

In June a circular from Councillor Hallas was ordered to lie on the table. This presumably was a BSP communication and is one of the few references to the British Socialist Party and Syndicalism to find its way on to the records of the ILP. At this meeting it was announced that the ILP had lost one of its Birmingham notables when Hubert Humphreys resigned.

In July it was the women's question again. Admiration was expressed at the protest of George Lansbury in the House of Commons over the forcible feeding of women and disgust of the ill-natured rebuke of Lansbury by Ramsay Macdonald in a letter to the *Daily Chronicle*. Such conduct was causing members to leave the party, it was claimed. At this meeting protests were also registered to Birmingham Education Committee for 'allowing the Navy League to enter the schools and push their propaganda. This violates the principle of non-bias in schools.'

From October to the end of the year local protest against the inactivity of Labour MPs on the Women's Franchise Question intensified. This began with a protest at the Franchise and Registration Bill 'trying to trick the advocates of votes for women' and asking Labour MPs to vote against it at the third reading. Then came another protest at the absence of a declaration that the Labour Party would vote against the third reading. This led on to the following exchange of correspondence. First a letter from J.S. Middleton, the national assistant secretary of the Labour Party to J.W. Kneeshaw:

> My dear Kneeshaw
> I have to acknowledge yours of the 11th. with resolution enclosed. We

note your Council approves the Party's attitude towards the circular issued regarding Woman's Suffrage policy. It is difficult to understand, however, why your Council is dissatisfied with the statement that the Party is determined to press for the inclusion of women in the Franchise Bill. You must allow the Parliamentary Party to shape their courses of action after deliberate discussion so long as they do not run counter to Conference decisions and pledges to their own constituencies. Would it not be better, if you do not believe the Party are intent on securing Woman's Suffrage, to say so? If you do believe they are intent on securing the Vote for women, you must allow them (to) handle the Parliamentary situation. It is doubtful whether your Council have any conception of what would follow any premature declaration by the Party.

The finance committee authorised the following reply:

Dear Middleton, I am requested by our Council to reply to your letter of November 13th. You ask if we do not believe the Party are intent on securing Womans' Suffrage. That is not the point. The point is *What are they prepared to do to secure it?* Whilst there are some members of the Party who we believe are prepared to go to the length of voting against the third reading of the Franchise Bill, there are others — and not a few either — who are not prepared to do *anything* that will endanger the position of the Government. Mr. Albert Stanley took the opportunity the other week of declaring from a *Liberal* platform that *he* would do nothing to endanger the Government. Is not *that* a rather premature declaration? If we may be candid — and you invite us to be — we *do not trust* the Party on this question and we are *not* prepared after their actions in connection with the Insurance Bill to leave them to do (what they think best?)

No reply to this letter is recorded.

From the end of 1912, the Minutes of the Finance Committee of the Birmingham ILP Federation are available and they immediately demonstrate that control of the purse strings brought with it political influence far beyond the purely financial. For instance, as we have seen, the above exchange of letters was authorised by the Finance Committee. Another illustration is that in December the Finance Committee received a letter from the Birmingham Fabians asking how best they could co-operate with the ILP. They were advised to affiliate to the Federation.

The advent of the BSP and Syndicalism brought a noticeable hardening of political attitudes. In January 1913 a letter from the BSP asking the Federation to co-operate with an Adult Suffrage Bull Ring demonstration would, in earlier years have been agreed without question; now it was resolved to take no action.

In February 1913, Sparkhill asked the Finance Committee to consider standing a candidate at a city by-election. Not content with stating whether finance would, or would not, be available for this contest, the Finance Committee laid down an organisational principle that no future contests would be authorised where sufficient preparations had not been made. It seems as though the Federation Council was voluntarily abdicating its powers on these matters for, in the same month, the Finance Committee, at the request of the Council, considered the possible formation of a Ladywood branch and resolved to let the matter stand for the present. A further resolution determined to concentrate on branches which were likely to contest elections. At the same time, efforts were made to start a strategic Central branch, and notices asking for support were to be placed in the *Labour Leader, Daily Citizen* and the *Daily Herald*. The Finance Committee's support was also sought in the mounting of a Health Week in Birmingham. The original intention was to confine the scope of the event to the habits of the poor, but the Finance Committee wanted to broaden it.

On the other hand, the increasing power of the Finance Committee could have been a reflection of the crisis in the ILP which afflicted the organisation from the second half of 1913. The main problem was the continuing dissatisfaction with the Parliamentary performance of the Labour MPs, and the organisational structure of the party which effectively limited rank and file control. The Labour Party held an annual conference, but this was of delegates of organisations affiliated to the local Labour Representation Committees. The question was complicated by the fact that the leading members of the Labour Party — Ramsay Macdonald, Snowden, Arthur Henderson etc. were also individual members of the ILP who were all moving from being youthful militants to respectable-responsible middle aged 'statesmen'.

The rot had begun in Birmingham in February 1913, when the Northfield branch took a decision to withdraw from the ILP and form a Socialist Society with members of the 'late BSP' and some Fabians. But, together with increased left militancy, there was also increased political apathy. In April there had been a special meeting of the Aston branch to consider the future. Only two members had attended, and a decision had been taken to close the branch.

In May 1913 a special Finance Committee meeting was called to review the state of the Party. Present were Mrs. Williams and Messrs Passey, Simpson, Neale, Tate, Margetts, Gittens, Greenway, Holloway, Sankey, and Watkins. Also, presumably, George Cook, who usually signed the minute book. Messrs Austin and Spires had also been invited 'in view of their past experience.' The meeting heard that the Party had consistently declined over the past three years from 25 branches to 15. Four years before, 58 comrades had been prepared to speak in the open-air; now it was down to 17. After a long discussion the meeting was adjourned at 10 pm. The next week the subject was renewed and the following resolutions passed:

1. A reunion of old and new members in September on a Saturday afternoon, to take the form of a Tea and Reunion. Philip Snowden, Keir Hardie or some other figure of importance would be asked to take part.
2. All branches to make Reports from special headings drawn up.
3. Branches to be asked to supply a list of members lapsed over the past three years and these to be invited to the Reunion. Mr. Spires volunteered to pay the postage on these.
4. Spires also volunteered to form a branch at Acocks Green, if a list of former members was provided.
5. An extension of the *Rotton Park Forward* was discussed and the secretary reported that this had already been discussed by Selly Oak and Handsworth branches.
6. The formation of a Literature Committee for house-to-house and other sales.
7. A Roll of Honour for collectors with the best record to be drawn up.
8. Visiting Committees to deal with lapsed members.

June was occupied in making arrangement for the Re-union. In July, the politics of the question were addressed. After a long discussion, a resolution of strong condemnation of the existing policy of the Labour Party was passed and the NAC was requested to take steps to ensure a more vigorous policy. Failing this, the NAC was asked to arrange a vote of all ILP branches regarding continued affiliation to the Labour Party. The same meeting was told that six former members of the Aston branch were willing to form a branch in All Saints ward and they were authorised to spend 5/-d. on an advertisement in the *Citizen* asking for members. Reports from branches were also accepted on the Coming of Age of the ILP.

At the end of August arrangements for the Coming of Age celebrations, which now seemed to be taking precedence of the Reunion, were authorised. Keir Hardie had agreed to speak at a Conference and also to visit branches. Cook was to chair the meeting. Spires was to speak on the local history of the ILP, and Keir Hardie would follow with Reminiscences of the ILP in the Country. Another national speaker F.C. Jowett was to be asked.to speak on the strict independence of the ILP in the parliamentary policy of the Labour Party. Fathers was to move a resolution to that effect and Passey was to second it. The Conference was to end with another resolution on securing the return of Labour councillors at the November local elections, the election of George Shann for East Birmingham in the parliamentary elections and for the Building of the ILP.

Unfortunately there was no record of any Finance Committee meeting in October and so no report of the Conference. Even more unfortunately, the Finance Committee minutes peter out at the end of 1913 and so we are unable to follow the fortunes of the ILP to the outbreak of war.

W. J. DAVIS, *Founder of the Brassworkers' Society, and a member of the T.U.C.'s Parliamentary Committee for over twenty years*

J. V. STEVENS, *President 1887–9 of Birmingham Trades Council*

Announcement Lloyd George Riot

The Ghosts of the Slain

R. L. Outhwaite: *The Ghosts of the Slain: A Vision of the Future,* with drawings by Joseph E. Southall, published by The National Labour Press, Manchester (1915).

Chapter Twenty-Four
THE WOMEN

The Economic & Social Condition of Women

It would be presumptious in these days for a man to attempt to write a
history of the women's movement; this women must do for themselves.
But there are special reasons accounting for increased social and political
activity of half the human race at the turn of the century which made
them more 'visible' and must be recorded here.

In the first place, the elemental forces rivetting the chains of women's
double oppression were being weakened. An enormously high death rate
gave biological as well as cultural justification to the ceaseless round of
child birth and child care throughout the reproductive period of a
woman's life which either killed her or reduced her to old age at 40.
Where the life of the vast majority of men was one of unremitting and
exhaustive physical toil for twelve hours of each day (including, usually,
a long walk to and from work), the ceaseless chores of washing, cooking,
cleaning and mending constituted a virtually inescapable division of
labour between husband and wife rendering female participation in the
labour movement almost impossible. If the working class male militant
had to be an exceptional man, the woman participant had to be a *very*
special woman.

By 1900 these circumstances were beginning to change. Death rates per
1000 in Birmingham moved as follows:

1890–94	1895–99	1900–04	1905–09	1910–14
20.7	20.3	19.3	16.9	14.4

And falling death rates were followed by falling birth rates:

32.7	33.7	31.4	28.7	26.5

Job opportunities for women were widening slightly, so that while, as we
have seen, the increase in schoolmistresses and nurses reflected little more
than the increase in population, clerical work did offer widening
opportunties. Female clerks in Birmingham rose from 41 in 1871 to 2687
in 1901. The advertisement of a primitive vacuum cleaner in a British
Socialist Party concert programme is a reminder that labour saving
inventions were also on the way.

Further straws in the wind were the better educational·standards of
both men and women which began to come through in the 1880s and
1890s as a result of the 1870 Education Act, and the limited emancipation
of the Edwardian era both in ideas and facilities (e.g. cycling) and the
development of the Women's Movement.

All this contributed to, but does not explain, the key role of women
during the years of the Great Unrest 1910–14. Women chainmakers in
the Black Country were the catalyst for the great movements which

spread to women workers in Birmingham and fuelled the mass strikes of the semi-skilled and unskilled throughout the area.

To find the underlying reasons for this one must start with the general condition of women in Birmingham. It has been lamented that there is no general study of poverty in Birmingham equivalent to the great studies of Booth for London and Rowntree for York. But the position is different with regard to the condition of working women, for here we have the unique study of working women carried out between 1904 and 1907 by Edward Cadbury, M. Cecile Matheson and George Shann published as *Women's Work and Wages*. The aims of this work were:

1. In one large city to give a complete survey of the conditions under which women are earning their livelihood ...
2. To provide some definite standard of comparison so that future investigators may be able to ascertain what progress has been made ...
3. To ascertain to what extent the present industrial and social conditions are helping forward or retarding the physical, mental and moral condition of the workers.
4. To indicate upon what lines they think reformers will obtain the best results in their attempts to raise and brighten the lives of those who are the future mothers of our race.

The material for the book came from personal interviews with nearly 6000 working women, interviews with about 400 trade union secretaries, managers and foremen, and interviews and correspondence with employers, members and officers of girls' organisations etc.

The first chapter reviews legislating affecting women workers up to the consolidation of the Factories and Workshops Act of 1901 and draws attention to the various strands of interests promoting or opposing such measures. These included humanitarian support for the restriction of hours of work and entry for women to dangerous or offensive trades; trade unionists who believed that such measures would eventually benefit men; trade unionists whose support for such measures was motivated mainly by a desire to restrict job opportunities for women and thus protect mens' wages and jobs. Opponents of such legislation included uncaring employers, and some Women's Rights activists who saw such relieving measures as a plot to restrict the sphere of women's work.

The book then turns to the general distribution of women workers as given in the 1901 Census. This has already been dealt with in this work in the chapter on the Great Depression and only additional figures will be given here. Of the total female population over ten years of age, 38% were at work. Most girls, it was found, 'drifted' into their first jobs from ignorance of alternative work, mental inertia, poor physique or lack of power to discriminate or even understand the advantages or disadvantages of different trades. Another cause was the economic one of taking work which was initially better paid e.g. unskilled, heavier, dangerous or obnoxious trades rather than work with prospects which entailed training. All choices, however, were heavily dependent on the section of the working class from which the girl came.

For the overwhelming majority of girls, once they were in work, the over-riding consideration was 'to keep themselves respectable.' But whether 'respectability' was attainable was largely dependent on this initial choice. The 'sectionalism' of the girls tended to be reinforced in the workplace. Warehouse girls, for instance, whose work was cleaner and might involve some clerical duties tended not to mix with the other factory girls. Similarly, there were divisions between girls on different processes. One employer claimed that he had been frustrated from opening a factory canteen by lacquerers refusing to sit with 'dippers.' A summary of the views of girls in the metal trades states:

> The majority tell you that 'the work is alright and they have no complaints to make.' They accept it as a kind of fate, never think of trying to understand their legal safeguards, and when an accident happens, rarely of their own initiative claim compensation. They are afraid of any new teaching or suggestion that could by any possibility offend the master. There seems to be a general vague idea that the work must be as it is, that 'what is to be will be', be it accident, infection or any other misfortune; that it is better rather to bear those ills we have than fly to others we know not of.
> On the other hand this acquiescence in monotony, danger or disease breeds an enviable freedom from worry and anxiety. The one dread is . to be out of work or on short time.

The subjection of women was, however, firmly rooted in their economic exploitation. An analysis of the wages of the 6000 Birmingham women under consideration covered 137 industries sub-divided into no less than 546 grades. An average wage was calculated for married women in factories 'for every grade of work ranging from bottle-washing or rag-sorting to gold laying-on and lacquering.' This average came to 9/1d per week (page 227). This amount was less than the subsistence level i.e. it was insufficient to keep a woman in food, clothing and shelter. This average was for a full week's work and it must be borne in mind that factory work was usually better paid than workshop or outwork, and that married women workers were older and often better paid because more reliable than single women. This figure of 9/1d. challenges a more general assumption that women's wages averaged 10/d. a week in Birmingham. It is likely that when the above considerations are taken into account the average wage for all full-time working women was around 8/-d a week, although considerable numbers of women earned more than this.

One of the main excuses buttressing this injustice has always been that most women do not need to work and that they work for 'pin money'. Cadbury Matheson and Shann (henceforward CM & S) examined the need for married women to work in Birmingham. According to the 1901 Census, 35% (22000 out of 62000) of working women in the County Borough of Birmingham were married or widowed. Of these married women CM & S show that nearly 26% were widows, most of whom would work from necessity. This accounts for 5700 women. In addition, there were large numbers of what would be called today 'one parent families' who also worked of necesssity and brought up a family. The only statistic I have found in CM & S relevant to this is that 46% of all women home workers were either widows or deserted wives. This would suggest that 20% of married women home workers were 'deserted' wives either in the sense that their husbands were temporarily either working away or looking for work, or had permanently 'deserted' their wives. This could be either in the perjorative sense in which the term was always used by the authorities as leaving their wives penniless to the cold comfort of the Poor Law, or that they had decided to live apart from their wives and would be providing various amounts for the upkeep of the wife and the children where there was a family. Outwork is obviously the most convenient form of work for married women with children, so in estimating the percentage of such women in all employments, this 20% should be reduced to, say, that 15% of all working married women were 'deserted' wives. This would amount to 3300 women.

We then have to ask how many married women worked because their husband's wages were insufficient to provide basic subsistence for a family. This we do not know. But CM & S tell us that 26% of married women at work had husbands who earned 25/-d. or more, which we can take as being the amount necessary to keep a family of five at a minimum level of comfort. Here are 5700 women who might be said to be working for pin money. The other category of married women who might be said to work only for pin money is those married women without children. We do not know either the total number of married women without children or the number of childless married women who worked. Again we must resort to indirect calculation. A national estimate of childless married women for the period 1900 – 1909 is 11.3%. If we accept this as roughly true for Birmingham we must then conjecture how many of these women worked. Given contemporary attitudes that 'woman's place was in the home' it is unlikely that more than half of these women would go out to work. If this is correct this gives us about 2420 childless married women of whom about 1200 were working for 'pin money'. By deducting those working for 'pin money' from the total married women at work we can deduce not only the numbers working from necessity but also the categories. These are:

Total Occupied Married Women	22000
Those working for 'pin money'	7000
Those working from necessity	15000
of which 5700 widows	
3300 'deserted' wives	
remainder 6000 women with	
husbands earning less than	
25/-d. per week.	

So it would seem that 70% of married women worked from necessity compared with 30% working for 'pin money'.

CM & S then discussed the wage necessary to maintain a 'mininum standard of health' estimating this for the unmarried factory girl to be 14/-d.

> The mass of unskilled workers have one alleviation. They rarely take thought for the morrow. They go on, spending about 7/-d. a week on their keep and the rest of what they earn on clothes and amusement.

When such workers were sick, unemployed or on short time they were forced on to the charity of their families and where this was not available they faced semi-starvation and physical deterioration. Such was the permanent fate of those families where the woman was the main wage earner.

The position was scarcely different for skilled or professional women. If their wages were higher their requirements were greater and each grade of women workers was kept 'one step below' their necessary cost of production and reproduction.

CM & S clearly identified the forces keeping women's wages below subsistence level. These were:

1. The normal condition of a large surplus of the supply of labour over its demand.
2. Most work was unskilled or semi-skilled so that whole labour forces could be replaced within a few weeks if female labour proved troublesome.
3. Birmingham employers were acutely aware of the 'rate for the job' over the whole range of hundreds of trades and thousands of grades. This negated the alleged beneficial effect of competition between employers.
4. The elasticity of supply of female labour was very high, but elasticity of demand was low (i.e. in times of mass unemployment among men the supply of female labour increased when the demand for their labour was falling.)
5. The rigid division between jobs that were men's jobs and 'women's work' limited the range of jobs available to women.
6. The acceptance by the majority of women of a lower status and the belief that 'men should receive more'; the acceptance of the pathetic drudgery of being a working man's wife and the double exploitation of paid work during the day and unpaid domestic work at night meant that comparatively few women recognised the need for political rights or trade union organisation.

The Great Unrest of the years 1910–14 owed much to the sudden refusal of masses of women to accept such traditional beliefs.

Birmingham Women and the Trade Unions.

CM & S give an account of womens' trade unionism in Birmingham. They first list the difficulties of organising women: most girls look forward to marriage and their paid work life span is seen as short; considerations of sex and family life make it much more difficult for women to organise than men; employers were ruthless in exploiting the surplus supply of women whenever a threat of trade union organisation arose.

In the 1880s attempts had been made to organise pen workers by Joe Tanner and others, as we have seen, but the problems of the women and the hostility of the employers frustrated most of these efforts. Among non-manual workers trade unions had, perhaps, a better chance of survival. This was because, despite middle-class prejudice against trade unions, such women were better paid, more aware of developing trends, and had marginally more time to organise.

Where trade unions were open to both men and women, and women constituted a large proportion of the work force, was probably the best basis for the development of trade unionism among women, and women teachers were among the first to organise. The Birmingham and District Clerks' Provident Association was also such a mixed union, and its success led to the formation in about 1900 of the Birmingham and District Lady Clerks' Society. By 1903 this Society had 190 members. The benefits it offered were an employment bureau, out of work pay, medical attendance, special distress grants, annuities to aged and disabled members, and funeral expenses. The Society was 'managed by a committee of lady clerks engaged in some of the largest establishments in the city.'

One of many attempts to organise the numerous and important pen-workers in Birmingham was begun in 1895, but had to be restarted in 1898. Agitation was started by Miss Tuckwell and Lady Dilkes who were at the Trade Union Congress which met in Birmingham in 1897. They held meetings with women workers resulting in the formation of at least three trade unions, of which only the Pen-makers survived. One of the reasons for its success was the small subscripton of 2d. per week. But the fate of trade unionists when patronised by the mighty might be seen from the sequel:

> ... the undisciplined character of the members necessitated careful action. On one occasion 200 women presented an ultimatum to the union officials saying that unless they allowed them to come out on strike they would leave the union. The officials wisely refused this permission and 150 tore up their cards.

The union continued in existence, however, and its successes again demonstrate that the main impetus to trade union organisation often comes, not from wages, but from bad conditions. During its existence the union was able to see that the clauses of the Factory Acts applying specially to the pen trade were better observed, that the scandalous fines and deductions from wages were reduced, and that better sanitary conditions were provided.

The National Amalgamated Union of Shop Assistants, Warehousemen and Clerks was another mixed union which began in Birmingham in 1898. Returns for about 1905 showed a total membership of 265 in a central branch of over 100 members and five other branches of 20-30 members each. Of the 265 members forty were women. But, considering the vast number of Birmingham shop assistants, the trade was virtually unorganised.

The two most influential women trade union leaders in Birmingham and the West Midlands were Julia Varley and Mary Macarthur. But earlier pioneers should not be forgotten. Emma Patterson was the leading figure in the Women's Trade Union League formed in 1874. It was Emma who clashed with W.J. Davis and the Birmingham brassworkers at the 1877 TUC and again in 1882 over proposed legislation excluding women from such trades as chain-making and certain brass processes as allegedly harmful or degrading to women. Another Birmingham pioneer was Miss Hurlston who was the Women's Trade Union League organiser for the West Midlands in the 1890s and organised Birmingham women in the bedstead and pen trades, among others.

Mary Macarthur became secretary of the Women's Trade Union League in 1903 during the period when men's trade unions were beginning to open up to women, although there was resistance from the craft unions such as the ASE and the Birmingham brassworkers. In 1906 the National Federation of Women Workers was founded by the Women's Trade Union League as a general labour union for women catering for skilled women unable to join craft unions, skilled women working in trades where their number was so small that they were difficult to organise, and also for the vast mass of unskilled and semi-skilled for whom there was no trade union. Miss Macarthur was the first president of the Federation, but became secretary in 1908 when she and Gertrude Tuckwell exchanged posts. Early in 1906 the *Daily News* Exhibition of Sweated Industries took place and in the autumn of that year the *Woman Worker* was launched. The policy of the paper was the Minimum Wage and Protective Legislation for Women. In 1908 Mary Macarthur gave up the editorship of this paper and started an Anti-Sweating Campaign. These activities brought her into contact with the movement in the Black Country where she, together with Julia Varley organised the epic Chain-makers' strike of 1910 to enforce the minimum wage of the chain-making Wage Board.

The *Woman Worker* which ended an initial spell of existence in 1908 records for Birmingham only that a Domestic Servants Branch of the National Federation of Women Workers was formed in September of that year. It was supported by the Rev. Arnold Pinchard.

Julia Varley's contact with Birmingham and the Black Country was more continuous. She was a working class girl, born in Bradford in 1871, who left school at twelve to become a part-time mill girl and trade union activist. She was involved in the famous Manningham Mill strike of 1890–91 and became the first woman member of Bradford Trades Council. Julia worked with Mary Macarthur in both the Women's Trade Union League and its offshoot the National Federation of Women Workers and was thus introduced to the movement in Birmingham and the Black Country.

In 1909 on the initiative of Edward Cadbury she moved to Birmingham to organise trade unionism among women in the area. She quickly established a Card Box Workers branch of the NFWW at Bournville. This affiliated to the Birmingham Trades Council in September 1909. She became the branch delegate in January 1910 and was elected to the executive. She thus became the first woman delegate to Birmingham, as well as Bradford Trades Council.

As a result of her election to the executive, Julia became involved in all the campaigns of the Trades Council. In 1910 it was a campaign to improve wages and conditions in Birmingham bakeries where male operatives frequently worked over 90 hours a week for a wage little more than 20/-d. Later in the year it was the campaign with Mary Macarthur of their own union the NFWW at Cradley Heath with the Black Country chain-makers. In 1911 it was the women's struggle through the Workers' Union in the Black Country which triggered off the Great Unrest of the whole area.

Work among women was extremely complex and frustrating. Joe Tanner's problems with the pen makers in the 1880s were repeated in the 1890s when Arthur Keegan, secretary of the Birmingham Pen-Makers was driven to actual despair. Menfolk disliked the 'go-to-meetings women' and the women bowed to the dictats of the men he claimed. Keegan considered the folly of women infinite:

There are yet other and greater difficulties in organising women which are fundamental and apparently ineradicable. First I would place their impatience. We have had hundred of instances where having paid 2d. a week for a month or two, they have torn up their contribution cards in disgust, saying that nothing was done for them. They are unstable to a degree ... We have had an inspiring and enthusiastic meeting one week, and the next the self-same women will be scandalising the union. We have had nearly 2000 names on our books, and we have an effective membership of about 350. But their uncharitableness to each other is probably the most biting and disintegrating force which works against their solidarity ... The evil is far-reaching, and I fear endemic.

Women organisers were better able to sympathise and cope with these problems. Another difficulty was that the increasing market for female clerks and other skilled occupations was recruited largely from the daughters of lower middle class families with an ingrained hostility to trade unionism. For instance, it wasn't until 1915 that the Birmingham and District Lady Clerks' Association affiliated to the Birmingham branch of the National Union of Women Workers. At that time its membership had risen to 227 and its representative F.C.T. Ring explained that the Lady Clerks' Association was 'not a trade union, but looked after the interests of its members'. On the other hand, the Birmingham Association of Women Teachers was founded in 1909 and affiliated to the NUWW the next year.

This brings us to the important role played by the National Union of Women Workers (not to be confused with the National Federation of Women Workers.)

It began life at least as early as 1890 as the Birmingham Ladies Union of Workers among Women and Girls with the object of being 'A common centre for all Ladies and Associations engaged in the work of helping and caring for Women and Girls.' It began therefore as a middle-class organisation co-ordinating charitable work in the city. In November 1890 it organised in Birmingham a three day national conference and issued a 216 page report at which delegates came from no less than 84 towns to listen to a vast range of papers on such subjects as the YWCA, Emigration, Night Shelters, Useful Work, Prisons, Right Use of Leisure, Town Mothers' Unions, Co-operation in Charitable Effort etc.

The most important purely Birmingham input to the Conference seems to have been a Young Ladies Meeting chaired by Mrs. A. C. Osler. After a general paper had been read, Mrs. Osler asked several young ladies to give an account of their work in Birmingham. These included Miss Geraldine Southall speaking on Girls' Evenings at Home, and Miss Isabell Kennard of the Girls' Letter Guild whose members undertook to write at least one letter a month to a working girl on such topics as health, cookery, home life, marriage etc. Miss Emma Cadbury told of the work of the Factory Helpers' Union whose members visited factories in the dinner hour for a hymn, a bible reading and a friendly talk! The representative of the Needlework Guild said that its members were expected to make at least two garments a year and these totalled 33,000 which were distributed through hospitals etc. And the newly formed Snowdrop Band aimed to help young girls who were just starting work in factories. 'The moral tone of some of these is fearful', the audience was told. It was modestly stated in the report that 'the Young Ladies meeting was well attended.' In fact, a staggering 600 people listened to these proceedings.

This middle class dominated organisation was powerful enough in Birmingham to sustain from 1891 to 1924 a quarterly magazine called *Women Workers*. In 1890 the Birmingham branch had affiliations from 45 organisations. None of these was a trade union. When Julia Varley came to Birmingham one of her first actions was to affiliate her Women Workers' Industrial Organisation to the NUWW in 1912. The object of Miss Varley's WWIO was given as 'the improvement of industrial conditions of women workers in Birmingham through Industrial and Social Education, and Trades Union Organisation.'

By 1910 this respectable, middle-class, non-political National Union of Women Workers ws inevitably being drawn into the political and social maelstrom which was raging around it. At the 1910 AGM, Mrs. Cadbury, from the chair, called attention to the broadminded attitude of the Union, which in that year had added both the Association of Women Teachers and the Anti-Suffrage League to its membership. During 1910 the Union was involved in the administration of Women's Employment Bureaux, and in December the *Women Workers* had even printed a cautiously favourable article on Socialism. In 1912 much of the work of the Union was concerned with local work on the National Insurance Act of 1911, and in 1913 the Break-up of the Workhouse was discussed at the AGM. Although reasonably progressive throughout the period 1890 to 1914, this radicalism became more marked from 1913. Officers for that year included Miss Ryland (secretary) and Mrs. W.J. Ashley (president). The nine vice-presidents included Mrs. W. Barrow, Mrs. C.G. Beale, Mrs. George Cadbury and Mrs. A. C. Osler all of them recognisable liberal radicals and Suffragists.

It was over the latter issue that a 'rift' in the Union occurred in 1913. The president outlined the situation and said that no change in policy had been made. This had first been determined in 1902 when a resolution in favour of Women's Suffrage had been passed with little comment. The policy was reaffirmed in 1909 but 'with some unease among some people' (due, no doubt, to the rising militancy of the WSPU — GB). By 1912 the Anti-Suffragists were affiliated to the Union. When support for Women's Suffrage was again reaffirmed, the Union 'was threatened with the secession of some valued members.' To avoid this, a proposition to change the Union's rules from a majority of two thirds before resolutions could be sent to the government to a majority of three quarters, was put. This was defeated. The president concluded 'The ardent anti-suffragists had endeavoured to alter the Constitution. When this failed it was natural that some of them should resign.' In fact a letter had been received signed by 57 women resigning in protest at the NUWW taking any attitude, pro or anti, on the question of Women's Suffrage. By June 1914 it was reported that 15 of these signatures had been withdrawn and the loss of members more than made up.

When war broke out in August 1914 the NUWW supported the war effort and both Mrs. Osler and Julia Varley joined the Birmingham Citizen's Committee as the Union's representatives.

Before going on to deal with Women's Suffrage at some length, mention should be made of other women's organisations connected with the labour movement in Birmingham which it has not been possible to deal with here or of whose activity no record can be found.

The 1908 Birmingham ILP Handbook lists the Women's Labour League, secretary Miss G. Shuttleworth. This was the ILP's women's organisation set up by Margaret Macdonald in 1906. There was also the Women's Freedom League whose secretary was Miss A. Schofield of Oak Tree Lane, Bournville. This was a 1907 split of democrats from the Women's Social and Political Union chafing under the autocratic rule of Mrs. Pankhurst. Strangely enough, the ILP Handbook does not mention the Co-operative movement at all nor the important Women's Co-operative Guild which, I fear, is likely to be the most important omission from this chapter on women's activities.

For women's activities in the trade union movement I have taken the Trades Council's 1914 Report. This shows Julia Varley to be the only woman on the executive committee. Affiliated to the Trades Council was a Women's branch of the National Society of Printers, Warehousemen and Cutters. Its secretary was Miss. E. Tyzzer of 1 Margaret Road, Harborne. Also affiliated to the Trades Council was two branches of the Women's Labour League — Saltley (sec: Mrs. M. Stevens of 22 Ash Rd. Saltley) and Central (sec: Miss Annie G. Evans of Pershore Road).

Women's Suffrage
A Birmingham and Midlands Women's Suffrage Society existed from 1868 and was affiliated to the National Union of Women's Suffrage Societies. The date indicates a reaction to the Reform Act of 1867 which gave the vote to male householders in towns, but not, of course, to women. The Birmingham activities of this Society are recorded in a small volume of annual reports from 1868. One of the particular merits of this volume is that it lists all subscribing members for each year and so gives a complete list of all women participating in the Birmingham suffrage movement up to 1903 when the more militant Women's Social & Political Union appeared on the scene.

The Birmingham Women's Suffrage Society was a highly respectable body of almost exclusively middle class women. Its activities in the nineteenth century can be written off as ineffective, but its role in keeping alive the cause of Votes for Women over those frustrating years when it appeared a forlorn hope probably cannot be over-estimated.

The historian of the Women's Suffrage movement from the beginning of the twentieth century is Michele Shoebridge who, in 1983 wrote the unpublished Wolverhampton Polytechnic MA thesis *The Women's Suffrage Movement in Birmingham and District 1903 – 1918*. My information on the Women's Social and Political Union which follows is based almost entirely on her account.

If the founders of the women's suffrage movement were Liberal radicals, the Women's Social and Political Union emerged straight from the Labour movement. It was founded in Manchester by Mr. & Mrs. Pankhurst together with supporters such as Leonard Hall, who were all members of the Independent Labour Party. The WSPU was founded in 1903 as a result of the political upsurge which followed the ending of the Boer War. The 1904 ILP Conference backed the introduction of a Woman's Enfranchisement Bill and the 1906 election with the return of 29 Labour MPs led to hopes that the issue would be quickly and peacefully resolved. But the talking out of the Bill of 1904, the rough

handling of Emmeline and Christabel Pankhurst by the police, the
hostility of many men in the Labour movement and the general
disillusionment with the activities of the Labour Party in Parliament
determined that events would take a different course, and the WSPU
turned to militancy and violence.

The Birmingham branch of the WSPU was not set up until the middle
of 1907 and the announcement in *Women Workers*, the quarterly magazine
of the Birmingham NUWW, suggests that it differed little from the
already existing Birmingham Women's Suffrage Society:

> A branch of the WSPU has been set up with Mrs. Burman, Hartop
> Cottage Four Oaks as secretary and Mrs. Rylands 19 Hermitage Road,
> Edgbaston as Hon. Treas. Miss Pankhurst, Mrs. Despard and Mrs.
> Pethick Lawrence have already conducted successful meetings in
> Birmingham and Edgbaston and convinced their audiences that they
> were physically and mentally incapable of the violent conduct imputed
> to them.

However, the Birmingham WSPU quickly developed a militancy one
result of which was increased activity of the older Birmingham Women's
Suffrage Society. The report of the BWSS for the year 1906–7 shows that
a much enlarged committee, which included men as well as women, was
elected. The men were the Rev. James Adderley, Dr. Huxley and
Professor Muirhead. The influences of the new, thrusting WSPU was
acknowledged thus:

> No doubt the question of Women's Suffrage has become one of practical
> politics largely due to the militancy of the WSPU. Their zeal and self-
> sacrifice have inspired the enthusiasm of hitherto indifferent on-lookers;
> but their methods have undeniably alienated many old supporters. Your
> committee desires to reiterate its resolve to continue their work with this
> Society as heretofore on strictly constitutional lines.

An early WSPU organiser was Elizabeth Redfern, a shorthand writer
employed at the Birmingham County Court, and in November 1907
Mrs. Pankhurst had asked Balfour, the prime minister, to receive a
deputation in Birmingham (where he was due to make a speech) on his
intentions regarding women's suffrage. For this the Birmingham branch
received from London two temporary helpers — Jennie Baines and Nellie
Kenney — which greatly helped local organisation. By 1908 Birmingham
was playing its part in the important national activities of the WSPU.
These included a Caxton Hall meeting in February and the first of the
great Hyde Park demonstrations in June.

The increased activity of the WSPU was again reflected in the activity
of the BWSS. Its report for 1907–08 stated that a Women's
Enfranchisement Bill had been passed by 271 votes to 91:

> It is satisfactory to note that only one (Lord Morpeth) of seven
> Birmingham MPs (none of whom we fear can be counted as real friends
> of the Cause) voted against. This was undoubtedly due to the pressure
> of women.

This report also recorded that at the national Conference of Conservative
Associations in Birmingham in November a resolution supporting

Women's Suffrage had been passed with enthusiasm and there had been a similar vote at the National Liberal Federation.

By this time the WSPU had opened a regional office in Birmingham with Gladice Keevil as organiser. She was 24, a middle class lady educated at the Francis Mary Buss School and Lambeth Art School who was well-travelled having spent some time in France and America as a governess. On her return to Britain she became involved with the WSPU travelling round the country organising new groups. She had been chosen as one of ten other women to accompany Mrs. Pankhurst on the deputation to Parliament in February 1908. This led to her arrest and a six week prison sentence.

Again the advances in the city were shared by the BWSS which in 1908 – 09 reported 'phenomenal progress'. The Society, however, found it necessary to stress its Objects and Methods. The former were to obtain the Parliamentary vote for Women on the same terms that it is or may be granted to men. On the latter it was stated that 'The Society relies on public discussion, the spread of education on the subject and ordinary constitutional methods of agitation'.

The BWSS report stated that very little progress had been made in Parliament during that year. The Geoffrey Howard Adult Suffrage Bill calling for Adult Suffrage for all men and women over 21 after three months residence had been repudiated by all Women's Suffrage Societies and its second reading had only been carried by a majority of 35. 'Suffragists are more than ever convinced that they must concentrate all their energies on one thing — the removal of the sex disability. This refusal of the women to combine with men and support Adult Suffrage was condemned by such organisations as the Socialist Labour Party which saw class issues as taking precedence over the sexual question and this view was also shared by some in the BSP and the ILP. But it was also used as an excuse by men who were completely opposed to the enfranchisement of women. Hannah Mitchell summed up the question by saying that if women were to have their heads broken it would be for votes for women, not to work for votes for all and then find that women were not given it. She also quotes George Bernard Shaw's incisive comment on opponents of women's suffrage who hid behind a professed allegiance to Adult Suffrage

> If a man owes you a sovereign, and being able to pay you fifteen shillings, refuses to do so, depend upon it ladies, he never intends to pay the lot.

The BWSS report also stated that a Franchise Club had been formed in Birmingham which had doubled the membership of the BWSS, but, on the other hand, one of its branches had been dissolved, as all of its leading members had joined the WSPU. It also reported the formation in that year, of the Anti-Suffrage Society.

By 1909, the Birmingham WSPU still resembled the BWSS in its organisational activities and middle class personnel. Elizabeth Redfern was honorary secretary, Bertha Ryland, a member of one of Birmingham's leading families, ran the office. Gladys Hazel, a school teacher, managed the speakers' classes, Evelyn Burkitt ran the advertising side of the campaign. Gladice Keevil had been busy organising evening drawing-room gatherings and 'at homes' at the Priory Rooms in the centre of the city, and at Edgbaston where the wealthy and the influential lived. But factory gate meetings were also being held and where the employees were largely women, as at Cadbury's, successes were recorded in attracting working class support. Also in 1909 another organiser was appointed for Birmingham. This was Laura Ainsworth. The premises were also moved from 14 Ethel Street to larger ones at 33 Paradise Street.

Increasing WSPU militancy in 1909 led to a national decision to mount a demonstration on 17 September when Asquith, the prime minister, was due to address a mass meeting at Bingley Hall on the Liberal budget. This event proved to be a milestone in both the national and local history of the WSPU.

Birmingham suffragettes were mobilised and militants from outside Birmingham came to the city. At the meeting, only 150 specially chosen women were allowed into Bingley Hall. So further activities were planned. Two women climbed on to the roof of a nearby building, dislodged slates and hurled these at the police and Asquith's car, when it arrived. When Asquith left from New Street station, a metal object was thrown at his train. The same evening the Liberal Club was attacked.

Ten women in all were arrested. Two of them, Evelyn Burkitt and Ellen Barnwell were from Birmingham, Charlotte Marsh was the Yorkshire WSPU organiser and the others gave their addresses as the WSPU headquarters in London. The women who were sentenced were sent to Winson Green gaol where they went on hunger strike. In response to this they were forcibly fed. Birmingham thereby gained the odious distinction of being the first place in Britain where this barbaric procedure was practised.

The issue became a national one as Keir Hardie raised the matter in Parliament. The WSPU, unsuccessfully, sued the Home Secretary.

Rallies were held outside Winson Green prison every night demanding an end to forcible feeding and the release of the prisoners. When Laura Ainsworth was released on 4 December she received a 'welcoming breakfast' with Mrs. Pethick Lawrence present; a campaign was launched called the Mary Leigh Defence League. At the end of November there was a large rally for the release of Charlotte Marsh, the last of the Winson Green prisoners. This led to more arrests, including the Birmingham women Laura Ainsworth, Gladys Hazell and Brette Morgan.

These mass protests took their toll, however. Gladice Keevil had to leave Birmingham because of a break down in health. Her successor as Birmingham organiser was Dorothy Evans a gymnastics teacher trained at Chelsea Physical Training College.

These activities of the WSPU eclipsed the efforts of the BWSS whose report for 1909–10 focussed attention on the December 1909 general election. On election day 150 BWSS workers had picketed the polling stations with a petition demanding Women's Suffrage. A glowing tribute was paid to the police which, one feels, would not be shared by members of the WSPU:

> They brought us tea and umbrellas and kept children and drunks at a distance . . .

The national situation after the elections was assessed as 'difficult', with 400 MPs pledged to support some form of suffrage bill but 38 MPs openly opposed to any form of women's enfranchisement.

The progress of the Society had been 'well maintained', 212 new members having joined during the year bringing total membership to 662. During the year 113 meetings had been organised including 23 drawing room and 52 outdoor meetings.

From January 1910 until November 1911 there was a partial truce while the so-called Conciliation Bills were under discussion. These were the result of an all- party Parliamentary Conciliation Committee which came into existence in 1910 and introduced three bills, all of which, in Lloyd George's words were 'torpedoed'. Many suspect that Lloyd George did some of the firing and he was certainly in the engine room of the submarine when they were fired. From these failures Mrs. Pankhurst and the WSPU turned to increased violence, and finally arson, directed by her from abroad, as the campaign for Votes for Women reached its climax.

In September 1910 the Birmingham WSPU moved again to larger premises at 97 Bright Street and Gladys Hazell joined Dorothy Evans as Birmingham organisers.

The 1910–11 BWSS report explained that hopes had been pinned on the July 1910 Conciliation Bill which had passed its second reading in the House of Commons by 110 votes and was then sabotaged by the refusal of the Liberal government to give facilities for the Committee stage of the bill. There had been another great Trafalgar Square rally which 150 Birmingham women had attended, travelling in a special decorated train.

Before that, at Easter, there had been a national WSS concentration on the annual ILP conference, held that year in Birmingham. Open-air and factory meetings had been held, but the most important work, it was maintained, had been visits to the ILP branches in the city. On Easter Sunday there had been a mass rally in the Bull Ring with F.C. Jowett, Leonard Hall, Eden Paul, Margaret Smith and Mrs. Robinson speaking and Julia Varley in the chair.

When the second Conciliation Bill of 1911 failed, the WSPU responded with a procession to the House of Commons and a window breaking campaign. Birmingham members were involved in this and Margaret Haly from Northfield was arrested for stone throwing and Mary Jones was also charged.

At the same time, the National League for Opposing Women's Suffrage held a meeting at the Birmingham Town Hall at which both the League's national chairman, Lord Curzon, and Austen Chamberlain were present. Chamberlain declared that women did not want the vote, seeing it as a potential disruption to family life. On the other hand, a Birmingham branch of the Conservative and Unionist Women's Franchise Association was formed. The Association nationally had been in existence since 1908 under the patronage of Lady Willoughby de Broke, but neither those Conservative leaders or such of the rank and file who supported Women's Suffrage had been able to get this accepted as Party policy, it was reported.

Following the above two meetings, a well-attended WSPU meeting took place where L.C.S. Amery, Birmingham's only real Women's

Suffrage supporter among the city's seven MPs, spoke together with Viscount Woolmer and Christabel Pankhurst.

The 1911–12 BWSS report recorded 'one of our most successful years'. Membership had risen by 138 to 700 and there had been 117 meetings. The 1911 Conciliation Bill had been passed by 167, the largest majority for any government measure that year. But Asquith, the implacable opponent of votes for women had announced his intention of introducing a Bill which would enfranchise practically all men, but no women. The annual national women's suffrage demonstration in London had attracted 40,000 to 50,000 people. 200 of these had come from Birmingham 'both rich and poor'. Twelve women had stood in the Poor Law Guardians election. All of them had been elected and all of them were Suffragists. During the year all local MPs had been approached, but with 'poor results'. On the general public reaction to suffrage agitation the BWSS reported that

> The generality of men, and especially women, were indifferent or anti-before having the case put to them. After this, they were then in favour.

1912 saw the WSPU campaign reach new heights of ferocity. Attention was turned from private property to commercial premises, and earlier attempts to enlist public sympathy abandoned in favour of trying to coerce the government. Dorothy Evans received a four months sentence for wilful damage during this campaign. The high point of WSPU activity was a town hall meeting in November with Emmeline Pankhurst as the main speaker and a rejuventated Gladice Keevil in the chair. In her speech Mrs. Pankhurst concentrated on the recent defeat of George Lansbury at a Bromley and Bow by-election which he had contested on a Women's Suffrage platform. Pillar box firings were organised in Birmingham city centre to coincide with Lansbury's defeat and Mrs. Pankhurst's visit.

The arson campaign began nationally in February 1913 and was well under way by July when the hated Asquith visited the city on the 21st. By then, Dorothy Evans, twice a hunger striker and twice forcibly fed, had left Birmingham to become Ulster WSPU organiser. Gertrude Francis was appointed the new Birmingham organiser, assisted by Elizabeth Redfern. On the day of Asquith's visit a large house at 47 Upland Road, Selly Park, was destroyed. It had been used as a Roman Catholic Charitable Institute but, like previous targets, was empty at the time. This incident was combined with window breaking, the burning of post boxes and false fire alarms. WSPU members arrested were Florence Ward and Louisa Shepherd (both Walsall WSPU organisers), Mary Hawksley, Nellie Hall (daughter of Leonard), Kathleen Nicholson, Mrs. Gray and a woman who refused to give her name. On 22 July an unoccupied building at Perry Barr was burned down.

Gertrude Francis seems to have been arrested about this time and Lilias Mitchell became Birmingham organiser. Lilias was a Scot, had previously organised Newcastle and district and had been imprisoned and forcibly fed. When she arrived the policy of arson was weakening the movement by waverers leaving the WSPU and the most militant members being in prison.

During the summer of 1913 the office closed for its usual annual break, but by October was open again and reported to be selling 450 to 500 copies of the *Suffragette*. On October 20th. Suffragettes invaded the Cathedral chanting their own liturgy, 'for the delivery from prison of Sylvia Pankhurst, Mary Richardson and all suffragette prisoners'. On the 27th. October Sir John Simon visited the Free Trade Hall and was met with pillar box burnings and general disorder. Two days later Philip Snowden was interrupted at a Temperance meeting, despite the fact that he was a life-long supporter of Women's Suffrage.

On December 10th. there was a large meeting to celebrate the release of Emmeline Pankhurst from prison, but Mrs. Drummond was the main speaker, Mrs. Pankhurst having retreated abroad to direct the arson campaign. On December 23rd. another large, empty mansion in Birmingham known as Alstone Lawn was burned.

All the elements of the Great Unrest were now in operation — industrial and trade union; Larkinism and the Carsonite reaction to proposed Home Rule for Ireland; and Women's Suffrage violence. This produced complex reactions in Birmingham. For instance, the militancy of the WSPU while alienating sections of the female and male population, also stimulated the work of the constitutional suffrage societies. Also, while concern for the overall problems of the Liberal government was inducing the ILP leaders of the Labour Party in Parliament to reformist caution which discredited them in the eyes of the militants, respectable 'non-party' organisations were moving leftwards. We have seen this in the case of the Birmingham National Union of Women Workers. It was also true of the BWSS. Its 1912–13 Report stated that national policy had been changed to supporting only a Government measure of electoral reform (as against all-party Conciliation Bills which were not government sponsored and therefore dependent on the government allowing parliamentary time to pass them). This meant that in future the BWSS would actively help the Labour Party as the only party which had officially adopted the cause of Women's Suffrage. This coincided with increased attention paid by the BWSS to the labour movement. Trade unions approached during the year had included the brass workers, bricklayers, cabinet makers, railwaymen, shop assistants and tool makers. A BWSS branch was also set up at Bournville, where the women workers and the Cadbury family had always presented a sympathetic environment. As a result of all this, BWSS membership stood at its highest point — 955. The outlook for the BWSS in 1913, however, was summed up as follows:

> The outlook for the immediate future is one which calls for steadiness of purpose, loyalty and courage in the face of temporary check and delay. Our task is to create a strong public opinion in favour of justice for women, and at the same time to deepen the sense of national responsibility in the minds of women themselves, that they may take pains to qualify themselves for a wise exercise of the vote when they get it by acquiring a sound knowledge of public matters, especially those affecting the lives of their own sex and of children and by training themselves to social and political work.

For the WSPU nationally 1914 was a year of gradually falling off of arson and destruction, but in Birmingham such activities rose to a peak and only the war put an end to them.

In Februay 1914 the Carnegie Library at Northfield was burned down and an abortive attempt made to blow up the residence of the late Arthur Chamberlain. In March, the refreshments pavilion in Canon Hill Park was destroyed together with an attempt to destroy the Old Golden Lion Inn, a medieval building within the park. Another attack did £300 worth of damage to the pavilion of the Lawn Tennis Club at Olton.

Also in March there occurred the event which most disturbed middle-class opinion — the attack on the Cathedral where slogans were daubed throughout the building, including the famous Burne-Jones windows. This action not only alienated some Suffragists but also resulted in retaliation when WSPU windows were broken by a group calling themselves the Mysterious 50 who threatened not only to bomb WSPU premises but also to disfigure Suffragettes. Nothing more was heard of their activities, however.

In May the Harborne Oratory School cricket pavilion was burned down and the grandstand at the Castle Bromwich Racecourse attacked. The latter was probably retaliation for the imprisonment of Lilias Mitchell for 'not keeping the peace'. Lilias began a hunger strike and was then released under the Cat & Mouse Act, but her health had been undermined and Phyllis Aryton was appointed Birmingham organiser in her place in the same month.

In June, Birmingham women were implicated in attacks on London targets. Attacks on works of art spread to Birmingham when Bertha Ryland slashed Romney's 'Master Thornhill' in Birmingham Art Gallery. The case of Bertha Ryland received widespread publicity, not only because she was Birmingham's most socially distinguished Suffragette (she was related to the Lord Mayor of the city), but also because she suffered permanent damage to her kidney which resulted from her imprisonment for this offence. Her doctor suggested that this disability went back to her previous prison sentence in 1912 when she had been on hunger strike and forcibly fed. On the 12th of June Lilias Mitchell was rearrested while addressing a large meeting in the Bull Ring.

In July an unoccupied house in Yardley was attacked and there were other disturbances, such as interruptions in local churches when the Bishop of Birmingham was present.

On the 4th of the next month war broke out and suffrage agitation ceased abruptly. Mrs. Osler, the veteran BWSS campaigner offered the services of that organisation to the city council. Two of the Pankhursts — Emmeline and daughter Christabel (who had both been moving steadily to the political right from their ILP origins) became violently jingoistic and the WSPU both nationally and locally supported the war.

Chapter Twenty-Five

THE BIG BANG.
1910 – 1914

1910

This extraordinary period opens on the first day of the year with a national miners' strike followed by a seemingly never ending series of strikes. The middle months of the year saw the return of Tom Mann to England and the growth of 'Syndicalism' in all its forms. The ending of mass unemployment made possible an offensive on the wages front and a new spirit was evident.

This spirit was shown within the Birmingham Trades Council. Julia Varley was elected to the EC almost immediately on her arrival in Birmingham in 1909; the energetic J.E. Berry the secretary, replaced W.J. Morgan who had become a labour exchange manager; J. Kesterton the progressive president, was strengthened by the uncompromising socialism of Fred Hughes as vice-president.

The first beneficiaries of this new spirit were the Bakers. Working hours of up to 100 for £1, night work, appalling conditions in unventilated bakeries and much else was attested to by the *Birmingham Post*. A union existed, but since most bakeries consisted of a master baker and one employee, organising was difficult. The great achievement of Julia Varley, Jack Beard and the trades council was the mobilising of public support for the bakers. This was to be the indispensible factor in future campaigns in Birmingham and the Black Country.

The campaign was launched at the January trades council meeting. Billy Banfield, the bakers' leader, described the bakers' lives and indicted the city Health Committee for giving a bread contract to a baker working his men 70 to 90 hours a week. The Fair Wages and Conditions Clause was obviously being broken and this had a devastating impact when it was revealed that the chairman of the Health Committee was himself a master baker working his men 70-80 hours a week. A refusal of the Health Committee to act in this matter led the trades council to set up an Enquiry, the report of which was published and widely circulated. The report had a sensational effect. Its main conclusion, that Birmingham people ate bread produced in bakeries where 80% of employees worked 70-80 hours a week and 10% one hundred hours, was accepted as correct by the *Birmingham Daily Mail* which published a leader headed 'The Bread of Affliction' and agreed that this state of affairs could not continue. Eventually the Bishop of Birmingham succeeded in getting the master bakers to negotiate with the men in a committee under his chairmanship. Agreement was reached in November that hours should be limited to 54 with paid overtime beyond that and a minimum wage of 26/-d. The agreement, of course, applied only to those master bakers who accepted it, and the refusal of the government to designate the trade as a sweated industry and set up a Wage Board to regulate hours and conditions or promote a Bakers' Eight Hours Bill, limited the beneficial effects of the agreement. It was a magnificent victory, nevertheless.

In the meantime an even more decisive struggle of the women chain makers in the Black Country had opened in which Julia Varley played a leading role and the Birmingham Trades Council was soon deeply involved. The Chain Makers, unlike the Bakers, did have a Trade Board with a minimum wage rate of 2½d. an hour! It was this puny rate that had to be fought for and agitation for more than the minimum sustained.

1911.

The Birmingham Trades Council annual report for the year ending December 1911 opened by stating that remarkable as had been the progress of the council in 1910 the last year had 'eclipsed all previous experience.' Industrial unrest had become universal, but highly significant was that accompanying the industrial upheaval, Labour had triumphed at the polls in Birmingham. It was hoped that this would not only improve the well-being of the community, but would prevent many of the grievances which had previously occupied so much of the time of the trades council. Arising out of the enlargement of the city, the Kings Norton, Northfield & District Trades Council had decided to join Birmingham and the enlarged trades council now had 72 societies with 127 branches representing 30,000 members affiliated to it.

During the year the trades council had been concerned with both local and national issues. The victory at the polls had led to the city Council accepting the Fair Wages Clause which stipulated that no firms tendering for Council work would be granted contracts unless they paid the trade union rate of wages and observed the hours and conditions of work agreed between employers and the local organised body of workers.

On the feeding of school children, Julia Varley had given a lecture on 'How Bradford feeds its Children' and urged the city council to send a deputation to Bradford to see how they operated their scheme. The Council had not considered this necessary, but the trades council now eagerly awaited the report of a special committee set up by the city Council on this subject.

With regard to educational matters, there had been two major issues. The first was the decision of the city Council to give increased aid to Birmingham University without adequate representation and better provision of maintenance scholarships to enable working class children to attend. The second was a decision to raise secondary school fees from £3 to £4. A resolution of protest from the trades council contended that these two matters taken together suggested that the city Council was concerned to limit still further the already poor prospects of working class children securing secondary and higher education; it proposed a return to the old Joseph Chamberlainite city Council policy of free education for all.

Another important matter had been the demand for the provision of baths fitted with hot and cold water in every house of weekly rental in the city, to which the reply had been that financial considerations prevented the adoption of the proposal at that time.

With regard to local industrial disputes, the BSA strike had been the most important dealt with. A deputation of strikers had visited the trades council and a motion had been passed supporting and congratulating the strikers. It urged all other workers to show solidarity and render every possible moral and material support. The response had been splendid and this, together with the exemplary conduct of those involved in the strike especially the loyalty of the women, which had been beyond praise, had resulted in a settlement which promised well for the future.

The 1911 Insurance Act was a national matter which had occupied much time and aroused much controversy in the trades council. The final expression of their opinion was that while standing for a non-contributory scheme, it approved the actions of the Labour Party in Parliament to eliminate the many features inimical to labour interests and believed that the whole case for labour could confidently be left in their hands. The trades council further resolved that the deduction of contributions from 'wages that do not offer the worker more than mere subsistence must injure public health' and that, in such cases, the worker's contribution should be paid by the employer; the council also strongly condemned the proposal to reduce the £160 per annum income limit for medical attention.

Another national issue had been the right of peaceful picketing. The successes attending the recent struggles had 'so alarmed the capitalist organisations that strenuous efforts are being made to repeal the Trades Dispute Act . . . The determination of trade unionists never to surrender their right to peaceful picketing is evidenced by the enthusiastic replies to the following resolution:'

> That in view of the efforts being made at the present time by benches of Magistrates, Chambers of Commerce and other capitalist organisations to take away from the workers the right to picket during a strike, this council calls on the various trade unions to organise such a counter-move as may be effective . . . and suggests that the whole of the UK be organised into convenient centres with responsible executives so that should any Bill be presented in the House of Commons with any hope of its being passed into law, that a General Strike may be declared with a view to compelling its immediate withdrawal.

Closely allied to the above matters had been an appeal for recruits to a special police reserve. 'By monetary bribes and other inducements it sought to induce a section of the community to take upon themselves the role of upholders of privilege and monopoly.' The attitude of the trades council to the police was not, however, one of complete hostility. They were supporting the demand made to the Watch Committee for One Day's Rest in Seven for the police.

John Corbett in his history of the trades council elaborates further on the events of 1911. After the excitements of 1910 the early part of 1911 was a period of consolidation. But in August the industrial scene again erupted, this time with the railwaymen. They had borne the brunt of the Taff Vale judgement and their funds had been mulcted of £30,000. But the Trades Dispute Act of 1906 had made their funds secure and the railway bosses had been persuaded to accept the Conciliation and Arbitration Act of 1907. The Concessions were grudgingly conceded, however. They still refused to recognise the railway unions and they insisted on the quasi-military discipline which they held was necessary to run a railway. In 1909 the railwaymen suffered another blow when Osborne, a member of the Amalgamated Society of Railway Servants, brought the action which led to trade union political expenditure being

declared illegal. By 1911 railwaymen had had enough. Liverpool and
Manchester struck and Birmingham followed. On August 17th the union
executive declared a national strike. The Birmingham movement was
enthusiastic. Picketing against black legs unloading from goods yards was
vigorous. The government sent troops to 'defend' the railways:

> Alderman Sawyer 'with the Riot Act sticking out of his pocket' and the
> Deputy Stipendiary with military escort, went from rail depot to rail
> depot, to ask the Railway Company officials if help was needed. And
> behind them were the Munster Fusiliers acting as an Army of
> Occupation.

On August 19th. agreement was reached by the classical device of setting
up a Royal Commission, and in December partial recognition of the
union was granted. Trade union resentment at the use of troops flared up
at the September trades council meeting. H.J. Sabin made some defence
of the use of troops to maintain food supplies. Jack Beard rejected this.
'The rights of workers ... have been won by men who took the risks in
their hands; aye, and were ready to be hanged on the gallows if necessary
for the cause.' Fred Hughes demanded that the railways be 'taken from
the profit mongers.' A motion protesting at the use of the Munsters was
carried overwhelmingly.

At the following trades council meeting when it was clear that proposals
were afoot to make picketing illegal. Sabin and the militants again clashed.
Jack Beard moved the resolution on regional organisation and a General
Strike to defeat these proposals. Julia Varley said that after her experiences
in the Black Country, the only peaceful picketing she cared for was 'with
a brick.' The dominant mood was shown in the elections to the trades
council executive when Julia Varley polled 99 votes to Sabin's 11.

The militant mood was carried even further in November when the
BSA workers struck. Piecework rates had been falling and the bonus
system was suspect. Male capstan lathe operators earning 23/-d. to 28/-d.
a week were being replaced by girls earning 11/-d. to 15/-d.. The strike
was carried on in colourful style. The women struck with the men, the
skilled with the labourers, the organised with the unorganised, 3,500
marched from Golden Hillock Road to the Bull Ring where there were
8,000 demonstrators in support. Soon after, the Lord Mayor intervened
and a conference settled the strike. Another victory had been won.

This strike had the two features which were central to the struggles
ahead. First, the unorganised workers who came out with those already
unionised had no strike pay to fall back on and the majority no savings
either. Relief funds therefore had to be rapidly organised. This task was
taken on by the Workers' Union and its organisers such as Jack Beard
and Julia Varley. The second was the support of the general public.
There was a general, widespread opinion that workers, 'ought not to have
to work for such starvation wages,' and that the minimum wage asked for
was modest and ought to be granted. The latter point was particularly
significant in such a complex dispute as the BSA when the settlement
reached after 4½ week's struggle gave skilled workers little more than
they were offered before the strike and, in fact, a slight reduction in their
hourly rate, but the wages of other workers were considerably improved
and piecework guaranteed a minimum weekly rate.

1912.

The trades council's report for 1912 reported soberly on the year's work. Trade had been good, trade unionism had increased by leaps and bounds and the determination to close the gap between rising prices and stationary wages had continued.

With 77 societies and 134 branches, the trades council represented 40,000 workers in the city. The solid block of Labour councillors from the 1911 elections had led to better implementation of the Fair Wages Clause in contracts and similar results had been achieved from victories on the Boards of Guardians.

Much of the work of the trades council had been occupied with the National Insurance Act and a resolution deploring the selfishness of the medical profession and demanding a national state medical scheme had been passed.

The trades council had strongly urged the enfranchisement of women and voiced the demand for Adult Suffrage.

The main national disputes which had engaged the attention of the trades council were the great strike in the Port of London in June and the simultaneous furnishing trades dispute in Liverpool, Manchester and Nottingham, together with the struggle of the National League for the Blind against scandalous starvation wages at Bristol. A total of £140 had been sent to these three disputes.

The most interesting local dispute had been that of women and girls in the tailoring trades at Hednesford where the intervention of the Birmingham trades council had the effect of terminating the strike.

> The most important strike had taken place at Messrs. Avery's Ltd. which, precipitated by the labourers belongings to the Workers' Union, was joined in by all the skilled and other workers in every department with the result of winning against an, at first, unbending opposition on the part of the firm, not only what the men had come out for, but resulted in the works being transformed from long-standing non-union to what bids fair to become an all-round Union establishment.

The hollow-ware strike in the Black Country and Birmingham had not required financial help from the trades council 'thanks to the splendid work of the *Daily Citizen.*'

The resolution which became the starting point of a national campaign had been passed demanding a minimum wage for factory workers of 23/-d. per week of 48 hours for men and 15/-d. for women.

Finally the year had seen the tragic death of J.E. Berry. His successor Joseph Kesterton had taken over on a full-time basis.

1912, although a year of considerable advance, was a relatively quiet year compared with what had gone before and what was to come in 1913 and 1914. It might be as well, therefore at this stage, to review the progress of 'Syndicalism' in the industrial movement in Birmingham, especially as the main debate on this subject which has, erroneously in my view, been adjudged to have 'killed' Syndicalism, took place at the 1912 TUC.

There never was an industrial presence of Syndicalism in Birmingham in any way comparable to the political presence represented by Leonard Hall and others. The leading Birmingham trade unionist at the TUC continued to be W.J. Davis who was chairman of the TUC Parliamentary Committee in 1912 and presided over the TUC in 1913. As leader of the Brassworkers, Davis was interested in Federation, which was one of the main planks of the Syndicalists, and he was actively involved in the affairs of the General Federation of Trades Unions. But the major local presence at the GFTU was the Midland Counties Trade Federation which, although it had links with Birmingham, was dominated by the leaders of the small trades of the Black Country.

Other delegates of Birmingham based trade unions (besides Davis) who were represented at the main 1912 TUC which discussed Syndicalism were two others from Davis' 9000 strong National Society of Amalgamated Brassworkers and Metal Mechanics, one delegate from the Bedstead Workers with 950 members, J. Cuthbertson JP from the 1000 strong Amalgamated Metal Wire and Tube Makers of which Davis was also secretary, W.F. Beston the secretary of the nearly 7000 members of the Amalgamated Toolmakers, and Julia Varley of the Amalgamated Bournville Women Workers. There were also three other Birmingham delegates from unions which were not Birmingham based — the Wire Drawers of GB, the Provincial Typographical Society and the Amalgamated Society of Tailors. None of these delegates was a leading Syndicalist, nor even, as far as can be adjudged, rank-and-file Syndicalists. At any rate no Birmingham delegate made any contribution to the debate on Syndicalism.

Similarly with the trades council; federation and industrial unionsim was strongly supported, but for 'pure' Syndicalism i.e. control of industry by the trades unions concerned and opposition to the political wing of the labour movement, the trades council gave little support.

The opponents of Syndicalism at the 1912 TUC did not choose openly to oppose the new movement, but framed the resolution in such terms that only extreme, sectarian Syndicalists could vote against it, and it was this that gave them an overwhelming vote at the conclusion of the debate.

The scene for the debate was really set by the prior visit of J. Ramsay Macdonald, the fraternal delegate from the Labour Party, who was rapturously received, gave one of his spell-binding orations, and left to a storm of applause. Macdonald dealt, once again with the dilemma of the 41 strong Labour group in Parliament. Politics were real. The Labour MPs had not only to oppose the Liberal goverment, but it had also to prevent the even more reactionary Conservative Party from coming to power. In a memorable sentence, which was to dominate the subsequent Syndicalist debate, Macdonald said: 'In the work we are doing in the House of Commons you have to remember that, while there is a morass on one side of the road, there is a wild beast waiting to devour us on the other, and in keeping out of the morass I am not going to put myself into the jaws of the wild beast'. The anti-Syndicalist motion when it was put read:

> That this Congress reaffirms its continued support for independent working class political action in helping the industrial fight for a more equitable share of the wealth produced, and also declares for a larger share of representation, national and local, in view of the continued centralisation of social and industrial questions in the hands of the Government and local authorities.

One of the main arguments of the supporters of the motion was that those opposed to parliamentary action were 'young men in a hurry' whose theories of direct action and control of industry could only be imposed by civil war. The main opponent of the resolution was Noah Ablett of the South Wales Miners' Federation who was closely connected with the influential pamphlet *The Miners' Next Step*, which had been published that year. Ablett deflected the force of the resolution by saying that Syndicalists stood for making the TUC the Industrial Parliament of the future and there was no work which could not be organised industrially. The motion therefore begged the question. Sydicalists were not opposed to political action, he concluded.

The subsequent debated ranged widely and seriously over the many issues raised by Syndicalism, but a vote for the motion was not necessarily a vote against Syndicalism, nor a vote of confidence in the action of the Labour MPs. The final result was overwhelmingly for the motion, 1,693,000 against 48,000. Despite this vote, the next year anarchy erupted with a vengeance and Syndicalists, industrial unionists, direct actionists and militants of all sorts grouping themselves around the *Daily Herald*, flourished.

1913.

When J.E. Berry, the trades council secretary met with a fatal motor cycle accident taking his family on holiday, the trades council lost not only an organiser of considerable ability, but one able to inspire by both his oratory and his writing. Consider, for instance, this from his last report:

> 1911 will ever be memorable as marking an epoch in industrial history, and to have been permitted to take part in such manifestions of the solidarity of Labour is a matter on which we may feel justly proud.

1913 was another such epoch making year, but the reports of the new secretary, Joseph Kesterton, were rather more prosaic:

> In our last report it was stated, 'The year 1912 has been an eventful one locally and nationally and it is certain that these words apply with even greater force to 1913.'

Kesterton did, however go on to say:

> The awakening of the unskilled worker has continued, and many thousands have at last recognised there is no hope for their desperate position except organisation and combination.

Kesterton reported first on the strike in the city and elsewhere in the midlands of the Navvies where previously employers had competed with each other to lower the rate for this 'laborious toil' to 5d. an hour. The attempt to organise the men was only partially successful mainly because of their poverty and their having no fixed home as they had to move to follow their work because of its 'shifty' character. A strike had occurred which, after two or three weeks 'had inevitably collapsed'. Nevertheless, much had been gained; the city council had adopted a rate of 6½d. an hour and it was hoped to establish a considerably higher rate.

The great Black Country and Birmingham strike for the 23/-d. weekly minimum wage was, 'The biggest we have seen in the midlands for some years', and arose directly, it was claimed, from the 1912 Conference of all unions for the unskilled called by the Birmingham Trades Council. The most gratifying feature had been the public support which raised £3500 for a central fund as well as funds raised by local strike committees and one opened by the *Evening Despatch*.

Three strikes running simultaneously which the trades council had supported had been the Dublin, Cornwall and Birmingham furnishing trades disputes:

> The brutal outrages of the police at Dublin and Cornwall were strongly condemned by the Council and great protest meetings were held in the Midland Institute and Town Hall.Vindictive sentences have been a scandalous feature of the Dublin strike and have aroused resentment throughout the country.

The Birmingham furnishing trades had made a long overdue effort to better their conditions and had been very successful. 'Wages and hours have been considerably improved, and the men and women have been completely organised, the several Unions involved making hundreds of new members.'

It was not only in Cornwall and Dublin that police brutality brought protests. 'Unprovoked outrages of a startling character in South Africa' brought the following resolution.

> This Council ... views with horror the latest outburst of capitalist tyranny, as evidenced by the shooting down of our fellow workers in Johannesburg whilst exercising the rights of citizenship by holding a public meeting to ventilate their grievances; and calls the attention of all sections of the working class to the fact that this brutal outrage was committed by British troops acting on the authority of the Governor-General of South Africa and of General Botha, at the bidding and in the interests of an unscrupulous gang of cosmospolitan financiers and mine owners, whose policy in the past led to the sacrifice of the lives of thousands of Britain's sons and the expenditure of millions of money, in order to consolidate their power to exploit labour, black and white alike.

The efficacy of trade union organisation in previously unorganised trades had been strikingly illustrated by the case of the Bakers' Union, where, during the year, a baker advertised for non-union men. The public were informed and meetings were arranged. But before these could take place, 'The Society's representative was sent for and Union men engaged.'

Several cases of the evasion of the Fair Wages Clause had been dealt with and 'in most cases adjusted.' A growing number of enquiries had been made to the trades council by government departments, Co-operative Societies and private firms seeking information regarding working conditions and wages of firms tendering for contracts, and one firm working for the government had been ordered to raise its wages to the agreed minimum.

A minimum wage had also been introduced for musicians and three of the city's four theatres had agreed to pay this. The remaining theatre had refused to pay the rate and, when the men went on strike, advertised for non-unionists. The aid of other trade unionists had been sought and the public asked to boycott the theatre. Within three days the management had capitulated and the standard rate conceded.

The joint efforts of the National League of the Blind and the trades council, (to which they were affiliated) had at least been successful in obtaining free transport on the corporation tramways for the blind.

The National Union of •Railwaymen had been formed by amalgamation during the year and a similar process had brought into existence the Gold, Silver and Kindred Trades Society. In conjunction with the trades council, they were 'now undertaking the long over-due process of reorganising the jewellery trade in Birmingham.'

1913 also saw political advances. Trade unionists had been elected at Duddeston (W.W. Saunders) and Rotton Park (Tom Hackett) while Councillors George Shann (Selly Oak) and J. Gregory (Saltley) had been re-elected. Progress had been been even more marked in Smethwick where Kesterton had been been elected, also G. Wilkinson (Ladywood Toolmakers) and A Morris (Workers' Union) and Labour now held half the seats on Smethwick Town Council.

This wide range of industrial, social and political action on the part of the trades council probably had the effect of blunting some of the edge of Syndicalism in the city and Joseph Kesterton ended his report with 'the Year's Lessons':

> While the strike weapon has been used during the year with some effect, and concessions won which seemed far off twelve months ago, the lesson has been driven home that it is not sufficient to have industrial unrest and industrial power — if the workers are to any extent to improve their present servile condition we must also have political power. The Capitalist classes are still the ruling classes and prepared to use all the civic and military forces to drive men to work under any conditions and to manipulate the law to their own advantage. If we would even 'hold that we have' we must have a stronger voice in the Legislature and in our local assemblies. We must give more attention to the political side of the question; we must fight more seats; we must have the money to do so with. The cause is worthy of the sacrifice.

For the full significance and impact of the revolt of the dispossessed which had begun in 1910 – 11 and reached its climax in 1913 – 14 we can turn to the pages of Richard Hyman's *The Workers' Union* and also the pamphlet *Nor Shall the Sword Sleep* by James Leask and Philomena Bellars. These strikes affecting mainly the Black Country but inevitably impinging on Birmingham take their place among the epics of our national working class movement.

The origins of this vast movement are disputed. George Askwith, the government's chief Industrial Commissioner, who was hastily dispatched to the Black Country in 1913, believed that it originated in Dudley with some women striking saying that they could no longer live on the wages paid, and likening this to the effect of the Match Girls strike in London in 1888 which had sparked off the New Unionism movement of 1888 – 90. Hyman locates the origins of the movement in Soho, the traditional heartland of the Birmingham engineering industry taking in parts of Handsworth, Smethwick and West Bromwich, with the November 1912 strike at Avery's. The chronology below, however follows in the main the narrative of Leask and Bellars who identify the morning of Tuesday 18th.

February 1913 as the decisive moment, when 500 men at Tangye's stopped work.

The Tangyes were 'enlightened' employers, but it was not until the end of February when 1600 of the 2400 workforce were on strike demanding the 23/-d. minimum wage for all adult male full-time workers, that the firm conceded. What followed was a veritable crusade, as much moral as economic, for the 23/-d. minimum.

Sterner opposition came from West Bromwich. Here the girls at United Hinges, Ltd. (a subsidiary of Kenrick's) struck on the grounds that they were only paid for the work after it had been dispatched from the works, and if the girls left the firm before then, they were liable not to be paid at all. A mass meeting of strikers, both men and women, demanded the 23/-d. minimum for unskilled male labourers and 12/-d. for women. The United Hinge strikers were soon joined by girls from the parent company, Kenrick's. A Worker's Union survey at this firm showed that 84% of the women were earning less than 12/-d. and 43% earning 6/-d. to 8/-d.

A major extension of the strike came on 19th April when some workers at the Birmingham Railway Carriage & Wagon Works came out. This works had only recently been organised by the Worker's Union. Many of the 'unskilled' were key workers such as stokers, and when they struck, the works came to a standstill. Eventually carriage workers in Oldbury, Smethwick, Wednesbury and Birmingham were all on strike. Dudley Docker at the annual meeting of Metropolitan Carriage, Wagon & Finance Co. complained that these actions were 'abominable breaches of contract', particularly as the Engineering & Allied Trades Federation, hastily being cobbled together to counteract the strikes, had agreements with 'certain trades unions.' This was countered by the Workers' Union pointing out that it was not one of those 'parties' and in any case, such agreements did not cover unskilled workers.

By now the strike had spread to all the Black Country and much of the Birmingham engineering trade. In Wolverhampton the management of Bayliss, Jones and Bayliss dug in for a long struggle; in Dudley the boiler firm of H & T Danks, with family links with the progressive movement going back to Reform and Chartist times, paid the 23/-d.

At the end of May the London *Times* was reporting 20,000 out in the Black Country, but this was little better than an educated guess; at its height, there were probably 40,000 idle in the Black Country.

The strikes were now a matter of national concern. The support of the local population led to large sums being raised, both locally and nationally, to support the strikes. Despite this, the hardships suffered were grievous; but the strikers were no strangers to semi-starvation and their resolve to win the minimum seemed to strengthen as their hardship increased.

In June moves were made to settle the strikes when the two employers' associations, the Midland Employers' Federation and the Engineering & Allied Trades Federation twice met with union representatives, but failed to reach an agreement. The employers attempted to divide the men by offering a 23/-d. minimum for Birmingham, but 21/-d. for the Black Country. A Workers' Union ballot of all members decisively rejected this tactic.

Towards the end of June matters came to a head when 12,000 men in the Birmingham metal trades joined the strike. Bitterness and violence were also spreading. On 30th June fifty or sixty police were sent to the Fellows works in Bilston to 'guard the premises.' Determined efforts were made by the strikers to storm the main gates and the police force was increased to 150.

Large numbers of employers were now conceding the rate. On the 2nd. July it was reported that only one firm in Birmingham had not conceded the 23/-d.

George Askwith, acting on behalf of the Board of Trade intervened, and negotiations began at the Birmingham Council House. The eventual agreement was signed on 7th July 1913. Its main provisions were

1. A 23/-d. a week minimum for able-bodied unskilled workers in the Birmingham District, which included Smethwick and Oldbury.
2. A 22/-d. minimum for the Black Country to rise to 23/-d. after six months.
3. A scale of payments for females and youths as follows:
    Females: 6/-d. at age 14 rising to 12/-d. at age 21.
    Youths: 7/-d. at age 14 rising to 23/-d. at age 21.

Elaborate consultation arrangement were also made to prevent future strikes. The trade unions concerned were deemed to have rules to deal with any breach of the agreement and assurance that they would so deal. The agreement was to last 12 months. It was signed by T. Horace Spencer on behalf of the Midland Employers' Federation and for the unions by H. Simpson of the Amalgamated Gas Workers, Brick Makers and General Labourers Union, J. Firth for the National Union of Gasworkers, and Julia Varley and John Beard on behalf of the Workers' Union. This agreement was by no means universally accepted by trade unionists, and it remains to be investigated to what extent the opposition of the militants, particularly in Bilston and Walsall, was carried.

In the meantime strikes and violence were sweeping Dublin, and anyone who thought that the 1912 TUC resolution had killed off 'Syndicalism' was to be quickly disillusioned as the Dublin transport strike put the movement back on centre stage.

James Larkin and James Connolly were the two main leaders of the Irish Transport & General Workers' Union. Connolly was recently returned from the USA and close contact with the IWW, de Leon and the American SLP. Larkin came from Liverpool and had clashed with James Sexton, the ILP moderate (who seconded the resolution against Syndicalism at the 1912 TUC), over the settlement of the Merseyside transport strike of 1912. This had accepted a 'rationalisation' scheme of employment of dockers which ended casualisation, but, in the opinion of Larkin and other militants restricted the rights of the labourer to work where and when he liked. For his opposition to the settlement, Larkin had been expelled from the National Union of Dock Labourers. Larkin had also clashed with Sexton when he was NUDL organiser in Ireland when Larkin had supported a strike of Dublin carters and the NUDL had refused to support it. This had led to the setting up of the Irish Transport & General Workers Union led by Larkin, who by then had removed himself permanently to Ireland. Neither Larkin nor Connolly were 'pure'

Syndicalists, but both were powerful industrial organisers and Larkin's particular contribution to industrial struggle was the spreading of the 'sympathetic' strike.

In the first half of 1913 a rash of strikes in Dublin was supported by Larkin who pointed out that the main opponents of trade unionism in Dublin were Guinness's and the Dublin United Tramways Company owned by W.M. Murphy who was also the Dublin financier and newspaper tycoon. Larkin began recruiting among the Dublin tramwaymen. By mid-August Murphy was alarmed and as part of the employer counter-attack throughout the UK, told his men to leave the union or be sacked. Larkin's reply was to organise sympathetic strike action, including a refusal of Dublin newsboys to sell Murphy's paper!

On 26th August the tramwaymen stopped work leaving the trams in the streets. Murphy manned them with scab crews. The police and army were mobilised to fight 'Larkinism' and leaders, including Larkin, were arrested. August 31 was Bloody Sunday when a meeting due to be addressed by the bailed Larkin was prohibited as 'unlawful and seditious'. Police attempts to arrest Larkin led to violence and deaths. Workers fought police to prevent blacklegs driving the trams. On 3 September 400 employers under the chairmanship of Murphy declared that they would not employ any member of the Transport & General Workers Union. So began the great Dublin Lock-out.

Larkin's response was to appeal to the TUC, then in session, for assistance, and so Birmingham became involved. The trades council collected £400 by the end of the year and assistance continued into 1914.

Sympathetic action was taken by militant members of the newly-formed National Union of Railwaymen. Nearly 10,000 were eventually involved, mainly from Liverpool, Crewe, Derby, Sheffield and Birmingham in blacking traffic to Dublin. Corbett's account for Birmingham is as follows:

> The railwaymen at Suffolk Street Goods Yard set the movement in motion. A dozen men refused to handle traffic for Dublin. They were sacked and the rest downed tools until the twelve were reinstated. The call flashed to all the rail depots in the city. The Lawley Street men marched to the Bull Ring. The walk-out became complete. The local Railway Union officials supported the stand and Guard Shakespeare took the lead. A strike committee was set up.
>
> The following day Walter Hudson MP and other members of the NUR Executive came to enquire into the situation. The ASLEF Headquarters sent telegrams to the men to remain firm. A Bull Ring rally called upon the unions to call a national strike.
>
> The EC of the NUR repudiated the strike as unjustified on the 19th, but the local committee rejected the EC manifesto and refused to order the return to work until the twelve men were reinstated.
>
> Feeling became frayed. Crowds of pickets attempted to rush Queens Drive where several carts were being loaded. The gates had to be locked and police cordons maintained. The police cleared Livery Street several times. There were numerous scuffles between strikers and the men in charge of vans. 6,000 rising to 7,000 were on strike and on September 20 a compromise was affected. The Company agreed to reinstate the twelve if they would agree to handle all traffic. There was still reluctance to accept the rider to the reinstatement, but W. Hudson MP, Assistant Secretary of the NUR persuaded the men ... to accept. Birmingham had made its militant gesture to bring new heart to the Dublin strikers.

Larkin came to England for a self-proclaimed 'fiery cross' campaign urging sympathetic action on behalf of the Dubliners. The Socialist groups around the Daily Herald and Clarion organised enthusiastic meetings including the one previously reported, at Birmingham Town Hall which brought on to the same platform George Lansbury, Jim Larkin and 'Big Bill' Haywood the legendary U.S. trade union leader. A special TUC Conference in December 1913 pledged itself to maintain support for the strikers and called on all unions to refuse to handle goods from or to firms which refused to recognise the Irish TGWU; but the wider sympathetic strike action requested by Larkin was refused.

1914.

It is almost impossible to gain a clear picture of the political and industrial scene for the first nine months of 1914 because the annual reports, so important for assessing activity over a year, are totally dominated in 1914 by the catastrophe that overwhelmed the country in August of that year.

It is clear that the general offensive of employers met with only limited success. The Dublin lock-out ended with temporary defeat as the starving men began to return to work in January 1914. On the other hand, Connolly and Larkin had lit the fuse which was to explode two years later in the Easter Uprising. The overwhelming defeats of Syndicalism at the 1913 TUC and the subsequent special conference in December were on paper and not on the ground. The spirit of revolt remained. It was shown by some considerable dissatisfaction at the settlement of the Black Country and Birmingham strikes of 1913. Militants such as Teddy Wilson of Bilston and Joe Thickett of Walsall were continuing to wage the class fight as energetically as were the employers. The Midlands Employers' Federation was constantly complaining of sabotage in the factories with shaft-belts cut and machinery damaged. The crowded Birmingham Town Hall meeting which brought onto the same platform George Lansbury of the Daily Herald, Jim Larkin, and the leading USA Syndicalist Bill Haywood, demonstrated the vitality of the broader aspects of Syndicalism and militant feeling. The Birmingham and Black Country branches of the Workers' Union were notably more militant than those in other parts of the country and in March 1914 the West Bromwich branch of the Workers' Union declared. 'We believe in the *Daily Herald*, Jim Larkin and Direct Action.'

As we have seen, the political movement in Birmingham was in disarray at the beginning of 1914 over the failure of Labour MPs to act in any decisive way to promote working class interests. New trends were appearing; it may be significant that it was from the papers of Dick Etheridge, the Communist militant of the next generation who was to spend most of his working life initiating and developing the shop stewards movement of Austin's and the midland car industry, that I first encountered copies of the Anarchist papers *Freedom, Herald of Revolt* and *The Syndicalist.*

In addition, the Suffragette movement was also reaching its climax of arson and seeming anarchy. The police and army were being deployed with increasing frequency and brutality. Even the ruling class was in revolt against the Liberal government with Carson and the army officers threatening mutiny if Home Rule were applied to Ulster. Finally, the economic situation was again deteriorating and slump and mass unemployment were returning. If there was a lull in the summer, there was the expectancy of renewed militancy, a 'Wait till Autumn' feeling was in the air. George Askwith the government's industrial trouble-shooter wrote at the time, 'Within a comparatively short time there may be movements ... coming to a head of which recent events have been a small foreshadowing.'

But with the autumn came war. The Big Bang was over — to be replaced by a yet Bigger Bang. The reality of an increasing understanding of the reasons for poverty and the possibility of ending it, gave way to the fantasy of the romanticism of war and the primitive appeal of jingoism. The working class returned to obedience, stood docilely in line to murder, and be murdered by, fellow proletarians abroad. They were officered by the traditional ruling class of the rich and privileged; but their NCOs were their own comrades, and those previously the most militant often now the most servile — Jack Beard, Julia Varley, W.J. Davis, Labour councillors and Suffragette leaders. It was indeed a very small minority on the trades council, in the trade unions and the political groups who led the struggle for the next return to reality. But that is another story.

JULIA VARLEY, *first woman delegate to the Birmingham Trades Council*

J. KESTERTON, *President 1910–12 and Secretary 1913–18 of Birmingham Trades Council*

Chapter Twenty-Six
CONCLUSION

This book has attempted to show that working people are the central core around whom the history of Birmingham has been made. The thread uniting these disparate masses through successive generations has been a radical tradition in Birmingham going back to the middle ages. This radical tradition insists that life has a higher purpose than the pursuit of individual wealth and self-interest. In the earliest years of the building of a community in Birmingham, Christianity was the most important element of this tradition, although one would like to know the extent to which medieval society continued to be pagan or secular.

What does seem clear from the earliest description of the religious life of the town by Hutton in the eighteenth century, is that organised Christianity failed to satisfy the needs and aspirations of the majority of working people. Christianity has always played a double role. On the one hand is the, usually dominant, conservative tradition of supporter of the state and thought controller of the plebian population; on the other hand is the radical tradition stemming from primitive Christianity, stressing the virtues of collectivist and socialist modes of living. The long crisis from the Reformation to the Restoration shattered the authoritarian Roman Catholic church and released the extraordinary Sectarian activity of Dissent which, in Birmingham joined with the earlier Christian tradition to develop further the radical tradition of the town.

From the period of the Industrial Revolution, key sections of the growing working class found it necessary to combat the conservative religious elements by developing its own Secular outlook, first through the critique of Christianity by Thomas Paine and then through the rational religion of Robert Owen. Subsequent developments led to the more robust Rationalism which affected Birmingham history as Secularism.

In the 1850s, Secularism was the bridge over which the Birmingham working class movement crossed from the revolutionary, innovative and pioneering structures created in the developing phase of capitalism 1815 – 50, to the re-emergence of Socialism in the 1880s. One of the local particularities was the religious configuration of the area. In Birmingham the established church was largely neutered; 'priestdom' was rarely the strong arm of local bourgeois control acting as religious terrorists peddling heaven and hell on Sundays, and temporal terrorists the rest of the week dispensing 'justice' in their role of JPs. This is in marked contrast to the adjacent Black Country. Nor was the hardly less terroristic mainstream Methodism with its bitter hostility to Chartism and working class organisation generally, the major religious influence that it was in some parts of the country. Nor was the Birmingham working class movement scarred by Protestant/Roman Catholic sectarianism as in Liverpool, Glasgow and elsewhere.

It was the more democratic sects — Quakers, Baptists, Unitarians, and the unique George Dawson (who found it necessary to build his own church) which dominated the religious life of Birmingham. Many of their adherents were 'rational religionists', allowing deists to co-exist with the natural religion of Robert Owen and these in turn sympathising with the atheism of the followers of Charles Bradlaugh.

Towards the left of this spectrum lay the 'religion of Socialism'. An irony of this development was that Arthur O'Neil, the most important Christian Chartist, closed the Birmingham Chartist church as early as 1845, and himself became a Baptist moving steadily to the political right. His later influence was as a peace campaigner and not as a Christian Socialist. O'Neil's influence, together with Joseph Sturge, the U.S. consul Elihu Burritt, and John Bright gives Birmingham a prominent place in the history of the international peace movement. The 'religion of socialism' resurfaces again only with the Labour and Socialist churches in Birmingham in the 1890s, and here, as we have seen, they were at their strongest when the national movement initiated by John Trevor was in decline, and survived until the first World War.

Secularism in its twenty five years dominance of the working class movement in Birmingham accommodated all the political and social movements of that period and culminated in the short-lived Republican-ism of the key years 1870 – 74 which saw the Paris Commune and also the last hectic years of Victorian 'prosperity'. Birmingham was an important centre of English Republicanism which can be seen as the culmination of the Administrative Reform movement initiated as a result of the Crimean disasters. It brought together emerging Socialism (land nationalisation), the still unfulfilled Chartists demands (male suffrage), and the two key Administrative Reforms (abolition of the House of Lords and universal, free, compulsory, secular state Education). The import-ance of Republicanism in Birmingham was enhanced by the adhesion of Joseph Chamberlain and his disciplined forces of Liberalism in the town.

Republicanism was broken by the Great Depression. Among other manifestations of the new Imperialism which this ushered in should be noted the transition from local state control and a local 'dictatorship of the bourgeoisie' to national state control. Birmingham exhibits this transition particularly clearly with Chamberlain's migration from local to national politics and his break-up of the Liberal Party. This transition from local to national state I have tried to trace for the Black Country; and this needs to be done for Birmingham also, but I have not been able to do it here.

The onset of the Great Depression brings us back to the economic field on which the development of capitalism and the class struggle are fought out. From the vantage point of the later 1980s, I have continued to use a 'long wave' analysis designating 1875 – 95 as the first of three Great Depressions, the other two being 1921 – 39 and the third, from 1974 onwards. Each of these depressions has a two-fold characteristic. The first is of being a profound crisis of capitalism, putting the very existence of the sytem at risk. The second characteristic of the Depressions is that they are also periods of the profound restructuring of capitalism; the modernising of businesses and the new branches of industry emerging, eventually providing the opportunity for higher rates of profit which create the possibility of overcoming the crisis. It should be noted, however, that even if the crisis is 'overcome' this only lays the basis for the next crisis.

It is the ever-present influence of the trade cycle which basically accounts for the corresponding cycles of belief in the immortality of capitalism and successive developments of socialist thought and action.

Two questions are particularly pertinent to this process. One is that of poverty, and the other of class consciousness.

An attempt has been made to measure poverty in Birmingham. In the second half of the eighteenth century the evidence suggests that despite the enormous increments of wealth created the general standard of living fell and the Hunger Riots were a reaction to periods when the cost of food rose above the level of wages, resulting in actual starvation. The period of the Napoleonic Wars was no better, and working class protest had to be repressed by violence.

After the Napoleonic Wars the three Long Depressions to 1844 brought into play the factor which is probably the most potent in perpetuating poverty — unemployment and short-time working. Attempts have been made recently by estimates of increased production, and wages falling less steeply than prices to suggest that the first half of the nineteenth century was one, despite the countervailing evidence of mass working class protest, of rising living standards. Such evidence ignores the existence of masses of unemployed with no income, the Birmingham plague of short-time working which took income below the level necessary to provide food and shelter, as well as the permanent mass of poverty from sickness and old age. Insufficient evidence has been found to make a definitive statement on the extent of Birmingham poverty in this period, but I suggest that it will be found to be comparable with the Black Country experience where each successive slump brought wages back to subsistence levels and there were insufficient years of prosperity to raise working class living standards more than marginally.

1845 until 1875 were the thirty years of undisputed British industrial supremacy in which Birmingham played such an important part. One might have expected working class living standards to soar. This did not happen. One reason was that these 'prosperous' years had a surprising number of number of depressed years. The reports of the Amalgamated Society of Engineers, which at this time represented the new high technology, bear witness to this. But the basic reason was the operation of the mechanism of capitalism which created ever greater extremes of wealth and poverty. This is testified to by Joseph Chamberlain and his 'doctrine of ransom'.

The result was that when the Great Depression struck, the limited gains that had been made were largely lost and in the worst years of 1876 – 9 and 1885 – 7 working class living standards plummeted to 1840s levels.

From 1895 to 1900 there was another boom. Living standards benefitted from this continuity of employment; but trade declined from this point to the mass unemployment of 1905 – 8. When prosperity returned, the unskilled and semi-skilled took the opportunity to organise and raise wages from semi-starvation to bare subsistence levels in the Great Unrest.

In summary, it is suggested that living standards rose substantially on only three occasions. On the first occasion, the gains of 1845–50 were retained because no large scale depression followed. During the Great Expansion living standards rose only marginally until the Great Boom of 1870–74. Much of this improvement was lost in the subsequent Depression. The other period of rapid improvement was from 1895 to 1900, the gains from which were not retained.

Why were working class conditions so deplorable in 1914? One conclusion is that the growth of productivity under capitalism was insufficient to support rising living standards for workers before the basic contradiction of widening extremes of wealth and poverty resulted in the inevitable depression.

The other basic question arising from the capitalist trade cycle is the fate of socialism and the development of class consciousness.

This narrative has shown (a) the virtual disappearance of Socialism from about 1845 until 1884 and (b) subsequent growths of Socialist influence each dashed either by economic depression or the sudden emergence of nationalism and jingoism. Such disjunctions can be followed by examining the strands and strength of class consciousness in Birmingham which have successively been built and demolished. 'First wave' class consciousness arose from the development of capitalism and the 'making' of the Birmingham working class through a radicalism of revolutionary traditions drawn from the English, American and French revolutions of the seventeenth and eighteenth centuries; this was driven underground by the repressive legislation of the Napoleonic wars. 'Second wave' class consciousness was built on a base of Owenite Socialist theory and Chartist political practice; it was broken by the virility of capitalism in its Workshop of the World phase. 'Third wave' class consciousness had a number of strands. One was the climacteric of Liberal radicalism with the Radical Programme of 1885 which endorsed a collectivist programme. It advocated land nationalisation, repudiated laissez-faire philosophy, accepted a much wider measure of government intervention, and agreed that this would be 'socialist' (but not Communist!). This programme was endorsed by Joseph Chamberlain (while not binding himself to all its features) in his preface to the published programme. The Radical Programme accepted that much of the new power given to the national state should be devolved to the local state. Here was a second strand of a tradition of the Civic Gospel inherited from Thomas Attwood in the 1830s, carried on by Joseph Chamberlain in the 1870s and taken up by the Fabians and others as Municipal Socialism in the 1890s.

When Joseph Chamberlain shattered the Liberal party in 1886 over Home Rule, the liberal radical tradition was taken over by Gladstonians led by George Cadbury, and the Birmingham working class moved from cloth-capped Chamberlainism to Lib-Labism. The key figure here in Birmingham was W.J. Davis, trade unionist extraordinary, as local leader of the Brassworkers and national TUC figure as member of the Parliamentary Committee. Lib-Labism was then transformed into what I have called Lab-Libism under constant harassment from the new unionists and the new Socialists of the SDF. Here the key figure was Joe Tanner, who, I would argue, was as important in his day as W.J. Davis, but who has a more abiding place in Birmingham and national working class history as the pioneer Marxist, putting down deep roots, which continue to exert a powerful influence.

The next strand of class consciousness was the development of the idea of the Right to Work. Socialists taught that mass unemployment was created by capitalism, that unemployment and mass misery had always been the lot of working people under capitalism, and that there was the valid and practicable alternative in Socialism. This was the message of the great orators of the labour movement at the mass Birmingham town hall rallies, whether it came from the wayward Victor Grayson, the great pragmatist Keir Hardie, the inspirational Tom Mann or the eventual trimmers, Snowden and Macdonald. But it was above all the message preached week by week on the street corners by the lesser lights of the local movement, and reinforced weekly by the working class newspapers.

Not only was it widely accepted that the Right to Work was a fundamental human right, but the means of providing that work was seen to be at hand. This was the locality, where public works and the provision of leisure amenities such as parks were urgently required; and if local provision of charitable and municipal funds dried up, then it was the duty of the national state to provide the money. The Right to Work campaign was strongest in the period of mass unemployment of 1903 – 08, but the groundwork for it has been laid earlier with struggles against the Poor Law and the provision of useful work as an alternative to the horrors of the Workhouse and its Stoneyard.

Another strand in the development of class consciousness was the long campaign for a Living Wage. The last outrageous effrontery of capitalism in distress is its claim that protection from competition at home and abroad can only be provided if wages are accepted that are lower than the cost of maintaining and reproducing the commodity labour. From the onset of the Great Depression when wages 'fell', workers made war on the Sweater and the Sweating System. It was the plight of the Black Country chain and nail makers which brought the national leaders of the SDF and Socialist League into Birmingham with subsequent local organisation. These early campaigns were sustained by the militancy and fortitude of hitherto hapless women workers and the organising ability of the early Socialists. These pioneering efforts of such outstanding women organisers as Julia Varley and Mary Macarthur combined with the actions of the trade unions, notably the Workers' Union culminated in the Great Unrest in which the vast mass of unskilled and semi-skilled men and women were in revolt against permanent semi-starvation and for a Living Wage.

The resultant class consciousness from the merging of these various strands led by 1914 to something approaching the classic revolutionary situation where the ruling class were no longer able of rule in the old way and the working class was no longer willing to be ruled in the old way. What was missing? What would have happened if the outbreak of the 1st. World War had not occurred and diverted working class feeling into nationalist and jingoist channels?

The political and trade union movement at that time exhibited an exceptional degree of fragmentation and disunity between the main working class ideologies of Anarchism (Syndicalism), Marxism, and Labourism. This suggests that British capitalism would have ridden the storm of 1910 – 14.

It took the war and the Russian revolution to create an actual revolutionary situation in many parts of the world between 1917 and 1921. This fostered the not entirely unjustified expectations that this could be extended to Britain. It did not occur. Instead, the movement here was restructured into Communist and Labourist trends. Birmingham played an important part in this process; the traditions of the Socialist Centre and co-operation between varying Socialist trends resisting the national Labour Party insistence that the Communists be outlawed and the movement split.

The inter-war years experience of mass unemployment, appeasement of fascism and the second World War itself led to another upsurge of class consciousness. It resulted in the Labour government of 1945 and, in Birmingham, the final laying of the ghost of Joseph Chamberlain with a Labour controlled local authority and Labour MPs in ten out of thirteen constituencies. This class consciousness extended to the city's factories resulting in important rises in living standards. The breaking of that class consciousness once again is a matter of recent history.

The role of working class consciousness in the future appears uncertain. But if the mechanism of capitalism is fundamentally unaltered despite its present transition from state monopoly capitalism to supranational monopoly capitalism, the old flaws will reappear — unsustainable extremes of wealth and poverty, cycles of mass unemployment, and conflicts generated by the uneven development of capitalism. Whatever the scenario of the future, working people will react, as they always have done, to protect and further their interests. In Birmingham there will be further twists in the development of the long-established democratic, radical and socialist tradition.

STATE OF TRADE & UNEMPLOYMENT IN BIRMINGHAM
1872 – 1900

Year	B'ham Chamber of Commerce Remarks	Scale	A.S.E. State	Index No.	B'ham Flint Glass Workers Unemploy %	Amalg Brassworkers Unemploy Benefit per head Members	Comments on Trade
1872	Developed so rapidly that usual relations supply & demand disturbed to inordinate degree	10			3.8%	6/10d	Expanding
1873	Remains fairly active	9	Mod	20	3.5	12/3d	
1874	Considerable depression some trades in town	8	Mod	18	5.4	11/-d	Depression
1875	-	-	Bad	11	3.5	7/4d	
1876	No relief of Depression from which staple trades & general industries of town suffer	5	Bad	10	2.8	6/7d	Unusual depth of depression of many trades
1877	No improvement. Depression great & almost universal	5	Bad	10	6.3	13/8d	Times are bad
1878	Depression still not reached its depth	5	Bad	10	5.4	20/6d	World wide Depression
1879	-	-	Bad	10	8.6	34/4d	Depression continues with ever greater severity
1880	Almost universal Depression	5	Bad	11	9.4	17/10d	Improved
1881	Gradual Improvement	6	Bad	14	5.5	15/3d	
1882	Improvement only partially maintained	6½	Mod	19	5.4	6/1d	
1883	Few prospects of developing trade	6	Bad	13½	8.6	10/10d	
1884	No improvement whatsoever	6	Bad	12	5.9	16/-d	Long prevailing Depression.
1885	-	-	Bad	12	4.4	19/4d	Exceptional severity of Depression.
1886	No material improvement	6	Bad	10½	5.0	16/1d	Most trying year Society ever experienced.
1887	Time not yet arrived to congrat. traders on return prosp. so long delayed & hopefully awaited	6½	Bad	10½	5.9	17/-d	Limited revival
1888	Gratifying increase	7	Bad	13	5.6	12/9d	Improved
1889	Very Considerable Increase	8	Mod	23	5.2	3/9d	
1890	Fair	7	Mod	23	3.7	15/6d	
1891	Increase home trade but fall foreign	7	Mod	19	2.6	12/2	
1892	Most Unsatisfactory	6½	Mod	15½	4.4	12/1d	
1893	Steady decrease volume trade	6	V.Bad	9	7.7	10/10d	
1894	Unsatisfactory	6	Bad	11	13.1	14/4d	Distress

Year	B'ham Chamber of Commerce Remarks	Scale	A.S.E. State	Index No.	B'ham Flint Glass Workers Unemploy %	Amalg Brassworkers Unemploy Benefit per head Members	Comments on Trade
1895	Opinions vary	6½	Mod	17½	11.0	11/1d	Terrible Distress
1896	Boom	8	Good	29	7.8	7/3	Severe depress 1st qtr
1897	-	-	Good	26	9.2	13/-	One of labour's fat years.
1898	Good	8	Mod	17	9.3	17/9d	
1899	Prosperity	9	Mod	19	-	13/4d	Trade Good.
1900	Weakness developed during the year	8	Mod	21½	-	14/-d	

NOTES: Chamber of Commerce Scale: 10 (high point of boom) to 5 (deepest Depression) Amalg. Society Engineers Index No: V.Bad – under 10: Bad 10 to 15: Moderate 15 to 25: Good 25 to 35: Very Good from 35 Upwards.
Number of A.S.E. branches reporting monthly: 1873 – 74 3: 1875 – 86 4: 1887 – 93 5: 1894 – 7 6: 1898 – 1900 7.

BIBLIOGRAPHICAL NOTES

Sources have normally been indicated in the text. The following is an elaboration and summary of those sources.

Chapter 1   EARLY RADICALISM

The main sources used for the political development of Birmingham from the sixteenth to the nineteenth century are the *Victoria County History of Warwick, City of Birmingham vol vii* and also William Hutton's *An History of Birmingham*.

For the eighteenth and early nineteenth centuries J.A. Langford's *Century of Birmingham Life* and R.K. Dent's *Old and New Birmingham* have been most useful.

For the early history of the government of Birmingham there is Toulmin Smith's *English Gilds* with its suggestive material on the origins, functions and significance of the gilds, particularly in the west Midlands and also J.T. Bunce's *vol i* of the *History of the Corporation of Birmingham*.

On the so-called food riots and 'mob politics' there is D.E. William's *Hunger Riots in 1766* (Midland History vol iii No.4), R.B. Rose, Langford; also E.P. Thompson's authoritative *Moral Economy of the English Crowd in the Eighteenth Century* (Past & Present No. 50 Feb 1971).

For the discussion on Wages, Prices, the amount spent on bread and food, and estimates of the standard of living in the eighteenth century the sources have been given in the text.

For the period 1760 – 1800 the indispensable source is John Money's *Experience and Identity*.

The Priestley Riots of 1791 are covered in detail by Hutton, Dent and Rose. The definitive summing up is R.B. Rose's *The Priestley Riots of 1791 (Past and Present* No. 18 Nov. 1960).

Full bibliographies for the whole period can be found in C. Gill's *History of Birmingham vol i*, and the detailed footnotes in the VCH vol vii; and for the 1760 – 1800 period in Money's *Experience and Identity*.

Chapter 2   WORKING CLASS CONSCIOUSNESS

R.B. Rose —   *Political History to 1832* (in *Victoria County History of Warwickshire vol vii, Birmingham*)

J.A. Langford —   *A Century of Birmingham Life.*

R.K. Dent —   *Old & New Birmingham.*

C. Behagg —   *Artisan Radicalism in Birmingham* (unpublished B.A. dissertation University of Birmingham 1971).

   – do –   *Custom, Class & Change; the Trade Societies of Birmingham* (in *Social History vol 4 no 3.*)

Asa Briggs —   *Presss & Public Opinion in Early Nineteenth Century Birmingham* (in *Dugdale Society Occasional Papers No. 8*)

Attwood's currency views have been dealt with by S.G. Checkland — *The Birmingham Economists 1815 – 50* (in the *Economic History Review 2nd. Series I (1948 no. 1).* and also Asa Briggs — *Thomas Attwood and the Economic Background of the Birmingham Political Union* (in the *Cambridge Historical Journal vol IX No. 2 1948*).

The history of the Birmingham Political Union has been dealt with in detail in most of the general histories of Birmingham, but special mention should be made of the most detailed of these Carlos Flick — *The Birmingham Political Union*

1830 – 39. This is something of a rogue item. Flick's thesis is that the reputation of the BPU as the national leadership of the fight for the Reform Bill was a figment of Attwood's imagination and a result of his propaganda machine. This would seem to take debunking too far; but the serious effect this 'myth of the BPU' has had on foreshortening the history of Chartism in Birmingham and the subsequent success of Joseph Chamberlain and his circle in creating similar myths regarding Birmingham history, indicate that Flick's ideas should not be dismissed too lightly.

George Griffith —   *Going to Markets and Grammar School vol I chap 3* for
                     Alexander Somerville and Birmingham during the later
                     stages of the Reform agitation.

The national working class newspapers used include Wooler's *Black Dwarf*, Cobbett's *Political Register*, Carlile's *Republican* and Hetherington's *Poor Man's Guardian*. For the local press see Briggs (above).

Chapter 3   OWENITE SOCIALISM

The main sources in this study of Owenite Socialism are:

History of the Birmingham Co-operative Society Ltd. 1881 – 1931 (Birmingham 1931). No author given.

George Jacob Holyoake — *History of Co-operation (1906)*

George Jacob Holyoake — *Sixty Years of an Agitator's Life. (1906)*

J.F.C. Harrison — *Robert Owen & the Owenites in Britain & America (1969)*

The Owenite newspapers *Crisis* and *New Moral World*.

The section on the Operative Builders' Union and the GNCTU is based on R.W. Postgate — *The Builders' History (1923)* chapters 3 to 5.

Chapter 4   CHARTISM

The prime sources used throughout are Feargus O'Connor's *Northern Star*, Ernest Jones's *People's Paper* and *Cabinet Newspaper*, R.C. Gammage's *History of the Chartist Movement 1837 – 54*, and Lovett's autobiography, *Life and Struggles of William Lovett*.

The main sources creating the three myths which it is hoped that this chapter will help to dispel viz. that Chartism in Birmingham was a middle-class led movement which expired when these leaders deserted the movement in 1839; that the basic differences within Chartism were between Moral and Physical Force adherents; and that Birmingham was the town that epitomised class collaboration and class peace were the *Birmingham Journal* and the Birmingham 'liberal' historians R.K. Dent *Old and New Birmingham chap. LXV, J.A. Langford, A Century of Birmingham Life,* and J.T. Bunce, *History of the Corporation of Birmingham.*

The modern myth perpetuators include Conrad Gill, *History of Birmingham vol 1 (1952)* but above all Trygve R. Tholfsen, *The Chartist Crisis in Birmingham (in the International Review of Social History 1958).*

The cautious challenging of the myths can be seen in the early work of Asa Briggs, *vol VII of the Victoria County History of Warwick* (1964) and *Chartist Studies* (1962). The considerable body of work on Chartism by Dorothy Thompson with references to Birmingham notably in *The Chartists* (1984) laid the basis of a more realistic approach to Birmingham Chartism, while the most forthright attack on class collaboration comes from the work of Clive Behagg, notably his *Birmingham Political Union and Early Chartism* (1982) in *The Chartist Experience* edited by James Epstein and Dorothy Thompson.

The definitive study so far of the Birmingham Chartist Church apears to be J. Ryan *Religion and Radical Politics in Birmingham* (unpublished Birmingham University MA thesis).

The best study of O'Connor's Land Plan is Alice Mary Hadfield's *The Chartist Land Company* (1970) with much detail on Great Dodford. An earlier study, Joy MacAskill's *The Chartist Land Plan* in *Chartist Studies* edited by Asa Briggs (1962), is inaccurate as far as Great Dodford is concerned. On Great Dodford itself there is Peter Searby's *Great Dodford and the later history of the Chartist Land Scheme* in *The Agricultural History Review vol 16, 1968* and a study of Great Dodford itself in Winifred Bond's *From Hamlet to Parish*. The latter was brought to my attention by Mr. J. Hunt of the Birmingham and Midland Institute.

The most comprehensive general bibliography of Chartism is *Bibliography of the Chartist Movement 1837–1976* by J.F.C. Harrison and Dorothy Thompson (1978). Mike Boddington's *Labour History in the West Midlands County: A Bibliography (1984)* is indispensable for Birmingham labour history.

Chapter 5 to 9   SECULARISM

As acknowledged in the text, the pioneer study of Birmingham Secularism was Christine Stephen's unpublished B.A. dissertation, *The Secularist Movement in Birmingham and District 1850–1885,* the material from which she has generously allowed me to use.

The 'Holyoake' period of the first decade of Secularism is covered in Holyoake's newspaper *The Reasoner* and his books *History of Co-operation* and *Sixty Years of an Agitator's Life.*

Sources for the subsequent Bradlaugh period are the newspaper *National Reformer,* Bradlaugh's *Autobiography* and his daughter Hypatia Bradlaugh Bonner's *Charles Bradlaugh, A Record of his Life and Work.* Also the centenary volume of 1933 *Champion of Liberty, Charles Bradlaugh.*

J.A. Langford's *Modern Birmingham and its Institutions* is essential reading as he was both historian and leading Co-operator.

General works which include local references are:

J.F.C. Harrison —   *Robt. Owen & the Owenites in Britain and America.*
Edward Royle —   *Victorian Infidels: The Origins of the British Secular Movement 1791–1867*
Edward Royle —   *The Infidel Tradition from Paine to Bradlaugh.*
David Tribe —   *100 Years of Freethought.*

An essential local source for the co-operative movement is *History of The Birmingham Co-operative Movement 1881–1931.* The modesty of the author of this highly competent study extends not only to the withholding of his name, but also to the fact that he supplies the best summary of the movement before 1881 back to Owenite Socialism.

Details of the Birmingham School Board elections are taken from A.F. Taylor — *Birmingham School Board 1870–1903* (unpublished Birmingham University M.A. thesis 1955)

For the formation of the Birmingham Trades Council and the importance of the Master & Servant Acts see John Corbett — *History of Birmingham Trades Council.*

All references to the International are taken from *The First International Documents vols I to V* which contain the minutes of the General Council as well as all other documents.

Chaps 10 to 14   THE GREAT DEPRESSION

The standard texts for Imperialism are J.A. Hobson — *Imperialism, a Study* and V.I. Lenin — *Imperialism, the Highest Stage of Capitalism.*

For the so-called myth of the Great Depression see S.B. Saul — *The Myth of the Great Depression 1873 – 96* and the bibliography in this booklet.

For the reality of the Great Depression see G.J. Barnsby — *Social Conditions in the Black Country 1800 – 1900* chap 7 The Standard of Living and response to this in E.H. Hunt — *British Labour History 1815 to 1914* pp 73 – 74 and also R. Church's review of Barnsby in *Economic History Review* vol 34 pp 484 – 5. A more general attack on the 'Optimistic' school who consider that working class living standards rose throughout the nineteenth century is G.J. Barnsby — *The Standard of Living in England 1700 – 1900.*

The analysis of occupations in Birmingham is taken entirely from the official ten yearly Censuses 1851 to 1901.

Employer responses to the Great Depression are taken from G.H. Wright — *Chronicles of the Birmingham Chamber of Commerce 1783 – 1913* and the Second Report of the *Royal Commission on the Depression of Trade and Industry 1885.*

Trade Union responses to the Great Depression are taken from W.E. Dalley — *The Life of W.J. Davis* (1916), W.D. Best — *Brass Chandelier*, W.E. Dalley — *An Historical Sketch of the Birmingham Trades Council 1866 – 1926.* E.J. Smith — *The New Trades Combination Movement* in *Economic Review 1898*, Alan Fox — *Industrial Relations in Nineteenth Century Birmingham* in *Oxford Economic Papers 1955*, H.A. Clegg, A. Fox & A.F. Thompson — *A History of British Trade Unions since 1889* and Eric Taylor — *The Midland Counties Trade Federation 1886 – 1914* in *Social History vol I No. 3 1972.*

The *Flint Glass Makers Magazine 1860 – 1897* (with some gaps) are at the present time (1988) in the possession of the general secretary of the union Mr. J.R. Price 4, Prospect Hill, Stourbridge. To Mr. Price I owe a considerable debt of gratitude not only for making these magazines available but also for his willingness to instruct me into the mysteries of the glass trade.

The main sources I have used for Joseph Chamberlain are the definitive multivolume biography of J.L. Garvin; Peter T. Marsh who has dealt with Chamberlain's business activities in — *Joseph Chamberlain, screw manufacturer* in *Dictionary of Business Biography vol 1 (1984)* and Charles W. Boyd (ed) *Mr. Chamberlain's Speeches* vol 1. Also *Life of Joseph Chamberlain* (Associated Newspapers Ltd) no date. This is a volume of seven essays. The two I have used are J.A. Spender — *Mr. Chamberlain as a Radical* and a brilliant essay by J. Ramsay Macdonald — *Mr. Chamberlain as a Social Reformer.* An interesting modern biography by a fellow betrayer of his own party over Ireland is Enoch Powell — *Joseph Chamberlain.* This book deals mainly with Ireland and Chamberlain's post-radical life, but it is magnificently illustrated.

Chaps 15 to 17   THE GREAT DEPRESSION (CONT.)

Contemporary sources reflecting hostility to the landed interest, speculation regarding the development of village communities and the existence of primitive communism included John Bateman — *The Great Landowners of Great Britain & Ireland* (1876), J.E. Thorold Rogers — *The Economic Interpretation of History* (1888) and *Six Centuries of Work & Wages* (1884), Max Beer — *Social Struggles in Antiquity* and, of course, F. Engels — *Origin of the Family, Private Property and the State* together with Lewis Morgan's *Ancient Society* on which Engel's book was based.

The working class newspapers and other sources for each of the socialist organisations were:

S.D.F. *Justice* and 3 articles in *Labour Mail* Dec 1906 to Feb 1907 by A.R. Burns
— *The 20th Anniversary of the Socialist Movement in Birmingham, some Early Recollections.*
Clarion. *Clarion* and Robert Blatchford - *Merrie England*
Socialist League *Commonweal.*
Fabian Society *Fabian News.*
Labour Church *Labour Prophet. Minutes* and *Labour*
Church Hymn Book.
Birmingham Socialist Centre *The Pioneer* (1899 – 1902)
and annual reports from 1901.

On the trade unions and socialism the sources used have been *Birmingham Trades Council Minute Books* and *Annual Reports* and *Birmingham & District Trades Journal* from April 1896 to 1899. Also John Corbett's excellent *Birmingham Trades Council 1866 to 1966* which is marred only by his persistent misspelling of Granger's name by 'Grainger' and mistaking the ASE stalwart Joe Tanner for the later Jack Tanner. Dalley's previously mentioned *Sketch of the B'ham Trades Council* and *Life of W.J. Davis.* There is also an important unpublished Birmingham University dissertation by H.E. Houghton — *The Birmingham Trade Union Movement and Political Action in the Eighteen Nineties.*

On the Trades Union Congress there are the *TUC Annual Reports* 1884 – 1900, W.J. Davis — *The British TUC, History and Recollections;* also B.C. Roberts — *The Trades Union Congress 1868 – 1921.*

For the last words on the Great Depression the two graphs in the text are supported by the full figures in Appendix 1. The admittedly fragile material on the standard of living in Birmingham is based on my Black Country approach in my previously quoted *Social Conditions* chap 7. and *Standard of Living in England* pp 38 – 42 supplemented by the national material in B.R. Mitchell and Phyllis Deane *Abstract of British Historical Statistics* particularly pp 64 – 65, 271 – 272 and p 9.

On Marx' Theory of Value there is Philip H. Wicksteed's *The Common Sense of Political Economy* with an Introduction by Lionel Robbins (1946) with Wicksteed's *The Marxian Theory of Value* in vol 2. which also gives George Bernard Shaw's contributions to the debate. Then H.M. Hyndman's *The Economics of Socialism* containing his seventh lecture *The Final Futility of Final Utility.*

Chap 18 TOWARDS SOCIALIST UNITY

The further development of the Socialist societies continues to be followed through the working class newspapers *Justice, Clarion* and for the S.L.P. *The Socialist.* For the ILP there is also the *ILP News* for the years 1897 – 1903 as well as the Birmingham ILP Federation *Minutes 1909 – 14,* Kings Heath ILP *Minutes 1906 – 19* and the Hay Mills ILP *Minutes 1908 – 11.* For activity of the trades council there are the Birmingham Trades Council's *Annual Reports,* the *Labour Mail* 1906 – 7 as well as Corbett. For the labour Churches there are the Central Labour Church *Minute Books 5 and 6* covering the period Nov. 1903 to Dec 1909, Kings Heath ILP *Minutes* and the Stirchley Labour Church *Programmes 1911 – 12* and *1913 – 14.* For the Socialist Centre its *Annual Reports 1901 – 10* are available and also its paper *The Pioneer* for 1899 – 1902.

Chap 19 THE LIBERAL DIMENSION

For Joseph Chamberlain's continued dominance of Birmingham politics I have continued to use the sources quoted for Chap 14, but his role as the leading Imperialist of his day is part of national politics. I have also dipped into the Chamberlain Papers in Birmingham University library sufficiently to confirm

that not too much of real significance found its way on to paper where
Chamberlain was concerned. Here I should acknowledge my indebtedness to the
genial erudition of Dr. B.S. Benedikz who presides over the Heslop Room where
these papers are kept.

For the role of Gladstonian Liberals in the town there is A.G. Gardiner's *Life
of George Cadbury* (1923); the activities of the Lib-Labs are followed through Trades
Council proceedings.

The Chamberlain business connection and the activities of Birmingham
business men during the Boer War is written almost entirely from a copy in my
possession of a Birmingham B.A. dissertation by W. T. Taylor — *Birmingham
Business and the Boer War*. Unfortunately, my copy lacks three Appendices and the
bibliography. Even more unfortunately, there is no copy of this dissertation in the
Birmingham University library.

Chap 20   TRADE UNIONISM & LABOUR POLITICS 1900 – 10
Cyril Collard is the historian of the Right to Work Movement in Birmingham.
See his *Unemployment in Birmingham, Policy & Reaction 1900 – 14* (unpub M. Soc.
Soc. thesis B'ham Univ 1979) and his *Unemployment Agitation in Birmingham
1905 – 10* in A. Wright and R. Shackleton (eds) — *Essays in Birmingham Labour
History*. Birmingham Corporation's feeble efforts to provide work are followed
through C.A. Vince's fourth volume of the *History of the Corporation of Birmingham*.
Working Class attitudes to emerging Welfare State measures e.g. Health and
Unemployment Insurance, Old Age Pensions etc. have been followed through
Trades Council reports and Gardiner's *Life of George Cadbury*.

Chap 21   POVERTY & SLUMP 1900 – 1910
Poverty in Birmingham has been analysed from The City of Birmingham Aid
Society *Annual Reports* from 1907 and the proceedings of the Distress Committee
of the Corporation. Attempts to quantify Birmingham poverty start from Charles
Booth's *Life and Labour of the People of London*, B.S. Rowntree's study of York —
Poverty, A study of Town Life (1902), Corbett's *The Birmingham Trades Council
1866 – 1966*, and G.J. Barnsby — *The Standard of Living in England 1700 – 1900*.

Chap 22   THE BRITISH SOCIALIST PARTY
Justice became the main organ of the BSP, although *Clarion* remained an
important source of information and, after 1912, the *Daily Herald*. There was also
a monthly, internal bulletin of the Party *Socialist Record* 1912 to 1916.

There is also the *Official Report of the Socialist Unity Conference 1911* on the birth
of the Party and *Annual Reports* thereafter.

For Leonard Hall there is a mimeographed biography by John Smethurst, the
existence of which I learned from Edmund Frow at the Frow's Working Class
Movement Library, Jubilee House, 51 Crescent, Salford M5 4WR. I have
consulted Eddie and Ruth over many matters in the past and never found them
wanting. For the special part played by Birmingham in the formation of the Party
there are the *B.S.P. (Birmingham Section) Papers* at the British Library of Political
and Economic Science at the London School of Economics with the
correspondence between Victor Grayson and Leonard Hall and other
Birmingham leaders of the BSP.

Chap 23   SYNDICALISM 1910 – 14

Probably the best introduction to the complexities of Syndicalism is the book of readings *Workers' Control* edited by Ken Coates and Tony Topham (Panther paperback 1970). Tom Mann's paper *The Syndicalist* from 1912 charts what little there was of mainstream Syndicalism in Birmingham.

Sources for the minor developments arising from Syndicalism such as Anarchism, Anarcho-Communism etc. have been detailed in the text and the further activities of the main stream socialist groups continue to be recorded from sources already quoted, mainly the working class press.

For futher enlightenment on Rutland Boughton and musical matters associated with the Clarion choir I am indebted to the distinguished Wolverhampton musicologist, author, Socialist and football fan Dr. Percy Young.

Chap 24   THE WOMEN 1900 – 14

The first sections on the economic and social conditions of working women and women in trade unions are based on the book *Women's Work and Wages* by Edward Cadbury, M. Cecille Matheson and George Shann.

Details of the lives of Mary Macarthur and Julia Varley are taken from *The Dictionary of Working Class Biography vols 2 and 5* and Mary A. Hamilton's biography *Mary Macarthur.*

The material on the Women's Social and Political Union is, as acknowledged in the text, based almost entirely on the unpublished Wolverhampton Polytechnic M.A. thesis of Michele Shoebridge *The Women's Suffrage Movement in Birmingham and District 1903 – 18* (1983) which she has kindly allowed me to use.

Chap 25   THE BIG BANG 1910 – 14

The Birmingham Trades Council's annual reports and John Corbett's history of the trades council have been supplemented by Richard Hyman — *The Workers' Union* (1971) and the splendid pamphlet by James Leask OBE and Philomena Bellars — *Nor Shall the Sword Sleep, An Account of Industrial Struggle* together with George Askwith *Industrial Problems and Disputes* (1920) for the militant struggles of the Big Bang.

TUC material comes from B.C. Roberts' *The Trades Union Congress 1868 – 1921* and the debate on Syndicalism from the TUC Report of 1912.

Additional material on Syndicalism has come from Bob Holton *British Syndicalism 1900 – 1914* and Alan Clinton — *The Trade Union Rank and File, Trades Council in Britain 1900 – 40.*

Chap 26   CONCLUSIONS

For Elihu Burritt's importance both as historian of the West Midlands and international peace campaigner see Vivian Bird's 'Foreword' to the 1976 reprint of Burritt's *Walks in the Black Country and its Green Borderland.*

For the transition from local state to national state see G.J. Barnsby — *Social Control in the 19th. Century Black Country,* Our History pamphlet No. 55 Communist Party History Group 1972.

For conclusions at variance with those expressed above see Eric Hopkins — *Birmingham The First Manufacturing Town in the World 1760 – 1840* (1989).

INDEX

SPONSORS OF THE BOOK

John Gabriel, Birmingham
Denis Howell MP, Birmingham
T & G W Union, Midland Region
Peter Lightfoot, Sutton Coldfield
Dr. J. M. Bourne, Birmingham
M & H Chatwin, Solihull
Rev Tom Rock, Wolverhampton
Pat McGovern, Kidderminster
Jon Raven, Wolverhampton
Kathleen Stredder, Pattingham
C. V. Collett, Sutton Coldfield
J. & R. Stewart, Birmingham
J. S. Rana, Wolverhampton
R. Hollyhock, Sutton Coldfield
Don Wilkins, Dudley
A & H Hale, Rickmansworth
J & K Ball, London
E. H. Davies, Droitwich
Harry Houghton, Birmingham
D & M Mackie, Cannock
C. Brady, Birmingham
R. H. W. Pemberton, Birmingham
Dr. Joan Lane, Leamington Spa
King Edward VI Camp Hill Girls' School
   Birmingham
Clare Short MP, London
Dr. Carl Chinn, Birmingham
Colin Hopkins, Wolverhampton
Handsworth Wood Girls' School,
   Birmingham
Ellen Rooney, Stoke-on-Trent
Haribhajan Singh, Birmingham
Tessa Bidgood, Birmingham
Ian Turner, Wolverhampton
Larry Moody, Wolverhampton
Mike Shilvock, Stourbridge
P. H. Page, Wolverhampton
Paul Mackney, Birmingham
Peter Morgan, Sutton Coldfield
Community College Bilston
Harold Marsh, Solihull
Joyce Pearce, Birmingham
Woodbrooke College, Birmingham
Frank McGee, Peterborough
C. M. Jones, Birmingham
Gordon Weaver, Birmingham
Richard Clements, Birmingham
Cherry Sewell, Birmingham
G & L Stevenson, Birmingham
Lynne Jones, Birmingham
M. G. Costello, Solihull

A. Smith, Birmingham
Bill Weale, Birmingham
John J. Moore, Solihull
David Grainger, Birmingham
Sonia Wright, Kidderminster
A & M Underwood, Amesbury
Stephen J. Haycock, Kingswinford
Mark Hayman, Birmingham
Dr. R. Gray, Southsea
V & T Jones, Birmingham
Gordon Will, Birmingham
Maisie Harris, Halesowen
Tina Mackay, Birmingham
Jerry Bartlett, Kidderminster
David Parsonage, Stourbridge
Timothy Amman, Birmingham
Geoff Beddow, Stafford
John Goodman, Coventry
W. Mids Graphical Society, Willenhall
Rev. A. Benton, Birmingham
C. F. Reeve, Birmingham
Dept Local Hist, Birmingham
Labour Movement Library, Denmark
C. Hall, Birmingham
Hiroshi Kano, Tokyo
Miss G. E. D. Hasler, Birmingham
B'ham NALGO, Birmingham
Dr. Simon Forde, Leeds
John Edwards, West Bromwich
Dudley & Dist Trades Council
Gerald Chaney, Norwich
Dr. D. G. Wright, Shipley
Stewart Maclennan, Glasgow
Working Class Movement Library,
   Salford
Peter C. Gould, Grimsby
Dr. Paul Richards, Kings Lynn
Dr. John Swift, Birmingham
Bill Moore, Sheffield
A. D. Atienza, Bury St. Edmunds
W. S. Ainsworth, Birmingham
Paul F. Tyler, London
N.U.P.E., Birmingham
John Gorman, Waltham Abbey
Noreen Branson, London
Sir David Perris, Birmingham
Derek Jones, Solihull
Richard Shackleton, Birmingham
C. F. Fitzer, Birmingham
Alan Sutton, Solihull
Sybil Shine, London

Dr. M. Mullings, London
Edwin H. Dare, Loughton
B. M. D. Smith, Birmingham
Stuart R. Perry, Birmingham
Brian Taylor, London
NCU(E) Int.Br., Birmingham
Marxist-Leninist Inst., Berlin
NUPE, Birmingham
Sandwell Libraries West Bromwich
Doreen Smith, Birmingham
Richard Hyman, Coventry
Reg Hall, Croydon
B'ham & Mid Soc for Geneology &
  Heraldry
G. E. Reed, Birmingham
Rodney Hilton, Birmingham
B & M Pearce, Cardiff
Rowland Dye, Birmingham
Dick Pratt, Birmingham
Lea Hall Victimised Miners 1984 – 5
Derek Perkins, Bristol
D. R. Yeomans, Bristol
Chris Darke, London
5/908 Branch T.G.W.U., Birmingham
Bishopsgate Institute, London
Christopher Dyer, Birmingham
David Crosher, Nuneaton
Peter Snape MP, London
D. E. Spilsbury, Birmingham
David C Mattocks, Birmingham
Steven Weale, Birmingham
W. A. S. Swale, Stroud
Susan Thomas, Birmingham
Andrew Newman, Oxford
Dr. Edward Royle, York
Colin Burden, Birmingham
Calvin Tattersall, Solihull
Alastair J. Reid, Cambridge
Robert Fyson, Newcastle-under-Lyme

Pauline Atienza, Birmingham
Ken Evans, Wolverhampton
Nick Matthews, Wolverhampton
Brian Lovett, Bilston
Dennis Turner MP, Bilston
Dr. Dave Morris, Stourbridge
Ruskin College, Oxford
Trades Council, Birmingham
David & Isabel Crook, Beijing, China
Richard Kisch, London
George Jelf, Birmingham
Keith Wymer, Birmingham
Local History Centre, Walsall.
Ray Garner, Wolverhampton
Michael S. Darby, Birmingham
Nancy Beattie, Birmingham
C, A, G & A Hale, Watford
Shelia Gillett, Rickmansworth
Mel Parker (Mrs), Birmingham
Robin Corbett, MP, London
Jez Vanes, Coseley
Vron Tyrrell, Birmingham
T. T. J. Capnerhurst, Birmingham
Mr M. Shafi, Wolverhampton
Esther Sterenberg, Birmingham
Science Museum, London
Baroness Fisher of Rednal, Birmingham
Dennis Haskey, Birmingham
Ted Brake, Winchcombe
Co-operative Union, Manchester
Max Bennett, Wolverhampton
Olwyn P. Powell, Birmingham
John Hazlehurst, Bristol
Robert Hazlehurst, Wolverhampton
Kate Berry, Worcester
F. & H. Crompton, Worcester
Dr. L. Mirejovsky, Prague
Frank Reeves, Wolverhampton
R. J. McCarthey, Birmingham